God's Saved Israel

God's Saved Israel

Reading Romans 11:26 and Galatians 6:16 in Terms
of the New Identity in Christ and the Spirit

Philip La G. Du Toit

◦PICKWICK *Publications* • Eugene, Oregon

GOD'S SAVED ISRAEL
Reading Romans 11:26 and Galatians 6:16 in Terms of the New Identity in Christ and the Spirit

Copyright © 2019 Philip La G. Du Toit. All rights reserved. Except for brief quotations in critical publications or reviews, no part of this book may be reproduced in any manner without prior written permission from the publisher. Write: Permissions, Wipf and Stock Publishers, 199 W. 8th Ave., Suite 3, Eugene, OR 97401.

Pickwick Publications
An Imprint of Wipf and Stock Publishers
199 W. 8th Ave., Suite 3
Eugene, OR 97401

www.wipfandstock.com

PAPERBACK ISBN: 978-1-5326-5359-9
HARDCOVER ISBN: 978-1-5326-5360-5
EBOOK ISBN: 978-1-5326-5361-2

Cataloguing-in-Publication data:

Names: Du Toit, Philip La G., author.

Title: God's saved Israel : reading Romans 11:26 and Galatians 6:16 in terms of the new identity in Christ and the Spirit / by Philip La G. Du Toit.

Description: Eugene, OR: Pickwick Publications, 2019 | Includes bibliographical references and index.

Identifiers: ISBN 978-1-5326-5359-9 (paperback) | ISBN 978-1-5326-5360-5 (hardcover) | ISBN 978-1-5326-5361-2 (ebook)

Subjects: LCSH: Bible. Romans, XI, 26—Criticism, interpretation, etc. | Bible. Galatians, VI, 16—Criticism, interpretation, etc. | Jews in the New Testament. | Christianity and other religions—Judaism. | Judaism—Relations—Christianity.

Classification: LCC BS2655.J4 D8 2019 (print) | LCC BS2655.J4 (ebook)

Scripture quotations marked (AMP) are taken from the Amplified Bible, copyright © 1954, 1958, 1962, 1964, 1965, 1987 by The Lockman Foundation. Used by permission.

Scripture quotations marked (ASV) are taken from the American Standard Version, public domain.

Scripture quotations marked (DST) are taken from the Dutch Staten Vertaling (Dutch State Translation), public domain.

Scripture quotations marked (ESV) are taken from the The Holy Bible, English Standard Version®, copyright © 2001 by Crossway, a publishing ministry of Good

News Publishers. All Rights Reserved.

Scripture quotations marked (GNB) are taken from the Good News Bible, copyright © 1994 by the Bible Societies/HarperCollins Publishers Ltd UK; American Bible Society 1966, 1971, 1976, 1992. Used by permission.

Scripture quotations marked (GW) are taken from the God's Word®, copyright © 1995 by God's Word to the Nations. All rights reserved.

Scripture quotations marked (ISV) are taken from the International Standard Version, copyright © 1996-2014 by the ISV Foundation. All rights reserved internationally. Used by permission of Davidson Press LLC.

Scripture quotations marked (KJV) are taken from the King James Version, public domain.

Scripture quotations marked (LITV) are taken from the Literal Translation of the Holy Bible, copyright © 1976-2000 by Jay P. Green, Sr. All rights reserved.

Scripture quotations marked (NAT) are taken from Die Bybel, Nuwe Vertaling (New Afrikaans Translation), copyright © 1975, 1979, 1983, 1986 by Bybelgenootskap van Suid-Afrika. All rights reserved.

Scripture quotations marked (NEB) are taken from the New English, copyright © 1961, 1970 by Oxford University Press and Cambridge University Press. All rights reserved. Used by permission.

Scripture quotations marked (NIV) are taken from the Holy Bible, New International Version®, NIV®, copyright © 1973, 1978, 1984, 2011 by Biblica, Inc.™ Used by permission of Zondervan. All rights reserved worldwide. www.zondervan.com. The "NIV" and "New International Version" are trademarks registered in the United States Patent and Trademark Office by Biblica, Inc.™

Scripture quotations marked (NJB) are taken from The New Jerusalem Bible, copyright © 1985 by Darton, Longman & Todd, Ltd. and Doubleday, a division of Random House, Inc.

Scripture quotations marked (NKJV) are taken from the New King James Version®, copyright © 1982 by Thomas Nelson, Inc. All rights reserved. Used by permission.

Scripture quotations marked (NLT) are taken from the Holy Bible, New Living Translation, copyright © 1996, 2004, 2007 by Tyndale House Foundation. Used by permission. All rights reserved.

Scripture quotations marked (NRSV) are taken from New Revised Standard Version Bible, copyright © 1989 National Council of the Churches of Christ in the United States of America. Used by permission. All rights reserved.

Scripture quotations marked (OAT) are taken from Die Bybel (Old Afrikaans Translation), copyright © 1957, 1996 by Bybelgenootskap van Suid-Afrika. All rights reserved.

Scripture quotations marked (REB) are taken from The Revised English Bible, copyright © 1989 by Oxford University Press and Cambridge University Press.

Scripture quotations marked (RSV) are taken from the Revised Standard Version, copyright © 1946, 1971 Division of Christian Education of the National Council of Churches of Christ in the United States of America. Used by permission.

Scripture quotations marked (RV) are taken from the Revised Version, public domain.

Scripture quotations marked (YLT) are taken from Young's Literal Translation, public domain.

Manufactured in the U.S.A.   05/13/19

To Carina

Contents

Acknowledgments | xi
Abbreviations | xiii

1 Introduction | 1
   Background   1
   Problem Areas and Focus   4
   Methodology and Demarcation of the Fields of Study   16

2 Israel, Israelites, and Judeans (A and AB) | 31
   Israel, Israelites and Judeans in Other Texts   31
   Israel According to the Flesh   39
   Israel According to the Flesh and Israel as Children of the Promise (AB)   45
   Schematic Presentation of People Sharing in Identity Modes A and AB   53
   Romans 2:17–29: Outward and Inward Judeans (AB?)   54
   Summary and Concluding Remarks   68

3 Faith in Christ, Abraham, and Law (ABC) | 71
   Romans 1:16–17   71
   Romans 4:1–25   77
   Galatians 3:1–29   87
   Galatians 4:21—5:1   100
   Ephesians 2:8–22   107
   Summary and Concluding Remarks   117

4 Faith in Christ, Israel, and the Judean (AC) | 119
   Faith in Christ in Discontinuity with Israel and the Judean (AC)   119
   The New Creation Versus Flesh (AC)   156
   Summary and Concluding Remarks   169

5 Spirit, Flesh and Identity | 174
   Spirit and the New Covenant Versus Flesh and
   the Old Covenant (AC)   174
   Spirit and Flesh as Modes and Markers of Identity (AC)   184
   Preliminary Conclusions and Implications   219

6 "All Israel" and "the Israel of God" | 231
   Introduction to Romans 9 to 11   231
   Romans 9 (ABC)   235
   Romans 10 (AC)   251
   Romans 11 (ABC)   262
   Galatians 6:7–16 (ABC)   334

7 Conclusions and Implications | 346
   Israel, Judeans, and Identity   348
   The Identity in Christ and the Spirit as Fulfilling the Identity
   According to the Flesh   350
   Universal and Particular   353
   Implications for Pauline Theology   354
   Paul and Christianity   356

Bibliography | 357
Subject Index | 379
Index of Modern Authors | 383
Index of Ancient Sources | 387

Acknowledgments

MOST OF THE RESEARCH presented here was done during my PhD studies at Stellenbosch University in South Africa. My love for exegeting the text of the New Testament, I owe to my father, Ben Du Toit, who was also one of my New Testament lecturers and supported me through all of my academic career. I would also like to thank my mother, Corrie Du Toit, for her godly attitude and love, especially for preparing meals on Wednesday afternoons in my post-doctoral years when I drove through to Stellenbosh and Somerset West for seminars and post-doctoral work. Much of the initial PhD research was refined and expanded over the past view years, most notably the section on tracing the idea of ancient, historical Israel's salvation in the rest of the New Testament and the Church Fathers. I owe my gratidute to Jeremy Punt, my doctoral supervisor, who guided me through the whole process of completing my PhD, for his valuable insights and input. I would also like to thank Marius Nel and Francois Wessels for reading through much of this study and for recommending it to the publishers.

Most of my gratitude goes to my wife, Carina, for her endless patience, love, prayer, and support through all these years. This work would not have been possible without her. It is to you I dedicate this book. Thanks to my daughters: Clara-Marié, Pippa, and Judy for loving their dad and for understanding that he sometimes had to work late into the evenings. I also want to thank Usher and Veronica Bell and Cliff and Stephanie Canipe for their friendship, spiritual support, and prayer in our lives, and for all the times of wonderful fellowship. Thank you Pieter and Liesel Roos for your friendship and for encouraging us in our work and ministry. Thank you Albert and Corné Theron for your invaluable spiritual input in our lives. Thank you Callie Joubert for your constant friendship and for motivating me through all of my academic career. Thank you Hannes Knoetze, Alfred Brunsdon, and Amanda Du Plessis for your friendship and for creating a friendly work environment wherein I could finish this work.

Lastly, I would like to thank the following academic journals for permission to incorporate material from published articles into this book: "Paul's Radicalisation of Law-obedience in Romans 2: The Plight of Someone Under the Law." *In die Skriflig/In Luce Verbi* 50/1 (2016) 1–8. Their journal website is at https://indieskriflig.org.za/index.php/skriflig. "The Salvation of 'All Israel' in Romans 11:25–27 as the Salvation of Inner-Elect, Historical Israel in Christ." *Neotestamentica* 49/2 (2015) 417–52. Their website is at https://journals.co.za/content/journal/neotest and at http://newtestament.org.za/neotestamentica.html. "Reading Galatians 6:16 in Line with Paul's Contrast between the New Aeon in Christ and the Old Aeon before the Christ Event." *Stellenbosch Theological Journal* 2/2 (2016) 203–25. Their website is at http://ojs.reformedjournals.co.za.

Philip La G. Du Toit
May 2019

Abbreviations

General

AB	Anchor Bible
ABD	*Anchor Bible Dictionary.* Edited by David Noel Freedman. 6 vols. New York: Doubleday, 1992
ACNT	Augsburg Commentaries on the New Testament
ANTC	Abingdon New Testament Commentaries
BDAG	Danker, Frederick W., Walter Bauer, William F. Arndt, and F. Wilbur Gingrich. *Greek-English Lexicon of the New Testament and Other Early Christian Literature.* 3rd ed. Chicago: University of Chicago Press, 2000
BDB	Brown, Francis, S. R. Driver, and Charles A. Briggs. *A Hebrew and English Lexicon of the Old Testament*
BDF	Blass, Friedrich, Albert Debrunner, and Robert W. Funk. *A Greek Grammar of the New Testament and Other Early Christian Literature.* Chicago: University of Chicago Press, 1961
BECNT	Baker Exegetical Commentary on the New Testament
Bijdr	*Bijdragen: Tijdschrift voor filosofie en theologie*
BJRL	*Bulletin of the John Rylands University Library of Manchester*
BNTC	Black's New Testament Commentaries
BSac	*Bibliotheca Sacra*
BZNW	Beihefte zur Zeitschrift für die neutestamentliche Wissenschaft
CBC	Cornerstone Biblical Commentary
CBQ	*Catholic Biblical Quarterly*

CE	Common Era
cf.	*confer* (Latin). Compare. In this book it refers to a *similar* or *complemantary* interpretation or text, although not identical to the view presented, including all references thereafter (separated by ";"). In other words, "cf." is used in support of *similar* views and not of opposing views. Additionally, Scripture references to disputed Pauline letters that convey a similar meaning to that which is argued, are marked in this manner.
CJET	*Caribbean Journal of Evangelical Theology*
ConcC	Concordia Commentary
CPNIVC	The College Press NIV Commentary
CTJ	*Calvin Theological Journal*
CurBR	*Currents in Biblical Research*
DLNT	*Dictionary of the Later New Testament and Its Developments.* Edited by R. P. Martin and P. H. Davids. Downers Grove, IL: InterVarsity Press, 1997
DPL	*Dictionary of Paul and His Letters.* Edited by Gerald F. Hawthorne and Ralph P. Martin. Downers Grove, IL: InterVarsity Press, 1993
EDNT	*Exegetical Dictionary of the New Testament.* Edited by Horst Balz and Gerhard Schneider. ET. 3 vols. Grand Rapids: Eerdmans, 1990–1993
EGT	*The Expositor's Greek Testament*, Edited by W. Robertson Nicoll. 5 vols. London: Hodder and Stoughton, 1902–1910
EKKNT	Evangelisch-katholischer Kommentar zum Neuen Testament
HThKNT	Herders Theologischer Kommentar zum Neuen Testament
HTR	*Harvard Theological Review*
HTS	*HTS Teologiese Studies/Theological Studies*
ICC	The International Critical Commentary
IDS	*In die Skriflig/In Luce Verbi*
Int	Interpretation: A Bible Commentary for Teaching and Preaching
IVPNTC	The IVP New Testament Commentary Series
JBL	*Journal of Biblical Literature*
JECH	*Journal of Early Christian History*

JETS	*Journal of the Evangelical Theological Society*
JQR	*The Jewish Quarterly Review*
JSHJ	*Journal for the Study of the Historical Jesus*
JSJ	*Journal for the Study of Judaism*
JSNT	*Journal for the Study of the New Testament*
JSNTSup	Journal for the Study of the New Testament Supplement Series
L&N	Louw, Johannes P., and Eugene A. Nida, eds. *Greek-English Lexicon of the New Testament: Based on Semantic Domains*. 2nd ed. New York: United Bible Societies, 1989
LXX	Septuagint (Ancient Greek translation of the Old Testament)
MSJ	*The Master's Seminary Journal*
MT	Masoretic Text
NA28	*Novum Testamentum Graece*, Nestle-Aland, 28th ed.
NAC	The New American Commentary
NCB	New Century Bible
NCBC	New Cambridge Bible Commentary
Neot	*Neotestamentica*
NGTT	*Nederduits Gereformeerde Teologiese Tydskrif*
NIBCNT	New International Biblical Commentary on the New Testament
NICNT	New International Commentary on the New Testament
NICOT	New International Commentary on the Old Testament
NIDNTT	*New International Dictionary of New Testament Theology*. Edited by Colin Brown. 4 vols. Grand Rapids: Zondervan, 1975–1978
NIGTC	The New International Greek Testament Commentary
NIVAC	The NIV Application Commentary
NovT	*Novum Testamentum*
NovTSup	Supplements to Novum Testamentum
NPP	New Perspective on Paul
NT	New Testament
NTL	New Testament Library
NTS	*New Testament Studies*

OT	Old Testament	
OTL	Old Testament Library	
PCNT	Paideia Commentaries on the New Testament	
PNTC	The Pillar New Testament Commentary	
RB	*Revue biblique*	
RelSRev	*Religious Studies Review*	
RNPP	Radical New Perspective on Paul	
SBJT	*The Southern Baptist Journal of Theology*	
SE	Studia Evangelica	
SP	Sacra Pagina	
STJ	*Stellenbosch Theological Journal*	
Str-B	Strack, Hermann Leberecht and Paul Billerbeck. *Kommentar zum Neuen Testament aus Talmud und Midrasch*. 6 vols. Munich: Beck, 1922–1961.	
TAP	Traditional Approach to Paul	
TDNT	*Theological Dictionary of the New Testament*. Edited by Gerhard Kittel and Gerhard Friedrich. Translated by Geoffrey W. Bromiley. 10 vols. Grand Rapids: Eerdmans, 1964–1976	
TNTC	Tyndale New Testament Commentaries	
TOTC	Tyndale Old Testament Commentaries	
TS	*Theological Studies*	
TynBul	*Tyndale Bulletin*	
WBC	Word Biblical Commentary.	
WEC	The Wycliffe Exegetical Commentary	
WUNT	Wissenschaftliche Untersuchungen zum Neuen Testament	
ZECNT	Zondervan Exegetical Commentary on the New Testament	

Ancient Sources

General

Cicero
Flac.   *Pro Flacco*

Dio Chrysostom
Disc.   *Discourses*

Epictetus
Diatr.   *Diatribai*

Epiphanius
Pan.   *Panarion*

Josephus
Ag. Ap.   *Against Apion*
J.W.   *Jewish War*
Ant.   *Jewish Antiquities*

Philo
Mos.   *De Vita Mosis*

Philostratus
Vit. Apoll.   *Vita Apollonii*

Polycarp
Mart. Pol.   Martyrdom of Polycarp

Seneca
Ira   *De Ira*

Suetonius
Claud.   *Divus Claudius*

Tacitus
Hist.   *Historiae*
Off.   *De Officiis*

Mishnah, Talmud and Related Literature

Sanh.   Sanhedrin
T. Benj.   Testament of Benjamin

OT Apocrypha/Pseudepigrapha

2 Bar.	2 Baruch
1 En.	1 Enoch
CD	The Cairo Damascus Document
Pss. Sol.	Psalms of Solomon

NT Apocrypha/Pseudepigrapha

1 Clem.	1 Clement
2 Clem.	2 Clement
Herm.	Shepherd of Hermas
Herm. Vis.	Shepherd of Hermas, Vision(s)
Herm. Sim.	Shepherd of Hermas, Similitude(s)

Church Fathers

Clement of Alexandria
Strom.   *Stromateis*
Diogn.   Diognetus

Ignatius
Magn.   *To the Magnesians*

Irenaueus
Epid.   *Demonstration of the Apostolic Preaching*
Haer.   *Against Heresies*

Justin
Dial.   *Dialogue with Trypho*

Tertullian
An.   *The Soul*

1

Introduction

Background

THE APOSTLE PAUL'S THEOLOGICAL understanding of Israel has been a controversial and debated topic since the beginning of Christianity, starting with the Church Fathers (e.g., Justin Martyr, Marcion of Sinope, Tertullian), through the Reformation (e.g., Martin Luther, John Calvin, Augustine of Hippo), until today. In Reformed circles the legacy of Martin Luther left a lasting impression on Pauline theology. He interpreted Paul's letters such as to establish the universal human plight and his or her need for divine grace. In terms of the relationship between Israel and the church, Luther's view was characterized by what has become known as "replacement theology" or "supersessionism," where the Christian church is understood as a replacement for Israel.¹ This view had the corollary of a negative view of the Torah. Luther understood the "works of the law" (ἔργων νόμου) in Paul's letters as the inadequate and hopeless means of trying to earn one's salvation. Christ was the solution for this human plight.²

Much of Luther's approach to Paul's letters and especially his "plight to solution" scheme became entrenched, constituting the *Traditional Approach to Paul* (TAP hereafter). One of the side-effects of the TAP is that the understanding of Paul has been perceived by many as being anti-Israel, and even antisemitic.³ Ever since World War II and the Holocaust in particular,

---

1. Luther, *Jews*, 265, had put forth his position as follows: "For such ruthless wrath of God is sufficient evidence that they [the Jews] assuredly have erred and gone astray. Even a child can comprehend this. For one dare not regard God as so cruel that he would punish his own people so long, so terrible, so unmercifully . . . Therefore this work of wrath is proof that the Jews, surely rejected by God, are no longer his people, and neither is he any longer their God."
2. Cf. Thiselton, *Hermeneutics*, 311–14.
3. E.g., Gager, *Paul*, 15.

theological notions that could be interpreted as anti-Jewish have been contested progressively.[4]

In New Testament Theology, the voices against the TAP have become gradually louder, especially from theologians such as Stendahl, Sanders, Dunn, and Wright.[5] These writers have accentuated the "Jewishness" of Paul,[6] and have especially reconsidered and reinterpreted the term "works of the law" in a more positive light. According to Sanders,

> [Paul's gospel] is thus not first of all against the means of being properly religious which are appropriate to Judaism that Paul polemicizes ("by works of law"), but against the prior fundamentals of Judaism: the election, the covenant and the law; and it is because these are wrong that the means appropriate to "righteousness according to the law" (Torah observance and repentance) are held to be wrong or are not mentioned. *In short, this is what Paul finds wrong in Judaism: it is not Christianity.*[7]

This view of Paul has developed in what has become known as the *New Perspective on Paul* (NPP hereafter), a term that was arguably coined by Dunn.[8] By implication, the NPP holds that Paul has been fundamentally misunderstood. In the same vein as Sanders, Dunn does not view Paul's reference to "works of the law" as denoting human achievement, since he views Paul's doctrine of justification by faith to be "a thoroughly Jewish doctrine." Rather, "works of the law" would denote "a concern to maintain Israel's covenant obligations and distinctiveness."[9] This understanding of Judaism has become known by the term "covenantal nomism."[10] According to Dunn, "continued adherence to works of the law on the part of Christian Jews is both unnecessary and itself a threat to the sufficiency of that faith."[11] In the NPP, "plight to solution" is turned around to "solution to plight," where the Old Covenant is re-interpreted from the perspective of the gospel of Christ.

With the proponents of the so called *Radical New Perspective on Paul* (RNPP hereafter),[12] Paul is pictured as completely "Jewish" without any

---

4. Cf. Cranfield, *Romans*, 1:448.

5. Stendahl, "Apostle Paul"; Sanders, *Palestinian Judaism*; Dunn, "New Perspective"; Wright, *Climax*.

6. Cf. esp. Casey and Taylor, *Jewish Matrix*.

7. Sanders, *Palestinian Judaism*, 551–52.

8. Dunn, "New Perspective."

9. Dunn, *Theology of Paul's Letter*, 75–76, 79, 100.

10. Sanders, *Palestinian Judaism*, 75.

11. Dunn, *Theology of Paul's Letter*, 80.

12. The term was coined by Johnson Hodge, *If Sons*, 9, 153, and later used by

connection to some of the main tenets of Christianity.[13] This view is also associated with a non-supersessionist position, often described as "Two-Covenant Theology" or "Dual-Covenant Theology." In this understanding, Israel remains in their original covenant with God by keeping the laws of the Torah, and

1. Gentiles may either believe in Christ to be saved, constituting a parallel covenant for gentiles,[14] or

2. they may be considered as "righteous gentiles" (not "Christians") and obtain a place in the world to come by observing the Noahide Laws, which is a minimum set of laws (excluding e.g. circumcision) or requirements (*halakhot*) that were expected of gentiles.[15] This implies that there are not "two different systems of redemption" with Paul,[16] but that Christ-believers adhered to a different set of requirements in order to be counted as "righteous" and as "potential Jews."[17]

In terms of Pauline scholarship, the NPP, and especially the RNPP by implication, tend to question the entire Pauline witness as evidence of "Christianity." Eisenbaum's book with the main title: *Paul was not a Christian*, is an example of this tendency.[18] Yet, the implications of this approach are even wider reaching. On the one hand, it challenges the way in which concepts of "Jewishness" or "Jewish identity" in Paul's letters are understood, and on the other hand, how the identity of the Christ-believers is defined.

Zetterholm, *Approaches*, 161.

13. E.g., Eisenbaum, *Paul*; Nanos, *Mystery*; idem., "Myth"; Zetterholm, *Formation*; Gager, *Reinventing*; Elliott, *Liberating*; Gaston, *Paul*; Stendahl, "Introsepctive Conscience"; idem., *Paul*.

14. E.g., Gager, *Reinventing*; Gaston, *Paul*; Stendahl, *Paul*.

15. E.g., Eisenbaum, *Paul*, 252; Campbell, *Paul*, 6; Nanos, *Mystery*, 50–56; cf. Tomson, *Paul*, 50. In this view, the admission of "righteous gentiles" is not understood as a separate covenant, and adherents of this view do not necessarily employ the term "Two-Covenant" or "Dual-Covenant." Even though Nanos, *Mystery*, 23, admits that the terms "Noahide Laws" and "halakhot" are strictly anachronistic, since these terms were coined in later Rabbinic Judaism (see below), he argues that this concept was present in the Qumran book of *Jubilees* 7:20–21: "And in the twenty-eight jubilee Noah began to command his grandsons with ordinances and commandments and all of the judgments which he knew. And he bore witness to his sons so that they might do justice and cover the shame of their flesh and bless the one who created them and honor father and mother, and each one love his neighbor and preserve themselves from fornication and pollution and from all injustice" (translation of O. S. Wintermute in Nanos, *Mystery*, 55).

16. Eisenbaum, *Paul*, 252.

17. Nanos, *Mystery*, 54.

18. Johnson Hodge, *If Sons*, 153, follows a similar approach in that she describes her agenda as "rescuing [Paul] *from* Christians, rather than *for* Christians."

Problem Areas and Focus

Two of the most prominent passages in Paul's conception of Israel are Romans 11:26 and Galatians 6:16. The interpretation of these passages can be considered as linchpins of Paul's conception of Israel. In addition, both of these passages normally have a profound influence on interpreters' view on Israel. The main aim of this study is to determine the respective referents of "all Israel" who "will be saved" (Rom 11:26) and "the Israel of God" whom Paul blesses (Gal 6:16).

In order to address this problem, one has to determine the way in which Paul relates to whom he calls Ἰσραήλ and/or the Ἰουδαῖοι in his letters, and whether the the way in which he relates to them is consistent with the way in which he refers to Israel in Romans 11:26 and Galatians 6:16. An important question beneath this kind of study is whether Paul views the Christ-believing community as a movement within the faith of Israel, or whether belief in Christ constitutes a new identity that transcends the faith and the way of life of the Old Testament. A second question that flows forth from the former is whether Paul sees Israel as a continuing entity within the new covenant with salvation-historical significance or whether he perceives historical Israel to end in Christ and thus as being replaced by believers in Christ.

According to Gager[19] there are apparent opposing passages in Paul's letters about the Torah and Israel, which he divides into "anti-Israel" and "pro-Israel" passages (the "pro-Israel" set: Rom 3:1, 31; 7:7, 12; 9:4; 11:1, 26; Gal 3:21 and the "anti-Israel" set: Gal 3:10, 11; 6:15; Rom 3:20; 9:31; 11:28; 2 Cor 3:14). He points out four main ways of addressing this apparent discrepancy:[20]

1. The psychological technique, which would provide for a change or inconsistency in Paul's approach to these issues.[21]
2. The resigned technique, which would simply leave the apparent contradictions as they stand without trying to resolve them.[22]
3. A removal of the "offending" passages that are explained as additions and/or corruptions of the text.[23]

---

19. Gager, *Reinventing*, 5–7.
20. Gager, *Reinventing*, 7–9.
21. E.g., Hamerton-Kelly, *Sacred Violence*.
22. E.g., Räisänen, *Paul*.
23. E.g., O'Neill, *Romans*.

4. The dominant technique, which subordinates one set of passages to the other (according to the interpreter's view), constituting Gager's own approach.

Bassler rightly notes that the latter technique carries the assumption that Paul's views remained consistent. She admits that even though one would ideally decide after looking at the evidence, "deep-seated convictions about inspiration often suggest the answer beforehand." If the interpreter decides that Paul is fundamentally consistent, he or she has to find a way of harmonizing the apparently different assertions, "allowing one passage to control the meaning."[24] A second decision that needs to be made is which passage(s) should count as evidence.

Deep-seated convictions are indeed an important factor in the Pauline debate. Scholars with stronger evangelical sentiments would tend to retain a certain discontinuity of faith in Christ with physical Israel[25] whereas theologians with stronger positive sentiments about or affiliations with Judaism (or with strong feelings against antisemitism) would tend to seek stronger continuity between the gospel of Christ and physical Israel.[26]

As approaching this topic from an evangelical pre-understanding, I cannot deny my own deep-seated convictions about Paul and Israel. Although the term "evangelical" can have a wide range of meaning and does not denote a homogenous approach, Fitch identifies at least three points of emphasis that is historically associated with evangelicalism. These are (1) a high view of the authority of Scripture, (2) a strong belief in a personal conversion experience and (3) an activist engagement with culture in ways peculiar to evangelicalism.[27] It is especially a high view of the authority of Scripture (1) that I share. Specific areas in Bloesch's definition of evangelical that form part of my own conviction are to uphold "the gospel of free grace as we see this in Jesus Christ" and being "Christocentric and not merely theocentric." As he states, "it is not the teachings of Jesus Christ that are considered of paramount importance but his sacrificial life and death on the cross of Calvary. The evangel is none other than the meaning of the cross."[28]

---

24. Bassler, *Navigating*, 71. The strongest contestant to this notion is arguably Räisänen (*Paul*) who does not view Paul's thought as consistent, especially in terms of his view of the law.

25. E.g., Wright, *Faithfulness*, 2:774–1265; *Climax*; Sanders, *Jewish People*, 207–10; *Palestinian Judaism*, 552.

26. E.g., Eisenbaum, *Paul*; Nanos, "Rethinking"; idem., "Inter-Christian Approaches"; idem., *Mystery*.

27. Fitch, *Evangelicalism*, 13; cf. Olson, *Westminster Handbook*, 9; Pierard and Elwell, "Evangelicalism," 406.

28. Bloesch, *Future*, 15.

While placing my "cards on the table," personal convictions about Paul and Israel, although inevitable,[29] have to be seen as an underlying problem on both sides of this debate. Preconceived notions may cause the interpreter to read a certain understanding "into" the text and hinder objectivity in the process.[30] Another factor with respect to the understanding of identity in Paul, which arguably strains objectivity, is the desire not to be mistaken for an "antisemite" by proposing an understanding that would impinge on the interest of national Israel. Kim goes so far as calling this a "theological *shibboleth* that hinders one from interpreting Paul's theology objectively."[31] The ideal will always be to strive to read Paul on his own terms, and to try and limit pre-understandings of postmodern, Western society to a minimum.

Social-Scientific and Theological Approaches to Identity

While this study relates closely to the study of identity, my approach to identity will be more theological than social-scientific. My presupposition is that Paul's theological portrayal of the identity in Christ within the Pauline corpus supersedes and transcends social and ethnic aspects of identity. Although ethnic identity can be understood as a cultural construct and a matter of self-ascription,[32] the term "ethnicity" or "ethnic" is normally applied in a more restricted way to denote "a group's shared biological origins" and in a broader way to resemble "the concept of nationality."[33] In this book it is used with a slight preference toward the biological side.

While appreciating the value of social-scientific approaches to aspects of identity, many contemporary approaches to identity in the New Testament utilize social-scientific categories as *master categories* to describe the *totality* of identity in the New Testament. Identity formation is normally seen as a process of negotiation between group norms and boundaries, which includes cultural phenomena such as ethnicity, honor and shame, patron and client relationship, and kinship language and relations.[34] In these approaches, Paul's "theologizing" is however often included within or subordinated to social categories. An example is where Tucker suggests that,

---

29. Cf. Thomas, "Trends," 249.

30. Cf. Thomas, "Trends," 251–52.

31. Kim, "Reading," 329; cf. Cranford, "Election," 27.

32. Punt, "1 Corinthians," 4; cf. Campbell, *Paul*, 3–5; Sechrest, *Former Jew*, 39; Wan, "Collection," 191–92.

33. Weeks, "Ethnicity," 681.

34. E.g., Tucker, *Remain*; *Belong*; Campbell, *Paul*; Johnson Hodge, *If Sons*; Buell, *New Race*.

rather than a prior theological reality displacing ethnic categories, "Paul's theologizing defines the Christ-movement in the context of social categories of identity, rather than to the exclusion of these."[35] Tucker is right that social identities including ethnicity are included within the in-Christ-identity in Paul, but by contrasting the defining of identity to a prior theological reality displacing ethnic categories, he creates the impression that social categories are in fact higher in priority in defining identity than theological categories. This impression is heightened when Tucker states that "Paul's theologizing provides ideological justification for the formation of Christ-movement *social* identity,"[36] and that "Paul's theologizing provides the social categories necessary for the formation of an 'in Christ' *social* identity."[37] A similar approach is that of Wan who states that

> [a]ll interpretations and all constructions of reality are ethnocentric. "Ethnocentricity" in this regard does not carry any pejorative sense but is the ineluctable hermeneutical condition from which no interpreter can escape and under which all interpretations are constructed—insofar as no interpreter could escape his or her own ethnicity.[38]

While it is not explicitly stated, Wan's approach implies that Paul's theology is subordinate to an ethnic program. While it is true that one's worldview is inevitably influenced by one's ethnicity, which Wan sees as a cultural construct, it is another question whether "ethnocentricity" is the right term to describe this notion. Although Wan disclaims his use of "ethnocentricity" from being pejorative, it suffers from the same totalizing tendency as that of Tucker and those with similar approaches, namely that a social or cultural category becomes the all-encompassing hermeneutic key through which identity in Paul is read: all other hermeneutic lenses are subordinated to it.

To work in the direction of subjecting Paul's "theologizing" to social-scientific categories as ultimate, controlling categories for identity in Paul, could however hold the danger of standing in too much tension with the theological core of Paul's gospel and thus tend to be reductionistic.[39] While some consider the new identity in Christ as a "third entity,"[40] Esler approaches identity in Paul with the "aid of" a social-scientific framework, and understands identity in Paul as a new, "superordinate" identity wherein

---

35. Tucker, *Remain*, 39.
36. Tucker, *Remain*, 39, emphasis added.
37. Tucker, *Remain*, 41, emphasis added, cf. Campbell, *Paul*, 158, 161.
38. Wan, "Collection," 196.
39. Cf. Wright, *Faithfulness*, 1:28; Watson, *Paul*, 347–48.
40. E.g., Sanders, *Jewish People*, 207.

the Ἰουδαῖοι and non-Ἰουδαῖοι as subgroups are incorporated yet enjoyed a "relative status."[41] Although the latter approach is a step back from viewing believers in Christ as a "third entity," it already seems closer to Paul's theological thought than an approach where Paul's "theologizing" is seen as being determined and controlled by a social category.[42] The approach of this study is thus to view the new identity in Christ as primarily a theological reality with effects in the social world rather than viewing the identity in Christ as primarily a socially created identity that directs theology.

On the one side of the debate, Campbell voices concerns against viewing the ἐκκλησία as (a) a "Third Race" or "third entity" that replaces both Ἰουδαῖος and Ἕλλην, (b) a "New Israel" or (c) a "Redefined Israel." His main objections to these models are that their universal nature holds the danger of superiority, dominancy and imperialism, and that these models display a lack of adequate awareness of "cultural indebtedness," particularity, and a real concern for diversity within the church.[43]

On the other side of the debate, from an evangelical perspective it can be argued that an over emphasis on particularities could neglect the broader, theological significance of those particularities. The Pauline theme of freedom from the law can be seen as laying down a permanent foundation for subsequent Christian communal identity in spite of historical particularities.[44] An over-accentuation of particularities might additionally hold the danger of giving rise to another form of universalism, that is that many different roads lead to Rome (religious pluralism).

Terminology and Identity

The next problem concerning research about Paul's position toward Israel is that pre-understandings of ancient cultures and societies and preconceived notions expressed by concepts that have gained currency in the academy and beyond, may also hinder an authentic understanding of a specific culture or group of people. A case in point is the interpretation and translation of the term Ἰουδαῖοι in the New Testament. For many, translations such as "Jews" and "Judaism" in New Testament scholarship have contributed to prejudice

---

41. Esler, *Conflict*, 144–45, 360; cf. Zoccali, *Whom God Has Called*, 176.

42. E.g., Tucker, *Remain*. Cf. also Zoccali, "1 Corinthians," 107, criticizing Tucker, *Remain*; idem., *Belong*. Although Esler, *Conflict*, 4–5, resists the notion to speak of Paul as a "theologian" (in terms of a systematic enterprise), he does leave room for "theology" in Paul in terms of the sum of the beliefs held by an individual or group in respect of their faith.

43. Campbell, *Paul*, 96–103; cf. Johnson Hodge, *If Sons*, 8.

44. Watson, *Paul*, 354–60.

against modern Jews.⁴⁵ As Mason points out, current understandings of terms like "Jews" or "Judaism" cannot uncritically be projected into the text of the New Testament and thus be equated with Paul's use of Ἰουδαῖοι.⁴⁶

Neusner maintains that Rabbinic Judaism as we know it was born when people came to believe that by studying the Torah and by keeping the commandments, they would play a critical role in the coming of the Messiah. He dates this period at about 70 CE, somewhat before the destruction of the Temple of Jerusalem. He understands Rabbinic Judaism as a gradual development mainly after 70 CE.⁴⁷ Even into the first century, he writes: "the principal institutions of Israel remained priesthood and monarchy, Scripture and its way of life, holy Temple, land, and people."⁴⁸

As a result of this hermeneutical distance between today's Judaism and the Ἰουδαῖοι in Paul's letters, Mason⁴⁹ and others⁵⁰ have suggested that a translation such as "Judeans" is a more appropriate translation for the Ἰουδαῖοι in Paul's letters in order to distinguish them from contemporary Jews. Mason argues that one cannot assign the full designation of "religion" to the Ἰουδαῖοι in the second temple period, but rather views them as an *ethnos*.⁵¹ He defines an *ethnos* as having a distinctive nature or character expressed in unique ancestral traditions, which reflected a shared ancestry or genealogy, with its own charter stories, customs, norms, conventions, mores, laws and political arrangements or constitution.⁵² This fundamental category of *ethnos* includes important elements of what we know today as a "religion," but the political-ethnographic category of *ethnos* cannot be equated with "religion."

---

45. E.g., Campbell, *Paul*, 2; cf. BDAG, Ἰουδαῖος.

46. Mason, "Jews."

47. Neusner, *Messiah*, 1–5; cf. Mason, "Jews," 502; Langer, "Jewish Understandings," 258.

48. Neusner, *Messiah*, 4.

49. Mason, "Jews."

50. E.g., BDAG, Ἰουδαῖος; Elliott, "Jesus"; Esler, *Conflict*; Malina and Rohrbaugh, *Synoptic Gospels*, 32.

51. Mason, "Jews," 483–88, warns against employing a term such as "religion" (not "religious") in connection with New Testament studies. He defines "religion" as a Western category with no counterpart in ancient culture. He identifies various elements that constitute "religion": *ethnos*, cult, philosophy, rites of passage (e.g., at birth, marriage and death), voluntary association (e.g., church or synagogue) and finally, astrology and magic. The term "religious" has to be distinguished from "a religion" as such. The term "religious" thus remains a valid term in describing aspects of biblical identities (p. 481), as will be the case in this book.

52. Mason, "Jews," 484.

Although the translation "Judeans" could be confused for people from the geographical Judea, Mason shows that "Judean" does not have a geographical restriction any more than other ethnic descriptions such as "Roman," "Egyptian" or "Greek."[53] He argues that such a restriction arises in our minds because of the absence of a geographic Judea today. Josephus, who can be considered as important in explaining Judean history, laws and customs, uses Ἰουδαῖοι as an *ethnos*,[54] especially when he juxtaposes Judeans with Babylonians, Egyptians, Chaldaeans, Athenians, and Spartans.[55] One of the underlying notions that drive this translation is a reaction against the perceived anti-Judaism that has been fostered by glossing Ἰουδαῖος with "Jew."[56] As Esler explains, it encourages the idea of "'the eternal Jew' who, it is alleged, killed Christ and is still around, to be persecuted if possible."[57] According to Esler, the translation "Judean" more appropriately reflects the territorial connotations inherent to the term Ἰουδαῖος, which only started to fade around the third and even the fourth century CE.[58]

Miller, however, follows a more fluid approach and points out that with many of the Ἰουδαῖοι in the second temple period a *concept* of "religion" was already present. He argues that there exists an overlap in what ancient people considered as distinct about the Ἰουδαῖοι and what is normally understood under the term "religious." He therefore resists restricting the Ἰουδαῖοι of the second temple to an *ethnos*. In spite of the above arguments against anti-Judaism he argues that the translation "Judaeans" would evoke "another form of anti-Semitism," namely that it would rob contemporary Jews of their Biblical heritage and their continuity with ancient Israel.[59] For Miller[60] and Levine[61] such a translation could additionally give rise to the idea that the Bible has been purified of Jews. Miller therefore prefers the translation "Jews" for the Ἰουδαῖοι of the New Testament in that it reflects for Miller the complexity of the term Ἰουδαῖοι in the New Testament, which carries both ethnic and religious connotations.

If both the translations of Ἰουδαῖοι ("Judeans" and "Jews") can be interpreted as anti-Jewish, it leaves the translator with a difficult choice.

53. Mason, "Jews," 504.
54. Esp. *Ag. Ap.* 1.6, 8–9.
55. See Mason, "Jews," 491–92.
56. BDAG, Ἰουδαῖος.
57. Esler, *Conflict*, 62–63.
58. Esler, *Conflict*, 66–69.
59. Miller, "Ethnicity," 255–59; cf. Campbell, *Paul*, 3; Johnson Hodge, *If Sons*, 13–14.
60. Miller, "Ethnicity," 258.
61. Levine, *Misunderstood Jew*, 160–65.

Notwithstanding the difficulty around these translations, Masons' recommendation to translate Ἰουδαῖοι with "Judaeans" (or "Judaean" for Ἰουδαῖος)⁶² will be followed in this book even where cited references do not. The two main reasons for opting for this translation are (1) to account for the hermeneutical distance between today's Judaism and the Ἰουδαῖοι in Paul, especially the fact that Ἰουδαῖος/Ἰουδαῖοι cannot be understood as a "religion" in the full sense of the word⁶³ and more naturally fits the category of *ethnos*,⁶⁴ and (2) to keep the nature and depth of the historical difference between contemporary Jews and the Ἰουδαῖοι in Paul under discussion. Terms such as "Jews" and "Judaism" (in reference to the Ἰουδαῖοι in the time of Paul) are however still prevalent in most of NT scholarly material that will be consulted in this research. I will employ "Judean(s)" in reference to them even where designations such as "Jews" or "Judaism" occur in the literature, unless where I quote directly. I will therefore leave terms such as "Jew" or "Jewish" *as is* in quotes of scholars in reference to the Ἰουδαῖοι in Paul's time, even though I would prefer translations such as "Judeans" or "a Judean way of life."

In the same way, since Christianity as we know it today was strictly speaking a later development after Paul, especially in terms of its institutional character as world religion, the terms "Christian" and "Christianity" can also be considered as anachronisms in terms of Paul's thought.⁶⁵ While the term "Christianity" in this Pauline study is avoided in the strict sense, Paul's continuity or discontinuity with Christianity remains under discussion. In my view, the terms "Jesus followers," "Jesus group(s)"⁶⁶ or "Jesus-movement"⁶⁷ lean toward an understanding of stronger discontinuity between Paul and Christianity. While being sensitive toward the anachronism of the term "Christian" in connection with Paul on the one hand,

---

62. Mason, "Jews."

63. Although Miller, "Ethnicity," argues against Mason, "Jews," in his perception of Ἰουδαῖοι not being a "religion," Miller does not describe the Ἰουδαῖοι of the New Testament as a full scale "religion" either. Miller, "Ethnicity," 255, argues that "some people had a *concept* of religion even though there was no generally accepted term for it" and that there existed "a middle ground between ethnicity and a fully-formed concept of religion."

64. I hereby don't deny that some of the Ἰουδαῖοι in the New Testament would have a concept of what is understood today as a "religion," but the possession of such a concept among some of these *people* does not in itself prove that such a connotation would necessarily be inherent to the *term* Ἰουδαῖος.

65. Donfried, "Jewish Matrix," 11–12; Eisenbaum, *Paul*; Campbell, *Paul*, 12; Mason, "Jews"; Lieu, *Neither Jew*, 191–209; *Christian Identity*; Gager, *Reinventing*.

66. E.g., Malina, *New Testament World*.

67. Gager, *Reinventing*, VIII.

and keeping Paul's continuity with a Christian identity under discussion on the other, I will employ the term "Christ-believers"[68] (or similar) in this book. The term "church" will be employed as a translation for ἐκκλησία in this book, a term that is abundant in the Pauline corpus. It has to be understood as the congregation or community of believers in Christ.[69]

The *overlapping nature* of identity-related terms with other theological concepts in Paul's thought that could carry other connotations apart from identity as such (e.g., his thought on σάρξ/πνεῦμα), would suggest that his thought on identity *cannot be isolated* from the rest of his theological thinking (e.g., eschatology, soteriology, etc.). The approach of this study will thus be primarily *theological-exegetical* with the aim to pursue Paul's conception(s) of identity along the constraints of Paul's own language and thought, even when these constraints do not correspond exactly to current etic identity-related terminology and definitions (e.g., ethnicity, race, nation, religion, Jews, Judaism, Judeans, Christians, etc.). In other words, the aim is to lay out some of Paul's main identity-related *constraints*[70] of the Christ-believer in relation to being a Ἰουδαῖος and/or especially being part of Ἰσραήλ, and not to attempt to make Paul's perception of identity fit precisely into current *terms* of identity. My approach therefore tends to be more emic than etic. A truly emic approach is not possible however, since precise identity-related categories were not known yet, or they were still in the process of development. Yet an etic approach is not possible either, because etic categories "are not precise, observer-independent, publicly arguable, or falsifiable" and they are therefore beyond the historian's reach.[71] It has to be pointed out though that, while my approach tends to be more emic, the aim is more toward outlining the appropriate theological constraints of identity in Paul's *thought* than to find appropriate sociological or anthropological categories or nomenclature to describe the *self-identity of the people* whom Paul addresses or represents (see below).[72]

---

68. Campbell, *Paul*, 12, who admits to employing this term earlier in his work, decided to switch to "Christ-followers" as a result of his fear of over-emphasising the place of belief over against good works. However, viewing faith as an (or the) important constitutive element of the identity in Christ does not necessarily imply an "old perspective" view on Paul (e.g., Wright, *Paul Really Said*, 1997; idem., *Climax*).

69. L&N §11.32; cf. BDAG, ἐκκλησία, §3b.

70. Cf. Mason, "Jews," 458.

71. Mason, "Jews," 459; cf. Elliott, "Jesus," 121.

72. Elliott, "Jesus," 121, points out that the "process of identification and self-identification is an issue of classification and categorization. As with all classification, it is essential to be clear on *who* is doing the classifying, according to what *criteria*, and for what *purposes*."

Apart from the understanding of language as such as put forth earlier, there are two main reasons for this approach. The first reason is that much of the current identity-related terminologies may verge on being *anachronistic*, where current categories are superimposed onto the New Testament perception(s) of identity. The second reason is that a measure of *uncertainty and fluidity* exists between the various identity-related terms in academic circles.

Anachronism

The historical distance between terms and conceptions of identity today and that of New Testament times is a complex problem. Current terminology of identity attempts to balance an authentic understanding of patterns of identity in the New Testament with current (mostly western) anthropological, social, and theological categories. This is at heart a hermeneutical problem.

Mason notes that there are no ancient Hebrew or Aramaic terms that correspond closely to today's "Judaism." The terms 'Ιουδαϊσμός and *Iudaismus* (Latin) have a different and peculiar history of their own. It was not until 200 to 500 CE that these terms have become established with a meaning that can be related more closely to today's "Judaism."[73] Among the terms "Jew," "Judaism" and "Judeans," there exists a complex set of connotations, ranging from ethnical and racial connotations,[74] to connotations relating to physical descent and geographical origin,[75] and to later connotations about being opposed to Jesus[76] or Christianity.[77] It was only around the third century CE when "Judaism" or "Jewishness" was associated with a "belief system and regimen of the *Ioudaioi*,"[78] and only viewed as a full-fledged "religion" and isolable category during the Enlightenment.[79] Boyarin argues that the term "Jewish" was instrumental in the self-definition of Christianity over against "Judaism," especially in a category such as "Jewish Christianity," a category that he largely attributes to modernity, and aims to dissolve.[80] All these different connotations are thus related to different insider and outsider groups

---

73. Mason, "Jews," 460–61.
74. E.g., Buell, *New Race*.
75. E.g., Mason, "Jews."
76. E.g., Johnson Hodge, *If Sons*, 12.
77. E.g., Buell, *New Race*, 28.
78. Mason, "Jews," 471.
79. Mason, "Jews," 512.
80. Boyarin, "Rethinking."

defining these categories over more than two millennia.[81] John H. Elliott summarizes that the "concepts 'Jew', 'Jewish' and 'Christian' *as understood today* are shaped more by fourth century rather than first-century CE realities and hence should be avoided as anachronistic designations for first-century persons or groups."[82] Even terms such as "ethnicity" and "ethnie"[83] carry a large amount of anachronistic baggage, as Duling points out:

> Should the relatively recent social-scientific terms *ethnicity* and *ethnie* be used to analyze ancient Mediterranean peoples? Yes, as long as one recognizes that they are loaded with outside observers' (etic) meanings and, for social-scientists, some extensive theoretical perspectives. The ancient Mediterraneans had no "ethnicity theory," but they certainly had a "selfconcept," a "group concept," and an "others concept."[84]

In the same manner, the term "Christianity" as one of the world religions stands in hermeneutical tension with the believers and followers of Christ whom Paul addressed. Categories that define a Christian today cannot be equated uncritically with Paul's conception of the identity of the believer of Christ.[85]

Uncertainty and Fluidity Among Terms of Identity

In recent New Testament studies of identity, there has been a tendency to redefine terms of identity in order to align them more closely with an authentic New Testament understanding of identity, especially in studies with social scientific overtones. One such approach is that of Buell.[86] In order to bring terms such as "race" and "ethnicity" into the self-understanding of early followers of Christ, she redefines these terms in fluid categories that include

---

81. Cf. F. Barth's, *Ethnic Groups*, definition of ethnicity as being both self-ascribed and other-ascribed. The insider-versus-outsider definitions for identity can also be viewed as an inherent problem to the categorization of identity. Self-definitions of identity are in tension with the definitions of outsiders. Outsider definitions for identity may tend to generalize or create stereotypes (Elliott, "Jesus," 124).

82. Elliott, "Jesus," 119.

83. "Ethnie" is a term commonly utilized by ethnicity theorists to refer to an ethnic group or community (Duling, "Whatever Gain," 803). Hutchinson and Smith, *Ethnicity*, 6, define it as "a named human population with myths of common ancestry, shared historical memories, one or more elements of common culture, a link with a homeland and a sense of solidarity among at least some of its members."

84. Duling, "Whatever Gain," 810.

85. Cf. Mason, "Jews," 488; Elliott, "Jesus," 143, 147.

86. Buell, *New Race*.

fictive kin, and do not necessitate natural descent. In a similar way, Johnson Hodge argues for "a new way to read kinship and ethnic language in Paul that dismantles the contrast between a universal, 'non-ethnic' Christianity and an ethnic, particular Judaism."[87] Similarly, Wan views the Christ-believing community in Paul as an *ethnos*, where he understands an *ethnos* as a flexible concept in which gentiles could be included.[88] While Sechrest's approach to ethnicity is similar in defining it in fluid categories, she understands the Christ-believing identity in Paul as constituting a new race.[89]

In the above approaches, nomenclature such as "ethnicity," "race," "religion" or "kinship" seems to be indispensable for their definitions of identity,[90] and rather than finding new terms or abandoning these terms, these terms are redefined within open and fluid categories (relative to traditional definitions of "ethnicity," "race," etc.) in order to fit their conception of identity and particularity.

With respect to the New Testament's own terms of identity, Duling recognizes the overlapping and fluid nature of terms such as ἔθνος and γένος, even though he defines ἔθνος broader (including e.g., mythical ancestral categories) and γένος narrower (focusing on birth and ancestry, yet expandable to broader categories).[91]

Judeans and Israel

One of the key presuppositions to this study is that it is not taken for granted that the designations Ἰουδαῖοι and Ἰσραήλ are necessarily pointing to the exact same identity(ies) in Paul. The areas of difference, overlap and sameness are kept open for further definition and refinement in view of the way in which Paul utilizes them.

---

87. Johnson Hodge, *If Sons*, 4.
88. Wan, "Collection," 192, 199.
89. Sechrest, *Former Jew*, 39, 123, 160, 164, 210.
90. Buell, *New Race*, 2, states: "The central argument of this book is that early Christian texts used culturally available understandings of human difference, which we can analyze in terms of our modern concepts of 'ethnicity,' 'race,' and 'religion.'" Johnson Hodge, *If Sons*, 3, writes: ". . . in Paul this new relationship is understood in terms of ethnicity and kinship." Her quest for the right terminology especially comes forth when she writes: "I have a clear idea of what we need: one term, not two, that operates in English the way *Ioudaios* . . . operate in Greek" (15).
91. Duling, "Whatever Gain"; cf. L&N §10.1, 10.32, 58.23.

Summary and Focus

The main focus of this book is to address Paul's definition and understanding of the identity of "Israel" in the light of belief in Christ, with a special focus on who "all Israel" is that will be saved in Rom 11:26 and to whom the "Israel of God" (Gal 6:16) refers to. This main focus needs to be addressed amidst two main categories of problems within the debate:

1. The quagmire of interpretations of the TAP, the NPP and the RNPP on the identity and ethnicity of God's people, and
2. Different views on membership in God's covenant(s) with His people.

Methodology and Demarcation of the Fields of Study

The notion to look deeper into Paul's theology to grasp his understanding of the identity in Christ, suggests that a methodology of the "dominant technique," where "one set of passages" are subordinated to "the other" (see Gager's fourth technique above), might be too simplistic. Rather than for example making some Ἰσραήλ passages dominant and other subordinate (in terms of "pro-Israel" and "anti-Israel"), my approach would rather be to interpret all these passages in relation to the deeper theological thrust around identity in Paul's letters. To pursue the latter, my approach will primarily be exegetical with a theological aim, working toward a coherent understanding of deeper theological aspects of identity in Paul's letters. The exegesis itself will comprise of four main aspects: semantic, structural, contextual and theological-exegetical. The latter will constitute the main body of this study.

Concerning the choices of specific Pauline passages and themes, the theological insight relating to deeper aspects of identity in Paul's letters as pursued within certain passages will progressively interact with other passages (as the bigger picture becomes clearer), even though some of the issues might relate to one another indirectly. In this regard, Thiselton's reference to "multiple horizons of meaning"[92] is helpful in terms of two kinds of hermeneutical horizons: (1) The "juxtaposition of a variety of mutually qualifying images, symbols, analogies, or even referential terms allows an understanding to 'come alive.'"[93] (2) We can see complex puzzles as a *Gestalt*,[94] that forms a coherent picture instead of the atomistic pieces that

---

92. Thiselton, *Hermeneutics*, 318–20.
93. Thiselton, *Hermeneutics*, 318.
94. *Gestalt* as a German psychological term refers to the essence or shape of an

we began with. This method therefore tends to be more deductive than inductive. Yet, the questions relating to an understanding of Paul's theology will always be correlated to the researcher's hermeneutical interests: his or her point of view and symbolic universe, including language and world view. Apart from this fact, it has to be taken into account that any understanding of an ancient text is incomplete.

One of the areas of study that is anticipated to contribute to Paul's understanding of Israel, is his πνεῦμα-σάρξ dichotomy. This can be derived from the close relationship between the concept of σάρξ and Israel. In 1 Corinthians 10:18, Paul uses the term Ἰσραήλ in close connection with σάρξ (Ἰσραὴλ κατὰ σάρκα). In Romans 9:3, the expression τῶν συγγενῶν μου κατὰ σάρκα is employed in close co-textual proximity to Ἰσραηλίτης in verse 4 and Ἰσραήλ in verse 6. The expression μου τὴν σάρκα in Romans 11:14 also points in this direction. Apart from passages that contain the term Ἰσραήλ (Rom 9:6, 27, 31; 10:19, 21; 11:2, 7, 25, 26; 1 Cor 10:18; 2 Cor 3:7, 13; Gal 6:16; Phil 3:5) and Ἰσραηλίτης (Rom 9:4; 11:1; 2 Cor 11:22), Paul's πνεῦμα-σάρξ dichotomy will be studied for its significance for his conception of identity (Rom 7:5-6; Rom 8:1-16; Gal 5:16-25; 1 Cor 12:12-13; cf. Col 2:11-13).

---

entity's complete form: that perception is the product of complex interactions among various stimuli (cf. Ramsey, *Religious Language*, 23-24).

Scope

While being aware of the dispute about Pauline authorship in respect of Ephesians and Colossians,[95] passages in these epistles[96] will in principle be incorporated within the field of study in addition to the passages occurring in the seven undisputed letters (Rom; 1 Cor; 2 Cor; Gal; Phil; 1 Thess; Phlm).

> 95. While this study concerns aspects of the identity of the Christ-believer in Paul, and by implication touches on "higher" vs. "lower" Christology in Paul's letters, this study might contribute indirectly to the reassessment of some arguments about Pauline authorship in Ephesians and Colossians (cf. Wright, *Fresh Perspective*, 19), even though it will not be a main focus area. An equally important reason why passages in Ephesians and Colossians are included is because many recent Pauline scholars view them as authentically Pauline despite arguments against Pauline authorship. Scholars who argue for the authenticity of Ephesians include the following: Wright, *Faithfulness*, 1:56–61; Gundry, *Survey*; Arnold, *Ephesians*, 50; Johnson, *Writings*, 364; Thielman, *Ephesians*, 5; Köstenberger et al., *Cradle*; Carson and Moo, *Introduction*, 486; Hoehner, *Ephesians*, 2–61; O'Brien, *Ephesians*, 5–47; Boles, *Ephesians*; Bruce, *Colossians*; Roberts, *Efesiërs*, 11–12; Wood, "Ephesians"; Barth, *Ephesians*, 41; Van Roon, *Authenticity of Ephesians*; Guthrie, *Introduction*, 527–28; Hendriksen, *Ephesians*; Foulkes, *Ephesians*. Those who argue for the authenticity of Colossians include the following: Wright, *Faithfulness*, 1:56–61; Gundry, *Survey*; Pao, *Colossians & Philemon*, 23; Johnson, *Writings*, 349; Köstenberger et al., *Cradle*; Moo, *Colossians*, 41; Carson and Moo, *Introduction*, 521; Thompson, *Colossians and Philemon*, 2–5; Garland, *Colossians and Philemon*; Melick, *Philippians*, 165–68; Bruce, *Colossians*; Roberts, *Efesiërs*, 11; O'Brien, *Colossians*; Vaughan, "Colossians"; Kümmel, *Introduction*, 342; Guthrie, *Introduction*, 572–77; Hendriksen, *Colossians*.
>
> 96. While I do not view the debate on authorship on 2 Thessalonians or the Pastoral Epistles as closed, they are not anticipated to contribute substantially to my enquiry, and will thus not form part of the main field of study. While many recent scholars defend Pauline authorship for 2 Thessalonians (e.g., Weima, *Thessalonians*, 83–85; Wright, *Faithfulness*, 1:56–61; Gundry, *Survey*; Shogren, *Thessalonians*, 29; Thiselton, *Thessalonians*; Johnson, *Writings*, 255; Köstenberger et al., *Cradle*; Fee, *Thessalonians*; Witherington, *Thessalonians*; Carson and Moo, *Introduction*, 542; Jones, *Thessalonians*; Nicholl, *Thessalonica*; Beale, *Thessalonians*; Green, *Thessalonians*; Malherbe, *Thessalonians*; 364–74; Martin, *Thessalonians*; Morris, *Thessalonians*, 17–23; Wanamaker, *Thessalonians*, 17–28; Jewett, *Anthropological Terms*, 3–18; Thomas, "2 Thessalonians," 302–3; Kümmel, *Introduction*, 268; Best, *Thessalonians*), the support for the Pastoral Epistles is more varied. Towner, *Timothy and Titus*, 87–88, argues for Pauline authorship with leaving the possibility open that Timothy and Titus may have contributed to the letter. Other scholars who endorse Pauline authorship include the following: Gundry, *Survey*; Köstenberger et al., *Cradle*; Belleville, *1 Timothy*, 8–9; Carson and Moo, *Introduction*, 554–68; Van Neste, "Titus"; Johnson, *Timothy*, 98–99; Mounce, *Pastoral Epistles*; Stott, *1 Timothy and Titus*, 33–34; Guthrie, *Pastoral Epistles*, 64; Oden, *Timothy and Titus*, 15; Fee, *Timothy, Titus*, 25–26; Knight, *Pastoral Epistles*. Prior, *Paul*, 37–39, asserts Pauline authorship in the Pastoral Epistles without an amanuensis, contra the undisputed letters. Although Wright, *Faithfulness*, 1:61 views 2 Timothy as Pauline, he is more hesitant about 1 Timothy and Titus. Occasional references to 2 Thessalonians and the Pastoral Epistles will thus function on a secondary level in this book, normally indicated by "cf."

The reason for including these three letters (Eph; Col) within the broader field of study is to integrate them into the Pauline theological discussion. In a strict sense the discussion about their authenticity will therefore be left open with the aim to reconsider some of the arguments pertaining to their authenticity or inauthenticity. The main focus and weight, however, will rest on the undisputed letters, and will be compared to the patterns of thought that will emerge from Ephesians and Colossians without treating these three letters as being indispensable to the main theses.

Semantic Approach and Selection of Passages

The underlying semantic approach of this study entails that a synchronic approach to language is higher in priority than a diachronic approach,[97] which largely builds on the work of Ferdinand De Saussure.[98] Köstenberger, Merkle, Plummer,[99] Botha[100] and Silva[101] rightly argue that the average speaker or writer is only conscious of the current state of a language and is thus not necessarily aware of how it developed. This would also have been the case with the Bible's first readers. Even if someone is aware of the development of language (e.g., a language professor), it does not necessarily influence the way in which such a person uses language. This approach is, however, not intended to disregard the development of language or concepts through time (diachronic), which will indeed be addressed below, but is based on the understanding that a synchronic approach to Paul's language as of primary importance.

The priority of synchrony above diachrony relates to an understanding of language as a *system* of naming (naming being something differential) rather than language being an *inventory* of naming (language as nomenclature). Words are more than labels that the one speaking or writing attaches to reality. In this understanding, language is not seen as merely a "bag of words," but rather a prism through which a non-linguistic system is viewed. Language creates someone's point of view and comprehension of reality.[102] One important implication of this approach to language is that the relationship between lexical definitions of words and their actual meaning within

---

97. Köstenberger et al., *Going Deeper*, 478–80; Kim, "Greek Study," 56; Wallace, *Grammar*, 4; Botha, *Semeïon*, 131–33; Silva, *Biblical Words*, 35–38; Barr, *Semantics*.

98. De Saussure, *General Linguistics*, 79–95.

99. Köstenberger et al., *Going Deeper*, 479.

100. Botha, *Semeïon*, 131–33.

101. Silva, *Biblical Words*, 35–38.

102. Botha, "Louw & Nida-Woordeboek," 16; Swanepoel, "Literêre Analise," 302–4.

a given text is fluid and dialectical. In the process of exegesis, lexical definitions are therefore not seen as fixed constraints in determining the meaning of certain words in certain texts. Although lexical definitions could help facilitate exegesis, exegetical conclusions in terms of the use of certain terms ultimately prompt a possible reassessment of lexical definitions.

Since Louw and Nida's lexicon is based on a similar approach to language,[103] their arrangement of words under semantic domains and subdomains is helpful in delimiting the appropriate passages to be studied in this book. Their approach is however not without difficulty. One could ask if Louw and Nida's arrangement of semantic domains is not influenced by certain preconceived notions or a western worldview. Since there are no first-century *koine*-Greek speaking individuals available today, an emic representation of a first-century view on reality remains a hermeneutical challenge.[104] Notwithstanding this inherent difficulty, their lexicon based on semantic domains is arguably the most appropriate point of departure in pursuing the Pauline passages pertaining to my enquiry. The actual *terms* occurring under the specific domains should however not be seen as primary with respect to a methodology that aims to gain a deeper understanding in Paul's thought, but rather as being *subjected to meanings or patterns of thought*. In other words, the terms discussed below and the passages that will be attached to these meanings have to be understood against the semantic domains and subdomains in which the terms occur, rather than understanding the terms as *carrying* (all) the meanings, concepts or patterns of thought that are pursued. In a strict sense, the identification of these passages thus has to be understood as both (1) a preliminary step in ascertaining the passages that pertain to identity, and (2) as an incomplete exercise in that Paul's thought on identity may occur in passages that do not contain any of these terms or that Paul's thought on identity overlaps with other concepts in his thought. Notwithstanding these limitations, the aim will be to cover the broadest possible initial scope of research pertaining to identity with the aim of extending the scope as new horizons open.

The procedure in this chapter will be to identify the initial appropriate semantic fields via Louw and Nida's Lexicon, and to supplement their definitions by other lexical definitions and contemporary discussions. The reasoning behind this approach is based on the presupposition that there exists a measure of overlap between the definitions (within the semantic domains)

---

103. See L&N 1:vi–xx.
104. Cf. Botha, "Louw & Nida-Woordeboek," 17.

in Louw and Nida's lexicon and the definitions of the various terms in more conventional lexicons[105] and even theological dictionaries.[106]

As suggested above, the discussion about identity in the Pauline corpus primarily involves passages where the terms Ἰσραήλ and Ἰσραηλίτης occur (Ἰσραήλ: Rom 9:6, 27, 31; 10:19, 21; 11:2, 7, 25, 26; 1 Cor 10:18; 2 Cor 3:7, 13; Gal 6:16; Phil 3:5; Ἰσραηλίτης: Rom 9:4; 11:1; 2 Cor 11:22). While the semantic domains in which Ἰσραήλ and Ἰσραηλίτης occur would serve as preliminary criterion for determining related terms, more specific criteria will be needed in order to identify some of the initial terms within the semantic domains and subdomains to address the problems at hand. While the terms Ἰσραήλ and Ἰσραηλίτης and the domains in which they occur are considered as primary criteria for determining related terms, the secondary criteria can loosely be described as having some bearing on *being part of God's people*, including being part of Israel and/or the believers in Christ. After considering related terms that occur in the same semantic domain as Ἰσραήλ and Ἰσραηλίτης, the next step will be to broaden the scope to other subdomains within the same domains, and lastly to extend the scope to terms in related domains.

In this semantic demarcation, four variables are considered: (1) semantic domains and subdomains (based on L&N), (2) terms relevant to my enquiry within the Pauline corpus, (3) definitions of terms (using L&N as point of departure, and expanded by BDAG and *EDNT*), and (4) the relevant passages within the Pauline corpus.

The semantic approach of this study implies an interrelation of lexical definitions and the actual meaning within the text. This relationship has to be seen as fluid and dialectical: semantic domains and subdomains, including the terms and their definitions (in discussion with lexical definitions and relevant literature), serve as point of departure in order to help facilitate exegesis, yet, the exegetical conclusions ultimately prompt a possible reassessment of lexical definitions.

The semantic domains and subdomains that can be considered as most relevant to my enquiry are the following domains in L&N:

"Names of Persons and Places" (93)

"Persons" (93.1–388)

Ἑβραῖος (93.105)

---

105. E.g., BDAG.
106. E.g., *EDNT*.

Ἰουδαῖος (93.172)

Ἰσραήλ (93.182)

Ἰσραηλίτης (93.183)

All of the above terms are specific titles pertaining to specific identities.

"Groups and Classes of Persons and Members of Such Groups and Classes" (11)

"Socio-Religious" (11.12-54)

λαός (11.12)[107]

ἀδελφός (11.23)

ἀδελφή (11.24)

ἀδελφός (11.25)

ἐκκλησία (11.32)

ἐκκλησία (11.33)

σῶμα (11.34)

οἱ ἐκ περιτομῆς (11.51)

The terms in this subdomain can be divided into the following classes: people who belong to God, whether Judeans or Christ-believers (11.12); fellow Christ-believers (11.23-24); fellow Judeans or countrymen (11.25); a group or groups of Christ-believers (11.32-34); people who insisted on circumcision (11.51).

"Socio-Political" (11.55-89)

υἱοὶ Ἰσραήλ (11.58)

ἔθνος, λαός (11.55)[108]

---

107. It is noteworthy that Paul mostly uses λαός in the context of Old Testament citations (except Rom 11:1, 2), which underlines the connotations derived from the Hebrew עַם. Yet, according to Rom 9:25 the "true λαός" is called from both the Ἰουδαίων and ἐθνῶν (cf. Frankemölle, "λαός," *EDNT*, 2:341).

108. It can be pointed out here that the term λαός in the New Testament is largely determined by its Hebrew counterpart עַם that normally denotes God's people, and ἔθνος in turn, by its Hebrew counterpart גּוֹי, denoting people outside Israel. The Septuagint translates עַם primarily with λαός and גּוֹי with ἔθνος. Yet, especially in the Pauline corpus, as a result of his inclusive gospel of both Judeans and Greeks, these terms (ἔθνος and λαός) are often used interchangeably (as this semantic domain suggests) and neutrally in terms of their relation to being God's people (Walter, "ἔθνος," *EDNT*,

INTRODUCTION

πατριά (11.56)

συμφυλέτης, συγγενής, ἀδελφός (11.57)

πολιτεία (11.67)

The terms in this subdomain denote the following: an ethnic designation (11.58); a socio-political community (11.55); people belonging to the same people group (11.57); a socio-political unit (11.67).

"Kinship Terms" (10)

"Groups and Members of Groups of Persons Regarded as Related by Blood but without Special Reference to Successive Generations" (10.1–13)

γένος, σάρξ (10.1)

σάρξ (earthly descent)[109]

φυλή (10.2)

The terms in this subdomain denote the following: an ethnic group (10.1); earthly decent; a biologically related subgroup or tribe within a nation (10.2).

"Hold a View, Believe, Trust" (31)

"Be a Believer, Christian Faith" (31.102–7)

πιστεύω, πίστις (31.102)

1:382–83). The term λαός, however, is more frequently used in Paul to denote God's people than ἔθνος. Ἔθνος also occurs in the semantic domain 11.37 of Louw and Nida: "those who do not belong to the Jewish or Christian faith—'heathen, pagans.'" Yet, a degree of uncertainty does exist between these two subdomains (11.55 and 11.37), admitted by Louw and Nida. They arguably overlap in Gal 2 and Rom 15 for example. In Eph 3:1, 6, ἔθνος is used in the context of "believing gentiles."

109. BDAG, σάρξ, §4. If "earthly descent" (natural birth) as opposed to "spiritual descent" (spiritual birth) is understood under σάρξ as suggested by BDAG's definition (§4), it seems to fall somewhat outside this particular subdomain (10.1) or any other subdomain provided for σάρξ in L&N. The closest semantic subdomain to "earthly descent" in L&N is probably somewhere between subdomains 9.12 ("human nature, with emphasis upon the physical aspects—'physical nature, human.'") and 58.10 ("human nature, particularly in reference to the physical aspect of human life—'human nature, physical nature of people'"). None of these subdomains exactly denote "earthly *descent*" as such.

"Behavior and Related States" (41)

"Particular Patterns of Behavior" (41:29–43)

ἰουδαΐζω (41.32)

Ἰουδαϊσμός (41.33)

While the terms in subdomain 31.102 (above) are self-explanatory, the terms in subdomain 41.32–33, which pertain to the behavior of the Judeans, are set up for further explanation and clarification.

When one intends to match the Pauline material to the specific subdomains listed above, including the various terms occurring in the particular subdomains, the same terms that occur in other subdomains (not listed above) have to be eliminated. While the latter process inevitably involves a measure of interpretation, the intention is to restrict interpretation to a minimum. When the co-text of the passages containing Ἰσραήλ and Ἰσραηλίτης are considered, the terms that relate to the above subdomains can be listed as will follow shortly. When some leniency is allowed before or after the occurrence of these terms to keep the train of thought intact where appropriate, the following seven passages emerge (terms included):

1. Rom 9–11 (main focus)

    Specific focus areas:

    9:3–8 (Ἰσραήλ, Ἰσραηλίτης, συγγενής, ἀδελφός, σάρξ)

    9:24–31 (Ἰσραήλ, υἱοὶ Ἰσραήλ, Ἰουδαῖος, λαός, πίστις)

    10:1–4 (ἀδελφός, πιστεύω)

    10:6–8 (πίστις)

    10:9–13 (Ἰουδαῖος, πιστεύω)

    10:17 (πίστις)

    10:19–21 (Ἰσραήλ, ἔθνος, λαός)

    11:1–2 (Ἰσραήλ, Ἰσραηλίτης, λαός, φυλή)

    11:7 (Ἰσραήλ)

    11:14 (σάρξ)

    11:20 (πίστις)

    11:25–27 (Ἰσραήλ, ἀδελφός)
2. 1 Cor 10:18 (Ἰσραήλ, σάρξ)
3. 2 Cor 3:5–16 (υἱοὶ Ἰσραήλ)

INTRODUCTION

4. 2 Cor 11:18–24 (Ἰσραηλίτης, Ἑβραῖος, Ἰουδαῖος, σάρξ)
5. Gal 6:7–8, 12–16 (Ἰσραήλ, σάρξ)
6. Eph 2:8–22 (Ἰσραήλ, οἱ ἅγιοι, σῶμα, πίστις)
7. Phil 3:1–9 (Ἰσραήλ, Ἑβραῖος, ἀδελφός, ἐκκλησία, γένος, σάρξ, φυλή, πίστις)

The next step is to identify passages that display a fairly high frequency of terms within the above semantic subdomains, including a few selected passages anticipated to have some bearing on being part of Israel and/or being a Judean, even though some passages might contain a single relevant term. The following passages are identified (allowing some leniency before or after the terms to keep the train of thought intact):

8. Rom 1:16–17 (Ἰουδαῖος, πιστεύω, πίστις)
9. Rom 2:17–29 (Ἰουδαῖος)
10. Rom 4:1–25 (ἔθνος, οἱ ἐκ περιτομῆς, σάρξ, πιστεύω, πίστις)
11. Rom 15:5–13 (ἔθνος, λαός)
12. 1 Cor 1:21–24 (Ἰουδαῖος, πιστεύω)
13. 2 Cor 5:14–21 (σάρξ)
14. Gal 1:11–14, 22–23 (γένος, ἐκκλησία, Ἰουδαϊσμός, πίστις)
15. Gal 2:11–16 (Ἰουδαῖος, οἱ ἐκ περιτομῆς, πιστεύω, ἰουδαΐζω)
16. Gal 3:1–29 (ἔθνος, ἀδελφός, πιστεύω, πίστις)
17. Gal 4:21–5:1 (σάρξ)
18. Col 3:9–15 (Ἰουδαῖος, σῶμα)
19. 1 Thess 2:13–16 (Ἰουδαῖος, συμφυλέτης, ἀδελφός, ἐκκλησία, πιστεύω)
20. Phlm 1:16 (ἀδελφός, σάρξ)

These Scripture passages (8–20) will be considered as secondary, and will not necessarily involve the same depth of study as passages 1 to 7.

Toward a Constraint-Driven Theological Approach

Any term- or category based approach to identity seems to suffer from the general hermeneutical dilemma that exists between today's perception(s) of identity and the perception(s) of identity in New Testament times. Such approaches therefore tend to be subjected to a quagmire of redefinitions or qualifications.[110]

The aim of this study is neither to precisely redefine these or similar terms to express Paul's understanding of identity nor to solve all the hermeneutical dilemmas involved in them. Neither is the aim to coin new terms to address conceptions of identity in Paul. Rather than aiming at finding essential categories or definitions, my approach will be constraint-driven. The aim is to identify the outer constraints[111] wherein a possible Pauline *theology of identity* can be perceived. In a sense these constraints will be employed to draw the outer picture of Paul's perception(s) of being God's people in the light of the work of Christ and his encounter with Christ. In attempting to identify some of these constraints within Paul's thought, Paul's own vocabulary or close equivalents will be utilized as far as possible without trying to reduce these terms in themselves to any essential category. In other words, these constraints will be *described or explained* rather than *labelled*.

Yet, while the aim of my approach is to understand Paul's theological thought and his self-definition of identity, it is not intended as a replacement for approaches that attempt categorization. A Pauline, theological perspective on identity, even though outlined by way of constraints, inevitably ought to influence our understanding and (etic) categorization of the terms we use to describe identity now and in the New Testament, but this is not a primary aim of my approach.

On a theological level, the aim will be to describe Paul's thought more deductively than inductively. In other words, rather than superimposing external models (e.g., social or anthropological theories) onto the text and make Paul's thought fit onto those models, the methodology will lean more toward explaining Paul's thought by the co-text or other Pauline texts. While this will not be done to the exclusion of inductive methodologies, and a dialectic between these two approaches is acknowledged, the approach will thus be more textually immanent than transcendent.

The theological exegesis on each passage will not attempt to be a comprehensive interpretation of all aspects or all possible problem areas within them. The approach is mainly to pursue the constraints in Paul's thought

---

110. The problematic nature of the current terms and categories for identity largely surfaces by this statement of Elliott, "Jesus," 125: "I will then show that specific terms of our current nomenclature are inaccurate, and deny advances in our understanding of ancient social relations within and beyond Israel of the first several centuries of the Common Era."

111. An attempt to draw the outer constraints of identity does not necessarily imply that these constraints are deemed to be broad. They may also be narrow.

pertaining to *being God's people*, and thus to focus on the main questions asked in the layout of the problem areas for this study. While Romans 9 to 11 will constitute the main focus and involve the most attention, the approach will be to interpret this section of Romans with a more profound grasp of Paul's theological understanding of identity at hand as gained through studying other Pauline material. Romans 9 to 11 will thus be subject to the larger pattern in Paul's thought on identity.

Approaching the Pauline Passages Under Three Anticipated Modes of Identity

The larger pattern that Romans 9 to 11 and all other identity-related passages pertaining to being God's people will be subjected to, can be described in terms of three anticipated *modes* of identity[112] that will follow shortly. These three modes of identity are not necessarily to be understood to the exclusion of one another. The aim is therefore not to classify them by essential nomenclature, but rather to describe them by way of constraints derived from Paul's own nomenclature.[113] The three proposed modes of identity are as follows:

A. Israel according to the flesh.

B. Israel as children of the promise and as partakers of election.

C. Believers in Christ as partakers of the new creation and the Spirit.

---

112. On the one side of this notion would be to imply "categories" or "types" of identity (e.g., Wright, "Romans," 448, 688). Yet, the designation "categories of identity" would risk an over emphasis on discontinuity or exclusion of other "modes" of identity and would hold the danger of essentialism. On the other side of this notion would be to imply "aspects of identity," but this term might risk underplaying discontinuity between these "modes" of identity and hold the danger of universalism. While aspects of continuity (and inclusivity) and discontinuity (and exclusivity) are anticipated among these different "modes," as will become clearer later on, the terminology "modes of identity" is intended to retain both aspects.

113. This methodology presupposes a preliminary understanding and thus initial deductions of the passages themselves to be tested later on. Although one could expect this kind of pattern to *follow* exegesis rather than to *precede* it, stylistically, the reader should note that the intention behind the current approach is to integrate a discussion of the various modes of identity within the theological exegesis rather than adding a lengthy process of systematization afterwards that would require the repetition of much of the theological discussion. Additionally, this approach is intended to help the reader to progressively gain insight into the various modes of identity during the course of the study rather than postponing the process and keep the reader wondering right until the end.

Israel according to the flesh (A) can be described as the broadest mode of identity relating to God's people in Paul's letters. This correlates largely to the whole nation of Israel, and can be described as the *outer Israel* (A). Mode B can be understood as *inner Israel*,[114] a mode *within* mode A. Mode A can be described without mode B, but mode B includes mode A. The differentiation between the outer (A) and inner (B) modes is anticipated to correlate mainly to aspects of descent, filiation[115] and election. The aspect of descent mostly relates to *outer Israel* (mode A), and election to *inner Israel* (mode B), with filiation more or less in the middle. Still, all three of these aspects display both inner and outer dimensions, as will become clearer later on.

Since the main focus of this book is on Israel, the main theses of this book are laid out along passages that have some connection to identity modes A and/or B. The third mode of identity that constitutes the identity of the Christ-believer (C) is therefore expected to show both aspects of *continuity* and *discontinuity* with A and/or B. It is expected that passages where faith in Christ is portrayed in *continuity* with Israel's patriarch Abraham would display all modes of identity (ABC), and in passages where the new creation and the indwelling of the Holy Spirit in Christ is set in *discontinuity* with Israel's old identity marked off by outward identity markers, would mainly display identity modes A and C. In other words, the new identity in Christ involves a new set of identity markers, which is anticipated to display both aspects of *continuity* and *discontinuity* with the identity markers of Israel.

The logic behind the proposed chronology of exegesis and the arrangement of the various passages under this pattern is to create a measure of progression, starting with texts that can be grouped under identity mode A, followed by AB, ABC, and then AC. Even though my approach is to align the content of these passages along these anticipated constraints of Paul's thought on identity, a measure of fluidity in the way in which the passages relate to the three modes of identity has to be acknowledged, in some passages probably more so than others. The arrangement of the various passages under A to C therefore is not intended as a watertight classification of the passages under Paul's thought on identity, but rather as an aid to help understand the points of emphasis among the various passages. This methodology in turn has the aim of facilitating a better appreciation for the coherency in Paul's pattern(s) of thought regarding identity.

---

114. Cf. the distinction Cranfield, *Romans*, 2:471, draws between the "general area of election" and the "inner circle of election" (see esp. pp. 45–52).

115. Filiation is to be distinguished from the etic category of "kinship." "Filiation" is intended as a theological term that holds the notion of being "children of," e.g., being "children according to the flesh" or "children of the promise" (Rom 9:8) and correlates to adoption (Rom 9:4).

Based on a preliminary understanding of the various passages as laid out in above, in conjunction with the three proposed modes of identity (A, B, and C), the passages will be dealt with in the following order:

A

Israel according to the flesh

1 Cor 10:18; 2 Cor 11:18–24

AB

Israel according to the flesh and Israel as children of the promise

Rom 9:3–8

Outward and inward Judeans

Rom 2:17–29

ABC

Faith in Christ in continuation with- and as fulfillment of the promises to Abraham

Rom 1:16–17; 4:1–25; Gal 3:1–29; 4:21–5:1; Eph 2:8–22

AC

Faith in Christ in discontinuity with Israel and the Judean

Rom 15:5–13; 1 Cor 1:21–24; Gal 1:11–14, 22–23; 2:11–16; Phil 3:1–9; 1 Thess 2:13–16; Phlm 1:16

The new creation in Christ versus flesh

2 Cor 5:14–21; Col 3:9–15

At this point, the spirit-flesh dichotomy in Paul will be pursued in more depth in order to better understand the role of the Spirit/spirit in identity over against flesh. This will involve assessing other Pauline passages where this theme surfaces: 2 Cor 3:5–16; Rom 7–8; Gal 5:16–18; 1 Cor 12:12–13; Col 2:11–13. The aim of this aspect of the study is to formulate a more precise description of these two aspects (Spirit/spirit and flesh) in terms of their connection to identity.

The two key passages of this book are saved for last, namely Romans 9 to 11 and Galatians 6:7–16, of which Romans 11 will occupy the most space. Romans 9 to 11 can be understood as climactic[116] in the structure and theology of Romans, and Galatians 6:11–16 can be seen as a summary and conclusion of Paul's message(s) in Galatians.[117] As pointed out earlier, the main problems to be addressed in Romans 11 and Galatians 6 are the referent and meaning of the salvation of "all Israel" (Rom 11:26) and "the Israel of God" who is blessed (Gal 6:16) respectively. Both passages are at the end of long treatises of Paul's understanding of his gospel, and build upon the understanding of the preceding co-textual material. In addition, the understanding of these two passages is expected to gain from a deeper understanding of identity in Paul's thought as laid out in all the other Pauline passages. These two passages are anticipated to display all three modes of identity (ABC), especially how Paul's portrayal of the new identity in Christ (C) has to be understood in relation to both the *inner* and *outer* Israel (AB).

---

116. See esp. Wright, *Climax*, who treats Rom 9–11 as the climax of Paul's thought (see p. 233 for others).

117. E.g., Fung, *Galatians*, 300.

2

Israel, Israelites, and Judeans (A and AB)

BEFORE VENTURING INTO THE Pauline passages themselves, a brief introduction on the occurrence of "Israel," "Israelites" and "Judeans" in other texts will serve the purpose of comparing the Pauline usage of these terms with the history and context in which they are employed in order to identify similar or unique aspects in the way Paul employs them.

Israel, Israelites and Judeans in Other Texts[1]

There are two aspects to keep in consideration when the terms "Israel," "Israelite" and "Judean" are considered in texts outside of Paul, namely their (1) historical development, which accounts for a *diachronic* aspect and (2), their meaning in surrounding texts in Paul's time (including the New Testament), which accounts for a *synchronic* aspect.

Diachronic

Von Rad states that יִשְׂרָאֵל ("Israel")[2] was originally a sacred term that denoted "the totality of the elect of Yahweh and of those united in the Yahweh cult. It thus embraces the central beliefs of the league."[3] This ended with David's

---

1. The term עִבְרִי/Ἑβραῖος is not discussed here, for rather than being a prevalent title for identity in Paul's time, the term was a honored title from the distant past. Paul therefore uses Ἑβραῖος in connection with identity only twice within a specific context (2 Cor 11:22, see pp. 41–45; Phil 3:5, see pp. 140–41).

2. Etymologically, יִשְׂרָאֵל consists of אֵל ("God") and שָׂרָה ("to prevail" or "to have power"; cf. BDB, יִשְׂרָאֵל), as explained in Gen 32:28. The name has been interpreted as "He who strives with God" or even "God strives" (Mayer, "Israel," *NIDNTT*, 2:305).

3. Von Rad, "Ἰσραήλ," *TDNT*, 3:357.

monarchy, and the name "Israel" became separated from the southern tribes. As a result of underlying tensions in the Davidic kingdom, the northern tribes later broke away from Rehoboam and formed the kingdom of Israel. The southern tribes returned to a separate existence and formed the kingdom of Judah (a secular, political name) under the Davidic dynasty. With the fall of the northern kingdom and their deportation, in a third phase Israel was adopted by the southern kingdom.[4] The title "Israel" was used as a *spiritual designation* that transcended the house of Judah. This name had deep roots even for the southern kingdom, and signified the people of God.[5]

After the exile, people were even more restricted to the province of Judah, and the people outside this province were non-Israelites.[6] The term יְהוּדִי ("Judean")[7] came into being after the exile. While the name had stronger territorial connotations initially, the territorial component receded and the religious component became predominant, especially with the appearance of proselytes.[8] In the latter sense, יְהוּדִי was used in a more general way for a member of the people of Israel.[9] Both terms (יִשְׂרָאֵל and יְהוּדִי) thus denoted the religious confession of these people, where יִשְׂרָאֵל was

> the fellowship of all those who worship the one true God. Thus this people describes itself as the chosen people, i.e., the people whom the one true God has chosen to worship and confess Him as distinct from the rest of the world.[10]

Mayer connects יִשְׂרָאֵל with God's irrevocable covenant with His people, and His faithfulness, where even His judgment is a part thereof.[11] According to Kuhn, there was a sense in which this right standing with God was inherited and salvation was granted to the believers. Someone else could

---

4. Von Rad, "Ἰσραήλ," *TDNT*, 3:357; cf. Moo, *Romans*, 561; Mayer, "Israel," *NIDNTT*, 2:305. The designation יִשְׂרָאֵל was later appropriated for the southern kingdom (Isa 5:7; 8:18; Mic 2:12; 3:1, 8, 9; 5:1) and the name יַעֲקֹב was transferred from the northern to the southern kingdom (Isa 2:5, 6; 29:22; Mic 2:7; 3:1, 8, 9; 5:6; Nah 2:2).

5. Von Rad, "Ἰσραήλ," *TDNT*, 3:357.

6. Kuhn, "Ἰσραήλ," *TDNT*, 3:359.

7. The term יְהוּדִי ("Judean") is etymologically derived from יְהוּדָה ("Judah"). Gen 29:35 suggests a link between and יְהוּדָה and יָדָה ("give thanks" or "praise") in Leah's remark: "This time I will praise the Lord" (Mayer, "Israel," *NIDNTT*, 2:305). Cf. Paul's play with words on this theme in Rom 2:29 (οὗ ὁ ἔπαινος οὐκ ἐξ ἀνθρώπων ἀλλ' ἐκ τοῦ θεοῦ).

8. Tomson, "Names," 124.

9. Although the term יְהוּדִי was not generally applied to God's people in the Old Testament, there are exceptions (e.g., Zech 8:23; Dan 3:8, 12; Von Rad, "Ἰσραήλ," *TDNT*, 3:358) Cf. the term's use in Nehemia and Esther in terms of indicating any member of the Israelite nation (Moo, *Romans*, 561).

10. Kuhn, "Ἰσραήλ," *TDNT*, 3:359–60.

11. Mayer, "Israel," *NIDNTT*, 2:307.

partake in salvation through faith, but they had to become a member of the people. The distinction between the two terms (יִשְׂרָאֵל and יְהוּדִי) was that יִשְׂרָאֵל signified the name that the people used for themselves, and יְהוּדִי was the non-Judean name for them.¹² Where יִשְׂרָאֵל *always* had a religious connotation pointing to the chosen people of God, יְהוּדִי was also used by non-Judeans and did *not always* carry this connotation. It even had a disrespectful or contemptuous sound on the lips of outsiders.¹³

Gutbrod indicates that the above notion is confirmed by the fact that pagan writers never used the term Ἰσραήλ for the Judean people.¹⁴ In contrast, the Qumran sect who was emphatically inner-Judean used the name "Israel" exclusively.¹⁵ Philo's usage of the term corresponds to the usage of the Old Testament.¹⁶ He used Ἰσραήλ as the "inside" name of his nation, whereas he used Ἰουδαῖος as referent to an adherent of the nation of the Judeans as present in Alexandria.¹⁷

It is significant that the use of Ἰσραηλίτης and Ἰουδαῖοι was largely influenced by the Exile. Ἰσραηλίτης generally described the pre-exilic period and Ἰουδαῖοι was used for people of the second temple.¹⁸ This tendency is especially recognisable with Josephus.¹⁹ Josephus uses Ἰσραηλίτης "for members of the people of God in past days. He does not use it for present members."²⁰ Josephus speaks of Ἰσραηλῖται 188 times in *Antiquities* 2 to 6 when he describes the ancient time, but predominantly employs Ἰουδαῖοι from *Antiquities* 6.6 onward and exclusively from 6.317 right up to the end.²¹ Kuhli writes:

> Ἰσραηλίτης was thus reserved for a part of history that was now closed. Its use by a contemporary Jew must, therefore, have been an archaism limited to specific occasions and rhetorical formulas of address (cf. 4 Macc 18:1).²²

Even Miller seems to admit to the tendency to view the term "Israel" as a term that predominantly denoted God's people of ancient, Old Testament times

---

12. Kuhn, "Ἰσραήλ," *TDNT*, 3:360; cf. Elliott, "Jesus"; Tomson, "Names."
13. Kuhn, "Ἰσραήλ," *TDNT*, 3:360.
14. Gutbrod, "Ἰσραήλ," *TDNT*, 3:371.
15. Tomson, "Names," 139.
16. Gutbrod, "Ἰσραήλ," *TDNT*, 3:372.
17. Tomson, "Names," 137.
18. Kuhli, "Ἰσραηλίτης," *EDNT*, 2:205.
19. Tomson, "Names," 123-24, 137-39; see esp. *Ant.* 11.169-73.
20. Gutbrod, "Ἰσραήλ," *TDNT*, 3:372.
21. Kuhli, "Ἰσραηλίτης," *EDNT*, 2:205.
22. Kuhli, "Ἰσραηλίτης," *EDNT*, 2:205; cf. Jewett, *Romans*, 561-62. 4 Macc 18:1 reads: "O Israelite children, offspring of the seed of Abraham" (NRSV).

when he ascribes the predominance of the term "Israel" in *Jubilees* "to the fact that the storyline in these two books retells ancient Israelite history."[23]

Synchronic

According to the New Testament lexicon of Louw and Nida, the term Ἰσραήλ could have three meanings: (1) "the patriarch Jacob (Ro 9.6)," (2) "the nation of Israel (Matt 2.6)" and (3) "a figurative reference to Christians as the true Israel (Ga 6.16)—'Israel.'"[24] These three meanings closely correspond to those of BDAG.[25] A main focus of this book is to determine whether the third meaning (3) can be established exegetically. There exists some initial uncertainty as to whether the meaning "true Israel" or "Israel as Christ-believers" (meaning 3 above) is warranted in texts like Galatians 6:16 and Romans 11:26, and has to be pursued further exegetically.

Louw and Nida list the term Ἰσραηλίτης under the meaning: "the ethnic name of a person belonging to the nation of Israel—'Israelite' (Acts 2.22)."[26] The term Ἰσραηλίτης does not seem to carry a direct spiritual or religious meaning (as Ἰσραήλ) in the Pauline corpus,[27] but a possible religious connotation cannot be disregarded either.

Louw and Nida list the term Ἰουδαῖος under the meaning: "the ethnic name of a person who belongs to the Jewish nation—'a Jew' (Mark 7.3)."[28] In BDAG Paul's use of Ἰουδαῖος is described as "one who is Judean (Jewish), with focus on adherence to Mosaic tradition, *a Judean*."[29] A possible exception to Paul's use of Ἰουδαῖος as indicated lexicographically, is Romans 2:28–29, where he describes a "true" Judean by way of inward circumcision of the heart in the spirit.[30]

In the Synoptic Gospels, the terms Ἰουδαῖος and Ἰουδαῖοι are rare, and are usually employed in connection with people and land.[31] In the Gospel of John, οἱ Ἰουδαῖοι is the common term for those with whom Jesus has dealings, where the Synoptists normally have ὁ ὄχλος or οἱ ὄχλοι ("multitude/s"), which is less frequent in the Gospel of John. Ἰουδαῖος is never used by the

---

23. Miller, "Other Group Labels," 109.
24. L&N §93.182.
25. BDAG, Ἰσραήλ, §1–3.
26. L&N §93.183; cf. BDAG, Ἰσραηλίτης.
27. Kuhli, "Ἰσραηλίτης," *EDNT*, 2:204–5.
28. L&N §93.172.
29. BDAG, Ἰουδαῖος, §2.
30. Cf. Kuhli, "Ἰουδαῖος," *EDNT*, 2:195; see pp. 54–68.
31. Kuhli, "Ἰουδαῖος," *EDNT*, 2:194; Mayer, "Israel," *NIDNTT*, 2:315.

Synoptists "as a proper name for the people to whom Jesus comes."³² It is significant that the expression βασιλεὺς τῶν Ἰουδαίων is never on Jesus' lips or on the Evangelists' lips themselves.³³ The term Ἰσραήλ is used for the people in the Synoptic Gospels (only used twice in Mark) by themselves, where the emphasis leans toward the religious side. It is often applied as denotation for the people of God (e.g., Matt 15:31; Luke 1:68). For the Judeans, Jesus is βασιλεὺς Ἰσραήλ (Matt 27:42; Mark 15:32—even though spoken in mockery), not βασιλεὺς τῶν Ἰουδαίων. Ἰσραήλ is similarly applied in Messianic context (e.g., Luke 2:25, 32; 24:21), when Jesus finds great faith (Matt 8:10; Luke 7:9), when he indicates that he was sent to the lost sheep of the house of Israel (Matt 10:6; 15:24), or where Jesus indicates that the disciples will judge the twelve tribes of Israel (Matt 19:28).³⁴ For Luke, the Judean people almost become those who refuse to believe in Jesus.³⁵ It is remarkable how the author of both Luke and Acts who probably was a non-Judean, "faithfully preserved the speech duality typical of Jewish texts."³⁶

In the Gospel of John, after Jesus was asked whether he was the king of the Judeans (18:33), he virtually denies this title by answering (v. 36) that his kingdom is not of this world. Gutbrod describes Ἰουδαῖος in John as "a matter of national and temporal remoteness," which provides the possibility of a Ἰουδαῖος who believes in Jesus (8:31; 11:45; 12:11).³⁷ In John, the Ἰουδαῖοι are often those who refuse to believe in Jesus and oppose him.³⁸ The term Ἰσραήλ occurs only four times in the Gospel, but is applied in a fixed sense, where Ἰσραήλ is the people of God as a whole.³⁹ Relation to Israel implies a relationship to God. Nathanael who is called an ἀληθῶς Ἰσραηλίτης (1:47), has to be understood in the same manner. Israel as God's people need not be understood as the living members of the day, but "almost as a supratemporal entity."⁴⁰ There is thus a bigger contrast between the terms Ἰουδαῖος and Ἰσραήλ in John.⁴¹

32. Gutbrod, "Ἰσραήλ," *TDNT*, 3:375; cf. Kuhli, "Ἰουδαῖος," *EDNT*, 2:194.

33. Kuhli, "Ἰουδαῖος," *EDNT*, 2:194. See e.g. Matt 2:2, where the question "Ποῦ ἐστιν ὁ τεχθεὶς βασιλεὺς τῶν Ἰουδαίων;" is asked by a foreigner (Gutbrod, "Ἰσραήλ," *TDNT*, 3:375).

34. Gutbrod, "Ἰσραήλ," *TDNT*, 3:384–85.

35. Eltester, "Israel," 119.

36. Tomson, "Names," 280.

37. Gutbrod, "Ἰσραήλ," *TDNT*, 3:378.

38. Gutbrod, "Ἰσραήλ," *TDNT*, 3:378–79; cf. Kuhli, "Ἰουδαῖος," *EDNT*, 2:195–96; Tomson, "Names," 281–83, 287.

39. Mayer, "Israel," *NIDNTT*, 2:315; Gutbrod, "Ἰσραήλ," *TDNT*, 3:385.

40. Gutbrod, "Ἰσραήλ," *TDNT*, 3:385.

41. Kuhli, "Ἰσραήλ," *EDNT*, 2:203.

In Acts, Ἰουδαῖος is used in a very similar way as in the Gospel of John. They are the inhabitants of Palestine and members of this religious community. The religious connotation varies in individual passages. They are committed to the law (10:28) and circumcision (16:3; 9:22; 18:28; 22:12). The Ἰουδαῖοι can oppose the preaching of Christ as in the Gospel of John (9:23; 12:11; 13:50; 17:5, 13; etc.) but this negative aspect is not inseparably linked to the term. There are Judeans who believe (14:2).[42] Although Ἰουδαῖος occurs as a self-designation in Luke's account of Paul's speech to Rome (21:39; 22:3), the fact that Romans (outsiders) among others are addressed, might accout for this usage. The term Ἰσραήλ is dominant in the first part of Acts, and Ἰουδαῖος in the second. Ἰσραήλ denotes the members of the people of God. They are called upon to recognize Jesus as the Christ (2:36; 4:10; 13:24).[43] There is therefore continuity between Ἰσραήλ and belief in Christ, especially in 13:23, where Jesus is identified as descendant of David and Savior in Paul's speech, and thus the fulfillment of the promise to Israel (2 Sam 7:12; 22:51).[44] The designation Ἰσραηλῖται is mostly used in the context of presenting the gospel to the Old Testament people, signifying a transitional situation (2:22; 3:12; 5:35; 13:16).[45]

In Revelation, Ἰουδαῖος is used twice in a pejorative context (2:9; 3:9) of imposters that masqueraded as Judeans, but lied and are called a συναγωγὴ τοῦ Σατανᾶ. In the context of the persecution of the believers in Christ, these people were probably Judeans who were antagonistic toward the Christ-believing community(ies) in that they rejected Jesus as the Messiah.[46] Ἰσραήλ is used in historical (2:14) and eschatological context where the twelve tribes of Israel feature (7:4; 21:12).[47] Despite the interpretative uncertainty of the symbolic imagery in the latter two references, Israel points to the historical nation of the Old Testament.[48]

42. Gutbrod, "Ἰσραήλ," *TDNT*, 3:379–80.

43. Gutbrod, "Ἰσραήλ," *TDNT*, 3:386.

44. Cf. Kistemaker, *Acts*, 474–75. Gutbrod, "Ἰσραήλ," *TDNT*, 3:386, when he refers to Acts 13:23 (which is erroneously indicated as 12:23), he argues that there "is more than agreement; there is identity" between "the people of the past" and "present Israel"—of which the latter is seemingly the Israel of that day. This interpretation however does not seem to be completely warranted by the context. The Savior of Israel can be interpreted salvation-historically, making "Israel" correspond to God's people of the Old Testament for whom God fulfilled His promise.

45. In 21:28 the term is on the lips of the Ἰουδαῖοι who reacted against Paul's gospel and wanted the people to retain their heritage.

46. Patterson, *Revelation*, 107, 139–40; Kistemaker, *Revelation*, 123–24; Roloff, *Revelation*, 48, 61, 78.

47. Cf. Mayer, "Israel," *NIDNTT*, 2:315.

48. Casurella, "Israel," *DLNT*, 542.

In approaching Paul's use of the terms Ἰσραήλ, Ἰσραηλίτης and Ἰουδαῖος, three distinctions thus apply:

1. J. H. Elliott argues that Ἰουδαῖος in the New Testament can mostly be viewed as an "outsider term"[49] over against Ἰσραήλ and Ἰσραηλίτης as mostly "insider terms."[50] For Elliott[51] the term Ἰσραήλ seems to reflect "self-identifiers when ingroup Israelites are addressing one another," in contrast to Ἰουδαῖος that largely reflects outsider language.[52] Tomson goes so far as stating that the designations "Jew" and "Israel" signal "different social identities: an 'outside' identity as a Jew in regard to the ancient world of nations, or alternatively, an 'inside' identity as one belonging to the 'people of Israel.'"[53] By borrowing from Kuhn,[54] Miller, however, questions Tomson's approach and points out that although outsiders only used Ἰουδαῖος to denote Judean people, Ἰουδαῖος was also used as a self-designation (e.g., 2 Macc 1:1–10; 8:32; 10:8; 3 Macc 4:21; Greek inscriptions).[55] Yet, even if Ἰουδαῖος as a self-designation is acknowledged outside the New Testament, it does not necessary follow that it was used in the New Testament in such a manner. While I generally accept the insider-outsider distinctions as proposed by Elliott[56] in terms of their use in the New Testament, including Paul, there is no need for these distinctions to be set in stone. Even Elliott does not set these distinctions in stone either:

---

49. Elliott, "Jesus," 123. Ἰουδαῖοι as an outsider designation for people associated with the land of Ἰουδαία, Jerusalem and the temple was especially prevalent in the Diaspora. Diaspora Israelites did accommodate the term Ἰουδαῖοι as a self-designation when addressing outsiders, and occasionally insiders. "Often, however, even in the Diaspora, as Paul demonstrates, preference for 'Israel' and 'Israelite' remained strong" (149). This corresponds to the Hebrew יִשְׂרָאֵל which "the people uses for itself," and יְהוּדִי which is "the non-Jewish name for it" (Kuhn, "Ἰσραήλ," TDNT, 3:360).

50. Elliott, "Jesus," 143; cf. Tomson, "Names," 120. Elliott, "Jesus," 129, disconnects the term Ἰουδαῖος from the mouth of Jesus and especially renders the term "king of the Ἰουδαίων" as an outsider definition (Matt 2:2; 27:11, 29, 37; Mark 15:2, 9, 12, 18, 26; Luke 23:3, 37, 38; John 18:33, 39; 19:3, 19, 21). This is strengthened by Jesus' referral to Ἰσραήλ in Matt 10:6 and 15:24 and the absence of Jesus appropriating the term Ἰουδαῖος (139).

51. Elliott, "Jesus," 129–30.

52. Similarly, Von Rad, "Ἰσραήλ," TDNT, 3:359, states: "Israelites also use it ["Israel"] of themselves in distinction from foreigners."

53. Tomson, "Names," 120.

54. Kuhn, "Ἰσραήλ," TDNT, 3:363–65.

55. Miller, "Other Group Labels," 100; cf. Dunn, Romans, 1:109.

56. Elliott, "Jesus."

The New Testament writings present a less uniform picture in regard to use of the terms Ἰσραήλ, Ἰσραηλίτης and Ἰουδαῖος as identifiers. On the whole, however, they manifest a continued preference for 'Israel' as chief self-designation, especially in Israelite insider-to-insider discourse.[57]

2. A more import distinction in connotation between the terms Ἰσραήλ and Ἰουδαῖος is arguably the religious-ethnic distinction. In Paul, the term Ἰσραήλ generally has stronger religious connotations whereas the term Ἰουδαῖος has stronger ethnic connotations. Kuhli states:

> It is indisputable that Ἰσραήλ has in Paul a specific religious meaning in comparison with Ἰουδαῖος. This fact is especially apparent in the distribution of both words in Romans, where chs. 1–8 use Ἰουδαῖος exclusively and from ch. 9 on Ἰσραήλ is consistently used.[58]

In a similar fashion, Campbell writes:

> When Paul uses the term [Israel] he is not using it simply as a general designation of those claiming physical descent from Abraham. Rather he uses it to designate them as the people of the covenant made with Abraham . . . One gets the impression that when Paul wants to stress ethnic affiliation, he uses the term Jew, but when he comes to reflect upon their spiritual heritage, Israel/Israelite alone can clearly designate this people as a religious entity.[59]

3. Apart from isolated passages in the writings of the Apostolic Fathers where the terms Ἰσραήλ and Ἰσραηλίτης are applied to ancient, historical Israel,[60] these terms hardly feature in Christian or fringe Christian writings until the middle of the second century (esp. Josephus).[61] They do not make much at all from literal Israel or the twelve tribes.[62] The term Ἰσραήλ was the first time applied to Christians in 160 CE when Justin stated: "We are . . . the true spiritual Israel."[63] There is thus a ten-

---

57. Elliott, "Jesus," 136–37.
58. Kuhli, "Ἰσραήλ," *EDNT*, 2:204.
59. Campbell, "Israel," *DPL*, 441.
60. Clement (1 Clem. 29.2–3) quotes Deut 32:8–9 from the Septuagint when he writes about how God elected historical, ethnic Israel. The Epistle of Barnabas urges its readers to understand the meaning of the OT text and Israel from the perspective of the church, often typologically (Casurella, "Israel," *DLNT*, 543; Mayer, "Israel," *NIDNTT*, 2:316).
61. Kuhli, Ἰσραηλίτης, *EDNT*, 2:205.
62. Casurella, "Israel," *DLNT*, 543.
63. *Dial.* 11.5; cf. 100.4; 123.9; Mayer, "Israel," *NIDNTT*, 2:316; Richardson, *Israel*, 12.

dency in Christian literature to apply the terms Ἰσραήλ and Ἰσραηλίτης to ancient, historical Israel, while the term Ἰουδαῖος is applied to Judeans in the time of the New Testament and the time of the early church, largely conforming to post-exilic distinctions (see above). This tendency even corresponds to the notion in common English today "to reserve 'Israelite' for the people of the Hebrew Bible, and 'Jew' for people of the last two millennia."[64]

If these distinctions between Ἰσραήλ/Ἰσραηλίτης and Ἰουδαῖος can be maintained (especially the latter two) in Paul, Gager's juxtaposition of "pro-Israel" and "anti-Israel" texts in Paul[65] (see above) becomes problematic and seems to suffer from misnaming. The above three distinctions between these terms will serve as *initial constraints* in approaching these terms in the Pauline corpus,[66] while guarding against making these distinctions too watertight. The ultimate difference among Paul's usages of these terms has to be determined exegetically.

Israel According to the Flesh (A)

This section marks the start of the main theological-exegetical body of this study, and represents the passages pertaining to identity mode A: Israel according to the flesh (1 Cor 10:18; 2 Cor 11:18–24).[67] These two passages are considered to display this mode of identity the clearest without implying much of the other modes.

1 Corinthians 10:18

This verse is set in the context of the practice of communion in the body of Christ (10:15–22), which might imply a contrast between Israel according to the flesh and believers in Christ. Yet, this verse is listed here, for Ἰσραὴλ κατὰ σάρκα seems to function here marginally[68] as a mere title for the people in the desert Paul is referring to without elaboration on its meaning or an explicit contrast to belief in Christ.

---

64. Langer, "Jewish Understandings," 257.
65. Gager, *Reinventing*, 5–7.
66. Cf. Elliott, "Jesus," 140–46.
67. See pp. 27–30.
68. Gutbrod, "Ἰσραήλ," *TDNT*, 3:387.

A popular interpretation on Paul's use of Ἰσραὴλ κατὰ σάρκα is that it implies an Ἰσραὴλ κατὰ πνεῦμα as counterpart.[69] Some interpreters go even further and, apart from implying an "Israel according to the Spirit," contrast "Israel according to the flesh" here to the church. It is argued that "our fathers" in verse 1 would point to the church as joint heirs of Israel that would correspond to an implied "Israel according to the Spirit" in verse 18.[70] Kistemaker (*First Epistle*, 345) interprets the phrase to indicate that the Israel Paul is referring to "lacked spirituality."

Even though one might want to contrast Ἰσραὴλ κατὰ σάρκα with a possible Ἰσραὴλ κατὰ πνεῦμα or understand Ἰσραὴλ κατὰ σάρκα with a negative connotation about their spirituality on the basis of Paul's dichotomy of σάρξ and πνεῦμα, the notion to construe an "Israel according to the Spirit/spirit" too hastily apart from a deeper understanding of Ἰσραὴλ in Paul, calls for caution, especially because of the fact that Paul never explicitly connects Ἰσραὴλ to πνεῦμα as such.[71] Ciampa and Rosner seem to take a safer route when they make a distinction between the

> Judaism which found its identity in the Jerusalem cult and believers who considered themselves the true heirs of Israel (and whom Paul elsewhere refers to as the true circumcision [Rom. 2:28-29], or the children of the Jerusalem above rather than the present Jerusalem [Gal. 4:25-26]).[72]

They connect this distinction to the distinction in the Old Testament between the "faithful remnant" and the citizens of Israel "who were considered unqualified as true members of God's covenant people."[73]

Still, even though Ἰσραὴλ κατὰ σάρκα can be rendered merely as the "earthly Israel,"[74] "the earthly nation . . . to which each belongs by natural descent,"[75] or historical Israel,[76] "some negativity may be implied in Paul's

---

69. E.g., Elliott, "Jesus," 141; Boyarin, *Radical Jew*, 74; Fee, *Corinthians*, 470.

70. Witherington, *Corinth*, 218.

71. Schweizer, "σάρξ," *TDNT*, 7:127; cf. Kuhli, "Ἰσραήλ," *EDNT*, 2:204; Mayer, "Israel," *NIDNTT*, 2:312.

72. Ciampa and Rosner, *Corinthians*, 477.

73. Ciampa and Rosner, *Corinthians*, 477-78.

74. BDAG, σάρξ, §4; Conzelmann, *1 Corinthians*, 172.

75. Schweizer, "σάρξ," *TDNT*, 7:127; cf. Thiselton, *Corinthians*, 771; Fee, *Corinthians*, 470.

76. Perkins, *First Corinthians*, 127; Collins, *First Corinthians*, 380; Horsley, *1 Corinthians*, 141; Sand, "σάρξ," *EDNT*, 3:231; Tomson 1986, "Names," 285; Conzelmann, *1 Corinthians*, 172; Barrett, *First Epistle*, 235; Pop, *Eerste Brief*, 213.

use of this term [Ἰσραὴλ κατὰ σάρκα]."⁷⁷ An implicit contrast to "true Israel" (Rom 4:1; 9:3) or even "the Israel of God" (Gal 6:16) is not impossible.⁷⁸ However, this notion does not necessitate a contrast between Ἰσραὴλ κατὰ σάρκα and belief in Christ. Fitzmyer is thus probably right when he states that Ἰσραὴλ κατὰ σάρκα is "ethnic or historical-empirical Israel of old, which Paul will distinguish in Rom 9:6 from those who are truly 'Israel,' the people of God in the OT."⁷⁹ Fitzmyer's contrast of Ἰσραὴλ κατὰ σάρκα with "Christians" as such⁸⁰ may however be reading too much into the text.⁸¹

That ancient Israel of the Old Testament is at stake, is confirmed by the context of 1 Corinthians 10. It starts with a reference to "our fathers" (v. 1), involving the "baptism" into Moses. In verse 7 the congregation is admonished not to be idolaters "as some of them were," pointing to historical Israel. The things that happened to them should serve as example and as an instruction for the congregation (v. 11). On the basis of these examples, Paul instructs them to flee from idolatry (v. 14). After referring to Lord's Supper (vv. 16–17), Paul then reverts back to ancient, historical Israel in verse 18. The idea that if they would eat the sacrifices they would be participants in the altar, is probably based on Leviticus 3:3 and 7:15.

In conclusion, Ἰσραὴλ κατὰ σάρκα in 1 Corinthians 10:18 can be considered as denoting the historical Israel of the Old Testament as a national, ethnic entity, in contrast to connotations about their faith, their state of heart, or the authenticity of their relationship with God.

2 Corinthians 11:18–24

This passage forms part of a larger section about Paul's suffering for the gospel (11:16–33). These verses probably indicate a reaction to some people in the congregation that questioned his apostleship (cf. 11:5), and form part of his defense of authority. Paul here sarcastically[82] or by "play[ing] the fool,"[83]

---

77. Collins, *First Corinthians*, 380; cf. Gutbrod, "Ἰσραήλ," *TDNT*, 3:387.

78. BDAG, σάρξ, §4.

79. Fitzmyer, *First Corinthians*, 392.

80. Fitzmyer, *First Corinthians*, 392.

81. While this notion is not considered as impossible, the same caution has to be applied here as by construing a possible Ἰσραὴλ κατὰ πνεῦμα as counter-concept (see above). It would be safer to be constrained by Paul's own thought on the concept of Ἰσραὴλ elsewhere (esp. Rom 11) than to construe too much from an argument of silence.

82. Matera, *II Corinthians*, 257.

83. Kistemaker, *Second Epistle*, 377.

turns to boasting (vv. 16–17) about his own heritage. This is in reaction to some within the congregation that boasted in their own external appearance (2 Cor 5:12),[84] which is equivalent to many that boast κατὰ σάρκα ("according to the flesh") here in 11:18.[85] In the same line of thought, Schweizer interprets the expression as boasting in which people have regard only to what may be seen and what counts with human beings.[86]

Focusing on external qualities like pedigree or descent would certainly be an aspect of this type of boasting. In this sense, the similarity to Ἰσραὴλ κατὰ σάρκα (1 Cor 10:18) is clear. In this context (2 Cor 11:18), κατὰ σάρκα thus can be rendered as "according to earthly descent."[87] The expression has been contrasted to κατὰ κύριον, parallel to the "foolishness" (ἀφροσύνη) of the boasting in verse 17,[88] without necessarily excluding the notions of "wealth, birth, or ancestry," which Chrysostom connected to κατὰ σάρκα here.[89] Lenski summarizes the general notion when he states: "'The flesh' sums up all such externals and non-essentials"[90] (cf. πρόσωπον in 2 Cor 5:12).

Paul indirectly gives an indication as to what his opponents[91] would typically boast about according to the flesh in verse 22 when he confirms his own pedigree in three expressions: Ἑβραῖος, Ἰσραηλίτης, and σπέρμα Ἀβραάμ.[92] There seems to be an ascending order in the three expressions Paul uses, "moving from racial purity, to religious identity, to Abrahamic descent."[93]

In the Bible, the term "Hebrew" is first mentioned in Genesis 14:13, where Abraham is called הָעִבְרִי ("the Hebrew").[94] According to the Egyp-

---

84. This is the notion of those boasting ἐν προσώπῳ and not in the heart in 2 Cor 5:12 (BDAG, πρόσωπον, §4).

85. Cf. κατὰ σάρκα στρατευόμεθα ("walking according to the flesh") in 2 Cor 10:3.

86. Schweizer, "σάρξ," *TDNT*, 7:130–31; cf. BDAG, σάρξ, §5.

87. BDAG, σάρξ, lists the meaning of κατὰ σάρκα in 2 Cor 11:18 under both §4 ("human/ancestral connection, *human/mortal nature, earthly descent*") and §5 ("the outward side of life as determined by normal perspectives or standards").

88. Cf. Harris, *Second Epistle*, 782; Furnish, *II Corinthians*, 496.

89. Thrall, *Corinthians*, 2:715; John Chrysostom, "Corinthians."

90. Lenski, *Corinthians*, 1262.

91. Paul identifies his opponents as "super apostles" (τῶν ὑπερλίαν ἀποστόλων) in 11:5 and 12:11, and those who masquerade as apostles of Christ (μετασχηματιζόμενοι εἰς ἀποστόλους Χριστοῦ) in 11:13 (Kistemaker, *Second Epistle*, 360–61; cf. Furnish, *II Corinthians*, 502–3).

92. Cf. Phil 3:5, albeit with variation in terminology (see pp. 135–47).

93. Matera, *II Corinthians*, 263.

94. The etymology of this word is uncertain. It denoted a people of equal standing without regard to their ethnic heritage and without a permanent home, who

tians, the term Ἑβραῖος indicated an offspring from Jacob.⁹⁵ Later on the term was applied as an honored title from the distant past rather than the "derogatory or even contemptuous" term Ἰουδαῖος.⁹⁶ In general, the term Ἑβραῖος denotes a Judean who retained their national language⁹⁷ and customs,⁹⁸ and signifies racial purity⁹⁹ distinct from proselytes.¹⁰⁰ Yet, Ἑβραῖος can simply denote Hebrew speaking Israelites over against Greek speaking Israelites,¹⁰¹ or Judeans of Palestinian descent (Acts 6:1).¹⁰² But in this context it seems more probable that Paul wants to confirm his ability to speak Hebrew/Aramaic together with the fact that he is a full Judean by birth and ancestry.¹⁰³

According Genesis 32:28, the patriarch Jacob was renamed יִשְׂרָאֵל ("Israel").¹⁰⁴ The association of Israel with being descendants of the patriarch is prominent in the New Testament (e.g., Luke 1:16; Acts 5:21; Rom 9:27; 2 Cor 3:7).¹⁰⁵ Technically, Jacob's offspring included the Samaritans, yet only the Judeans were called "Israelites."¹⁰⁶ The most likely connotation to Paul's use of the term Ἰσραηλίτης here, is that Paul identifies himself as

---

contractually entered the settled population. They penetrated the arable land. The word "Hebrew" was thus used by other people in old stories, even sometimes in a derogatory or self-deprecating manner (Mayer, "Israel," *NIDNTT*, 2:305).

95. Kistemaker, *Second Epistle*, 385.

96. Kuhn, "Ἰσραήλ," *TDNT*, 3:367–68; cf. Kistemaker, *Second Epistle*, 385–86.

97. This is not beyond dispute though. An inscription "συναγωγή Ἑβραίων" ("Synagogue of the Hebrews") in Corinth indicates that Ἑβραῖος might have been used as a self-identification of Greek speaking Judeans in the Diaspora (Thrall, *Corinthians*, 2:725; Kruse, *Corinthians*, 194). The difference between Palestinian and Diaspora Judeans must thus not be exaggerated (Hengel, *Judaea*, and others—see Harris, *Second Epistle*, 794).

98. Harris, *Second Epistle*, 794; Tomson, "Names," 128; Plummer, *Corinthians*, 319; Bernard, "Corinthians," *EGT*, 3:105; cf. Mayer, "Israel," *NIDNTT*, 2:309.

99. Matera, *II Corinthians*, 263; Kruse, *Corinthians*, 194.

100. Furnish, *II Corinthians*, 514.

101. BDAG, Ἑβραῖος, §1.

102. Harris, "2 Corinthians," 390; Gutbrod, "Ἰσραήλ," *TDNT*, 3:389.

103. Thrall, *Corinthians*, 2:730.

104. Von Rad, "Ἰσραήλ," *TDNT*, 3:356, views the transfer of the name of the patriarch as a secondary process after the tradition constituted by the sacral league of the twelve tribes, narrated in Jos 24.

105. Kuhli, Ἰσραήλ, *EDNT*, 2:203.

106. Cf. Matt 10:5–6, where Jesus advised his disciples not to enter a town from the Samaritans, but to go the "the lost sheep of Israel" (Kistemaker, *Second Epistle*, 386).

a member of God's chosen people[107] as part of his *heritage*.[108] This would accord with a long tradition of viewing the term (Ἰσραηλίτης) as designating the people of God.[109]

The expression σπέρμα Ἀβραάμ ("seed of Abraham") can technically be broader than the previous two, for it can include the offspring of Isaac, Ishmael, and Keturah (Gen 25:1-6; 12-18).[110] But this connotation seems unlikely for the fact that (1) Paul is bringing the terms (all three) nearer to being a servant of Christ (v. 23), which constitutes progression,[111] and (2) that Paul uses σπέρμα Ἀβραάμ elsewhere in connection with *inner* Israel (Rom 9:7, see pp. 51-52) or faith in Christ (Rom 4:13, 16, 18; Gal 3:29). A connotation to faith in Christ or even being part of *inner* Israel is, however, not present here, for Paul shares these identity markers with his opponents. In this context, σπέρμα Ἀβραάμ primarily denotes physical descent from Abraham and probably that Paul shares in the promises that God made to Abraham,[112] which included the Messianic promises (cf. Rom 9:4-5, see pp. 48-49).[113]

When Paul (v. 23) asks whether his opponents are servants of Christ (διάκονοι Χριστοῦ), this designation is treated in a similar fashion to the other titles that constituted Paul's opponents' boasting in externalities (κατὰ σάρκα in v. 18), and thus does not have a direct bearing on being a Christ-believer. This designation was rather a disguise and "one of the self-designations of Paul's rivals,"[114] and might have had to do with making a claim on meeting or knowing Christ in person before his ascension.[115]

In verse 24, Paul introduces a fourth term in close proximity to the three honored titles that constituted his heritage (v. 22),[116] namely Ἰουδαῖοι,[117] but in a negative context, which suggests that Ἰουδαῖος does

---

107. Harris, *Second Epistle*, 795; Matera, *II Corinthians*, 263; Thrall, *Corinthians*, 2:727; Furnish, *II Corinthians*, 514; Plummer, *Corinthians*, 320.

108. Cf. Dunn, "Paul Think," 193.

109. Cf. Von Rad, "Ἰσραήλ," *TDNT*, 3:357.

110. Kistemaker, *Second Epistle*, 387.

111. Cf. Matera, *II Corinthians*, 263; Plummer, *Corinthians*, 320.

112. Harris, *Second Epistle*, 795; Matera, *II Corinthians*, 263-64; Thrall, *Corinthians*, 2:727-29; Kruse, *Corinthians*, 195; Furnish, *II Corinthians*, 514; Barrett, *Second Epistle*, 293-94; Plummer, *Corinthians*, 320.

113. Plummer, *Corinthians*, 320; Bernard, "Corinthians," *EGT*, 3:105; cf. Matera, *II Corinthians*, 263.

114. Harris, *Second Epistle*, 796.

115. Cf. Furnish, *II Corinthians*, 535.

116. Cf. Dunn, "Paul Think," 193.

117. This is the first and only time Paul uses this term in 2 Cor (apart from a

not carry the same value as the other three for Paul. Here the word might imply "the opposition to Christ which these people have displayed in their actions."[118] Paul's use of Ἰουδαῖος here seems to correspond to the distinction that Elliott makes between Ἰουδαῖος as mostly an outsider term and Ἰσραήλ as mostly an insider term of self-identification[119] (see above). This is probably the reason why Paul does not use the term in verse 22 when he gives an account of his own heritage.

In the context of 2 Corinthians 11, all four titles, even though applied in positive and negative contexts (positive: Ἑβραῖος, Ἰσραηλίτης, and σπέρμα Ἀβραάμ; negative: Ἰουδαῖος), can be described as titles Paul uses to describe physical heritage or ethnic membership of a people,[120] without direct connotations of faith or devoutness to God, in other words, "according to the flesh" (v. 18).

Israel According to the Flesh and Israel as Children of the Promise (AB)

The next mode of identity to be explored is identity mode B: Israel as children of the promise and as partakers of election, or to invoke the terms introduced earlier, identity mode AB.[121] Although Romans 9 to 11 will be dealt with later, the modes of identity in Romans 9:3-8 will be addressed here in order to help define identity mode AB more precisely in relation to identity mode A.

Romans 9:3-8

In 9:3-8, Paul will lay out specific distinctions about the identity of Israel that will prove to be key in comprehending his salvation-historical exposition that formally ends in 11:32.[122] Paul expects close attention to the distinctions he draws in the opening part of his exposition, which will be the building blocks of his eventual conclusions. In other words, everything in 9:3-8 has to be kept in mind and serves as reference to the scenario's that will

---

reference to the geographical Ἰουδαία in 1:16).

118. Gutbrod, "Ἰσραήλ," *TDNT*, 3:381.

119. Elliott, "Jesus," 140-46.

120. Collins, *Second Corinthians*, 229; Danker, *II Corinthians*, 181.

121. As previously mentioned, identity mode B implies identity mode A (see pp. 27-30).

122. Cf. Longenecker, *Introducing Romans*, 412, and Moo, *Romans*, 564-65, who see 9:5-11:28 as an "inclusio" that surrounds Paul's discussion.

be playing out toward the end of this whole diachronic, salvation-historical scene portrayed by Romans 9 to 11.

Kindred According to the Flesh and Their Eight Privileges (vv. 3-5)

Similar to 1 Corinthians 10:18 and 2 Corinthians 11:18 (see above), κατὰ σάρκα in verse 3 denotes the whole nation of Israel by natural, earthly descent[123] or blood relationship,[124] and in this case, those of his kindred who do not believe in Christ.[125] The latter constitutes part of the reason for his sorrow and anguish (v. 2) for them and Paul's desire for them to accept Christ, as will come to the forefront later on (e.g., 10:1; 11:14). Yet his anguish might in addition point to something deeper, as will come to the surface as Paul progresses in his exposition.

It is noteworthy that Paul introduces in verse 4 the designation Ἰσραηλίτης (in this case the plural Ἰσραηλῖται) for the first time in the letter to the Romans. The terms Ἰσραηλίτης and Ἰσραήλ only occur in chapters 9 to 11. It can be argued that Paul is drawing the circle closer, starting with more outsider terminology (mostly Ἰουδαῖοι in 1-8) to more insider terminology (Ἰσραηλίτης and Ἰσραήλ) here in 9 to 11.[126] As will become more clear later on, it is of even further significance that Paul refers to his kindred according to the flesh as Ἰσραηλῖται (v. 4) and not Ἰσραήλ (v. 6) where he provides a more precise distinction (see below).

Even while the designation Ἰσραηλίτης can be considered an insider term for the people of God[127] of the Old Testament, the privileges of being an Ἰσραηλίτης that Paul will soon be highlighting (vv. 4-5), can all be understood as identity markers of the identity κατὰ σάρκα (v. 3), identity mode A, the *outer Israel*.[128] From the content of these privileges and the context (esp. vv. 9-17) it can be derived that Paul primarily has *historical*

---

123. BDAG, σάρξ, §4.

124. Zerwick and Grosvenor, *Grammatical Analysis*, 479.

125. Hultgren, *Romans*, 356; Jewett, *Romans*, 561; Moo, *Romans*, 559; cf. Wright, "Romans," 627.

126. Cf. Jewett, *Romans*, 562; Kuhli, Ἰσραήλ, *EDNT*, 2:204.

127. Elliott, "Jesus," 123; Jewett, *Romans*, 562; Dunn, *Romans*, 2:526.

128. Cf. Wright, "Romans," 629; Moo, *Romans*, 559-60; Gutbrod, "Ἰσραήλ," *TDNT*, 3:386-87.

Israelites in mind,¹²⁹ although unbelieving Judeans in Paul's present would stand in continuity with them.¹³⁰

To these Ἰσραηλῖται (κατὰ σάρκα) belong the following eight privileges (vv. 4-5):

1. *The adoption* (ἡ υἱοθεσία). In line with Paul's anguish (v. 2) and the fact that he appeals to his kindred κατὰ σάρκα (v. 3), the adoption (literally "sonship") here "must mean something different than the adoption of Christians in chap. 8."¹³¹ God's adoption here "conveys to that nation all the rights and privileges included within the Old Covenant."¹³² Contra Jewett,¹³³ this filiation or mode of being part of God's people is not the same as being "children of the promise" (v. 8) and does not necessarily entail salvation.¹³⁴

2. *The glory* (ἡ δόξα). This refers to God's presence with the Israelites in the Old Testament,¹³⁵ particularly the theophanies that were the Israelites' privilege as God's people (Exod 16:10; 24:5-17; 40:34-35; Lev 9:23; Num 14:10; etc.).¹³⁶ The glory that Paul has in mind here can be compared to the glory of the temporal ministry of Moses that was abolished (2 Cor 3:5-16, see pp. 174-85).

3. *The covenants* (αἱ διαθῆκαι). It is not clear to which covenants Paul is referring to. He could be referring to covenants with Abraham and the other patriarchs,¹³⁷ the Mosaic covenant and its various ratifications,¹³⁸

---

129. Käsemann, *Romans*, 258; Ridderbos, *Romeinen*, 207; cf. Moo, *Romans*, 560; Mounce, *Romans*, 196; Dunn, *Romans*, 2:535.

130. Dunn, *Romans*, 2:535.

131. Moo, *Romans*, 562. In Rom 8:15 and 23, υἱοθεσία points to adoption as a result of receiving the Spirit and not as something obtained by physically being part of a nation. Cf. also υἱοθεσία in Gal 4:5 (see p. 100).

132. Moo, *Romans*, 562.

133. Jewett, *Romans*, 563.

134. Osborne, *Romans*, 238; Moo, *Romans*, 562.

135. Hultgren, *Romans*, 357; Moo, *Romans*, 563; Bruce, *Romans*, 185; Cranfield, *Romans*, 2:462. Contra Jewett, *Romans*, 563, who connects the glory as revealed in 8:18 to the glory of Israel.

136. Dunn, *Romans*, 2:526, 534.

137. Dunn, *Romans*, 2:527.

138. Barrett, *Romans*, 177.

or the several covenants mentioned in the Old Testament,[139] of which the latter is probably the best option.[140]

4. *The legislation* (ἡ νομοθεσία). While this can refer to the act of giving a law or the laws that were made, the legislation, the second option is preferred.[141] It would here thus be equivalent to the law to Moses,[142] and would correspond to the preceding αἱ διαθῆκαι, the covenants made.[143] This interpretation would additionally correspond to Paul's later referral to the law (9:31, 32; 10:4, 5).

5. *The service* (ἡ λατρεία). This service refers to the sacrificial system (or cultus) of the Israelites[144] and not necessarily to their deeper worship such as their praying.[145] It is likely that ἡ λατρεία thus refers to their ritual acts of worship in general (cf. Josh 22:27; 1 Chr 28:13) and the entire Yahwistic religious system.[146] Although the meaning of ἡ λατρεία as religious system does not necessarily imply a sharp contrast between "internal" and "external" worship, the ritual practice in general is not to be understood as a barometer of the condition of their heart (cf. Isa 29:13; Matt 15:7–9; Mark 7:6).

6. *The promises* (αἱ ἐπαγγελίαι). These promises refer to the promises to the fathers.[147] Dunn notes that Paul deliberately excludes the land in this list, which would be included in the promise to Abraham[148] (cf.

139. A fourth possibility would be that Paul could refer to all the covenants including the New Covenant (e.g., Jewett, *Romans*, 564; Ellison, *Mystery*, 36–37), but that would not fit the current context, which is about Israelites according to the flesh (cf. Moo, *Romans*, 562).

140. Osborne, *Romans*, 239; Moo, *Romans*, 563; Bruce, *Romans*, 186; Cranfield, *Romans*, 2:462. This can especially be derived from the fact that the intertestamental passages that use the plural "covenants" normally refer to all the covenants that God had made with the "fathers" (Sir 44:12, 18; Wis 18:22; 2 Macc 8:15; Moo, *Romans*, 563).

141. BDAG, νομοθεσία; contra Moo, *Romans*, 564.

142. Hultgren, *Romans*, 357; Osborne, *Romans*, 239; Bruce, *Romans*, 186. Hultgren, *Romans*, 357, mentions 2 Macc 6:23 that refers to the law of Moses as "the holy God-given law" and 4 Macc 17:16 that refers to it as "the divine legislation."

143. Cranfield, *Romans*, 2:462–63.

144. Moo, *Romans*, 564; Dunn, *Romans*, 2:527; Käsemann, *Romans*, 259; Sanday and Headlam, *Romans*, 231. All nine occurrences of λατρεία in the Septuagint carry this notion (Moo, *Romans*, 564).

145. Contra Cranfield, *Romans*, 2:463. My view is also contra Jewett, *Romans*, 564–65, who extends this "worship" to include the worship of the Christ-believers—a notion that does not seem to fit the context.

146. Hultgren, *Romans*, 358; Osborne, *Romans*, 239; 1 Macc 1:43; 2:19, 22.

147. Cf. ἐπαγγελίας τῶν πατέρων in 15:8; Moo, *Romans*, 564; Dunn, *Romans*, 2:528.

148. Dunn, *Romans*, 2:528; cf. Hultgren, *Romans*, 358.

4:13), together with the blessing to the nations. This could even include God's promise through David that he would raise up a kingdom from one of his descendants to rule over an everlasting kingdom (2 Sam 2:4–17),[149] or more specifically ὁ Χριστὸς τὸ κατὰ σάρκα (v. 5a), the Messianic promise.[150]

7. *The fathers* (οἱ πατέρες). Moo points out that "[d]escent from the patriarchs is valid both for them and for their descendants. The meaning and extent of these promises constitute the linchpin in Paul's interpretation of salvation history"[151] (see esp. 9:6b–13; 11:15, 28). The fathers need not be limited to Abraham, Isaac and Jacob, but could be meant in a more general sense (4 Macc 13:17).[152]

8. *From whom the Christ [is] according to the flesh* (ἐξ ὧν ὁ Χριστὸς τὸ κατὰ σάρκα). Christ, the Messiah is from ethnic Israel.[153] This is the highest of all privileges. Jesus the Christ is *their* awaited Messiah.[154] Yet, the Israelites' share in Christ is limited to κατὰ σάρκα, indicating natural, ethnic descent[155] from David,[156] which would logically correspond to the same meaning of κατὰ σάρκα in verse 3 (cf. 1:3–4).[157]

The translation of verse 5 is subjected to punctuation. While it is grammatically possible to translate ". . . according to the flesh, is the Christ. God who is over all be blessed for ever"[158] or similar, the translation ". . . from them is traced the human ancestry of Christ, who is God over all, forever praised!"[159] or similar[160] is preferred. This latter translation implies a comma (not a period) after σάρκα, and is both grammatically and exegetically justified.[161] In this preferred translation the Israelites' Messiah is considered

---

149. Hultgren, *Romans*, 358.

150. Käsemann, *Romans*, 259.

151. Moo, *Romans*, 564; cf. Hultgren, *Romans*, 358; Osborne, *Romans*, 239.

152. Hultgren, *Romans*, 358; cf. Cranfield, *Romans*, 2:464.

153. Wright, "Romans," 629; Moo, *Romans*, 565; cf. Osborne, *Romans*, 240; Mounce, *Romans*, 196.

154. Osborne, *Romans*, 240; Wright, "Romans," 634; Dunn, *Romans*, 2:528, 535; Sanday and Headlam, *Romans*, 231; contra Gaston, *Paul*, 7.

155. Hultgren, *Romans*, 358; Witherington and Hyatt, *Romans*, 251; cf. Osborne, *Romans*, 240.

156. Bruce, *Romans*, 186.

157. Cf. Wright, "Romans," 630–31; Dunn, *Romans*, 2:535.

158. RSV.

159. NIV.

160. E.g., NRSV.

161. Jewett 2007, *Romans*, 567–68; Seifrid, "Romans," 649, 653; Osborne, *Romans*,

God. That Paul would see Christ as the Israelites' own Messiah and even as their Lord (10:13) and God (v. 5), would accentuate Paul's immense pain and anguish (v. 2) for them not accepting Christ, and would make the irony almost unbearable.[162]

Paul's reference to Christ furthermore signifies the most central point of continuity between the Israelites and the gospel, later to be elaborated upon in 9:24 to 10:21 (see below). In this context, however, Paul has mentioned the way in which they relate to Christ as κατὰ σάρκα, which would keep the entire mode of identity of the Ἰσραηλῖται (v. 4) within a natural, physical identity, signifying identity mode A, the *outer Israel*. That includes all the 8 privileges mentioned above. In Paul's exposition, none of these privileges necessarily imply salvation or even faith or devoutness to God as such and can all be considered as *external* privileges that all physical descendants of the patriarch Israel would share in by default.[163] This does not mean that second temple Judeans generally made such a distinction between salvation and inherited privileges. The kind of distinctions between an "outer" and "inner" Israel as implied in Romans 9 to 11 seem to be very much unique to Paul (see below).

240–41; Witherington and Hyatt, *Romans*, 251–52; Wright, "Romans," 630–31; Moo, *Romans*, 565–68; Mounce, *Romans*, 197; Bruce, *Romans*, 186–87; Guthrie, *Theology*, 340; Cranfield, *Romans*, 2:464–70; Cullmann, *Christology*, 312–13; Sanday & Headlam, *Romans*, 233–38; contra Dunn, *Romans*, 2:529; Käsemann, *Romans*, 259. The first translation method would place a period after σάρκα and takes what follows as an independent praise to God, while the preferred translation that places a comma after σάρκα means that the words after the comma would modify ὁ Χριστὸς. Some arguments that favor the latter, preferred translation method are the following (Moo, *Romans*, 567–68; cf. Bruce, *Romans*, 186–87; Guthrie, *Theology*, 339–40; Cranfield, *Romans*, 2:466–69): (1) The ὁ ὤν is most naturally taken as a relative clause that modifies the preceding co-text (Robertson, *Grammar*, 1108). (2) Paul's doxologies are always tied to the preceding context (e.g., 1:25; 11:36; 2 Cor 11:31; Gal 1:5). (3) Normally, independent blessings of God take the word "blessed" in the first position (except Ps 67:19, LXX), not after "God," which suggests that the blessing must be tied to the previous co-text (Cranfield, *Romans*, 2:468 views this argument in itself as strong and almost conclusive). (4) An antithesis is expected after "according to the flesh." (5) The exalted language about Jesus (e.g., κύριος in 10:13 is identical to Joel 2:32 in the Septuagint, a translation for יְהוָה—see Bruce, *Romans*, 187 and Cranfield, *Romans*, 2:468; see also "in the form of God" in Phil 2:6) and the activities ascribed to him (e.g., dispensing of grace in Rom 1:7; judging sins in 1 Cor 4:4–5 and 2 Cor 5:10; creation in Col 1:16 and Eph 3:9; forgiving of sins in Col 3:13) attest to Paul's belief in Christ's deity. Yet, while this translation and interpretation is preferred, one has to acknowledge that this aspect of Paul's understanding of Christ is mostly subtle with delicate distinctions.

162. Cf. Moo, *Romans*, 568.

163. Gutbrod, "Ἰσραήλ," *TDNT*, 3:387; cf. Wright, "Romans," 629; Moo, *Romans*, 559–60.

They Are Not All Israel that Are From Israel (vv. 6-8)

Paul now moves on to arguably the most decisive statement of the entire Romans 9 to 11 in unlocking the rest of his exposition. For the first time in the letter Paul now uses Ἰσραήλ. As previously indicated, he could have used the term Ἰσραήλ in verse 4, but deliberately used Ἰσραηλίτης in the context of his kindred according to the flesh, identity mode A. Paul reserved the term Ἰσραήλ for this very significant definition and distinction about the true identity of "Israel."[164] Paul here defines the meaning of "Israel" as he will apply it in the rest of Romans 9 to 11. This thesis will be tested as the study progresses toward the end of Romans 11 (see esp. pp. 314-19).

In the phrase οὐ γὰρ πάντες οἱ ἐξ Ἰσραήλ, οὗτοι Ἰσραήλ, there are a few translation possibilities. It can be translated "For not all those of Israel are Israel,"[165] "For they are not all Israel which are from Israel,"[166] or even more precisely, "For all those from Israel, these are not Israel."[167] Whichever translation one chooses, the notion stays more or less the same: Israel is not to be defined in terms of those who are ἐξ Ἰσραήλ the patriarch[168] or those who are his physical descendants.[169] In other words, the Ἰσραηλῖται as described in 9:4-5 would represent those ἐξ Ἰσραήλ (the physical descendants), the *outer Israel* (identity mode A), while Ἰσραήλ denotes the *inner Israel* (identity mode AB, see pp. 27-30).[170] The important point here is that the *inner Israel* is the real Israel or the "true Israel,"[171] or at least what Paul will have in mind when he refers to "Israel" without qualification in the rest of Romans 9 to 11.[172]

164. Cf. Gutbrod, "Ἰσραήλ," *TDNT*, 3:386-87.

165. LITV.

166. KJV.

167. Dunn, *Romans*, 2:539; Piper, *Justification*, 47-48.

168. BDAG, Ἰσραήλ, §1; Moo, *Romans*, 573; Gutbrod, "Ἰσραήλ," *TDNT*, 3:383; cf. Dunn, *Romans*, 2:538.

169. Kuhli, "Ἰσραήλ," *EDNT*, 2:204; cf. Zerwick and Grosvenor, *Grammatical Analysis*, 479.

170. Some take Ἰσραήλ to refer to the church, which would include the gentile Christ-believers, in analogy to the interpretation that "the Israel of God" in Gal 6:16 is a reference to the church. But apart from the fact that the latter interpretation can be contested (see pp. 338-45), such a notion in respect of Rom 9:6 is not warranted given the current context (Moo, *Romans*, 574).

171. Osborne, *Romans*, 242; Wright, *Climax*, 238.

172. Wright, "Romans," 636, has a similar approach when he writes in connection with verse 6: "Paul has put down a marker that from this point on the word 'Israel' has two referents . . ." Even though this might be true in a general sense in the Pauline material, here in Rom 9:6 Paul seems to (re)define the term "Israel" as such to only point to *inner Israel*.

Paul now (vv. 7-8) defines Ἰσραήλ (*inner Israel*): "not all of Abraham's children are his seed."[173] To be Abraham's physical descendant therefore does not make you a real descendant (σπέρμα) of what Paul calls Ἰσραήλ. The real descendants are called or reckoned (καλέω) in Isaac. The τοῦτ' ἔστιν (v. 8) explains: the children of the flesh (τῆς σαρκός) are not even called "children of God," only the children of the promise (τέκνα τῆς ἐπαγγελίας) are descendants (σπέρμα). In verses 9 to 23 Paul elaborates on God election of (v. 11) the children of the promise amidst the broader category of national, historical Israel.

The terms Paul uses in Romans 9:3-8 can now be arranged under the two modes of identity (A and AB) as follows:

Identity mode A:

τῶν ἀδελφῶν (my brothers, v. 3)

μου τῶν συγγενῶν μου κατὰ σάρκα
(my kindred according to the flesh, v. 3)

Ἰσραηλῖται (Israelites, v. 4)

οἱ ἐξ Ἰσραήλ (those from [the patriarch] Israel, v. 6)

Ἀβραάμ . . . τέκνα (Abraham's children, v. 6)

τέκνα τῆς σαρκός (children of the flesh, v. 8)

Identity mode AB:

Ἰσραήλ (Israel, v. 6, second occurence)

σπέρμα (seed/descendants, vv. 7 [x2], 8)

ἐν Ἰσαάκ (in Isaac, v. 7)

τέκνα τοῦ θεοῦ (children of God, v. 8)

τέκνα τῆς ἐπαγγελίας (children of the promise, v. 8)

---

173. Wright, "Romans," 636; Moo, *Romans*, 575; Dunn, *Romans*, 2:540; cf. NRSV. This translation takes the ὅτι with οὐδ' as the introduction to the whole sentence. Alternatively, the ὅτι can be read with εἰσὶν σπέρμα Ἀβραάμ, which would translate "Nor because they are his descendants are they all Abraham's children" (NIV). Yet the σπέρμα is exegetically and co-textually the significant term (vv. 7b, 8), which makes the translation that takes ὅτι with οὐδ' more preferable (Moo, *Romans*, 575). Even in the alternative translation, the central point stays the same: the real descendants of Abraham are not merely national Israel (Dunn, *Romans*, 2:540).

ISRAEL, ISRAELITES, AND JUDEANS (A AND AB) 53

The theological implications of these two modes of identity in this passage will be elaborated upon on pp. 235-51.

Schematic Presentation of People Sharing in Identity Modes A and AB

People sharing in identity modes A and B as put forth above can be represented schematically as follows:

```
Outer Israel        (People sharing in identity mode A)              Judean
Identity defined "according to the flesh": ethnicity, law, circumcision

         Inner Israel  (People sharing in identity mode AB)    Israel
         Identity defined by promise and election




         Inner Election                              Children of God

Outer Election                                                People of God
```

The outer frame represents the totality of the people of God as defined in Old Testament terms. Simultaneously, this outer frame marks people sharing in identity mode A. People whose identity is defined in this way are either Israel according to the flesh of the Old Testament (Ἰσραηλίτης) or unbelieving Judeans in Paul's present (Ἰουδαῖος). Israel according to the flesh (national Israel) was the national people of God in the Old Testament and formed part of God's outer election. Their identity was marked off by physical descent, law and circumcision. Judeans in Paul's present defined their identity as God's children on the same basis as national, historical Israel according to the flesh (identity mode A).

While the totality of Israelites in the Old Testament shared in identity mode A, not all would share in identity mode B. Identity mode AB constitutes the real or true Israel in Old Testament times that Paul identifies with the term Ἰσραήλ in Romans 9:6 (second occurrence). People sharing in both identity modes A and B (identity mode AB) are indicated by the solid frame, which exists *within* the totality of God's people (within people sharing in identity mode A). They are the *children* of God (Rom 9:8) and form part of God's inner election. In the Old Testament, their identity is marked off by both the identity markers of identity mode A and by being children of the promise (identity mode B: being part of God's inner election). Identity mode B could not exist on its own and necessarily implies identity mode A. The question about the criteria for someone to share in identity mode AB will be addressed later on (esp. pp. 235–51).

Romans 2:17–29: Outward and Inward Judeans (AB?)[174]

The main question behind Romans 2:17–29 for this study is to what or to whom Paul is referring to in verse 29 when he mentions the "inward" Judean whose circumcision is from the heart and the S/spirit. Does Paul intend a spiritual, inward identity as an identity *within* ethnic Judeans, similar to the "true Israel" in Romans 9:6? Is he referring to Christ-believers? Or is Paul referring to an actual identity or is his aim purely rhetorical?

In Romans 2, Paul makes extensive use of the diatribe style.[175] For Paul there is no difference in the way God treats sin, whether Judean or gentile (3:4, 9–12, 19).[176] Romans 2:1–16 can be seen as a critique of the Judeans' presumption about their inherited privileges (esp. vv. 1–5), where Paul relativizes their possession of the law in terms of the effect it has on God's judgment (vv. 12–15), and Paul "levels the playing field" between Judean and gentile,[177] especially in terms of the overall redemptive work of Christ.[178] The Judeans cannot assume that they will escape God's wrath any more than gentiles.[179]

In verses 17–29, Paul directly addresses a Judean interlocutor.[180] With his statement σὺ Ἰουδαῖος ἐπονομάζῃ ("you call yourself a Judean") in verse

---

174. This section largely corresponds with an article that was published in *In die Skriflig/In Luce Verbi* 50.1 (2016) 1–8, titled "Paul's Radicalisation of Law-obedience in Romans 2: The Plight of Someone Under the Law."

175. E.g., Moo, *Romans*, 125; Dunn, *Romans*, 1:108.

176. Moo, *Romans*, 126.

177. Moo, *Romans*, 127.

178. Hultgren, *Romans*, 131.

179. Moo, *Romans*, 157.

180. E.g., Wright, "Romans," 446; Moo, *Romans*, 159; Dunn, *Romans*, 1:109. The notion that Paul would address a gentile who wants to be called a Judean and believes he has become a Judean (Theissen, "Paul's Argument," 373–91), or a gentile who wants to become a Judean but behaves hypocritically (Nanos, "Paul's Non-Jews," 26–53) is unlikely. To reduce the inability of the Judean in 2:17–29 to being a gentile who cannot comply with the true requirement of circumcision (Theissen, "Paul's Argument"), suppresses the force of the examples of sinful conduct that Paul lists in 2:21–24 (e.g., stealing, adultery). The criticism of the law-observance of the Judean in this passage

17, he confronts the Judean identity at its core. Paul's dialogue is not with any specific Judean, but with a typical Judean[181] or the Judeans as a nation.[182]

Criticizing the Judean Identity (vv. 17-22)

In verses 17 to 22, Paul lists 5 blessings, 4 prerogatives and 3 violations,[183] which can be seen as part of the Judean identity:

5 Blessings (vv. 17-18). (1) Paul does not normally appropriate the name Ἰουδαῖος (v. 17) as a self-designation.[184] Although the term Ἰουδαῖος is generally regarded as an outsider term with some exceptions (see pp. 34-39), in Paul's dialogue with his Judean interlocutor he specifically uses the term Ἰουδαῖος when he addresses Judean pride and presumption.[185] He arguably reserves the terms Ἰσραήλ and Ἰσραηλίτης for when he explains God's dealings with His people in the context of salvation history in Romans 9 to 11. It does not necessarily mean that Paul is anti-Judean,[186] but rather that he wants to relativize any Judean privilege.[187] (2) The possession of the law (v. 17) was certainly a blessing, but many Judeans thought that their reliance on the law would exempt them from judgment[188] or secure their salvation.[189] (3) Even though boasting in God (v. 17) is not inherently

---

is thus hardly that proper circumcision is lacking. Or if Paul merely wanted to correct the hypocritical behavior of gentiles who wanted to become like Judean without becoming full Judeans (Nanos, "Paul's Non-Jews"), why would it be necessary to put so much emphasis on obeying the law, and how would such a notion relate to 3:21 that uncouples righteousness from law-observance? Further, if the position of the Judean in relation to the law has not fundamentally changed in Christ (Nanos, "Paul's Non-Jews"), what is Christ's real significance for *them*, and what is then so "revelational" about righteousness by faith (φανερόω, 3:21)? In light of these notions it makes more sense to see the Judean in 2:17-29 as representing an actual Judean.

181. Dunn, *Romans*, 1:109.
182. Wright, "Romans," 445, 447.
183. Moo, *Romans*, 161-62.
184. Rather Ἰσραηλίτης: Rom 11:1; 2 Cor 11:22. For Gal 2:15, see pp. 131-35.
185. Dunn, *Romans*, 1:108. This still fits into the same pejorative pattern in which Paul utilized the term Ἰουδαῖοι in contrast to terms such as Ἰσραήλ, Ἰσραηλίτης or Ἑβραῖος in 2 Cor 11:22-24 (see pp. 41-45).
186. Cf. 3:1-2 where Paul commends the Judeans as guardians of the oracles of God.
187. Cf. Dunn, *Romans*, 1:108.
188. Moo, *Romans*, 160; Cranfield, *Romans*, 1:164; cf. Dunn, *Romans*, 1:110.
189. Barrett, *Romans*, 55. This notion can be derived from Mic 3:11, where Micah says to Israel's leaders that they "lean on" (ἐπαναπαύομαι, LXX, same as Rom 2:17) the Lord, saying that calamity will not come upon them (Moo, *Romans*, 159-60).

wrong[190] and Paul boasts in this way himself (e.g., Rom 5:11; 1 Cor 1:31; 2 Cor 10:17), he rather condemns an exclusive claim on God on the basis of ethnicity.[191] (4) By knowing God's will (v. 18), Paul alludes to a "too easy assumption of a privileged knowledge by virtue of being instructed in the law."[192] (5) To distinguish the things that really matter (v. 18)[193] is, as the former, a privilege derived from the possession of the law.

4 Prerogatives (vv. 19–20). (1) Paul addresses the Judean as being convinced (πέποιθάς)[194] that he or she is a guide to the blind, (2) a light for those who are in darkness, (3) an instructor of the foolish, and (4) a teacher of the immature.[195] Many expositors recognize language borrowed from the Diaspora synagogue here,[196] which served as Judean propaganda directed to the Hellenistic world.[197] Paul addresses typical Judean attitudes toward gentiles in that he continues to confront the Judeans' reliance on their privileged status over against the gentiles.[198]

3 Violations (vv. 21–22). Paul names three violations of the law as evidence of the Judeans' failure to teach themselves.[199] (1) Stealing and (2) adultery are part of the Decalogue. (3) Paul lastly asks the Judeans who detest idols (ὁ βδελυσσόμενος τὰ εἴδωλα)[200] if they rob temples (cf. ἱερόσυλος in Acts 19:37).[201]

---

190. Moo, *Romans*, 160; Dunn, *Romans*, 1:110; Cranfield, *Romans*, 1:165.

191. Cf. Dunn, *Romans*, 1:110.

192. Dunn, *Romans*, 1:111.

193. Dunn, *Romans*, 1:111. The phrase δοκιμάζεις τὰ διαφέροντα can also be rendered "approve those things that are best" or "distinguish the things that differ [from God's will]" (Moo, *Romans*, 160–61).

194. Zerwick and Grosvenor, *Grammatical Analysis*, 463.

195. Moo, *Romans*, 161–62.

196. E.g., Moo, *Romans*, 162; Käsemann, *Romans*, 70; cf. Dunn, *Romans*, 1:113.

197. Moo, *Romans*, 162.

198. Cf. Dunn, *Romans*, 1:112.

199. Moo, *Romans*, 163.

200. Zerwick and Grosvenor, *Grammatical Analysis*, 463

201. BDAG, ἱεροσυλέω, §1; Zerwick and Grosvenor, *Grammatical Analysis*, 463; Moo, *Romans*, 163. The verb ἱεροσυλέω, a *hapax legomenon*, could also mean "to commit sacrilege" (BDAG, ἱεροσυλέω, §2; Cranfield, *Romans*, 1:168; Barrett, *Romans*, 57). Dunn, *Romans*, 1:114–15, argues that while Paul might have Mal 1:14 in mind where funds and gifts intended for the temple were misappropriated, it is more probable that he had pagan temples in view—"the danger being that of actual plunder . . . or of use of items taken from idol shrines" (cf. Wright, "Romans," 447; Bruce, *Romans*, 99). The exact practice Paul is referring to remains unclear, however (cf. Moo, *Romans*, 163).

Criticizing Boasting in the Law and Disobeying It (vv. 23–27)

Verse 23 sums up the notion of verses 21 to 22: the Judeans' boasting in the law as mark[202] of God's favor becomes a dishonor to God if their actions contradict the law.[203] Yet, Paul equally criticizes both their boasting in the privilege of possessing the law and their disobedience to the law.[204] Dunn is at pains to accentuate the NPP here when he argues that boasting in the possession of the law would be Paul's main target and disobedience to the law would be its result.[205] Gathercole, however, convincingly argues for Paul's equal critique of both boasting in the possession of the law and the disobedience thereof, where "God's election and Israel's obedience are consistently held together, and neither is emphasized at the expense of the other."[206] On the basis of various Judean texts[207] Gathercole shows that final vindication based on works was prevalent in Judean thinking.[208] His final conclusion differs from Dunn in that "the relationship between obedience and reliance on the Law in the texts above might be better described as reliance upon the Law *presupposing* or *including* obedience to it."[209] In Moo's dialogue with the NPP, he concludes that disobedience to the law remains part of the deeper problem that Paul addresses in 2:1–29.[210] Moo argues for viewing the notion of merit in salvation as universal and "part of the broader realm of anthropology" that stretches wider and deeper than salvation history or even the Judean understanding of faith, law, and covenant.[211] For Westerholm, Paul's point is that "sinners cannot be declared righteous

---

202. Wright, "Romans," 446–47, refers to "badges that marked out" Judeans from their pagan neighbors rather than "marks."

203. Dunn, *Romans*, 1:115; cf. Wright, "Romans," 446–47. For Wright and Dunn, both NPP proponents, the problem that Paul has with the Judean nation is not so much their sin and their breaking of the law, but that they dishonored God.

204. Longenecker, *Introducing Romans*, 327; Westerholm, *Perspectives*, 444; Gathercole, *Boasting*, 200–215; Moo, *Romans*, 214.

205. Dunn, *Romans*, 1:115. E.g., "it needs to be said repeatedly that Paul regards the doing of the law as something desirable and necessary . . . His criticism of the Jewish interlocutor is that his national pride in the law has resulted in his *failing* to do what the law requires."

206. Gathercole, *Boasting*, 203.

207. E.g., Sirach, Tobit, Baruch, Enoch, 1 and 2 Maccabees, Jubilees, Psalms of Solomon, Testaments of the Twelve Patriarchs, Pseudo-Philo, 2 [Slavonic] Enoch, Apocalypse of Zephaniah, Testament of Job and Sibylline Oracles.

208. Gathercole, *Boasting*, 37–90.

209. Gathercole, *Boasting*, 215, emphasis original.

210. Moo, *Romans*, 214; cf. Hong, "Law," 154.

211. Moo, *Romans*, 217.

on the basis of a law whose requirement to do what is right they have not met."[212] Finally, Longenecker makes the following remark:

> For the same rabbinic writings that Sanders uses for an understanding of Palestinian Judaism also contain some Jewish teachings, refer to some Jewish teachers, and report some Jewish situations that reflect an outlook that can only be called "legalistic" and not "nomistic"—and which, at times, some of the leading rabbis of the period denounced.[213]

Blasphemy against the name of God (v. 24) is thus the result of both their attitude[214] and conduct.[215]

In verse 25, Paul criticizes circumcision *per se*,[216] the ultimate Judean mark of distinctiveness, the mark of the covenant. Membership of the people of the covenant without circumcision was unimaginable. It was obligatory and fundamental to their core identity,[217] even to the point that some would regard it as "a passport to salvation."[218] That the transgression of the law would cause their circumcision to become uncircumcision would have been controversial, but in Paul's view such a sharp challenge "to undermine so central a pillar of Jewish self-understanding and identity" was necessary.[219]

That Paul by implication awards covenant status and judgment over against Judeans to uncircumcised persons who fulfill the law (vv. 26–27),[220] relativizes the importance of circumcision even more.[221] Paul's direct con-

---

212. Westerholm, *Perspectives*, 444.
213. Longenecker, *Introducing Romans*, 327.
214. Dunn, *Romans*, 1:116.
215. Moo, *Romans*, 166.
216. Moo, *Romans*, 167.
217. Dunn, *Romans*, 1:119–20; cf. Wright, "Romans," 448.
218. Barrett, *Romans*, 58; adopted by Cranfield, *Romans*, 1:172; cf. Mounce, *Romans*, 100.
219. Dunn, *Romans*, 1:121.
220. This notion would have been beyond the bounds of what was legally permitted within the Judean tradition and boundary markers (Hultgren, *Romans*, 131). It may be asked if Paul is creating an altogether new mode of identity here. Against the bigger picture of Paul's discourse in Rom 1–3, however, the possibility of either gentiles or Judeans who fulfill the law remain more ideal than real. The point Paul is working toward, is that he does not consider adherence to the law (even if possible) or possessing the law as warrant for salvation or as constitutive of belonging to God's people in the New Testament, a status that is only accessed and marked by faith in Christ (Rom 3–4).
221. While this is true in an absolute sense, one has to acknowledge that circumcision also has to be understood as historically and contextually positioned. In other words, circumcision was not insignificant in itself. It indeed served the timely purpose of confirming God's covenant and appropriating His promises (Gen 17:10). Paul did

nection of circumcision (that is in itself part of the law)²²² with the obedience of the law, makes circumcision and possession of the law almost synonyms, as if circumcision in itself places you under the obligation to fulfill the law, a mutuality indeed confirmed in Galatians 5:3.²²³

In summary, Paul's rhetoric in verses 17 to 27 mainly relativizes the name Ἰουδαῖος, their possession of the law and their circumcision, and places a Judean on an equal level with anyone else in terms of (1) obedience to the law and (2) their privileged status as covenant people of God. Paul will soon be contrasting the inability of both Judeans and gentiles to fulfill the law and their inherent corruptness (3:9–20) to the revelation of righteousness by faith in Christ apart from the works of the law (3:21–31).

All the privileges of the Judeans mentioned in verses 17 to 27 (e.g., their name, possession of the law, circumcision) can be regarded as external or *outward* privileges, which constituted the externalized identity²²⁴ of the typical Judean.²²⁵ The Judean identity described in verses 17 to 27 can thus be described as identity mode A, very similar to Israel according to the flesh, or in Cranfield's words: "outside that Israel within Israel, to which Paul refers in 9.6ff."²²⁶

The True Judean (vv. 28–29)

In verses 28 to 29, Paul now identifies a "true" Judean as one whose circumcision is not outward but *inward*. The real circumcision that counts is καρδίας ἐν πνεύματι οὐ γράμματι: of the heart, in the (human) spirit²²⁷ or spiritual,²²⁸ and not in the written Torah itself.²²⁹ It is unlikely that Paul is referring to the Holy Spirit here or that he alludes to be "in the Spirit" as a Christ-believer,²³⁰ for the expressoin ἐν πνεύματι is used together with

---

however question its significance when it was understood as making circumcised persons exempt from judgment, or as ensuring their salvation.

222. Barrett, *Romans*, 58.

223. Bruce, *Romans*, 99.

224. Cf. Barrett, *Romans*, 60.

225. Cf. Dunn, *Romans*, 1:123.

226. Cranfield, *Romans*, 1:172.

227. KJV; LITV; Zerwick and Grosvenor, *Grammatical Analysis*, 464; Ervin, *Conversion-Initiation*, 113; Sanders, *Jewish People*, 127; Calvin, *Romans*, 82, 85.

228. RSV; NRSV; Hultgren, *Romans*, 130–31; Du Toit, "Translating Romans," 591; Barrett, *Romans*, 60.

229. Hultgren, *Romans*, 130; Dunn, *Romans*, 1:124; Käsemann, *Romans*, 77.

230. Contra Wright 2002, "Romans," 449; Moo, *Romans*, 174–75; Dunn, *Romans*, 1:127–28.

καρδίας, which would rather place both terms in an anthropological domain (see below). Even Paul's allusion to the meaning of their name ("praise") in the words: οὗ ὁ ἔπαινος οὐκ ἐξ ἀνθρώπων ἀλλ' ἐκ τοῦ θεοῦ, underscores the notion that Paul is still within the domain or the Judean identity.[231]

Circumcision of the Heart in the Old Testament

When Paul is speaking of the circumcision of the heart (v. 29), his Judean interlocutor certainly derived his or her conception of such an expression from the Old Testament. This concept is specifically mentioned in Leviticus 26:41; Deuteronomy 10:16; 30:6; Jeremiah 4:4, and 9:13-14, 25-26. Yet, the context of all of these passages links the circumcision of the heart closely to *conduct* according to God's law: actual obedience and doing the law.

In Leviticus 26, the people's uncircumcised heart (v. 41) is set within the context of confessing their iniquity and the trespassing of their fathers (v. 40). A humbling attitude is certainly part of what is intended in realizing the uncircumcision of their hearts (v. 41), but the humbling of their uncircumcised heart entails that they shall, in God's words, "make amends of their iniquity, because they dared to spurn my ordinances, and they abhorred my statutes" (v. 43).[232] In verse 46 the people are then commanded to adhere to "the statutes and ordinances and laws that the LORD established between himself and the people of Israel."[233]

The urging to God's people to "circumcise the foreskin" of their hearts in Deuteronomy 10:16 is preceded by God who told the Israelites what is required of them: they should fear God, walk in all His ways, love Him and serve Him with all their heart and soul (v. 12). Fundamental to this requirement is that they should keep the commandments and decrees of God (v. 13). Circumcising their hearts (v. 16) would by implication enable them to fulfil God's commandments and decrees. Yet, the circumcision of their hearts is also built on the basis of God's lordship (v. 17), His justice and His love for strangers (v. 18). The circumcision of their hearts thus implies that His people should replicate these divine characteristics: they should also love strangers (v. 19), they should fear the Lord, worship Him alone, hold fast to Him, and swear by His name alone (v. 20), for He is their praise and their God who has done awesome things for His people and multiplied them (vv. 21-22).

---

231. Cf. Hultgren, *Romans*, 130-31; Ervin, *Conversion-Initiation*, 113-15; Gutbrod, "Ἰσραήλ," *TDNT*, 3:381; Ridderbos, *Romeinen*, 69. Paul's pun on the meaning of the Judean name required some Judean insider knowledge (cf. Wright, "Romans," 449).

232. NRSV.

233. NRSV.

Deuteronomy 11 then reiterates the practical execution of the circumcision of their hearts: "You shall love the LORD your God, therefore, and keep his charge, his decrees, his ordinances, and his commandments always" (v. 1).[234] And again they are instructed: "Keep, then, this entire commandment that I am commanding you today" (v. 8).[235] The context of Deuteronomy 10 to 11 thus grounds the circumcision of the heart in both (1) an attitude of reverence, love and commitment to God, and (2) in the actual keeping of God's decrees, ordinances and His commandments.[236] The keeping of God's commandments is thus part of the "covenant requirements."[237]

Deuteronomy 29 ends by pointing to God's anger and every curse in this book that would result from the people's idolatry (vv. 26–28). Verse 29 states that the secret things belong to the Lord and that the revealed things belong to God's people forever "to observe all the words of this law."[238] Deuteronomy 30 directly follows with urging the people to call the blessings and curses to mind, to return to the Lord and to obey Him with all their heart and soul, just as the Lord commands them (vv. 1–2). Verses 3 to 5 give an account of how God will restore the people's fortunes and gather them from where they are exiled. Part of what God will do is to circumcise the people's hearts in order that they would love God with all their heart and soul (v. 6). God's enemies and those who persecute God's people will, however, be cursed (v. 7). Then follows the result of God's circumcision of the heart: they will obey the Lord and observe His commandments (v. 8). God's blessing on His people and the prosperity they will receive (v. 9) are on the basis of obeying the Lord and, in the Deuteronomist's words, "by observing his commandments and decrees that are written in this book of the law, because you turn to the LORD your God with all your heart and with all your soul" (v. 10).[239] In verse 16, the love for God is again connected to obeying God's commandments: by walking in His ways and by observing His commandments, decrees and ordinances. The keeping of the commandments in turn results in "life" (חָיָה; cf. Lev 18:5). There is thus an inseparable relationship between life (vv. 6, 16), the circumcision of the heart (v. 6), the love for God (vv. 6, 11), and the keeping of God's commandments (vv. 8, 10, 16). Yet Merrill refers to the requirement to love God with all your heart and soul (which by implication involves obedience to God's commands) as an "impossible

---

234. NRSV.
235. NRSV.
236. Cf. Merrill, *Deuteronomy*, 203; Craigie, *Deuteronomy*, 364.
237. Merrill, *Deuteronomy*, 203.
238. NRSV.
239. NRSV.

standard," and being "the ideal of covenant behaviour, the one to be sought but never fully achieved."[240]

In Jeremiah 4 and 9, the connection between the circumcision of the heart and the keeping of the law is even more explicit. Jeremiah 4 starts with urging Israel to return to God and to put away their abominations from God's presence (v. 1). If they change their conduct by swearing "As the LORD lives"[241] in truth, justice and in uprightness, then the nations shall be blessed by God and boast by Him (v. 2). The people are urged to break up a fallow ground and not to sow among thorns (v. 3). Then in verse 4, the people are commanded to circumcise themselves to God and to remove the foreskins of their hearts in order to avoid God's wrath because of the evil of their "doings."

In Jeremiah 9:13–14, God's people are reprimanded for forsaking the law that God has set before them, for not obeying His voice, and for not walking in accordance with it. They have stubbornly followed their own hearts (which are uncircumcised by implication) and committed idolatry. In the same context, God says in verses 25 to 26 that days are coming when He will attend to all those who are circumcised but are [actually] uncircumcised [in heart], or to "all those who are circumcised only in the foreskin" (v. 25).[242] In verse 25, Israel is depicted as "uncircumcised in heart" and compared to the gentile nations who are (literally) uncircumcised. The comparison of Israel with the gentiles is obviously on the basis of their sinful conduct. Harrison writes that the Judaeans "though circumcised in body, had no real inner dedication to the spiritual ideals of Sinai."[243]

Apart from the close connection between the circumcision of the heart and the doing of the law in the Old Testament, the concept of the human spirit (רוּחַ) is not foreign to the Old Testament either (e.g., Gen 41:8; 2 Kgs 19:7; Job 7:11; Num 16:22; Isa 42:5). 2 Chronicles 28:12 reports of David's plans for the temple that he had "in spirit" (ἐν πνεύματι, LXX). While the human "heart" (לֵבָב) is used together with רוּחַ as human quality in Joshua 2:11 and 5:1, רוּחַ in these instances denotes human courage. Yet, in Psalm 77:6, the terms לֵבָב ("heart") and רוּחַ ("spirit") are used together as human properties that God must communicate with and search. The best example of where the terms לֵבָב ("heart") and רוּחַ ("spirit") are used together, is probably Deuteronomy 2:30, which reports of King Sihon of Heshbon who did not allow the Israelites to pass through, for the Lord "had hardened

---

240. Merrill, *Deuteronomy*, 421.
241. NRSV.
242. NRSV.
243. Harrison, *Jeremiah*, 92.

his spirit and made his heart defiant."²⁴⁴ An exceptionally clear example of where there exists a close link among obedience, the circumcision of the foreskin of the heart, God's creation of "a holy spirit" in people, repentance, the cleaving to God and all His commandments, and the fulfilling of God's commandments, is found in *Jubilees* 1:22–25.

> And the Lord said unto Moses: "I know their contrariness and their thoughts and their stiffneckedness, and they will not be *obedient* till they confess their own sin and the sin of their fathers. And after this they will *turn to Me* in all uprightness and with all (their) heart and with all (their) soul, and I will *circumcise the foreskin of their heart* and the foreskin of the heart of their seed, and I will create in them a *holy spirit*, and I will cleanse them so that they shall not turn away from Me from that day unto eternity. And their souls will cleave to Me and to all *My commandments*, and they will *fulfil My commandments* . . ." (*Jubilees* 1:22–25).²⁴⁵

Both the concepts of the human "spirit" and the human "heart," which have to be in line with God's will or commandments, are significant within the frame of reference of the Old Testament. Since Paul addresses a Judean in 2:17–29, he would certainly anticipate an understanding of these concepts from an Old Testament point of view. By implication, the human "heart" and "spirit" must not be hardened or uncircumcised, but these human qualities or properties must be in line with God's law. Rather than circumcision being something in the external, physical sphere, the true *Ioudaios* should be spiritually and inwardly capable of doing the law.

Paul's Rhetoric: Doing the Law

The theme of *obeying* or *doing* the law is prominent in the whole of Romans 2. Verse 1 starts with reprimanding those who judge people who "do the same things" as described in Romans 1:18–32. God's judgment is on those who "do" such things (vv. 2–3). The "hard and impenitent heart" lies beneath this sinful conduct and is connected to God's repaying "according to each one's deeds" (vv. 5–6; see above). Verse 13 states that God justifies the "doers of the law." Even the gentiles are subjected to God's law in some way (vv. 15–16). The depth of Paul's critique against the claim on righteousness or justification before God on the basis of Judeans who possess the law is that

---

244. NRSV.
245. Charles, *Apocrypha*, 12, emphasis added.

their *conduct* is not in line with (vv. 21–23) the "requirements of the law" (δικαιώματα τοῦ νόμου, v. 26)[246] on which they lay claim. If they do not obey the law, their claim on the law or circumcision is worthless (v. 25). Doing the law is so central in Paul's argument that even gentiles who live according to the law are considered as "circumcision" (v. 26)—even to the point that they would judge Judeans who don't do the law (v. 27). In line with the whole context of doing the law, and the Old Testament connotations attached to being circumcised in heart (see above), it is thus quite likely that what Paul is describing in verses 28–29 is simply a Judean who *does* the law. It may be objected that Paul's reference to οὐ γράμματι (v. 29) would go against such an interpretation, but οὐ γράμματι in this context alludes to the possession of the written law rather than to its observance.[247]

Several problems can be identified with the interpretation that the one who is circumcised in heart in the spirit, is a believer in Christ:[248] (1) It would mean that Paul uses the term Ἰουδαῖός in verse 28 in a metaphorical way for Christ-believers, which transcends it normal use and has no counterpart in the rest of the Pauline corpus. (2) Paul later states that by the works of the law no one will be justified (3:20), which he contrasts to the righteousness of God that has "now" been disclosed (3:21): the righteous of God through faith, which entails that everyone without distinction is justified by faith in Christ apart from the works of the law (3:22; cf. 3:28).[249] Justification through faith in Christ apart from the works of the law is however at odds with the notion in 2:13 that "doers of the law" will be justified. As discussed above, the rest of Romans 2, including the circumcision of the heart in verses 28–29, echoes the importance of the doing of the law, which even exemplifies the circumcision of the heart in the human spirit (see above). If a Christ-believer is implied in 2:28–29, it would seem as if a Christ-believer is still subjected to the law or "under the law"—something that Paul later denies (6:14–15; 7:6). (3) In view of Paul's accentuation of all people's inherent corruptness (3:1–20) and the fact that faith only enters Paul's main discourse in 3:22 (after the introductory "title" statement in 1:16–17), to imply that a "true Judean" is someone who is regenerated in Christ and believes in him seems out of place in terms of the build-up

---

246. Osborne, *Romans*, 77; Moo, *Romans*, 170; cf. NRSV. Cf. also BDAG's (δικαίωμα, §1) definition: "a regulation relating to just or right action, *regulation, requirement, commandment*."

247. Hultgren, *Romans*, 130; Moo, *Romans*, 174; Dunn, *Romans*, 1:124; cf. γράμμα in v. 27.

248. E.g., Osborne, *Romans*, 78–79; Moo, *Romans*, 175.

249. It could be objected here that Paul claimed law abidance himself on the basis of Phil 3:6, but see pp. 135–47.

of Paul's argument. Even Wright seems to cover the awkwardness of his interpretation (who reads the Christ-believer in here) when he states that "Paul has introduced this brief description of the new covenant people in his argument without full explanation"[250] and then goes to great pains to make it fit into the bigger structure of Romans.

But if Paul has a law-abiding Judean in mind with his reference to being circumcised in heart in the spirit (2:28-29), it can be asked if Paul considers it *possible* to do the law. Did Paul envision people in his past, present or future who *can* do the law? This is exactly the question that he addresses in 3:9-20. There he emphatically places all people under sin without distinction (v. 9). No one is righteous (v. 10), seeks God (v. 11), shows kindness (v. 12) or lives righteously, peacefully or fearfully as the law requires (vv. 13-18). In verse 20, Paul states that "now we know that whatever the law says, it speaks to those who are under the law, so that every mouth may be silenced, and the whole world may be held accountable to God."[251] The human impossibility to perfectly adhere to the law thus renders its ability to serve as instrument or mark of righteousness null and void. Only faith can bring about or mark off righteousness (3:21-31). With this larger picture of Paul's thought in mind, an allusion to circumcision in the heart (2:28-29) as fulfilling the law would be indeed ironic and even paradoxical.

Yet such a paradox would precisely fit into Paul's argument. Paul would then create a deliberate irony: he contrasts the Judean's inability to adhere to the law (as with the gentile) with an *ideal* Judean[252] or even a non-Judean (v. 27) who can. In other words, a Judean who lays claim on the possession of the law (οὐ γράμματι, v. 29) *should also be* "circumcised in heart" and therefore would possess the inward moral capability in his or her spirit to fulfill the law.[253] Such Judeans would live up to their claim, and they would honor and praise God (v. 29). Although this ideal image of a Ἰουδαῖος could hint on the inner Israel (identity mode AB),[254] it does not become an actual mode of identity or term to identify the inner Israel, but rather point to an *unattainable ideal*. The *ideal* Judean would then make the contrast with the total corruptness of all people and their inability to fulfill the law in Rom 3:1-20 even more stark and effective. Such an ideal picture of how Judeans ought to be, would implicitly prompt for a solution: firstly to repent of their inability to fulfill the

250. Wright, "Romans," 449.
251. NRSV.
252. Cf. Hultgren, *Romans*, 130.
253. Cf. Ervin, *Conversion-Initiation*, 113-15; Gutbrod, "Ἰσραήλ," *TDNT*, 3:381. Ervin, *Conversion-Initiation*, 113-15, points to the notion in Deut 10:16, where the circumcision of the heart is something the people was called upon to do for themselves.
254. Cf. Cranfield, *Romans*, 1:175.

law, which is real humbleness (Lev 26:41, see above), and secondly to accept Christ as Messiah in faith. Understood in this way, Paul's image of the ideal Judean would be an implicit rhetorical appeal to accept Christ, for he is the only one who fits that ideal picture (cf. 3:25-26).

To see the "true Judean" as someone who can do the law, which Paul later argues to be impossible, would also fit a pattern in Paul's thought of eschatological contrast between (1) the old way of existence under the law and sin that awaits completion, and (2) the new way of existence by faith in Christ (esp. Rom 7:5-6; 8:1-16, see pp. 189-206). This eschatological and salvation-historical contrast between the two ages is especially indicated by the νυνί ("now") in 3:21,[255] which indicates the disclosure of the righteousness of faith in Christ of the *new era in Christ* (cf. the epiphany of faith in Gal 3:23, 25; 4:4-5). If the νυνί indicates the *eschatological turning point* in Paul's exposition, that would place the preceding (esp. 1:18-3:20, including 2:28-29) and all identities involved within the domain of the old age before Christ, and the subsequent 3:21-31 and the involved identities in the new age in Christ.

The old age would additionally be indicated by the expression "under the law" in 2:12 and 3:19. It is noteworthy in this regard that Paul seems to widen the domain of the law in that he depicts gentiles as having "a law to themselves" (2:14). Moreover, in sequence of 3:9, which speaks of both Judeans and Greeks being under sin, 3:19-20 denotes that gentiles are included ("the whole world") in those "under the law," which pertains to "whatever the law speaks" (cf. the "we" language in Gal 3:23).[256] The gentiles in the old era before the Christ event can thus be understood as being subjected to the same conditions for justification as Israel of the Old Testament, which awaited fulfillment in Christ. Such an idea is complemented by the fact that there was only one divinely revealed law in the Old Testament available. The era of the Spirit in Christ is certainly anticipated beneath 2:28-29, where the "just requirement of the law" is fulfilled in those who walk according to the Spirit (8:4), but as secondary layer of meaning rather than a primary one.

In 3:1, Paul asks what the advantage of the Judean is, and what the value of circumcision is. But if the Judean in Romans 2:28-29 pointed to a believer in Christ and not to an actual Judean in the Old Covenant as such, Romans 2:28-29 would be an interruption to Paul's argument. It fits the rhetorical flow of Paul's argument more naturally if Romans 2:28-29 remains within the identity of the Judean right up to 3:3. Additionally,

255. Cf. Longenecker, *Epistle to the Romans*, 399; Matera, *Romans*, 96; Osborne, *Romans*, 92-93; Schreiner, *Romans*, 180; Moo, *Romans*, 221-22.

256. Gispen, *Leviticus*, 264, argues that Lev 18:5 was probably understood as representing the standard for more than Israel—a principle that implicated all people.

the type of questions asked in 3:1 implies that the preceding (including 2:28-29) sketches a picture of being a Judean that is *not* more advantageous than being a gentile, a notion that would stand in conflict with the idea that someone in Christ is a kind of true Judean. The questions in 3:1 thus strengthens the notion that 2:17-29 pictures the unattainable ideal of the identity of a Judean before or without faith in Christ. The logic between the lines would thus be as follows: Since the Judeans do *not* keep the whole Torah (2:17-27), which implies that they are *not* circumcised in heart in their spirit (2:28-29), Paul in 3:1 asks what is then the advantage of the Judean or what the value of circumcision is.

It has to be indicated here that Paul is not trying to portray the *whole* of the Old Testament teaching on justification or salvation as if the *only* prevalent understanding in the time of the second temple was that the law must be fully obeyed in order to obtain eternal life or vindication. Yet, although Paul's focus on obeying the law for vindication was *not against* the teaching of the Old Testament on these subjects, because texts such as Leviticus 18:5, Deuteronomy 30 and Ezekiel 20:11, 13 and 21 could be understood in this way (see above), that was probably not the main point of Paul's rhetoric. The main point of Paul's rhetoric was rather to radicalize law-obedience to such an extent that it would make faith in Christ for salvation or vindication absolutely indispensible for all people, including *all Judeans*. In addition, Paul would want to contrast the means of salvation and justification of the old era before Christ (works and law-obedience) with the means of justification in the new era in Christ (faith). If understood in this way, Romans 2 to 3 could form part of an apologetic response to some who might have questioned the validity of his all-inclusive gospel of faith, including *Judeans*.[257]

It could be objected that such a reading of Romans 2 to 3 would portray the Judeans in a too negative way. Yet, such a reading could hardly be interpreted as against the *Judeans exclusively*, because gentiles are included in Paul's exposition: they are also subjected to the requirement to do the law (2:14, 26 and 3:19 by implication). Paul is not arguing against the identity of the Judeans as such, but against *any identity* before or outside Christ. The whole world is accountable to God (3:19). All people have sinned and fall short of God's glory (3:23). All people are affected by the old era under the law and are in need of salvation and justification by faith.

---

257. Although the letter to the Romans is generally seen as being written to gentile believers, most agree that some Judeans were present in the congregation (see pp. 231-35). Yet, the logic behind a more general apologetic could lie in Paul's relative unfamiliarity with the congregation (15:21-24) and the possibility of the letter also being intended to be read by other Judeans.

My approach thus has to be differentiated from an approach that understands 2:1-29 as still being applicable to Judean Christ-believers as if they are still expected to do the law.[258] Since complete obedience to the law is required to obtain righteousness (2:13), which is impossible (3:1-20), Paul's view of the law cannot be understood such as that "full Torah submission continues to function as an appropriate expression of ethnic identity and faithfulness towards God."[259] Being "under the law," which would involve that one continues to be submitted to the requirements of the law (2:12), rather represents an *eschatologically old way of relating to God* that is contrasted with the new way of relating to God in 3:21-31.

Zoccali's comparison of Judean Christ-believers who would "fulfill" the law with gentile believers who "as a matter of theological logic . . . keep the law" although being uncircumcised,[260] is hardly convincing. How are both groups considered to fulfil/keep the law in Christ if Judean believers are required to still submit under the Torah while gentile believers are not? There exists an inconsistency between the idea of fulfillment of law in Christ, which would be applicable to *all*, over against the idea that to "continue to submit to" the requirements of the law would *only* be applicable to Judean Christ-believers. Zoccali argues that circumcision would still have value in that Judean believers would be considered as obeying the law (citing 2:25) while both Judean and gentile would be justified on the basis of faith (citing 3:30). What exactly would then be the *value* of circumcision in obeying the law (2:25) if both Judean and gentile are justified on the *basis of faith* (3:30)? Such value would then have to be something other than justification. Paul already connected the obedience of the law with justification in 2:13 (which has to pertain to the eschatologically old situation, otherwise it would contradict 3:20), but Zoccali seems to disconnect the value of circumcision in obeying the law from justification. The other danger that lurks behind Zoccali's interpretation is a kind of perpetuation of Judean exclusivity (see further pp. 131-35 and pp. 281-84).

Summary and Concluding Remarks

When the terms Ἰσραήλ, Ἰσραηλίτης and Ἰουδαῖος are considered in texts other than Paul, there are roughly three constraints that come to the fore: (1) The term Ἰουδαῖος is mostly used as an outsider term whereas Ἰσραήλ and Ἰσραηλίτης are mostly used as insider terms. (2) While the term Ἰσραήλ

---

258. E.g., Zoccali, "Children"; *Whom God Has Called*, 67; cf. Nanos, "Myth," 4.
259. Zoccali, "Children," 270.
260. Zoccali, *Whom God Has Called*, 66-68.

has stronger religious connotations, the term Ἰουδαῖος has stronger ethnic connotations. (3) Until 160 CE (Justin), the terms Ἰσραήλ and Ἰσραηλίτης hardly feature in Christian or fringe Christian writings. When they do occur, they point to ancient, historical Israel.

The way in which Paul uses Ἰσραήλ in 1 Corinthians 10:18 seems to confirm the third constraint above in that it points to ancient, historical Israel of the Old Testament. In combination with κατὰ σάρκα, Ἰσραήλ denotes Israel as a national, ethnic entity without connotations to their faith or their state of heart (identity mode A). The expression Ἰσραήλ κατὰ σάρκα does not necessitate an "Israel according to the Spirit" as counterpart but is merely a reference to earthly or ethnic Israel.

The titles Paul uses in 2 Corinthians 11:18–24 to describe is heritage, Ἑβραῖος, Ἰσραηλίτης, and σπέρμα Ἀβραάμ, all carry connotations about his physical heritage or ethnic connection to historical Israel. In the way Paul applies them, neither of the designations carry specific spiritual connotations. In this way they correspond to the way Ἰσραήλ is used in 1 Corinthians 10:18: "according to the flesh." The pejorative context in which the term Ἰουδαῖος is used, corresponds to the insider-outsider distinction of applying Ἰσραηλίτης more as an insider term and Ἰουδαῖος more as an outsider term (1 above).

The eight privileges listed in Romans 9:3–5 (adoption; glory; covenants; legislation; service; promises; fathers; from whom Christ according to the flesh) can all be considered as external privileges, for none of them imply salvation and all of national Israel shared in them (identity mode A). Paul makes an important distinction in 9:6, where he differentiates inner, elect Israel (identity mode AB) from outer, national Israel (identity mode A). This distinction can be considered as definitive in respect of the rest of Paul's exposition in Romans 9 to 11. As the diagram on p. 53 shows, inner, elect Israel can be considered as a group of people *within* national Israel whose identity is defined by promise and election: they are the "true Israel."

Romans 2:17–29, which addresses the Judean, criticizes their claim on the law in terms of their standing before God. If they laid claim on circumcision and the possession of the law they ought to completely obey the law as well. Paul argues that it is only on the basis of perfect obedience of the law that such a claim would be considered as valid. In view of the close association between circumcision of the heart and obedience of the law in the Old Testament (esp. Lev 26:41; Deut 10:16; 30:6; Jer 4:4 and 9:13–14, 25–26), Paul's reference to being circumcised in the heart in the spirit (Rom 2:29) can be interpreted as the inward ability to obey and fulfill the law. In view of 3:9–20 the latter notion is, however, considered as an impossible ideal for both Judean and gentile. Hereby Paul problematizes the Judean identity (and unbelieving gentile identity) at its core, which anticipates a solution: righteousness through faith in Christ alone (3:21–31). Romans 2:17–29 can be considered as describing the identity of the Judean under the old way of existence under the law, before the Christ event. This is especially indicated by the "now" in 3:21, which indicates the salvation-historical turning point in Paul's exposition, placing 1:18 to 3:20 and all the identities involved in it under the old age before Christ (identity mode A and non-believing gentiles) and 3:21–31 and all the identities involved in it in the new age in Christ (identity mode C). The prerequisite to do the whole law is thus not understood as theoretical or hypothetical as in the regular reformed view, but as actual, yet as redundant due to its salvation-historical fulfillment in Christ. The contradiction between 2:13 and 3:21 is thus retained, but explained as pertaining to two separate salvation-historical eras—a distinction that is not always articulated or developed to its full consequence within the structure of Romans 1–3 in reformed approaches.

An allusion to identity mode AB or even C is not impossible in 2:28–29 (cf. Rom 8:4), but if so, it probably features on an implicit or secondary level. The whole of Romans 2 rather focuses on the literal doing of the whole law, which Paul portrays as principally being applicable to all people, including gentiles (esp. 2:14, 26). Because of the impossibility for anyone to do the whole law and the effects of sin on all people under the the law (3:4–20), the scenario Paul sketches in Romans 2 thus necessitates faith in Christ. The latter can be understood as being part of Paul's rhetorical strategy, constituting the plight of someone under the law, necessitating a solution. In Paul's rhetoric he radicalizes obedience to the law in the Old Testament to the point of obtaining salvation and justification by doing it. Yet, while such a teaching is not inconsistent with the Old Testament itself, it serves the purpose of portraying the means of justification and salvation of the Old Testament as impossible and therefore as redundant. Being a rhetorical strategy in the build-up of the letter to the Romans, such a reading of Romans 2 does not imply that Paul does not teach that doing good is part of a Christ-believer's life. Yet, such doing is not originating from an old existence under the reign of the law, but originates from a new existence in the Spirit within the new eschatological existence in Christ (6:14–18; 8:1–14, see pp. 199–206), which is free from the law (7:1–6, see pp. 189–99).

A further implication of the above reading of Romans 2:17–19 is that Paul creates the impression that historical Israel who lived under the law has been rejected for their inability to perfectly do the whole law, a notion that he later makes more explicit in 9:27–33.

3

Faith in Christ, Abraham, and Law (ABC)

THE NEXT MODE OF identity to be addressed is identity mode C. In principle, this identity mode can stand on its own, without A or B. In the texts that will be discussed in this chapter and the next, however, all of them display some or other relation to A or AB. As indicated on pp. 27-30, ABC passages can be understood as displaying mostly *continuity* with Israel (ch. 3), whereas the AC passages can be understood as mostly displaying *discontinuity* between Christ-believers and Israel (ch. 4).

With the exception of Galatians 4:21-5:1, faith in Christ is a central theme in the passages in this section, and is together with the Spirit[1] (Gal 3:2-5; 4:29; Eph 2:18, 22) constitutive of the identity in Christ. The connection of the believer in Christ to Abraham and/or the promise to him is especially predominant in Romans 4:1-25; Galatians 3:1-29 and 4:21-5:1, and is probably implied in Romans 1:16-17 and even in Ephesians 2:12. Identity in terms of the law is a prominent theme in most of these passages (except Rom 1:16-17), especially Romans 4 and Galatians 3.

Romans 1:16-17

Apart from the modes of identity that are represented here, some aspects pertaining to Christology, righteousness (δικαιοσύνη), salvation (cf. Rom 11:26), and faith will be elaborated upon. This will help to sketch some of the outer constraints of much of Paul's understanding of the believer in Christ (identity mode C) in relation to the Judean and/or Israel, especially in his letter to the Romans.

---

1. While faith will be a constant theme in most of the chis chapter and the next, Paul's understanding of Spirit/spirit in terms of the identity of the Christ-believer will eventually climax in chapter 5.

In Paul's introduction to his letter to the Romans, he indicates that the gospel of God (v. 1), which was promised by the prophets in the Holy Scriptures (v. 2) concerning His Son, came ἐκ σπέρματος Δαυὶδ κατὰ σάρκα (v. 3). The qualification κατὰ σάρκα primarily refers to Jesus' physical, Davidic descent,[2] which alludes to his Messianic stature.[3] The phrase secondarily carries overtones of Jesus' natural human existence.[4] His natural earthly existence would be the counterpart of his pre-existence, signified by τοῦ γενομένου.[5] For Käsemann Christ is the "decisive content" of the gospel and the "theme of the epistle," where the περὶ τοῦ υἱοῦ αὐτοῦ (v. 3) refers back to the εὐαγγέλιον θεοῦ (v. 1) and replaces an objective genitive, equivalent to εὐαγγέλιον τοῦ Χριστοῦ.[6] Moo extracts no less than four Christological titles in verses 1 to 4: "Son of God," "Seed of David," "Messiah" and "Lord." Christ's centrality to the gospel is for Paul also signified by the phrase εὐαγγελίῳ τοῦ υἱοῦ αὐτοῦ in 1:9 (cf. 15:19, 29), which constitutes a high Christology.[7]

Most commentators regard 1:16-17 as a title statement and as thematic of the whole letter.[8] Possible accusations against Paul's gospel that would have been anti-Judean may lie behind Paul's statement that he is not ashamed[9] of the gospel.[10] Paul's pride for the gospel is rooted in the power of God to salvation (v. 16). The power of God and salvation itself go hand in hand, and define the gospel as an actualized message[11] in the life of its recipients.[12]

---

2. Wright, "Romans," 417; Dunn, *Romans*, 1:13; Barrett, *Romans*, 18; Ridderbos, *Romeinen*, 25; L&N §10.1.

3. Osborne, *Romans*, 30; Wright, "Romans," 415-16; Moo, *Romans*, 46; Cranfield, *Romans*, 1:58; Barrett, *Romans*, 20.

4. L&N §58.10; cf. Moo, *Romans*, 47; Käsemann, *Romans*, 11; Ridderbos, *Romeinen*, 25.

5. Osborne, *Romans*, 30; Moo, *Romans*, 46; cf. Cranfield, *Romans*, 1:59; Barrett, *Romans*, 20-21; contra Dunn, *Romans*, 1:12.

6. Käsemann, *Romans*, 10, 24.

7. Moo, *Romans*, 50-51; cf. Ridderbos, *Romeinen*, 25-26.

8. E.g., Wright, "Romans," 423; Moo, *Romans*, 63; Dunn, *Romans*, 1:37; Cranfield, *Romans*, 1:87; cf. Osborne, *Romans*, 39.

9. Hultgren, *Romans*, 71, thinks that some people may have found the gospel abhorrent, since it is about a crucified "savior" that was rejected by the Roman authorities, which in itself could have been perceived as obscene (cf. Jewett, *Romans*, 137).

10. Moo, *Romans*, 66; Grayston, "Not Ashamed." Some Greek witness include τοῦ Χριστοῦ after εὐαγγέλιον (D2 K L P Ψ 104. 630. 1175. 1241. 2464 𝔐).

11. Käsemann, *Romans*, 22.

12. Cf. Witherington and Hyatt, *Romans*, 56; Mounce, *Romans*, 70.

While the deliverance of a broad range of evils is signified by σωτηρία and its cognates[13] in the New Testament, as inherited from its use in the Old Testament,[14] "Paul uses the words only of spiritual deliverance"[15] with an eschatological focus, especially as deliverance from eschatological "judgment that is finalized on the last day" (Rom 5:9–10; 13:11; 1 Thess 5:9).[16] Although salvation often carries a negative meaning (deliverance from something), it can denote "restoration to wholeness,"[17] the restoration of the glory that sinful people lack,[18] or "God's provision for a person's spiritual need."[19] Apart from the eschatological dimension of salvation, anyone who believes already shares in salvation,[20] which entails "a present peace and joy as a state of openness before God" and people.[21] While Jewett[22] and Wright[23] both understand salvation as having a current effect apart from final judgment, they tend to put more emphasis on the social effect of salvation to the possible expense of inner, spiritual transformation.[24] In terms of the effect

13. L&N additionally list σώζω, σωτήριος and σωτήριον through semantic subdomains 21.25–30.

14. In the OT, salvation is normally attributed to God who delivers his people from their enemies (e.g., Exod 14:13; 15:2) or from physical peril (e.g., Judg 15:18; 1 Sam 11:9). Among other uses (e.g., historical/temporal; spiritual/eternal), it can denote God's eschatological deliverance (e.g., Isa 12:2; 25:9; 46:13; 49:6; 52:7, 10) of His people (Moo, *Romans*, 66; Sanday and Headlam, *Romans*, 23).

15. Moo, *Romans*, 67; contra Jewett, *Romans*, 138–39.

16. Moo, *Romans*, 67; cf. Dunn, *Romans*, 1:39; Cranfield, *Romans*, 1:89; Käsemann, *Romans*, 22.

17. Dunn, *Romans*, 1:39.

18. Cranfield, *Romans*, 1:89.

19. Moo, *Romans*, 67—see esp. the notion of "saved by hope" (ἐλπίδι ἐσώθημεν) in Rom 8:24.

20. Moo, *Romans*, 67; cf. Osborne, *Romans*, 40; Dunn, *Romans*, 1:39; Cranfield, *Romans*, 1:89; see e.g. νῦν ἡμέρα σωτηρίας in 2 Cor 6:2 (cf. Rom 8:24).

21. Käsemann, *Romans*, 22.

22. Jewett, *Romans*, 138;

23. Wright, "Romans," 424.

24. Jewett, *Romans*, 138–40, 143, understands salvation as present, and sees salvation more as a transformation of the Roman imperial power structure of honor and shame. Similarly, for Wright, "Romans," 424, "'salvation' had far more to do with the rescue of Israel from pagan oppression, from Egypt or Babylon or, now, Rome, than with 'life after death.'" While the gospel would indeed affect the understanding of the imperial power structure and would prompt a transformation thereof, this would not be salvation itself, but rather a result of a new Spirit-filled life (Rom 8; Gal 5:25), a new understanding of the worth of people as equals (Gal 3:28), and love poured out in the hearts of people in Christ (Rom 5:5) that worked through to the community. In other words, I would neither argue for disconnecting the experience of spiritual realities from social realities in the first-century person, nor would I dislodge the social effect of

of the power of salvation, Dunn brings this power in connection with a "marked effect on people, transforming them—as evident particularly in conversion," and to "a visible and marked alteration in a current condition that could not be attributed to human causation."[25] Similarly, Mounce connects salvation to "justification (being set right with God), sanctification (growth in holiness), and glorification (the ultimate transformation into the likeness of Christ . . .)."[26] All of these aspects place salvation right in the center of the human relationship with God.[27]

Salvation is for παντὶ τῷ πιστεύοντι (v. 16). In terms of the nature of faith in Paul, faith can be viewed as a reaction to God's grace without merit.[28] It signifies "trust in a person"[29] and "total reliance upon God."[30] As for the status or role of faith, it can be seen as both the initial and continuing access point to the saving power of God[31] (cf. προσαγωγή in Rom 5:2) and as mark or badge of those in the New Covenant.[32]

Just after Paul accentuated the universal nature of the gospel (for everyone), he strikes a particular note:[33] Ἰουδαίῳ τε πρῶτον καὶ Ἕλληνι (v. 16). Most commentators recognize a sense of Judean priority from this phrase.[34] As for the nature of this priority, it is at least chronological and historical in that the gospel came to the Judeans first and then to the nations.[35] At a deeper level, Paul might have their priority in God's saving purposes in mind.[36] Yet since Paul accentuates the responsibility to believe in verse 17,[37] their priority seems to include their *responsibility* toward the gospel (1:16; 2:10) as people to whom God's words have been entrusted (3:2). There even appears to be some form of priority with respect to judgment (2:8–9).

---

salvation from the spiritual reality of salvation in Paul's gospel. But social transformation *follows* inner, spiritual transformation rather than preceding it.

25. Dunn, *Romans*, 1:39.
26. Mounce, *Romans*, 71; cf. Bruce, *Romans*, 87.
27. Cf. Witherington and Hyatt, *Romans*, 50; Cranfield, *Romans*, 1:87–91.
28. Moo, *Romans*, 67; Cranfield, *Romans*, 1:90.
29. Moo, *Romans*, 67.
30. Dunn, *Romans*, 1:46.
31. Dunn, *Romans*, 1:40.
32. Wright, *Fresh Perspective*, 113, 121; *Paul Really Said*, 125–29.
33. Moo, *Romans*, 68; cf. Käsemann, *Romans*, 22.
34. Moo, *Romans*, 68; Dunn, *Romans*, 1:40.
35. Cf. Moo, *Romans*, 69; Mounce, *Romans*, 71; Hendriksen, *Romans*, 1:61.
36. Dunn, *Romans*, 1:40; Cranfield, *Romans*, 1:91; cf. Ridderbos, *Romeinen*, 33–34.
37. Cf. Moo, *Romans*, 67.

The righteousness (δικαιοσύνη, v. 17) can firstly denote the status of the believer given by God,[38] which is the classic Protestant interpretation. Luther viewed the righteousness as purely forensic without denoting moral transformation, which he described with the phrase: *simul iustus et peccator* ("simultaneously righteous and sinner").[39] Cranfield notes that the Catholic scholars traditionally included moral regeneration as part of righteousness.[40] By taking θεοῦ as an objective genitive, righteousness can secondly denote an attribute or attitude of God such as His faithfulness[41] to His promises.[42] It can thirdly point to an activity of God, where θεοῦ is taken as a subjective genitive, and denote the saving action of God.[43]

Other than Cranfield who views righteousness as the status of the believer[44] or Jewett who sees it as God's activity,[45] Dunn rightly argues for an approach that embraces both God's action (subjective genitive) and the gift bestowed by God (objective genitive):

> Since the basic idea of *relationship* in which God acts even for the defective partner, an action whereby God sustains the weaker partner of his covenant relationship within the relationship, the answer again is really *both* ... It is God's righteousness which enables and in fact achieves man's [sic] righteousness.[46]

Moo has a similar approach, and writes that righteousness includes both theology (God's acting) and anthropology (the human being who receives).[47] For Paul, the righteousness of God is thus a relational concept, "the act by which God brings people into right relationship with himself"[48] and with one another.[49]

---

38. Cranfield, *Romans*, 1:99–100; adopted by Mounce, *Romans*, 73.

39. In Moo, *Romans*, 71.

40. Cranfield, *Romans*, 1:95.

41. As Dunn, *Romans*, 1:43 points out, this is one of the possible meanings of πίστις (cf. Rom 3:3; Gal 5:22; 2 Thess 1:4).

42. Fitzmyer, *Romans*, 262.

43. Roberts 1981, "Righteousness," 18; Barrett, *Romans*, 29.

44. Cranfield, *Romans*, 1:99–100; cf. Ridderbos, *Paulus*, 175–76, who views righteousness in Paul as a human quality that is attributed/granted (Dutch: "toegekend") by God.

45. Jewett, *Romans*, 142.

46. Dunn, *Romans*, 1:41–42.

47. Moo, *Romans*, 74; cf. Barrett, *Romans*, 29; Sanday and Headlam, *Romans*, 24–25.

48. Moo, *Romans*, 74.

49. Jewett, *Romans*, 141; Dunn, *Romans*, 1:40–41.

The phrase ἐκ πίστεως εἰς πίστιν (v. 17) has been variously interpreted.⁵⁰ It can be interpreted as "faith from start to finish"⁵¹ or "altogether by faith."⁵² Yet Dunn notes that the ἐκ is most naturally understood as denoting the source of the revelation and the εἰς as denoting "that to which the revelation is directed."⁵³ Because of the apparent oddness of seeing both the ἐκ and εἰς as referring to human appropriation of God's righteousness, many commentators tend to see the ἐκ as denoting God's faithfulness, and the εἰς as denoting human faith.⁵⁴ There might remain some ambiguity in how faith is portrayed in Paul's reference to Habakkuk 2:4 (in Rom 1:17)⁵⁵ in that it might involve both God's faithfulness and human faith.⁵⁶ While all these interpretations are possible, there might be a much simpler solution to the problem. The solution I propose is that Romans 4 is largely the explanation of ἐκ πίστεως εἰς πίστιν, where the the ἐκ πίστεως would denote Abraham's faith (Rom 4:3, 9, 13, 16, 17, 20) and the εἰς πίστιν would denote the faith of the Christ-believers (Rom 4:24). These two aspects of faith would perfectly fit Dunn's source/direction distinction⁵⁷ (see above). The phrase ἐκ πίστεως εἰς πίστιν would then have salvation-historical significance.⁵⁸

If the expression ἐκ πίστεως denotes the faith of Abraham, the faith of the Christ-believer (εἰς πίστιν), which signifies identity mode C, can be understood as in *continuity* with the original righteousness and faith of Abraham. The net result would be that all three modes of identity are being represented here: ABC, where A represents the Ἰουδαῖος (v. 16), B as pointing to Abraham's faith and righteousness (ἐκ πίστεως), and C as pointing to anyone's faith and righteousness in Christ (εἰς πίστιν). This continuity is enhanced by (1) the priority of the Judean in terms of their position in salvation history, and (2) by Paul's comparison of his current

---

50. Cranfield, *Romans*, 1:99, lists eight possibilities, of which "from the faith of the OT to the faith of the NT" (Tertullian), "from present faith to future" (Aquinas), "from God's faithfulness to man's [sic] faith" (originally Ambrosiaster; see main text), and the idea of growth in faith (Sanday and Headlam, *Romans*, 28) are probably the most noteworthy.

51. Barrett, *Romans*, 31.

52. Cranfield, *Romans*, 100. These interpretations of Barrett and Cranfield can be seen as an expression of the concept of *sola fide* (Jewett, *Romans*, 144; Cranfield, *Romans*, 1:100; cf. Ridderbos, *Romeinen*, 35).

53. Dunn, *Romans*, 1:44.

54. E.g., Witherington and Hyatt, *Romans*, 48; Wright, "Romans," 425; Manson, "Romans"; Gaston, *Paul*; Barth, *Romans*, 41–42; Herbert, "Faithfulness."

55. Cf. Wright, "Romans," 426.

56. Osborne, *Romans*, 44; Dunn, *Romans*, 1:44.

57. Dunn, *Romans*, 1:44.

58. Cf. Käsemann, *Romans*, 31.

motivation of his gospel (constituted by ἐκ πίστεως εἰς πίστιν) with Habakkuk 2:4 (Ὁ δὲ δίκαιος ἐκ πίστεως ζήσεται, v. 17), which signifies that Paul anchors the current principle(s) of faith pertaining to the gospel firmly in the Old Testament.

Romans 4:1–25

In Romans 3, Paul explained that in the light of the work of Christ, all people have an equal status before God in terms of sin, and that covenant membership is not defined in terms of natural descent or law (3:1–20). Faith in Christ has become the equalizing access point and mark of covenant membership (3:21–26). In 3:27–31, which can be seen as a summary of what will be explained in 4:1–25,[59] Paul sums up the new situation in Christ with respect to the "[law of] works" (τῶν ἔργων, v. 27) that stands opposed to the "the law of faith" (νόμου πίστεως, v. 27). Dunn paraphrases νόμου πίστεως as "law understood in terms of faith"[60] or the law as "'done' by faith."[61] He understands νόμος in this whole passage (esp. 3:27–31) as referring to the Old Testament and not to the Sinai-Torah.[62] Dunn thus interprets "law of faith" as not the law of the Judeans alone. Wright seems to understand νόμος here more in the direction of Sinai-Torah throughout 3:27–31, but then as a response to grace.[63] To see νόμος throughout 3:27–31 as Torah, whether defined in broader terms (Dunn) or narrower terms (Wright, Cranfield), appears somewhat strenuous.[64] In the context of 3:27–31, it makes more sense to take νόμος in verse 27 as referring to a principle[65] or system,[66] which can then be interpreted as a principle or basis of righteousness: either by works or by faith. Even in this interpretation, it does not have to contradict the NPP or even the TAP, especially when τῶν ἔργων and πίστεως can still be understood as both *entrance to* and *mark of* the Old and New Covenants respectively.[67]

---

59. Jipp, "Rereading"; Moo, *Romans*, 244–45.
60. Dunn, *Romans*, 1:184, 186.
61. Dunn, *Romans*, 1:192.
62. Dunn, *Romans*, 1:191.
63. Wright, "Romans," 479–80; cf. Cranfield, *Romans*, 1:220.
64. Wright, "Romans," 480, admits that it is "controversial to take νόμος . . . here as 'Torah' throughout."
65. Zerwick and Grosvenor, *Grammatical Analysis*, 466; Newman and Nida, *Translator's Handbook*, 70; NJB; NIV; RSV; NEB.
66. BDAG, νόμος, §1b; Barrett, *Romans*, 82.
67. It is esp. circumcision that would serve as both *entrance to* and *mark of* the

The "universal monotheism"[68] that Paul sets forth in Rom 3:29 alludes to the *Shema*,[69] and is thus deeply rooted in the Torah (in the broader sense). The privileged position of the Judeans in terms of covenant membership in reality undercuts this universal monotheism, which is more effectively safeguarded by justification by faith.[70] The Torah is no longer the dividing wall between Judean and other nations.[71] Osborne writes: "But now a salvation-historical change has occurred. Relationship with God is based no longer on Torah but on faith in the Son of God."[72] This important theme underlies much of Paul's motivation for the inclusion of the gentiles in Rom 4:1–25 and the rest of his gospel. By God's justification of both circumcised and uncircumcised on the basis of faith in Jesus (3:24–26), the νόμος (3:31), referring to the whole of the Old Testament,[73] is confirmed (ἵστημι, v. 31)[74] or validated,[75] not in the sense that those who partake in the covenant through faith in Christ have to adhere to the stipulations and outward rituals of the Torah as such, but that the Old Testament remains the foundation on which the gospel is built.[76] Another aspect of the validation of the law is that the law is fulfilled in and through faith in Christ[77] in that the believer is accounted as really having "done the law" on the basis of Christ's fulfillment of the law (cf. 8:4).[78]

From Faith to Faith

The phrase ἐκ πίστεως occurs frequently throughout Romans (1:17; 3:26; 3:30; 4:16 [x2]; 5:1; 9:30, 32; 10:6; 14:23). While ἐκ πίστεως occurs 9 times in the direct context of faith in Christ, the only exception is in 4:16 (second occurrence), where it occurs in the phrase ἐκ πίστεως Ἀβραάμ, the "father

---

covenant in the OT (cf. Rom 2:17–29).

68. Dunn, *Romans*, 1:188.
69. Wright, "Romans," 482.
70. Dunn, *Romans*, 1:188.
71. Moo, *Romans*, 251.
72. Osborne, *Romans*, 102.
73. Dunn, *Romans*, 1:191.
74. Zerwick and Grosvenor, *Grammatical Analysis*, 467; Cranfield, *Romans*, 1:224; Newman and Nida, *Translator's Handbook*, 72.
75. BDAG, ἵστημι, §4; L&N §76.20; Newman and Nida, *Translator's Handbook*, 72.
76. Cf. D'Angelo, *Moses*, 194.
77. Moo, *Romans*, 255; Mounce, *Romans*, 120; Cranfield, *Romans*, 1:240; cf. Barrett, *Romans*, 84.
78. Moo, *Romans*, 484.

of us all." Here, faith in Christ is identified with the faith of Abraham,[79] the forerunner and father of the faith of both Judean and non-Judean. The whole of Romans 4:1–25 is an exposition of the origin of the principle of ἐκ πίστεως, and where it finds its root,[80] namely, in the faith of Abraham that was counted to him for righteousness (vv. 3, 5).

Many commentators seem to miss how verses 4 to 5 describe the nature of faith. Faith is per definition opposed to work for a reward,[81] which ran contrary to much of the Judean perception of obtaining God's promise (cf. 2:13)[82] and especially of Abraham's reception of the promise[83] and David's acceptance by God.[84] The notion that an element of merit was present in the Judean perception of obtaining God's promise is much debated in the TAP versus the NPP. While much has been put on the table in favor of an understanding of the faith of Judeans of the second temple that was not based on salvation by merit, and did indeed incorporate an understanding of grace,[85] many scholars in response identified various instances within the religious understanding of Judeans of the second temple (or in its proximity) where final vindication based on works and merit was prevalent.[86] The notions of final vindication by merit (TAP) and staying within the covenant by the marks of the covenant, which included the observance of the law

79. O'Brien, "Converted," 387.

80. Cf. Mounce, Romans, 126.

81. Dunn, Romans, 1:203. The expression ἐργαζομένῳ ὁ μισθός probably alludes to the business world, where λογίζεται would then be "a reckoning of payment for work done" (ibid; cf. Hultgren, Romans, 180; Wright, "Romans," 491).

82. Hultgren, Romans, 184; O'Brien, "Converted," 379; Gathercole, Boasting; Moo, Romans, 263; Käsemann, Romans, 107; Cranfield, Romans, 1:227, 229.

83. O'Brien, "Converted," 384; Gathercole, Boasting, 235–40; Bruce 1985, Romans, 115; Sir 44:19–20; 1 Macc 2:52; Jub 19:8–9; 23:9–10; CD 3:2–4; cf. Barrett, Romans, 86, 91. The allusion to Abraham as being ungodly (ἀσεβῆ, v. 5) and being more of a gentile (before being circumcised, v. 10) than an Israelite, would be extreme in terms of the Judean perception of Abraham (Hultgren, Romans, 181; Wright, "Romans," 492).

84. O'Brien, "Converted," 381, 389; Gathercole, Boasting, 246–48; CD 5:5; 4QMMT, C 24–25.

85. E.g., Sanders, Palestinian Judaism; Dunn, "New Perspective"; idem., Romans, 1:335–40; idem., Theology of Paul's Letter; Wright, Climax; Paul Really Said.

86. E.g., Gathercole, Boasting; Carson et al., Variegated Nomism (2 vols.). Maston, Divine and Human Agency, points to the centrality of the obedience of God's commandments in people's relationship with God from the writings of Ben Sira (second century BCE). He concludes that "Ben Sira defines everything about the divine-human relationship in terms of obedience to the commandments" (57). Against Sanders, Palestinian Judaism, who presented Ben Sira as an example of covenantal nomism, Maston, Divine and Human Agency, 73–74, shows that Ben Sira depicted God as reacting to human obedience or disobedience. In other words, God's response to the individual is determined entirely by whether a person has kept the Torah.

(NPP), do not have to contradict each other though. Both these notions could be held together.[87] Moo, who works in this direction, sees the Judean perception of faith as synergistic.[88]

Paul defines faith as not accumulating debt (ὀφείλημα, v. 4) and thus as void of any inherent merit. Faith is inherently according to grace (κατὰ χάριν, v. 4). In other words, faith is to acknowledge that God's favor cannot be earned or worked for.[89] Faith is to trust (πιστεύοντι, v. 5)[90] God's grace (κατὰ χάριν, v. 4) and promise (ἐπαγγελία, vv. 13, 14, 16, 20),[91] and to cease with all human self-reliance[92] and effort. Faith is for Paul "something qualitatively distinct from any human-originated endeavor,"[93] but can simultaneously be described as "the act and decision of the individual person."[94] The verbs επίστευσεν (v. 3) and πιστεύοντι (v. 5) are active indicative: it is Abraham that believed,[95] not God that imparted Abraham's faith or believed "through" Abraham in Himself. In this context it is thus unnecessary to see faith as being "imparted" irrespective of the human response. Faith ultimately relates to both God's grace in Christ and the human freedom to react to that grace. This understanding of faith underscores both the unmerited and relational aspect of righteousness, where faith constitutes both (1) the entrance into[96] (cf. Rom 5:2) and the mark of [97]Abraham's spiritual family, and (2) the reciprocal character of the relationship between God and His people.

Additionally, the understanding of Abraham's faith as a human reaction on God's grace, provides content to the ἐκ πίστεως of 1:17 (see esp. ἐκ πίστεως in 4:16). Abraham's belief in the promise that was fulfilled in Christ (4:3) and especially God's grace in the promise to Abraham, is foundational

---

87. Hagner, *New Testament*; Longenecker, *Galatians*; see pp. 89-94.

88. Moo, *Romans*, 263.

89. Dunn, *Romans*, 1:215, notes that the function of the law was to bring people to consciousness of their transgression and to "the same unconditional dependence and reliance on God which man [sic] in general had abandoned (1:19-25) and which Abraham displayed so clearly."

90. Hultgren, *Romans*, 185; O'Brien, "Converted," 387; Wright, "Romans," 499; Mounce, *Romans*, 123; cf. Zerwick and Grosvenor, *Grammatical Analysis*, 46.

91. Cf. Cranfield, *Romans*, 1:231.

92. Bruce, *Romans*, 117.

93. Moo, *Romans*, 264.

94. Käsemann, *Romans*, 109.

95. This can also be seen in πιστεύοντι δέ (v. 5) being contrasted to μὴ ἐργαζομένῳ, a present middle, which indicates reflexivity and the subject's participation in the action (Wallace, *Grammar*, 414-16).

96. Moo, *Romans*, 267.

97. Wright, "Romans," 496; Käsemann, *Romans*, 109.

to belief in Christ that *has come* in a salvation-historical sense (Gal 3:23, 25; cf. Rom 3:21).[98] This belief in Christ corresponds to εἰς πίστιν in 1:17, which is the access and mark of the new identity in Christ (identity mode C). This understanding thus explains both the ἐκ πίστεως (promise to Abraham) and the εἰς πίστιν (faith in Christ) of 1:17. The identification of Abraham's faith with the faith of the believer in Christ constitutes an aspect of the profound *continuity* between the two.[99]

Abraham, Faith and Identity

One of the important questions pertaining to Romans 4:1-25 is which modes of identity are represented here. Romans 4:1 indicates Abraham as τὸν προπάτορα ἡμῶν κατὰ σάρκα. This primarily designates Abraham as the "father of race, in view of his place within salvation-history"[100] as opposed to spiritual generation.[101] The designation κατὰ σάρκα (v. 1) can be viewed in *continuity* with ὁ Χριστὸς τὸ κατὰ σάρκα in 9:5 (see pp. 46-52), and constitutes a dimension of physical descent in the promise to Abraham, signified by circumcision (τοῖς . . . ἐκ περιτομῆς, v. 12), which was fulfilled and ended in Christ κατὰ σάρκα (cf. σπέρματί σου, ὅς ἐστιν Χριστός, Gal 3:16). Yet, to Abraham circumcision was a seal of the righteousness of faith (v. 11)—a deeper meaning that was also fulfilled in Christ, where the "just/righteous requirement of the law might be fulfilled in" Christ-believers (8:4). Therefore, Christ's fulfillment of the promise had both a natural, physical dimension in that Christ was Abraham's physical descendant (9:5), and a spiritual dimension in that the righteousness of God has been revealed apart from the law for all who believe in Christ without differentiation (3:21-22). In Christ, the physical dimension of the promise ended (cf. 10:4), and the phrase "Abraham, our father according to the flesh" (4:1) thus stands in *ultimate discontinuity* with both the concepts σπέρμα and ἐπαγγελίας (cf. Gal 3:7-9, 16).

Abraham received the circumcision as seal of righteousness of faith when he was still uncircumcised, constituting the basis on which he could become the father of all gentiles who believe (4:11). But Abraham's faith as uncircumcised was also the basis on which he could become the father of

---

98. Käsemann, *Romans*, 109, understands faith in Rom 4 as similar to the epiphany of faith in Gal 3:23, 25.

99. Käsemann, *Romans*, 118; cf. Moo, *Romans*, 257.

100. Dunn, *Romans*, 1:199; cf. Hultgren, *Romans*, 179; Wright, "Romans," 489-90; Cranfield, *Romans*, 1:227.

101. Moo, *Romans*, 260.

those circumcised who walked in the steps of their (physical) father Abraham by believing in addition to being circumcised (v. 12).[102] It is important to note here that Abraham is not portrayed in verse 12 as physical father of Israel, but as father of those of them that believe. But the question arises if faith is in Christ or apart from Christ. The same question applies to verse 16, and will thus be discussed below.

The promise to inherit the world was preserved for Abraham's seed on the basis of faith, and not on the basis of law (v. 13).[103] The promise is to be inherited on the basis of faith in order to be sure to all the seed (v. 16),

a. οὐ τῷ ἐκ τοῦ νόμου μόνον

b. ἀλλὰ καὶ τῷ ἐκ πίστεως Ἀβραάμ, ὅς ἐστιν πατὴρ πάντων ἡμῶν.

Several questions can be asked here. (1) The question can be asked whether two groups, (a) and (b), are envisioned (e.g., Judean believers and gentile believers) or one group: physical Judeans (a) who additionally believe (b). (2) It can be asked whether these believers in (b), whether the second group or the only group, believe in Christ as such. (3) One can ask if physical descendants of Abraham can be counted as heirs and children of the promise apart from faith in Christ.

As for the first question (1), the first possibility to be eliminated is that group (a) would denote a group that would inherit the promise on the basis of law apart from faith. Paul has already established in verse 12 that Abraham is the father of those who are not only heirs on the basis of circumcision, but additionally believe. That a group would inherit apart from faith would be contrary to what Paul has said from 3:19 up to this point.[104] Regarding the identity of (a) and (b) there is difference of opinion. Some view the first group as Christ-believing Judeans and the second group as Christ-believing gentiles.[105] Others (probably correctly) see (a) and (b) as overlapping, where (a) represents Christ-believing Judeans and (b) represents both Christ-believing Judeans and gentiles.[106] Still others view (a) and (b) as constituting one group of either Christ-believing Judeans[107] or

---

102. Moo, *Romans*, 270; Dunn, *Romans*, 1:210-11.

103. Wright, "Romans," 496.

104. Wright, "Romans," 498; Käsemann, *Romans*, 121.

105. Moo, *Romans*, 279; Mounce, *Romans*, 128; Hendriksen, *Romans*, 152, 156-57; Cranfield, *Romans*, 1:242.

106. Jewett, *Romans*, 331; Kühl, *Römer*, 147; Weiss, *Römer*, 203-5; cf. Käsemann, *Romans*, 121. Jewett, *Romans*, 331, leaves room for some ambiguity here and includes "all of Paul's fellow believers, no matter which cultural and theological tendency they represent."

107. Longenecker, *Epistle to the Romans*, 515.

believing Judeans apart from Christ.[108] The implication of the latter view is that believing Israel in the past and believing Judeans in Paul's present are/remain God's people.

In answer to the second question (2), the way in which faith is qualified in verse 24 has to be taken into account. Belief is in God ("Him") who raised Jesus from the dead. While faith is not portrayed as being in Christ as such, Paul does not separate belief in God from the work of Christ. Although faith throughout Romans 4 cannot unambiguously be connected to Christ, faith cannot unambiguously be disconnected from Christ either. The measure of uncertainty regarding faith in Romans 4 is however diminished if the immediate context (Rom) and the rest of Paul's letters (e.g., Gal 3) are considered. On both sides of Romans 4, faith is qualified in gospel terms. In 3:22–26, those believing are being justified through the redemption and faith in Christ Jesus, and in 5:1–2, justification by faith is through Christ, through whom there is access by faith into the grace wherein believers stand.

One of the stronger arguments in interpreting faith in Romans 4 Christologically, is the possibility advanced by Jipp[109] that Romans 3:27–4:1 previews Paul's narration of the Abraham account in 4:2–25, centring on four issues: the exclusion of works in justification (3:27–28 // 4:2–8), Abraham's justification as preceding his circumcision (3:29–30 // 4:9–12), the continuity between the law and faith (3:31 // 4:13–15) and the nature of Abraham's paternity (4:1 // 4:16–25). In this interpretation, the Abraham narrative is to be understood in terms of Paul's "prior Christological commitments" where "Abraham functions for Paul as a representative figure whose story typologically portrays features of Paul's gospel."[110]

It thus seems likely that Paul has faith in the gospel in view in 4:24, which by implication applies to faith in both verses 12 and 16.[111] This understanding is strengthened by the main thrust of Paul's argument in Romans 4, which is that "believers in Christ are legitimate children of Abraham."[112] It is thus doubtful whether Paul would want to establish faith apart from Christ in such ambiguous terms amidst the unambiguous references to faith in the rest of the letter. Furthermore, if the bigger picture is considered (esp. Rom 9–11 where Paul addresses profound yet potentially sensitive issues), the measure

---

108. Hultgren, *Romans*, 186; Dunn, *Romans*, 1:216.

109. Jipp, "Rereading."

110. Jipp, "Rereading," 239.

111. Wright, "Romans," 492, 502; Moo, *Romans*, 270, 277–79, 287; Käsemann, *Romans*, 121; cf. Jewett, *Romans*, 331, 342.

112. Jewett, *Romans*, 320.

of uncertainty surrounding faith in Romans 4 might have something to do with Paul's subtle rhetoric, rather than with intended ambiguity.

As for the third question (3), it has to be noted that Paul identifies Abraham as both the father κατὰ σάρκα (Israelites/Judeans of physical descent, v. 1) and Abraham as the father of "us all" (v. 16), which seems to be pointing to all in Paul's present who believe in Christ. In view of Paul's bigger salvation-historical scheme (esp. Rom 9:1-10) it is most unlikely that the physical children of Abraham would be reckoned as heirs to the promise,[113] for they would only be Abraham's children κατὰ σάρκα, constituting identity mode A (*outer* Israel, cf. Rom 9:6, see pp. 51-54). Abraham's ambivalent status as gentile[114] who became both the father of national Israel (according to the flesh, v. 1) and the father of faith of "us all" (including gentiles), might relate to the fact that the promise (vv. 13, 14, 16, 20) was ultimately fulfilled by Christ (see esp. 15:8).[115] Abraham's ambivalent status thus does not only legitimate the acceptability of gentiles who responded to the gospel in Christ,[116] but it indicates that Abraham's true descendants were in fact not so much those who imitated his circumcision, but those who imitated his faith,[117] an understanding that really comes into full force in Christ. Yet if Paul would allude to believing Israel apart from Christ in verses 12 and 16 (which would indicate identity mode AB, *inner* Israel), they would have to point to historical Israel, for they could hardly point to Judeans in Paul's present whose belief is not directed to the gospel in Christ. Depending on one's interpretation of Romans 11, the latter idea would not fit the larger context and would have no parallel elsewhere in Paul's letters.

---

113. Wright, "Romans," 490, 496; Cranfield, *Romans*, 1:242; Hendriksen, *Romans*, 157-58.

114. Jewett, *Romans*, 319.

115. Cf. Sanday and Headlam, *Romans*, 107.

116. Jewett, *Romans*, 319.

117. Sanday and Headlam, *Romans*, 107; cf. Wright, "Romans," 494. This notion undermines the notion that water baptism could be a replacement for circumcision or that such baptism could be understood in terms of baptismal regeneration (cf. Mounce, *Romans*, 126). In addition, this interpretation goes against the notion that Paul "restructures *genealogical lines* in order to reconfigure the boundaries that unite and divide people" (Eisenbaum, "New Abraham," 142, emphasis added). For Eisenbaum, Paul does not assume that Judeans are biological descendants (κατὰ σάρκα) while gentiles become descendants by adoption (υἱοθεσία). Rather, she contends that Paul "simply means that the Gentiles are now in the process of claiming their inheritance, whereas Jews have already received it" (140). In Eisenbaum's approach, she does not understand genealogy as being based purely on biology, but sees genealogy as interrelated with kinship relations. Notwithstanding these distinctions, her reading seems to circumnavigate the central criterion for *true descent* from Abraham, which is faith.

It is noteworthy that Paul neither mentions anything of the inheritance of land that was part of the promise to Abraham and formed part of Israel's expectation (e.g., Gen 12:7; 13:15-17; 15:7; Isa 57:13; 60:21; Jer 24:6; 30:3; 32:41; Ezek 36:10-12; 37:25; Ps 25:13; 37:9), nor of Israel's national reign over the nations (e.g., Isa 11:10-14; 42:1, 6; 49:6; 54:3; Jer 4:2; 23:5; Zech 9:10) through the worldwide earthly dominion of the Messiah (Ps 72:8-11; Isa 9:7; Jer 23:5). Rather, believers now inherit the whole cosmos (Rom 4:13), which points to all of humanity,[118] which is Abraham's seed,[119] or points to the restoration of the whole created order that transcends a territorial understanding of the promise of the land to Israel.[120] The Messiah's reign is now of a different *kind*:[121] he reigns over the dead and the living (Rom 14:9; cf. 15:12; 2 Cor 5:16).[122] The promises to Abraham in terms of the one new family of Judean and Greek believers in Christ (15:8)[123] is therefore fulfilled in a way different from prevalent Judean messianic expectations in terms of (1) Abraham's seed, (2) the land and (3) the reign of God through His people. Rather than being a physical, political reign, Christ's reign can be described as non-material.[124]

In light of Romans 4 then, identity mode B is most certainly constituted by Abraham himself as believing God's promise (v. 3). Abraham's faith is portrayed as foundational to the promise that has been fulfilled in Christ, and as a type[125] or paradigm[126] of the faith in Christ. Abraham's faith thus constitutes the *continuity* between Abraham (identity mode AB) and the believer in Christ (identity mode C). Believers in Christ, whether Judean or non-Judean, become heirs of the promise[127] to Abraham, and identity modes B (Abraham) and C (Christ-believers) thus become one in Christ. Those of law (Israel according to the flesh, identity mode A)

---

118. BDAG, κόσμος, §6a.

119. Wright, "Romans," 496.

120. Dunn, *Romans*, 1:213.

121. Wright, *Faithfulness*, 2:911, 1065.

122. Wright, *People of God*, 408, and Danker, *II Corinthians*, 81, understand οὐδένα οἴδαμεν κατὰ σάρκα in 2 Cor 5:16 such as that the Corinthians do not know Jesus as a national Messiah any longer.

123. Wright, "Romans," 535.

124. Du Toit, "Christian Zionism"; cf. Witherington, *Jesus*, 57; Fitzmyer, *The One*, 183.

125. Hultgren, *Romans*, 190.

126. Dunn, *Romans*, 1:223.

127. In Rom 4, inheritance (κληρονόμος, vv. 13, 14) and promise (ἐπαγγελία, vv. 13, 14, 16, 20) are closely linked.

cannot inherit the promise apart from faith (4:14) and are by implication excluded from inheritance.

The other aspect of faith in the promise to Abraham that Paul highlights is his description of God's activity as "making the dead alive, and calling the things that are not as if they were" (4:17). The calling of the things that are not as if they were probably alludes to God's *creatio ex nihilo*, which was part of the Judean tradition.[128] Apart from the revival of Abraham's "dead" body (σῶμα ἤδη νενεκρωμένον, v. 19), Paul might have something more in mind with his referral to the revival of the dead (v. 17), which will probably be better understood in his repetition of the same notion in 11:15 (see pp. 267-71).

In the light of Paul's salvation-historical[129] exposition in Romans 4, the *continuity* that believers in Christ have with Israel can now be described more precisely. The continuity of faith neither flows *through* Israel or the Judean nation, nor are Christ-believers an *extension* of them as a nation. Faith, whether being a believing Judean or gentile, connects in a *punctiliar* way (cf. Gal 4:21–5:1, see pp. 100-107) onto Abraham through Christ *apart from* Israel according to the flesh (4:14; cf. 9:3-5). With belief in Christ there is therefore not continuity in terms of the works of the law, including circumcision (3:20, 28), for the law in fact stands antithetical to faith in 4:13-16.[130] Rather, the law and its works have been fulfilled in Christ.[131] Even while Christ himself was for Paul a physical descendant of the patriarchs (1:3; cf. 9:5), the only connection of any Christ-believer to being God's people, regardless of ethnicity, is via faith in Christ, and not physical (κατὰ σάρκα). Käsemann thus rightly identifies the actual continuity with Abraham as "the power of God."[132] Belief in Christ therefore renders any claim on covenant membership based on law, circumcision or any other external identity marker ineffective.[133] Käsemann correctly states that "[t]he polemic which runs through the whole chapter [4] shows that we are dealing here not with an extension or modification of the Jewish view, but with its contrast."[134]

---

128. Hultgren, *Romans*, 189; O'Brien, "Converted," 385-86; Moo, *Romans*, 281; Käsemann, *Romans*, 122; Cranfield, *Romans*, 1:244; cf. BDAG, καλέω, §4; Mounce, *Romans*, 128; Barrett, *Romans*, 97; Macc 7:28.

129. Käsemann, *Romans*, 116.

130. Hultgren, *Romans*, 184; Käsemann, *Romans*, 118.

131. Moo, *Romans*, 255; cf. Barrett, *Romans*, 84.

132. Käsemann, *Romans*, 117.

133. Cf. Bruce, *Romans*, 119.

134. Käsemann, *Romans*, 79.

Galatians 3:1-29

Galatians, which some consider to be one of the oldest of Paul's letters,[135] has traditionally been viewed as the fountainhead for reflection about justification by faith.[136] Many of the NPP versus TAP debates revolve around the understanding of the "works of the law" (ἔργων νόμου) and faith (πίστις; πιστεύω) in Galatians 3. Whereas the understanding of these concepts certainly converges with the enquiry of this book, my aim is not to repeat the whole of this debate here, but to focus on the modes of identity represented in this chapter.

The Opponents and Recipients

The identity of Paul's opponents has to be inferred by a mirror reading of the letter,[137] but not without awareness of its dangers.[138] The traditional identification of Paul's opponents as "Judaizers," has been contested for the main reasons that (1) it would imply a conflict in Galatia between Judean and anti-Judean factions, and (2) that the verb Ἰουδαΐζω (2:14) is more correctly translated as "to adopt Judean practices"[139] or to "live like a Judean" (see pp. 131-35), rather than "to Judaize." These Missionaries,[140] Teachers[141] or Preachers[142] were probably Judean Christ-believers.[143] These Teachers of

---

135. Some who accept the South Galatian theory date the origin of the letter as early as 48 CE (e.g., Hagner, *New Testament*, 437; Carson and Moo, *Introduction*, 464; Fung, *Galatians*, 28) or 49-50 (e.g., George, *Galatians*, 48; Guthrie, *Introduction*, 479).

136. Hays, "Galatians," 183.

137. George, *Galatians*, 60.

138. Barclay, *Obeying*, 37-41, shows that mirror reading inevitably involves circularity. One of the biggest problems in mirror reading Galatians is its polemical rhetoric, which may result in partial accounts, or accounts that state one side of an issue. The overarching danger in mirror reading Galatians is that it could become an arbitrary exercise. More specifically, mirror reading can become selective instead of focussing on the whole. It can be dangerous to focus on particular words that are taken to represent the vocabulary of the opponents, which could result in "a fragile chain of assumptions" (p. 39). Barclay finally warns against the danger of over-interpretation. For example, not every statement that Paul makes is necessarily a rebuttal of counter-statements of his opponents.

139. Cf. Hays, "Galatians," 185; Barclay, *Obeying*, 36.

140. Dunn, *Epistle to the Galatians*, 11.

141. Martyn, *Galatians*, 117-26.

142. De Boer, *Galatians*.

143. Since most scholars refer to them as "Jewish Christians" (e.g., Carson and Moo, *Introduction*, 465; Hays, "Galatians," 185; Hong, "Law," 88; Barclay, *Obeying*, 185; Fung, *Galatians*, 8) this seems to be the consensus view among most scholars.

the Law[144] urged the other believers in Christ (a) to be circumcised (2:3; 5:2–3), (b) to observe Judean sabbaths and feast days (4:8–11), (c) to obey everything in the Torah (3:10), to be wanting to be under the law (4:21), to try to be justified by the law (5:4), to promise that those who keep the commandments would find life (3:12),[145] and lastly (d) that the Torah of Moses was divinely ordained to provide moral perfection (ἐπιτελέω, v. 3) in order to restrain the impulses of the flesh (5:16, 24).[146] While the Teachers of the Law may have thought of themselves as believers in Christ, Paul was ready to challenge the authenticity of their belief in Christ.[147] Dunn argues that their tactics might have been "underhand and seductive."[148]

While most scholars agree that the original recipients of the letter are gentile Christ-believers,[149] apart from using the first person singular in terms of his own death to the law and his new found identity in Christ (2:19–21), Paul frequently uses the first person plural when he addresses his recipients concerning the work of Christ, the content of the gospel, or the law (1:4; 2:15, 16, 17; 3:13, 14, 23, 24, 25; 4:3, 5, 26, 28, 31; 5:1, 5, 25, 26; 6:9, 10). The first person plural includes Paul, a Judean Christ-believer, and all Judean and gentile believers by implication.[150] In other words, even though (1) the addressees are gentile Christ-believers, (2) much of Paul's rhetoric[151] in the letter is aimed at the Teachers of the Law, and (3) his style

---

144. This term that I will employ is a combination of the term Martyn, *Galatians*, 117–26, uses ("Teachers") and the crux of their agenda (see main text).

145. For a–c, see Carson and Moo, *Introduction*, 466; Hays, "Galatians," 185, 252.

146. Martyn, *Galatians*, 292–93, shows this motive from CD 2:14–16: "Hear now, my sons, and I will uncover your eyes so that you may see and understand the works of God . . . so that you may walk *perfectly* in all his ways and not be drawn *by the thoughts of the Guilty Impulse* and by lustful eyes" (Vermes, emphasis added). 1QS 5:5 speaks of circumcising the Impulse.

147. Cf. Carson and Moo, *Introduction*, 466.

148. Dunn, *Epistle to the Galatians*, 152. This is suggested by Paul's direct and open approach (see esp. 3:1, where Christ is depicted as being openly exhibited before the Galatians' eyes), which might have been contrary to the approach of the Teachers of the Law.

149. E.g., De Boer, *Galatians*, 5; Hays, "Galatians," 184; Betz, *Galatians*, 4; Bruce, *Heart Set Free*, 182.

150. Hays, "Galatians," 262; Wright, *Climax*, 143; Dunn, *Epistle to the Galatians*, 176, 179; Fung, *Galatians*, 148–49.

151. Betz, *Galatians*, has made a significant contribution in arguing that Galatians is an "apologetic letter" that is structured in accordance with the conventions of ancient judicial rhetoric, even though later reviewers have observed that Galatians does not fit the apologetic letter genre as neatly as Betz proposed (Hays, "Galatians," 188). It would be more likely that Paul's rhetoric was not judicial but deliberative, which aim is to persuade the recipients toward a certain course of action (Kennedy, *Rhetorical*

is thus tailored for a specific context, the propositional content underlying his rhetoric in Galatians can be applied to all the people groups with whom Paul had contact.[152]

Antitheses in Galatians 3

Paul's rhetoric in Galatians 3 contains several antitheses that relate to identity. These antitheses can be divided into three main groups:

1. πνεῦμα versus σάρξ (v. 3)

   πνεῦμα versus ἐξ ἔργων νόμου (vv. 2, 5)

2. ἐξ ἀκοῆς πίστεως versus ἐξ ἔργων νόμου (vv. 2, 5)

   ἐκ πίστεως (vv. 7, 8, 9, 11, 12) versus ἐξ ἔργων νόμου (v. 10), ἐν νόμῳ (v. 11) and ὁ νόμος (v. 12)

3. ἐξ ἐπαγγελίας versus ἐκ νόμου (v. 18)

Expressions containing the terms πίστις, ἐπαγγελία, or πνεῦμα belong propositionally together, and are opposed to expressions containing νόμος or σάρξ, which in turn belong together.

Galatians 3:2 contains Paul's first mention of the Spirit in the letter. The reception (λαμβάνω, v. 2) of the Spirit accompanies the beginning (ἐνάρχομαι, v. 3) of the new identity in Christ.[153] This happens at conversion[154] (cf. Rom 8:15; 1 Cor 2:12; 2 Cor 6:4) and corresponds with justification.[155] In reference to verses 1 to 5, Hansen writes that "Paul teaches that the presence of the Spirit is the distinguishing mark of belonging to the

---

Criticism, 144–52).

152. Cf. Donfried, *Thessalonica*, 196, 198; Thiselton, *New Horizons*, 239; Beker, *Paul the Apostle*, 351.

153. Moo, *Galatians*, 182; Dunn, *Epistle to the Galatians*, 152–53, 156; cf. Hays, "Galatians," 251.

154. Dunn, *Epistle to the Galatians*, 152–53; Longenecker, *Galatians*, 102. Conversion does not imply that the believers in Christ converted from one religious system to another (e.g., from "Judaism" to "Christianity"), but it does point to the acquirement of a new core identity in Christ. This does not necessarily mean that previous ethnic designations such as "Judean" were eradicated, but that they were not definitive in marking off identity as God's people any longer. The issue of conversion and more specifically Paul's conversion will be addressed in more depth on pp. 125–30.

155. Fung, *Galatians*, 152; Bruce, *Galatians*, 149; cf. George, *Galatians*, 215. Bruce, *Galatians*, 149–50, argues that the Spirit belongs for Paul to the foundation of the gospel. The Spirit's link to justification can especially be derived from the Spirit's function as guarantee for final salvation (2 Cor 1:22; 5:5).

family of God's people."[156] The Spirit is being supplied to (ἐπιχορηγέω, v. 5)[157] the believer, and is characterized by working works of power (ἐνεργῶν δυνάμεις, v. 5) in them. The promise to Abraham (ἐπαγγελίας, vv. 14, 17, 18, 19, 22, 29) is closely linked to the Spirit (v. 14),[158] which constitutes its eschatological fulfillment,[159] and arguably its main content.[160] Both Judean and non-Judean alike ("we," v. 14)[161] who believe (vv. 2, 5, 14)[162] in Christ (2:16; 3:14, 22, 26)[163] partake in the Spirit. Apart from Christ, neither Ju-

156. Hansen, *Philippans*, 221.

157. Dunn, *Epistle to the Galatians*, 157; Zerwick and Grosvenor, *Grammatical Analysis*, 569.

158. Hays, "Galatians," 261; Martyn, *Galatians*, 322.

159. Silva, *Interpreting Galatians*, 176; Fee, *People of God*, 60; cf. Moo, *Galatians*, 182. Fee, *People of God*, 51–61, explains the eschatological dimension of the messianic age as commencing with the outpouring of the Spirit. For believers in Christ who partake in the Spirit, salvation is both a present (e.g., Rom 8:24; cf. Eph 2:5, 8) and future (e.g., Rom 5:9, 10; 1 Cor 15:2) reality that principally has been effected in Christ's resurrection from the dead.

160. Cf. De Boer, *Galatians*, 167, 216; Silva, "Faith," 237; Dunn, *Epistle to the Galatians*, 180; Bruce, *Galatians*, 168. Paul's understanding of the promise is thus spiritual and not material, and therefore makes nothing of the inheritance of the land (Dunn, *Epistle to the Galatians*, 183; Wright, *Climax*, 174; Bruce, *Galatians*, 172).

161. Fee, *People of God*, 60; Martyn, *Galatians*, 322. Paul's use of the first person plural (λάβωμεν) includes himself, a Judean Christ-believer.

162. The genitival phrase ἀκοῆς πίστεως (vv. 2, 5) proves difficult to translate, for both terms are lexically ambiguous. Many scholars agree that πίστις refers to the human act of believing (*fides qua creditur*), and does not have Jesus as its referent (Meyer, *Law*, 145–46; Silva, "Faith," 235; Longenecker, *Galatians*, 103; Fung, *Galatians*, 131; Bruce, *Galatians*, 149). It can be translated as "believing what you heard" (Longenecker, *Galatians*, 103). Silva, "Faith," 218, 235, argues that even in the translation of Martyn, *Galatians*, 281, 286–88), "the proclamation that has the power to elicit faith" (adopted by De Boer, *Galatians*, 175), does not eliminate the human act of believing. In verse 14, faith is to be understood as a human act (cf. Dunn, *Epistle to the Galatians*, 179) and as the means by which the Spirit is being received (λαμβάνω), for it stands in the context of Abraham's faith (3:6) and the righteous that will live by faith (v. 11).

163. The phrase πίστεως Ἰησοῦ Χριστοῦ (2:16 [x2]; 3:22) can be understood either as a subjective genitive ("[the] faith[fulness] of Jesus Christ": De Boer, *Galatians*, 193, 239; Hays, "Galatians," 239–40; Longenecker, *Galatians*, 145; ISV; LITV; KJV) or an objective genitive ("faith in Jesus Christ": Moo, *Galatians*, 40–48, 160–61; Fee, *Philippians*, 325; George, *Galatians*, 107, 188–89, 251; Dunn, *Epistle to the Galatians*, 164, 195; Fung, *Galatians*, 165; Bruce, *Galatians*, 181; Betz, *Galatians*, 117, 175; ESV; NRSV; ASV). Since both translations are grammatically possible, the decision has to be determined exegetically. Silva, "Faith," 227–34, (adopted by Carson and Moo, *Introduction*, 473) convincingly argues for viewing the phrase as an objective genitive, for the following main reasons: (1) The witness from the Greek fathers (e.g., Chrysostom) who understood it as "faith in Christ" shows that native Greek speakers had no difficulty in understanding the phrase as an objective genitive, and that such an understanding was not unnatural (cf. Luke 6:12; Rom 3:3; contra Hays, "Galatians," 147). (2) The

dean nor gentile had received the Abrahamic blessing, which is the Spirit.[164] Those who believe in Christ are frequently referred to as ἐκ πίστεως (vv. 7, 8, 9, 11, 12, 22, 24), which Martyn translates as "those whose identity is derived from faith."[165] Longenecker[166] views those ἐκ πίστεως as denoting "a specific mode of existence." They constitute identity mode C.

The Spirit (corresponding to faith and promise) is being contrasted with the flesh (σάρξ, v. 3), and by implication with the works of the law (ἐξ ἔργων νόμου, vv. 2, 5).[167] All other constructions with νόμος would by implication resort under σάρξ. In this context then, σάρξ refers to a mode of living (ζάω, v. 12), propagated by the Teachers of the Law whereby perfection (ἐπιτελέω, v. 3) is achieved in resistance to the "Impulsive Desire of the Flesh," which in turn is closely related to circumcision as commencement of law observance.[168] All other requirements from the Teachers of the Law, for example, observance of Judean sabbaths and feast days (4:8-11) or to obey everything in the Torah (3:10),[169] would form part of deriving "their identity from observance of the Law."[170] Dunn correctly argues that their

---

human response of believing is undeniably present in the New Testament (e.g., ἔχω with πίστις: Matt 17:20; 21:21; Mark 4:40; 11:22; Luke 17:6; faith contrasted with doubt: Mark 11:23). (3) In Paul's other letters, he uses πίστις in reference to faith in Christ rather than as an attribute of Christ (e.g., Rom 4:5, 9), and never *unambiguously* refers to πίστις that belongs to Christ. The idea that faith(fulness) belongs to Christ is thus not characteristic of Paul. (4) In Gal 2-3, when Paul uses the verb πιστεύω, he seems to use it mostly in connection with our faith in God or Christ (Paul refers to active, human faith in Gal 2:16; 3:6 and 22; cf. Dunn, *Theology of Paul's Letter*, 57-58). In Gal 2:16, the clause εἰς Χριστὸν Ἰησοῦν ἐπιστεύσαμεν exegetes the phrase πίστεως Ἰησοῦ Χριστοῦ (similarly τοῖς πιστεύουσιν in 3:22). Paul's language about faith thus has to be understood against the contrast between the notions of law-works (as human action) over against the act of faith, which remains a prominent theme in Paul (cf. note 239, p. 146). That Paul was capable of using a subjective genitive or that he might have used the genitive with some ambiguity in relation to Christ is however not hereby denied.

164. Martyn, *Galatians*, 322.

165. Martyn, *Galatians*, 299, 302; adopted by Hays, "Galatians," 255-56; cf. Dunn, *Epistle to the Galatians*, 163.

166. Longenecker, *Galatians*, 116.

167. Fung, *Galatians*, 134.

168. De Boer, *Galatians*, 179-80; Martyn, *Galatians*, 290-94; cf. George, *Galatians*, 213; 1QS 5:5.

169. cf. Carson and Moo, *Introduction*, 466.

170. Martyn, *Galatians*, 299; cf. De Boer, *Galatians*, 215; Hays, "Galatians," 257. Being a dedicated NPP proponent, Hays, "Galatians," 257-58, drops Martyn's, *Galatians*, 299, "observance," and reformulates: "those whose identity is derived from works of Law" (cf. De Boer, *Galatians*, 215). Wright, *Climax*, 149, expresses a similar notion when he refers to "'doing the law' as the covenant boundary marker."

emphasis was on "ethnic identity," which stands in contrast to the Spirit.[171] In view of the antithesis of Spirit and flesh, their identity can be described as fundamentally being derived from flesh (σάρξ, v. 3).[172] Everything that the Teachers of the Law insisted upon was outward and external, including the observance of the law. There is thus an overlap in meaning in the way Paul employs σάρξ here with κατὰ σάρκα elsewhere.[173] This identity in the flesh Paul is portraying here represents identity mode A.

By expressing the contrast of the Spirit, faith and the promise to the law (esp. ἐξ ἔργων νόμου, 2:16; 3:2, 5, 10) in terms of different modes of identity, largely corresponds to a NPP-understanding of the law in this context, yet not to the exclusion of elements of merit in the Judean perception of their identity and the Torah.[174] Circumcision was for the Judean people the way they entered into the covenant people and inherited the blessing spoken to Abraham.[175] Law was thus central to God's covenant with Israel.[176] Yet, for Paul, his statement that righteousness "is not found in the realm of the Law [v. 11] is true of every human being" and not merely for the Judean.[177] De Boer rightly states that the "overall point is that observing the law is totally irrelevant to God's activity of providing the Spirit to the Galatians."[178] Martyn further argues that Paul therefore "erase[s] the distinction" between Judean and gentile (esp. v. 28).[179] In Paul's exhortation to the Galatians, "he is now a former Jew, so they are former Gentiles . . . in Christ humanity is becoming a liberated unity."[180] Paul, by rejecting the Teachers of the Law's covenantal nomism, is thus not suggesting a modified form of covenantal nomism,[181] but a "new identity [in Christ] that lies beyond ethnic, social and sexual

---

171. Dunn, *Epistle to the Galatians*, 155.

172. Cf. Hays, "Galatians," 253; Dunn, *Epistle to the Galatians*, 155–56.

173. See esp. κατὰ σάρκα in Rom 9:3; 1 Cor 10:18; 2 Cor 5:12 and 11:18.

174. Moo, *Galatians*, 178; Hagner, *New Testament*, 366–74; Longenecker, *Galatians*, 102–6; cf. George, *Galatians*, 217–18; Rom 2:17–29, see pp. 54–68). For Longenecker, *Galatians*, 102, the phrase ἐξ ἔργων νόμου refers to "the whole legalistic complex of ideas having to do with winning God's favor by a merit-amassing observance of the Torah" (see also Longenecker, *Galatians*, 86).

175. Martyn, *Galatians*, 291; cf. Longenecker, *Galatians*, 109; Bruce, *Galatians*, 155.

176. Dunn, *Epistle to the Galatians*, 169.

177. Martyn, *Galatians*, 322; cf. De Boer, *Galatians*.

178. De Boer, *Galatians*, 181.

179. Martyn, *Galatians*, 335–36.

180. Martyn, *Galatians*, 336.

181. Martyn, *Galatians*, 347; Wright, *Climax*, 156.

distinctions."¹⁸² Judean or gentile "identity markers no longer matter."¹⁸³ Longenecker states that this new identity is inherited by "faith alone apart from righteous deeds or circumcision."¹⁸⁴ "[A]ll people are accepted on the same basis of faith and together make up the one body of Christ."¹⁸⁵ In Lategan's words: "Christ . . . is the only way through which Jews, the physical descendants of Abraham, can come to God again."¹⁸⁶

The law as mark that distinguished Judeans and gentiles consequently prevented the blessing of Abraham from reaching its destination, which is all nations. The law constituted a barrier between Judean and gentile.¹⁸⁷ The gospel of Christ therefore marks off two "contrasting epochs"¹⁸⁸ characterized by law and faith respectively,¹⁸⁹ and lends an eschatological character to Paul's exposition in Galatians 3.¹⁹⁰ The "coming" of faith (3:23, 25) and the eschatological Spirit (3:2, 3, 5, 14) meant that the "period of the law came to an end."¹⁹¹ Regarding verse 3, Fee correctly remarks that

> the ultimate contrasts in Paul are eschatological: life "according to the flesh," lived according to the present age that has been condemned through the cross and is passing away; or life "according to the Spirit," lived in keeping with the values and norms of the coming aeon inaugurated by Christ through his death and resurrection and empowered by the eschatological Spirit.¹⁹²

---

182. Martyn, *Galatians*, 374.

183. De Boer, *Galatians*, 247.

184. Longenecker, *Galatians*, 114; cf. George, *Galatians*, 217; Dunn, *Epistle to the Galatians*, 179; Bruce, *Galatians*, 155.

185. Longenecker, *Galatians*, 157; cf. Hays, "Galatians," 187; Wright, *Climax*, 173-74.

186. Lategan, *Galasiërs*, 62-63 (all translations of this source are my own); cf. Hong, "Law," 154; Sanders, *Jewish People*, 208.

187. Cf. Dunn, *Epistle to the Galatians*, 169; Eph 2:11-16 (see pp. 107-17).

188. This is especially signified by the "faith that was revealed" (πίστιν ἀποκαλυφθῆναι, v. 23) and faith that "came" (ἐλθεῖν, v. 23) or "has come" (ἐλθούσης, v. 25).

189. Dunn, *Epistle to the Galatians*, 198; see also, 196, 205; De Boer, *Galatians*, 172, 237; Silva, *Interpreting Galatians*, 177-78; Fee, *Empowering Presence*, 395; Bruce, *Galatians*, 152, 181; *Heart set Free*, 190.

190. Bruce, *Galatians*, 154; cf. Hays, "Galatians," 270; Silva, *Interpreting Galatians*, 177-78.

191. De Boer, *Galatians*, 237; cf. Silva, *Interpreting Galatians*, 179.

192. Fee, *Empowering Presence*, 385; cf. Jewett, *Anthropological Terms*, 110; 2 Cor 5:14-17 (see pp. 156-64).

Similarly, Silva states that Paul's contention in verse 3 is "that *the mode of existence based on the works of the law is eschatologically obsolete*. Faith, on the other hand, is the way to new life."[193]

Although Paul rejects external identity markers and envision one new humanity in Christ,[194] it does not imply that he is anti-Judean as such: (1) Paul shifts the focus away from a covenant identity and preoccupation with law, back to its original focus: the grace of God (cf. Rom 4:7–12).[195] (2) Paul does not deny Judeans their ethnic identity as such, but he equalizes the playing field between Judean and non-Judean in terms of being children of Abraham (3:7), and at a deeper level, of being children of God (v. 26). In Christ, ethnic, physical or social identity (v. 28: Judeans/Greeks, male/female, slave/free) does not cease to exist, but is relativized in terms of the new identity of all in Christ.[196] Paul thus reformulates the Judean's claim on Abraham specifically, away from national or ethnical terms and away from claims based on the works of the law, toward spiritual terms (faith and the Spirit). In other words, being a Judaean is no longer constitutive of someone's covenant-identity in Christ. Paul thus reduces being a Judean to being a mere socal or ethnic identity without constitutive power in respect of one's relationship with God. Paul shows the Teachers of the Law that gentile inclusion was part of the original intention of the promise to Abraham (v. 8b),[197] and by implication, that if they understood the promise they laid claim on, they would see its fulfillment in Christ as a blessing to all nations. Dunn in fact states that Paul's "*mission to the Gentiles was nothing other than the fulfilment of Israel's mission*"[198] (contra Marcion). This understanding constitutes the heart of the profound *continuity* between Israel and the Christ-believers.

Abraham's Faith, Law and Identity: Galatians 3 and Romans 4

Paul's account of the promise to Abraham in Galatians 3 is similar to that of Romans 4, but with important differences. Since Paul has a stronger reprimanding approach in Galatians 3, his style is more direct and his contrasts more pronounced. While the time gap between Galatians and

---

193. Silva, *Interpreting Galatians*, 176, emphasis original.
194. Martyn, *Galatians*, 336.
195. Dunn, *Epistle to the Galatians*, 163.
196. George, *Galatians*, 243; Dunn, *Epistle to the Galatians*, 207; cf. 1 Cor 12:13 (see pp. 212–15); Col 3:11 (see pp. 164–68).
197. Dunn, *Epistle to the Galatians*, 164–65.
198. Dunn, *Epistle to the Galatians*, 165, emphasis original.

Romans remains uncertain, depending largely on the dating of Galatians (see note 134, p. 87), the differences between Galatians and Romans are more likely to be attributed to different contingent situations, than to a fundamental shift in Paul's thought.[199] Yet a measure of development in Paul's thought cannot be ruled out either. But the development arguably pertains mostly to a greater measure of finalization in his thought and a more nuanced approach in Romans.

As in Romans 4:3, 9, and 13, Abraham's faith[200] was reckoned (λογίζομαι) to him as righteousness (Gal 3:6), and as in Romans 4:16 and 24, the faith of believers in Christ is identified with the faith of Abraham (Gal 3:7, 9).[201] Similarly, as the believers in Christ are reckoned as non-physical descendants (σπέρμα) of Abraham in Romans 4:13, 16, and 18, they are considered in Galatians 3 as his children by believing in Christ (Gal 3:7) or as his descendants (σπέρμα) by belonging to Christ (v. 29). Contrary to the perception of the Judeans and the Teachers of the Law in particular that Judean people were heirs of the promise to Abraham, apart from Christ himself, Paul does not consider biological Israelites as heirs of the promise.[202] Therefore, the promise to Abraham becomes completely spiritual, and a matter of faith only.[203] This emphasis is similar to Romans 4, except for the explicit reference to the Spirit (see below).

As for the differences, Christological[204] and Pneumatological aspects are more pronounced in Galatians 3. While Christ as Abraham's physical descendant is implied elsewhere in Romans (Rom 9:5), it does not form part of Paul's exposition in Romans 4. Here in Galatians 3, Christ is portrayed as the single, physical (cf. Rom 9:5) seed (σπέρμα) of the promise (ἐπαγγελίας)

---

199. Witherington, "Contemporary Perspectives," 260; Hong, "Law," 155; Beker, *Essence*, 44–59; *Paul the Apostle*, 94–108. Räisänen, *Paul*, 82–83, also argues against development in Paul's thought between Galatians and Romans, and recognizes the similarity of Paul's position on faith and the law in the two letters. But, contrary to my approach, he does not view Paul's thought on the law as consistent. He sees laxity in Paul's attitude toward the Torah and a tension in Paul's answer whether the law is still in force. He even rejects the view that the law was abolished as standard, while remaining in force as prediction, promise and "paraclesis," which would constitute the "letter" of the law (e.g., 2 Cor 3; D'Angelo, *Moses*, 194).

200. Abraham's "subsequent faithfulness under trial" after his trust in God, was considered as part of the Judean understanding of Abraham's faith and his reckoning as righteous (Dunn, *Epistle to the Galatians*, 161; cf. George, *Galatians*, 218). Fung's, *Galatians*, 135, reference to the Judean perception of Abraham's faith as being "a meritorious work," is an overstatement, however (Dunn, *Epistle to the Galatians*, 161).

201. Betz, *Galatians*, 143.

202. Longenecker, *Galatians*, 126.

203. Cf. Dunn, *Epistle to the Galatians*, 179; Bruce, *Galatians*, 155.

204. Cf. Lührmann, *Galatians*, 64–65.

to Abraham (vv. 16, 19), contrary to the Judean view of Abraham's seed.[205] Baptism (v. 27) confirms the "new identity"[206] in Christ. By belief in Christ and identification with him in his death and resurrection as enacted in baptism,[207] the believer becomes a spiritual descendant (σπέρμα) of Abraham (v. 29)[208] and partaker of a "new spiritual existence."[209] Paul, therefore, converges a physical and spiritual meaning of the σπέρμα of the promise to Abraham in Christ himself.[210] In terms of the inheritance of the promise to Abraham, there is thus correspondence in the way Paul employs the terms σπέρμα and ἐπαγγελίας in both Galatians 3 and Romans 4, where both terms are ultimately designated for believers in Christ only. Here is a double fulfillment of the promise:[211] (1) Christ himself, the only physical descendant (σπέρμα) of Abraham, (2) fulfilled the law in all respects. In becoming cursed by God (v. 13),[212] Christ removed the curse of the law[213] and brought all people back to the original, spiritual intention of the promise.

The other explicit difference between Romans 4 and Galatians 3, is the prominence of the Spirit in Galatians 3:2, 3, 5, and 14, who is not mentioned in Romans 4. Yet, in Romans 5 to 8, the role of the Spirit in identity

---

205. Dunn, *Epistle to the Galatians*, 160, shows that Abraham was naturally regarded as the father of the Judean people, the founder of the Judean race (Gen 12:24; Isa 51:2; Matt 3:9; cf. George, *Galatians*, 217–18), and that Israel naturally thought of itself as Abraham's seed (Ps 105:6; Isa 41:8; cf. Lührmann, *Galatians*, 57, 66; Longenecker, *Galatians*, 131).

206. De Boer, *Galatians*, 243.

207. As argued elsewhere, baptism itself is not the actual entrance into spiritual descent, but only enacted therein (contra De Boer, *Galatians*, 243). The decisive point of entry into the New Covenant remains faith (Du Toit, "Die 'beklee-' Metafoor," 47–48). The "clothe" metaphor in Paul has a reflexive function (mainly derived from the prominence of the medium form of ἐνδύω and cognate terms: Rom 13:12, 14; 1 Cor 15:49, 53, 54; 2 Cor 5:2, 3, 4; Gal 3:27; 1 Thess 5:8; cf. Col 2:11, 15; Col 3:8, 9, 10, 12; Eph 4:22, 24, 25; 6:11, 14, 15), and is employed in close connection to the stripping of the old identity and the actualization of the new identity in Christ (Rom 13:12-14; Gal 3:27-29; cf. Eph 4:22-25; Col 3:5-12). The notion of identity change in the baptismal practice of the early church is especially evident in the practice where baptismal candidates divested themselves of old clothes before baptism, symbolising the "putting off" of the old person, and clothed themselves with new clothes afterwards, symbolising the "putting on" of the new person in Christ (Du Toit, "The 'Clothe' Metaphor"; cf. esp. Martyn, *Galatians*, 374).

208. Fung, *Galatians*, 138, 172; cf. Hays, "Galatians," 273.

209. Fung, *Galatians*, 172; cf. Ridderbos, *Paulus*, 223, 253.

210. Both dimensions are present in Rom 4, but less pronounced.

211. Cf. Fung, *Galatians*, 177–78.

212. Longenecker, *Galatians*, 122; George, *Galatians*, 241–42; Hong, "Law," 60; see Deut 21:23; cf. 2 Cor 5:21.

213. Hays, "Galatians," 260; Fung, *Galatians*, 147.

is addressed in a more comprehensive way in comparison to Galatians. In Galatians, Paul paints his pictures quicker and with broader strokes. For example, the gospel is preached to Abraham (3:8), the promise to Abraham becomes the Spirit (v. 14, see above) and runs in close parallel with Christ himself, the single seed of Abraham (vv. 16, 19). In terms of the fulfillment of the gospel as rooted in the Torah and the promise to Abraham, the link between Abraham and the Christ-believer thus seems to run deeper and harder in Galatians 3, almost to the point of becoming anachronistic, as if Paul's gospel can be read directly in God's promise to Abraham, and Christ (physically) and the Christ-believers (spiritually) become the only heirs to the promise, without regard to ancient Israel. This is probably the reason why Martyn makes the following remark:

> If, then, we had only Paul's letter to the Galatians, we would have no reason to credit the apostle with a belief in the divine election of the ancient people of Israel. Indeed, precisely the opposite.[214]

In terms of the contrast between the law and faith, and by implication between identity modes A (Israel according to the flesh) and C (Christ-believers), the overall *discontinuity* is sharper in Galatians 3 (cf. Eph 2:11–22), compared to Romans 4 and the rest of Romans.[215] The law in Galatians 3 implies a curse and verges on becoming God's enemy, and the contrast between the works of the law and faith is more pronounced, especially in view of Paul's polemical approach toward the Teachers of the Law (cf. Gal 5:12). While the theme of circumcision is not explicitly mentioned in Galatians 3 (as in Rom 4), Paul's critique against circumcision as work of the law and as identity marker is harsher in Galatians (5:1–11).

In spite of Paul's negative evaluation of the law and its works in defining a righteous identity (Gal 3), he does not view the law as inherently against God[216] or His promises (3:21), but rather that God is the Originator[217] of both the law and the promise.[218] The difficult ὁ δὲ μεσίτης ἑνὸς οὐκ ἔστιν, ὁ δὲ θεὸς εἷς ἐστιν (v. 20) is probably best understood where the ἑνὸς οὐκ denotes "*a duality of parties* involved in a mediated arrangement,"[219]

---

214. Martyn, *Galatians*, 350.

215. Lincoln, *Ephesians*, 134, compares the same matter in Galatians, Romans and Ephesians, and perceives a greater stress in discontinuity in both Galatians and Ephesians.

216. Contra De Boer, *Galatians*, 230–32; Martyn, *Galatians*, 312, 326, 358.

217. The law was added (προστίθημι, v. 19) and given (δίδωμι, v. 21).

218. Hays, "Galatians," 267; Dunn, *Epistle to the Galatians*, 191; Hong, "Law," 155; Longenecker, *Galatians*, 143; Bruce, *Galatians*, 180.

219. Longenecker, *Galatians*, 141, emphasis original.

and does not indicate the origin of the law as if not from God.[220] But where Longenecker[221] and others[222] view the involved parties as God on the one hand and Israel on the other, I would modify their view as follows: The phrase ἑνὸς οὐκ probably refers to Moses as mediator of the law for many (Israel), while the θεὸς εἷς, apart from pointing to the *Shema*, might additionally point to the single seed of the promise (vv. 16, 19), which is Christ (v. 16) and God (by implication).[223] The basic contrast would then be between the law (designated for many) and the promise (designated for One) and repeat or summarize Paul's prior comparisons between these two (vv. 16-19) in different words.[224]

Nevertheless, even while Paul views the law as imposing a curse[225] (vv. 10, 13) on Judean and gentile alike[226] (cf. v. 22), as it compelled all who rely on the works of the law[227] to fulfill everything in the written Torah (v. 10), the law is not intrinsically evil, but rather a curse for the reason that no one is able to fulfill the law.[228] The law did not provide a basis by which one

---

220. Contra De Boer, *Galatians*, 228; Martyn, *Galatians*, 358

221. Longenecker, *Galatians*, 141.

222. E.g., Burton, *Galatians*, 191-92; Lightfoot, *Galatians*, 146-47.

223. See pp. 49-50n161 for Christ's deity in Paul.

224. Wright's, *Climax*, 157-74, view probably comes closest to my own interpretation, especially in terms of his connection of ἑνός in v. 20 to the single (ἑνός) seed (Christ) in v. 16, but Wright views the contrast in v. 20 as a contrast between a single family (Judeans and gentiles together) and two separate families (Judeans and gentiles separately). While the former side of Wright's proposal is conceivable, the "two families" to which he opposes the contrast, is not evident from the text of Galatians itself, and supposes a "family of gentiles" in the Old Testament.

225. In connection with the curse of the law (vv. 10-14), Wright, *Climax*, 141, understands that "in the cross of Jesus, the Messiah, the curse of exile itself reached its height, and was dealt with once and for all, so that the blessing of the covenant renewal might flow out the other side, as God always intended." This can be seen as another layer to the understanding of the law in Gal 3, which Wright labels a "*messianic christology*" (146, emphasis original).

226. George, *Galatians*, 233, 263-64; Dunn, *Epistle to the Galatians*, 176-78; Fung, *Galatians*, 148-49. Bruce, *Galatians*, 167, 182, observes that both Judeans and gentiles were confined under the law, since the law was a restrainer of all people (vv. 16, 22; cf. Rom 2:14). Contra Gager, *Reinventing*, 103, who argues that the curse of the law and circumcision, which have been transcended by Christ, only applies to gentiles.

227. Longenecker, *Galatians*, 116; cf. Dunn, *Epistle to the Galatians*, 170-71; Bruce, *Galatians*, 157.

228. Moo, *Galatians*, 204; George, *Galatians*, 230-32; Dunn, *Epistle to the Galatians*, 171; Lührmann, *Galatians*, 61; Fung, *Galatians*, 146; Lategan, *Galasiërs*, 62; contra Hays, "Galatians," 257. Dunn, *Epistle to the Galatians*, 171-73, correctly states that Paul's "hidden presumption is that complete or perfect obedience to the law is beyond human capacity." Dunn however hastily qualifies this obedience of the law in terms

could be declared righteous.²²⁹ If it was possible to fulfill the law, it could have given life (vv. 12, 21; cf. Rom 7:10).²³⁰ Cranfield argues that Christ did just that: by his perfect obedience, he provided redemption from the curse of the law.²³¹ In terms of Paul's salvation-historical exposition in Galatians 3,²³² the law had an important function.²³³ To converge the parallel verses 22 to 23, the law concluded (συγκλείω, v. 22, 23) and guarded (φρουρέω, v. 23)²³⁴ all people (πάντα, v. 22; ἐφρουρούμεθα, v. 23, 1 pl.) under the power of sin (v. 22) and under the law (v. 23), for the promise to be given (δίδωμι, v. 22) to all believers in Christ (v. 22) by the revelation of faith (v. 23). All people being under sin includes both Judean and gentile,²³⁵ which implies that faith has come as revelation for all people, including Judeans. The law was the supervising guardian²³⁶ or disciplinarian,²³⁷ only until Christ came (v. 24).²³⁸ In other words, the law preserved and necessitated the promise (Christ) and the revelation of faith to all.

As in Romans 4, identity mode AB is constituted by Abraham himself who believed in God's promise and was counted as righteousness (Gal 3:6). Since Christ is the descendant of Abraham (physically), Christ-believers are connected to Abraham through faith (spiritually), just as Abraham was reckoned as righteous through faith. Christ as physical descendant of Abraham and faith in Christ, which is identified with Abraham's faith, constitute the points of *continuity* between identity modes A, B and C. Just

---

of covenantal nomism: in assuming the Judeans were safe under the law, they were blinded to the seriousness of their sin. As noted earlier though (Rom 2:17–29), Paul views disobedience to the requirements of the law just as important as boasting about possessing the law.

229. Westerholm, *Perspectives*, 380, 383, 444. Cf. Wright, "Romans," 649, who mentions Gal 3:21 in his discussion of Rom 9:31. He states: "Covenant membership would indeed have been defined by Torah had that been possible, just as the Torah would have given life had it been capable of doing so, instead of having to work with material that was doomed to die ([Rom] 7:10; cf. Gal 3:21)."

230. Cf. Räisänen, *Paul*, 95.

231. Cranfield, *Romans*, 2:522.

232. George, *Galatians*, 217, 272; Dunn, *Epistle to the Galatians*, 151; Fung, *Galatians*, 146, 153; Bruce, *Galatians*, 154; contra Martyn, *Galatians*, 343–44.

233. Cf. Betz, *Galatians*, 169.

234. NRSV.

235. De Boer, *Galatians*, 235.

236. Longenecker, *Galatians*, 149; cf. Dunn, *Epistle to the Galatians*, 197.

237. NRSV.

238. According to Longenecker, *Galatians*, 139, Paul here deviates widely from the Judean view. Wis 18:4 speaks of the "imperishable light of the law," and Josephus states that the law is immortal (*Ag. Ap.* 2.277; cf. Philo, *Mos.* 2.14).

as in Romans 4, the line of continuity between the Christ-believer (identity mode C) and Abraham (identity mode AB) in Galatians 3 does not follow *through* physical Israel apart from Christ himself, but *directly* connects to Abraham through Christ.[239] In Paul's salvation-historical exposition in Galatians 3, it is thus not clear what his view is on historical Israel. It is only in 6:16 where Paul uses the term Ἰσραήλ, where he possibly addresses some aspects on this topic (see pp. 334–45).

Galatians 4:21–5:1

Galatians 4:1–9 connects closely to the preceding. Paul continues to build upon and elaborate on the theme of inheritance. The sending of God's Son achieves cosmic significance[240] in that the epoch under the law is described as being under bondage to the "basic principles" (στοιχεῖα, vv. 3, 9)[241] of the world (v. 3). But when the fullness of time had come, God sent His Son, born ἐκ γυναικός and born ὑπὸ νόμον (v. 4; cf. Rom 9:5), to redeem those ὑπὸ νόμον so that all people, regardless of being Judean or non-Judean, can receive (ἀπολάβωμεν, 1 pl.) adoption as children (v. 5).[242] Being under the law or deriving one's identity from law and ethnicity,[243] constitutes identity mode A, and corresponds to "flesh" (3:3). This mode of identity is contrasted to being an heir (κληρονόμος, v. 7) and child (υἱός, vv. 6, 7). In terms of descent, being a υἱός (vv. 6, 7) corresponds with God's own Son (υἱός, v. 4). Because of adoption (υἱοθεσία, v. 5) through Christ, God has sent the Spirit of His Son (cf. πνεῦμα υἱοθεσίας in Rom 8:15) in believers' (Gal 3:26) hearts, crying Αββα ὁ πατήρ (4:6). The Spirit is the final, ultimate contrast to an identity according to the flesh, and is indispensable to the identity in Christ (identity mode C).[244]

Verses 10 to 11 elaborate on what Paul means by living under the "basic principles" (vv. 3, 9) or under the law (vv. 4, 5) by some practical examples. Verses 12 to 20 contain a personal appeal to his recipients whom Paul perceives to being led astray by the Teachers of the Law.

---

239. Cf. Lategan, *Galasiërs*, 66.

240. Cf. Hays, "Galatians," 281.

241. ISV; Zerwick and Grosvenor, *Grammatical Analysis*, 571.

242. Hays, "Galatians," 284; Fung, *Galatians*, 183. It is noteworthy that the concept of adoption (υἱοθεσία) is reset in Christ and not something that Judeans obtain by physical birth, other than with historical Israel (Rom 9:4, see p. 47)

243. Cf. Dunn, *Epistle to the Galatians*, 155.

244. Cf. Hays, "Galatians," 285; Fung, *Galatians*, 185.

Verses 21 to 31 once again connect to many of the themes in verses 1 to 9: (1) The υἱός (vv. 6, 7) is repeated in verses 22 (pl.) and 30 (sing.), and correlates closely to the τέκνα in verses 25, 27, 28 and 31. (2) An identity ὑπὸ νόμον (vv. 4, 5) is repeated in verse 21. (3) Jesus was born (γίνομαι, v. 4) ὑπὸ νόμον, which is similar to the child from the slave woman who was born (γεννάω) κατὰ σάρκα (vv. 23, 29). (4) Jesus, being born ἐκ γυναικός (v. 4) is paralleled by the two women in verses 22 to 31.

Additionally, many of the themes in Galatians 4:21–5:1 correspond to the same themes in Galatians 3: (1) The term ἐπαγγελίας (v. 23, 28) is used in 3:14, 17, 18, 19, 22 and 29. (2) The phrase ὑπὸ νόμον (v. 21) occurs in 3:23. (3) The term Ἀβραάμ (v. 22) appears in 3:6, 7, 8, 9, 14, 16, 18 and 29. (4) The expression κατὰ σάρκα (vv. 23, 29) corresponds to σαρκί in 3:3. (5) One of the two διαθῆκαι (v. 24) corresponds to the διαθήκη in 3:15 and 17. (6) The phrase κατὰ πνεῦμα (v. 29) agrees with πνεῦμα in 3:2, 3, 5 and 14. The contrast between κατὰ πνεῦμα and κατὰ σάρκα (v. 29) is especially close to the contrast of πνεῦμα and σάρξ in 3:3.

The correspondence of themes and concepts in 4:21–5:1 with those in Galatians 3 and 4:1–9 strongly suggests that Paul addresses very much the same issues here in 4:21–5:1 as in 4:1–9 and especially 3:1–29, although from another angle. Rather than viewing this passage as a supplementary argument to the previous arguments to reinforce what he argued earlier,[245] Betz correctly understands 4:21–5:1 as Paul's strongest argument in 3:1–4:31.[246]

Most scholars agree that Paul's allegory of the two women (v. 24) is "fundamentally tempered by typology."[247] Longenecker correctly notices that the manner in which Paul applies allegory is more Palestinian than Alexandrian (e.g., Philo). Paul is not emancipating the meaning of the passage from its historical content in order to transmute it into a moral sentiment or philosophical truth (Alexandrian). Paul rather refers to the original historical content and interprets it typologically. Paul's allegory is thus an aid to typology and regards history as meaningful.[248]

---

245. E.g., Bruce, *Galatians*, 214; Burton, *Galatians*, 251; John Chrysostom, "Galatians."

246. Betz, *Galatians*, 238–40; adopted in part by Longenecker, *Galatians*, 198–99, who differs from Betz who sees 4:31 as the conclusion of Paul's entire argumentative *probatio*. Longenecker rather sees it as part of Paul's appeals and exhortations headed by "become like me" (4:12).

247. Martyn, *Galatians*, 436; adopted by Moo, *Galatians*, 295; cf. De Boer, *Galatians*, 296; Hays, "Galatians," 301; George, *Galatians*, 338–40; Longenecker, *Galatians*, 209–10; Bruce, *Galatians*, 217; Betz, *Galatians*, 239; Lightfoot, *Galatians*, 180.

248. Longenecker, *Galatians*, 209–11; cf. De Boer, *Galatians*, 296; Bruce, *Galatians*, 218.

In 4:21–5:1 Paul draws up two contrasting columns that represent two covenants (διαθῆκαι, v. 24). The main contrasts can be arranged as follows:

Two covenants

Slave woman (v. 22)	Free [woman] (vv. 22, 23, 26, 30, 31)
Slavery (v. 24, 25)	
Hagar (vv. 24, 25)	
Present Jerusalem (v. 25)	Jerusalem above is free (v. 26)
Mount Sinai (vv. 24, 25)	
Under the law (v. 21)	
Born according to the flesh (vv. 23, 29)	[Born] by promise (v. 23)
	[Born] according to the Spirit (v. 29)
Born into slavery with her children (v. 24)	Children of the promise, like Isaac (v. 28)
Son of the slave woman (v. 30)	Son of the free [woman] (v. 30)
The yoke of slavery (5:1)	Freedom in Christ (5:1)

Hays, Martyn, and Dunn argue for viewing the two columns as one covenant in terms of two different understandings, the left column as representing the gospel of Paul's opponents (Teachers of the Law) in terms of law and flesh, and the right column as the right understanding of the covenant in terms of freedom and promise.[249] They additionally view the giving birth of children (γεννῶσα, pres. part., v. 24) as pointing to present churches rather than to individuals, where the left column would then point to Paul's opponents (Teachers of the Law) rather than to ethnic Israel. Consequently, the slave woman who has to be cast out (v. 30) is also identified with Paul's opponents.[250]

This line of argumentation, however, becomes strenuous in context of the birth of the two sons of Abraham (vv. 23, 29) who each represent

---

249. Hays, "Galatians," 302; Martyn, *Galatians*, 446; Dunn, *Epistle to the Galatians*, 249. De Boer's, *Galatians*, 286–310, approach is similar in that he understands the two columns in terms of correcting "wrong exegesis." He does, however, connect the left column to physical descent and circumcision specifically.

250. Hays, "Galatians," 306; Martyn, *Galatians*, 446; Dunn, *Epistle to the Galatians*, 258.

one of two actual covenants (v. 24), and thus has salvation historical significance.[251] It is more in line with the overall context[252] and the progression of Paul's argument in 3:1–4:31[253] to understand the left column as representative the Old Covenant and the right column of the New Covenant.[254] The argument in 4:21–5:1 still has to be viewed in salvation-historical context.[255] One of the stronger arguments in viewing the two covenants as representative of two epochs (old and new) is the close proximity of 4:21–5:1 with 4:4–6, including the corresponding themes (see above), where the dividing salvation-historical moment (πλήρωμα τοῦ χρόνου, v. 4) is portrayed by the sending of God's Son[256] who was also "born of a woman, born under the law" to redeem those under the law, that all people (ἀπολάβωμεν, 1 pl., v. 5) might receive the adoption as children (v. 5) and the Spirit (v. 6) in Christ. The phrase ὑπὸ νόμον occurs in 3:24; 4:4–5 and 4:21, which seems to bind the salvation-historical discourse in chapters 3 to 4 together.

More fundamentally, these two covenants can be broken down into two modes of identity, an identity according to the flesh that is defined by law and its consequential slavery (identity mode A), versus an identity that is birthed from the Spirit according to promise and freedom (identity mode C, see below). Yet, Paul undeniably alludes to the Teachers of the Law who insisted on "perfecting" (ἐπιτελέω, 3:3) their identity according to the law and flesh, which is all about external markers and outward performance. As Bruce notes, Paul inverts the argument of the opponents. Where they would argue for true descent from Isaac through physical ancestry and circumcision, Paul in fact connects their line of argumentation to Ishmael, the son of Hagar, the slave woman.[257] But Paul's refutation of his opponents is not the only aim of his argument in 4:21–5:1. He concludes his salvation-historical exposition as put forth in 3:1–5:1 by

---

251. Cf. how "Abraham" (Rom 4; 9:7; 11:1; 2 Cor 11:22; Gal 3) and "Isaac" (Rom 9:7, 10) feature elsewhere in the context of the Old Covenant.

252. Cf. the corresponding terms and concepts as discussed above.

253. See Betz, *Galatians*, 238–40; cf. Longenecker, *Galatians*, 198.

254. Meyer, *Law*, 129, 136–37; Fee 1994, *Empowering Presence*, 413, 416; George, *Galatians*, 340; Longenecker, *Galatians*, 211; Fung, *Galatians*, 206–07; Lategan, *Galasiërs*, 91; Bruce, *Galatians*, 218; Betz, *Galatians*, 243. Even though Longenecker, *Galatians*, 211, views the two covenants as the Old and the New, he understands the casting out of "the slave woman and her son" (v. 30) as the casting out of the Teachers of the Law (217).

255. Longenecker, *Galatians*, 213; cf. Bruce, *Galatians*, 217.

256. Cf. Fung, *Galatians*, 184; Lategan, *Galasiërs*, 79.

257. Bruce, *Galatians*, 218–19; cf. De Boer, *Galatians*, 292, 298; Hays, "Galatians," 306.

denying inheritance on the basis of law (ὑπὸ νόμον, v. 21) or ethnicity[258] (vv. 23, 29-30) and ties inheritance only to children of the promise and the Spirit who are free from the law (vv. 28-30). The contrast between κατὰ σάρκα γεννηθείς (v. 29; cf. κατὰ σάρκα γεγέννηται, v. 23) and κατὰ πνεῦμα [γεννηθείς] (v. 29) is to be understood as a contrast between natural birth and birth from the Spirit, which, apart from pointing to the promise (v. 28), probably alludes to regeneration (cf. 3:2-5).[259]

Paul hereby does not reject Judean people indiscriminately, neither is he anti-Judean. Paul in fact connects inheritance directly to their ancestors Isaac and Abraham, who typologically represent the New Covenant. The New Covenant is therefore firmly rooted in the Old[260] and is dependent on Christ as being born under the law (4:4). The work of Christ (see Gal 3:22-29) is the initial fulfillment of God's covenant with Abraham, awaiting the final eschatological fulfillment.[261] With respect to Paul's overall salvation-historical scheme, the two covenants do not co-exist in parallel, and there is in this sense indeed one covenant that has been fulfilled, that resulted in a new mode of existence.[262] Meyer is therefore correct to refer to

---

258. This notion can be derived from κατὰ σάρκα γεννηθείς, which signifies an ethnic identity derived from natural descent (cf. George, *Galatians*, 335-38), which in turn stands in contrast to a spiritual identity: birth ἐκ τῆς ἐλευθέρας δι' ἐπαγγελίας (v. 23) or birth κατὰ πνεῦμα (v. 29).

259. Cf. Meyer, *Law*, 140; Hays, "Galatians," 305; Fee, *Empowering Presence*, 414-16. It can be asked if Paul assigns an actual identity according to the Spirit to Isaac and by implication to historical Israel (v. 29). In v. 28, Paul compares "us" (believers in Christ) with Isaac. As Betz, *Galatians*, 249, points out, Paul does not have Isaac and Ishmael as individuals so much in mind in v. 29 than "the types they represent." In other words, Paul is at this point in deep typological-allegorical language. As Fee, *Empowering Presence*, 415-16, notes, Isaac's birth κατὰ πνεῦμα might be "simply an analogy and nothing more." Yet, as is suggested in Rom 9:18-22, Paul did see Isaac's birth as supernatural, which probably conveys much of Paul's allusion here (cf. Betz, *Galatians*, 243; Fung, *Galatians*, 214; Hendriksen, *Galatians*, 187; Burton, *Galatians*, 252-53). But in terms of Paul's main rhetoric, he opposes the Old Covenant ("Ishmael") according to flesh to the New Covenant ("Isaac") according to the Spirit (see main text), for the reception of the Spirit is associated with the beginning of belief in Christ (3:2-5; 4:6) and not with an identity under the law (4:4-5, 21). Given Paul's typological-allegorical language, an implied designation of historical Israel as "Israel according to the Spirit" is therefore unlikely.

260. Contra Bultmann, "Significance," 31-32, who states: "To the Christian faith the Old Testament is no longer revelation as it has been, and still is, for the Jews . . . The events which meant something for Israel, which were God's Word, mean nothing more to us . . . To the Christian faith the Old Testament is not in the true sense God's Word" (cf. Marcion).

261. Cf. Dunn, *Epistle to the Galatians*, 243.

262. Longenecker, *Galatians*, 116.

the portrayal of the Old and New Covenants here in terms of an *eschatological contrast* because

> a new entity comes on the scene and replaces the former and because it fulfills what the former provisionally anticipated or accomplishes what the former failed to do. Therefore, the new thing replaces the former thing because the emergence of the new has rendered the existence of the former outdated and thus eschatologically old.[263]

The New Covenant stands in both *continuity* and *discontinuity* with the Old. What is cast out (v. 30) is therefore not the Judean people *per se*, but the Old Covenant, or more specifically, the old mode of filiation to God that was marked off by outward identity markers, constituted mainly by natural descent from Isaac, circumcision and possession of the law.[264] By implication, the Judean people who resist the gospel and Christ[265] are not counted as children of the promise, but children of the slave woman, and they are denied inheritance and their status as God's people. Burton puts it simple: "Allegorically interpreted the expulsion of Ishmael points to a rejection of the children of Abraham according to the flesh in favour of the sons of Abraham by faith."[266] Even if one chooses the view that Paul casts out the Teachers of the Law or an "Ishmael-church"[267] it is hard to avoid the latter conclusion, since a mode of identity marked by outward identity markers (identity mode A), represented much of the claim of Paul's opponents in terms of "a perfected" identity as well. The point here is not so much that unbelieving Judean people as such are being disinherited, but that by implication, all who do not find their identity through faith in Christ only, are in fact not "children of the promise" (v. 28) and therefore denied inheritance (cf. 3:26, 29).[268]

In terms of the casting out of "the slave woman and her son" (v. 30), Bruce is probably right that Paul does not envision an active casting out of some members of the congregation but rather describes "the fate of each

---

263. Meyer, *Law*, 137.

264. Cf. De Boer, *Galatians*, 285–310; Martyn, *Galatians*, 441; Dunn, *Epistle to the Galatians*, 257. Even though De Boer, Martyn and Dunn (as cited) do not view the two covenants as pointing to the Old and New Covenants, they do share these notions about identity in terms of the Teachers of the Law.

265. Cf. Bruce, *Galatians*, 219.

266. Burton, *Galatians*, 267; cf. Fung, *Galatians*, 215; Lategan, *Galasiërs*, 93; Betz, *Galatians*, 251; Hanson, *Studies*, 95.

267. Cf. De Boer, *Galatians*, 308; Martyn, *Galatians*, 446; Dunn, *Epistle to the Galatians*, 250.

268. Cf. Bassler, *Navigating*, 76; Lührmann, *Galatians*, 93.

party."²⁶⁹ Apart from scholars who do not identify those to be cast out with unbelieving Judean people,²⁷⁰ many scholars are hesitant on admitting outright denial of inheritance to Judeans on the basis of ethnicity without faith in Christ, and attempt to temper the apparent harshness of such a conclusion by comparing it with Paul's exposition in Rom 9 to 11.²⁷¹ Betz, however, resists such moderation and suggests a revision of Paul's thought in Romans 9 to 11 in comparison with Galatians 4.²⁷² Longenecker, despite seeing the two covenants as the Old and New Covenants, rejects the view that the "the slave woman and her son" may point to a casting out of unbelieving Judean people in general, for he argues that Romans 11:13-21 and 14:1-15:13 negate such a view.²⁷³ It remains a question how much of the various interpretations on the table are regulated by the "dominant technique," where one passage controls the meaning of another (see pp. 4-16). Nevertheless, the measure of contrast between Paul's view in Romans 9 to 11 and his exposition in Galatians 4:21-5:1 ultimately depends on (1) the amount of time one allows for development in Paul's thought between Galatians and Romans (esp. the dating of Galatians), (2) if acknowledged, what the nature or extent

---

269. Bruce, *Galatians*, 225.

270. E.g., Hays, "Galatians," 302; Martyn, *Galatians*, 446; Dunn, *Epistle to the Galatians*, 258; Longenecker, *Galatians*, 217; contra De Boer, *Galatians*, 308.

271. E.g., Lategan, *Galasiërs*, 93. Cf. Bruce, *Galatians*, 225, who displays overall hesitance here. He identifies the "the slave woman and her son" as "those who, being 'under law', are still in bondage," and as "theologically, Ishmaels," but he resists an interpretation of expelling some people in the congregation on the basis of his interpretation of Romans 11:13-21 and 14:1-15:13 (see note 273, p. 106).

272. Betz, *Galatians*, 251.

273. Longenecker, *Galatians*, 211, 217 (see however pp. 267-76). In respect of 14:1-15:13, rather than Christ-believers that are accommodated within "Judaism," Christ-believers are accommodated that still adhere to food laws or feast days, whether Judean or gentile (Wright, "Romans," 731; cf. Ridderbos, *Romeinen*, 302), but more probably, Judean believers that needed liberation from Old Testament or Judean ritual requirements (Schreiner, *Romans*, 712; Moo, *Romans*, 836; Mounce, *Romans*, 251; cf. Dunn, *Romans*, 2:797-98; Bruce, *Romans*, 244-45; Cranfield, *Romans*, 2:697; Barrett, *Romans*, 256). This understanding argues additionally for a measurable Judean Christ-believing audience of Romans, even though they might be a minority (see pp. 231-35). These believers are identified as "weak persons" (14:1, 2; 15:1), but more specifically, "those who are weak in faith" (τῇ πίστει προσλαμβάνεσθε, 14:1). These weak persons are thus not unbelieving "Jews" (contra Nanos, *Mystery*, 85-165; see Gagnon, "Why"). The "strong persons" (15:1) have to bear the weak. Paul is persuaded that nothing is "unclean in itself" (14:14). The reason Paul can make these exceptions is that Paul views these laws as peripheral and in fact superfluous in defining the identity of God's people in the new eon in Christ. Rather, "the kingdom of God is not food and drink but righteousness, peace and joy in the Holy Spirit" (14:17), which is the theological center of Romans 12 to 15 (Dunn, *Romans*, 2:823).

of such development is, and ultimately (3) one's understanding of Romans 9 to 11, especially 11.

Regarding the modes of identity, the left column in the above table represents identity mode A and the right column identity mode C. As in Romans 4 (see pp. 77-86) and Galatians 3 (see pp. 87-100), identity mode AB is once again represented by Abraham and Isaac as representatives of promise (Gal 4:23, 28) and Spirit (vv. 6, 29). Although faith is implied in the context of the preceding Galatians 3, it is not explicitly mentioned here in 4:21-5:1. Martyn is essentially correct in his view that

> the Galatians . . . have been included in a line extending through the centuries from Abraham, Isaac, and Jacob. His [Paul's] exegesis is thoroughly *punctiliar*, in the sense that he sees a divine correspondence between two *points*, God's action in the birth of Isaac and God's action in the birth of the Galatian congregations.[274]

The difference in my interpretation is that I perceive this correspondence to stretch wider than the Galatian congregations so that it can be applied to all the people in the New Covenant. This correspondence would then represent the spiritual[275] aspect of God's covenant with Abraham, which is fulfilled through Christ in the believer. The physical aspect of the covenant has been fulfilled in Christ who was "born under the law" (4:4) as a physical descendant of Abraham and Isaac. This physical aspect was fulfilled and ended in Christ himself. The *continuity* of identity mode C to that of A can therefore be described as: (1) a physical, natural continuity with Abraham and Isaac in the Person of *Christ only*, and (2) a punctiliar continuity with Abraham through *belief only* in Christ, the intended recipient of the promise.

Ephesians 2:8-22

While my own position would be to defend Pauline authorship for Ephesians,[276] space does not allow for venturing into a discussion on the debate. The current passage in Ephesians will thus be treated with awareness of the dispute about authorship. Many defenders of Pauline authorship see Ephesians as being written in Roman prison in the early 60s CE.[277] Those who reject Pauline authorship normally date the letter

---

274. Martyn, *Galatians*, 444, emphasis original.
275. Cf. George, *Galatians*, 345.
276. See note 95, p. 18 for a list of scholars who defend this position.
277. E.g., Thielman, *Ephesians*, 19; Carson and Moo, *Introduction*, 486-87; Hoehner,

at around 90 CE.[278] Pursuing a specific setting for the letter seems to run against the literary genre of the letter,[279] which looks more like a tract than an epistle.[280] The letter is predominantly destined for gentile Christbelievers (2:11; 3:1),[281] although not to the exclusion of Judean believers (1:11–14).[282] The letter was probably destined for Asia Minor,[283] and was probably meant as a circular letter.[284]

The thoughts of earlier Pauline letters is carried to a new stage in Ephesians,[285] which probably led to the description of Ephesians as "the crown of Paulinism."[286] It is for this exact reason that many have argued against Pauline authorship, which they in fact view as a departure from Pauline thought. One of the crucial areas in this equation is the way in which the new creation and the new entity of believers in Christ are understood in Ephesians. In Perkins' words: "[r]eading Ephesians . . . [o]ne would infer . . . that the entire heritage of Israel had passed into the church."[287] This notion is normally contrasted to commentators' interpretation of the salvation of Israel in Romans 11[288] and arguably contributes to the tendency to reject Pauline authorship of Ephesians.[289] The extent of this "contrast" in turn obviously depends on one's interpretation of both Romans 11 and Ephesians 2.

Ephesians establishes powerful images of the identity of the Christbeliever.[290] Lincoln suggests that by mirror reading, it can be inferred

---

Ephesians, 96; O'Brien, *Ephesians*, 57.

278. E.g., Muddiman, *Ephesians*, 35; Lincoln, *Ephesians*, lxxiii; Schnackenburg, *Ephesians*, 25.

279. Perkins, "Ephesians," 352.

280. Bruce, *Colossians*, 229; Fuller, *Introduction*, 66.

281. O'Brien, *Ephesians*, 50, 176; Schnackenburg, *Ephesians*, 125; Lincoln, *Ephesians*, 112; Bruce, *Colossians*, 230.

282. O'Brien, *Ephesians*, 50.

283. Perkins, "Ephesians," 361; O'Brien, *Ephesians*, 48; Bruce, *Colossians*, 230. This deduction would be reasonable given the reference to the recipients' hearing of God's grace that was given to Paul to minister to gentiles (3:2; 4:21; O'Brien, *Ephesians*, 48).

284. Carson and Moo, *Introduction*, 488; O'Brien, *Ephesians*, 47, 183; Guthrie, *Introduction*, 520, 530–31; Roberts, *Efesiërs*, 12. The absence of "in Ephesus" in some of the best manuscripts (1:1), the impersonal tone of the letter, and the more general content would suggest such a conclusion (O'Brien, *Ephesians*, 47).

285. Bruce, *Colossians*, 229.

286. Dodd, "Ephesians," 1224–25.

287. Perkins, "Ephesians," 404.

288. Cf. the same tendency regarding Gal 4:21–5:1 (see above).

289. E.g., Muddiman, *Ephesians*, 120; Perkins, "Ephesians," 404; Schnackenburg, *Ephesians*, 110; Lincoln, *Ephesians*, 134.

290. Cf. Perkins, "Ephesians," 352.

from the prayers to the readers (3:14-19) and appeals in the conclusion of the paraenesis (cf. 4:1-16; 6:10-20) that the main problems for the readers were "powerlessness, instability and a lack of resolve, and [that] these are related to an insufficient sense of identity."[291] Ephesians 2 is central in defining the new identity of the believers in Christ. These gentile believers were once dead through their trespasses and sin (v. 1). They lived in the lusts of their flesh, following its desires and senses (v. 3). In contrast, God made them alive with Christ[292] through His love and mercy (vv. 4-5). They are saved by grace (vv. 5, 8) through faith, not of themselves (v. 8). This salvation is the gift of God.[293] While many who are sceptical about Pauline authorship expect justification in verse 8 (δικαιόω, e.g., Rom 3:20, 24, 28; Gal 2:16-17; 3:11, 24),[294] Marshall points out that salvation terminology is quite normal in the rest of the Pauline corpus (e.g., Rom 1:16; 5:10; 10:9-10; 1 Thess 2:16; 1 Cor 15:2).[295]

This salvation is οὐκ ἐξ ἔργων (v. 9), lest anyone boast (καυχήσηται). The letter indeed contrasts salvation to merit.[296] Yet, as pointed out earlier, this notion is not foreign to Paul, and is implied in the context of boasting in addition to pride in identity and ethnicity (Rom 2:17-19, 4:1-25). Marshall states that human effort in general "does not exclude but includes the practices required by Judaism."[297] As here in Ephesians 2:9, "works" (ἔργων) without the immediate qualification, "of the law" (νόμου),[298] is comparably contrasted in the letter to the Romans with grace (Rom 4:4;

---

291. Lincoln, *Ephesians*, 82-83; cf. Perkins, "Ephesians," 352.

292. The clause "you being dead to sin, God has raised together in Christ Jesus" is authentically Pauline (cf. Rom 6:11, 13; Muddiman, *Ephesians*, 100).

293. Cf. Hoehner, *Ephesians*, 343; O'Brien, *Ephesians*, 175; Lincoln, *Ephesians*, 112. The τοῦτο refers to the preceding clause (τῇ γὰρ χάριτί ἐστε σεσῳσμένοι διὰ πίστεως) as a whole, where the διὰ πίστεως modifies the verb σεσῳσμένοι. This means that faith itself is not necessarily portrayed as being imparted, for faith intrinsically "involves the abandonment of any attempt to justify oneself and an openness to God which is willing to accept what he has done in Christ" (Lincoln, *Ephesians*, 111; cf. Rom 4:4-5).

294. See e.g., Perkins, "Ephesians," 392-93; Schnackenburg, *Ephesians*, 98; Luz, "Rechtfertigung," 365-83.

295. Marshall, "Salvation"; adopted by O'Brien, *Ephesians*, 174.

296. O'Brien, *Ephesians*, 174; Lincoln, *Ephesians*, 111; Bruce, *Colossians*, 290; cf. Muddiman, *Ephesians*, 111.

297. Marshall, "Salvation," 345-46; cf. O'Brien, *Ephesians*, 176-77.

298. Many who reject Pauline authorship (e.g., Muddiman, *Ephesians*, 111; Lincoln, *Ephesians*, 112; cf. Perkins, "Ephesians," 392; Schnackenburg, *Ephesians*, 98) expect ἔργων νόμου (e.g., Gal 3) here.

11:6), faith (Rom 4:5) and election (Rom 9:11). This shorter form is thus thoroughly Pauline.[299]

The terms ποίημα and κτίζω (v. 10) signify the new creation in Christ,[300] created in Christ unto ἔργοις ἀγαθοῖς. While this notion about good works has been described as "scarcely Pauline" in that it is perceived to contract Paul's teaching of justification into a moralistic direction,[301] O'Brien argues that such an understanding fails to understand this statement (v. 10) within the flow of the argument. Good works are designed for God's new creation as fruit or consequence, and are thus neither meritorious nor a prerequisite for redemption (cf. Rom 13:3; Gal 5:6; 6:10; 2 Cor 5:10; 9:8; 1 Thess 5:15; 2 Thess 2:17).[302]

Verse 11 urges the gentile Christ-believing readers to remember (μνημονεύετε). In terms of cultural memory, Punt writes: "Collective memory provides a centripetal force for a group, and concomitantly serves as powerful marker of social differentiation . . ., and boundary-drawing and self-identification is what constitutes identity."[303] This memory of the readers' past helps them to have a greater appreciation and gratitude for what God has done to change their past,[304] and contrasts their new found identity in Christ to their old identity, which was labelled with the derogatory designations τὰ ἔθνη ἐν σαρκί and ἀκροβυστία.[305] Their previous identity apart from Christ, which is described as being "in the flesh" (v. 11), portrays the gentiles as being ethnically predispositioned.[306]

This ethnic predisposition made these gentiles strangers (ξένοι, v. 12) to several privileges (v. 12), which can be compared to the privileges of Israel according to the flesh in Romans 9:3-5 (see pp. 47-49):[307] (1) They were without Christ (χωρὶς Χριστοῦ), the Messiah who belonged to Israel whom they hoped for.[308] This correlates to the eighth privilege in Romans 9:5 (cf. Rom 9:3), Christ according to the flesh (designating ethnic descent). (2) They

299. Cf. Thielman, *Ephesians*, 144; Hoehner, *Ephesians*, 344-45; O'Brien, *Ephesians*, 176.

300. O'Brien, *Ephesians*, 178.

301. Lindemann, *Aufhebung*, 138.

302. O'Brien, *Ephesians*, 180; cf. Hoehner, *Ephesians*, 349-50.

303. Punt, "Identity, Memory and Scriptural Warrant," 154.

304. Lincoln, *Ephesians*, 135.

305. Perkins, "Ephesians," 397.

306. Cf. Muddiman, *Ephesians*, 115; Lincoln, *Ephesians*, 135; Bruce, *Colossians*, 291.

307. Muddiman, *Ephesians*, 119; Perkins, "Ephesians," 397; O'Brien, *Ephesians*, 188; Schnakenburg, *Ephesians*, 109; Bruce, *Colossians*, 293.

308. O'Brien, *Ephesians*, 188-90; Bruce, *Colossians*, 294; cf. Hoehner, *Ephesians*, 355; Roberts, *Efesiërs*, 66-67.

were alienated from (ἀπηλλοτριωμένοι)³⁰⁹ the citizenship or membership (πολιτεία)³¹⁰ of Israel, which corresponds to the adoption (first privilege) of Romans 9:3. (3) Being strangers to the covenants of the promise (τῶν διαθηκῶν τῆς ἐπαγγελίας) parallels the third (αἱ διαθῆκαι) and the sixth privileges (αἱ ἐπαγγελίαι) in Romans 9:4. The primary covenant of promise in Paul is the Abrahamic covenant (Rom 4; Gal 3; 4:23, 28). In comparison with Romans 9:4-7 (v. 7 mentions Abraham explicitly), τῶν διαθηκῶν τῆς ἐπαγγελίας here in Ephesians 2:12 includes at least the covenant promise to Abraham.³¹¹ The genitive (τῆς ἐπαγγελίας) probably refers to the Abrahamic promise as the foundation promise.³¹² (4) The gentiles were having no hope (ἐλπίδα μὴ ἔχοντες). This logically flows from being strangers to the covenants of the promise³¹³ and the fact that they were without a Messiah. (5) Finally, they were without God in the world (ἄθεοι ἐν τῷ κόσμῳ). They were predispositioned in terms of their relationship with God.³¹⁴ These last two privileges that they were estranged from summarize the lowest point of their predicament. But in Christ all Judean privilege has been abolished.³¹⁵

The reference to Ἰσραήλ (v. 12) refers to the Old Testament depiction of Israel as God's people.³¹⁶ At the deepest level, in the gentiles' past they were not in a covenant relationship with God. They were outside the sphere of God's election.³¹⁷ Yet, even the position of Israel is described as "the so called circumcision" (τῆς λεγομένης περιτομῆς, v. 11).³¹⁸ Apart from the gentiles' old identity "in the flesh," the circumcision of the Judean people is

309. Perkins, "Ephesians," 397.

310. Hoehner, *Ephesians*, 356-57; Perkins, "Ephesians," 397; Lincoln, *Ephesians*, 137. While πολιτεία can refer to the "commonwealth" (e.g., Bruce, *Colossians*, 292) of Israel, the notion of citizenship or membership is preferred in the context, for it is more inclusive. One can be a resident of a state and not be a citizen. Apart from the fact that Israel was not an independent state as such, but part of the commonwealth of Rome in the time of Paul (Hoehner, *Ephesians*, 357), the status of the gentiles as strangers from Israel in this context pictures the situation in the Old Testament (cf. Perkins, "Ephesians," 397). The gentiles would not want membership of the political state of Israel so much as they would want the special privileges God bestowed on Israel (Hoehner, *Ephesians*, 357).

311. Hoehner, *Ephesians*, 359; Muddiman, *Ephesians*, 121; Lincoln, *Ephesians*, 137.

312. O'Brien, *Ephesians*, 189.

313. Hoehner, *Ephesians*, 360.

314. Cf. O'Brien, *Ephesians*, 190.

315. Lincoln, *Ephesians*, 149.

316. Perkins, "Ephesians," 397; Gutbrod, "Ἰσραήλ," *TDNT*, 3:387.

317. Lincoln, *Ephesians*, 137.

318. BDAG, λέγω, §4; Hoehner, *Ephesians*, 354; Schnackenburg, *Ephesians*, 108; OAT.

also described as ἐν σαρκὶ χειροποιήτου (v. 11). So, even *their* identity is depicted as being in the realm of flesh, signifying identity mode A. Circumcision was one of their primary identity markers that marked the Judean people off from other nations. Ephesians 2 thus does not merely establish salvation (vv. 5, 8) as counterpart of merit (see above), but contrasts the identities of both Judean and gentile outside Christ with the identity in Christ (identity mode C), which in turn fits much of the contentions about identity in the NPP.[319] Both the identities of Israel and the gentiles are being transcended in Christ.[320]

This new, shared identity in Christ is portrayed by several metaphors that stand in stark contrast with an identity defined by flesh and with the division between Israel and the gentiles before Christ (vv. 13–18). The gentiles who were "far" have come "near" in Christ (v. 13, 17; see below). This new identity in Christ of both Judean and gentile is being described by several positive and negative images:

Positive images: Both Judean and gentile have been made one entity (εἷς, v. 14)[321] through the blood of Christ. Christ constitutes peace (εἰρήνη, v. 14; εὐηγγελίσατο εἰρήνην, v. 17) between God and human beings and between the nations.[322] Christ created both nations in himself into one new person (ἕνα καινὸν ἄνθρωπον, v. 15), which signifies the new creation[323] (cf. 2 Cor 5:17) "where neither circumcision nor uncircumcision counts for anything" (Gal 6:15).[324] Both Judean and gentile (ἀμφότερος, v. 16) are reconciled to God in one body of believers[325] by the cross (v. 16), and together[326] have access (προσαγωγή) to God by one Spirit to the Father (v. 18).

Negative images: This new unity has been established in removing the middle wall of division (v. 14)[327] by abolishing the enmity (ἔχθρα, v.

319. See esp. Lincoln, *Ephesians*, 141–42; cf. Schnackenburg, *Ephesians*, 108; O'Brien, *Ephesians*, 177; Bruce, *Colossians*, 296.

320. O'Brien, *Ephesians*, 209; Lincoln, *Ephesians*, 144, 149; Bruce, *Colossians*, 290, 295.

321. Hoehner, *Ephesians*, 363.

322. Lincoln, *Ephesians*, 148, 161; Bruce, *Colossians*, 295.

323. Muddiman, *Ephesians*, 133; O'Brien, *Ephesians*, 199–200; Schnackenburg, *Ephesians*, 115; Lincoln, *Ephesians*, 143.

324. O'Brien, *Ephesians*, 178.

325. Hoehner, *Ephesians*, 382; Schnackenburg, *Ephesians*, 16; O'Brien, *Ephesians*, 201–2. The phrase ἐνὶ σώματι (v. 16) can also refer to the body of Christ. While there might have been a certain porosity between Christological and ecclesiological connotations here (Muddiman, *Ephesians*, 135), the latter connotation would be more likely in this context.

326. Hoehner, *Ephesians*, 388; O'Brien, *Ephesians*, 209.

327. The expression μεσότοιχον τοῦ φραγμοῦ is a redundant construction, which

14, 16)³²⁸ in Christ's flesh (ἐν τῇ σαρκὶ αὐτοῦ, v. 14), that is, by his death³²⁹ (cf. Col 1:22). This middle wall is qualified as the law (v. 15)³³⁰ of commandments contained in ordinances,³³¹ which He rendered inoperative (καταργέω, v. 15).³³² The law functioned "as a fence to protect Israel from the impurity of the Gentiles, the law became such a sign of Jewish particularism that it also alienated Gentiles and became a cause of hostility."³³³ Perkins points out that the law referred to here is neither just ceremonial, nor refers merely to those elements that are "in decrees" made by those who interpret the law (e.g., the elders, Matt 23:1-4, 15-24; Mark 7:5-8).³³⁴ That the law would be divisible into rites and customs over against Moses' legislation has little support in Judean texts.³³⁵ The reference to the law in Ephesians 2:15 rather signifies the whole law.³³⁶ Perkins concludes: "Ephesians leaves no opening for the continuing observance of the law by Jewish Christians."³³⁷ Similarly, Thielman writes that "Christ did away with every facet of the Jewish way of life."³³⁸ The enmity or alienation caused by the law was thus twofold in that there was a rift between Judeans and gentiles and hostility between both of them and God.³³⁹

---

constitutes a stylistic feature (not un-Pauline; cf. e.g., Rom 1:23) that created "liturgical sonority and special emphasis, and allows extra time for the hearer to register the image and reflect upon it" (Muddiman, *Ephesians*, 126). The term μεσότοιχον is a *hapax legomenon* and refers to a shared wall between terraced houses. The term φραγμός refers to a dry stone wall. The combination μεσότοιχον τοῦ φραγμοῦ might have referred to the dividing wall between Israel and the gentiles in the temple (Muddiman, *Ephesians*, 127; Lincoln, *Ephesians*, 141; Zerwick and Grosvenor, *Grammatical Analysis*, 582), which is applied metaphorically here.

328. The corresponding concepts in Rom 5:10 (ἐχθρός) and 8:7 (ἔχθρα) respectively, signifies the term to be Pauline.

329. O'Brien, *Ephesians*, 196.

330. Arnold, *Ephesians*, 162; Thielman, *Ephesians*, 170–71; Hoehner, *Ephesians*, 371–74; Perkins, "Ephesians," 399; O'Brien, *Ephesians*, 196; Lincoln, *Ephesians*, 141; Roberts, *Efesiërs*, 64.

331. KJV.

332. Hoehner, *Ephesians*, 374; ISV; cf. BDAG, καταργέω, §2.

333. Lincoln, *Ephesians*, 141.

334. Perkins, "Ephesians," 399–400; cf. Hoehner, *Ephesians*, 376; O'Brien, *Ephesians*, 199; contra Barth, *Ephesians*, 287–91.

335. E.g., Josephus; CD-A 19.29; 4QMMT.

336. Arnold, *Ephesians*, 162; Thielman, *Ephesians*, 169; Perkins, "Ephesians," 400.

337. Perkins, "Ephesians," 402–3.

338. Thielman, *Ephesians*, 169.

339. O'Brien, *Ephesians*, 205; cf. Roberts, *Efesiërs*, 62.

The new identity in Christ that unites both Judean and gentile as portrayed in Ephesians 2, looks very similar to the same new identity portrayed in Galatians 3, (1) where the curse of the law has been removed, and the law's function as marking off the Judean people from other nations has been rendered redundant,[340] and (2) where one new identity in Christ relativizes the differentiation between Judean and gentile. This new identity in Christ can be described as a *third entity*[341] or people-group[342] that supersedes both Judean and non-Judean identities.[343] This new identity in Christ provides the only access (προσαγωγή, v. 18) to the Father by the Spirit, and both Judean and gentile alike have thereby become fellow-citizens of all believers (συμπολῖται τῶν ἁγίων, v. 19)[344] and of all people of God of all ages.[345] Fellow-citizenship is thus not merely with Judean Christ-believers or with Judeans in particular.[346] In Perkins' words, it is "impossible to use Ephesians to support theories of an ongoing covenant with Israel that will bring it to salvation outside of Christ."[347]

This sharp *discontinuity* between the new creation and Israel has led writers such as Lincoln to construe a progressive pattern of discontinuity (Galatians), toward stronger continuity (Romans), and back again toward stronger discontinuity (Ephesians) when "Paul's position on admission of Gentiles had been established."[348] At this point it could be asked why Ephesians 2 would fall under this section (ABC). Identity mode A can be detected in Israel as "the so called circumcision [the people] made in the flesh by hands" (v. 11) and identity mode C is recognized by the new creation in

---

340. Cf. Arnold, *Ephesians*, 163; Fee, *Empowering Presence*, 683.

341. Perkins, "Ephesians," 400.

342. Cf. Roberts, *Efesiërs*, 65. While agreeing with the intent to designate a new entity by the term "third race" (e.g., Sechrest, *Former Jew*, 123; Lincoln, *Ephesians*, 144) or a "new race" (e.g., Moo, *Galatians*, 143; Hoehner, *Ephesians*, 379), as Clement himself referred to them (*Strom.* 6.5.41.6; Diogn. 1), I do not prefer this terminology because of its ethnic connotations. As Crook, "Former Jew," 60, states, this approach is "limited by the heavy baggage the term 'race' carries in the contemporary world." The designation "new creation" is more descriptive and in line with Paul's own nomenclature (cf. Sanders, *Jewish People*, 173, 207).

343. Cf. Arnold, *Ephesians*, 164; Perkins, "Ephesians," 404; O'Brien, *Ephesians*, 209; Bruce, *Colossians*, 296.

344. Perkins, "Ephesians," 402; O'Brien, *Ephesians*, 211; Fee, *Empowering Presence*, 683.

345. Bruce, *Colossians*, 302.

346. O'Brien, *Ephesians*, 200; contra Faust, *Pax Christi*, 184–88; Kirby, *Ephesians*, 168.

347. Perkins, "Ephesians," 402–3; cf. Roberts, *Efesiërs*, 69.

348. Lincoln, *Ephesians*, 134.

Christ. But what about identity mode AB? Amidst the discontinuity, several aspects of an equally profound *continuity* between the new identity in Christ and Israel can be detected. While "the circumcision" (the people) can be described as identity mode A, the "membership of Israel" (τῆς πολιτείας τοῦ Ἰσραήλ, v. 12) is not so clear. This might refer to *inner* Israel or *true* Israel (identity mode AB; cf. esp. Rom 9:6). Even while the first four of the five privileges (v. 12, see above) do not necessarily constitute the inner Israel (cf. Rom 9:4–5), being without God (ἄθεος) can hardly be seen as a mere external or ethnical privilege. For the gentiles, to be without God signified "that they had no relationship with the true God, the God of Israel."[349] Israel as portrayed in verse 12 is thus probably a conflation of identity modes A and AB. This notion is strengthened by the following five indicators, all of which indicate the *continuity* between Israel and belief in Christ:

1. That the gentiles were previously "far" (μακράν, vv. 13, 17), alludes to a previously positive ("near," ἐγγύς, vv. 13, 17) relationship of Israel with God (cf. Ps 148:14).[350] Perhaps the continuity of the new identity in Christ with Israel is implicitly indicated the strongest by the fact that Israel was never "far." They were by implication always near.[351] Since Christ was theirs (v. 13), their relationship with God continued uninterrupted with belief in their Messiah. Yet, Lincoln rightly notes that "the language of coming near undergoes a transformation. Because of Christ's work, it can be used of Gentiles in general, not simply of proselytes to Judaism."[352] In Christ, the gentiles could share in a "newly created community whose privileges transcend those of Israel."[353] Christ thus created "one new person which transcends the two"[354] identities (Israel/Judean and gentile), which means that Israel's identity was transformed in Christ as well (cf. Rom 11:25–27, see esp. pp. 309–14). The church was thus not incorporated into historical Israel as such,[355] but formed a new entity in continuity with historical Israel and as fulfillment of their history.

---

349. O'Brien, *Ephesians*, 190.

350. Cf. Bruce, *Colossians*, 13.

351. Cf. Muddiman, *Ephesians*, 137.

352. Lincoln, *Ephesians*, 139.

353. Lincoln, *Ephesians*, 139; cf. O'Brien, *Ephesians*, 191; contra Tomson, "Names," 285, who argues that the gentiles are "no longer 'estranged from the citizenship of Israel.'" The estrangement of the gentiles from the citizenship of Israel, however, pertains to the former eschatological eon (see main text).

354. Lincoln, *Ephesians*, 144.

355. O'Brien, *Ephesians*, 203; cf. Lincoln, *Ephesians*, 144; contra Barth, *Ephesians*, 270.

2. The use of Scripture in Ephesians itself signifies the continuity between belief in Christ and Israel. In O'Brien words: "The use of the Old Testament Scriptures in this key paragraph [Eph 2:11-22], both explicitly (cf. vv. 13, 17) and by way of allusion or echo (cf. vv. 19-22), underscores the note of continuity between Gentile Christians and the promises of God to Israel (cf. Gen 12:1-3; Isa 49:5, 6)."[356] As mentioned earlier, the promise (ἐπαγγελίας, gen., v. 12) probably alludes to the foundation promise to Abraham.

3. The continuity of the new creation with Israel is additionally confirmed by the gentile Christ-believers' membership of the saints and the household of God (τῶν ἁγίων καὶ οἰκεῖοι τοῦ θεοῦ, v. 19), which signifies all people of God of all ages.[357]

4. Was it not for Israel and their Messiah (see above) who became the Messiah of the world (cf. ἐν τῷ κόσμῳ, v. 12), the gentile people could never become part of God's new creation. Christ himself, Israel's Messiah, remains the cornerstone[358] (ἀκρογωνιαῖος, v. 20) of the new creation, which is the corporate body of believers in Christ that constitutes the temple (v. 21) and the dwelling place of God in the Spirit (v. 22).[359] The overarching notion here is that the new creation fits into God's history of salvation.[360]

5. The Spirit (πνεῦμα, vv. 18, 20) describes the nature of the new identity in Christ, and stands in contrast to an identity defined by flesh (σάρξ, vv. 11, 15) apart from Christ. This contrast can be identified as typically Pauline. As pointed out by Suh, this pneumatic dimension of Ephesians 2 shows remarkable parallels with Ezekiel 37, together with many other parallels.[361] Ezekiel 37 and Ephesians 2 both begin

---

356. O'Brien, *Ephesians*, 183-84.

357. Bruce, *Colossians*, 302.

358. The term ἀκρογωνιαῖος could just as well refer to the crowning stone or capstone that held the building in place (see BDAG, ἀκρογωνιαῖος; Zerwick and Grosvenor, *Grammatical Analysis*, 582), but Hoehner, *Ephesians*, 402-5, shows that "cornerstone" would fit the current context better in conjunction with the foundation (θεμέλιος) of apostles and New Testament prophets, especially in its possible allusion to Isa 28:16 that depicts God as laying in Zion "a foundation stone, a tested stone, a precious cornerstone [ἀκρογωνιαῖος, LXX], of a sure foundation" (RSV; cf. Thielman, *Ephesians*, 182; Fee, *Empowering Presence*, 687-88; Schnackenburg, *Ephesians*, 122-24; Lincoln, *Ephesians*, 153-55; Bruce, *Colossians*, 304-6).

359. Hoehner, *Ephesians*, 414-15; cf. Muddiman, *Ephesians*, 143-44; Lincoln, *Ephesians*, 158.

360. Lincoln, *Ephesians*, 133, 159.

361. Suh, "Ezekiel 37." Some of the corresponding concepts (between Ezek 37 and

their chapters with God's bringing back of dead people to life. The prophet Ezekiel anticipates the day when God will bring forth the New Covenant (Ezek 37:26; cf. Jer 31:31). The one new people in Christ (Eph 2:15–16) can be compared to the "one stick" (Ezek 37:17, 19), the one new nation wherein God will unite the northern and southern kingdoms of Israel. Whatever the nature and the depth of this correspondence between Ezekiel 37 and Ephesians 2 is, it seems safe to say that the notion of God creating a new covenant (that Suh interprets as the new creation) of different people into one family, is firmly rooted within Old Testament prophecy. This further emphasizes the strong *continuity* between the new creation and Israel, the people of God.

Summary and Concluding Remarks

Faith as such can be understood as the most prominent point of continuity of Christ-believers with Abraham and by implication with historical Israel. While faith in Romans 4 is portrayed in a more general way than in Galatians 3, I have argued for an understanding of faith that involves faith in Christ in both passages. Although the possibility remains in Romans 4 that faith could be applied to Israel apart from Christ, this notion cannot be established beyond doubt. If such a notion could be established, it would most probably refer to historical (ancient) Israel. In Galatians faith is pictured explicitly as faith in Christ. Even though faith in Romans 4 is referred to in more general terms, it is doubtful whether Paul would have shifted from ultimately defining faith onto salvation away from faith in Christ in Romans 4 as opposed to Galatians 3, especially if the context of Romans is taken into account.

In the last four passages that were discussed (Rom 4:1–25; Gal 3:1–19; 4:21–5:1; Eph 2:8–22) the law (including the "works of the law," descent and circumcision) is portrayed as being opposed to faith or the identity in Christ. The law or circumcision is thus not to be understood as constitutive of the identity in Christ. Faith in Christ is the marker of identity in Christ, which is apart from the law and opposed to the law, including works and circumcision.

Eph 2) that Suh (ibid,. 718) lists include the following: "Spirit/spirit" (Ezek 37:1, 5, 6, 8, 9, 10, 14; Eph 2:18, 22), "covenant" (Ezek 37:26; Eph 2:12), "peace" (Ezek 37:26; Eph 2:14, 15, 17), "one" (Ezek 37:16, 17, 19, 22, 24; Eph 2:14, 15, 16, 18), "two" (Ezek 37:22; Eph 2:15), "dwelling place" (Ezek 37:27, 28; Eph 2:21, 22), "hope" (Ezek 37:11; Eph 2:12); "law" (Ezek 37:24; Eph 2:15), "dead" (Ezek 37:9; Eph 2:1, 5), "sin" (Ezek 37:27; Eph 2:1), "make alive" (Ezek 37:3, 5, 9, 14; Eph 2:5) and "joining" (Ezek 37:7; Eph 2:21).

The continuity in which the believer in Christ thus stands to Abraham is not defined ethnically but through faith only (spiritually), regardless of ethnic background. This continuity is *punctiliar* in that Christ himself who shares in an ethnic identity ("flesh-identity") with Israel (as Abraham's Seed in Gal 3), is the sole connection point for believers to Abraham and historical Israel. Christ fulfilled the law by both (1) completing the era under the law in being the physical heir to the promise to Abraham, and (2) by fulfilling its demands. An identity in Christ represents the free Covenant in the Spirit as opposed to a Covenant of slavery under the bondage of the law (Gal 4:21–5:1).

The letter to the Ephesians provides evidence for both the continuity of the Christ-believing identity with historical Israel's privileges, and believers' discontinuity with the law and the covenant with Israel. The identity in Christ is portrayed as a *third entity* that replaces the old entity (Israel), where ethnic differentiation is superseded.

4

Faith in Christ, Israel, and the Judean (AC)

Whereas chapter 3 had the continuity between Israel/Judeans and belief in Christ in view, this chapter is concerned with the *discontinuity* between Israel and the Christ-believers. Pages 119–56 focus on the discontinuity between Israel/Judeans and Christ-believers in general while pages 156–68 focus on the new creation specifically.

Faith in Christ in Discontinuity with Israel and the Judean (AC)

The passages to be discussed in this section are approached with the distinctions between the designations Ἰσραήλ and Ἰουδαῖος in mind as laid out in pp. 37–39. These distinctions are however not to be understood as ridged constraints. Yet these passages are expected to show mostly discontinuity between the identity in Christ and the Judean identity. Naturally, an important question that will be addressed in this section is whether the Christ-believing community in Paul is to be understood as being a movement *within* the Judean identity or whether it *transcends* it in forming a new identity.

Romans 15:5–13

Romans 15:1–13 is the final climax of the letter,[1] which can be divided into two parts: verses 1 to 6 and verses 7 to 13. Each part starts with a command relating to Romans 14 (βαστάζω, v. 1; προσλαμβάνω, v. 7), summoning the "strong" to support the "weak."[2] At the end of the first part (vv. 5–6), Paul

---

1. Wright, "Romans," 744.
2. Wright, "Romans," 744; cf. Moo, *Romans*, 871.

focuses on the unity among believers in Christ. He prays that God will give them "to think the same" (τὸ αὐτὸ φρονεῖν, v. 5)[3] that they may with one mind or purpose (v. 6)[4] and with one mouth (ἐν ἑνὶ στόματι) glorify God. Their worship with one mouth points to their "common worship,"[5] which originates from one united community of believers in Christ, consisting of both Judeans and gentiles.[6] The "dividing line between these two groups" constituted by the law has been removed in the New Covenant, signifying *discontinuity* between an ethnic identity and the identity in Christ. This inclusion of Judeans and gentiles was the theological basis for the "strong" and the "weak" to receive one another.[7]

The receiving of one another (v. 7) is based on the Messiah's receiving of them, whose work was on behalf of the whole world. Just as the Messiah welcomed them, they should welcome one another in order that God may be glorified.[8] Christ was the minister of the περιτομή (v. 8),[9] which points to the Judeans according to the flesh[10] or ethnic Israel,[11] signifying identity mode A. Both the truthfulness (ἀλήθεια, v. 8)[12] or covenant faithfulness[13] of God, and the promises of the fathers (v. 8) point back to these same themes in Romans 9:4-6 (see pp. 47-50).[14] Christ confirmed these promises to the fathers, which includes the promise to Abraham to include gentiles (v. 9a; cf. Gal 3:14, 22)[15] who would glorify God for His mercy (v. 9b). Cranfield argues that the Judean Christ-believers should thank God for his faithfulness to have called gentiles for the sake of His mercy.[16] The notion behind Paul's statement in verses 8 to 9a is that Israel's history was brought to a climax through their Messiah and opened the way to all nations, wherein God's

---

3. BDAG, φρονέω, §1; Wright, "Romans," 746; Moo, *Romans*, 871.
4. BDAG, ὁμοθυμαδόν; cf. Moo, *Romans*, 871.
5. Wright, "Romans," 746.
6. Cf. Dunn, *Romans*, 2:841; Moo, *Romans*, 874.
7. Moo, *Romans*, 874.
8. Wright, "Romans," 746; Bruce, *Romans*, 256; Barrett, *Romans*, 270.
9. Barrett, *Romans*, 271, takes περιτομή to refer to the act of circumcision in the sense that Christ carried out the promises implied in the covenant of which the seal was circumcision, or that Christ has been instrumental in admitting the gentiles to the privileges promised to the Judean believers of which circumcision was the symbol.
10. Cranfield, *Romans*, 2:741.
11. Wright, "Romans," 747.
12. Wright, "Romans," 747; Mounce, *Romans*, 261.
13. Dunn, *Romans*, 2:847.
14. Cf. Wright 2002, "Romans," 746; Cranfield, *Romans*, 2:741-42.
15. Dunn, *Romans*, 2:847.
16. Cranfield, *Romans*, 2:743.

mercy was always designed for all,[17] Judeans and the nations alike. Dunn correctly senses an echo here of the principle of "to the Judean first, but also to the Greek" (1:16).[18] Israel's Messiah ministered *their* gospel to His own people first (cf. Matt 15:24), and extended it to the nations, who was always intended in the promise (or gospel, cf. Gal 3:8) to Abraham.

In verses 9b to 12, Paul introduces a series of Old Testament quotations in support of his "solemn declaration (vv. 8–9a) as a whole,"[19] which Dunn summarizes as "the inclusion of the Gentiles within the promises to his people."[20] Paul quotes four Scriptures:

1. Verse 9b is a verbatim quote from Psalm 17:50 (LXX) or 2 Samuel 22:50. Paul probably reads the Psalm typologically,[21] pointing to the Messiah.[22] Moo argues that David's praise of God among the gentiles comes from his God-given victory over the gentile nations. God has made David the head of nations so that people whom David did not know, served him. This would typologically fit Paul's purposes if he attributed to Christ this praise of God for the subduing of the nations under the messianic rule.[23]

2. In verse 10, Paul quotes from Deuteronomy 32:43, following the Septuagint (differing markedly from the MT). Here the nations rejoice together with God's own people, which in the context of Deuteronomy is Israel.[24] The Greek of the Septuagint here allows for a much more universal perspective than the MT.[25]

3. Paul quotes Psalm 116:1 (LXX) in verse 11, which almost follows the Septuagint and is a close rendering of the Hebrew (Ps 117:1, MT).[26] This is a call on the nations to praise "the Lord," which alludes to the same identification of Jesus with Yahweh as in Romans 10:13 (see pp. 253–62).

---

17. Wright, "Romans," 747; cf. Osborne, *Romans*, 382; Mounce, *Romans*, 262; Barrett, *Romans*, 272.
18. Dunn, *Romans*, 2:848.
19. Cranfield, *Romans*, 2:745; cf. Dunn, *Romans*, 2:848.
20. Dunn, *Romans*, 2:848.
21. Moo, *Romans*, 878.
22. Wright, "Romans," 748; Moo, *Romans*, 878–79; Cranfield, *Romans*, 2:745.
23. Moo, *Romans*, 879; cf. Sanday and Headlam, *Romans*, 398.
24. Moo, *Romans*, 879; Cranfield, *Romans*, 2:746.
25. Dunn, *Romans*, 2:849.
26. Dunn, *Romans*, 2:850.

4. Isaiah 11:10 is quoted in verse 12. Wright argues for this fourth quote as the climax of the series, and even as the climax of the whole 14:1 to 15:13.[27] The nations will come to hope in the Davidic Messiah,[28] the "root of Jesse" (cf. Rev 5:5; 22:16). His rising up (ἀνιστάμενος) probably alludes to Christ's resurrection.[29] "Isaiah speaks here of God's purpose to renew the whole created order, and to gather the remnant of Israel, together with the Gentile world, into the one community of salvation."[30]

There exists a marked progression in these four quoted Scriptures (1–4). It starts with David's praise (1) and moves on to the inclusion of the nations in praise (2). The call on the nations to praise the Lord (3) includes the Judeans.[31] In the last quote (4), Israel's Messiah is also the Lord and Ruler of all nations. The term ἔθνος thus seems to undergo a transformation to include Judeans.[32] There is now only one people of God[33] where there is no ethnic differentiation any longer. Similarly, the term λαός (vv. 10, 11) displays fluidity between being a designation for a socio-political community (v. 11)[34] and for God's people (v. 10).[35] In verse 10, other nations are invited to rejoice with God's people (λαός). Conversely, in verse 11, λαός is applied in parallel with ἔθνος: all nations (πάντα τὰ ἔθνη and πάντες οἱ λαοί) are invited to praise the Lord as one people of God. Moo contends that the "new people of God" in Christ should experience piece and joy as joint participants in the kingdom of God (cf. 14:17) while they praise him with a united voice by the power of the Holy Spirit (15:13).[36] The uniting function of the Spirit corresponds to the identity of the new united people of God (identity mode C), which transcends all other identies.

---

27. Wright, "Romans," 748.

28. Wright, "Romans," 748; Moo, *Romans*, 880; Dunn, *Romans*, 2:850; Bruce, *Romans*, 257; Cranfield, *Romans*, 2:747; cf. Osborne, *Romans*, 383; Barrett, *Romans*, 272.

29. Wright, "Romans," 748; Moo, *Romans*, 880.

30. Wright, "Romans," 748.

31. Cf. Bruce, *Romans*, 257.

32. Cf. Walter, "ἔθνος," *EDNT*, 1:382–83. This possible shift in meaning is not accounted for in L&N.

33. Cf. Wright, "Romans," 748; Barrett, *Romans*, 272; Ridderbos, *Romeinen*, 325. Cf. also Dunn, *Romans*, 2:853, who writes: "All of them are united by their references to the nations/Gentiles, with the theme of praise a further strong linking factor."

34. L&N §11.55.

35. L&N §11.12; see Walter, "ἔθνος," *EDNT*, 1:382–83.

36. Moo, *Romans*, 881.

1 Corinthians 1:21–24

These verses lie amidst Paul's positioning of the gospel of the cross (vv. 17, 18, 23) among categories of worldly or human wisdom (vv. 17, 19, 20, 22, 25), God's wisdom (vv. 21, 24), and foolishness (vv. 18, 20, 21, 23, 25, 27). The aim here is not to expound the depth of meaning of these categories of wisdom and foolishness, but to identify and describe the modes of identity.

In verse 21, there is a direct relationship between salvation and belief (σῶσαι τοὺς πιστεύοντας). Belief, in turn, is closely related to preaching (τοῦ κηρύγματος). These close connections among these concepts are comparable to the same connections in Romans 10:9–17 (see pp. 253–62). While hearing is not explicitly mentioned here (1 Cor 1:21), it is implied.[37] Similar to Romans 10:9–10, faith here (1 Cor 1:21) can be identified as saving faith, constituting a "positive salvific relationship" between the believer and God.[38] Faith can be described as "confidence and trust."[39] Salvation itself is ultimately effected by God and transcends all human strength, wisdom, piety and self-praise, even toward God.[40]

Christ crucified is the content of the preaching (v. 23). For the Judeans, a crucified Messiah would have been "a contradiction in terms."[41] He was therefore a stumbling block[42] or a trap[43] for the Judeans. Similar to Romans 9:33 (cf. Rom 11:11–12), the stumbling block is opposed to salvation[44] and thus seems to be "fatal and deadly."[45]

---

37. Collins, *First Corinthians*, 105.
38. Collins, *First Corinthians*, 105.
39. Lenski, *Corinthians*, 63; cf. Ciampa and Rosner, *Corinthians*, 98.
40. Käsemann, *Paul*, 40; cf. Pop, *Eerste Brief*, 42.
41. Morris, *Corinthians*, 45.
42. Ciampa and Rosner, *Corinthians*, 100; Fitzmyer, *First Corinthians*, 159; Collins, *First Corinthians*, 107; Mare, "1 Corinthians," 195; Morris, *Corinthians*, 46. BDAG, σκάνδαλον, §3, describes this general meaning as "that which causes offense or revulsion and results in opposition, disapproval, or hostility, *fault, stain* etc."
43. Abbott-Smith, *Lexicon*, 408. Lenski, *Corinthians*, 66, argues in favor of retaining this meaning in its metaphorical application. Although this is one of the listed meanings in BDAG (σκάνδαλον, §1), 1 Cor 1:23 is not listed under that meaning. Thiselton, *Corinthians*, 171, however warns against establishing this meaning too firmly for its weak attestation outside biblical Greek. It thus remains one of several possible meanings.
44. Ciampa and Rosner, *Corinthians*, 100; cf. Mare, "1 Corinthians," 195.
45. Lenski, *Corinthians*, 66, argues that a "σκάνδαλον . . . is the stick of a trap to which the bait is fixed and by which the trap is sprung, metaphorically an offense, but always one that is fatal in its effects."

Judeans and the nations⁴⁶ (vv. 22–24) represent "the totality of humankind . . . from the perspective of salvation history."⁴⁷ Those who are called are both (τε καί) Judeans and non-Judeans (v. 24). There is therefore not a notion of priority of Judeans over non-Judeans present in 1 Corinthians, as opposed to the letter to the Romans (Rom 1:17; 2:9–10). Collins writes:

> The division of humanity into two camps by means of the message of the cross, a manifestation of the power of God, is an eschatological reality that transcends the natural social division of humanity into two "races," Jews and Gentiles. In vv. 22–24 Paul describes the message about Christ crucified in the presence of all humankind.⁴⁸

The cross is central to the gospel for Paul. In the cross the divisions between ethnic identities are relativized (cf. Eph 2:8–22). In Christ the crucified, the gospel thus has a universal appeal, and is a call to all people to fellowship in the one single church without distinction.⁴⁹ Thiselton argues that Christ here constitutes a cosmic turning point, which casts essential light on the Christological and cosmic significance of Jesus Christ.⁵⁰

In summary, those who believed the preaching of the gospel are saved (v. 21) and consist of both Judeans and non-Judeans (vv. 22–24). They represent identity mode C. This community of believers stand in *discontinuity* with ethnic or cultural distinctions, or with non-believing people groups, whether Judean or non-Judean.

Identity mode A would be constituted by Judeans who hear the gospel and become believers, transforming them into identity mode C. In the light of the gospel, identity mode C thus seems to deconstruct identity mode A, especially with respect to defining God's people. This is especially evident in 1 Corinthians 10:32, where the "church [ἐκκλησία] of God" represents a third entity apart from Judeans or the nations.⁵¹

---

46. Paul's alternation between ἕλλην (vv. 22, 24) and ἔθνος (v. 23) signifies the identification of these terms with each other (Collins, *First Corinthians*, 107–8; cf. Barrett, *First Epistle*, 55).

47. Collins, *First Corinthians*, 106.

48. Collins, *First Corinthians*, 92.

49. Ciampa and Rosner, *Corinthians*, 100; Collins, *First Corinthians*, 108; Sanders, *Jewish People*, 208; cf. Conzelmann, *1 Corinthians*, 46–47; Pop, *Eerste Brief*, 46.

50. Thiselton, *Corinthians*, 170.

51. Barrett, *First Epistle*, 245.

Galatians 1:11–14, 22–23

These verses form part of Paul's autobiographical defense for his gospel and apostleship (1:11–2:14). According to Paul, his gospel did not have a human origin (vv. 11–12a),[52] but came directly to him through a revelation of Jesus Christ (v. 12b) on his road to Damascus. The phrase ἀποκαλύψεως Ἰησοῦ Χριστοῦ (v. 12b) is probably an objective genitive: Christ was revealed.[53] The notion here is that of a personal encounter and the beginning of a personal relationship with Christ.[54] That which Paul has learned from Jerusalem's leaders confirmed his own convictions, which stemmed from his encounter with the risen Christ and his commissioning on the Damascus road.[55] He was thus never discipled by the Jerusalem authorities, neither has he ever been under their jurisdiction.[56]

Paul writes about his earlier life ἐν τῷ Ἰουδαϊσμῷ (v. 13). The term Ἰουδαϊσμός is a *hapax legomenon* in the New Testament. BDAG defines the term as "the Judean way of belief and life."[57] Hays compares the use of the term with its occurrences in 2 Maccabees 2:21;[58] 8:1;[59] 14:38;[60] 4

---

52. De Boer, *Galatians*, 75; Hays, "Galatians," 210; George, *Galatians*, 108; Dunn, *Epistle to the Galatians*, 52; Longenecker, *Galatians*, 23; Lategan, *Galasiërs*, 26; Bruce, *Galatians*, 88; Betz, *Galatians*, 62; cf. Fung, *Galatians*, 51. The above translation is preferred rather than "in a human way," "from a human standpoint" (BDAG, ἄνθρωπος, §2b; discussed by Dunn, *Epistle to the Galatians*, 52) or "according to the thought of man [sic]" (listed by Burton, *Galatians*, 37).

53. Moo, *Galatians*, 95; Martyn, *Galatians*, 144; Dunn, *Epistle to the Galatians*, 54; Fung, *Galatians*, 54; Bruce, *Galatians*, 89; Burton, *Galatians*, 41. George, *Galatians*, 111, argues that there is deliberate ambiguity in the text in that both objective and subjective genitives are intended.

54. Dunn, *Unity and Diversity*, 205; Bruce, *Galatians*, 89.

55. Cf. Dunn, *Unity and Diversity*, 71; Bruce, *Galatians*, 88.

56. Hays, "Galatians," 210; cf. George, *Galatians*, 110, 113; Lategan, *Galasiërs*, 33.

57. BDAG, Ἰουδαϊσμός. Dunn, *Epistle to the Galatians*, 55, does not even include "beliefs" as constitutive of the Judean identity.

58. The context is about the driving out of barbarian masses ὑπὲρ τοῦ Ἰουδαϊσμοῦ, which signifies "a certain kind of activity over against a pull in another, foreign direction" (Mason, "Jews," 466).

59. Here, Judas called for the support of his relatives and those who had remained ἐν τῷ Ἰουδαϊσμῷ. The term Ἰουδαϊσμός seems to be a slogan for a Maccabean counter movement to bring back other Judeans and to reinstate the ancestral law (Mason, "Jews," 467).

60. Similar to Macc 8:1, the notion in Macc 14:38 is related to a program "of striving to restore Judaean law and custom against a powerful counter-current" (Mason, "Jews," 468).

Maccabees 4:26,[61] and the letters of Ignatius of Antioch (second century CE)[62] where its usage

> strongly suggests that it designates a body of practices that distinguish Jews from Gentiles, particularly with reference to circumcision, dietary laws, sabbath observance, and the system of sacrifices and feasts. That is to say, "Judaism" refers not so much to a set of beliefs or doctrines as to a culture; it designates a network of habitual observances that characterize the Jewish people as members of a distinctive society set apart for God in the midst of the pagan world.[63]

Similarly, Mason argues that Paul's employment of the term Ἰουδαϊσμός is similar to the kind of "Judaizing" found in the Maccabean texts, indicating "a violent harassment of Jesus' followers (Gal 1:13) out of zeal, as he [Paul] puts it, for the ancestral traditions (1:14)"[64] (cf. Acts 9:1-3; 22:3-5). This implies a restricted meaning to the term in 1:13. The Ἰουδαῖοι has to be understood as largely an ethnic-geographical entity until at least about 70 CE, and thus not yet as a fully developed "religion" as such.[65]

Paul contrasts his former life ἐν τῷ Ἰουδαϊσμῷ to the ἐκκλησία τοῦ θεοῦ, which he persecuted (v. 13b). The ἐκκλησίαν τοῦ θεοῦ refers to "the universal Church as the messianic people of God in its entirety."[66] George compares the church to "the special people of the Holy One of Israel, 'the community of God.'" He argues that "[t]his expression was used in the Old Testament to describe the children of Israel who stood in a special covenantal relationship to God."[67] While Paul is referring to Judean believers in this context, the "church of God" has relevance to Paul's gentile converts

---

61. The context is about Jason's radical attempt (advanced by Antiochus IV) to dissolve Judean law and temple service. He tried to compel every member of the nation (ἔθνος) to eat polluted food and to swear off Ἰουδαϊσμός. The sense is that Antiochus reacted against opposition, a kind of "Judaizing" (Mason, "Jews," 468).

62. Mason, "Jews," 470, shows that in Ignatius *Magn.* 10, Ἰουδαϊσμός is applied in the context of movement from one group to another. "Whereas the author of 2 Maccabees had championed Ἰουδαϊσμός as response to the threat of Ἑλληνισμός, Ignatius coins Χριστιανισμός as remedy for a threatening Ἰουδαϊσμός."

63. Hays, "Galatians," 213; cf. Dunn, *Epistle to the Galatians*, 56.

64. Mason, "Jews," 466-69.

65. Mason, "Jews," 493-96, 511. Yet, Dunn, *Epistle to the Galatians*, 56, sees "Judaism . . . as a description of the religion of the Jews" as emerging already in the Maccabean revolt (second century BCE). Cf. Miller, "Ethnicity," 255-59, who argues that many Ἰουδαῖοι did have a concept of "religion."

66. Fung, *Galatians*, 55; cf. Moo, *Galatians*, 100; Longenecker, *Galatians*, 28; Burton, *Galatians*, 45.

67. George, *Galatians*, 114; cf. Lategan, *Galasiërs*, 28.

as well, "so indicating in Paul's thinking the union of Jewish and Gentile believers in Christ."⁶⁸ Fung convincingly argues that Saul persecuted the church because he had stumbled over the stumbling block himself (1 Cor 1:23). He contends that a crucified Messiah must have been an "incomprehensible absurdity" for Saul, where the cross would have been the "decisive refutation" of the claim that Jesus was the Messiah (cf. Matt 27:42; Luke 24:20–21; John 12:34). Fung maintains that Saul saw a fundamental incompatibility between life ἐν τῷ Ἰουδαϊσμῷ and faith in Christ, especially in terms of the threat that faith posed for the supremacy of the law.⁶⁹ The affirmation by Christ-believers of Christ as the crucified Messiah would have been blasphemous for Judeans: "a crucified man could not conceivably be the elect one of God."⁷⁰

Paul explains his advance ἐν τῷ Ἰουδαϊσμῷ on the basis of his exceeding⁷¹ zeal⁷² for the traditions of his ancestors (v. 14). Bruce links Paul's ancestral traditions to "the ancestral law" (τοῦ πατρῴου νόμου) of Acts 22:3, and to Philippians 3:5, where Paul describes himself as "a Hebrew born of Hebrews, as to the law a Pharisee . . . as to righteousness under the law blameless"⁷³ (cf. Acts 23:6; 26:5).⁷⁴ The "ancestral traditions" are thus closely linked to the Torah itself.⁷⁵

---

68. Longenecker, *Galatians*, 28.

69. Fung, *Galatians*, 57–62; cf. George, *Galatians*, 115; Bruce, *Heart Set Free*, 70–72; Godet, *Corinthians*, 105.

70. Bruce, *Heart Set Free*, 71.

71. Dunn, *Epistle to the Galatians*, 59, links Paul's progress in the Judean way of life (προέκοπτον ἐν τῷ Ἰουδαϊσμῷ, v. 14) to "a sense of superiority."

72. Hays, "Galatians," 214, and Dunn, *Epistle to the Galatians*, 61–62, connect Paul's "zeal" (ζηλωτής, v. 14) to the willingness to employ violence against those against the law, similar to Elijah's slaughter of Baal prophets (Sir 48:2; 1 Macc 2:58) and the Maccabean revolts (1 Macc 2:15), and thus connect "zeal" to the persecution of the early Judean believers in Christ (cf. Phil 3:5).

73. Bruce, *Galatians*, 91.

74. Paul's reference to being a Pharisee, once in the present tense (Acts 23:6) and one in the aorist tense (26:5), has to be understood within a polemical context where Paul rhetorically wanted to divide the crowd on the resurrection in order to win them over for the gospel (cf. 1 Cor 9:22–23) and that his belief in resurrection shares roots with Pharisaism, especially in terms of resurrection (see Du Toit, "Was Paul Fully Torah Observant," 7).

75. Martyn, *Galatians*, 155; Fung, *Galatians*, 57; Betz, *Galatians*, 68.

In the light of Paul's law-free gospel,[76] where the new identity in Christ is constituted by faith in Christ only and the indwelling of the Holy Spirit[77] over against an identity derived from the law (2:19; esp. 3:1-29), Paul's Damascus experience can be understood as a *conversion*[78] rather than merely a call.[79] Although Paul did not convert to a religious system called "Christianity" at the time, he did undergo a fundamental *change of identity*.[80] In 2:20,

76. Hays, "Galatians," 186, 210, 300; Longenecker, *Galatians*, 23-24, 26; Bruce, *Galatians*, 88; cf. note 11, pp. 232-33. Longenecker, *Galatians*, 26-27, discusses some of Paul's opposition among Judean Christ-believers. This opposition to Paul's law-free gospel was often bitter and intense. The *Ascension of James* (middle second century CE) speaks of Paul's law-free approach: "he [Paul] . . . began to write against circumcision, the sabbath, and the law" (cf. Epiphanius, *Pan.*). In the *Kerygmata Petrou* (late second century CE), Paul is referred to as "the enemy man" who proclaimed "lawless and absurd doctrine." Although we do not know of any such attacks against Paul in the first century, these kind of opposition "undoubtedly had roots in earlier times," and it is possible that Paul's opponents in Galatia insinuated something similar.

77. Paul mentions the Holy Spirit in Gal 3:3 as constituting the beginning of belief in Christ (cf. 3:14).

78. I could opt for a term such as "transformation" (which lies semantically close to "conversion"), but "conversion" is still the prevalent term within New Testament scholarship (see main text) despite its possible connotations about conversion to a religious system.

79. Das, *Galatians*, 125-29; Moo, *Galatians*, 102; De Boer, *Galatians*, 77; Segal, "Aspects of Conversion," 184-86; *Paul the Convert*, 285-300; George, *Galatians*, 29-33, 107, 110, 113; Longenecker, *Galatians*, 26, 28; Fung, *Galatians*, 59, 71; Lategan, *Galasiërs*, 29-30; Bruce, *Galatians*, 88; *Heart Set Free*, 74-76; Burton, *Galatians*, 44, 49; cf. Dunn, *Unity and Diversity*, 71; contra Eisenbaum, *Paul*, 132-149; Stendahl, *Paul*, 3-27. While Dunn, *Epistle to the Galatians*, 53, 63, often refers to Paul's "conversion" unqualified (as cited), he problematizes the term in connection with Paul if conversion from one "religion" to another is thereby implied, which comes close enough to my own position on the application of this particular term. But see also note 80 below.

80. Wright, *Fresh Perspective*, 113-121; Hays, "Galatians"; cf. Segal, "Aspects of Conversion," 185; Fung, *Galatians*. Cf. also Sanders, "Jewishness," 68-69, who, although acknowledging Paul's "new identity," he still understands Paul as being "Jewish." Yet he states that Paul "was Jewish as well as a new person in Christ, but his congregations did not constitute 'Judaism,' which was a separate entity." It might be asked, however, if this tension that Sanders holds on to does not become untenable in the light of Paul's desire to win Judeans for example (1 Cor 9:20) or the fact that Paul's converts are never presented as "Judeans" or "Israel" as such (cf. Donfried, "Jewish Matrix," 14). Yet Sanders, *Jewish People*, 207-8, states that "the church, in both his [sic] understanding and practice, became in effect a third entity" for Paul. In Sanders' understanding, Paul denies the election of "Israel" (which he equates with "Jews"): entrance to the people of God is not by accepting the law, but through faith in Christ. Dunn, *Epistle to the Galatians*, 57, also seems to work is this direction, albeit more hesitantly. He writes: "it was precisely the identity of the 'Jew' which was at issue . . . If Paul's use of 'Judaism' here [1:13] indicates a certain distancing of himself from the characteristic self-understanding of most of his fellow Jews, he still regarded himself as a Jew." While Dunn's understanding of Paul is that of a critique of the Judean identity and its self-understanding, our ways part when

Paul states: "I no longer live, but Christ lives in me,"[81] whereby he affirms his "death" to the old identity defined by the law (2:19).[82] His statement: "the life I now live in the flesh[83] I live by faith in[84] the Son of God" (2:20),[85] declares his new identity defined by faith in Christ,[86] which is no longer defined ethnically or by the possession of the law.[87] Since his encounter with the risen Jesus Christ, Paul's identity is therefore not defined by ethnicity and the law any longer, but by faith and a personal relationship with Christ. This change of identity arguably constitutes the core of his gospel.[88] With Paul's change of identity "his historical attachment to Israel is being relativized"[89] and can hardly be understood as merely a movement *within* the Judean identity.[90] The new identity in Christ (identity mode C) thus stands in *discontinuity* with the identity constituted by the Judean way of life (identity mode A).

In 1:15-16, Paul elaborates on his calling (v. 15), the Son that was revealed to him, and his consequential proclamation of Christ among the gentiles (v. 16). In verses 17 to 21 he outlines his travels and course of action, which was removed from any instruction or revelation from any human being. When he was in Syria and Cilicia (v. 21), he was unknown to the churches of Judea (v. 22). The churches of Judea were probably believers who were forced to leave Jerusalem in the persecution that followed Stephen's death, together with others that formed through the outreach of Jerusalem disciples before that. These churches might show some similarity to those in 1 Thessalonians 2:14, where the believers suffered persecution at the hands of their fellow "countrymen,"[91] but this notion remains only a pos-

---

he contends that "Christians" is another "Jewish movement."

81. ISV.

82. Hays, "Galatians," 244; cf. Wright, *Fresh Perspective*, 117; Fung, *Galatians*, 122.

83. Σάρξ here refers to bodily life here on earth (BDAG, σάρξ, §2b; cf. Abbott-Smith, *Lexicon*, 403; Moo, *Galatians*, 171; NLT; GNB; NAT; NIV).

84. Some render this as a subjective genitive: "the faithfulness of the Son" (e.g., Hays, "Galatians," 244; Longenecker, *Galatians*, 93–94; ISV; cf. KJV). A subjective genitive is, however, not characteristic of Paul when πίστις is mentioned in connection with Christ (see note 163, p. 90), and is thus not preferable here (Dunn, *Epistle to the Galatians*, 146; Fung, *Galatians*, 122; Lategan, *Galasiërs*, 52; Betz, *Galatians*, 125; ESV; GW; GNB; NRSV; REB; NIV; NAT; RSV; OAT; cf. NLT).

85. NRSV.

86. Hays, "Galatians," 244.

87. Wright, *Fresh Perspective*, 118.

88. This notion corresponds to "justification by faith," a feature of the gospel highlighted by some commentators (e.g., George, *Galatians*, :112; Fung, *Galatians*, 54).

89. Lategan, *Galasiërs*, 29.

90. Contra Dunn, *Epistle to the Galatians*, 57; Betz, *Galatians*, 64.

91. Bruce, *Galatians*, 103; cf. Longenecker, *Galatians*, 41.

sibility due to the uncertainty surrounding the identity of these countrymen (see pp. 147–54). Bruce argues that Paul was "unknown personally,"[92] for he might have had underlings who handled the day-to-day activities of the churches in Judea so that he had no direct dealings "with the rank and file." All Judean Christ-believers did, however, know him as "the persecutor" (v. 23)[93] or rather, "the one who formerly persecuted us."[94] This kind of title for Paul probably became established among all Judean Christ-believers, which would affirm Paul's change of core-identity.

Paul describes belief in Christ as "the faith" (τὴν πίστιν, v. 23; cf. 3:23, 25), which can be interpreted "objectively, to the movement itself"[95] and thus signifies its "objective content."[96] Hays argues that the "substantive content" of the gospel is summarized in kerygmatic formulas such as 1:3-4 and 1 Corinthians 15:3-5.[97] These formulas of faith arguably point in the direction of a new faith-identity that was in the process of becoming entrenched, separate from Judean beliefs and customs.[98] While Hays and Longenecker[99] connect "the faith" here to the gospel, and Moo to the "movement,"[100] Lightfoot is probably correct that its meaning "seems to hover between the Gospel and the Church."[101] De Boer rightly views this faith as definitive for the Christ-believing identity even for those who are Judeans by birth.[102]

---

92. Bruce, *Galatians*, 104. So BDAG, πρόσωπον, §1b, regarding ἀγνοούμενος τῷ προσώπῳ in v. 22 (lit. "unknown by face"). In respect of v. 22, Fung, *Galatians*, 82, suggests that Paul was "unknown *in his new identity as a Christian*" (emphasis original).

93. Dunn, *Epistle to the Galatians*, 83.

94. Martyn, *Galatians*, 177.

95. Moo, *Galatians*, 114.

96. George, *Galatians*, 132; cf. Hays, "Galatians," 217; Dunn, *Epistle to the Galatians*, 84.

97. Hays, "Galatians," 217.

98. Dunn, *Epistle to the Galatians*, 84, seems somewhat surprised with this formula ("the faith") "at such an early stage" of what he calls "the Christian movement." Such a sense, he argues, has no parallel either in Paul's background or in the Greek usage of the time.

99. Hays, "Galatians," 217; Longenecker, *Galatians*, 42.

100. Moo, *Galatians*, 114.

101. Lightfoot, *Galatians*, 86; adopted by Bruce, *Galatians*, 105.

102. De Boer, *Galatians*, 103.

Galatians 2:11-16

The Antioch incident has been a much debated topic in recent scholarship, especially in terms of the TAP and the NPP. The difference in opinion is due to Paul's concise account in this passage and the lack of crucial information as to what the exact circumstances were. The whole of the debate will not be repeated here. Outlining some of the main positions will have to suffice, with the focus being on Paul's theological thought behind his narration of the incident. Lategan states that Paul's account of the Antioch incident is not "for the sake of telling the story, but to illustrate the theological principle that he holds."[103]

Most commentators hold that even though Peter would normally eat with gentile believers in Christ and declared both Judean and gentile believers as free from the law, certain people who came from James wanted the Judean believers to observe the obligations akin to a Judean way of life, especially food laws, and/or advise Peter to detest from eating with gentiles. This would imply that gentile believers who wanted to enjoy fellowship with Judean believers had to adhere to these laws as well. This made Peter to draw back from the table fellowship, separating himself from gentile Christ-believers:[104] (1) for fear of conservative Judean Christ-believers who wanted to retain dietary laws,[105] or (2) for fear of Judean non-believers.[106]

Dunn, however, does not draw such defined distinctions between the Christ-believing and non-believing Judeans. He understands the Antioch incident more in terms of "intra-Jewish polemic," where faith in Jesus Christ would be an "intra-Jewish possibility."[107] But the deeper issue has to do with "the truth of the gospel" (v. 14) and the status and identity of a believer in Christ (v. 16). Martyn points out that the designations "the uncircumcision," "the Gentiles" and "the circumcision" are all linked to ethnicity: "once

---

103. Lategan, *Galasiërs*, 44.

104. Schreiner, *Galatians*; Hays, "Galatians," 232–34; Fung, *Galatians*, 106–11; George, *Galatians*, 167–86; Lategan, *Galasiërs*, 43–44; Betz, *Galatians*, 104–7; cf. Longenecker, *Galatians*, 71–78.

105. Lategan, *Galasiërs*, 43; cf. Moo, *Galatians*, 143; De Boer, *Galatians*, 133; Hays, "Galatians," 234; Martyn, *Galatians*, 234; Betz, *Galatians*, 109; Burton, *Galatians*, 107. Fung, *Galatians*, 108–9, takes the notion further and argues that this would ultimately lead to the requirement for gentiles to circumcise.

106. Longenecker, *Galatians*, 73, substantiates this reading from 2:7–9, where ἡ περιτομή refers simply to Judeans, and not to believers in Christ. This would imply that believers in Antioch were pressured by Judean nationalism and its antagonism against Judeans who had gentile sympathizers. Similarly, Bruce, *Galatians*, 131, hesitantly identifies them to be "Jewish militants."

107. Dunn, *Epistle to the Galatians*, 115–41.

a person enters the church, ethnic origin becomes for Paul and his fellow workers a matter of no importance"[108] (cf. 3:28). Martyn is thus probably correct that there was "a party . . . whose members derive their basic identity from their ethnic . . . heritage and who are sure that all members of the church have to be taken into this ethnic heritage, at least to some degree."[109] Since the ethnic heritage of the Judean believers was closely linked with the Torah, it would be safe to say that Torah observance was the ultimate "dividing wall" between the Judean and gentile believers in Christ.[110]

To "live like a Judean" (Ἰουδαϊκῶς ζῇς and Ἰουδαΐζω, v. 14)[111] is thus a matter of law observance, and distinguishes their way of life from that of a gentile.[112] To live like a Judean ran contrary to the gospel itself, for it deprived gentile believers of fellowship with Judean believers on equal terms and marred the grace that has been effected through Christ.[113] Any distinction between Judean and gentile believers would go against the grain of Paul's understanding of the gospel (esp. 3:28),[114] which points to the new creation in Christ (esp. 6:15). Paul thus "never wavered in his conviction that God was making a new creation by drawing into one church both Jews and Gentiles"[115] (cf. 2:7-10; Rom 15:25-31). De Boer is therefore essentially right when he states that Paul's rebuke "was meant to bring Cephas back to his sense, to help him . . . rediscover his (and their) true Christian identity."[116]

---

108. Martyn, *Galatians*, 233.

109. Martyn, *Galatians*, 234. Martyn identifies the party as a party within the Jerusalem church, but as he indicates in a footnote, it might have been in the Antioch congregation. This is not of crucial importance though.

110. Hays, "Galatians," 234; cf. Martyn, *Galatians*, 235; Bruce, *Galatians*, 137.

111. BDAG, Ἰουδαΐζω; Ἰουδαϊκῶς. Those referring to living like ". . . a Jew" or ". . . Jews" are the following: Betz, "ἰουδαΐζω," *EDNT*, 2:192; "Ἰουδαϊκῶς," *EDNT*, 2:192; "Ἰουδαϊσμός," *EDNT*, 2:192; Fung, *Galatians*, 111; Zerwick and Grosvenor, *Grammatical Analysis*, 567; Lategan, *Galasiërs*, 46; Mayer, "Israel," *NIDNTT*, 2:310; ISV; NRSV; RSV; KJV. Although there is overlap in meaning between these expressions, Longenecker, *Galatians*, 78, recognizes in Ἰουδαΐζω a slight leaning toward the notion "to become a Jew" rather than just "to live like a Jew." Similarly, Betz, *Galatians*, 112, argues that the term Ἰουδαΐζω would include more than submitting to Judean dietary laws for Paul: "it describes forcing one to become a Jewish convert obliged to keep the whole Torah (cf. 5:3)" (cf. George, *Galatians*, 181).

112. De Boer, *Galatians*, 137; Martyn, *Galatians*, 235; cf. Moo, *Galatians*, 144.

113. De Boer, *Galatians*, 136; Hays, "Galatians," 231, 234-35.

114. Bruce, *Galatians*, 137.

115. Martyn, *Galatians*, 236; cf. George, *Galatians*, 183.

116. De Boer, *Galatians*, 137.

In verse 15, Paul expresses a sharp distinction between the Judean and gentile identities.[117] The self-definition of the Judean Christ-believers[118] was instrumental to the circumstances leading up to the Antioch incident. Paul's language in verse 15 and his inclusion of himself as a Judean "by birth" (φύσει)[119] serves to place himself in the place of a typical Judean who perceived the rest of the world as outside the realm of God's covenant righteousness.[120] Paul's inclusion of himself is thus part of his rhetorical strategy,[121] rather than a description of his own identity. Gutbrod states that Paul "could not call himself simply a Ἰουδαῖος in this sense [remaining within the limits prescribed by the law], with no supplementary explanation," which he argues is proved by 2 Corinthians 11:22.[122] In Paul's expression φύσει Ἰουδαῖοι (Gal 2:15), the accent is thus more on Paul's ethnic heritage than on his current identity.[123]

Longenecker suggests that "sinners[124] of the Gentiles" (ἐξ ἐθνῶν ἁμαρτωλοί) is a colloquialism used by Judeans in reference to gentiles and probably carries a note of irony in this context.[125] The term φύσει (v. 15), which can be connected to the status of Judeans by birth (see above), "is different now from what it was when they lived under the law" and "constituted a barrier between them and the Gentiles." In "the way of faith in Christ, the barrier is down and there is no distinction between Jew and Gentile either in respect of sin (Rom. 3:22) or in respect of access to God's justifying grace (Rom. 10:12)."[126]

The content of the "truth of the gospel" (v. 14) is stated in verse 16. No person will be justified or rectified[127] (δικαιόω) by observing the law (ἐξ

---

117. Hays, "Galatians," 236; cf. Fung, *Galatians*, 113.

118. Betz, *Galatians*, 115; adopted by Longenecker, *Galatians*, 83; cf. Dunn, *Epistle to the Galatians*, 132.

119. Longenecker, *Galatians*, 83; Bruce, *Galatians*, 137; Betz, *Galatians*, 115; ESV; NIV; ISV; NRSV; GW; GNB; NAT.

120. Dunn, *Epistle to the Galatians*, 133.

121. Cf. Longenecker, *Galatians*, 83; Betz, *Galatians*, 115.

122. Gutbrod, "Ἰσραήλ," *TDNT*, 3:381.

123. Cf. De Boer, *Galatians*, 142.

124. "Sinners" would also be a synonym for gentiles (e.g., Isa 14:5; Macc 2:44; Matt 26:45; Luke 6:32–33; Longenecker, *Galatians*, 83; cf. George, *Galatians*, 188; Betz, *Galatians*, 115).

125. Longenecker, *Galatians*, 83; cf. Hays, "Galatians," 236.

126. Bruce, *Galatians*, 137.

127. Martyn, *Galatians*, 247, 249; adopted by Hays, "Galatians," 237; De Boer, *Galatians*.

ἔργων νόμου),[128] but by Christ only[129] or by faith in Christ only.[130] The verb δικαιόω points both to the right relational status of the believer (forensic),[131] and an ethical renewal.[132] If the verb is read in conjunction with the noun δικαιοσύνη and the adjective δίκαιος in Paul, which also have behavioral nuances, such a reading shows how Paul merges forensic and ethical categories.[133] Longenecker rightly points out that the

> watershed in all discussions about Paul and the law has to do with Paul's view of the Mosaic law as a religious system. And the principal question here is: Is Paul's polemic directed against the law itself or against a particular attitude toward the law that sees the law as a means of winning favor with God (i.e., "legalism")?[134]

In answer, Longenecker writes that Paul's polemic "is not only against legalism . . . but against even the Mosaic religious system, for he saw all of that as preparatory for and superseded by the relationship of being 'in Christ.'"[135] As Longenecker correctly concludes, the "works of the law" thus points *both*[136] to the badges of covenantal nomism (NPP)[137] *and* to the "whole legalistic complex of ideas having to do with winning God's favor by a merit-amassing observance of Torah" (TAP).[138]

---

128. Martyn, *Galatians*, 247; Fung, *Galatians*, 113.

129. De Boer, *Galatians*, 139; Longenecker, *Galatians*, 84; Martyn, *Galatians*, 247. While theologically agreeing with the notions put forth by Longenecker and Martyn on this point, I would be inclined to understand the πίστεως Ἰησοῦ Χριστοῦ as an objective genitive ("faith in Christ") rather than a subjective genitive ("the faith[fullness] of Christ"). While faith in Christ would imply trusting in the complete work of Christ (cf. Lategan, *Galatians*, 48), human faith would stand in direct contrast with "works of the law" as human action, which is a fundamental Pauline contrast (cf. note 136, p. 90).

130. George, *Galatians*, 188; Fung, *Galatians*, 113–15; Lategan, *Galatians*, 43, 48; Sanders, *Jewish People*, 172; Hendriksen, *Galatians*, 96–97; Burton, *Galatians*, 120–21; cf. Bruce, *Galatians*, 139–40.

131. This aspect additionally has an eschatological dimension and correlates to salvation (George, *Galatians*, 191–96).

132. Longenecker, *Galatians*, 84–85; Bruce, *Galatians*, 138; cf. Hays, "Galatians," 237–39.

133. Longenecker, *Galatians*, 85.

134. Longenecker, *Galatians*, 85.

135. Longenecker, *Galatians*, 85–86.

136. Longenecker, *Galatians*, 86; cf. Hagner, *New Testament*, 366–74.

137. So Dunn, *Epistle to the Galatians*, 136–37; Hays, "Galatians," 238–39.

138. So Moo, *Galatians*, 159; George, *Galatians*, 191–92, 194; Fung, *Galatians*, 114; Lategan, *Galatians*, 47–48; Betz, *Galatians*, 117.

The new identity in Christ through faith only (identity mode C) is portrayed as being in *discontinuity* with an ethnic identity derived from adherence to the law (identity mode A),[139] which has to be understood as inadequate means of justification.[140] Peter's hypocrisy (ὑπόκρισις, v. 13) would perpetuate the distinction between Judean and gentile, which Paul argues against,[141] and reduce the gentile believers into "second-class" believers.[142] For Paul, the principle of justification by faith in Christ applies to all human beings (σάρξ, v. 16)[143] and is thus a universal principle[144] without differentiation in terms of ethnicity or heritage.[145] In this passage, the change of identity in Christ of both Judean and gentile alike apart from the law is further accentuated by Paul's death to the law and his old identity, and by Christ who now lives in him (vv. 19-20, see pp. 128-29).[146]

Philippians 3:1-9

In this passage, Paul contrasts his former life as a Judean with his present righteousness based on faith (esp. vv. 4a-9).[147] Verses 2 to 21 have a

---

139. Cf. esp. De Boer, *Galatians*, 152-55; Martyn, *Galatians*, 229, 233, 251, who states: "as regards salvation, observance of the Law and the faith of Christ constitute a genuine antinomy" (p. 251). Similarly Fung, *Galatians*, 116; Lategan, *Galatians*, 47-49.

140. Fung, *Galatians*, 114; cf. George, *Galatians*, 190-91.

141. Cf. Martyn, *Galatians*, 248-49.

142. George, *Galatians*, 182.

143. BDAG, σάρξ, §3a.

144. George, *Galatians*, 191; Fung, *Galatians*, 117-18. This universality is indicated in v. 16 by the first person plurals (ἐπιστεύσαμεν, δικαιωθῶμεν, and esp. καὶ ἡμεῖς— the καὶ making the ἡμεῖς emphatic), which implies the inclusion of Judean believers (Longenecker, *Galatians*, 88; cf. Lategan, *Galatians*, 48). The principle of justification by faith is in fact part of the self-definition of a Judean Christ-believing theology (Betz, *Galatians*, 115), and thus simultaneously constitutes a profound element of *continuity* with the Judean heritage, especially in terms of Abraham's faith (cf. Rom 4).

145. Lategan, *Galatians*, 48-49; Bruce, *Galatians*, 135, 138; cf. De Boer, *Galatians*, 154-55; Martyn, *Galatians*, 249. While De Boer and Martyn (as cited) share similar notions about the "the works of the law" or ethnic identity not being constitutive of the Christ-believing identity, their accent is more on the *faithful work* of Christ than on belief *in* him.

146. This understanding is contrary to an approach where Gal 2:15-16 is to be understood as merely "intra-Jewish religious discourse" (Ruzer, "Paul's Stance," 84). If the "works of the law" denotes both defining identity on the basis of the law (NPP) and obedience to the law (TAP), the notion to keep righteousness (δικαιόω, v. 16) based on faith in Christ [alone] (διὰ πίστεως Ἰησοῦ Χριστοῦ, v. 16) within a Judean identity (let alone a "Jewish" identity), becomes untenable.

147. Fee, *Philippians*, 285.

markedly different tone than the rest of the letter. While Paul's friends are commended in 2:19-30, dangerous "dogs" are condemned in 3:2. Apart from this contrast, 3:2-21 seems to break the rhythm between the appeal to "finally rejoice" in 3:1 and the tender words of 4:1-3 that would smoothly follow on 3:1.[148] It has for these reasons been suggested that 3:2-21 is an interpolation[149] or that Paul originally ended the letter at 3:1 and came back later to add a doctrinal discussion to it.[150] But Reed has shown that the following three elements can be labelled as an "epistolary hesitation formula" and constitute a transition from one subject to the next:[151] (1) γράφειν (to write), (2) οὐκ (negative particle) and (3) ὀκνηρόν (expressing hesitation) in verse 1.

The whole of 3:2-21 is strongly Christ-centered[152] (see vv. 3, 7, 8-10, 12, 14, 18, 20, 21), which probably signifies the strongest point of continuity with the preceding part of the letter.[153] The repeated theme of "rejoicing" (χαίρω, 1:18; 2:17, 18, 28; 3:1; 4:4, 10)[154] is essentially "in the Lord" (3:1; 4:4) as the object and source of joy,[155] which complements the high Christology. Although the tone of 3:2-4 is thus negative toward Paul's opponents, his focus on intimate, personal knowledge[156] of Christ and participation in his resurrection and suffering (3:7-10; cf. 1:29-30; 2:17) qualifies the rejoicing as a deep, Christ-centered rejoicing, which is not directed toward oneself (cf. 2:21).[157] As applied often by Paul (e.g., Rom 4:24; 5:11, 21; 10:13; 1 Cor 1:3), Jesus as "Lord" (Phil 3:1, 8, 20) corresponds with the Septuagint's translation of Yahweh (MT, see pp. 256-57). The personal "my Lord" (v. 8) signifies Paul's existential identification with Christ who humbled himself

---

148. Cf. Hansen, *Philippians*, 212.

149. E.g., Beare, *Philippians*, 101.

150. Silva, *Philippians* (BECNT), 167.

151. Reed, "Epistolary Hesitation"; cf. Hansen, *Philippians*, 213.

152. Hansen, *Philippians*, 211; cf. Fee, *Philippians*, 285.

153. This high Christology is esp. evident in 2:5-11, where both the humble, serving character of Christ and his Lordship are accentuated.

154. This repeated theme goes against Beare's, *Philippians*, 100, notion to translate v. 1 as "Finally, my brethren, I bid you farewell in the Lord" (Hansen, *Philippians*, 214).

155. Hansen, *Philippians*, 214.

156. Paul's use of γνῶσις probably follows the Old Testament understanding of the knowledge of God (e.g., Jer 9:23, 24; 31:34; Hos 4:1; 6:6), which is based on His self-revelation and signifies a personal relationship (Hooker, "Philippians," 527; O'Brien, *Philippians*, 388; Hawthorne, *Philippians*, 137-38; cf. Hansen, *Philippians*, 235; Bockmuehl, *Philippians*, 205).

157. Fee, *Philippians*, 285; O'Brien, *Philippians*, 349-50, 362.

and suffered (2:6–11).[158] The theme of having the same mind (φρονέω) in verse 15 fits well with the same theme earlier (2:2, 5) and later (4:2) in the letter. These notions in turn underscore the intricate relationship of 3:2–21 with the rest of the letter.

Paul's opponents whom he addresses in verses 2 to 3 are most likely Judean believers in Christ[159] who accentuated circumcision and Judean credentials[160] and might have wanted to make full Judean proselytes of the gentile believers.[161] Their attitude would thus be that of superiority.[162] The very derogatory connotation to them as "dogs" (κύνας, v. 2) is ironic in that the term is normally applied to impure gentiles[163] (cf. Matt 7:6). Paul reverses the term and applies it to these Judean believers who seem to threaten his gospel. The same irony is evident in the term κατατομή (v. 2), denoting "the mutilation" or "cutting in pieces,"[164] which is a play on περιτομή (v. 3).[165] Paul thus applies a term that is normally used in a pagan context (κατατομή) to describe those who focus on circumcision, as if he pictures their focus on circumcision as being equal to the pagan rite of cutting one's own flesh[166] (cf. Gal 5:12). These ironical designations for Paul's opponents might suggest that the expression in the middle, κακοὺς ἐργάτας (v. 2), is derived from the Septuagint expression οἱ ἐργαζόμενοι τὴν ἀνομίαν ("those who work iniquity," e.g., Ps 5:6; 6:9; 58:3), and that Paul changed the "iniquity" into "evil" in order for the assonance to work.[167] Silva (*Philippians* [BECNT],

158. Cf. Hansen, *Philippians*, 235; Bockmuehl, *Philippians*, 206.

159. Although the opponents' identity is not certain, in analogy of Paul's opponents elsewhere (esp. Galatians), it seems more probable that they were Judean believers than being pure Judeans (contra Hawthorne, *Philippians*, 125). It has not been characteristic of Judean people to pressure gentiles to become circumcised (Silva, *Philippians* [BECNT], 147).

160. Hansen, *Philippians*, 217; cf. Bockmuehl, *Philippians*, 183; Fee, *Philippians*, 294; O'Brien, *Philippians*, 355–56; Silva, *Philippians* (WEC), 169.

161. Hooker, "Philippians," 525; Bockmuehl, *Philippians*, 184.

162. Bockmuehl, *Philippians*, 187, 194–95; O'Brien, *Philippians*, 352, 356.

163. Hooker, "Philippians," 524; Fee, *Philippians*, 295; O'Brien, *Philippians*, 354–55; Hawthorne, *Philippians*, 125; Vincent, *Philippians*, 92. It is interesting to note that Rabbi Aqiba (although from later Rabbinic Judaism) named his two dogs Rufus and Rufina to indicate the manner of life of the gentiles (*Midrash Tanhuma* 107b; cited in the Targum, Str-B, 1:725; Fee, *Philippians*, 295). Reumann, *Philippians*, 461, argues that κύνας can also refer to "lapsed Jews" (referring to Matt 15:26–27).

164. BDAG, κατατομή.

165. Zerwick and Grosvenor, *Grammatical Analysis*, 598.

166. Hansen, *Philippians*, 220; Reumann, *Philippians*, 462; Fee, *Philippians*, 296; O'Brien, *Philippians*, 357–58; Silva, *Philippians* (WEC), 169–70; cf. Hooker, "Philippians," 524; Bockmuehl, *Philippians*, 189; Hawthorne, *Philippians*, 126.

167. Fee, *Philippians*, 296.

147) suggests that the expression κακοὺς ἐργάτας is intended to refute the opponents' claims that they were doing the works of the law (cf. Gal 3:10; 5:3; 6:14). It seems then that Paul turns his opponents' own derogatory or outsider terms against them and thereby changes them into outsiders. This is how serious Paul sees their agenda.

At this point it has to be acknowledged that part of Paul's rhetoric strategy was probably influenced by the politics of identity of the first century where the formation of identity was influenced by the "other." The politics of "othering" was indebted to the classic anti-democratic discourses of Plato and Aristotle.[168] In this process of "othering," the new identity of Christ-believers was partly influenced by defining their boundaries in reference to the Judean way of life. This may have led to the release of negative energy in relation to the "other," which in turn encouraged a measure of stereotyping and even vilification or aggression.[169] The extent to which the dynamics of "othering" can be applied to Paul's rhetoric however remains a matter of debate.[170]

Paul's ironical rhetoric is further enhanced by designating believers in Christ (ἡμεῖς, v. 3) as the [true] περιτομή (v. 3),[171] a term normally denoting Judeans.[172] But Paul redefines περιτομή in this context: they are those who serve[173] in the Spirit of God and boast in Christ Jesus and have no

---

168. Schüssler Fiorenza, "Paul," 45.

169. Punt, "Politics of Difference," 199-225; Schüssler Fiorenza, "Paul," 45, 50. This dynamics of "othering" in Paul may be identified in reviewing the frequency of terms such as ἔξω ("outside": 1 Cor 5:12, 13; 1 Thess 4:12; cf. Col 4:5) and ἕτερος ("other"). The latter term describes different categories (Rom 7:3, 4; 1 Cor 3:4; 12:9, 10; 14:7; 15:40), an "other commandment" (Rom 13:9), "other law" (Rom 7:23), "other spirit/gospel" (2 Cor 11:4; Gal 1:6), or "other apostle" (Gal 1:19). The term is also applied in reference to any other entity (Rom 8:39) or other people. It could denote another person on the inside (Rom 2:1, 22; 1 Cor 4:6; 6:1; 10:24, 29; Gal 6:4) but also someone in general (Rom 13:8; 1 Cor 14:21; 2 Cor 8:8; Punt, "Politics of Difference," 213).

170. Cf. Punt, "Politics of Difference," 219-20.

171. Fee, *Philippians*, 298; O'Brien, *Philippians*, 358; Silva, *Philippians* (WEC), 170; Lightfoot, *Philippians*, 145. Paul's application of περιτομή here can be compared to Rom 2:25-29. But as discussed on pp. 59-68, the Judean who ought to be circumcised in heart in Rom 2:25-29 does not designate an actual believer in Christ, but rather pictures the ideal Judean who can fulfill the law (which is impossible) and arguably serves as appeal to accept Christ who fits this ideal picture and who is the solution to the dilemma. Reumann, *Philippians*, 474-75, argues for viewing περιτομή here as "an 'Israel term' for the church," but the polemical context rather suggests a unique application that cannot be standardized. While the church fulfilled much of the intent of the Old Testament promise to Israel (esp. Gal 3 and the seed of Abraham), that the church is in fact the "Israel of God" (Gal 6:16), is not that evident (see pp. 338-45).

172. BDAG, περιτομή, §2a.

173. Paul probably follows the Septuagint's use of λατρεύω, which denotes the

confidence in the flesh (v. 3; cf. Gal 3:1–5; Col 2:11). For Paul, physical circumcision as such is by implication not a sign of covenant membership[174] any more.[175] The phrase ἐν σαρκὶ πεποιθότες occurs once in verse 3 and twice in verse 4, and stands antinomical to "we ... who serve in the Spirit of God and boast in Christ Jesus" (see below). The verb πείθω is typically Pauline (cf. Rom 2:8, 19; 8:38; 14:14; 15:14; 2 Cor 1:9; 2:3; 5:11; 10:7; etc.) and means to "trust in" or to "depend on."[176] The object of this verb is σάρξ, which denotes "physical advantages" or "earthly things."[177] This "trust in physical advantages" both denotes the attitude of Paul's adversaries and his own attitude within his former life as unbelieving Judean. The term σάρξ is used in denoting that which is outward[178] and was part of Paul's former life.[179] In this context, ethnic heritage[180] and the circumcision itself seem to resort under this term.[181] Hooker is probably right that the law itself "operates in the sphere of flesh"[182] (cf. Rom 7, see pp. 189–99). Although σάρξ carries overtones of the eschatologically old way existence before Christ[183] (cf. esp. Rom 7:5–6; Rom 8:1–16, see pp. 189–206), such a notion is not primary in this context and rather figures on a deeper, underlying level (see below). Paul then lists 7 concrete examples (vv. 5–6) of what would typically constitute the grounds for trusting in the flesh. The former 4 of these seven examples are privileges inherited by birth and the latter 3 are his own accomplishments in his former life:[184]

Levitical service. In Paul's use here, it would then stand in ironical contrast to v. 2. Those who "served" were forbidden to κατατομή. Additionally, the serving in the Spirit stands in contrast with the "workers of iniquity" who engaged in such illegitimate "service" (Fee, *Philippians*, 300).

174. In the traditional Judean understanding, physical circumcision would signify covenant membership (Bockmuehl, *Philippians*, 189; Gen 17:10–24; cf. Hawthorne, *Philippians*, 125).

175. Cf. O'Brien, *Philippians*, 358–59; Silva, *Philippians* (WEC), 171; Hawthorne, *Philippians*, 127.

176. BDAG, πείθω, §2a; Zerwick and Grosvenor, *Grammatical Analysis*, 599.

177. BDAG, σάρξ, §5.

178. BDAG, σάρξ, §5; Silva, *Philippians* (WEC), 171.

179. O'Brien, *Philippians*, 366.

180. Hansen, *Philippians*, 222.

181. Hansen, *Philippians*, 222; Silva, *Philippians* (BECNT), 149; O'Brien, *Philippians*, 363–64.

182. Hooker, "Philippians," 525.

183. Fee, *Philippians*, 300–302.

184. Cf. O'Brien, *Philippians*, 364, 368; Silva, *Philippians* (BECNT), 150; Silva, *Philippians* (WEC), 174.

Four Privileges Inherited by Birth (v. 5)

1. Paul was circumcised on the eighth day. The construction περιτομῇ ὀκταήμερος is probably a dative of respect or reference,[185] which may indicate that Paul's circumcision was superior to the circumcision of a gentile proselyte.[186]

2. Paul is ἐκ γένους Ἰσραήλ: from the nation[187] or the race[188] of Israel the patriarch.[189] This denotes ethnic Israel[190] by implication. Paul therefore claims genealogical purity.[191] His use of Ἰσραήλ together with ἐκ γένους can be compared to Romans 9:6 ("all those from Israel, these are not Israel," see p. 51), denoting the (first) broader category: "those from Israel" (Rom 9:6), which is similar to "Israel according to the flesh" (1 Cor 10:18; cf. Rom 9:3).

3. Paul is φυλῆς Βενιαμίν: from the tribe of Benjamin. This denotes Paul's specific bloodline.[192] Apart from the fact that Benjamin as a child of Jacob's cherished Rachel was loved, Benjamin was the only child born in the promised land (Gen 35:16-18). Additionally, the first king of Israel came from the tribe of Benjamin (1 Sam 9:1-2).[193]

4. Paul is a Ἑβραῖος ἐξ Ἑβραίων: a Hebrew of Hebrews (cf. 2 Cor 11:22). While this designation arguably implies that the Aramaic language was Paul's mother tongue,[194] this is not beyond dispute (see note 97, p. 43). In this context it seems to indicate that Paul was brought up in the Hebrew culture.[195] The term Ἑβραῖος was a honorary title from

---

185. BDF §197.

186. Hansen, *Philippians*, 223.

187. BDAG, γένος, §3.

188. Hansen, *Philippians*, 223; Reumann, *Philippians*, 482; Hooker, "Philippians," 526; O'Brien, *Philippianis*, 370; L&N §10.1; Zerwick and Grosvenor, *Grammatical Analysis*, 599; Vincent, *Philippians*, 96.

189. BDAG, Ἰσραήλ, §1.

190. L&N §10.1.

191. Hansen, *Philippians*, 223.

192. BDAG, φυλή, §1; cf. Hansen, *Philippians*, 224; contra Reumann, *Philippians*, 483.

193. Hansen, *Philippians*, 224; Bockmuehl, *Philippians*, 196; O'Brien, *Philippians*, 370; Hawthorne, *Philippians*, 132.

194. Hansen, *Philippians*, 224; Reumann, *Philippians*, 483; O'Brien, *Philippians*, 371; Vincent, *Philippians*, 97; cf. Silva, *Philippians* (BECNT), 153-54; Hawthorne, *Philippians*, 133.

195. Hansen, *Philippians*, 225; cf. Bockmuehl, *Philippians*, 196; O'Brien, *Philippians*, 372; Hawthorne, *Philippians*, 133; Lightfoot, *Galatians*, 147.

the distant past, which can be contrasted to the more general term Ἰουδαῖος.[196]

Three Accomplishments in Paul's Former Life (vv. 5–6)

5. Paul was according to the law a Pharisee. Josephus writes that they were "esteemed most skilful in the exact explication of their laws."[197] They assigned special significance to purity laws, stressing the distinction between clean and unclean, and therefore distanced themselves from "unclean" persons.[198] They were considered as great moral leaders who sought to reform Judean society with their purity rules and sabbath observance. Much of their legal requirements were based on their "oral law."[199]

6. Concerning zeal, Paul was a persecutor of the church (cf. Gal 1:13). This zeal is similar to the zeal for the law in the Maccabean revolt (1 Macc 2:26-27, 50). Paul's referral to zeal has to do with an "intense dedication to keeping the law."[200] The term is "closely linked with a fervent commitment to defending the purity of Israel's religious practice and of her communal institutions, even at the cost of life itself."[201] Saul's persecution of the church thus can be understood as defending the identity of God's people as faithfully keeping the law over against what was preached by the church.[202] According to Paul's definition of the church as the "[true] circumcision" (v. 3), Saul by implication persecuted the true people of God.[203]

7. Paul claims to have been blameless concerning the righteousness in the law. At first glance, this claim seems to contradict Paul's other statements that all who rely on the works of the law are under a curse (Gal 3:10, 13), which made it impossible to adhere to the standard the law has set (Rom 3:20; 7:6; 8:3; Gal 3:21). But Paul's reference to being blameless in terms of the righteousness in the law has to be understood

---

196. Kuhn, "Ἰσραήλ," *TDNT*, 3:367–68.

197. Josephus, *J.W.* 2.8.14.

198. Bockmuehl, *Philippians*, 197; cf. O'Brien, *Philippians*, 373. This is probably the reason why they were known as "the separated ones" (BDAG, Φαρισαῖος).

199. Hansen, *Philippians*, 225–26.

200. Hansen, *Philippians*, 226; cf. BDAG, ζῆλος, §1; Hawthorne, *Philippians*, 134.

201. Bockmuehl, *Philippians*, 199.

202. Hansen, *Philippians*, 227.

203. Hansen, *Philippians*, 228.

in its specific polemical context, which functions as a pre-conversion assessment[204] of Paul's life. Paul presents this specific accomplishment in terms of the *pharisaic interpretation* of the law.[205] He therefore did not claim to be sinless.[206] Paul's claim has to do with observable and verifiable aspects of his portrait,[207] and can mainly be connected to sabbath observance, food laws and ritual cleanliness.[208] The whole of this claim is being put into perspective in Paul's assessment of the righteousness from the law being ineffective in terms of his righteous status before God (v. 9, see below) and his rejecting of all 4 privileges and 3 accomplishments as σκύβαλον (v. 8).

Does Paul Continue to be a Pharisee? Answering the RNPP

In terms of Paul's reference to his Pharisaic background (v. 5), Bockmuehl argues that Paul "may well continue to hold Pharisaic views, even if his practice of purity laws and table fellowship was now more lenient."[209] This approach, which forms part of the RNPP, implies that the Judean and gentile Christ-believers remain in distinct subgroups within the Christ-believing community. The Judean believers thus retain their distinct identity derived from the observance of the Torah, including circumcision, the observance of specific days and dietary restrictions. They are to be distinguished from gentile Christ-believers who do not have to follow all the latter restrictions.[210] The gentile

---

204. Westerholm, *Israel's Law*, 161; adopted by Hansen, *Philippians*, 229. Contra Bockmuehl, *Philippians*, 202, who also seems to qualify the possibility of keeping the law in terms of Pharisaic interpretation: "it was perfectly possible to lead a life that was righteous and did not contravene this system—especially with the benefit of Pharisaic legal interpretation." Paul's focus on the human depravity and his or her inability to fulfill the law and be righteous on the basis of law (see above), however, constitutes a deeper understanding of the law than a "Pharisaic legal interpretation." Bockmuehl's mention of the possibility to keep the 613 commandments that would have been part of the Pharisaic system is strictly speaking anachronistic in terms of the origin of these 613 commandments (being part of Rabbinic Judaism), even though there might have been signs in Pharisaic groups that the system was underway.

205. Fee, *Philippians*, 309; O'Brien, *Philippians*, 374, 380; Silva, *Philippians* (WEC), 174, 176.

206. O'Brien, *Philippians*, 380; Silva, *Philippians* (BECNT), 151; *Philippians* (WEC), 175. Rather than denoting "sinlessness," the word ἄμεμπτος is a standard way of expressing "exemplary conformity to the way of life prescribed the OT" (Silva, *Philippians* [BECNT], 151).

207. Hansen, *Philippians*, 229; Silva, *Philippians* (BECNT), 151.

208. Fee, *Philippians*, 309; cf. Hawthorne, *Philippians*, 123.

209. Bockmuehl, *Philippians*, 198.

210. Cf. Nanos, "Paul's Relationship to Torah," 123–24; *Mystery*, 50–56; Rudolph,

subgroup of believers is thus accommodated within the social community on the basis of "Jewish" halakha. This limited set of requirements for gentile believers is sometimes referred to as the "Noahide Commandments"[211] or "Noahide Laws,"[212] a set of requirements that is often identified with the so called "Apostolic Decree" in reference to Acts 15:19-32; 16:1-5 and 21:25.[213] Accordingly, gentile believers are called "Noachians"[214] or "Noahides."[215] However, a halakhic model that appeals to the Noahide laws is strictly anachronistic, and the notion that an earlier form of such a model can be identified with Paul cannot be established beyond doubt.[216]

Further, the above approach would imply that Paul still partly defines his identity by "flesh" and not purely by God's Spirit (v. 3). It would further imply a kind of exclusivity for Judean believers over against gentile believers. Wan writes that "while Gentiles are fully incorporated into a Jewish milieu, they are nevertheless placed in a subordinate position."[217] He refers to the "priority of the Jewish people" in Paul.[218] However, the latter notion is difficult to reconcile with the way in which Paul relativizes any distinctions between Judean and gentile Christ-believers (Rom 3:22; 10:12; 1 Cor 1:24; 12:13; Gal 3:28-29).[219] Although Paul continues to acknowledge Judean and Greek in Christ in Galatians 3:28 and thus acknowledges that "differences remain for these dyads,"[220] these ethnic designations can hardly be seen as still being definitive in marking off Abraham's offspring, just as male/female or slave/free are social identities that are irrelevant in terms of marking off Abraham's offspring. Being a Judean thus lost its definitive power in marking off God's people in the light of the new age that was inaugurated by the "coming" of faith (Gal 3:23, 25). Faith and the Spirit are now the only markers of identity in the new faith-era in Christ that mark off Abraham's

---

Jew; Tucker, *Remain*, 62-114; Eisenbaum, *Paul*, 252; Campbell, *Paul*, 89-93; Bockmuehl, *Jewish Law*; Wan, "Collection."

211. Nanos, *Mystery*, 366; cf. Tomson, *Paul*, 271.
212. Nanos, *Mystery*, 51; cf. Campbell, *Paul*.
213. Nanos, *Mystery*, 52; Tomson, *Paul*, 273-74 (see note 15, p. 3).
214. Tomson, *Paul*, 272.
215. Nanos, *Mystery*, 50. In Rabbinic Judaism, all descendants of Noah are considered as *b'nei Noah* or "Noahides" (Foley, "Noachide Laws," 45).
216. I have argued this in some length elsewhere (Du Toit, "Noagitiese Wette"; see note 368, pp. 283-84).
217. Wan, "Collection," 208.
218. Wan, "Collection," 214.
219. Cf. Wright, *Faithfulness*, 2:1435; Sanders, *Jewish People*, 33, 40-41.
220. Nanos, "Myth," 4.

children or God's children (Gal 3:7, 9, 26, 29).²²¹ A halakhic understanding of identity in Christ, however, argues for keeping gentile believers and believers from the Judeans in an uneven relationship in terms of their relation to the law, which would imply a difference in status as God's people. While the social identities listed in Galatians 3:28 would indeed perpetuate a different *social* status in the case of the slave/free binary for example, this difference has to be differentiated from the status as *God's people*, wherein male/female or slave/free would be irrelevant (cf. Phlm 16).

Horrell lists several other difficulties in trying to fit Paul's ethic to a halakhic model: (1) Since the halakhic model presupposes equal participation in salvation, one may ask how sharply the distinction between the soteriological and ethical function of the law may be drawn. (2) It can be asked if Paul's distancing from his former way of life as a Ἰουδαῖος (Gal 1:13; Phil 3:7-8) so that he is now longer ὑπὸ νόμον (e.g., Rom 6:14-15; 1 Cor 9:20-21) can be harmonized with a halakhic model.²²² Being no longer "under the law" would imply both a soteriological and ethical stance. (3) The halakhic model necessitates that Paul addresses exclusively gentile believing audiences or at least that Paul is exclusively an apostle to the gentiles. It is however clear that there were Jews among the congregations to whom Paul writes (e.g., Rom 16:3, 7, 11, 21, 23; 1 Cor 1:1, 14; 7:18-19; 16:19).²²³ Paul's use of the first person plural in addressing the Galatians, which includes himself, a Judean believer, also strongly argues against the RNPP on this point.²²⁴

Paul's New Identity as Superseding his Previous Judean Identity

Paul's four privileges and three accomplishments in Philippians 3:5-6 (see above) is rather to be understood as defining Paul's earlier identity ἐν σαρκί (vv. 3-4). The privileges inherited by birth (1-4 above) can all be connected to Paul's Judean descent and pedigree²²⁵ in which Paul could indeed claim

---

221. Du Toit, "Galatians 3"; cf. Wright, *Faithfulness*, 2:875; De Boer, *Galatians*, 244; Hays, "Galatians," 187; Martyn, *Galatians*, 335; Longenecker, *Galatians*, 157.

222. E.g., Tucker, *Remain*, 103, and Bockmuehl, *Jewish Law*, 171, argue that ὑπὸ νόμον could denote a "strict interpretation of the law" in 1 Cor 9:20 while denoting something totally different in Rom 6:14-15; Gal 3:23; 4:4-5, 21; and 5:18, which seems like special pleading (see Du Toit, "Keeping of the Commandments").

223. Horrell, *Solidarity*, 17-18.

224. Du Toit, "Galatians 3."

225. Hansen, *Philippians*, 222; cf. Hawthorne, *Philippians*, 130.

superiority (v. 4).²²⁶ But trust in these Judean "identity markers"²²⁷ would imply "trust in the flesh" that is juxtaposed to the identity in Christ,²²⁸ constituted by righteousness based on faith (v. 9).²²⁹ The three accomplishments (5-7 above) are in some way connected to the law, or more specifically, righteousness based on the law (v. 9),²³⁰ which also constitutes an aspect of "trust in the flesh."²³¹ The law could however not bring true righteousness²³² (cf. Rom 3:21-31). "Trust in the flesh" thus ranges from a focus on descent (1-4 above) to human accomplishments based on law (5-7 above). In summary, trust in the flesh denotes "what is physical, external, visible, and temporal, in contrast to the spiritual, internal, invisible, and eternal."²³³

Paul's use of the verb λατρεύω (v. 3) has to be connected to righteousness (vv. 6, 9).²³⁴ "Service" in the Spirit (v. 3) stands antithetical to righteousness based on Torah observance (v. 9). The deeper, underlying contrast in 3:1-9 can thus be expressed as between σάρξ (vv. 3-4) and πνεῦμα (v. 3), which ultimately

> stand juxtaposed as *eschatological realities* that describe existence in the overlap of the ages. One lives either "according to the Spirit" or "according to the flesh." These are mutually incompatible kinds of existence; to be in the one and then to revert to the former is spiritual suicide from Paul's point of view.²³⁵

Paul defines the righteousness based on the law as his "own" (ἐμός) righteousness (v. 9) and opposes it to "the righteousness of God [based] on faith," which implies a contrast between two sources of righteousness²³⁶ (cf. Rom 10:3, see pp. 253-54). The connotation of accomplishment or merit is hard to deny in this context (TAP),²³⁷ but not to the exclusion of

---

226. Cf. Hansen, *Philippians*, 225.
227. Reumann, *Philippians*, 474; Fee, *Philippians*, 294.
228. Cf. Hansen, *Philippians*, 220.
229. Cf. Silva, *Philippians* (BECNT), 152.
230. Cf. Fee, *Philippians*, 296.
231. Cf. Hooker, "Philippians," 525.
232. Hooker, "Philippians," 528.
233. Hooker, "Philippians," 526; cf. BDAG, σάρξ, §5; Silva, *Philippians* (WEC), 171.
234. Fee, *Philippians*, 300.
235. Fee, *Philippians*, 302, emphasis added.
236. Moo, *Romans*, 635; O'Brien, *Philippians*, 396-97; Bruce, *Romans*, 199; Käsemann, *Romans*, 281; cf. Hansen, *Philippians*, 240; Hawthorne, *Philippians*, 141-42.
237. Hansen, *Philippians*, 239; Silva, *Philippians* (BECNT), 160-61; *Philippians* (WEC), 187; Westerholm, *Perspectives*, 312; Gathercole, *Boasting*, 181-82; Fee, *Philippians*, 323; O'Brien, *Philippians*, 394-96; Hawthorne, *Philippians*, 125, 127, 141.

pride or trust in physical identity markers (NPP).[238] Both these aspects are present here.

The righteousness of God based on faith (τὴν ἐκ θεοῦ δικαιοσύνην ἐπὶ τῇ πίστει, v. 9) comes through faith in Christ (διὰ πίστεως Χριστοῦ, v. 9)[239] and is received by dependence on Christ.[240] This righteousness reflects one's right relationship with God.[241] This notion is especially accentuated in verses 7 to 8 by Paul's portrayal of intimate, personal knowledge of Christ[242] as only gain, in contrast to all external, ethnic privileges and human accomplishments in terms of the law, which he all considers as loss and even as refuse.[243]

The identity in Christ defined by serving in the Spirit, which signifies identity mode C, stands in stark *discontinuity* with the identity outside of faith in Christ, which in Paul's case represents identity mode A. Identity mode A is here described as placing trust in the flesh, and consists of confidence in external, ethnical identity markers (e.g., circumcision, tribe, and lineage) and in observable adherence to the law. The contrast between these modes of identity (A and C) constitutes a complete transformation[244] or conversion experience[245] in Paul's life. The transformation implies the tak-

---

238. Bockmuehl, *Philippians*, 188; cf. Dunn, *Romans*, 2:588.

239. As elsewhere (e.g., Gal 2:16; 3:22), πίστεως Χριστοῦ could be rendered as a subjective genitive (e.g., Hooker, "Philippians," 528; Bockmuehl, *Philippians*, 210–11; O'Brien, *Philippians*, 398–99), indicating Christ's faith[fulness] (see note 163, p. 90). But it is more likely an objective genitive ([human] faith in Christ), for (a) there is no analogy for "based on faith" to refer to Christ's activity other than human faith, (b) the contrast between "my own righteousness" with "through faith" seems to fit an objective genitive more naturally (rather than if it would refer to Christ's faith), and (c) faith in connection with suffering is human faith in 1:29, which makes it likely that human faith is intended here in 3:9 too where it stands in close proximity to suffering (vv. 10–11; Fee, *Philippians*, 325–26). Silva, *Philippians* (BECNT), 161, notes that Paul never speaks unambiguously of Jesus as faithful, and that it is always safer to interpret ambiguous grammatical forms in the light of the unambiguous ones. Opting for the objective genitive takes nothing away from the unmerited character of God's righteousness, for faith as human response is "the act of counting as loss all those things that may be conceived as grounds for self-confidence before God" (Silva, *Philippians* (WEC), 188).

240. Hansen, *Philippians*, 242; cf. Silva, *Philippians* (WEC), 180.

241. Hansen, *Philippians*, 240; Fee, *Philippians*, 324; Hawthorne, *Philippians*, 142.

242. Cf. O'Brien, *Philippians*, 386; Silva, *Philippians* (WEC), 189.

243. BDAG, σκύβαλον. Σκύβαλον could mean "dung" or "excrement" (e.g., O'Brien, *Philippians*, 390), but in 1 Cor 4:13, similar language is used to refer to "off-scouring and refuse" (Fee, *Philippians*, 319), which makes the translation "refuse" or "garbage" preferable (ESV; ISV; NRSV; ASV).

244. Hansen, *Philippians*, 231.

245. O'Brien, *Philippians*, 383–84; Silva, *Philippians* (WEC), 179, 181; Hawthorne, *Philippians*, 136.

ing on of a whole *new* identity[246] as part of a "new order" or "new age of salvation"[247] (cf. 2 Cor 5:17, see pp. 156–64) where "citizenship" (πολίτευμα, v. 20) is not defined in earthly terms (cf. ἐπίγεια φρονοῦντες, v. 19), but is in heaven (v. 20).

1 Thessalonians 2:13–16

This passage is arguably one of the most controversial passages in the Pauline corpus, and has often been left out of church liturgy because of fear for its possible "anti-Jewish" or "antisemitic" implications.[248] This is partly the reason why some scholars view this passage as unacceptable, based on the understanding that Paul held an "antisemitic" position,[249] or as un-Pauline and thus as an interpolation.[250] It is noteworthy that there is no manuscript support for the theory that this is an interpolation.[251] Arguments against authenticity on the basis of structural difficulties are not insurmountable either.[252]

Verse 13 starts with the second thanksgiving report after 1:2–3. Paul thanks God for the Thessalonians' original reception of the gospel as the word of God. Paul wanted to emphasize the divine origin of the message,[253] even in the midst of suffering and persecution (v. 14). It was the word of

---

246. Hansen, *Philippians*, 220.
247. O'Brien, *Philippians*, 361; Silva, *Philippians* (WEC), 171.
248. Cf. Fee, *Thessalonians*, 103.
249. E.g., Best, *Thessalonians*, 122.
250. E.g., Schmidt, "1 Thessalonians"; Pearson, "1 Thessalonians."
251. Smith, "Thessalonians," 703; cf. Malherbe, *Thessalonians*, 174.
252. There is seemingly a lack of connection of 2:13–16 with the preceding and a disruption of the narrative flow (Wanamaker, *Thessalonians*, 109). But 2:13–16 is probably best understood as a rhetorical device known as digression in the *narratio*, to provide a transition to the next issue to be discussed, and like the *exordium* functions to favor the audience (Wuellner, "Greek Rhetoric," 180–81; adopted by Wanamaker, *Thessalonians*, 109). This would explain the renewal of thanksgiving (going back to 1:2–3), forming a conclusion to the preceding 2:1–12, constituting the response to the missionary proclamation of Paul and his co-workers. 1 Thess 2:13–16 also forms the transition to the second stage of narration (2:17–3:10). Additionally, the digression thus has a paraenetic function and confirms the Thessalonians' current pattern of faithfulness in the midst of opposition as being part of a wider apocalyptic pattern of oppression of God's people (Wanamaker, *Thessalonians*, 109; cf. Malherbe, *Thessalonians*, 168, 176). Weima, *Thessalonians*, 197, argues that this passage is also connected to the subsequent material in that it (1) constitutes a defense for Paul's absence from the Thessalonian believers (2:17–20) and (2) connects to the theme of persecution in 3:1–5.

253. Green, *Thessalonians*, 140; Martin, *Thessalonians*, 88.

God that transformed their lives.[254] In terms of the flow of the letter, Paul's focus has changed from their ongoing faithfulness to their conversion itself.[255] As Paul explained earlier (1:5), "it is the power of God at work in the believers that validates the gospel message and distinguishes the people of God."[256] At the deepest level, Paul's polemic in this passage is against those who oppose this gospel.[257]

The persecution that the Thessalonians have endured (v. 14) is one of the evidences that they received the word of God.[258] Wanamaker argues that the opposition of the Judeans to Paul's mission has been "the will of God in terms of his apocalyptic framework."[259] Their suffering in fact "proves that they are fellow-members of the same body as the [regional] Judean[260] churches."[261] In this sense, the Thessalonian believers have become the paradigm for the other congregations[262] by way of passive[263] imitation of the congregations in Judea through suffering.[264] The first believers in Judea, in turn, can be understood as the "first fruits" of God in establishing the New Covenant (Rom 15:26–27; Gal 1:17–24; 2:1–10).[265] In summary, Paul's polemic that will follow, has to be understood against the contextual background as put forth above, especially (1) the importance of the reception of the word of God for Paul (v. 13), and (2) Paul's understanding of the formation of the church as being amidst opposition (v. 14).

---

254. Green, *Thessalonians*, 141.

255. Fee, *Thessalonians*, 86; Green, *Thessalonians*, 140, 146; cf. Malherbe, *Thessalonians*, 167.

256. Martin, *Thessalonians*, 88.

257. Weima, *Thessalonians*, 208; Van Houwelingen, *Tessalonicenzen*, 91; Green, *Thessalonians*, 138; Malherbe, *Thessalonians*, 169; Martin, *Thessalonians*, 90–91; Wanamaker, *Thessalonians*, 115–18; cf. Smith, "Thessalonians," 703.

258. Green, *Thessalonians*, 141.

259. Wanamaker, *Thessalonians*, 116; cf. Malherbe, *Thessalonians*, 176.

260. Commentators refer to the Judean believers in Christ from the geographical Judea (Ἰουδαία, v. 14) as "Judean churches" (Green, *Thessalonians*, 141; Smith, "Thessalonians," 704; Bruce, *Thessalonians*, 45), "Jewish people of Judea" (Fee, *Thessalonians*, 94) or "Judean Christians" (Malherbe, *Thessalonians*, 168; Wanamaker, *Thessalonians*, 112). These designations must not be confused with "Judeans" (Ἰουδαῖοι).

261. Bruce, *Thessalonians*, 45.

262. Green, *Thessalonians*, 142.

263. They were not actively seeking martyrdom as e.g., Polycarp (Mart. Pol. 19.1) later on (Green, *Thessalonians*, 141).

264. Green, *Thessalonians*, 141; Wanamaker, *Thessalonians*, 112.

265. Green, *Thessalonians*, 141–42.

Paul writes that the Thessalonians have suffered the same things from their own countrymen (συμφυλέτης, v. 14)²⁶⁶ or compatriots²⁶⁷ than the congregations in Judea. Fee argues for the Thessalonians being predominantly gentile, suffering at the hands of fellow gentiles.²⁶⁸ While Fee's proposal seems reasonable given the comparison Paul puts forth (καθὼς καὶ αὐτοὶ ὑπὸ τῶν Ἰουδαίων), it is not all that clear who exactly caused the Thessalonians to suffer.²⁶⁹ Some clarification is needed. If the account of Acts 17:5–10 is considered as valid means to determine the original history of the Thessalonian church, as many interpreters do,²⁷⁰ Paul and his compatriots would have to leave Thessalonica because of Judean opposition.²⁷¹ The extent to which one allows for the "theological agenda" of Acts' author in terms of presenting "an idealistic picture of the pristine period of early Christianity,"²⁷² which would correspond to the dynamics of "othering,"²⁷³ however, complicates the debate.

Notwithstanding the difficulty in this debate, if the opposition to the Thessalonians were Judean in the current context (1 Thess 2:13–16), it neither fully explains the hostility that a largely gentile community would experience, nor the use of the term συμφυλέτης.²⁷⁴ Meeks contends that the exclusivism of early believers in Christ led to the persecution of the Thessalonians with whom they had "shared ties of kinship and racial or local origins."²⁷⁵ Additionally, their exclusivism might have been tied to opposition to the decrees of Caesar by their belief that Jesus is Lord (over against Caesar) and thus considered as a direct challenge to the sovereignty of Caesar, and as a breach of the oath of loyalty that was required of all citizens within the Empire. The Thessalonians would then have been a political threat for their refusal to participate in the imperial cult. This would in

---

266. L&N §11.57; LITV; KJV.

267. BDAG, συμφυλέτης; NRSV.

268. Fee, *Thessalonians*, 94, 99–100, bases this conclusion on 1:9 ("You turned from idols to serve the living and true God").

269. Cf. Wanamaker, *Thessalonians*, 112.

270. E.g., Hagner, *New Testament*, 419–25; Fee, *Thessalonians*, 92–93; Green, *Thessalonians*, 143; Malherbe, *Thessalonians*, 175; Martin, *Thessalonians*, 89–90; Wanamaker, *Thessalonians*, 113.

271. Fee, *Thessalonians*, 92; Martin, *Thessalonians*, 90; Wanamaker, *Thessalonians*, 113.

272. Park, *Jew or Gentile*, 3.

273. Cf. Punt, "Politics of Difference," 203–4.

274. Wanamaker, *Thessalonians*, 113.

275. Meeks, "Apocalyptical Language," 691.

turn lead to their persecution by their own compatriots.²⁷⁶ For this reason, although the Thessalonians were probably predominantly gentile, the congregation might have consisted of both gentile and Judean believers.²⁷⁷ The term συμφυλέτης (v. 14) can thus be rendered as "fellow-Thessalonians."²⁷⁸

The original congregations in Judea (Ἰουδαία, v. 14) to whom Paul compares the Thessalonians' suffering, suffered from "the Judeans" (Ἰουδαῖοι, v. 14). An important factor in the understanding of verses 15 to 16 is how one understands the participial modifier of "the Judeans" (τῶν, v. 15). Is it best understood as restrictive or non-restrictive, and is the reference to the Judeans thus general or specific? If one translates by inserting a comma after "the Judeans" (non-restrictive), verses 15 to 16 have to pertain to Judeans in general. If the translation is without the comma (restrictive), verses 15 to 16 would refer to specific Judeans. Although both (restrictive and non-restrictive) are grammatically possible, many commentators opt for the restrictive sense here.²⁷⁹ Yet, whether one understands the τῶν (v. 15) as restrictive or non-restrictive ultimately has to be determined by the context itself (see below). In verses 15 to 16, Paul ascribes to "the Judeans" several actions and consequences:

1. They killed the Lord Jesus and the prophets (v. 15). The reference to the killing instead of the crucifixion of Jesus is probably because Paul does not connect a salvific dimension to Christ's death here but states the fact of who were responsible for his death.²⁸⁰ That God's own people would have killed and/or crucified Jesus is certainly not a new idea to the New Testament (Luke 24:20; John 5:18; 7:1; 8:59; 11:45–53; 18:14, 31; Acts 2:23, 36; 3:13–15; 4:10; 5:30; 7:52; 10:39; 13:28; cf. Matt 27:25; Mark 12:1–9). Similarly, the theme of the killing of the prophets by their own people in the Old Testament (1 Kgs 19:10, 14; 2 Chr 36:15; Neh 9:26; Jer 2:30) is carried over to the New Testament (Matt 5:12;

---

276. Jewett, *Thessalonian Correspondence*, 123–25; adopted by Wanamaker, *Thessalonians*, 113–14; cf. Van Houwelingen, *Thessalonicenzen*, 87–88.

277. Donfried, *Thessalonica*, 202; Martin, *Thessalonians*, 90.

278. Martin, *Thessalonians*, 90; Bruce, *Thessalonians*, 46; cf. Van Houwelingen, *Thessalonicenzen*, 90.

279. E.g., Weima, *Thessalonians*, 208; Van Houwelingen, *Thessalonicenzen*, 86; Malherbe, *Thessalonians*, 169. Fee, *Thessalonians*, 95, argues for the restrictive sense on the basis that the particular grammatical construction is "rarely, if ever" non-restrictive in Paul, and that there have been 6 modifiers up to this point in the letter, which are all restrictive (1:7, "all who believe, (living) in"; 1:10, "Jesus who rescues us"; 2:4, "God who tests"; 2:10, "you who believe"; 2:12, "the God who calls you"; 2:14, "the churches of God which are in Judea").

280. Fee, *Thessalonians*, 96–97.

23:31-35, 37; Luke 11:48-51; 13:33-34; Acts 7:52), including Paul (Rom 11:3; 1 Thess 2:15). This intertextual evidence[281] would suggest that Paul adopted these traditions and have Old Testament prophets in mind[282] rather than New Testament prophets.[283] Wanamaker suggests that "Paul saw continuity in the pattern of Jewish rejection of God's agents from OT times to his own."[284] If continuity between Paul and the Old Testament tradition about killing the prophets by God's own people is acknowledged, it is hard not to understand Paul's reference to "the Judeans" in some general sense. In addition, Paul's unqualified, general reference to "the Judeans" (a) in 2 Cor 11:24-26 within the context of suffering at their hands (see pp. 44-45) and especially (b) his reference to them (in contrast to Greeks) in 1 Cor 1:22-23 within the context of seeking a sign and stumbling at the crucified Christ (see pp. 123-24), might suggest a more general reference to them here in 1 Thessalonians 2:15-16 too.[285]

2. According to verse 15, they persecuted[286] "us" (ἡμᾶς, v. 15). It is not certain to whom ἡμᾶς refers, whether to Christ-believers in general[287] or to Paul and his fellow missionaries.[288]

3. That they displease God (v. 15) is probably connected to the fact that they did not accept Jesus as their Messiah or as agent of their salvation,

---

281. Cf. Robbins, *Texture*, 3.

282. Weima, *Thessalonians*, 211-12; Malherbe, *Thessalonians*, 169; Martin, *Thessalonians*, 91; cf. esp. Paul's quote of 1 Kgs 19:10 in Rom 11:3.

283. Contra Fee, *Thessalonians*, 98.

284. Wanamaker, *Thessalonians*, 115; cf. Weima, *Thessalonians*, 207.

285. That Paul would not have Judeans in general in mind because many Christ-believers were "Jews" (Weima, *Thessalonians*, 209), is problematic, because (a) Paul never unambiguously, or in an unqualified way, refers to Christ-believers as Ἰουδαῖοι, (b), Paul does not see a Judean ethnic identity as constitutive of being a Christ-believer (esp. Gal 3:28), and (c) it circumvents the close connection between the Ἰουδαῖοι in this context and those who oppose the gospel—just as the Old Testament prophets were opposed by their own people.

286. BDAG, ἐκδιώκω, §2; L&N §39.45; Carson and Moo, *Introduction*, 534; Wanamaker, *Thessalonians*, 115; Best, *Thessalonians*, 116. It is equally possible to understand ἐκδιώκω as "drive out" (BDAG, ἐκδιώκω, §1; L&N §15.159; Zerwick and Grosvenor, *Grammatical Analysis*, 616).

287. If the clause κωλυόντων ἡμᾶς τοῖς ἔθνεσιν λαλῆσαι (v. 16) alludes to the Pauline mission, then "who persecuted us" would include a wider opposition to the Christian movement (Wanamaker, *Thessalonians*, 115).

288. Paul himself did experience hostility from Judeans (Gal 5:11; 2 Cor 11:24-26). If ἐκδιώκω (v. 15) is translated as "drive out," ἡμᾶς would more likely refer to Paul and his co-workers (Green, *Thessalonians*, 144-45; Wanamaker, *Thessalonians*, 115).

and that they went against God's will in hindering the spreading of the gospel by persecuting Judean Christ-believers.[289]

4. They oppose everyone (v. 15). This notion would reflect the general anti-Judeanism of the Greco-Roman world[290] where Judeans opposed other people on the basis of Judean exclusivism.[291]

5. They hinder "us" from speaking to the gentiles so that they may be saved (v. 16). Unlike the antagonism constituted by the anti-Judeanism of the Greco-Roman world (4 above), for Paul the antagonism of the Judeans toward the non-Judeans ultimately has to be connected to their hindering of his mission to the gentiles whom he wanted to lead to salvation[292] (see Acts 13:45-50; 14:2, 19; 17:5-9, 13; 18:12). This probably forms the background of Paul's beatings by the Judeans (2 Cor 11:24).[293] The opposition of the Judeans was in essence opposition to the purposes of God and an attack against humanity in that they blocked the way to the hope of salvation.[294]

6. They have constantly been filling up their sins to the limit (v. 16). The filling up of sins echoes the same theme in the Old Testament (Gen 15:16; Dan 8:23; cf. 2 Macc 6:14). They have resisted the divine initiative throughout their history.[295]

7. God's wrath has come upon them at last (v. 16). The expression εἰς τέλος can also be translated as "completely" (LXX: Josh 8:24; 2 Chr 12:12)[296] or "forever" (LXX: 1 Chr 28:9; Ps 9:18; 77:8), but the translation "at last"[297] or "finally"[298] is preferable, for the temporal use of

---

289. Martin, *Thessalonians*, 92; Wanamaker, *Thessalonians*, 115, 118; Frame, *Thessalonians*, 112; cf. Green, *Thessalonians*, 145; Bruce, *Thessalonians*, 47.

290. Tacitus, *Hist.* 5.5, wrote that the Judeans were loyal to one another "but toward every other people they feel only hate and enmity" (cf. Philostratus, *Vit. Apoll.* 5.33). Josephus, *Ag. Ap.* 2.121, claimed that Apion falsely maintained that Judeans swore to God to "show goodwill to no foreigner, especially Greeks."

291. Wanamaker, *Thessalonians*, 115; cf. Green, *Thessalonians*, 145; Bruce, *Thessalonains*, 47.

292. Green, *Thessalonians*, 146; Martin, *Thessalonians*, 90-91; Wanamaker, *Thessalonians*, 115.

293. Wanamaker, *Thessalonians*, 116.

294. Green, *Thessalonians*, 146; cf. Martin, *Thessalonians*, 90.

295. Green, *Thessalonians*, 147-48; cf. Wanamaker, *Thessalonians*, 116; Bruce, *Thessalonians*, 48.

296. BDF §207.3; cf. Zerwick and Grosvenor, *Grammatical Analysis*, 616.

297. E.g., NRSV; NIV.

298. BDAG, τέλος §2bγ.

πάντοτε (v. 16) requires a temporal sense for εἰς τέλος.²⁹⁹ Although God's wrath has already begun to be realized in the present (Rom 1:18), the final culmination of wrath lies in the future (Rom 2:5; cf. 2 Thess 1:7–10). The reference to God's wrath thus constitutes His present judgment to be completed in the future.³⁰⁰

1 Thessalonians 2:15–16 shows remarkable similarities with Matthew 23:31–36. In the Gospel of Matthew, the scribes and Pharisees are depicted as descendants of those who murdered the prophets (Matt 23:31; cf. 1 Thess 2:15a) and they are said to fill up the measure of their father's deeds (Matt 23:32; cf. 1 Thess 2:16b). This will lead them in the judgment to their condemnation in hell (Matt 23:33, 35; cf. 1 Thess 2:16c). Both passages refer to Judean opposition to the gospel mission (Matt 23:34; 1 Thess 2:15b). The latter is the most striking parallel.³⁰¹ The correspondence between these two passages suggests that Paul has adopted a pre-Synoptic tradition of the believers in Christ.³⁰²

One of the best explanations for Paul's attack on the Judeans is probably that it was a stock feature of ancient rhetoric called *vituperatio*, "which functioned in the context of social conflict between individuals or groups with competing interests and claims"³⁰³ and ranged from issues regarding status to difference in values within symbolic universes. These differences in values in turn helped to demarcate and define a new group while simultaneously casted doubt on the legitimacy of the rival group³⁰⁴ (cf. Rev 2:9; 3:9). Here in 1 Thessalonians 2:13–16, Paul contrasts the new identity in Christ (identity mode C) with the Judean identity (identity mode A), where the Judeans' claim on being God's people is implicitly being problematized. In addition, this serves as demarcation of the new identity in Christ, which constitutes a new, separate identity (identity mode C) in *discontinuity* with the non-believing Judean identity (identity mode A).³⁰⁵

---

299. Malherbe, *Thessalonians*, 171; Wanamaker, *Thessalonians*, 117; cf. Frame, *Thessalonians*, 114.

300. Fee, *Thessalonians*, 102; Green, *Thessalonians*, 149; Donfried, *Thessalonica*, 204–7; Malherbe, *Thessalonians*, 171, 177.

301. Wanamaker, *Thessalonians*, 116.

302. Malherbe, *Thessalonians*, 174–75; Bruce, *Thessalonians*, 43, 49; cf. Wanamaker, *Thessalonians*, 116.

303. Wanamaker, *Thessalonians*, 118; cf. Du Toit, "Vilification"; Freyne, "Vilifying," 118–19.

304. Wanamaker, *Thessalonians*, 118; Collins, "Vilification," 314; cf. Punt, "Politics of Difference."

305. Cf. Wanamaker, *Thessalonians*, 118–19. In essence, this approach argues against an approach where Paul's attack on the Judeans can be reduced to an "'in-house'

Focusing on the process of establishing the new identity in Christ over against the Judean identity does not completely resolve Paul's polemic against the Judeans in terms of possible anti-Judeanism, but it places Paul's rhetoric within a larger perspective. The sharpness of Paul's rhetoric is probably enhanced within the context of persecution, which formed part of the identity of both Paul and the Thessalonians. At the deepest level, however, it has to be noted that Paul was not indiscriminately "anti-Judean" in the sense that his rhetoric was directed against race or ethnicity,[306] but against those who oppose the gospel, especially among the gentiles. This stood for Paul in a prophetic tradition of opposition to God's agents by His own people,[307] and formed part of God's apocalyptical framework of people's hardening[308] (cf. Rom 9:11-23, see pp. 239-42). Paul's critique against the Judeans was thus more theological than social.[309]

A relationship of interdependence between opposition and identity has to be acknowledged. Paul's rhetoric was directed toward those who have chosen to remain a separate identity in opposition to belief in Christ as Savior and Messiah and remained claiming covenant membership of God's people on the basis of ethnicity and outward identity markers defined by the "works of the law." The term Paul uses for this group of people is Ἰουδαῖος. Paul never applies the term Ἰσραήλ in the context of opposition to the gospel or persecution of the church. This would suggest that "Israel" whose salvation-historical path Paul lays out in Romans 9 to 11 (esp. Rom 11)[310] is not exactly the same entity as the people who opposed the gospel and persecuted the early believers in Christ, which Paul here calls "the Judeans."[311] Although further clarification is needed between these designations in view

---

Jewish debate" (Smith, "Thessalonians," 703; cf. Van Houwelingen, *Thessalonicenzen*, 87, 90; Malherbe, *Thessalonians*, 179). If Paul strives for establishing a new identity in Christ that stands opposed to an unbelieving Judean identity, Paul's identity in Christ and that of his fellow-believers cannot be restricted to a Judean identity, let alone a "Jewish" identity.

306. Van Houwelingen, *Thessalonicenzen*, 87; Martin, *Thessalonians*, 93.

307. Green, *Thessalonians*, 149; cf. Martin, *Thessalonians*, 93-94.

308. Wanamaker, *Thessalonians*, 116-17; cf. Malherbe, *Thessalonians*, 170, 176.

309. Cf. Malherbe, *Thessalonians*, 170.

310. Two important factors to keep in mind here is Paul's restrictive definition of Ἰσραήλ in Rom 9:6 (see pp. 51-52) and the fact that Paul never uses the term Ἰουδαῖος in Romans 11 where he explains "Israel's" destiny (see pp. 262-334). Furthermore, the negative statements about the Judeans in 1 Thess 2:13-16 corresponds with similar statements in Romans (Rom 9:22-24; 10:3, 21; Donfried, *Thessalonica*, 208).

311. Cf. Bruce, *Thessalonians*, 49.

FAITH IN CHRIST, ISRAEL, AND THE JUDEAN (AC)

of Romans 11, it has to suffice to say at this point that a possible tension between 1 Thessalonians 2:13–16 and Romans 11 is not warranted.[312]

Philemon 1:16

Paul's plea to Philemon to accept Onesimus, a slave of Philemon that probably trespassed,[313] climaxes when Paul writes that Onesimus is "a beloved brother" (v. 16).[314] This title signifies both Philemon and Onesimus' new relationship to the Lord and to each other.[315] This new relationship constituted by the new identity in Christ[316] corresponds with the new creation of God (2 Cor 5:17)[317] and conversion.[318] Fitzmyer relates this new reality to the "fundamental appeal that Paul is making to Philemon."[319]

Yet, there remains a duality in terms of Onesimus' identity and the relationship he has with Philemon.[320] This duality is constituted by (1) Paul's acknowledgement of Onesimus' status as a slave, although more than a slave, and (2) Paul's portrayal of Onesimus as "a brother . . . both in the flesh and in the Lord." The expression ἐν σαρκί points to the "outward side of life" and "the external relationship"[321] or "natural human relationship"[322] between master and slave (or patron and client).[323] Moo renders the duality as a relationship on both "earthly level" (ἐν σαρκί) and "spiritual level" (ἐν κυρίῳ).[324] There is a clear priority of the status in the

---

312. Many commentators find difficulty in reconciling 1 Thess 2:13–16 with Rom 9–11 (e.g., Marshall, *Thessalonians*, 82–83; Green, *Thessalonians*, 143; Van Houwelingen, *Thessalonicenzen*, 85; cf. Malherbe, *Thessalonians*, 178; Bruce, *Thessalonians*, 47–48), which is one of the reasons why some reject the authenticity of 1 Thess 2:13–16 (cf. Zoccali, "All Israel," 314).

313. Felder, "Philemon," 899, argues that this can be deducted from the "if" in v. 18, which is probably more than rhetorical and implies some form of wrongdoing.

314. Fitzmyer, *Philemon*, 114.
315. Thompson, *Colossians*, 219.
316. Cf. Thompson, *Colossians*, 219; Lohse, *Colossians*, 203.
317. Fitzmyer, *Philemon*, 114.
318. Thompson, *Colossians*, 220.
319. Fitzmyer, *Philemon*, 114.
320. Cf. Dunn, *Colossians*, 336.
321. BDAG, σάρξ, §5.
322. O'Brien, *Colossians*, 298; cf. Fitzmyer, *Philemon*, 115.
323. Dunn, *Colossians*, 336.
324. Moo, *Colossians*, 423.

Lord over the natural status in the flesh, which is described in terms of the master-slave relationship.³²⁵

While σάρξ in this context does not point to "Israel in the flesh" or the non-believing Judean identity (identity mode A), this occurrence of σάρξ (Phlm 1:16) is included here to demonstrate an aspect of the larger understanding of σάρξ, namely the human side of human beings' existence, which is "constrained by human appetites and ambitions"³²⁶ (cf. Rom 7:5; 8:8; 2 Cor 4:11; 10:3; Gal 2:20; Phil 1:22; 3:3-4). The new identity in Christ stands in *discontinuity* with all natural human identities, including ethnic identities, social identities or identities defined by outward, earthly markers (i.e., the works of the law). From the perspective of the new identity in Christ, there is thus a sense in which all aspects of identity outside of a relationship with Christ are considered as being in the sphere of σάρξ. Similarly, Jewett understands σάρξ here as depicting "the old aeon which remains in opposition to the new aeon even though it is being transformed by it."³²⁷ This broader application of σάρξ helps to pave the way to one of the most decisive aspects of Pauline theology: the new creation in Christ.

The New Creation Versus Flesh (AC)

In both of the next two passages, the "old" is being contrasted to the "new." The "new creation" (2 Cor 5:17) constitutes one of the most central aspects of discontinuity between the identity in Christ and the identity before or outside of Christ. Colossians 3:9-15 echoes similar themes.

2 Corinthians 5:14-21

In 2 Corinthians 5:12, Paul writes against self-recommendation (οὐ . . . ἑαυτοὺς συνιστάνομεν) based on external appearance (ἐν προσώπῳ),³²⁸ which was characteristic of Paul's opponents (10:12, 18).³²⁹ Their boasting focused on physical heritage and ethnic membership of God's people (11:12, 18-24), and can be described as boasting κατὰ σάρκα (11:18; cf. 10:3). Paul counters with providing an opportunity (ἀφορμὴν διδόντες, v.

---

325. Dunn, *Colossians*, 336; Melick, *Philippians*, 365; O'Brien, *Colossians*, 298.
326. Dunn, *Colossians*, 336.
327. Jewett, *Anthropological Terms*, 135.
328. BDAG, πρόσωπον, §4; cf. Zerwick and Grosvenor, *Grammatical Analysis*, 544.
329. Keener, *Corinthians*, 183; Matera, *II Corinthians*, 131.

12) for boasting on his behalf.³³⁰ The term ἐξίστημι (v. 13)³³¹ corresponds with the notion of Paul's own boasting (cf. παραφρονέω in 11:23).³³² Even though Paul later boasts in his own pedigree in reaction to his opponents' boasting (11:18-22), he supersedes it with boasting in his own weakness (11:30; 12:5, 9).³³³ Boasting essentially ought to be in the Lord (10:17) and in the cross³³⁴ (cf. Gal 6:14). The real ground for boasting thus lies within a new identity in Christ (vv. 15-21), where one's life is not directed to oneself (μηκέτι ἑαυτοῖς ζῶσιν, v. 15) but to Christ (τῷ ὑπὲρ αὐτῶν, v. 15; cf. Gal 2:19-20). Christ's purpose was to bring an end to the self-centered existence of humanity with the risen Christ at the center.³³⁵ This new identity and outlook on life corresponds to the knowledge of the fear³³⁶ of the Lord (v. 11) and the constraining effect (συνέχω, v. 14)³³⁷ of the love of Christ (v. 14)³³⁸ that enables one to "judge" (κρίνω, v. 14) and "know" (εἴδω, γινώσκω [x2], v. 16) differently.

For Paul (v. 15), Christ's death has to be understood as having a universal scope,³³⁹ especially if the context is considered. The universal scope of Christ's work is evident from πάντων and πάντες in verse 14, πάντων in verse 15, κόσμον in verse 19, and possibly ἡμῶν and ἡμεῖς in verse 21. Although "us" (x2) in verse 21 would include Paul and his apostolic associates,

---

330. Matera, *II Corinthians*, 131; cf. NRSV.

331. BDAG, ἐξίστημι, §2a, defines the term as being out of one's senses.

332. To "be beside oneself" (BDAG, παραφρονέω).

333. Cf. Pop, *Tweede Brief*, 163.

334. Furnish, *II Corinthians*, 333.

335. Thrall, *Corinthians*, 1:411-12; Kruse, *Corinthians*, 123; Barrett, *Second Epistle*, 169.

336. The element of fear probably has to be understood against the background of Paul's awareness of "the judgment seat of Christ" (5:10; Matera, *II Corinthians*, 130).

337. Zerwick and Grosvenor, *Grammatical Analysis*, 544; Matera, *II Corinthians*, 133; Kruse, *Corinthians*, 121-22; Lenski, *Corinthians*, 1027; KJV; cf. BDAG, συνέχω, §8; Harris, *Second Epistle*, 419; Thrall, *Corinthians*, 1:409; Barrett, *Second Epistle*, 167; Pop, *Tweede Brief*, 162; Plummer, *Corinthians*, 173; REB; ISV. The term συνέχω can also be translated as "impel" or "urge on" (BDAG συνέχω, §7; Sampley, "Corinthians," 91; Thrall, *Corinthians*, 1:408; NRSV).

338. It is preferable to understand the phrase ἀγάπη τοῦ Χριστοῦ as a subjective genitive: "the love of Christ" in view of other Pauline texts such as Rom 5:5, 8; 8:35 and 2 Cor 13:13 (cf. Harris, *Second Epistle*, 418; Matera, *II Corinthians*, 132-33; Sampley, "Corinthians," 92; Thrall, *Corinthians*, 1:408; Furnish, *II Corinthians*, 309; Barrett, *Second Epistle*, 167; cf. Lenski, *Corinthians*, 1027, 1034; Plummer, *Corinthians*, 173).

339. Harris, *Second Epistle*, 422; "2 Corinthians," 352; Thrall, *Corinthians*, 1:411; Furnish, *II Corinthians*, 327; Barrett, *Second Epistle*, 174; cf. Matera, *II Corinthians*, 134; Lenski, *Corinthians*, 1028-30.

the principle is applicable to all believers.[340] This understanding stands in contrast to the view of *Limited Atonement*.[341] Lenski argues that Christ's death "counts for all time: for the entire future time, for all the prior time" and that "[a]ll in the Old Testament who believed were saved by that death just as all are in the New Testament who believe."[342] This thesis will be revisited later on (see pp. 309–14). Paul connects the "death" of all people to Christ's death (v. 14). But in what sense did all people die? To answer this question, one has to look deeper into Paul's thought behind this statement and thus look at 5:14–21 as a whole (see below).

"Those who live" (οἱ ζῶντες, v. 15) is best understood as those in whom the new creation has come into effect, which are not all people.[343] Such a shift from the universal ("all have died," v. 14; "he died for all," v. 15) to the particular ("those who live," v. 15) would correspond to the particular "if anyone" (εἴ τις) in verse 17 and the command "be reconciled to God" in verse 20. These particular notions however seem to stand in some tension with the idea that Christ "reconciled the world to himself" (v. 19). On the one hand, the "world" seems to point to the idea that God's reconciliation in Christ is *intended for* the whole world and not that each and every individual are effectively reconciled with God. The context here is the *ministry* of reconciliation (v. 18), which sets the tone and approach to such a ministry: "we" (v. 18) who received the ministry of reconciliation should minister to the world in a way where Christ's love compels or restrains us to minister a message that entails that Christ died for all, that all died with him, and that his reconciliation is for all (vv. 14–15, 19). On the other hand, there seems to be an inherent cosmic dimension attached to this idea as well (see below).

In terms of its application in the life of the believer, the death and resurrection of Christ signifies the death of the old identity (or person) and the resurrection of the new identity (or person) in Christ[344] (see Gal 2:19–20; 1 Cor 15:53; cf. Eph 4:24; Col 3:10–14). The death and resurrection of Christ did not only redefine human identity, it also redefined the purpose of living. Christ is both the source of life (implied by ἵνα οἱ ζῶντες) and the goal of life (τῷ ὑπὲρ αὐτῶν). The life-ethic of the person in Christ has been realigned

---

340. Harris, *Second Epistle*, 422, 425; "2 Corinthians," 354; Keener, *Corinthians*, 187.

341. E.g., Hodge, *Corinthians*, 135; Owen, *Death of Death*.

342. Lenski, *Corinthians*, 1031–32.

343. Collins, *Second Corinthians*, 119; Harris, *Second Epistle*, 421, 423; "2 Corinthians," 352; Furnish, *II Corinthians*, 311.

344. Cf. Keener, *Corinthians*, 184; Pop, *Tweede Brief*, 169.

FAITH IN CHRIST, ISRAEL, AND THE JUDEAN (AC) 159

with Christ himself[345] whose death and resurrection was an exemplification of such a self-denying life-ethic (see Rom 15:1–6 and esp. Phil 2:5–21).[346]

But more fundamentally, Christ's death and resurrection changed the way in which those in Christ know (εἴδω, γινώσκω [x2], v. 16) or perceives[347] Christ and other people, in that neither Christ nor other people are known κατὰ σάρκα any longer (v. 16). While most define the expression κατὰ σάρκα broadly in terms of that which pertains to the outward or external side of life,[348] Paul seems to contextualize this expression against the background of how his opponents defined their identity.[349] Paul's opponents defined their identity and status by way of external criteria pertaining to pedigree, descent and cultural heritage[350] (11:12, 18–24, see pp. 41–45).[351]

Even Christ's identity could be described in terms of σάρξ (v. 16), as the Messiah from ethnic Israel (Rom 9:5, see p. 49). In view of his death and resurrection though, Christ is not known any more in terms of his ethnic descent or pedigree, which pertains to his natural, earthly identity (σάρξ). Wright and Danker[352] take this one step further. They understand οὐδένα οἴδαμεν κατὰ σάρκα in 2 Cor 5:16 such as that the Corinthians do not know Jesus as a national Messiah any longer.[353]

Christ's identity is now defined in terms of his position in God's reconciliation of humankind to Himself (vv. 18–20), which was effected through the cross.[354] As counterpart of the same reality, the understanding of Christ's relationship with humankind is shifted away from natural, outward or physical terms (i.e., ethnic, genealogical, cultural) toward an understanding that

345. Cf. Harris, *Second Epistle*, 424; Thrall, *Corinthians*, 1:420.

346. Cf. Pop, *Tweede Brief*, 162.

347. Matera, *II Corinthians*, 135.

348. BDAG, σάρξ, §5; Harris, *Second Epistle*, 427, 429; "2 Corinthians," 353; Keener, *Corinthians*, 183–84; Plummer, *Corinthians*, 176.

349. Cf. Schweizer, "σάρξ," *TDNT*, 7:131.

350. Pedigree, descent and cultural heritage would be included in what is understood under the outward or external side of life (cf. Harris, *Second Epistle*, 427), but is more specific. A broader scope of "outward appearances" would also include things such as intellectual capability, physical attributes or even charismatic endowment and pneumatic displays (Harris, *Second Epistle*, 427), but not all of these necessarily fit the overall context of the letter that well.

351. Sampley, "Corinthians," 92–93; cf. Keener, *Corinthians*, 183.

352. Wright, *People of God*, 408; Danker, *II Corinthians*, 81.

353. Cf. Bruce, *Heart Set Free*, 99.

354. Furnish, *II Corinthians*, 331–32, rightly argues that the counterpart of "according to the flesh" (v. 16) in this context is not so much "according to the Spirit" (cf. Pop, *Tweede Brief*, 169) as it is "according to the cross" (see 1 Cor 2:2), which the world regards as weakness (1 Cor 1:17–18, 23–25; 2 Cor 13:4).

correlates with the new creation. A similar notion is found in Galatians 3:28, where Paul writes that in Christ there is no difference between Judean or Greek, slave or free, and male or female, which lies beneath the new creation in Christ. In Galatians 6:15 (see p. 338), the same principle is even more pronounced, where Paul states that neither circumcision nor uncircumcision means anything, but that a new creation is everything.[355]

In answer to the earlier question about the meaning of the "death" of all people in Christ (v. 15), the best answer is probably that all people died to any affiliation with God based on external, natural criteria. A claim on righteousness (δικαιοσύνη, v. 21) or reconciliation (καταλλαγή, vv. 18, 19; καταλλάσσω, vv. 18, 19, 20) with God based on ethnicity, pedigree[356] or even the works of the law (see Rom 7:4; Gal 2:19)[357] is rendered redundant in the death of Christ. In his death, all people died to any *claim on being God's people* apart from the reconciliation that Christ himself accomplished. This does not necessarily mean that people's cultural heritage is forgotten or denied in Christ, but it means that one's cultural heritage is *not constitutive* of their *filiation to God* any longer. In other words, in Christ, no cultural marker is constitutive of their "childhood" (υἱοθεσία, Gal 4:5; Rom 8:15, 23) any longer. This would imply that their new identity in Christ supersedes and relativizes social identities. In Christ, people are not known in terms of their *social identity*, but in terms of their *theological identity* (see below). Otherwise, there would have been a basis for boasting or superiority in terms of external (v. 12) particularities, or it would even mean that not everyone completely died in Christ (v. 15).

The new creation (καινὴ κτίσις, v. 17)[358] is thus the definitive point of *discontinuity* between the old order and the new order[359] (cf. 2 Cor 3:1–4:6).

---

355. Sampley, "Corinthians," 93; Furnish, *II Corinthians*, 329, 333; Barrett, *Second Epistle*, 174; Plummer, *Corinthians*, 180.

356. Cf. Harris, *Second Epistle*, 427; Furnish, *II Corinthians*, 329, 332.

357. Cf. Furnish, *II Corinthians*, 311; Plummer, *Corinthians*, 180.

358. The concept of "newness" is central to Pauline theology (cf. Harris, *Second Epistle*, 433). Other Pauline terminology that would correspond to the new creation are "new testament" (καινὴ διαθήκη[ς], 1 Cor 11:25; 2 Cor 3:6), "new life" (καινότητι ζωῆς, Rom 6:4), "newness of the Spirit" (καινότητι πνεύματος, Rom 7:6) and if considered Pauline, the "new humanity" (καινὸν ἄνθρωπον, Eph 2:15; 4:24; νέον τὸν ἀνακαινούμενον, Col 3:10).

359. Harris, *Second Epistle*, 424, 433, 434; idem., "2 Corinthians," 353; Thrall, *Corinthians*, 1:421, 423, 424; REB; NEB; cf. Matera, *II Corinthians*, 136; Sampley, "Corinthians," 94; Barnett, *Corinthians*, 1997:297; Furnish, *II Corinthians*, 316. The idea of a new order that replaces the old order is especially prevalent in Isa 43:18–19. The terms τὰ ἀρχαῖα, ἰδού and καινά are verbally parallel in Isa 43:18–19 (LXX) and 2 Cor 5:17. Isa 65:17 and 66:22 allude to a new cosmos that the Lord creates (Thrall, *Corinthians*, 1:410–21).

That which was lost in Adam was restored in Christ (Rom 5:12-21).³⁶⁰ At heart, the new creation in Christ constitutes a new eschatological reality,³⁶¹ which consists of both a (1) cosmic and (2) an individual dimension:³⁶²

1. Firstly, the cosmic dimension pertains to the reconciliation of humankind in Christ, where all of humankind are *principally* being reconciled in Christ³⁶³ solely on the basis of God's work (vv. 17-18)³⁶⁴ in Christ's death and resurrection (vv. 14-15). The reconciliation implies that the barrier that alienated people from God has been broken down³⁶⁵ (cf. Eph 2:13-16, see pp. 112-13). Christ who was "made to be sin" (v. 21) provides a substitutionary function to his death for all people.³⁶⁶ Secondly, the reconciliation of the whole world accentuates the divine nature of reconciliation: it is solely a work of God and not something that human beings can establish or "negotiate" in and by themselves. Thirdly, the new eschatological era that has begun in Christ, pertains to the transformation of the entire universe (v. 19).³⁶⁷ This new era will be fully inaugurated at the parousia.³⁶⁸

---

360. Keener, *Corinthians*, 185; cf. Thrall, *Corinthians*, 1:411; Furnish, *II Corinthians*, 326.

361. Fee, *Empowering Presence*, 330-32; cf. Keener, *Corinthians*, 185-86; Barnett, *Corinthians*, 298; Thrall, *Corinthians*, 1:428; Barrett, *Second Epistle*, 173.

362. Cf. Harris, *Second Epistle*, 423, 449; Barnett, *Corinthians*, 297; Fee, *Empowering Presence*, 331; Thrall, *Corinthians*, 1:411.

363. Cf. Matera, *II Corinthians*, 129, 136; Thrall, *Corinthians*, 1:436; Kruse, *Corinthians*, 126; Furnish, *II Corinthians*, 319, 335-36.

364. Furnish, *II Corinthians*, 336; cf. Lenski, *Corinthians*, 1045-46.

365. Kruse, *Corinthians*, 126.

366. Harris, *Second Epistle*, 421; Matera, *II Corinthians*, 134; Furnish, *II Corinthians*, 335; Lenski, *Corinthians*, 1029-31). In the phrase ἡμῶν ἁμαρτίαν ἐποίησεν (v. 21), there is a sense in which Christ takes the place of humanity (cf. Gal 3:13, where Christ became a "curse"). Christ is also the representative of humanity, the new Adam who does God's will. Christ's death is "on behalf of" and "for the sake of" humanity (Matera, *II Corinthians*, 134; cf. Harris, *Second Epistle*, 421; Kruse, *Corinthians*, 122). This view is contra Sampley, "Corinthians," 92, and Sanders, *Palestinian Judaism*, 463-72, who view Christ's death as "being for" or as "siding with" people.

367. Sampley, "Corinthians," 92; Thrall, *Corinthians*, 1:427-28; Furnish, *II Corinthians*, 315. Cf. Rom 8:21-23, where the whole of creation longs for the freedom that God's children already experience.

368. Cf. Matera, *II Corinthians*, 145; Kruse, *Corinthians*, 125-26.

2. Individual reconciliation is *effected* by belief[369] in Christ's completed work.[370] Individual reconciliation involves a fundamental transformation[371] or conversion[372] of the believer's identity[373] and status[374] before God: the old person that died with Christ and the new person that lives because of the resurrection, becomes actualized and realized.[375] "Paul is saying that if anyone exists 'in Christ', that person is a newly-created being,"[376] which implies regeneration[377] (cf. Titus 3:5; John 3:7; 1 Pet 1:3, 23). In this anthropological dimension of the new creation,[378] the believer has to respond (καταλλάγητε, v. 20)[379] in that he or she has to personally identify with Christ in his death and resurrection.[380] This identification with Christ is enacted in baptism[381] (cf. Rom 6:1–5; Gal 3:27; see esp. note 207, p. 96), but the human response to God's work of reconciliation is ongoing.[382] The transformation and reconciliation of the individual ultimately corresponds with the establishment of a right relationship with God.[383]

Paul's understanding of the new identity in Christ that follows his conversion, can be seen as a direct result of his Damascus encounter with the risen Lord, where some profound changes had been brought about in Paul's

---

369. Harris, *Second Epistle*, 422; Matera, *II Corinthians*, 137; Sampley, "Corinthians," 93; Thrall, *Corinthians*, 1:433; Pop, *Tweede Brief*, 163, 168; cf. Furnish, *II Corinthians*, 314.

370. Cf. Harris, *Second Epistle*, 432; Matera, *II Corinthians*, 138; Kruse, *Corinthians*, 126.

371. Cf. Matera, *II Corinthians*, 145; Sampley, "Corinthians," 92–93; Garland, *2 Corinthians*, 286–87; Lenski, *Corinthians*, 1042.

372. Harris, *Second Epistle*, 423; Thrall, *Corinthians*, 1:415, 420, 422; cf. Kistemaker, *Second Epistle*, 193.

373. Keener, *Corinthians*, 184.

374. Thrall, *Corinthians*, 1:443.

375. Cf. Matera, *II Corinthians*, 137. Although there is an aspect of the new creation that is still awaited (e.g., Rom 8:24) that aspect is not accounted for here.

376. Thrall, *Corinthians*, 1:427.

377. Harris, *Second Epistle*, 432–34; "2 Corinthians," 353.

378. Harris, *Second Epistle*, 432.

379. Harris, *Second Epistle*, 424; Kruse, *Corinthians*, 126–27.

380. Sampley, "Corinthians," 96; cf. Thrall, *Corinthians*, 1:401.

381. Barrett, *Second Epistle*, 169; cf. Thrall, *Corinthians*, 1:425; Furnish, *II Corinthians*, 329.

382. Matera, *II Corinthians*, 142.

383. Harris, *Second Epistle*, 436; "2 Corinthians," 353; Sampley, "Corinthians," 93, 95; Kruse, *Corinthians*, 129; cf. Thrall, *Corinthians*, 1:431, 443.

identity and attitude. He now recognized and proclaimed Jesus as Lord and Messiah (Rom 10:9; cf. Acts 9:22; 17:3) and now viewed Judean and gentile believers alike as Abraham's offspring through faith (Gal 3:26–29; Rom 4; 10:1–4, 12–13; cf. Eph 2:11–19). The new attitude toward Christ prompts a new outlook on those for whom Christ died (cf. 1 Cor 8:11).[384] The new identity is therefore thoroughly Christologically defined. Christ is represented in each verse of this passage (vv. 14–21), each highlighting another aspect of the new order that has come into being through his death and resurrection. Paul arranges themes of creation, reconciliation, righteousness, flesh, sin, death, life, knowledge and love around the Person and work of Jesus Christ. All of these themes are ultimately defined through the death and resurrection of Christ.

It is important to note here that both the cosmic and individual dimensions of the new creation are completed works of God in Christ. Paul does not set the idea of a new creation within the context of a process of negotiation of a new, upcoming social identity. Neither does he expect people to actively reconcile themselves with God. The reconciling work of God in the new creation is portrayed as acts that God does in Christ (esp. v. 18). The *passive* imperative (καταλλάγητε, v. 20) is also telling, which points to the divine origin of God's reconciliation.

2 Cor 5:14–21 arguably contains the most pronounced account of *discontinuity* in Paul's thought between the identity according to the flesh (identity mode A) and the *new* identity in Christ (identity mode C). But although the new creation suggests a strong discontinuity in the old and the new order, this does not imply an actual discontinuity in salvation history, contra Thrall.[385] The new creation is not so much a *replacement* of "the old salvation-history"[386] as it is a *culmination* of salvation history (cf. Rom 9–11, esp. Rom 9:30–33, see pp. 245–51). Paul would have found continuity with the concept of a new creation in the Old Testament (e.g., Isa 43:18–19; cf. 42:9; 48:6) and in contemporary Judean thinking.[387] Paul's thinking on the new creation, however, cannot be equated to similar notions in later Rabbinic Judaism.[388] The new creation, although it supersedes or transforms the "old creation" thus does not imply "a complete

---

384. Cf. Harris, *Second Epistle*, 429–30; "2 Corinthians," 353; Kruse, *Corinthians*, 124, 127.

385. Thrall, *Corinthians*, 1:427.

386. Thrall, *Corinthians*, 1:427.

387. Cf. Thrall, *Corinthians*, 1:428; Furnish, *II Corinthians*, 332; Barrett, *Second Epistle*, 173.

388. Cf. Barrett, *Second Epistle*, 173–74; contra Pop, *Tweede Brief*, 169.

disjuncture with all that preceded it."[389] Yet if Paul's theological notions of (1) a new way of knowing others (not "according to the flesh"), (2) the death of all people in Christ, and (3) the centrality of Christ in the new creation are accepted in terms of its full force, it is inevitable that the Christ-believing community has to be understood as a *third entity* (cf. 1 Cor 10:32; Eph 2:8-22, see pp. 107-17, esp note 342).[390]

Campbell resists understanding the new creation as constituting a third entity. He refers to converts as continually changing being in Christ, yet with retention of ethnicity. He argues that in "Paul, there can be no separation between theology and social reality. It is on the *basis of the latter* and in ongoing conversation with it that he makes his theological statements concerning the new life in Christ."[391] Although the theological reality of the new identity should manifest on a social level and ultimately define how believers interact socially, according to 2 Corinthians 5:14-21, social realities is hardly the "basis" of Paul's theology. Precisely the opposite is true. The theological reality of death and reconciliation in Christ causes "us" not to know anyone in terms of their social identity any longer (2 Cor 5:16). Although the believing community is multi-ethnic (as Campbell argues) and retains their social/ethnic identity in Christ in some way, social/ethnic identity in Pauline terms has to be understood as an aspect of identity that is not constitutive in *marking off filiation to God* or *covenant membership* any longer.

Colossians 3:9-15

Although I would defend Pauline authorship for Colossians[392] (as with Ephesians), due to space limitations the letter will be treated with awareness of the dispute about authorship. Although the majority of the recipients were probably gentile (see esp. 1:12), there is good reason to think that there were a substantial number of Judeans in Colossae.[393]

---

389. Campbell, *Paul*, 141, seems to imply that such an implication is connected to approaches that accentuate the new creation as *superseding* the old.

390. Cf. Wright, *Faithfulness*, 2:1443-49; Sechrest, *Former Jew*, 15; Lincoln, *Ephesians*, 14; Sanders, *Jewish People*, 173, 178-79, 207.

391. Campbell, *Paul*, 158, emphasis added.

392. See note 95, p. 18 for a list of NT scholars defending Pauline authorship of Colossians.

393. Moo, *Colossians*, 27, shows that according to Josephus, Antiochus II had settled 2000 Judean families in the general area around 213 BCE (*Ant.* 12.3.4). Cicero, the Roman (first century BCE), refers to the Roman seizure of a substantial amount of money contributed by Judeans in the area to support the temple of Jerusalem (*Flac.* 28).

Colossians 3:1–3 echoes the Pauline themes of having died with and being raised with Christ (Rom 6:4–5; 2 Cor 5:15; Gal 2:19–20; cf. Col 2:12–13). The notion of Christ who is "our life" (v. 4) is equally Pauline (Gal 2:20; Phil 1:21). These themes constitute the new identity in Christ in contrast to an identity without or before Christ. The practices and attitudes in verses 5 to 9 characterize "things that are on earth" (τὰ ἐπὶ τῆς γῆς, vv. 2, 5), where the values in verses 12 to 17 are indicative of "things that are above" (τὰ ἄνω φρονεῖτε, v. 2).[394] That which is on the earth corresponds with τὸν παλαιὸν ἄνθρωπον (v. 9; cf. Eph 4:22; Rom 6:6) and that which is above is parallel to τὸν νέον [ἄνθρωπον] (v. 10; cf. Eph 4:24).[395] There is difference of opinion regarding the meaning of the old/new ἄνθρωπος. Many recent translators and commentators translate the phrases with "old/new self."[396] BDAG lists its occurrence in verse 9 under the main rubric of "a being in conflict at a transcendent level"[397] and explains it as a being "from another viewpoint."[398] The expression παλαιὸν ἄνθρωπον is explained in Louw and Nida as an idiom, "literally 'old person' or 'former person'" that denote "the old or former pattern of behavior, in contrast with a new pattern of behavior which people should conform to."[399] Others understand the contrast as being between the old and new "nature" of a person.[400] But Ridderbos is probably right that the old ἄνθρωπος points to an "old way of existence outside of Christ,"[401] which is essentially a way of existence under the rule of sin. He contrasts this with "a different way of existence,"[402] which is a "new life-reality in Christ."[403]

As with the new creation in 2 Cor 5:17 (see above), the old and new ἄνθρωπος are probably best understood in terms of both (1) a corporate (or cosmic) and (2) an individual sense:[404]

394. Thompson, *Colossians*, 74.

395. Even though the expression νέον ἄνθρωπον does not occur in the undisputed Pauline letters, the concepts of "old" and "new" is thoroughly Pauline (Barth and Blanke, *Colossians*, 411; see note 358, p. 160).

396. Moo, *Colossians*, 252; Melick, *Philippians*, 294–95; Wright, *Colossians*, 137; L&N §41.43; NRSV; NIV.

397. BDAG, ἄνθρωπος, §5.

398. BDAG, ἄνθρωπος, §5b.

399. L&N §41.43; cf. Lincoln, *Ephesians*, 643.

400. E.g., Bruce, *Colossians*, 146; Schweizer, *Colossians*, 198.

401. Ridderbos, *Kolossenzen*, 211 (all translations of this source are my own).

402. Ridderbos, *Kolossenzen*, 213.

403. Ridderbos, *Kolossenzen*, 214.

404. O'Brien, *Colossians*, 190; cf. Thompson, *Colossians*, 77–78; Lincoln, "Colossians," 644; Dunn, *Colossians*, 222. This view is preferable rather than some who tend to lean toward either the corporate (Moo, *Colossians*, 267–70) or individual (Schweizer,

1. The corporate dimension of the new ἄνθρωπος points to a new humanity that has been created in Christ, which stands in contrast with the old humanity, which in turn corresponds with the "in Adam" concept (Rom 5:14; 1 Cor 15:22, 45).[405] This new humanity in Christ denotes a "new order of existence inaugurated by Christ's death and resurrection."[406] The old humanity is "the embodiment of the unregenerate humanity," and the humanity in Christ is the "recreated humanity in the Creator's image" (v. 10).[407] This new humanity corresponds to the new creation in Christ[408] (cf. 2 Cor 5:17) where there is no distinction between "Greek and Judean, circumcised and uncircumcised, barbarian, Scythian, slave and free" (v. 11; cf. Rom 10:12; Gal 3:28; 1 Cor 12:13). In this context, the expression "Greek and Judean" describes the whole of humanity.[409] The corporate identity in Christ is not defined in terms of ethnicity, race or social status. Talbert is correct in noting that according to the so called "household code" in 3:18–4:1, the slave-master relationship still exists, which implies that Greek and Judean still exist as social/ethnic indicators even within the new community in Christ. Yet all identity markers pertaining to ethnicity, race or social status have been rendered *ineffective* in terms of *defining one's position* in Christ.[410] Christ has become "all in all" (v. 11), which probably indicates Christ as the only, universal source of deriving one's *identity as God's people* in the new creation.[411]

2. Although the new identity in Christ is already accomplished by Christ's death and resurrection (vv. 1, 3) it has to be actualized in the life of the believer:[412] (a) There has to be an individual regeneration or transformation by the power of God, where the "new person" in Christ becomes

---

Colossians, 197–98) significance of the old and new humanity/person.

405. Dunn, *Colossians*, 221–22; Barth and Blanke, *Colossians*, 412; Wright, *Colossians*, 138; Bruce, *Colossians*, 147–48; O'Brien, *Colossians*, 190–91; cf. Ridderbos, *Kolossenzen*, 211–14.

406. Lincoln, *Ephesians*, 643; adopted by Thompson, *Colossians*, 78; cf. Ridderbos, *Kolossenzen*, 213–14.

407. O'Brien, *Colossians*, 191; cf. Moo, *Colossians*, 268; Dunn, *Colossians*, 222.

408. Moo, *Colossians*, 2008:269; Wright, *Colossians*, 139; O'Brien, *Colossians*, 192; Lohse, *Colossians*, 142.

409. Moo, *Colossians*, 267–68, 270; O'Brien, *Colossians*, 192.

410. Talbert, *Ephesians*, 229; cf. Thompson, *Colossians*, 79–81; Lincoln, "Colossians," 644; Dunn, *Colossians*, 223, 225, 227; Wright, *Colossians*, 139–40; O'Brien, *Colossians*, 192; Lohse, *Colossians*, 144; Abbott, *Ephesians*, 285.

411. Cf. Moo, *Romans*, 272, 275; Melick, *Philippians*, 298; Wright, *Colossians*, 140.

412. Cf. Lohse, *Colossians*, 142.

an actual ontological reality in the life of the believer.[413] (b) This new identity was enacted by "clothing" oneself (ἐνδυσάμενοι, v. 10) with the new ἄνθρωπος, which probably points to baptism[414] (cf. 2:11-13, see pp. 215-20). In this context, baptism can be understood as a conscious identification with Christ's death and resurrection,[415] and signifies the unity of all believers in Christ (cf. Gal 3:27-28). (c) The new identity in Christ has to be actualized continually[416] in the life of the believer[417] by "putting on" (ἐνδύσασθε, v. 12) the virtues and values corresponding to the new identity. Dunn refers to conversion as embracing "a new way of life."[418] This "putting on" is a process that primarily takes place in the realm of the mind (φρονεῖτε, v. 2; cf. Rom 12:2).[419]

The Colossians are described as God's chosen people (ἐκλεκτοὶ τοῦ θεοῦ, v. 12), holy (ἅγιοι, v. 12) and beloved (ἠγαπημένοι, v. 12). All three these designations are standard ways of describing Israel in the Old Testament.[420]

---

413. Cf. Thompson, *Colossians*, 78; Melick, *Philippians*, 296; O'Brien, *Colossians*, 192. This reality is probably best portrayed by 2:11-13, which signifies the removal of the flesh of the individual and the regeneration of the new person through faith (cf. Moo, *Colossians*, 266).

414. Moo, *Colossians*, 266; Lincoln, "Colossians," 644; Dunn, *Colossians*, 221; Fee, *Empowering Presence*, 647; Wright, *Colossians*, 138; Bruce, *Colossians*, 146; O'Brien, *Colossians*, 189; Schweizer, *Colossians*, 196; Lohse, *Colossians*, 142.

415. In Col 2:11-15, the baptismal candidate is portrayed as being buried "with" Christ and raised "with" him through faith, a theme that parallels the meaning of baptism as put forth in Rom 6:3-6. The identification with Christ is conscious, as can be derived from the high frequency of the medium form of the "clothing" metaphors in the Pauline literature (see Du Toit, "The 'Clothe' Metaphor"), which signifies reflexivity and the subject's participation in the action (Wallace, *Grammar*, 414-16).

416. The aorist participle (ἐνδυσάμενοι, v. 10) is followed by an aorist imperative (ἐνδύσασθε, v. 12), constituting the ongoing process of actualization.

417. O'Brien, *Colossians*, 190.

418. Dunn, *Colossians*, 220-21; cf. Lincoln, "Colossians," 643.

419. The fundamental renewal of a person is not a gradual process (contra Lincoln, "Colossians," 643; Dunn, *Colossians*, 221; Schweizer, *Colossians*, 202), but a fully completed work of Christ (1:21-22; cf. Phil 2:15; Eph 5:27). But the actualization, the "putting on" (v. 12) or the "living out" of the new identity in Christ and the renewal of the mind (v. 2; cf. Rom 12:2). is a continuous process (cf. Lohse, *Colossians*, 142, 145). The object of renewal in v. 10 is thus not the human person itself, but [true] "knowledge" (ἐπίγνωσις; Moo, *Colossians*, 269; cf. Melick, *Philippians*, 297).

420. Moo, *Colossians*, 275-76; Thompson, *Colossians*, 81; Lincoln, "Colossians," 647; O'Brien, *Colossians*, 197; Lohse, *Colossians*, 146; Lightfoot, *Colossians*, 219; cf. Bruce, *Colossians*, 153). Although the concept of Israel as God's *chosen* people in the Old Testament is widespread, the term ἐκλεκτοί appears in the following (LXX): 1 Chr 16:13; Ps 105:6, 43; 106:5; Wis 4:15; Isa 43:20; 45:4; 65:9 (Moo, *Colossians*, 275; cf. Rom 9:24-25; 8:30; Eph 1:4). In terms of God's people as *holy*, Deut 14:2 is significant: "For

The use of these terms does not necessarily imply that believers in Christ *are* the "new/true Israel,"[421] but that these three *privileges* have been transferred to the Christ-community.[422] Christ-believers therefore participate in the heritage of Israel of the Old Testament[423] and they are hereby identified as *God's people*,[424] just like Israel in the Old Testament.

The peace of Christ (v. 15) underscores the unity of all believers in Christ in one body (ἐν ἑνὶ σώματι, v. 15),[425] and the fact that there is no differentiation on the basis of ethnicity, circumcision, or social status.[426] The body of Christ corresponds to the new ἄνθρωπος (v. 10)[427] and the new creation.

The contrast between the old (παλαιός, v. 9) and the new (νέος, v. 10) is similar to the "new creation" and the "old things" of 2 Corinthians 5:17. The "new person" in Colossians 3:10 portrays the new identity in Christ (identity mode C) that stands in stark *discontinuity* with the "old person," which indicates the person whose core-identity is defined by earthly things (v. 2) and by social and ethnical identity markers (including identity mode A). It can be noted here that the contrast of the "new person" is not with "Israel according to the flesh" (identity mode A) in verses 8 to 9, but rather with a carnal, sinful person. But the "new person" is simultaneously contrasted with distinctions constituted by ethnicity and circumcision (v. 11), including "Israel according to the flesh" by implication. In the light of Christ, there is thus a sense in which identity mode A is reduced to the same level as any other identity before or outside (belief in) Christ. A prominent marker in defining the identity of the "old person" is circumcision (v. 11). These distinctions have been done away with in the "new person" in Christ. Christ himself is the new source of deriving one's fundamental identity, that is, your identity as God's elect, holy and beloved (v. 12).

---

you are a people holy to the LORD your God; it is you the LORD has chosen out of all the peoples on earth to be his people, his treasured possession" (NRSV; cf. Col 1:2; Eph 1:4). God's *love* for His people is often the fundamental basis for their election (e.g., Deut 4:37; 10:15; 1 Kgs 10:9; Ps 78:68; Isa 41:8; Hos 11:1; Moo, *Colossians*, 276; cf. 1 Thess 1:4; 2 Thess 2:13). All three concepts (election, holy, beloved) occur together in Deut 7:6–8 (Thompson, *Colossians*, 81).

421. E.g., Wright, *Colossians*, 141.
422. Wright, *Colossians*, 141; O'Brien, *Colossians*, 197; Lightfoot, *Colossians*, 219.
423. Dunn, *Colossians*, 228.
424. Wright, *Colossians*, 141; cf. Thompson, *Colossians*, 82.
425. Lincoln, "Colossians," 648; Dunn, *Colossians*, 235; Barth and Blanke, *Colossians*, 425–26.
426. Cf. Thompson, *Colossians*, 85.
427. Cf. Moo, *Romans*, 285.

Summary and Concluding Remarks

In faith in Christ, the differentiation between ethnic identities is relativized. In Romans 15:5-13, the way in which the terms ἔθνος and λαός are applied, convey a kind of fluidity between Judean and gentile identities in Christ. While ἔθνος seems to include Judeans, λαός seems to include gentiles. All people groups are invited to Praise the Lord as one people (Rom 15:5-13).

In 1 Corinthians 1:21-24, Paul indicates the cross of Christ to be central to the gospel. In Christ, the crucified, ethnic identities are relativized and united into one single church without distinction. The identity in Christ therefore supersedes the Judean identity in terms of defining membership of God's people.

Paul's Damascus experience can be understood as a conversion rather than merely a call (cf. Gal 1:11-14), yet not in terms of conversion from one religion to another, but rather as a change of identity. In Christ, Paul has died to the old identity under the law (Gal 2:19-20). His core identity is now defined by a personal relationship with Christ. Paul was probably known among the Judean Christ-believers as "the one who formerly persecuted us" or something similar (cf. Gal 1:23), which would confirm Paul's change of core-identity. The expression "the faith" (τὴν πίστιν, Gal 1: 24) seems to point to the faith-identity as becoming entrenched. To keep living as Judeans (Ἰουδαϊκῶς ζῆς and Ἰουδαΐζω, Gal 2:14) in Christ would perpetuate the distinction between Judean and non-Judean and run contrary to Paul's inclusive gospel. The "works of the law" to which most of Paul's rhetoric is directed, refers to *both* (1) badges of covenantal nomism and (2) a legalistic complex of ideas having to do with winning God's favor by merit-amassing observance of the law.[428]

The 4 privileges and 3 accomplishments that Paul lists in Philippians 3:3-4 can be understood as defining his identity in the flesh. His former identity in the flesh relates to his descent from physical Israel, his pedigree, and the centrality of the law in defining that identity. An identity defined by law stands in discontinuity with an identity constituted by faith in Christ. The deeper contrast in Paul's new identity over against his old identity relates to the Spirit against flesh (Phil 3:3), which can be understood as eschatological realities. This theme will be pursued in more depth in chapter 5.

In 1 Thessalonians 2:13-16, Paul refers to his "brothers" in the context of their persecution from Judeans. Although an element of "othering" may be identified with respect to identity, Paul's rhetoric is arguably not so much directed at Judeans *per se*, but rather to those who oppose the gospel.

---

428. Esp. Longenecker, *Galatians*, 86.

It may additionally be derived from these verses that Paul understood persecution as an ever present characteristic of God's people through the ages. The new identity in Christ that constitutes a new, separate identity (identity mode C), stands in *discontinuity* with the non-believing Judean identity (identity mode A).

Paul employs σάρξ in Philemon 1:16 in an extended meaning. The term correlates with all natural identities, including social (e.g., slave/client) and ethnic identities. All identities outside of Christ seem to be in the sphere of flesh.

The new creation in Christ (2 Cor 5:14–21) arguably represents the deepest aspect of the *discontinuity* between an identity in Christ and the old order, yet not as a replacement of salvation history, but as the culmination thereof. That which was lost in Adam was restored in Christ. The new reality in Christ constitutes a new eschatological reality that has been realized already, although awaiting final completion. This reality consists of both a cosmic (universal) and individual dimension. The cosmic dimension pertains to the principal "death" and reconciliation of humankind in Christ, which are being ministered to all people. The individual dimension pertains to the actualization and appropriation of the new creation in the lives of believers, bringing them into a right relationship with God. The new creation implies a new identity that fulfills and supersedes ethnic identities.

The old and new person as portrayed in Colossians 3:9–15 echoes much of the same notions as 2 Corinthians 5:14–21, especially the notions of having "died" with Christ and being raised with him. The old and new persons also point to two ways of existence. The old person denotes both unregenerate humanity and the unregenerate individual person. Likewise, the new person pertains to the new humanity in Christ and the new, regenerate individual person. The reality of this new identity in Christ has to be actualized in the life of a believer on a continual basis.

My approach goes further than an approach where Paul is merely seen as a "bicultural mediator," which implies that both Judean and gentile identities would largely stay in tact in Christ.[429] The new creation implies that cultural or social identities have been relativized to such an extent that those in Christ are not known "according to the flesh" any longer (2 Cor 5:16), that is, that people are not known in terms of their *social identity* (including ethnicity, culture, and even law),[430] but in terms of their *theological identity* in Christ. Their theological identity in Christ does not have to be socially

---

429. Tucker, *Remain*, 231.

430. For the connection between the concept of "flesh" and law, see esp. Rom 7:5 and Rom 8:3 (see pp. 189–212).

negotiated, but is already created by God in Christ as part of the new creation. The new identity in Christ is thus a God-given reality that involves all people (esp. 2 Cor 5:18). An approach that includes Paul's "theologizing" under an ideological, social agenda[431] in fact reverses the latter new reality in Christ. It implies that people in Christ are still known "according to the flesh," or according to their social identity, or that people's social identity is still constitutive of their filiation to God.[432]

My approach to the new identity in Christ, where the identity of the person "in Christ" is *defined* by Christ himself and his work, thus has to be distinguished from an approach that understands the identity in Christ as *inclusive* of various sub-identities. The latter includes approaches where sub-identities are perceived in a nested hierarchy of identity of which being in Christ is primary,[433] or where identity is seen as a new "superordinate" identity wherein Judeans and Greeks are incorporated yet enjoys a relative status.[434] In other words, the new identity in Christ does not merely *accommodate* all social/ethnic identities; it *redefines* the core identity of the believer in Christ.[435] As Moo states, "the Christian community is comprised of people who maintain their gender, familial, and social identities" (e.g., Judean/gentile; male/female). "But these earthly identities are no longer what is most important: solidarity in Christ is now the ruling paradigm for the new community."[436] "Whatever our worldly background or status, we all now have our fundamental identity determined by Christ."[437] Although Paul still acknowledges Judeans and Greeks in Christ in some way (e.g., Gal 3:28), these identities seem to *have become mere cultural and ethnic designations* in Christ. These cultural identities have lost their *constitutive ability* in defining either *filiation* to God (Judeans) or *separation* from God (gentiles). That is why a Judean Christ-believer has left a Judean "way of life," including law observance and circumcision, for the latter *was* in fact constitutive of their filiation to God under the law, and cannot continue to be so. If gentiles were merely to join God's people without having to keep the law or undergo circumcision while Judeans were still required to do so, the law and circumcision would still divide the way in which they related to God: their "childhood" (υἱοθεσία) would still be expressed in different, un-

---

431. E.g., Tucker, *Remain*, 39.
432. It seems telling that 2 Cor 5:16 is not mentioned in Tucker's, *Remain*, work.
433. E.g., Tucker, *Remain*, 188; Campbell, *Paul*, 157.
434. Esler, *Conflict*, 144–45, 360; Zoccali, *Whom God Has Called*, 176.
435. Cf. Thompson, *Colossians*, 79–80.
436. Moo, *Colossians*, 272; cf. Garland, *Colossians*, 42–43.
437. Moo, *Colossians*, 275.

equal terms, which would perpetuate Judean exclusivity. Judeans have thus died to (cf. 2 Cor 5:15) any aspect of identity pertaining to their filiation with God in the realm of "flesh" (that which is outward/external, including ethnicity, circumcision and law observance). There is thus a sense wherein the "old identity," that is, everything in their core-identity pertaining to the "old creation," dies in Christ. This does not mean that any person's cultural heritage is not remembered or acknowledged, but it has become irrelevant[438] and non-determinative in Christ.

A delicate yet important distinction has to be drawn here. My approach to identity is not to negate or devalue the dynamics of social identity formation *per se*. While acknowledging the dynamics of social identity formation, I do not see such dynamics as the primary controlling factor in Paul's *theology* of identity. Paul's theological portrayal of identity is rather part of the new creation itself and part of the revelation of the gospel given to him by God. This theological reality should affect people's perceptions of themselves and their relationships with one another in Christ. It is thus a matter of priority. In stead of a social agenda that ought to determine "theologizing," the theological reality in Christ ought to determine social dynamics.[439] A noteworthy example of a scholar that utilizes social formation theory yet seems to approach such formation from the predetermined new identity in Christ, is Kar Yong Lim.[440] His article occurs in an edited work about social identity in the New Testament, together with scholars such as J. Brian Tucker, Coleman A. Baker, Philip F. Esler and others.[441] In Lim's article on 2 Corinthians, he identifies the main problem in the Corinthian community as "their continual identification with their previous social identity."[442] He later argues that "by associating with the rivals, the Corinthians are in essence moving away from their 'in-Christ-new-creation' identity."[443] Paul's solution would be that they are reminded of "salience of their 'in Christ' identity."[444] The Corinthians have to

> evaluate their current status "in Christ" (which is "the new") against their own past (which is "the old") . . . The underlying question is this: is the group behaviour of the Corinthians compatible with their new identity in Christ as a new creation

---

438. Cf. De Boer, *Galatians*, 181.
439. Holmberg, "Jewish *Versus* Christian Identity," 421.
440. Lim, "New Creation."
441. Tucker and Baker, *T. & T. Clark Handbook*.
442. Lim, "New Creation," 296.
443. Lim, "New Creation," 300.
444. Lim, "New Creation," 298.

where the old is gone, and the new has come? ... If what they are now is incompatible with their status as being in Christ as a new creation, then decisive actions need to be taken to *align themselves* to it.[445]

If I understand Lim correctly, his approach implies that the "in Christ" identity is considered a predefined theological reality that has to *come into effect* in their social behavior and the way in which the Corinthian community relate to others. The identity in Christ in itself is less something that has to be negotiated than it is something that requires social and *practical alignment* to the truth of this new reality. The ultimate controlling factor for identity is thus not one's social or cultural identity, but the identity one receives through the completed reality of Christ's work on the cross.

With respect to Paul's own identity, Paul seems to identify himself as a descendent of Ἰσραήλ (Phil 3:5) or born Ἰσραηλίτης (Rom 11:1; 2 Cor 11:22), rather than being a Judean.[446] Yet Paul uses the term Ἰσραηλίτης more in connection with descent or ethnicity than denoting status as God's people (see also Rom 9:4). Similarly, being ἐκ γένους Ἰσραήλ (Phil 3:5) does not identify Paul as currently being part of elect "Israel" as such (identity mode AB), but denotes his line of descent. These designations are therefore not *definitive* with respect to Paul's current identity as God's child. With the exception of Romans 11:1 (see p. 263), Paul's reference to both terms (Ἰσραήλ and Ἰσραηλίτης) in connection with his own identity is within a polemical context against his opponents (Phil 3:5; 2 Cor 11:22). Paul's core-identity is now derived from being in Christ in discontinuity with his old identity where descent *was* (partly) constitutive in defining God's people (esp. Gal 2:19-20; Phil 3:8).

Regarding Paul's view of historical Israel, it is not clear at this point if Paul considers historical Israel as saved. Paul acknowledges God's salvation-historical plan with them in its culmination in Christ, but seems to view Christ as the end of the era under which they lived. It can thus be asked if Paul by implication does not view Israel as continuing to be God's people (in some way) in Paul's present. But the final answer to this question has to be derived from Romans 11.

---

445. Lim, "New Creation," 299, emphasis added.

446. As argued on pp. 131-35, Paul's inclusion of himself as Judean "by birth" in Gal 2:15 is part of his rhetorical strategy rather than an ultimate description of his own identity.

5

Spirit, Flesh and Identity

As has become evident from the passages discussed up to this point, πνεῦμα often stands in opposition to σάρξ in terms of identity (Rom 15:13; Gal 3:2, 5; 4:29; Phil 3:3; cf. Eph 2:18), and is thus an important notion in Paul's definition of identity from a theological perspective. This is a good example of how a mutually qualifying term "allows an understanding to 'come alive'"[1] (see pp. 16–30).

Although much of the spirit-flesh dichotomy has been discussed, this chapter aims to describe Paul's understanding of identity in terms of this dichotomy more precisely.

Spirit and the New Covenant Versus Flesh and the Old Covenant (AC)

2 Corinthians 3:5–16 signifies the last passage indicated on pp. 27–30 to be examined exegetically, pertaining to being God's people. The expressions "New Covenant/ Testament" (καινῆς διαθήκης, v. 6)[2] and "Old Covenant/ Testament" (παλαιᾶς διαθήκης, v. 14) occur together only here in Paul. As I will argue, this passage is fundamental to Paul's understanding of the identities of ancient Israel and believers in Christ.

2 Corinthians 3:5–16

In 2 Corinthians 3:1–18, πνεῦμα is mentioned six times (vv. 3, 6, 8, 17 [x2], 18) and can be regarded as one of the most significant passages about πνεῦμα in the Pauline corpus. The old and the new (covenants and ministries) are set in sharp contrast with each other: the letter against the Spirit/

---

1. Thiselton, *Hermeneutics*, 318.
2. The phrase καινὴ διαθήκη on its own occurs only in 1 Cor 11:25.

spirit (v. 6), death against life (v. 6), and condemnation against righteousness (v. 9).³ Paul's underlying concern in this passage is the defense of his apostleship, but not so much the *fact* of it, as its *character*.⁴ In Furnish's words, "[t]hese paragraphs are most accurately described as theological exposition with a polemical edge."⁵

The Corinthian congregation is Paul's "letter" of commendation to be known and "read" by all people, written with the Spirit of God, not on tablets of stone, but on tablets of human hearts (vv. 2–3).⁶ The πλαξὶν λιθίναις (v. 3) signifies insensitive hearts, while the πλαξὶν καρδίαις σαρκίναις denote sensitive, responsive hearts. Paul's use of πλάξ and λίθινος allude to the πλάκας λιθίνας of Exodus 31:18 and 34:1 (LXX), which is associated with Moses and the Old Covenant,⁷ or more specifically, with the written Mosaic law.⁸ The phrase πλαξὶν καρδίαις σαρκίναις alludes to the καρδίαν σαρκίνην that is contrasted to the καρδίαν τὴν λιθίνην in Ezekiel 11:19 and 36:26 (LXX), where the heart of flesh corresponds to the new spirit that the Lord will give to humankind.⁹

The Old and New Covenants and Salvation History

Verses 4 and 5 confirm the divine origin of Paul and¹⁰ the Corinthians' qualification (ἱκανότης, v. 5)¹¹ or competence.¹² God qualified them to be ministers (διάκονος, v. 6)¹³ of the New Covenant (διαθήκη, vv. 6, 14).¹⁴

3. Fee, *Empowering Presence*, 297.
4. Fee, *Empowering Presence*, 298.
5. Furnish, *II Corinthians*, 243.
6. NRSV.
7. Harris, *Second Epistle*, 265.
8. Wright, *Faithfulness*, 2:982; Meyer, *Law*, 77; Thrall, *Corinthians*, 1:226.
9. Meyer, *Law*, 80; Fee, *Empowering Presence*, 303; Thrall, *Corinthians*, 1:226.
10. The plural ἱκάνωσεν includes Paul himself. The aorist probably refers to Paul's Damascus encounter with the risen Christ, where he was filled with the Spirit and became a chosen instrument (Harris, *Second Epistle*, 270; Acts 9:15, 17–19).
11. BDAG, ἱκανότης; Zerwick and Grosvenor, *Grammatical Analysis*, 539; Harris, *Second Epistle*, 269.
12. NRSV.
13. Zerwick and Grosvenor, *Grammatical Analysis*, 539; Fee, *Empowering Presence*, 304; Barrett, *Second Epistle*, 111. Or "agents" (BDAG, διάκονος, §1; Harris, *Second Epistle*, 270).
14. BDAG, διαθήκη, §2; Harris, *Second Epistle*, 270; Fee, *Empowering Presence*, 304; Barrett, *Second Epistle*, 111. Διαθήκη can be rendered as "testament" (in BDAG, διαθήκη, §1 [not applied to 2 Cor 3:6, 14]; Zerwick and Grosvenor, *Grammatical*

The expression καινὴ διαθήκη, although appropriated in the Last Supper tradition (1 Cor 11:25), is ultimately derived from Jeremiah 38:31 (LXX; MT: 31:31).[15] If the interlaced[16] allusions to Scripture in Paul's language are taken into account (esp. Jer 38:31–33, LXX and Ezek 36:26–27) together with his reference to the Spirit in verse 3, the New Covenant can be described as a "covenant of Spirit" (ἀλλὰ πνεύματος, v. 6) that breathes life (ζῳοποιεῖ, v. 6; cf. Ezek 37:14; Rom 4:17; 8:11; 1 Cor 15:45) into the hearts of God's people.[17] The meaning of verse 6 can hardly be better described than in the words of Fee:

> In light of this kind of intertextuality, one can scarcely miss the eschatological implications of Paul's understanding of the Spirit—as fulfillment of God's promised gift of Spirit at the end of the ages, which according to 1 Cor 10:11 he understands already to have come. Thus the Spirit is the key to both continuity and discontinuity with the OT people of God. The continuity lies with God and his promises, especially the promise of the new covenant of "Spirit" with his people; the discontinuity lies with the Spirit's coming so as to fulfill the promise and thus usher in a new day, which includes the Gentiles, since they, too, have received the same Spirit by faith (see esp. Gal 3:6–14).[18]

Paul opposes the "covenant of Spirit/spirit" to the "covenant of the letter" (γράμμα, v. 6), which signifies the written law of Moses[19] (cf. Rom 2:27, 29, see pp. 54–68; Rom 7:6, see pp. 189–99),[20] the "hallmark of the old covenant."[21] Fee rightly remarks that it is not so much the law in itself that is "letter," but the fact that it constitutes "specific demands requiring obedience" that is mere "letter."[22] In contrast to the Spirit that gives life, the

---

Analysis, 539), but in the Septuagint, διαθήκη mostly (around 270 times) translates the Hebrew בְּרִית, so that the broad connotations of בְּרִית became attached to διαθήκη (Harris, *Second Epistle*, 270; cf. Barrett, *Second Epistle*, 112; Plummer, *Corinthians*, 86).

15. Harris, *Second Epistle*, 270–71; Wright, *Climax*, 176.
16. Sampley, "Corinthians," 64.
17. Fee, *Empowering Presence*, 304.
18. Fee, *Empowering Presence*, 304–5; cf. Barnett, *Corinthians*, 176.
19. Harris, *Second Epistle*, 273; Barnett, *Corinthians*, 176–77; Thrall, *Corinthians*, 1:234; Kruse, *Corinthians*, 92; Barrett, *Second Epistle*, 113; cf. Lenski, *Corinthians*, 921; Plummer, *Corinthians*, 87.
20. Contra Gaston, *Paul*, 156, who argues that the "letter" does not refer to the law or Scripture, but to rival missionaries.
21. Harris, *Second Epistle*, 273.
22. Fee, *Empowering Presence*, 306; cf. Meyer, *Law*, 83; Garland, *2 Corinthians*, 156–57. Barrett, *Second Epistle*, 113, is probably right that the deeper contrast here is

"letter" kills (ἀποκτείνω, v. 6; cf. θάνατος, v. 7). As elsewhere (Rom 7:5-9; 8:2; 1 Cor 15:56), Paul by implication associates the law with death and sin. Garland also connects the "killing" of the letter to the curse of the law (Gal 3:10-14).[23] These connotations additionally correspond with the notions of imprisonment (Gal 3:23) and slavery (Gal 4:21-5:1). The law aroused sin that led to death (Rom 7:10-11). Even though the law was intended to give life (Gal 3:12, 21; Rom 10:5; cf. Rom 2:27-29), it could not attain life (cf. Rom 7:10) without the Spirit that gives life (πνεῦμα ζῳοποιεῖ, v. 6).[24] Similarly, Meyer states that "the letter/Spirit dichotomy represents a fundamental contrast between the outward/ineffectual and the inward/effectual. This contrast between the ineffectual and the effectual reinforces the eschatological nature of the contrast between old and new covenants."[25]

Rather than constituting a contradiction in Paul's view(s) of the law, contra Räisänen,[26] the law that kills does not render the law intrinsically unspiritual (Rom 7:14) or against God's promises (Gal 3:21; cf. Rom 3:31), but states the inevitable result of an eschatological era where life and righteousness were sought after by law, and the identity of God's people was defined by law.[27] The life-giving Spirit thus both *fulfills* and *replaces* and the law, constituting both *continuity* and *discontinuity* with the law.[28] The "covenant of Spirit" is equivalent to a new "law" that frees people from the law of sin and death (Rom 8:2). As in Galatians 3 where faith and law are contrasted, the "covenant of the letter" and the "covenant of Spirit/spirit" here signify two "contrasting epochs"[29] or two forms of eschatological existence.[30] This understanding would allow for translating πνεύματος in verse 6 as "of spirit,"[31]

---

between human and divine action.

23. Garland, *2 Corinthians*, 157.

24. Harris, *Second Epistle*, 273; Garland, *2 Corinthians*, 157; Fee, *Empowering Presence*, 306-7; cf. Barrett, *Second Epistle*, 116.

25. Meyer, *Law*, 82; cf. Garland, *2 Corinthians*, 157; Hays, *Echoes*, 131.

26. Räisänen, *Paul*, 82-83.

27. Cf. Fee, *Empowering Presence*, 306, 814-15; Kruse, *Corinthians*, 92-93. Exactly what the killing entails, is not specified. Being contrasted with life, which has to point to eternal life (Fee, *Empowering Presence*, 307), the killing seems to point to the opposite of salvation. Allusions to physical death being the result of the breaking of many of the commandments of the Mosaic law (e.g., Lev 20; 24) cannot be ruled out (cf. Plummer, *Corinthians*, 88). The law that kills thus arguably carries connotations of both physical and spiritual death (Harris, *Second Epistle*, 273).

28. Fee, *Empowering Presence*, 813-14.

29. See Dunn, *Epistle to the Galatians*, 198, on Gal 3:23; cf. Meyer, *Law*, 84.

30. Fee, *Empowering Presence*, 816-17, 820.

31. E.g., Lenski, *Corinthians*, 919; NRSV; OAT; KJV; RV.

not to denote the human spirit *per se*, but this new eschatological existence in Christ (see pp. 199-206).

The letter that kills (v. 6) is rephrased in verse 7 as the "ministry of death" (διακονία τοῦ θανάτου), which is contrasted with the "ministry of the Spirit" (διακονία τοῦ πνεύματος, v. 8). In relation to διάκονος in verse 6, διακονία in verse 7 carries both the connotations of personal ministry[32] and the law as a system.[33] Paul must have his own ministry in mind and those who oppose his ministry. His rival missionaries are later described as διάκονοι Χριστοῦ (11:23). Paul's use of διακονία thus probably has a polemical bearing.[34]

In most of verses 7 to 11, Paul contrasts the glory of the ministry of the law with the ministry of the Spirit. The glory of the ministry of the Spirit, which corresponds with Paul's own ministry, is superior to that of Moses.[35] The Mosaic covenant was a ministry of death (θάνατος, v. 7) and condemnation (κατάκρισις, v. 9), where the ministry of the Spirit brings righteousness (δικαιοσύνη, v. 9) and life (ζωοποιέω, v. 6). The verb ἔσται (v. 8) is best understood as a logical future,[36] which means that it is future from the Sinai-event and subsequent to the glory of Moses.[37] Additionally, the Mosaic ministry or covenant[38] is being abolished[39] (καταργούμενον, v. 11; cf. Rom 10:4, see pp. 253-62) or annulled,[40] whereas the ministry of the Spirit is permanent

---

32. BDAG, διακονία, §3, describes διακονία in this context as functioning in the interest of a larger public, and proposes the translation "service" or "office." Zerwick and Grosvenor, *Grammatical Analysis*, 539, render the term as "administration."

33. Harris, *Second Epistle*, 281; Thrall, *Corinthians*, 1:241; Furnish, *II Corinthians*, 202.

34. Thrall, *Corinthians*, 1:232; Kruse, *Corinthians*, 93; cf. Harris, *Second Epistle*, 281; Sampley, "Corinthians," 65.

35. Thrall, *Corinthians*, 1:240; Kruse, *Corinthians*, 94; cf. Garland, *2 Corinthians*, 161; Lenski, *Corinthians*, 931.

36. Harris, *Second Epistle*, 286; Thrall, *Corinthians*, 1:245; Zerwick and Grosvenor, *Grammatical Analysis*, 539; Bultmann, *Corinthians*, 81; Furnish, *II Corinthians*, 227-28; Collange, *Corinthians*, 77-78; cf. Matera, *II Corinthians*, 83; Plummer, *Corinthians*, 91.

37. Thrall, *Corinthians*, 1:245. This does not necessarily exclude a future eschatological reference (Thrall, *Corinthians*, 1:245; Furnish, *II Corinthians*, 228).

38. Although the object of abolition in v. 7 is the glory, the neuter participle (καταργούμενον) in v. 11 is probably best understood as referring to the Mosaic covenant in general (Thrall, *Corinthians*, 1:252).

39. BDAG, καταργέω, §3; Matera, *II Corinthians*, 83, 86, 89; Garland, *2 Corinthians*, 165; Wright, *Climax*, 178, 181; Hays, *Echoes*, 133-36; Barrett, *Second Epistle*, 109, 118; cf. Thrall, *Corinthians*, 1:252-53; Schreiner, "Abolition," 51; Lenski, *Corinthians*, 934.

40. Furnish, *II Corinthians*, 229.

(μένω, v. 11).⁴¹ The ministry of death was powerless to lead to life since it was not accompanied by the Spirit. The ministry of the Spirit (v. 8), which is simultaneously the ministry of justification (v. 9), replaced the old ministry and rendered the old obsolete.⁴² The contrast between that which is being abolished and that which is permanent (v. 11) thus epitomizes Paul's view of salvation history in the light of the cross of Christ: the Old Covenant, its ministry and its economy is being abolished, while the New Covenant began in splendor and will always be invested with glory until the parousia when its implications will be fully realized.⁴³

Paul incorporates the account of Exodus 34:29-35 in his comparison of the glory of the new and the old. He repeats the expression "sons of Israel" (Exod 34:32, 34, 35) in verses 7 and 13, which is national, ethnic Israel,⁴⁴ but he abbreviates the verb δοξάζω (Exod 34:29, 30, 35, LXX) to the noun δόξα (vv. 7, 8, 9, 10, 11, 18) to fit his syntactical structure. Paul interprets the glory on Moses' face as a diminishing glory, an implication implicit to the text of Exodus 34:29-35.⁴⁵ This diminishing glory is an indication of the temporal character of Moses' ministry and thus symbolic of the provisional character of the Mosaic covenant.⁴⁶ The veil over Moses' face prevented Israel from seeing the end (τέλος) of that which was being abolished (v. 13). This symbolizes the impermanence of the Mosaic system based on the law.⁴⁷ Moses concealed⁴⁸

---

41. BDAG, μένω, §2; NRSV.

42. Fee, *Empowering Presence*, 307-8; cf. Hong, "Law," 154.

43. Cf. Harris, *Second Epistle*, 291; Thrall, *Corinthians*, 1:258. Contra Sampley, "Corinthians," 66-67, who argues against a salvation-historical understanding or superseding covenants. Yet he refers to the "new covenant," "being transformed" and "God's unfolding purposes," which does not seem entirely consistent.

44. L&N §11.58.

45. Thrall, *Corinthians*, 1:244, explains that the covering of Moses' face when he did not speak to Israel might imply a diminishing glory that had to be renewed when Moses came in the presence of the Lord.

46. Cf. Garland, *2 Corinthians*, 164; Thrall, *Corinthians*, 1:244.

47. Nathan, "Paul," argues for the ministry of Moses as the most likely referent of τὸ καταργούμενον in v. 11 and the glory of Moses' face as the most likely referent of τοῦ καταργουμένου in v. 13. Even if different referents are acknowledged for καταργέω (vv. 7, 11, 13, 14) or even if terms such as καταργέω, τέλος, κάλυμμα, and δόξα are interpreted such as to accentuate Paul's continuity with the Old Covenant, Paul's *juxtaposition* of the ministry of "the New Covenant" (v. 6), the "Spirit that gives life" (v. 6), and the "ministry of the spirit" (v. 8) *to* a "letter [that] kills" (v. 6), a "ministry of death" (v. 7), and a "ministry of condemnation" (v. 9), seems to stand in too much tension with a notion that Paul would (merely?) operate within a "post-Damascus view of Judaism" (227).

48. It is doubtful whether a measure of deception should be ascribed to Moses himself (contra Räisänen, *Paul*, 57), which would presuppose disillusionment or surprise

the ultimate redundancy of the Old Covenant and that it served only an interim function by God's salvation-historical design.[49] Following Havemann,[50] Garland argues that the veil protected Israel from the judgment of God.[51] If the veil was removed and God's glory was reflected, it would destroy them. The veil was thus also a sign of God's grace.

The Removal of the Veil in Christ

Parallel to Moses' veiled glory, the minds of the *historical people* of Israel were hardened (ἐπωρώθη, v. 14).[52] This historical hardening of Israel is well accounted for in the Old Testament[53] and corresponds to the same theme elsewhere in Paul (Rom 9:18, see pp. 239-48; Rom 11:7-10, see pp.

---

that Moses' radiance began to fade the longer he was removed from the source of glory (Garland, *2 Corinthians*, 172). Moses would rather be co-operating with God's divine purposes for Israel (Thrall, *Corinthians*, 1:258).

49. Seifrid, *Corinthians*, 163-65; Garland, *2 Corinthians*, 172; Thrall, *Corinthians*, 1:255-58; Barrett, *First Adam*, 52; cf. Meyer, *Law*, 90; Matera, *II Corinthians*, 92-93; Furnish, *II Corinthians*, 232; Barrett, *Second Epistle*, 119. Contra Cranfield, *Romans*, 2:855, arguing against that which is passing away (τοῦ καταργουμένου, v. 13) being "the whole religious system based on the law" (Barrett, *First Adam*, 52). Cranfield, *Romans*, 2:856, contends that the removal of the veil and the turning to the Lord *merely* suggest that the people will be able to "understand the true meaning" of the law or "discern the true glory of the law." But this line of interpretation neither fully accounts for the pejorative allusions to the system of law in verses 3 (πλάξ, λίθινος), 6 (γράμμα ἀποκτέννει) and 7 (διακονία τοῦ θανάτου ἐν γράμμασιν ἐντετυπωμένη λίθοις), nor for the meaning of διακονία (v. 7), which carries both connotations of personal ministry and that of a system or administration (see above). Wright, *Climax*, 182, shows that *both* positions on this matter should be held together: (1) an *incorrect understanding* of the law is removed in Christ, and (2) by not being under the law any longer, membership in the New Covenant is *not being demarcated* by the law any more.

50. Havemann, *Paul*, 207, 209, 223.

51. Garland, *2 Corinthians*, 174-75.

52. Seifrid, *Corinthians*, 166-67; Meyer, *Law*, 93; Garland, *2 Corinthians*, 176; Barnett, *Corinthians*, 194-95; Thrall, *Corinthians*, 1:261-62; Kruse, *Corinthians*, 97; Gutbrod, "Ἰσραήλ," *TDNT*, 3:386; Lenski, *Corinthians*, 938-39. The aorist indicative (ἐπωρώθη) points to historical Israel. Paul probably would have used the perfect tense if his contemporaries were included in the hardening (Thrall, *Corinthians*, 1:262). See also note 388, p. 288.

53. Textual references containing the term σκληρύνω (LXX; cf. Rom 9:18) in connection with Israel's hardening on various occasions are Deut 10:16; 2 Kgs 17:14; 2 Chr 30:8; Neh 9:16, 17; 9:29; Ps 95:8; Isa 63:17; Jer 7:26; 17:23; and 19:15. Some prominent references that echoes the hardening of Israel in different words are Num 14:11, 22-23; Deut 9:22-24; 29:4; Ps 78:56; Isa 6:9-11; 29:10-12; 44:18; 56:10; Jer 3:17; 5:21; 7:24; 11:8; 13:10; 23:17; Ezek 3:7, 9, and 12:2. Meyer, *Law*, 93, argues that Paul primarily has Deut 29:4; Isa 6:9-11; and Isa 29:10-12 in mind.

262-67). Their hardening probably denotes their rebellion against God's word, their inability to endure God's voice and their wayward hearts.[54] This historical condition is probably best summarized by Isaiah 6:9-11, which reports of the people's failure to comprehend and their unrepentant hearts. Paul compares Israel's historical hardening to his present day (σήμερον, vv. 14-15). Most commentators have contemporary unbelieving Judeans in mind as those who Paul refers to as having a veil over their hearts when the Old Covenant is read (vv. 14-15).[55] Although there is continuity in terms of Israel's situation with the Judeans in Paul's day, the continuity lies more in the *veil itself* as subject of that which is to be removed (καταργέω and ἀνακαλύπτω, v. 14; περιαιρέω, v. 16), than with historical Israel. While unbelieving Judeans would certainly be included in those with a veil over their hearts at the reading of the Old Covenant,[56] there are several reasons that would suggest more generality with respect to the people who read the Old Covenant outside Christ and the Spirit:

1. The abolishing of the veil "in Christ" (v. 14b) signifies the universal entrance to the New Covenant (cf. "if anyone is in Christ" in 5:17).[57]

2. The contrast of the Old and New Covenants, including their levels of glory, goes against the notion that Israel would remain (cf. καταργέω vs. μένω, v. 11) God's people in Paul's present day. The same notion of discontinuity is echoed in 5:14-21 where Paul explains the significance of the identity in Christ defined by the new creation in contrast to an identity defined by flesh.

3. Although the public reading (ἀνάγνωσις, v. 14; ἀναγινώσκω, v. 15)[58] of the Old Covenant might point to the reading of the Pentateuch in the synagogue,[59] Scripture was read in the early church as well (ἀνάγνωσις, 1 Tim 4:13),[60] which does not restrict this practice to Judeans. The term ἀναγινώσκω (v. 15) is elsewhere applied by Paul in

---

54. Seifrid, *Corinthians*, 167.

55. E.g., Harris, *Second Epistle*, 305; Sampley, "Corinthians," 68; Thrall, *Corinthians*, 1:261; Kruse, *Corinthians*, 97; Furnish, *II Corinthians*, 233; Lenski, *Corinthians*, 940.

56. The αὐτῶν in both verses 14 and 15 corresponds.

57. Cf. Harris, *Second Epistle*, 309; Furnish, *II Corinthians*, 210-11, 234.

58. BDAG, ἀνάγνωσις, §1; idem., ἀναγινώσκω, b.

59. Harris, *Second Epistle*, 305; Sampley, "Corinthians," 68; cf. Wright, *Climax*, 182; Barrett, *Second Epistle*, 121; Lenski, *Corinthians*, 940; Pop, *Tweede Brief*, 95; Plummer, *Corinthians*, 99.

60. BDAG, ἀνάγνωσις, §1. In 1 Tim 5:18, the term γραφή is applied to Deut 25:4, which is part of the Pentateuch.

the context of reading his own letters to the Christ-believing congregations (1 Thess 5:27; cf. Eph 3:4; Col 4:16). None of these terms thus necessitate application to unbelieving Judeans.

4. Verse 16 has no subject. Collins and Furnish translate verse 16 as follows: "Whenever *anyone* turns to the Lord the veil is removed"[61] Harris concurs: "though he [Paul] was deeply grieved by the general unresponsiveness of his compatriots to the gospel he proclaimed . . . the veil of ignorance concerning the new covenant and its glory could still be lifted from *anyone's* heart provided there was 'conversion to the Lord.'"[62]

Paul's Hermeneutic of the Old Covenant

Despite the measure of generality one would allow for the people in whose hearts the veil of ignorance remain in reading the Pentateuch outside of Christ (vv. 14-16), the whole of 2 Corinthians 3 displays a profound Spirit-centered and Christ-centered hermeneutic.[63] The entire history of salvation and especially the era under the Mosaic law is evaluated in terms of the New Covenant in Christ and the Spirit. Kistemaker writes: "The veil represents a refusal to accept the fulfillment of God's revelation in Jesus Christ."[64] Similarly, Guthrie writes that "in the synagogues of the first century, when people hear the old covenant read and understand it as the apex of God's intentions for his people, they are blinded to the significance of Christ's new covenant."[65] The eschatological letter-spirit contrast is thus equivalent to a Christ-Old-Covenant contrast. The "letter" of the Old Covenant, constituted by the Mosaic law, contained in the Pentateuch, has to be "read" through Christ.

Although this Christological and Pneumatological hermeneutic is probably not applied to the whole of the Old Testament Scripture in 2 Corinthians 3, Paul seems to have applied this hermeneutic principle in interpreting the whole of Old Testament Scripture elsewhere.[66]

---

61. Collins, *Second Corinthians*, 88; Furnish, *II Corinthians*, 202, emphasis added; cf. Kistemaker, *Second Epistle*, 123; Harris, *Second Epistle*, 306; Matera, *II Corinthians*, 95; Fee, *Empowering Presence*, 310; NIV.

62. Harris, *Second Epistle*, 306, emphasis added; cf. Furnish, *II Corinthians*, 210-11, 234.

63. Cf. Pop, *Tweede Brief*, 93.

64. Kistemaker, *Second Epistle*, 122.

65. Guthrie, *2 Corinthians*, 224.

66. See esp. Paul's use of Scripture in Rom 9-11 (see pp. 251-53); cf. Sampley, "Corinthians," 68; Barrett, *Second Epistle*, 122.

The Lord as the Spirit

The term κύριος (v. 16) is interpreted as pointing either to "Christ"[67] or "Yahweh."[68] Even if the term would designate "Yahweh," the turning to "the Lord" should not be isolated from Christology. For Paul, "turning to the Lord means accepting the gospel of Christ."[69] As with Romans 10:9-13, one probably has to acknowledge a measure of fluidity and continuity between "Yahweh" and "Christ" in view of the way in which Paul appropriates Scripture.[70] All the same, Paul contextualizes "the Lord" in verse 17 as "the Spirit."[71]

In the notion to turn to the Lord, Paul probably had his own conversion in mind where "something like scales" had fallen from his eyes at conversion (Acts 9:18).[72] In Paul's conversion, however, the filling with the Spirit was instrumental (Acts 9:17). The unexpected reference to the Lord as the Spirit that constitutes freedom (2 Cor 3:17) is thus key to Paul's ministry and the Corinthians' conversion vis-à-vis his opponents who relied on "letters" and law.[73] The Spirit is indeed the hallmark of the New Covenant.[74]

Discontinuity and Identity

In conclusion, one has to acknowledge the *discontinuity* between the Old and New Covenants as portrayed in this passage. The Mosaic ministry or the Old Covenant, which is defined by Mosaic law, is portrayed as a temporal ministry of death and condemnation with lesser glory, which was destined for abolition. This Old Covenant is being replaced and superseded with the

---

67. BDAG, κύριος, §2bγא; Lenski, *Corinthians*, 945; Plummer, *Corinthians*, 102; Meyer, *Corinthians*, 477.

68. Harris, *Second Epistle*, 308; Thrall, *Corinthians*, 1:272; Kruse, *Corinthians*, 98; Furnish, *II Corinthians*, 211-12; cf. Sampley, "Corinthians," 71. It has been argued that in Paul, κύριος without the definite article denotes Yahweh and ὁ κύριος denotes Christ (Zerwick and Grosvenor, *Grammatical Analysis*, 540; Harris, "2 Corinthians," 339). Zerwick and Grosvenor, *Grammatical Analysis*, 540, argues by implication that ὁ κύριος in v. 17 would be an exception to this rule, for it would point to κύριος of the previous verse. However, it is doubtful whether this rule can consistently be applied to Paul.

69. Furnish, *II Corinthians*, 235; cf. Bassler, *Navigating*, 75; Harris, *Second Epistle*, 309; Kruse, *Corinthians*, 98.

70. Cf. Sampley, "Corinthians," 71; see also p. 257.

71. Fee, *Empowering Presence*, 311.

72. Harris, *Second Epistle*, 309.

73. Fee, *Empowering Presence*, 311.

74. Harris, *Second Epistle*, 273; Sampley, "Corinthians," 73.

permanent New Covenant with superior glory for all humankind, effected by the Spirit that qualifies believers and brings eternal life and freedom.[75]

The abolition of the covenant defined by law and its supersession by the covenant of Spirit has to have profound consequences for defining the identity of God's people. Wright correctly sees the deeper contrast in this passage as between Israel and believers in Christ.[76] The law cannot serve as identity marker for God's people in the light of Christ's work through the Spirit, but has to be replaced by another identity marker (or other identity markers). In view of all of the Pauline passages discussed up to this point, the Spirit can be understood as central in defining the identity of God's people in the New Covenant, but further exploration is needed to describe πνεῦμα as opposed to σάρξ in terms of identity more precisely.

The modes of identity that are represented in this passage are identity mode A (national Israel) and identity mode C (those who have turned to the Lord), which are in *discontinuity* with each other. In the light of the New Covenant, there is a sense wherein identity mode A overlaps with the identity of all unbelievers. For Paul, Christ and the Spirit have become so central in redefining the identity of God's people (identity mode C), that he seems to universalize all people outside of Christ (identity mode A). In other words, the universality of God's people in Christ has universal implications for all people outside of Christ. In this sense, the ministry of death (v. 7) might be described as the destined "death" of identity mode A (together with all other unbelievers) in the death of Christ (esp. 5:15). This notion of universalization of all people outside of Christ in terms of identity will be examined and qualified further in the next section.

Spirit and Flesh as Modes and Markers of Identity (AC)

At this point in the exegetical study, it has come to the fore that there is a close relationship of both the concepts πνεῦμα and σάρξ with identity in Paul. In the passages consulted, the expression κατὰ σάρκα often denotes natural, ethnical descent (Rom 1:3; 4:1; 9:3, 5; 1 Cor 10:18; 2 Cor 5:16 [arguably]; 11:18; Gal 4:23, 29; cf. τέκνα τῆς σαρκός, Rom 9:8). Σάρξ is often contrasted

---

75. Cf. Seifrid, *Corinthians*, 163–65; Collins, *Second Corinthians*, 82–86; Wright, *Faithfulness*, 2:980–84; idem., *Climax*, 181, 192; Meyer, *Law*, 73–94; Barnett, *Corinthians*, 197; Fee, *Empowering Presence*, 307–8; Hong, "Law," 154; Kruse, *Corinthians*, 97–99; Furnish, *II Corinthians*, 207; Harris, "2 Corinthians," 338; Barrett, *Second Epistle*, 118–19; Pop, *Tweede Brief*, 91.

76. Wright, *Faithfulness*, 2:983; *Climax*, 180.

to πνεῦμα, which indicates the beginning of the life of the believer in Christ (Gal 3:2-3) and arguably those who are regenerated (Gal 4:29). Πνεῦμα can indicate a kind of existence in a new eschatological eon that is incompatible with σάρξ, which in turn can indicate an eschatologically obsolete way of existence (Gal 3:3; Phil 3:3). Spirit constitutes life, freedom and justification in the New Covenant, and is contrasted with the "letter" and with death, which indicates the ministry of the Old Covenant defined by the law that is abolished in Christ (2 Cor 3).

These meanings attached to πνεῦμα and σάρξ strongly suggest that the πνεῦμα-σάρξ dichotomy is central to the understanding of identity in Paul. This contrast is most prominent in Romans 7 to 8 (esp. 7:5-6; 8:1-16) and Galatians 5:16-25, which will constitute the main focus of this section. In 1 Corinthians 12:12-13, which contains a similar formula than Galatians 3:28 and Colossians 3:11 (Judeans, Greeks, slaves, free), Paul associates πνεῦμα with the "one body" of believers, which is closely related to identity. The strong language in Colossians 2:11-13, where "the body of" σάρξ is "put off" in the circumcision of Christ and where "the uncircumcision of" σάρξ is addressed, marks this passage as possibly contributing to the debate.

Romans 7 to 8

It can be argued that Romans 7 and 8 form the latter part of the second major section of the letter that starts in Romans 5.[77] The main reasons for this view are that many themes reoccur in Romans 5 through 8 and correspond especially in 5:1-11 and 8:18-39,[78] together with the fact that much of the subject matter in Romans 5 differs from 1 to 4.[79] The themes of "death," "law" and "sin" are associated with σάρξ (7:5-6; 8:2-3), while "life" is associated with πνεῦμα (8:2, 6, 10, 13). Since these themes (death, law, sin, life) are abundant throughout Romans 5 to 8:16, Romans 5 and 6 are anticipated as laying much of the ground work for understanding πνεῦμα and σάρξ in 7 to 8:16. A brief overview of Romans 5 to 6 (esp. Rom 6) pertaining to Paul's main thought around these themes (death, law, sin, life) will thus follow.

---

77. Wright, "Romans," 508; Moo, *Romans*, 292.

78. E.g., "love of God/Christ" (5:5, 8; 8:35, 39), "justify" (5:1, 9; 6:7; 8:30, 33), "glory" (5:2; 6:4; 8:18, 21, 30), "peace" (5:1; 8:6), "hope" (5:2, 4, 5; 8:20, 24, 25), "tribulation" (5:3; 8:35); "save" (5:9, 10; 8:24) and "endurance" (5:3, 4; 8:25; see Moo, *Romans*, 292-93).

79. Wright, "Romans," 508.

Romans 5

After establishing faith in Christ as the only means of righteousness (4:1–25, see pp. 77–86), Paul now confirms faith as the access to the grace in which believers stand (v. 2) amidst suffering (vv. 3–4). The Spirit and God's love assure believers and give them hope (v. 5). In 5:6–11, Paul focuses on Christ's death and the objective reconciliation that his death has established.

In the latter part of Romans 5 (vv. 12–21), Paul's approach is once again deeply salvation-historical[80] focusing especially on sin and death from Adam to Christ as representatives of humanity. Adam and Christ represent two respective epochs or eons.[81] Whereas the epoch of Adam is described as an epoch where death (v. 14, 17) and sin *reigned* (v. 21), the epoch of Christ is pictured by the *reign* of life (v. 17) and grace (v. 21). But the reign of Christ is pictured as surpassing the reign of Adam (πολλῷ μᾶλλον, περισσεύω/ περισσεία in vv. 15, 17). Christ's obedience, causing many to be righteous, is set over against Adam's disobedience (v. 19). Within the reign of death (from Adam to Moses, v. 14), the law was additionally brought into the equation, resulting in disastrous consequences (v. 20),[82] causing the trespass to multiply (πλεονάσῃ τὸ παράπτωμα, v. 20).[83] The reign of sin "in death" is finally contrasted to the reign of grace through righteousness unto eternal life through Jesus Christ as Lord (v. 21).

Wright correctly argues that Paul's basic thesis is that "Israel according to the flesh" is "in Adam,"[84] which Paul will be elaborating upon in Romans 7. The universal scope of Christ's work in terms of its effect on all people (see τοὺς πολλούς, v. 15; πάντας ἀνθρώπους, v. 18; οἱ πολλοί, v. 19) might even suggest having an effect in some way on historical Israel.[85] The gift of grace that abounded for many (v. 15), in Wright's words, "is nothing short of a new creation, creation not merely out of nothing but out of anti-creation, out of death itself."[86] Wright's notion is confirmed by the correspondence in themes between 5:12–21 and 2 Corinthians 5:14–21.[87]

---

80. Ridderbos, *Romeinen*, 112, 123; cf. Osborne, *Romans*, 143; Moo, *Romans*, 352.

81. Moo, *Romans*, 315, 352; Dunn, *Romans*, 1:288, 294–96; Ridderbos, *Romeinen*, 112; cf. Osborne, *Romans*, 143.

82. Wright, "Romans," 525.

83. Cf. NRSV.

84. Wright, "Romans," 525.

85. Although such a notion might seem premature in Romans 5, Paul's universal language in 5:12–21 seems to serve the purpose of assigning even deeper significance to Christ's death later on (see pp. 354–56).

86. Wright, "Romans," 528.

87. Corresponding themes: righteousness (Rom 5:17–19, 21; 2 Cor 5:21), the

Romans 6

The respective realms of sin and death in Adam, and that of righteousness and life in Christ that Paul has sketched in 5:12-21, form the foundation of Romans 6.[88] The whole of Romans 6 constitutes the Christ-believer's "transfer from the realm of sin to that of righteousness."[89] The transfer of believers from the old eon in Adam to the new eon in Christ results in a new relationship to sin.[90] Romans 6 concentrates on the subduing of sin, which is used in the singular throughout the chapter.[91] The *reign* of sin is still a prevalent theme (vv. 9, 12, 14), but now as a *former* reign to which the believer has died to (vv. 2, 6, 7) in the death of Christ (v. 3-4, 10). The transfer from the old age in Adam to the new age in Christ thus constitutes a change in masters. A believer in Christ is not under the "lordship" of sin or under the "power of" the law any longer, but under the "power of" grace (vv. 14, 15).[92] The believer died to the first "kingdom" and belongs to the second (cf. 5:21).[93]

The corporative dying to sin (v. 2) in Christ (v. 3) is therefore best understood as a salvation-historical reality, which has implications on both forensic and ethical levels.[94] The "old way of existence" is especially contrasted to the new in verses 5 to 6 where the salvation-historical divide carries eschatological significance.[95] The old ἄνθρωπος that has been crucified with

---

death of all people (Rom 5:12, 14, 15, 17; 2 Cor 5:14) and the power of sin that has been broken (Rom 5:13; 2 Cor 5:19, 21).

88. Moo, *Romans*, 352.

89. Moo, *Romans*, 351.

90. Moo, *Romans*, 352; Barrett, *Romans*, 122. Although Paul (vv. 3-4) refers to water baptism (Wright, "Romans," 533; Moo, *Romans*, 355, 359; Mounce, *Romans*, 149; Bruce, *Romans*, 140; Cranfield, *Romans*, 1:301; if anything other than water baptism is intended [e.g., metaphorical] the context is normally indicative, Ferguson, *Baptism*, 148) as enactment or portrayal (see note 207, p. 96; Wright, "Romans," 534; Mounce, *Romans*, 149; Dunn, *Romans*, 1:311; rather than representing a divine act trough baptism or a divine instrument, contra Moo, *Romans*, 634; Käsemann, *Romans*, 162-63; Cranfield, *Romans*, 1:304) of the death and resurrection of Christ and the transition from the old way of existence to the new (esp. Barrett, *Romans*, 122), baptism itself is not the main theme of the passage. Paul's reference to baptism here rather represents the conversion experience as a whole (Moo, *Romans*, 355).

91. Moo, *Romans*, 350.

92. Moo, *Romans*, 352, 358; cf. Hultgren, *Romans*, 243; Wright, "Romans," 540; Mounce, *Romans*, 162-63; Ridderbos, *Romeinen*, 125.

93. Wright, "Romans," 534.

94. Ridderbos, *Romeinen*, 125.

95. Ridderbos, *Romeinen*, 129; cf. Hultgren, *Romans*, 243; Osborne, *Romans*, 147; Moo, *Romans*, 374-75.

Christ (vv. 6-8) corresponds with similar notions elsewhere in Paul (Gal 2:20; 5:24; 6:14; cf. Eph 4:22; Col 3:9-10), and constitutes a realized eschatology where one is already alive in Christ (v. 11).[96] Both the "old person" (v. 6) and the implied "new person"[97] thus echo the contrast between the epoch in Adam and Christ or "the two contrasting ages of salvation history"[98] (cf. 5:21).

The respective reigns "under the law" (ὑπὸ νόμον, vv. 14, 15) and "under grace" (ὑπὸ χάριν, v. 15) once again constitute the old (law) and new (grace) salvation-historical (eschatological) realms or powers.[99] The law here is best understood as a system or body that exercises a binding force.[100] To be "under the law" describes a state of powerlessness outside of Christ where there is a command to do "good" but the power to fulfill it is lacking[101] (cf. 8:3). The notion to be slaves either of sin or righteousness (vv. 16-20) accentuates the change of master between the old reign of sin and the new reign of righteousness.[102]

Although the term σάρξ occurs once in Roman 6 (v. 19), it points to the lack of ability to grasp the deepest, spiritual realities,[103] and thus "simply denotes potential slowness of understanding" and not "moral disability."[104]

In terms of identity, the old eon in Adam corresponds to identity mode A (Israel according to the flesh), while the new eon in Christ corresponds to identity mode C (believers in Christ). As with 2 Corinthians 3 (see above), there seems to be universality in the identity outside of Christ. The identity of those outside of Christ is defined by sin and death, which is enhanced by the law. The identity in Christ is characterized by life, grace and freedom from the law.

---

96. Cf. Wright, "Romans," 538; Ridderbos, *Romeinen*, 131.

97. See the theme of "life" esp. in vv. 4, 8, and 13.

98. Moo, *Romans*, 374; cf. Osborne, *Romans*, 147; Dunn, *Romans*, 1:315-21. Although Barrett, *Romans*, 127, 129, recognizes the new eschatological age that is inaugurated in Christ, his emphasis is more on being "between the times." E.g., he stresses the Lutheran notion of *simul iustus et peccator*. Similarly, Dunn, *Romans*, 1:315-21, acknowledges the epoch in Adam as "life under the age prior to Christ, the old covenant" (p. 318) and Christ's death and life as "decisive eschatological events" (p. 321). Yet he states that the "new epoch of Christ does not mean an end to the old, but neither does its realization in the lives of believers await the complete end of the old" (p. 315).

99. Moo, *Romans*, 389.

100. Moo, *Romans*, 390; Schreiner, "Abolition," 54-59.

101. Ridderbos, *Romeinen*, 137.

102. Hendriksen, *Romans*, 206.

103. Ridderbos, *Romeinen*, 141.

104. Wright, "Romans," 545.

Even though both Romans 5 and 6 thus contain strong elements of *discontinuity* in terms of the identity of Israel and believers in Christ, the new eon that stands in contrast to the old in the whole of Romans 5 to 8 can also be understood as a *fulfillment* of the old and therefore in *continuity* with the old:[105] (1) The one family of Judean and gentile believers has to be understood as a fulfillment of the promises to Abraham (Rom 4). (2) The Old Testament promises pertaining to land and reign over the nations are fulfilled in Abraham's seed (believers in Christ) that inherit the whole world (4:13).

Romans 7

The main topic of Romans 7 is the Mosaic law. Paul makes two main points in this chapter. The first point is that the bondage to the law must be severed in order for people to be put into a new relationship with Christ (vv. 1–6). This gives rise to questions about the origin and nature of the law. In verses 7 to 25, which constitute the second point, Paul answers these questions by showing that the law came from God, but became the unwitting tool of sin, which confirmed and imprisoned in death. The law could neither justify nor sanctify.[106] Romans 8:3 sums up the whole point of 7:7–25: "God has done what the law, weakened by the flesh, could not do."[107] Romans 7 is not so much about the content of the law or whether the law is an expression of the will of God, as it is about the *regime* of the law. According to verses 1 to 6, a new reign has come in effect: that of πνεῦμα. Under the reign of the law, fulfillment of God's will is not possible (vv. 7–25).[108]

Although Paul's image of the "husband" that dies and enables the "wife" to remarry (vv. 2–4) is difficult to follow,[109] the main point is clear: The "marriage" to the first "husband" represents the regime under the law and its binding authority (κατέχω, v. 6).[110] The new relationship is with the resurrected Christ (v. 4), free from the reign of the law, to bear fruit (v. 4) and serve in the newness of πνεῦμα and not in the oldness of γράμμα (v. 6).

---

105. Cf. Wright, "Romans," 535.
106. Moo, *Romans*, 409.
107. NRSV; cf. Moo, *Romans*, 409.
108. Ridderbos, *Romeinen*, 143.
109. There exists an inherent difficulty to this image. The "husband" that dies seems to represent humanity, which corporately died in Christ (cf. 6:2–11). In other words, in Paul's explanation of the image in v. 4, the "you" in the first half of the image represents the husband. But there is a shift in the second half of the image, where the believer in Christ can only represent the wife (Wright, "Romans," 559).
110. Moo, *Romans*, 415; cf. Fee, *Empowering Presence*, 503; BDAG, κατέχω, §4.

The contrast between πνεῦμα and γράμμα (v. 6) echoes the same contrast of 2 Corinthians 3 (see above) where the Old and New Covenants are contrasted.[111] The New Covenant is set to take account of the problems inherent to the Old Covenant.[112] Where the Old covenant was ruled and defined by the law (γράμμα), the New Covenant is ruled and defined by πνεῦμα.[113] In the context of Romans, the πνεῦμα-γράμμα contrast evokes 2:29. As argued on pp. 54–68, πνεῦμα in 2:29 is unlikely to refer to the Holy Spirit in view of the build-up of Paul's argument, but rather refers to an *ideal* Judean who *ought to have* the ability in his or her spirit to fulfill the law, but in fact *does not have that ability* due to the corruptness of all people (3:1–20). In Christ, however, this *ideal* becomes a *reality*, but not as a possibility within the old way of existence under the law. A new existence in Spirit is needed to overcome the curse of the law, which required perfect obedience (cf. 2:13, 17–29). The way in which the ideal is realized thus surpasses the ideal person that the Old Covenant required. A whole new mode of existence and way of relating to God was required, other than being under law, sin and death. Now, through Christ's body (7:4) "we" are discharged (κατηργήθημεν, v. 6)[114] from the law and died to it (vv. 4, 6) to serve in the newness of πνεῦμα and not in the oldness of the "letter" any longer. Πνεῦμα is here (v. 6) without the article (as in 2:29), which might suggest that it denotes the human spirit. Translators and commentators are however divided between the translations of πνεῦμα here, alternating between translating it as God's Spirit[115] and the human spirit.[116]

Before deciding on an appropriate translation for πνεῦμα, one has to consider its contrast to σάρξ (v. 5), which constitutes the deeper contrast in verses 5 to 6 (which includes γράμμα, v. 6). The ὅτε ("when") in verse 5 stands in contrast to the νυνί ("now") in verse 6, and points to the contrast between two eschatological and salvation-historical realities or eons:[117]

111. Kruse, *Romans*, 296; Wright, "Romans," 560–61; Dunn, *Romans*, 1:366; cf. Bruce, *Romans*, 149–50.

112. Wright, "Romans," 560–61.

113. For Dunn, *Romans*, 1:371, Paul does not assign the law to the realm of the old epoch of sin and death "*simpliciter* as though the law was simply one with sin and death."

114. BDAG, καταργέω, §4; NRSV.

115. E.g., Osborne, *Romans*, 172; Wright, "Romans," 560; Moo, *Romans*, 410, 420; Fee, *Empowering Presence*, 503; Ridderbos, *Romeinen*, 146; ISV; NRSV; NIV.

116. E.g., Bruce, *Romans*, 54; REB; LITV; RV; DST; KJV.

117. Cf. Longenecker, *Epistle to the Romans*, 636–67; Jewett, *Romans*, 436–37; idem., *Anthropological Terms*, 145; Osborne, *Romans*, 173; Moo, *Romans*, 422; Fee, *Empowering Presence*, 504, 821; Käsemann, *Romans*, 190, 210; Cranfield, *Romans*, 1:337, 340; Schweizer, "σάρξ," *TDNT*, 7:133–35; "πνεῦμα," *TDNT*, 6:419, 424, 428; Ridderbos,

1. "Existence in the domain of the flesh," which "is determined by the three other 'powers' of the old age: sin, the law, and death."[118]

2. Existence in πνεῦμα, which stands opposed to an existence in the domain of σάρξ (which includes, law, sin and death), and is characterized by "newness."

The phrase ἐν τῇ σαρκί in verse 5 is thus an indication of a *way of existence* outside of Christ and the Spirit,[119] and points to the human existence as a "supra-individual reality to which the individual human-being-outside-of-Christ has lapsed into"[120] (cf. Gal 5:13, 17, see pp. 207–12). In Fee's words, "both the Law and the flesh belong to the past, on the pre-Christ, pre-Spirit side of eschatological realities."[121] Similarly, πνεῦμα in verse 6 denotes the new way of existence and eschatological reality in Christ where the Spirit is God's replacement of law observance.[122] The Spirit is the essential element of the New Covenant.[123] Ridderbos is therefore correct to suggest that σάρξ (v. 5, corresponding to γράμμα, v. 6) and πνεῦμα (v. 6) in this context essentially denote two separate salvation-historical categories[124] (cf. Gal 5:17). Life in the flesh thus does not belong to the believer's eschatological present.[125] Both πνεῦμα and σάρξ are therefore used in verses 5 to 6 in an *extended sense*.[126]

Romeinen, 145–47.

118. Moo, *Romans*, 419.

119. Fee, *Empowering Presence*, 510–11; Ridderbos, *Romeinen*, 145; cf. Osborne, *Romans*, 171; Guthrie, *Theology*, 172–73; Käsemann, *Romans*, 188–89; Cranfield, *Romans*, 1:337; Jewett, *Anthropological Terms*, 145; Sanday and Headlam, *Romans*, 176. While Dunn, *Romans*, 1:364, understands ἐν σαρκί and ἐν Χριστῷ as contrasting the two epochs (Adam/Christ), he understands σάρξ as "a condition or *attitude* which is in contrast to, at odds with, or *places restraints upon* the ἐν Χριστῷ" (emphasis added). Barrett, *Romans*, 137, works in this direction by stating that σάρξ here denotes "the state in which men [sic] are dominated by law, sin, and death," but argues that believers are "both in and not in the flesh."

120. Ridderbos, *Romeinen*, 145 ("Het 'zijn in het vlees' duidt deze meselijke existentie aan als een boven-individuele wekelijkheid, waaraan de individuele mens-buiten-Christus vevallen is"); cf. Schweizer, "σάρξ," *TDNT*, 7:133.

121. Fee, *Empowering Presence*, 504; cf. Sanders, *Jewish People*, 70.

122. Fee, *Empowering Presence*, 507; Käsemann, *Romans*, 210; cf. Schweizer, "πνεῦμα," *TDNT*, 6:416, 419, 425, 428.

123. Fee, *Empowering Presence*, 508.

124. Ridderbos, *Romeinen*, 146–47; cf. Moo, *Romans*, 422.

125. Fee, *Empowering Presence*, 505.

126. This *extended sense* in which both πνεῦμα and σάρξ (denoting two salvation-historical epochs) in Paul is a figurative use that pushes the boundaries of their normal range of meaning. Normally, πνεῦμα can denote things such as God's Spirit (e.g. Phil

Although the above mentioned authors understand πνεῦμα and σάρξ in terms of salvation-historical (and eschatological) categories, they still opt for translating πνεῦμα as "Spirit" (divine, see above) as opposed to "spirit" (human). This is however an inappropriate contrast. If πνεῦμα here denotes a salvation-historical *way of existence*, both God's Spirit and the human spirit are part of the definition, as Paul suggests in 8:16: "The *Spirit* Himself witnesses with our *spirit* that we are children of God."[127] The translation "spirit" thus seems more appropriate, but then not to denote the *human* spirit *per se*, but to denote a *way of existence* where the human spirit has been made alive and human existence and identity is defined by God's Spirit (see below).

The bondage that the law caused might create the impression that the law is inherently evil or against God, a line of reasoning that was indeed followed by Marcion. But in Romans 7:7-25 Paul defends the divine origin of the law (God's law, v. 22) by stating that it is inherently good (vv. 12, 17), just (v. 12) and "spiritual" (v. 14). Additionally, Paul seeks to explain how the law, although inherently good, could have such a deleterious effect.[128] Romans 7:7-25 can be divided into two sections, verses 7 to 12 and verses 14 to 25, where verse 13 forms a bridge in between.[129] In verses 7 to 12, Paul shows in the past tense how sin has utilized the law to bring death. Verses 14 to 25 describe in the present tense the constant battle between the will that agrees with God's law, and the flesh, which succumbs to the law of sin. The net result is that the law of God is impotent to break the power of sin,[130] but is necessary to drive people to Christ (see below).

One of the most important questions in understanding 7:14-25, is the identity of the "I" (ἐγώ). Does it refer to someone before or outside of Christ, or does it refer to a general struggle of a believer in Christ? Although both positions are well accounted for, it is more likely that the "I" represents the person before or outside of Christ.[131] More specifically, the "I" can be

---

1:19), the activity of God's Spirit in the community (e.g., 1 Cor 12:10), a spirit that is not from God (e.g., 1 Cor 12:10), or a part of the human personality (e.g., 1 Cor 5:3-5), which is potentially sensitive and responsive to God (L&N §26.9). Σάρξ can normally point to bodily flesh (e.g., Rom 2:28), the human body (e.g., 1 Cor 5:5), a human being (e.g., Rom 3:20), earthly descent (e.g., 2 Cor 11:18), or the outward/external side of life (e.g., Phil 3:3-4).

127. LITV, emphases added.

128. Moo, *Romans*, 423, 453.

129. Wright, "Romans," 565; Moo, *Romans*, 423-24.

130. Moo, *Romans*, 424.

131. Sanders, *Apostle's Life*, 653-55; *Jewish People*, 76; Kruse, *Romans*, 298, 305-11; Matera, *Romans*, 167; Jewett, *Romans*, 462-73; idem., *Anthropological Terms*, 147; Westerholm, *Perspectives*, 144-45; Wright, "Romans," 551-53; Moo, *Romans*, 447-49;

understood as a rhetorical device[132] that arguably points to Israel under the law from the perspective of a believer in Christ.[133] The reference to sin (vv. 8-9) evokes 5:12-14, which explained sin as "coming" into the world between Adam and Moses (the Mosaic law; cf. Gal 3:17). Paul probably rhetorically identified himself with Israel as the prophets did by using "I" in denoting Israel collectively (Jer 10:19-20; cf. Mic 7:7-10).[134]

Among others, the best arguments for viewing 7:14-25 as denoting the person before or outside of Christ are probably the following: (1) The strong connection of the "I" with the "flesh" (vv. 14, 18, 25) suggests that Paul has the unregenerate person or the person in Adam in mind (v. 5, see above).[135] (2) The questions Paul asks have to do with the law and thus with life under the law, and not with life in Christ, which is decisive for Fee.[136] (3) Romans 8:5-8 corresponds with 7:5-6 in terms of its contrast between two salvation-historical epochs and stands in contrast with 7:7-25, which might be understood as something of a digression. There is no hint in Romans 8:5-8 of an internal struggle[137] (see pp. 199-206). (4) The language of 7:7-25 describes the unregenerate existence that stands in contrast to the existence in Christ. The statement "I am of the flesh, sold into slavery under sin" (v. 14b)[138] can be contrasted to 6:2, 6, 11, and 18-22, where the release from the power of sin is described, and especially to Romans 8:9, which explicitly states that "you are not in flesh, but in spirit" (see pp. 199-206). To be a "prisoner of the law of sin" (v. 23) stands in contrast with 8:2, which

---

Fee, *Empowering Presence*, 511-15; Lambrecht, *Wretched*, 90, 136; Guthrie, *Theology*, 173-74; Beker, *Paul the Apostle*, 105-6, 216-17; Käsemann, *Romans*, 199-212; *Perspectives*, 443; Schweizer, "σάρξ," *TDNT*, 7:133; Ridderbos, *Paulus*, 132-39; idem., *Romeinen*, 154; Kümmel, *Römer 7* (see Moo, *Romans*, 446; Guthrie, *Theology*, 173; and Beker, *Paul the Apostle*, 388, for more references to proponents of this view); contra Hultgren, *Romans*, 285-92; Osborne, *Romans*, 173-91; Dunn, *Romans*, 1:357-413; Cranfield, *Romans*, 1:340-71.

132. Paul uses the first person impersonally in 3:7 (cf. 1 Cor 11:31-32; 13:1-3; 14:11; Gal 2:18), but this use is not frequent in Paul (Moo, *Romans*, 427). Yet various sources have been identified where "I" is used rhetorically and impersonally outside of Paul (see Lyons, *Pauline Autobiography*; Kümmel, *Römer 7*).

133. Wright, "Romans," 553, 558, 565; Lambrecht, *Wretched*, 84-85; cf. Kruse, *Romans*, 298.

134. Cf. Lambrecht, *Wretched*, 84-85. Moo, *Romans*, 427-31, argues that autobiographical elements has to be retained in Rom 7, and understands the "I" as Paul "in solidarity with Israel."

135. Moo, *Romans*, 445.

136. Fee, *Empowering Presence*, 511-14, explains that the implicit questions that Paul asks in v. 13 are: (a) Is the law sinful? (b) Was the law responsible for "my" death?

137. Fee, *Empowering Presence*, 514-15.

138. NRSV.

depicts believers as being free from the law of sin and death. Although believers continue to sin (e.g., 6:12-13; 13:12-14), 7:14-25 do not describe a struggle with sin, but a defeat by sin. The "I" struggles with the need to obey the Mosaic law, but Paul has declared a release from the dictates of the law (6:14; 7:4-6).[139] (5) Matera points to the problematic nature of reconciling Paul's statement in verse 9 to the autobiographical interpretation. How could there have been a time when "I" (Paul) lived apart from the law, since Paul was circumcised on the eighth day? This time Paul is referring to, fits better within a salvation-historical context when the law "came"[140] (ἐλθούσης, v. 9; cf. 5:12-14; Gal 3:17).

As argued on pp. 141-42, Paul's autobiographical account in Philippians 3 is different from what is portrayed in Romans 7. Paul's reference to being blameless in terms of the righteousness of the law (Phil 3:6) does not denote a general condition of Israel under the law from the perspective of the Christ-believer (as in Rom 7), but Paul's own achievements from a Pharisaic perspective. It has to do with outward, visible aspects of the law and not with the desire to do God's will in terms of the inmost being (7:15-23, 25).[141]

Although the tense is changed from past in 7:7-12 to present in 7:14-25, the change in tense alone cannot account for a change of topic.[142] The question about the law in verse 13a pertains to the preceding salvation-historical exposition of the law that was given to Israel, which in turn made sin to have revived (ἀναζάω, v. 9).[143] Verse 9a thus describes the time of Adam before the Mosaic law.[144] The law that was intended to give life (v. 10), which is inherently holy, just and good (vv. 12, 13a), corresponds with verse 14: "for we know that the law is spiritual."[145] Verses 14 to 25 can therefore be understood as an elaboration of the way in which the law functions with respect to enhancing sin, in spite of an understanding of the law as good or the intention to observe the law.

The contrast between πνευματικός and σάρκινος in verse 14 cannot have the same significance as the πνεῦμα-σάρξ contrast in verses 5 to 6.

---

139. Moo, *Romans*, 445; cf. Westerholm, *Perspectives*, 143; Wright, "Romans," 551-53.

140. Matera, *Romans*, 166.

141. Cf. Wright, "Romans," 552-53; Moo, *Romans*, 456.

142. Cf. Wright, "Romans," 565; Käsemann, *Romans*, 199.

143. NRSV.

144. Wright, "Romans," 563.

145. Cf. Wright, "Romans," 566.

Here in verse 14, πνευματικός probably indicates the law's divine origin.[146] It corresponds with the notions that the law is good (vv. 12, 17) and just (v. 12), and that it is God's law (v. 22). The use of πνευματικός here is similar to that of 1 Corinthians 10:3-4, where Paul describes the "spiritual" food and drink of the Israelites as given by God.[147] The πνευματικός-σάρκινος contrast can also be compared to the πνεῦμα-σάρξ contrast of Romans 2:29, where both aspects are characteristic of an existence before or outside Christ. Although the law is good and "spiritual," it remains an *ideal* to fulfill the law (see pp. 54-68). The term σάρκινος (7:14) probably describes a person's "cosmic fallenness to the world"[148] or his or her opposition to God.[149] Although the term σάρκινος in itself can be assigned to the regenerate (e.g., 1 Cor 3:1-3), an existence described as "of the flesh, sold into slavery under sin" (v. 14)[150] can only point to the person outside of Christ,[151] especially when it is compared to verse 5 (see above). The designation πνευματικός, which defines the law and not the "I," therefore stands independent of the way of existence in the flesh.

Verses 15 to 20 primarily portray the conflict between "willing" (θέλω, 7 times) and "doing" (ποιέω; κατεργάζομαι; πράσσω).[152] This conflict leads to defeat (v. 23) and despair (v. 24), a conflict that is akin to someone under the Mosaic law. The perspective on this conflict is, however, retrospective from Paul's position in Christ.[153] It is interesting that Paul's description of the unregenerate person in verse 15 is similar to others found in the ancient world,[154] which strengthens the notion that Paul here has the unregenerate person in mind. In the clause, "sin that dwells in

---

146. BDAG, πνευματικός, §2αβ; Moo, *Romans*, 453; Fee, *Empowering Presence*, 510; Cranfield, *Romans*, 1:355; Ridderbos, *Romeinen*, 155.

147. Moo, *Romans*, 453; Sanday and Headlam, *Romans*, 181.

148. Käsemann, *Romans*, 199; cf. Schweizer, "σάρξ," *TDNT*, 7:144.

149. Jewett, *Romans*, 461. Rather than understanding the term as denoting human weakness or frailty as in 1 Cor 3:1-3 (contra Moo, *Romans*, 453-54).

150. NRSV.

151. Wright, "Romans," 552; Moo, *Romans*, 454; Schweizer, "σάρξ," *TDNT*, 7:144; Ridderbos, *Romeinen*, 154; contra Cranfield, *Romans*, 1:356-57. Although Dunn, *Romans*, 1:388, recognizes the expression's ("of the flesh, sold into slavery under sin") allusion to the old epoch in Adam, he understands it as the believer's *current* "belongingness to the epoch of Adam."

152. The desire to "do" what the law dictates once again accounts for an understanding of the law that is more than marking off identity (cf. 2:13, 23-25).

153. Wright, "Romans," 571; Moo, *Romans*, 455-56.

154. E.g., Ovid's *Metamorphoses* 7:21: "I see and approve the better course, but I follow the worse"; Epictetus, *Diatr.* 2.26.4 (see Moo, *Romans*, 457; Käsemann, *Romans*, 200).

me" (v. 17), sin seems to be personified as a reigning authority in the life of someone outside of Christ.[155] In verse 18, σάρξ probably carries a simple material meaning, denoting physical human existence.[156] An element of anthropological dualism thus has to be acknowledged in Paul's view of the human being. It is not so much the "flesh" that is inherently evil as it is the material body that is particularly susceptible to sin.[157] This contrast is probably deliberate to show the "dividedness" of the Judean existence under the law "as a way of explaining how sincere respect for that law could be combined with failure to perform it."[158] There is thus always a dichotomy in the existence of the unregenerate between the will to do good and the ability to perform it. The will remains under the power of sin.[159] It is noteworthy that both the "I" (denoting primarily Israel under the law) and the law itself is being exonerated in a sense (vv. 15-20). The blame essentially rests on sin (vv. 17b, 20b). Although serious charges are laid against Israel (esp. 9:32-33; 10:21) the problem is not to be an Israelite in itself,[160] but rather that their identity has been defined by law, sin and death, which would include even inner, elect Israel.

The law in verse 21 is best understood as a "principle" rather than denoting the Mosaic law.[161] The "law" underlines the dichotomy between the "willing" and the "doing" of verses 15-20 as an ever present principle in the life of the person outside of Christ. In verse 22, the law is qualified as "the law of God," which denotes the Mosaic law.[162] Although the "inner person" (ἔσω ἄνθρωπον, v. 22) elsewhere describes the anthropology of a believer in Christ (2 Cor 4:16; Eph 3:16) the phrase is not a technical description of a Christ-believer,[163] and corresponds to a similar notion in verse 18.[164]

155. Cf. Wright, "Romans," 588; Moo, *Romans*, 458.
156. Cf. BDAG, σάρξ, §2ca; Moo, *Romans*, 459.
157. Moo, *Romans*, 459; cf. Cottrell, *Romans*; Boyarin, *Radical Jew*, 83.
158. Moo, *Romans*, 459; cf. Ridderbos, *Romeinen*, 169.
159. Cf. Moo, *Romans*, 459.
160. Wright, "Romans," 567-68.
161. Hultgren, *Romans*, 290; Moo, *Romans*, 460; Hendriksen, *Romans*, 234; Cranfield, *Romans*, 1:361-62; Ridderbos, *Romeinen*, 158; Sanday and Headlam, *Romans*, 182; cf. Käsemann, *Romans*, 205; contra Dunn, *Romans*, 1:392. The accusative τὸν νόμον is more naturally taken as the direct object of εὑρίσκω. The ὅτι introduces the content of τὸν νόμον and thus rules out the possibility of pointing to the Mosaic law. Additionally, the qualification "the law of God" (v. 22) suggests that this νόμος is distinguished from the previous one (Moo, *Romans*, 460).
162. Wright, "Romans," 570; Moo, *Romans*, 461.
163. In the Greek literature, this phrase was used to denote the "Godward" or immortal side of a human being (Jeremias, "ἄνθρωπος," *TDNT*, 1:365).
164. Moo, *Romans*, 462; cf. Ridderbos, *Romeinen*, 158.

In verse 23, the "other law" (ἕτερον νόμον) has to point to a "law" other than the Mosaic law. The alternative view (to understand it as the Mosaic law) would make the chief protagonists in verses 22 to 25 both God's law. This cannot be, for it is not the law that is "in the flesh," but sin (v. 18).[165] The "other law" rather refers to an authority or demand that is like, but opposed to the Mosaic law. It is best to take the "law of God" and the "law of my mind" as corresponding, and the "law of sin" as corresponding to "another law."[166]

The cry for deliverance from "the body of this death" (v. 24) echoes the notion of death in verses 9 and 10, which is the result of an existence that is "fleshly, sold under sin," outside of Christ (v. 14b).[167] Verse 25a already anticipates the solution to an existence under the law and sin, which is God's work in Christ. But it does not mark the beginning of Paul's discussion of the life in Christ just yet,[168] for verse 25b summarizes and recapitulates the "dividedness" of the "I" that Paul has put forth in verses 15 to 23: between the will to do God's law against the "flesh" that serves the "law of sin."[169] Σάρξ here (v. 25) rather has a material than an ethical meaning.[170] The whole of Romans 7 accentuates the fact that the Mosaic law cannot deliver anyone from the power of sin.[171] But although the Mosaic law could not in itself break the power of sin, the inherent virtue and purpose of the law is in fact vindicated in two ways: (1) It caused people to "die" in their own striving to do good and to realize "the body of this death" (v. 24) and their inability to do God's will, because of their existence in the flesh (v. 5). This "death" corresponds in a sense to the notion of the death of all people with Christ in his death (2 Cor 5:15; cf. Rom 5:15; 6:2-6). (2) The "death" of the "I," the complete self,[172] facilitated by the law is necessary in order to drive people to Christ who is the only One who can deliver (ῥύομαι, v. 24) them from their wretched situation and by implication save them "from themselves" (cf. Gal 2:20).[173]

---

165. Moo, *Romans*, 463; cf. Fee, *Empowering Presence*, 512; Ridderbos, *Romeinen*, 159.

166. Moo, *Romans*, 464; Cranfield, *Romans*, 1:364; Ridderbos, *Romeinen*, 159.

167. Cf. Moo, *Romans*, 465; Ridderbos, *Romeinen*, 154, 160, 162. In this interpretation, σῶμα is understood as metaphorical (cf. Nash, *Christianity*, 60).

168. Wright, "Romans," 571; Moo, *Romans*, 466-67.

169. Moo, *Romans*, 467; Fee, *Empowering Presence*, 521.

170. Moo, *Romans*, 467.

171. Moo, *Romans*, 467.

172. Cf. Witherington and Hyatt, *Romans*, 212.

173. Käsemann, *Romans*, 209, summarizes the "heart of Paul's teaching" in Rom 7 in terms of the limits that a "religious person" encounters after the fall (cf. Barrett,

It has to be noted here that although Paul primarily has Israel under the law in mind in Romans 7, one has to take the universal dimension of the law, sin and death into account.[174] Even though gentiles did not receive the Mosaic law as such, it remains the only standard of God for all humanity prior to the coming of Christ.[175] Since gentiles "are a law to themselves" (2:14–15), and since sin (3:10–24) and death have affected all of humanity in Adam (5:12–21), gentiles outside of Christ are in principle included in an existence that can be described as "the body of this death" (7:24). The scenario of Romans 7 (esp. vv. 7–25) can thus be applied to *all of unregenerate humanity* that would want to do God's will but cannot because of being under the law and being in a flesh-existence.[176] In other words, for someone *outside* of Christ, although living subsequent to Christ's death and resurrection, that person still lives in the old eon in the flesh. In terms of eschatology, one thus has to acknowledge the fact that even believers live "between the times."[177] Although the old eon constituted by an existence in the flesh has come to an end in Christ's death and resurrection, and becomes effective for those who are in Christ, the complete eradication of the old existence *for all of humanity* will only be realized at the parousia.

In the same line of thinking, there might be an even deeper perspective or layer to the understanding of Romans 7. Schreiner, while acknowledging the strength of the arguments of both the views that understand Romans 7:7–25 as denoting those in Christ and those outside of Christ, argues that Paul's purpose is "to communicate the inability of the law to transform human beings." For Schreiner, this scenario would include both unbelievers and believers in so far as they would rely on "their own capacities for moral transformation."[178] The implication of Schreiner's view

---

Romans, 138). Although the religious person agrees with God's will and delights in it, as long as salvation is strived for by obeying the commandments, that person becomes entangled in their own desire for life "which tries to snatch what can only be given" (Käsemann, *Romans*, 209).

174. Cf. Westerholm, *Perspectives*, 144–45; Dunn, *Romans*, 1:383; Käsemann, *Romans*, 195, 201, 205; Cranfield, *Romans*, 1:341.

175. Although it might be objected that it is unlikely that a gentile living before Christ might "delight in the law"; if one considers (1) the fact that Paul is largely defending the Mosaic law as such in Rom 7 as inherently good rather than accounting for many that do not obey it, and (2) that Paul who was born an Israelite looks at the law from the perspective of the new identity in Christ, the only reality that could define people's status and relation to God before Christ, regardless of ethnicity, can only be the Mosaic law (cf. Westerholm, *Perspectives*, 145).

176. Cf. Fee, *Empowering Presence*, 820; Ridderbos, *Romeinen*, 167.

177. Fee, *Empowering Presence*, 820–22.

178. Schreiner, *Paul*, 266–67.

would be the inverse of the view that I have argued for: that someone *in* Christ would be (or ought to be) *outside* of seeking transformation or deliverance through the law.

Romans 8:1–16

Romans 8:1 marks the beginning of Paul's response to the wretched (ταλαίπωρος, 7:24) existence before or outside of Christ as portrayed in 7:7–25. The νῦν (v. 1) is clearly temporal and not logical if Paul's use of the term elsewhere is taken into account (5:9, 11; 6:19, 21; 11:30, 31) and if the context is considered[179] (see above). The νῦν denotes the new era of salvation history inaugurated by Christ's death and resurrection (3:21; 5:9; 6:19, 22; 7:6).[180] The term κατάκριμα (v. 1) only occurs elsewhere in 5:16 and 18 in the New Testament and thus binds 8:1 to 5:12–21, where the reality and finality of life in Christ is depicted as the product of righteousness.[181] A measure of finality in Christ is constituted by the fact that God has already condemned[182] or punished (κατακρίνω, v. 3)[183] sin in Christ. To be free from condemnation thus bears eschatological significance.[184]

Verses 2 to 4 sketch the solution to the dilemma of the split "I" in 7:7–15. It is the work of Christ that is mediated by the Spirit that frees the "I" from "the law of sin and death." Romans 8 serves to reiterate and expand on the Christ-believer's eschatological life.[185] Some understand νόμος in verse 2 to refer to the Mosaic law in both occurrences, in that it would have a dual (paradoxical) role. This would imply that the Spirit puts the Mosaic law in its proper focus[186] or that it facilitates a correct understanding of the law.[187] But this line of interpretation is unlikely, since Paul often arranges the law on the opposite side of πνεῦμα (7:6; Gal 3:2, 5; 5:18), and Paul nowhere else envisions a new empowering of the Mosaic law. The "law of the Spirit" rather refers to the "law written on the heart" (Jer 38:31–34, LXX) or the "law" of the New Covenant (Ezek 36:24–32), which is closely

---

179. Fee, *Empowering Presence*, 521.
180. Moo, *Romans*, 472; cf. Barrett, *Romans*, 154.
181. Moo, *Romans*, 469.
182. Wright, "Romans," 575–76.
183. BDAG, κατακρίνω; Bruce, *Romans*, 161; cf. Mounce, *Romans*, 175.
184. Wright, "Romans," 575–76.
185. Moo, *Romans*, 469–70.
186. Wright, "Romans," 577.
187. Dunn, *Romans*, 1:416–18.

related to the Spirit[188] (cf. Ezek 37; 2 Cor 3:6-9). The "law of sin and death" could denote the Mosaic law, a description that can be deducted from 7:7-25 and 1 Corinthians 15:56. Although the law was not in itself sinful, it became an instrument of sin and death. But although this interpretation fits the context, it is not preferable. Νόμος here rather denotes a binding authority or power, for a similar expression ("the law of sin") denotes the "other law" in distinction from the Mosaic law in 7:23.[189] The phrase "law of sin and death" is specifically chosen by Paul, for it summarizes the total situation of the sinner.[190]

The "law of the Spirit of life in Christ Jesus" has done what the Mosaic law could not do because it was weakened by the flesh (v. 3). God condemned sin that exists in the flesh by sending His Son in the likeness[191] of "sinful flesh" (v. 3).[192] Σάρξ here denotes the human condition and human weakness and as such shows that Christ exposed himself to the power of sin.[193] Fee correctly argues that Christ has rendered the law obsolete and fulfilled the very purpose for which the law existed but was unable to accomplish: to provide righteousness[194] (δικαίωμα, v. 4; cf. 3:21; 4:13), which includes a right standing with God. Through the work of the Spirit, God has brought "the time of the Law to an end."[195] Matera and Moo argue for viewing τὸ δικαίωμα τοῦ νόμου πληρωθῇ (v. 4) as God's dealing with the demands of the law by the perfect obedience of Christ.[196] Christ was perfectly obedient to the law (cf. 2:13; 3:26) and has made many righteous by his obedience (cf. 5:19). Christ thus fulfilled the law through his work "by"

188. Moo, *Romans*, 475; cf. Fee, *Empowering Presence*, 521-27.

189. Matera, *Romans*, 191; Moo, *Romans*, 476; cf. Fee, *Empowering Presence*, 522.

190. Moo, *Romans*, 477.

191. Christ participated in this realm, but did not become imprisoned "in the flesh" (Moo, *Romans*, 480; cf. Cranfield, *Romans*, 1:381).

192. "Sinful flesh" probably refers to sinful humanity (Hultgren, *Romans*, 299; Matera, *Romans*, 192; cf. BDAG, σάρξ, §4).

193. Moo, *Romans*, 479-80.

194. Fee, *Empowering Presence*, 530; KJV; cf. Wright, "Romans," 580; Bruce, *Romans*, 147-48; Barrett, *Romans*, 157.

195. Fee, *Empowering Presence*, 530.

196. Matera, *Romans*, 193; Moo, *Romans*, 482-85. Although several renderings of τὸ δικαίωμα τοῦ νόμου is possible (e.g., "just decree," "righteousness"), the generality of Paul's language probably requires a general definition: "the right requirement of the law" (BDAG, δικαίωμα, §1; Moo, *Romans*, 481-82; Bruce, *Romans*, 163; Ridderbos, *Romeinen*, 173). Moo, *Romans*, 484, understands the "just requirement" of the law as a satisfaction of God's eternal moral demands and not in the sense that the specific demands of the Mosaic law must be met. The "just requirement" of the law thus has to be understood in a broad sense, which makes it applicable to all people.

(descriptive, not instrumental) those not walking κατὰ σάρκα but κατὰ πνεῦμα (v.4). Christ has both "done the law" and signifies the end of the law to bring about righteousness in those who believe (cf. 10:4).

Whichever understanding of δικαίωμα τοῦ νόμου (v. 4) one chooses (righteousness, just requirement of the law, or both), verses 2 to 4 essentially portray an eschatological realm transfer between two realms of salvation history, where the realm before or outside of Christ under the law is described by the expression κατὰ σάρκα (v. 4) and the realm in Christ[197] is described by κατὰ πνεῦμα (v. 4).[198] Σάρξ and πνεῦμα in this context can therefore not be understood as anthropological categories or even impulses or powers within a person. To walk "according to" the flesh is essentially to exist outside of Christ[199] where one's life is directed by this world.[200] In other words, σάρξ in opposition to πνεῦμα does not describe some kind of internal warfare in the life of the believer, but depict "two mutually exclusive ways of life"[201] or ways of existence.[202] The eon of πνεῦμα has replaced the eon under the law, and did not merely bring a better understanding of the law.[203] This does not mean that the believer does not struggle with sin or commit sin, but it means that the struggle is essentially in the realm of the mind and in terms of how the believer aligns himself or herself in accordance with their new found identity in Christ (cf. 12:1-2). Believers have to reckon themselves dead to sin (6:11) by putting to death the deeds of the body by the Spirit (8:13).[204]

In verses 5 to 7, Paul describes to believers what characterizes an existence κατὰ σάρκα and κατὰ πνεῦμα respectively. Those who exist κατὰ σάρκα (outside of Christ) set their minds on the things of the "flesh," and those who exist κατὰ πνεῦμα (in Christ) set their minds on the things of

---

197. Käsemann, *Romans*, 221-22, shows the close connection between ἐν πνεύματι (8:9) and ἐν Χριστῷ (8:1, 2), which he regards as interchangeable (cf. the smooth transitions from ἐν πνεύματι [v. 9a] to πνεῦμα Χριστοῦ [v. 9c], to Χριστὸς ἐν ὑμῖν [v. 10a]).

198. Jewett, *Romans*, 486; Moo, *Romans*, 477, 478, 485; cf. Wright, "Romans," 581; Fee, *Empowering Presence*, 537; Bruce, *Heart Set Free*, 203; Käsemann, *Romans*, 212-13, 219-20; Dodd, *Romans*, 133-34. Although Dunn, *Romans*, 1:424-25, understands the πνεῦμα-σάρξ dichotomy as a contrast between two epochs, he understands them "not as mutually exclusive conditions," but as "opposed alternatives" and thus in the context of exhortation to believers.

199. Cf. Jewett, *Romans*, 486; Fee, *Empowering Presence*, 537.

200. Moo, *Romans*, 485.

201. Fee, *Empowering Presence*, 537.

202. Jewett, *Romans*, 486; Ridderbos, *Romeinen*, 174.

203. Käsemann, *Romans*, 216; cf. Moo, *Romans*, 475; Fee, *Empowering Presence*, 507; contra Dunn, *Romans*, 1:417.

204. Fee, *Empowering Presence*, 537-38; cf. Wright, "Romans," 582.

the "Spirit" (v. 5).²⁰⁵ Death and life are juxtaposed to each other as mutually exclusive characteristics of an existence κατὰ σάρκα and κατὰ πνεῦμα respectively (v. 6). The "mind of the flesh" is enmity against God in that an existence in the flesh is under the law, cannot submit to the law (v. 7), and cannot please God (v. 8).

Verse 9 reiterates the mutual exclusivity of these two ways of existence, which is essentially that of a believer and unbeliever:²⁰⁶ "you [believers] are not ἐν σαρκί, but ἐν πνεύματι since the Spirit of God dwells in you." Moo correctly notes that ἐν σαρκί and ἐν πνεύματι denote "the old age of sin and death" and "the new age of righteousness and life" respectively.²⁰⁷ Paul indeed pictures "two ages or realms" and the believer's transfer into the new age of life and peace. But when Moo translates the first two occurrences of πνεῦμα (v. 9) both as God's Spirit and explains this translation as metaphorical language,²⁰⁸ he seems to miss the qualification Paul makes in this sentence. The expression ἐν πνεύματι clearly describes the existence of the believer in Christ as opposed to an existence ἐν σαρκί, which is the existence of someone outside of Christ.²⁰⁹ The notion in the first sentence of verse 9 is rather that Paul qualifies the existence ἐν πνεύματι by the indwelling of the Spirit *of God* (εἴπερ²¹⁰ πνεῦμα θεοῦ οἰκεῖ ἐν ὑμῖν). As in Romans 7:6 (see above) it would be more appropriate to translate ἐν πνεύματι (v. 9a) as "in spirit,"²¹¹ but not to denote the human spirit *per se*, but to denote the *new existence*²¹² where "being spiritual" is defined or characterized by the indwelling of God's Spirit. Paul's intention with the expression ἐν πνεύματι is arguably that he wants to incorporate both the human spirit and God's Spirit into this expression and leaves a measure of ambiguity within the expression on purpose. This is exactly the reason why I have left κατὰ πνεῦμα in verses 4 to 5 untranslated until now. Since κατὰ πνεῦμα in both verses 4 and 5 can be understood as describing a *way of existence* in the new eschatological age in Christ, it can be translated as "according to spirit" with a similar meaning to the one suggested for ἐν πνεύματι in verse 9a.

---

205. Cf. Moo, *Romans*, 486; Fee, *Empowering Presence*, 540–41.
206. Cf. Fee, *Empowering Presence*, 547.
207. Moo, *Romans*, 489–90.
208. Moo, *Romans*, 490.
209. Cf. Käsemann, *Romans*, 222–23.
210. "[I]f indeed, if after all" (BDAG, εἰ, §6l).
211. REB; Sanday and Headlam, *Romans*, 196.
212. Cf. Wright, "Romans," 583, who comes close to this understanding by describing ἐν πνεύματι as a "state" rather than having precise locative force.

One has to acknowledge a certain fluidity in Paul's language. He seems to stretch the inherent meaning of terms such as πνεῦμα and σάρξ to cover new ground.[213] In Wright's words, Paul "is carving out language to say what had not been said before."[214] Similarly, Paul's rhetorical play on words with νόμος (7:21, 23; 8:2)[215] stretches the meaning of the term beyond its normal use. Paul indeed seems to use language to say more than the words he uses would normally permit.

With Paul's seamless, trinitarian move from "God's Spirit" to "the Spirit of Christ" (v. 9b), Paul's high Christology is evident.[216] The absence of Christ's Spirit in someone's life shows that that person does not belong to God (v. 9b). This statement has profound implications for the identity in Christ (identity mode C). Believers in Christ receive their new way of existence[217] or new identity through their belonging to Christ. The indwelling of the Spirit is indeed the *identity marker* for the Christ-believer.[218] Similarly, from the perspective of belief in Christ, "flesh" as a way of existence outside of Christ (esp. ἐν τῇ σαρκί in 7:5; κατὰ σάρκα in 8:4, 5; ἐν σαρκί in 8:8–9) is characterized by natural impulses and physical performance,[219] and is defined by law, sin and death (8:2). "Flesh" can thus be understood as characterizing or *marking off the identity* of someone outside of Christ.[220]

The body that is dead (v. 10) seems to have an anthropological bearing[221] in that the body must be considered dead because of sin and is destined for death.[222] This understanding is strengthened by verse 11, which confirms the resurrection of the physical body. Within the anthropological vein, πνεῦμα, which is "life" (v. 10), therefore seems to be best understood as

---

213. Cf. note 126, p. 192.

214. Wright, "Romans," 583.

215. Fee, *Empowering Presence*, 522; cf. Käsemann, *Romans*, 209.

216. Fee, *Empowering Presence*, 547–48; cf. Moo, *Romans*, 491.

217. Ridderbos, *Romeinen*, 176.

218. Fee, *People of God*, 88; idem., *Empowering Presence*, 469–70, 553; cf. Hansen, *Philippians*, 221, on Gal 3:2.

219. Cf. the will to do good and the attempt to put this will into practice, but the inability to execute what is willed (7:15–20).

220. Cf. Fee, *Empowering Presence*, 553–54.

221. Jewett, *Romans*, 491; Moo, *Romans*, 492.

222. Fee, *Empowering Presence*, 550.

the human spirit,[223] which is [being made] alive[224] by the life-giving Spirit of God,[225] constituting a present reality.[226] The notion would be that the human spirit is transferred from the domain of death to the domain of life by the righteousness brought about by the indwelling of Christ's Spirit (cf. v. 11). If understood in this way, the eschatological, salvation-historical overtones of the two ways of existence (old and new) ring at the background. Similar to verse 9a, the qualified "Spirit of Him who raised Jesus from the dead" who dwells within the believer (v. 11), seems to differentiate the "Spirit" (v. 11 [x2]) from the "spirit" (v. 10).

Believers are debtors, not τῇ σαρκί (v. 12a), to live κατὰ σάρκα (v. 12b, 13a). Σάρξ again refers to the "old situation,"[227] the former sphere of existence of the unbeliever.[228] Paul's point is that believers are now "Spirit people" and not in the realm of flesh any longer and therefore ought to live accordingly. There is no hint of an inward struggle between two conflicting natural inclinations[229] or natures[230] within the believer. Paul rather grounds the imperative in the indicative of the gift of righteousness (v. 10).[231] The believer should put to death the deeds of the "body" in order to live (v. 13b). Here, σῶμα is used in an extended sense as an equivalent to σάρξ,[232] and denotes the "human way of existence" that is under the rule of sin.[233] The "mortification" (θανατόω, v. 13) of the works of the old human existence once again neither indicates an internal struggle nor triumphalism, but the renewal of the mind.[234] As "Spirit

---

223. Cottrell, *Romans*; Mounce, *Romans*, 172, 179; Fitzmyer, *Romans*, 491; Bruce, *Romans*, 165; Dodd, *Romans*, 138; Sanday and Headlam, *Romans*, 198; cf. NLT; AMP; NIV; RSV; NEB; OAT; ASV; DST. Moo, *Romans*, 492, argues against translating πνεῦμα as "spirit" for it would require changing ζωή (noun) to an adjective and adding "your" to the sentence. The latter is not necessary however (e.g., OAT; DST: "the spirit," [all translations of this source are my own]). In terms of changing ζωή into an adjective, Paul's compact and yet flexible language makes provision for such a rendering, especially in view of the fact that he does not supply a verb here. Even so, some ambiguity in Paul's use of πνεῦμα arguably remains.

224. NIV; RSV.

225. Bruce, *Romans*, 165.

226. Bultmann, *Theology*, 247; cf. Cranfield, *Romans*, 1:390.

227. Ridderbos, *Romeinen*, 179.

228. Fee, *Empowering Presence*, 557; cf. Moo, *Romans*, 494; contra Dunn, *Romans*, 1:448.

229. Contra NJB.

230. Fee, *Empowering Presence*, 556; contra NIV; NAT; Mounce, *Romans*, 178, 181.

231. Fee, *Empowering Presence*, 556.

232. Moo, *Romans*, 495.

233. Ridderbos, *Romeinen*, 179.

234. Fee, *Empowering Presence*, 559; cf. Barrett, *Romans*, 162.

people" believers have to learn not to heed to old habits but to rely on the empowering Spirit. By "the Spirit's help they are to 'become what they are.'"²³⁵ What they are is spelled out in verses 14 to 17.²³⁶

Verse 14 provides the new description of the "state of salvation"²³⁷ that has been granted to the church: that of being a child (lit. "son") of God. To be "led" (ἄγω, v. 14) by the Spirit does not so much describe personal, everyday "guidance" of the Spirit as it denotes the *identity*²³⁸ of those under the New Covenant, which stands opposed to a "Spirit of slavery" (πνεῦμα δουλείας, v. 15) but closely corresponds with the "Spirit of adoption" (πνεῦμα υἱοθεσίας, v. 15).²³⁹ The "Spirit alone identifies the people of God in the new covenant."²⁴⁰ In other words, being "led" by God's Spirit is a "distinguishing sign" of being God's child.²⁴¹ The expression "son of God" (singular) is often used in the Old Testament to identify Israel as God's own people (e.g., Exod 4:22; Jer 3:19; 31:9; Hos 11:1). Although less often, the expression "sons of God" (plural) is used similarly (e.g., Deut 14:1; Isa 43:6; Hos 2:1, LXX), which makes it likely that Paul borrowed the expression υἱοὶ θεοῦ from the Old Testament.²⁴² The cry to God: Αββα ὁ πατήρ (v. 15), underlines the close, personal relationship to God as child of God.²⁴³ Paul uses τέκνον (vv. 16, 17, 21; cf. Gal 4:28; Phil 2:15) and υἱός (vv. 14, 19; cf. 9:26; Gal 3:7, 26; 4:6, 7) in almost the same way to denote the people of God in the New Covenant.²⁴⁴

Verse 16 states the relationship between God's Spirit and the human spirit with respect to being God's children most unambiguously: "The *Spirit*

---

235. Fee, *Empowering Presence*, 559; cf. Moo, *Romans*, 496.

236. Fee, *Empowering Presence*, 559.

237. Ridderbos, *Romeinen*, 180 (all translations of this resource are my own).

238. This notion resembles the OT usage of "being led." E.g., the "leading" of God in paths of righteousness for the sake of God's name in Ps 23:3 shows evidence that they are children of God (Fee, *Empowering Presence*, 563).

239. Fee, *Empowering Presence*, 563–64. Paul's rhetorical style is best understood when πνεῦμα in both instances in v. 15 is translated with "Spirit." Understood in this way, the Spirit, which believers received, does not cause them to return to slavery, but rather issued in the adoption as children (Fee, *Empowering Presence*, 565–66; cf. GNB; NAT; DST). The verb λαμβάνω, which functions as verb for both occurrences of πνεῦμα, makes it likely that Paul contrasts two possible understandings of the function or character of the received Spirit.

240. Fee, *Empowering Presence*, 564.

241. Moo, *Romans*, 499.

242. Moo, *Romans*, 449.

243. Cf. Moo, *Romans*, 502–3.

244. Cf. Moo, *Romans*, 504; Bruce, *Romans*, 168.

Himself witnesses with our *spirit*[245] that we are children of God."[246] Here Paul clarifies much of the inherent ambiguity between God's Spirit and the human spirit inherent to his use of the term πνεῦμα, especially in Romans 8:1–15.[247] This close relationship between the human spirit and God's Spirit explains much of the understanding of πνεῦμα *in opposition to* σάρξ in Paul as pertaining to *both* God's Spirit and the human spirit (e.g., 7:6; 8:4, 5, 9a; cf. 2 Cor 3:6). Although Fee admits to this exact same ambiguity in other Pauline passages (e.g., 1 Cor 6:17; 14:14–15),[248] this ambiguity is probably more prevalent in Pauline thinking than often acknowledged, especially if full strength is given to the eschatological, salvation-historical understanding of both πνεῦμα and σάρξ. In the latter understanding of πνεῦμα, the focus is more on the *way of existence* and ultimately the *mode of identity* in the new eon in Christ, where the Spirit witnesses with the human spirit that they are children of God (v. 16), than on either God's Spirit or the human spirit *per se* (see above). Conversely, in the extended understanding of σάρξ as understood from an eschatological perspective, the focus is more on the objective *way of existence* and *mode of identity* before or outside of Christ than on the "humanness" or even the "weakness" of the individual human being.

Galatians 5:16–25

Paul starts Galatians 5:1 by emphasizing the *discontinuity* of the believer with the law. He encourages his readers to stand firm in the freedom from the slavery of the law (4:21–5:1).[249] Christ is central in defining their identity over against the identity marker of circumcision (5:2–3). In terms of justification, there is close correspondence between an identity defined by law and circumcision (v. 4). Christ and the law represent "separate spheres of power, such that anyone who chooses the Law's sphere of power has been cut off from access to Christ."[250] Similarly, faith (vv. 5–6) is portrayed as being opposite to an identity defined by circumcision (vv. 6–12) and law (by implication), and correlates with the Spirit (v. 5) and with love (v. 6).

---

245. In terms of Pauline anthropology, the human spirit is distinguishable from the body (cf. vv. 10–11), which is comparable to the "inner person" in 2 Corinthians 4:16 (Fee, *Empowering Presence*, 568). This once again accounts for a measure of duality in Paul's anthropology (see 273 pp. 226–230).

246. LITV, emphasis added.

247. Cf. Fitzmyer, *Romans*, 491.

248. Fee, *Empowering Presence*, 25–26.

249. Fee, *Empowering Presence*, 426.

250. Hays, "Galatians," 312.

Yet, to love others (vv. 13–14) is the fulfillment of the law "in one word," constituting *continuity* with the law. To walk[251] according to πνεῦμα corresponds with love for others (v. 16), which fulfills the love command and in turn fulfills the law.[252] This can especially be derived from Paul's expressing of love in terms of the fruit of the Spirit (v. 22). The Spirit replaced the law by fulfilling the aim of the law, which was love, not to "sum up" the law.[253]

By marking off identity by outward identity markers (e.g., circumcision), one could be "religious" without being "righteous."[254] But, as Fee states,

> Christ brought an end to Torah observance in part for that very reason. The Spirit replaced Torah so that God's people, Jew and Gentile alike, would have a new "identity": the indwelling of the Spirit of the living God himself.[255]

The new identity in Christ, marked by the indwelling of the Spirit, coheres with the commencement of a new era in redemptive history and the end of the old era of salvation history under the law.[256] The Spirit is fully sufficient and enables the believer to practice love and to live a life that does not go along with "the flesh."[257]

Walking in πνεῦμα is set up against ἐπιθυμίαν σαρκός (v. 16). As noted above, σάρξ is one of the more fluid words Paul employs. It generally does not describe an individual's physical desires or "sinful nature."[258] The ἐπιθυμίαν σαρκός (v. 16) is parallel to τὰ ἔργα τῆς σαρκός (v. 19). Most of these works of the flesh (vv. 19–21) lie apart from one's individual physical desires, rendering such a view ("sinful nature") unlikely.[259] Similar to Romans 7:5–6 and 8:4–5 and 9a (see above), both σάρξ and πνεῦμα are here essentially "eschatological realities, denoting the essential characteristic of

---

251. Περιπατέω (vv. 16, 25) probably follows the OT הָלַךְ (Hays, "Galatians," 325; Dunn, *Epistle to the Galatians*, 295; Longenecker, *Galatians*, 244), which is often employed in connection with observing the law (e.g., Lev 26:3; Deut 26:17; 30:16).

252. Fee, *Empowering Presence*, 429.

253. Fee, *Empowering Presence*, 426; cf. Hays, "Galatians," 322–23; Fung, *Galatians*, 246; LITV; RSV; RV; KJV; contra Hendriksen, *Galatians*, 211–12; NLT; NRSV; NIV.

254. Fee, *Empowering Presence*, 427.

255. Fee, *Empowering Presence*, 427.

256. Schreiner, *Paul*, 263.

257. Fee, *Empowering Presence*, 436; cf. Schreiner, *Paul*, 263.

258. Contra NLT; NAT; NIV.

259. Das, *Galatians*, 594; Fee, *Empowering Presence*, 430.

the two ages, before and after Christ."[260] This understanding can be derived from several elements in the context:

1. Faith in Christ[261] and the works of the law are mutually exclusive categories (3:2–26; 5:6)[262] and correspond to the πνεῦμα-σάρξ dichotomy (3:3–5; cf. 6:8–15). Πνεῦμα in this context thus denotes "the way of existence in the faith and is described as *by the Spirit* (6:1), *by . . . faith* (3:26)" while σάρξ "represents the way of existence outside the faith and is described as (literally) 'of human origin' (1:11), *in own power* (3:3), *under the supervision of the law* (3:25)."[263] Verse 17 reiterates the incompatibility of life in the Spirit with life in the flesh: "they belong to different worlds"[264] or realms.[265] There is thus no hint of a battle between two parts of the human constitution.[266] The Spirit and the flesh that "desire" against each other are rather on a supra-individual level between two antithetical realities, pertaining to two salvation-historical epochs within the realm of eschatology.[267] The clause "you may not

---

260. Fee, *Empowering Presence*, 431; cf. Silva, *Interpreting Galatians*, 183; Bruce, *Galatians*, 246.

261. Faith in Christ and the Spirit are in close relationship: the one implies the other (3:14; 5:5).

262. Fee, *Empowering Presence*, 431; cf. Das, *Galatians*, 593; De Boer, *Galatians*, 336.

263. Lategan, *Galasiërs*, 105, emphasis original. Peculiarly, although Lategan holds a strong position about the mutual incompatibility of the ways of existence of πνεῦμα vs. σάρξ, he interprets σάρξ as "sinful nature." Yet he does not understand it as having continued existence in believers' lives (pp. 102, 105, 109, 113).

264. Fee, *Empowering Presence*, 434–35; cf. Martyn, *Galatians*, 495.

265. De Boer, *Galatians*, 336; Jewett, *Anthropological Terms*, 102–5.

266. Cf. Fee, *Empowering Presence*, 435. Although Dunn, *Epistle to the Galatians*, 298–99, does not exactly view the battle as between parts of the human constitution, he describes the condition as a condition "of inward contradiction, of an individual pulled in two different directions" and as an "inner warfare." He argues that a believer is still "in the flesh" on the basis of 2:20. But ἐν σαρκί in 2:20 rather refers to bodily life on earth (see note 83, p. 129).

267. Cf. Silva, *Interpreting Galatians*, 183; Fee, *Empowering Presence*, 435; Fung, *Galatians*, 249–50; Schweizer, "σάρξ," *TDNT*, 7:133; Ridderbos, *Paulus*, 298–99; *Romeinen*, 145, on Rom 7:5). Martyn, *Galatians*, 493–94, 529–30 (adopted by Hays, "Galatians," 326–27 and De Boer, *Galatians*, 350) has a similar idea, but understands "Spirit" and "Flesh" as actors within an apocalyptical war of the end time (cf. Das, *Galatians*, 593; Bruce, *Galatians*, 243). Longenecker, *Galatians*, 245, sees πνεῦμα and σάρξ as "ethical forces" that seek to control a person's thought and activity (cf. Burton, *Galatians*, 297–01). Longenecker compares this ethical dualism to that found in the Johannine literature (e.g., John 3:6), and explains it as "the complex product of Paul's Old Testament background and his Rabbinic training" (adopted from Davies, *Paul*, 17). But this explanation, esp. in terms of Paul's alleged "Rabbinic training," is anachronistic

do whatever you want" (v. 17) in this context is best understood as not having "*the privilege* of doing whatever they wish,"[268] otherwise they would carry out the desire of the flesh.[269]

2. Being led by the Spirit is simultaneously contrasted to the flesh (vv. 16–19, 24) and being "under the law" (v. 18), which refer to the epoch before and outside of Christ (3:23; 4:5).[270] Life "under the law" (3:23; 4:5; 5:18) and the flesh are thus identified with each other.[271] Fee writes:

> [E]verything before Christ, which was fundamentally eliminated by his death and resurrection and the gift of the eschatological Spirit, belongs to the same "old age" sphere of existence. In that sense the Spirit stands over against both the flesh and the Law, in that he replaces the latter and stands in opposition to the former.[272]

Similarly, Das writes:

> Those who stand in the community of the flesh express their identity by an adherence to the Mosaic Law, which is, like the flesh, part of the old era.[273]

3. The "works of the flesh" (vv. 19–21) are described in terms of not inheriting the kingdom (v. 21).[274] The latter points to the eschatological consummation of God's kingdom, which has already become a present reality (Rom 14:17; 1 Cor 4:20).[275] Whether one inherits the kingdom or not pertains to being a believer or not, or being in Christ or not.[276] The conduct described in verses 19 to 21 thus describes the conduct akin to "the former way of life."[277] Dunn notes that "inheritance" was fundamental to Judean self-identity. Paul hereby emphasizes that

---

at best (Segal, "Jewish Presuppositions," 162).

268. Fee, *Empowering Presence*, 436, emphasis added.

269. Fee, *Empowering Presence*, 436.; cf. Jewett, *Anthropological Terms*, 106–7; John Chrysostom, "Galatians."

270. Cf. Fee, *Empowering Presence*, 438; Lategan, *Galasiërs*, 106; Bruce, *Galatians*, 256.

271. Westerholm, *Perspectives*, 379; cf. Fung, *Galatians*, 252.

272. Fee, *Empowering Presence*, 438.

273. Das, *Galatians*, 593.

274. Das, *Galatians*, 431.

275. Cf. Hays, "Galatians," 327.

276. Fee, *Empowering Presence*, 443.

277. Cf. Fee, *Empowering Presence*, 431.

inheritance of God's promises is now primarily "a matter of the Spirit and not of the flesh (including fleshly circumcision)."[278]

4. Verse 24 describes someone belonging to Christ as having crucified the flesh[279] (cf. 2:20). To "belong to Christ" is to be Abraham's seed and to be an heir (3:29), which correspond to being "in Christ" (3:28). The life in Christ is juxtaposed to a former way of life or the old order under the law in the flesh, to which the "I"[280] have died to (2:19; cf. Rom 5:15; 6:2-6; 7:9, 10, 24; 2 Cor 5:15).[281] The new creation (6:15) has come by implication[282] (cf. 2 Cor 5:17). The Spirit is the source of the new life in Christ (v. 25)[283] and replaces the self-centered "I."[284] This means that Christ and the Spirit mark the eschatological turning of the ages, and that life according to πνεῦμα and σάρξ are mutually incompatible options.[285] The end of the old way of existence and the start of the new in faith contain finality of death and the beginning of a new life.[286]

Although there are points of overlap, my approach has to be distinguished on certain points from the way in which Martyn and De Boer approach the πνεῦμα-σάρξ dichotomy in Galatians. Although both of them view πνεῦμα and σάρξ as 2 exclusive realms or powers, and the Spirit as an eschatological new reality, they do not so much see "Flesh" as belonging to the previous salvation-historical epoch. Both of them connect "Flesh" to an evil inclination or impulse. The opposition of πνεῦμα and σάρξ Galatians 5:16-25 is thus understood as being in the midst of an *ongoing cosmic battle*, rather than denoting excluding *salvation-historical* realities (πνεῦμα denoting the new age in Christ and σάρξ the former age before the Christ event).[287] De Boer rather sees the πνεῦμα-σάρξ dichotomy as a result of God's invasion of

---

278. Dunn, *Epistle to the Galatians*, 307.

279. Some sees here an allusion to the language of baptism (e.g., Hays, "Galatians," 328; Dunn, *Epistle to the Galatians*, 315; Fung, *Galatians*, 274; cf. Col 2:11-12).

280. The paradigmatic "I" in 2:18-20 invites his readers to join with Paul in his confessional statements (Hays, "Galatians," 243) and thus includes all true believers in Christ (Fung, *Galatians*, 122; BDF §281).

281. Fee, *Empowering Presence*, 455-56.

282. Fee, *Empowering Presence*, 455.

283. Fee, *Empowering Presence*, 456.

284. Bruce, *Galatians*, 256.

285. Fee, *Empowering Presence*, 431, 455-56; cf. De Boer, *Galatians*, 336; Ridderbos, *Paulus*, 298-99.

286. Lategan, *Galasiërs*, 109; cf. Longenecker, *Galatians*, 264.

287. Martyn, *Galatians*; De Boer, *Galatians*.

"the human sphere of the flesh": "Jesus Christ has actually *inaugurated* the eschatological conflict between Flesh and the Spirit."[288] Their view of σάρξ is, however, hard to make fit to Paul's statement that those who belong to Christ have "crucified the flesh" (v. 24),[289] which rather fits the salvation-historical interpretation of πνεῦμα and σάρξ.

The point of convergence in my understanding with that of Martyn and De Boer is that if people practice these "works of the flesh" (v. 19), it is as if they put themselves outside of Christ, the Spirit and belief in Christ.[290] Such a person in fact acts as an unbeliever. But I would contend that a person not living by the Spirit is also like someone placing himself or herself under the *old salvation-historical epoch*. The salvation-historical contrast between the flesh and the Spirit is therefore ultimately absolute.[291] The latter can especially be derived from 6:8 where eternal life as the end result of sowing in the spirit is contrasted with corruption as the end result of sowing in the flesh. The net result of such an understanding is that "flesh" denotes *both* the previous epoch under the reign of law, sin and death, *and* a position outside of Christ and the Spirit.

Even though an understanding that opposes the realm of "flesh" *before or outside* of Christ over against the realm of "Spirit/spirit" in Christ, excludes an understanding where an "ever present sinful nature" is in constant battle with the "indwelling Spirit," it does not result in triumphalism either. The tension between the "already" and the "not yet" is rather between the reality of the new life in the Spirit against the present weakness and suffering that still mark the existence of humanity that await the resurrection.[292]

Although I have consistently translated πνεῦμα with "Spirit" in Galatians 5:16–25, an eschatological understanding of πνεῦμα that points to the realm in Christ and the Spirit as opposed to the realm of flesh before or outside of Christ, would once again (cf. Rom 7:6; 8:4, 5, 9a) make provision for translating πνεῦμα with "spirit" (not anthropological *per se*) in at least

---

288. De Boer, *Galatians*, 336, 354, emphasis added; cf. Martyn, *Galatians*, 539; see also note 267, p. 209.

289. De Boer, *Galatians*, 367, implicitly admits to the inherent problem of his view when he states: "Paul declares that the Flesh was put to death sometime in the past, with the undeniable implication that it can no longer pose a threat to the freedom of the Galatians in the present. A primary concern of this passage to this point, however, has been to alert the Galatians to the ongoing danger of the Flesh to this freedom!" By pointing to "the juncture of ages" and the "dialectical interplay of the indicative . . . and the imperative" hardly rescues the inherent incompatibility of this view with 5:24.

290. Cf. Schreiner, *Paul*, 145.

291. Schreiner, *Paul*, 145.

292. Cf. Fee, *Empowering Presence*, 432.

verses 16, 18 and 25 (esp. where it occurs without the article).²⁹³ But even with the article in verse 17, although πνεῦμα primarily denotes the Spirit of God and should be translated accordingly, the eschatological understanding of πνεῦμα remains underneath the surface, especially in its opposition to σάρξ (cf. Rom 8:6), which in turn demonstrates the considerable fluidity in which Paul applies these terms.

1 Corinthians 12:12–13

After Paul's elaboration on the diversity of the gifts of the Spirit (vv. 7–10), which are "activated by one and the same Spirit" as the Spirit chooses (v. 11),²⁹⁴ he proceeds in typical Pauline style with consecutive γάρ-sentences²⁹⁵ (3 here: vv. 12–14), thereby connecting them to the former (vv. 1–11). In verse 12, Paul returns to the body metaphor (cf. 10:17; 11:29).²⁹⁶ This metaphor, which Paul applies to Christ (v. 12), was part of the "rhetorical topos of the body politic."²⁹⁷ It was in fact the most common topos for unity.²⁹⁸ But where contemporary writers used it to show order and hierarchy,²⁹⁹ Paul's usage was different in that he attributed the diversity of the members and the order among them to God rather than to nature. Additionally, Paul urged the members of the body (believers) to utilize their gifts in order to be mutually beneficial (v. 7; Rom 12:3–8).³⁰⁰

Paul grounds the unity of the body in verse 13. The relation of "baptism" to the Spirit has been variously interpreted. The ἐν (in ἐν ἑνὶ πνεύματι) can mainly³⁰¹ be understood as either instrumental, indicating sphere:

293. Bruce, *Galatians*, 243, has a similar idea regarding the translation of πνεῦμα and σάρξ. But he understands σάρξ in this context as "the power that opposes God" and suggests that one translates both πνεῦμα and σάρξ with capital letters: "Spirit" and "Flesh" (cf. Martyn, *Galatians*, 494).

294. NRSV.

295. E.g., Rom 1:16, 17, 18; 10:10, 11, 12, 13; 15:2, 3, 4; 1 Cor 11:5, 6, 7, 8, 9.

296. The term σῶμα was also identified on p. 22 as a significant term in identifying the believing congregation in Christ.

297. Collins, *First Corinthians*, 458.

298. Collins, *First Corinthians*, 458. Dio Chrysostom affirms that Aesop used it (*Disc.* 33.16). It occurs in Plato's *Republic*, was used by Cicero (*Off.* 3.5.22–23; 3.6.26–27) and was applied by Paul's contemporary, Seneca (*Ira* 2.13.7). Thiselton, *Corinthians*, 995, in addition lists Livy, Plutarch, Dionysius of Halicarnassus and Epictetus.

299. Collins, *First Corinthians*, 459; cf. Thiselton, *Corinthians*, 995.

300. Collins, *First Corinthians*, 460.

301. More alternatives are "with one Spirit" (NAT; in Thiselton, *Corinthians*, 13; note in NIV; in Ciampa and Rosner, *Corinthians*, 591) and even "for one Spirit" (in Thiselton, *Corinthians*, 13).

"by one Spirit,"[302] or as locative, indicating agency: "in one Spirit."[303] The choice of translation is largely a matter of interpretation.

Most interpreters understand the verb βαπτίζω as a technical term pointing to water baptism.[304] The reference to "baptism" is, however, not in isolation (which would certainly bear a technical meaning), but is modified by ἐν ἑνὶ πνεύματι.[305] Although baptism in water and partaking in the Spirit are often assumed to be at the beginning of the experience of the Christ-believing community in Paul, there is not a direct or causal connection between baptism and the Spirit.

Paul refers to the common reception of the Spirit by two clauses: (1) ἐν ἑνὶ πνεύματι ἡμεῖς πάντες ἐβαπτίσθημεν, and (2) πάντες ἓν πνεῦμα ἐποτίσθημεν. The first clause (1) is qualified by the prepositional phrase εἰς ἓν σῶμα, which in turn is modified by the parenthetical phrase εἴτε Ἰουδαῖοι εἴτε Ἕλληνες, εἴτε δοῦλοι εἴτε ἐλεύθεροι.[306] For the lack of Scriptural support, the second clause (2) hardly points to Spirit baptism,[307] the Lord's Supper[308] or to confirmation.[309] The two clauses (1 and 2) rather constitute a Semitic parallelism where both clauses carry the same notion,[310] which is a common device in Paul (cf. vv. 15–16, 17, 21, 22–23; 10:23). This view argues strongly for a metaphorical understanding of "baptism" in the first clause.[311]

302. Fitzmyer, *First Corinthians*, 473; Garland, *1 Corinthians*, 722; Thiselton, *Corinthians*, 997; ISV; NIV; RSV; OAT; KJV.

303. Taylor, *1 Corinthians*, 363; Collins, *First Corinthians*, 457; Fee, *Empowering Presence*, 175; Barrett, *First Epistle*, 288; Dunn, *Baptism*, 128–29; ESV; RV; "in the one Spirit": NRSV; REB; "in a single Spirit": NJB.

304. E.g., Ciampa and Rosner, *Corinthians*, 593; Fitzmyer, *First Corinthians*, 477; Sampley, "Corinthians," 945; Collins, *First Corinthians*, 463; Conzelmann, *1 Corinthians*, 212; Beasley-Murray, *Baptism*, 169; Lenski, *Corinthians*, 514.

305. Cf. Fee, *Empowering Presence*, 179.

306. Cf. Fee, *Empowering Presence*, 178–79.

307. A traditional Pentecostal view sees the first clause (1) as referring to conversion and the second clause (2) as referring to Spirit baptism as a second experience after conversion (e.g., Cottle, "Baptized," in Fee, *Empowering Presence*, 180). But the εἰς ("into") in v. 13 largely guards against such an interpretation (cf. Dunn, *Baptism*, 128).

308. To see an allusion the Lord's Supper in the verb ποτίζω is not accounted for in the New Testament. Neither is there evidence that the Lord's Supper would involve "drinking" the Spirit (Fee, *Empowering Presence*, 180; cf. Thiselton, *Corinthians*, 1001; contra Collins, *First Corinthians*, 463; Conzelmann, *1 Corinthians*, 212; Calvin, *Corinthians*, 341).

309. This is a traditional Roman Catholic view (e.g., Schnackenburg, *Baptism*, 84).

310. Fee, *Empowering Presence*, 180; *Corinthians*, 604–5; adopted by Ciampa and Rosner, *Corinthians*, 592; Gillespie, *First Theologians*, 120.

311. Paul applies "baptism" in a metaphorical sense in 1 Cor 10:2 (Dunn, *Baptism*,

Within the context of the work of the Spirit (vv. 4-11, see above) and Paul's reference to those who confess Jesus' lordship as partaking in the Spirit (v. 3), Paul in verse 13 most likely refers to their conversion and their receiving of the Spirit.³¹² The Spirit marks the true beginning of the new identity in Christ, which is accompanied by the demonstration of the Spirit and of power (2:4-5; Gal 3:2-5). The ἐν (in ἐν ἑνὶ πνεύματι) is thus probably locative: "in one Spirit."³¹³ The metaphor of baptism is thus drawn from water baptism but it does not include the act of water baptism itself. The metaphor rather denotes "spiritual transformation."³¹⁴ Similarly, "we were made to drink"³¹⁵ (ἐποτίσθημεν)³¹⁶ points metaphorically to the "experience of the Spirit in conversion."³¹⁷ Verse 13 thus neither directly denotes water baptism nor does it imply a direct connection between water baptism and the receiving of the Spirit.³¹⁸

The main point of verses 12 to 14 revolves around the unity of the body of believers constituted by the Spirit.³¹⁹ The phrase "whether Judeans or Greeks, slave or free" echoes the same theme of Galatians 3:28 and Colossians 3:11, where the new identity in Christ has relativized ethnic, racial or social identities. In Christ all ethnic or external identity markers (including the "works of the law") marking off God's children have been eradicated.³²⁰ Here in the context of 1 Corinthians 12, even God's diverse gifts are added

---

129).

312. Cf. Fee, *Empowering Presence*, 181; Kistemaker, *First Epistle*, 430; Dunn, *Baptism*, 130.

313. Taylor, *1 Corinthians*, 363; Fee, *Empowering Presence*, 181; Dunn, *Baptism*, 128. The "Spirit baptism" elsewhere in the NT is probably to be understood similarly, and is always contrasted with baptism in water (Matt 3:11; Mark 1:8; Luke 3:16; John 1:33; Acts 1:5; 11:16; Fee, *Empowering Presence*, 181).

314. Dunn, *Baptism*, 130.

315. Or "[we were] being watered, saturated, or *drenched in*" (Thiselton, *Corinthians*, 1000-1001).

316. NRSV; KJV; cf. Thiselton, *Corinthians*, 1000; Zerwick and Grosvenor, *Grammatical Analysis*, 522.

317. Dunn, *Baptism*, 130; cf. Gillespie, *First Theologians*, 120.

318. Taylor, *1 Corinthians*, 363; Fee, *Empowering Presence*, 179-82; *Corinthians*, 604-6; Gillespie, *First Theologians*, 120; Kistemaker, *First Epistle*, 429-31; Ladd, *Theology*, 587; Mare, "1 Corinthians," 264-65; Dunn, *Baptism*, 129-31; Best, *One Body*, 73. Although Thiselton, *Corinthians*, 997, 1000-1001, essentially shares the same view here, he renders ἐν ἑνὶ πνεύματι as "by one Spirit" in contrast to Fee and Dunn who render it as "in one Spirit." This view is contra Beasley-Murray, *Baptism*, 168-70. It has to be noted though that even while Beasley-Murray sees a close connection between water baptism and the Spirit, he does not view this association as automatic.

319. Cf. Dunn, *Baptism*, 130.

320. Esp. Wright, *Colossians*, 139-40; cf. idem., *Fresh Perspective*, 113-19.

to the list by implication. Membership to the body and status before God is not defined by any human quality, even if given by God, but by the "one Spirit" that "all were made to drink of" at conversion, who unifies all into one new identity.[321]

Colossians 2:11–13

Colossians 2:1–10 is thoroughly Christ-centered. In Christ, all the treasures of wisdom and knowledge are hidden (v. 3). The Colossians' firmness of faith in Christ is being commended (v. 5). They are encouraged to live in him (v. 6) and to be rooted in this faith in Christ (v. 7). Philosophy, empty deceit and human tradition "according to the elements of the world"[322] are being contrasted to Christ (v. 8). In Christ the fullness of the Godhead dwells bodily (v. 9). The Colossians have come to the fullness in Christ, who is the head of every ruler and authority (v. 10). The centrality of Christ is maintained in the rest of Colossians 2, especially in defining the concepts portrayed around the death and resurrection with Christ in verses 11 to 13.

A close correspondence between Colossians 2:11–13 and Romans 6:2–8 can be noted in terms of (1) the death of Christ and the believer's identification with his death, wherein the old "self"[323] or old humanity dies (Col 2:11; Rom 6:3–5, 7–8), (2) the resurrection of Christ and identification with his resurrection by faith, which enables new life (Col 2:12–13; Rom 6:4, 8), (3) the release from the "body of flesh" (Col 2:11) or the "body of sin" (Rom 6:6) in Christ (see below), and (4) baptism that signifies the death and resurrection of both Christ and the believer (Col 2:12; Rom 6:3–4). The three main differences between the two passages are (a) the notion of "flesh" in Colossians 2, which is absent in Romans 6, (b) the theme of circumcision in Colossians 2, which is absent in Romans 6, and (c) the tense of new life or resurrection of the believer, which is future in Romans 6

---

321. Cf. Thiselton, *Corinthians*, 997; Fee, *Empowering Presence*, 182. Although Ciampa and Rosner, *Corinthians*, 596, understand "baptism" as water baptism, they ground the unity of believers not in water baptism as such, but in conversion, which is "a universal experience for all believers and . . . is rooted in the activities of the one Spirit of God" (p. 593, quoting Fape, *Concept of Baptism*, 133; cf. Lenski, *Corinthians*, 514). Although applied to water baptism, not conversion *per se*, Fitzmyer, *First Corinthians*, 475, shares similar notions about identity.

322. LITV. The notion is probably that the Colossians' preoccupation with rules about material things (e.g., sabbaths, festivals, new moons, 2:16) was as if they treated them as cosmic powers that needed to be placated (Moo, *Colossians*, 191–92).

323. Moo, *Colossians*, 200.

(ἐσόμεθα, v. 5; συζήσομεν, v. 8) and aorist in Colossians 2 (συνηγέρθητε, v. 12; συνεζωοποίησεν, v. 13).

Flesh and Circumcision

In Christ, believers were circumcized with a circumcision not made by hands (Col 2:11). On one level, this non-physical circumcision probably alludes to the circumcision of the heart (Deut 10:16; 30:6; Jer 4:4; Ezek 44:7),[324] which is a spiritual circumcision,[325] and probably alludes to conversion.[326] On a second level, non-physical circumcision evokes its counterpart, namely, physical circumcision.[327] As Judean, ethnic "badge of identity,"[328] physical circumcision signified covenant membership (Gen 17:1-14).[329] Circumcision was a sign of belonging to the people of God.[330]

This contrast between literal and metaphorical circumcision echoes Paul's use in Philippians 3:3 (cf. Rom 2:28-29)[331] where the identity in Christ (identity mode C) is contrasted with an identity defined by that which is physical, external, visible and temporal (identity mode A). Here in Colossians 2, this spiritual circumcision is described in terms of "putting off the body of flesh in the circumcision of Christ" (v. 11). The "circumcision of Christ" most likely points to his whole body and thus his death on the cross and not to baptism as such.[332]

---

324. Moo, *Colossians*, 197; Melick, *Philippians*, 257; Pokorný, *Colossians*, 124; Bruce, *Colossians*, 103; Schweizer, *Colossians*, 147; contra Barth and Blanke, *Colossians*, 366.

325. BDAG, περιτομή, §1c; Harris, *Colossians*, 103; Melick, *Philippians*, 257, 259; Pokorný, *Colossians*, 124; Ridderbos, *Paulus*, 451; NLT; NRSV.

326. Moo, *Colossians*, 198, 200; Dunn, *Colossians*, 156; cf. Melick, *Philippians*, 258.

327. Cf. Lincoln, "Colossians," 624; Harris, *Colossians*, 103.

328. Dunn, *Colossians*, 154-56.

329. Cf. Moo, *Colossians*, 197; Dunn, *Colossians*, 155; Barth and Blanke, *Colossians*, 367.

330. Dunn, *Colossians*, 154; Pokorný, *Colossians*, 124.

331. As argued on pp. 63-68, the circumcision of the heart that Paul pictures in Rom 2:28-29 would constitute the ideal Judean identity.

332. Thompson, *Colossians*, 56-57; Lincoln, "Colossians," 624; Dunn, *Colossians*, 157-58; Hunt, "Colossians," 241, 243; O'Brien, *Colossians*, 117; Beasley-Murray, *Baptism*, 153. This interpretation takes ἐν (in ἐν τῇ περιτομῇ) as instrumental and τοῦ Χριστοῦ as an objective genitive (in Harris, *Colossians*, 102). The implication of this view is that baptism cannot be understood as replacing circumcision. Baptism is rather a new and different kind of sign within a new covenant (see esp. Hunt, "Colossians"; Du Toit, "The 'Clothe' metaphor"; idem., "Die 'beklee-' Metafoor," 52-53).

The "putting off [of] the body of the flesh" is not primarily the physical body[333] but the "body" that "serves sin,"[334] which denotes "the domination of sin."[335] This notion corresponds to "the body of this death" of Romans 7:24 (see pp. 189-99) and "the body of sin" of Romans 6:6, which in turn correspond with the old ἄνθρωπος of both Romans 6:6 (see pp. 187-89) and Colossians 3:9 (see pp. 164-68). The old "self" is being stripped off[336] and being buried in Christ. Dunn sees a variation of Paul's Adam Christology in the imagery in Colossians 2:11, where the flesh of the first Adam was stripped off, signifying a "cosmic circumcision of human flesh," which was "a preliminary to cosmic rule."[337]

The spiritual circumcision and the putting off of "the body of the sins of flesh" (Col 2:11) is signified[338] by the believer's "burial" in baptism (v. 12). Together with this spiritual burial, baptism portrays the reality of the believer's resurrection with Christ through faith in the working of God that raised Christ from the dead (v. 12). The believer's (spiritual) resurrection (v. 12) is the result of being made alive by God, after being dead in trespasses and in uncircumcision of flesh (v. 13). If one looks at this whole picture (vv. 11-13), it is not hard to detect notions of eschatological fulfilment,[339] where those in Christ represent a new humanity with a new status who belong to a new world, a new age[340] and a new order.[341] In Beasley-Murray's words: "The believer, risen with Christ and living in Christ, has become a new creature and lives in the new creation." This new life refers to "a

333. Allusions to the physical body is not completely transcended either. A similar expression in 1:22 (σώματι τῆς σαρκὸς) denotes the physical body of Christ (Moo, *Colossians*, 141; cf. Zerwick and Grosvenor, *Grammatical Analysis*, 605), and the context of baptism involves the physical body. The notion here, however, cannot primarily denote the physical body, for the stripping of the physical body would mean physical death (cf. Dunn, *Colossians*, 157).

334. Zerwick and Grosvenor, *Grammatical Analysis*, 606.

335. Moo, *Colossians*, 200; cf. Schweizer, *Colossians*, 143.

336. Moo, *Colossians*, 200.

337. Dunn, *Colossians*, 158.

338. Baptism is not the spiritual circumcision itself (contra Barth and Blanke, *Colossians*, 364; Melick, *Philippians*, 259-60; Pokorný, *Colossians*, 124; Lohse, *Colossians*, 101). Both the individual burial and resurrection with Christ is realized by faith (v. 12) and not by baptism as such. In baptism, the believer enacts burial and resurrection (see note 207, p. 96). Lincoln, "Colossians," 624, shows that ἐν ᾧ (v. 12) is best translated as "in Him" (NLT; NAT) rather than "in it" (contra ESV; GNB; REB; RSV; OAT; KJV), which would parallel the same phrase in v. 11.

339. Dunn, *Colossians*, 158; Pokorný, *Colossians*, 124; Schweizer, *Colossians*, 142; cf. O'Brien, *Colossians*, 115.

340. Wright, *Colossians*, 108; cf. Dunn, *Colossians*, 159; Pokorný, *Colossians*, 124.

341. Cf. Bruce, *Colossians*, 105.

new existence in the eschatological order, introduced in the resurrection of Christ and mediated by His Spirit."[342]

The uncircumcision of the flesh (v. 13) can be compared to the exclusion from the citizenship of Israel of Ephesians 2:11-12, which also bears the notion of being spiritually dead and being alienated from God.[343] Being "dead" in trespasses (v. 13) signifies more than having died with Christ, but signifies the *entire period prior to Christ* as being under the dominion of death, which was the result of sin and the uncircumcision of the flesh.[344] This notion becomes especially evident if σάρξ is understood in the extended sense (see note 126, p. 192) in both verses 11 and 13, denoting an existence outside of Christ (cf. Rom 7:5; 8:4, 5, 8, 9, see pp. 199-206). By extension, this metaphorical notion attached to the uncircumcision of their flesh (v. 13) includes even those who were God's people ethnically but were uncircumcised spiritually (v. 11).[345]

Colossians 2:11-13 thus constitutes the new criteria for the identity of God's people, which is defined Christologically. God's people are now those whose identity is not defined by ethnicity or outward identity markers such as physical circumcision, but by spiritual circumcision in Christ. Spiritual circumcision already lays the basis for the new humanity where all are one in Christ (3:10-11). As with the old and new ἄνθρωπος in 3:9-10, there exist in 2:11-13 both an individual and corporate, cosmological dimension in the transfer from the old existence outside of Christ to the new existence in Christ:[346] (1) The cosmic dimension is constituted by the death and resurrection of Christ that inaugurated the new eon where identity is not defined by flesh, but by faith and resurrection life. (2) The individual dimension involves the believer's identification with Christ's death and resurrection in faith and baptism, which signifies the burial of the old identity and the old "self" ("the body of flesh"), and the resurrection onto new life by faith.

Realized Resurrection and Life

By faith (διὰ τῆς πίστεως, v. 12) the resurrection and the new live is already a reality (aorist: συνηγέρθητε, v. 12; συνεζωοποίησεν, v. 13). The old epoch, its rule(r)s, and its practices had already passed, and believers already share

---

342. Beasley-Murray, *Baptism*, 140.

343. Dunn, *Colossians*, 163; Wright, *Colossians*, 109; O'Brien, *Colossians*, 122-23.

344. Lohse, *Colossians*, 107; cf. Lincoln, "Colossians," 625.

345. Cf. Moo, *Colossians*, 206-7. In principle Judean believers could thus be included here.

346. Cf. Thompson, *Colossians*, 57; Ridderbos, *Kolossenzen*, 179, 181.

in the resurrection life.³⁴⁷ This realized resurrection with Christ thus signals "the arrival of a new age (e.g., Rom 1:4; Gal 1:1), a new era in which sin and the powers no longer hold sway."³⁴⁸

Although some contrast the "realized" eschatology of Colossians 2:12-13 to the "future" eschatology of Romans 6 (ἐσόμεθα, v. 5; συζήσομεν, v. 8) as one of the reasons why Paul would not have written Colossians,³⁴⁹ this objection cannot hold:³⁵⁰ (1) Romans 6 is not that future orientated, especially if the present dimension of the new life in Christ (ζῶντας, vv. 11, 13), the past of the old life (συνετάφημεν, v. 4; συνεσταυρώθη, v. 6), and the reality of already being slaves of righteousness (ἐδουλώθητε, v. 18) are considered. It is this logic that has caused many scholars to consider one or both of the future tenses in Romans 6:5 (ἐσόμεθα) and 6:8 (συζήσομεν) as "logical futures."³⁵¹ (2) Within the context of Colossians, it would be natural to focus on the realized aspect of new life in view of the false teaching that was opposed. It is exactly the new life in Christ that counteracts the false teachers' insistence that believers must add something to their experience in order to attain spiritual fullness and liberation from the powers.³⁵² (3) The eschatology of Colossians is not "over-realized."³⁵³ Believers still have to "unclothe" themselves of the vices of the old humanity and actively "clothe" themselves with the new humanity, which represents the new identity in Christ (3:5-11).³⁵⁴

Preliminary Conclusions and Implications

In approaching Romans 9 to 11 and Galatians 6, this section serves to achieve a measure of coherency in the concepts relating to identity that have been discussed up to this point. In a study of this nature that pursues Paul's

---

347. Dunn, *Colossians*, 161.

348. Moo, *Colossians*, 205; cf. Wright, *Colossians*, 108.

349. Cf. Schweizer, *Colossians*, 145; Lohse, *Colossians*, 103-4.

350. Cf. Moo, *Colossians*, 204; O'Brien, *Colossians*, 119-20.

351. Kruse, *Romans*, 262; Jewett, *Romans*, 406; Wright, "Romans," 539, 540; Cottrell, *Romans*; Mounce, *Romans*, 150, 152; Frid, "Römer," 198-99; Cranfield, *Romans*, 1:307, 312, 313; Frankemölle, *Taufverständnis*, 51; Thyen, *Südunvegebung*, 206-8; Larsson, *Vorbild*, 71; Lagrange, *Paul*, 145; Plummer, *Corinthians*, 1915:91; Beet, *Romans*, 182; cf. Fitzmyer, *Romans*, 435; Beasley-Murray, *Baptism*, 139-40; Ridderbos, *Romeinen*, 131; Kühl, *Römer*, 204-5, 207; Hodge, *Romans*, 307, 312; Godet, *Romans*, 1:413. The importance of the logical future will be discussed further on pp. 295-302.

352. Moo, *Colossians*, 204; cf. O'Brien, *Colossians*, 120-21.

353. Cf. O'Brien, *Colossians*, 121.

354. Cf. Wright, *Colossians*, 110.

thought around certain concepts, there is always a measure of overlap with adjacent concepts. Depending on the level of insight one desires, the pursuit could carry on much longer. The interrelated nature of theological concepts in Paul's writings (or any propositional thought) makes a clean extraction of any such concept impossible. On the one hand there will always be limits with respect to the researcher's understanding of these concepts as well as the range of passages or texts that can be studied. On the other hand, some boundaries have to be drawn in order to gain insight. Apart from Romans 9 to 11 and Galatians 6, there is certainly more in the Pauline corpus to be explored in terms of Paul's thought on identity. The amount of passages that have been discussed at this point of the study, especially those pertaining to Ἰσραήλ, Ἰσραηλίτης and Ἰουδαῖος and their relation to Christ-believers, which constitute the main focus, are in my view adequate in order to move on to the final main aspect of the study.

The study has thus reached the stage where some of the loose ends around the main concepts pertaining to identity have to be tied together in order to facilitate a meaningful approach toward Romans 9 to 11 and Galatians 6. As put forth on pp. 16–30, the motive behind this methodology is to approach these passages with a deeper understanding of Paul's conception of Israel and identity at hand. This deeper understanding is intended to impose certain constraints on the possible interpretations of these passages. This methodology in turn attempts to counter for the "dominant technique," where one set of passages are subordinated to other passages (i.e., so called "pro-Israel" vs. "anti-Israel" passages, see pp. 25–27). This process of integration and systematization, however, has to be understood as tentative and incomplete. While the spirit-flesh dichotomy constitutes an underlying, overarching aspect in Paul's thought on identity, most of the concepts around identity as discussed in chapters 2 to 5 will be incorporated here.

Spirit and Flesh as two Distinct Eschatological Tealities: The Deepest Principle Behind Marking Off Identity

Both the terms πνεῦμα and σάρξ have a wide semantic range in Paul. The focus was not to unravel the complete range of meaning wherein these terms are employed, but to focus on the πνεῦμα-σάρξ dichotomy and its relation to identity. It was argued that the *eschatological* understanding of the terms πνεῦμα (esp. Rom 7:6; 8:4, 5, 9a; Gal 5:16, 25) and σάρξ (esp. Rom 7:5; 8:4, 5, 8–9; Gal 5:17) within the framework of *salvation history* in Paul constitutes the deepest principle behind Paul's thought on the identity of God's children in the light of Christ's work. This understanding can be summarized as follows:

1. Σάρξ in its extended application constitutes an eon and way of existence in Adam prior to or outside of Christ, which is defined by and under the control of the Mosaic law (see pp. 225-26), sin[355] and death.[356] Σάρξ thus stands for a *mode of identity* marked off by external, observable, human markers of identity.

2. Πνεῦμα in its extended application constitutes an eschatological eon and way of existence in Christ and the Spirit, which is defined by and under the control of the indwelling Spirit, which is a consequence of the new creation (having both corporate and individual significance). Πνεῦμα thus stands for a *mode of identity* marked off by the internal work of the Spirit, which constitutes adoption as God's children.[357]

On another level, σάρξ largely correlates with natural human possibility and πνεῦμα with divine possibility.[358] For Paul, σάρξ constitutes the *inability* in obtaining righteousness, which involves a right standing before God (cf. Rom 8:3-4). Πνεῦμα in contrast denotes the divine *ability* of God in providing righteousness (cf. Rom 8:10; 14:7) and adoption as children (Rom 8:15). In the same vein, πνεῦμα correlates with faith (esp. Rom 15:13; Gal 3:2, 5, 14; 5:5; cf. 2 Cor 4:13) while σάρξ correlates with the works of the law (esp. Rom 8:13; Gal 3:2-3; 5:19). In other words, σάρξ correlates to that which is subjective and πνεῦμα to that which is objective.

It is noteworthy that the expression κατὰ σάρκα is used in Romans 8:4, 5, 12, 13 in its extended sense, denoting an old way of existence, which opens the possibility for understanding the same expression similarly elsewhere. Within the exegetical study, κατὰ σάρκα has been interpreted as denoting ethnic or natural human descent (Rom 1:3; 4:1; 9:3, 5; 1 Cor 10:18; 2 Cor 11:18; Gal 4:23, 29). In the light of an understanding of σάρξ from an eschatological perspective, it is conceivable that Paul might have intended notions of the old existence outside of Christ in many of these instances of κατὰ σάρκα, even if this connotation might have existed in part. This extended meaning of σάρξ has already been implied in the expression

---

355. Although Paul often uses σάρξ in relation to sin (e.g. Rom 7:14; 8:3; Gal 5:19) it not so much as if σάρξ equals inherent sinfulness in human beings ("sinful nature"), but rather that σάρξ denotes a way of existence under the reign of sin.

356. Cf. Moo, *Romans*, 49-50.

357. Esp. Fee, *People of God*, 88; *Empowering Presence*, 469-70, 553; cf. Das, *Galatians*, 593; Hansen, *Philippians*, 221; Moo, *Romans*, 49-50.

358. Cf. Guthrie, *Theology*, 172.

ἐν σαρκί in Philemon 1:16 where the master-slave relationship can be understood as forming part of the old way of existence before our outside of Christ.[359] Similarly, the expression "Israel according to flesh" (1 Cor 10:18) might indicate God's people before Christ under the reign of law, sin and death (cf. Rom 8:2–4). In the same way, the meaning of "Christ according to flesh" (Rom 9:5) might (partly) correspond to Christ "born under the law" (Gal 4:4), or if paraphrased, Christ born under the eon ruled by law, sin and death. As discussed, the same flexibility in Paul's use of the term shines through in 2 Corinthians 5:16, where there seems to be an overlap in denoting natural human existence and descent. Within the context of the new creation in Christ, σάρξ in verse 16 (esp. first occurrence) might additionally carry overtones of an existence before Christ, before the new creation came into effect. This understanding would in turn open up new horizons of interpretation in this passage that cannot be pursued here.

Further implications of an identity marked off by Spirit/spirit in contrast to an identity marked off by flesh will be addressed in the discussion of Romans 9 to 11 below.

Spirit and Regeneration

Within the understanding of πνεῦμα in Paul, a notion that has surfaced sporadically is that of regeneration (Gal 4:28; 2 Cor 5:17; cf. Col 3:9–10) as implied counterpart of being unregenerate (e.g., Rom 7:14–25; Phil 3:3–4; cf. Col 3:9–10). Although this constitutes a topic on its own, some general remarks and references will have to suffice.

Apart from the theme of regeneration (παλιγγενεσία) in Titus 3:5, of which Pauline authorship is disputed by most (see note 96, p. 18), Paul never directly refers to "regeneration" or "rebirth" as such (compared to e.g., John 3:3–5; 1 Pet 1:3, 23). But although expressed in different terms, this notion is implied and in fact thoroughly Pauline,[360] as can be derived from the exegeted passages:

1. The reception of the Spirit in believers' lives corresponds with the beginning of life in Christ. Apart from Galatians 3:2–5 that states this explicitly, the new identity in the body of Christ effected at conversion is echoed in 1 Corinthians 12:13 by the metaphor of "baptism in one Spirit into one body." A similar notion is evident in Romans 8:1–16.

---

359. Esp. Jewett, *Anthropological Terms*, 135.

360. Fee, *Empowering Presence*, 857–59; cf. Bruce, *Romans*, 51; Guthrie, *Theology*, 166.

In Romans 8, the work of the Spirit is described as making the unregenerate person ("me") free from the "law" of sin and death (v. 2) and accomplishes what the Mosaic law could not accomplish (v. 3). Life in the Spirit, which constitutes a new way of existence and a new identity in the new eschatological eon outside of the realm of flesh, corresponds with being God's children (vv. 9–10, 14–15). The effect of this new identity is an actual experience where the human spirit witnesses together with God's Spirit that he or she is God's adopted child (v. 16). This new experienced identity implies the concrete transforming work of the Spirit within the life of the individual believer.

2. In close connection with the above, the theme of "life" in contrast to "death" in Christ and in the old humanity in Romans 5 to 8, correlates with the renewing work of the Spirit in the lives of people. The ability to walk in the new life, which is compared to the resurrection of Christ from the dead, is especially striking in this regard (Rom 6:4). The theme of the identification of the believer in the death and resurrection of Christ and the reality of the new life of the believer is paralleled in 2 Corinthians 5:15. A similar notion occurs in Galatians 2:20, where the crucifixion and death of the "self" is contrasted to Christ living in the life of the believer.

3. The removal of the veil in Christ (by God) that happens when someone turns to the Lord who is the Spirit of freedom (2 Cor 3:16–17) implies regeneration.

4. The new creation in Christ (2 Cor 5:17) involving both a corporate/cosmic and individual dimension, which effects transformation and reconciliation in the life of the believer, is equivalent to regeneration.

5. As noted in the exegetical discussion, Galatians 4:29, which contrasts birth according to the Spirit to birth according to the flesh (cf. v. 23), probably alludes to regeneration.

6. In Colossians 2:11–13 and 3:9–11, which was argued to represent Pauline teaching, regeneration is implied by the circumcision of the heart (2:11–13) and the new humanity that has been put on (3:9–11).

Other Pauline passages that imply regeneration include the following:

7. 1 Corinthians 2:12–16 account for the reception of the Spirit (v. 12). The received Spirit enables a spiritual understanding (v. 13, 15–16)

that is not possible for the natural, unregenerate person (v. 14).³⁶¹ This implies regeneration.

8. The notion of washing (ἀπολούω) in 1 Corinthians 6:11 stands in connection with the washing of sins (listed in v. 10), being sanctified (ἁγιάζω, v. 11), and being justified (δικαιόω, v. 11). This washing that has been effected by the Spirit (v. 11) probably describes "the conversion experience that had changed his [Paul's] readers' lives"³⁶² and thus alludes to regeneration.³⁶³

9. Levison argues that the language of Romans 5:5, 2 Corinthians 1:22, and 2 Corinthians 5:5 pertaining to the Spirit being given to the believers, is reminiscent of the language about the Spirit in Ezekiel's vision of the dry bones (esp. Ezek 36:26–27; 37:6, 14).³⁶⁴ For Levison the "early church takes precisely the same tack as the community at Qumran by transforming this vision of corporate recreation into an expression of *individual re-creation*."³⁶⁵

In all of the above Scripture references, the work of regeneration and the abiding presence of the Spirit in the lives of people correspond with the new identity in Christ, and constitutes the only true *mark of identity* of being God's people in the light of Christ's work (esp. Rom 8:16).

Spirit and Law

Paul describes the epoch of the Mosaic law and its reign as bringing the knowledge of sin (Rom 3:20; 7:7–12), as arousing sin (7:5), and as causing trespasses to increase (5:20). Being under the law is to be in prison and under slavery (Gal 3:23; 4:1; 4:21–5:1). The law, even though it was supposed to give live (Gal 3:12, 21; Rom 7:10), in fact brought death (Rom 7:10) and was

---

361. Taylor, *1 Corinthians*, 93; Ciampa and Rosner, *Corinthians*, 134–35; Collins, *First Corinthians*, 135–36; Fee, *People of God*, 88; *Empowering Presence*, 106–7; Guthrie, *Theology*, 164; Lenski, *Corinthians*, 115–17; cf. Witherington, *Paul Quest*, 211.

362. Barrett, *First Epistle*, 143.

363. Fee, *Empowering Presence*, 857.

364. Levison, *Filled*, 253–55.

365. Levison, *Filled*, 254, emphasis added. This implied interpretation of Ezek 36–37, however, does not necessarily deny a more general notion to the salvation of historical Israel, which arguably pertains to historical Israel's salvation and eschatological future (cf. Rom 5:12–21, see pp. 354–56; 11:26–27, see below). Although having a different interpretation of the eschatological fulfillment of this vision from my own, Levison acknowledges an implied dual understanding of Ezekiel's vision in Paul (pertaining to both the receiving of the Spirit and a "grand act of salvation" in Romans 5:12–21).

unable to obtain a right standing with God (cf. Rom 8:3-4). Therefore, the era under the law has been superseded eschatologically in Christ (esp. 2 Cor 3:5-16; Rom 7:4-5; 8:2-4). For those who believe, Christ has become the termination of the law (Rom 10:4, see p. 254). The Spirit has thus replaced the law in marking off the identity of God's children. All these aspects constitute the *discontinuity* between the law and the Spirit.

Yet, Paul never sees the Mosaic law as inherently evil or against God. The law is in fact inherently good and "spiritual" (Rom 7:12, 14). As noted in the discussion of Romans 7, it can be argued that the law was necessary in causing people to "die" in their own striving to do good and realize the "body of this death" (v. 24) and inability to do God's will because of their existence in the flesh (v. 5). Additionally, the reign of the law that caused the "I" (the complete self) to "die," drove people to Christ, the only Deliverer from the wretched existence under the law (v. 24). In Galatians 3, the law is pictured as the guardian until Christ came (v. 24). The law necessitated and preserved the promise (Christ) and the revelation of faith. The law thus had *salvation-historical significance*. The *continuity* between the Spirit and law lies in the Spirit's fulfillment of the law (esp. Rom 8:2-4). Since the Spirit and faith correlates, the same continuity between faith and the law can be seen in Abraham's faith (esp. Rom 4; Gal 3; 4:21-5:1).[366]

The Spirit's fulfillment of the law is both on the level of (1) achievement and (2) identity. (1) In terms of achievement, the Spirit constitutes the just requirement and fulfillment of the law (Rom 8:2-4; cf. Gal 3:2-6). In Galatians 5, the *fruit* of the Spirit (v. 22) is contrasted with the *works* of the flesh (v. 19). Through the Spirit, the believer rests in the objective work of God in Christ. That which a person "wills" but cannot achieve (Rom 7:15-20) is now achieved through the believer's unity with the Spirit. This aspect largely corresponds with the TAP. (2) In terms of identity, the Spirit is identified with righteousness (Rom 8:4, 10), which includes a right standing and relationship with God. The believer receives the Spirit of "sonship" (Rom 8:15; Gal 4:5) and his or her identity as God's children is marked off by the Spirit and not by the law. This aspect largely corresponds with the NPP.

Spirit and Israel

It is noteworthy that Paul never mentions "Israel according to spirit" as the counterpart of "Israel according to flesh" (1 Cor 10:18; cf. Rom 9:3). Paul in fact never directly associates Ἰσραήλ with πνεῦμα. The reason for this is probably because of the eschatological connotations Paul attaches

---

366. Cf. Fee, *Empowering Presence*, 813-16.

to πνεῦμα in its extended application. In terms of salvation history, the eschatological era of "spirit" in Christ and the mode of existence it denotes is incompatible with an existence in the old eon according to "flesh" (Rom 8:8–9; Gal 5:17; Phil 3:3).

The general concept of Ἰσραήλ thus seems to be identified with the existence before Christ that is indicated with κατὰ σάρκα in Romans 8:4, 5, 12, and 13. As noted in the discussions of especially 2 Corinthians 3:5–16 and 2 Corinthians 5:15, the counter-effect of the unification of all people into one identity in Christ (regardless of ethnic or social status: Gal 3:28; 1 Cor 12:13; cf. Col 3:11) is that all people before or outside of Christ, including Israel, have been identified with an unregenerate existence in the old eon in the flesh. Further implications of this understanding will be discussed and tested on pp. 262–319.

Spirit, Flesh and Anthropology

The fluid nature of the term σάρξ in Paul (which involves bodily existence), the "death" of all people in Christ (e.g., 2 Cor 5:15) and the regenerating work of the Spirit in the actual lives of human beings on the level of the human spirit (Rom 8:16), inevitably involves anthropology. In spite of the intriguing nature of this topic in Paul, some brief and concluding remarks (pertaining mainly to flesh, spirit and body) have to be made in order to tie together some of the hanging notions presented in this regard.

In as far as the flesh-existence of the old eon involves external, bodily existence whereas the existence in spirit involves internal, "spiritual" existence, it can be asked if a measure of duality is implied in terms of Pauline anthropology. It has to be noted that Paul never understands existence in the realm of spirit as ultimately disembodied. The difference lies in identity. Within the existence in σάρξ in the old eon, external, bodily existence *determines* identity (e.g., ethnicity and "works of the law,"[367] including circumcision). In contrast, within the eschatological existence in spirit, the internal regeneration and indwelling of the Spirit *determines* identity. This distinction is essentially a distinction of *priority*, and correlates with lordship. In the old eon, human beings reigned within the sphere of natural bodily existence, whereas in the new eon God's Spirit reigns in and through

---

367. A corollary of this understanding is that the "works of the law" as co-constituting factor in the old existence in flesh, can be understood as external and observable, whereas the Spirit is internal and non-observable. Similarly, in his interpretation of Paul, Boyarin, *Radical Jew*, 84–85, understands the law as belonging to the physical, outward sphere. For him, flesh means giving in to the body and observing the literal Torah.

the human spirit over the body. The mind and body is thus subjected to the Spirit/spirit (Rom 8:7-10; 12:1-2; cf. Eph 4:22-24; Col 3:1-3, 9-10).

The human spirit in the New Testament seems to denote an immaterial faculty of the human being that potentially interacts with God's Spirit.[368] In view of 1 Corinthians 2:11-14, this ability seems to be inactive or absent with the unregenerate person.[369] The new life (regeneration) and adoption as children that God's Spirit accomplishes, seem to quicken this faculty (Rom 8:16; 1 Cor 2:13, 15, 16). The death in Christ (2 Cor 5:15) and the death of the "self" (Rom 7:24; Gal 2:20) thus arguably involves the inability of the natural human spirit to interact with God. Yet in the unregenerate state, there exists a conflict between "willing" and "doing" (Rom 7:15-20). The latter is evidence of a form of anthropological dualism between the "inward" human will and "outward" bodily existence under the reign of the law, where the law is imposed on humanity from outside.[370] The inward part of the human constitution is, however, unable to accomplish God's will. In the existence ruled by the Spirit in Christ, God enables the human spirit to accomplish God's will (esp. Rom 8:1-16).

The inability of the material human body in its present form (σὰρξ καὶ αἷμα, 1 Cor 15:50)[371] to inherit God's kingdom arguably describes the kind of anthropological dualism that Paul holds in the best way. The need for a "resurrection body" (1 Cor 15:44, 52-54;[372] Phil 3:21) in the eschatological kingdom implies that the *continuity of personal identity* from the current existence to the existence in the coming kingdom cannot be tied to the current physical human body. The "dead in Christ" who will be raised (1 Thess 4:13, 16) seems to imply an intermediate state where personal identity has to remain intact in spite of the death of the body.[373] According to Cooper the "unclothed" (ἐκδύω) existence (2 Cor 5:4), which Paul wants to avoid, constitutes the same intermediate, disembodied existence between death

---

368. Cf. L&N §26.9; Witherington, *Paul Quest*, 204.

369. Cf. Witherington, *Paul Quest*, 204; Guthrie, *Theology*, 166.

370. Boyarin, *Radical Jew*, 84-85. Boyarin, however, takes this in another direction. For Boyarin, Paul's aim with his spirit-flesh dualism was "to erase all distinction between ethnos and ethnos, sex and sex and become one in Christ's spiritual body" as part of Paul's "political and theological program" (p. 85; cf. p. 107).

371. Fee, *Corinthians*, 798-99.

372. The difficult σῶμα πνευματικόν (1 Cor 15:44) is not necessarily to be understood as immaterial but rather as supernatural (Fee, *Corinthians*, 786) or transcendent (BDAG, πνευματικός, §2aβ). Yet a measure of Hellenistic vocabulary is difficult to deny (cf. Schweizer, "πνεῦμα," *TDNT*, 6:421).

373. Cooper, *Body*, 137-38, 167-69; by implication: Thomas, "1 Thessalonians," 276; Frame, *Thessalonians*, 175; cf. Bruce, *Thessalonians*, 101; Guthrie, *Theology*, 838-39; Plummer, *Thessalonians*, 76.

and final resurrection.³⁷⁴ Romans 8:19–23 constitute the transformation at the final resurrection of the current creation (v. 21), including the current bodily existence (v. 23), which is subject to corruption or decay (φθορά, v. 21). From this passage it can be argued that the body does not experience the new creation yet.³⁷⁵ The new creation is already a *spiritual* reality, but the new creation of the *physical* world is still awaited. The tension between the "already" and the "not yet" can thus be expressed in terms of *spiritual* ("already") and *physical* regeneration ("not yet").

2 Corinthians 12:2–4 arguably constitutes the strongest evidence for the dualism of spirit/soul and body in Paul's thought. This ecstatic experience constitutes an experience of temporal disembodiment that Paul sees as a possibility.³⁷⁶

Although these remarks by no means are intended as final, one cannot deny a measure of dualism (in terms of spirit/soul and body) in Paul's anthropology. Whatever the extent is to which one acknowledges dualism in Paul's anthropology, it has to be differentiated on crucial points from Hellenistic anthropology:

1. Paul never envisions disembodiment as ultimate destination. If disembodiment is acknowledged in Paul's thought, it is temporary or intermediate.

2. Even while Paul derives identity in the new eschatological existence in Christ from spirit (immaterial and internal) and not from the bodily existence (material and external), he never views the body (or flesh) as intrinsically evil or as without value.³⁷⁷ The body is not a prison to be freed from. The body is in fact a "temple" of the Holy Spirit (1 Cor 6:19) and must be presented unto God as a living, holy and acceptable sacrifice (Rom 12:1).

3. An understanding of σάρξ as the way of existence in the old eon is preferred over an understanding of σάρξ as "sinful nature" (as discussed).

374. Cooper, *Body*, 142; cf. Thrall, *Corinthians*, 1:381–82; Guthrie, *Theology*, 836; Hughes, *Corinthians*, 171. Barrett, *Second Epistle*, 156, works in the same direction by stating that Paul would be afraid of death, for he would desire the substitution of the spiritual body for the natural body (expected at the parousia) in his lifetime rather than to die beforehand. Harris, *Second Epistle*, 386, 388, also understands ἐκδύω as being disembodied, but not specifically in terms of the intermediate state between physical death and final resurrection, but rather that Paul resists ultimate disembodiment (cf. Kruse, *Corinthians*, 115).

375. Cf. Witherington, *Paul Quest*, 212.

376. Harris, *Second Epistle*, 839; Cooper, *Body*, 149–50; Barrett, *Second Epistle*, 308–9; Bruce, *Corinthians*, 247.

377. Cf. Witherington, *Paul Quest*, 204, 212.

Amidst the fluidity between the terms σῶμα and σάρξ in Paul, the former understanding of σάρξ (way of existence) is further removed than the latter understanding (sinful nature) from Epicurean thought where σάρξ is identified with the seat of cravings and lusts.³⁷⁸ The connection of σάρξ to sin in Paul has more to do with the reign and dominion of sin in the old eon than with a resident part of the human constitution.

4. Paul nowhere endorses the view of the soul's pre-existence.³⁷⁹

5. Paul does not have a monistic view as in Greek thought that spirit is identified with all matter. He rather differentiates between that which is material (body) and immaterial (spirit). The constitutive factor of πνεῦμα in the Greek world is that it always pertains to the material world, and is thus considered as a substance.³⁸⁰ It is never "spiritual" in the strict sense as in much of the New Testament.³⁸¹ In Greek thought, there is no differentiation between matter and the supernatural. All have πνεῦμα. It is a natural force, which is immanent and impersonal. The spirit is considered as a mode or action of the air, which indwells the organism of the cosmos in all its parts, and is therefore considered as a substance of the soul that regulates intellectual and spiritual functions. In Stoic monism, πνεῦμα is connected with the power of deity in as much as it permeates the universe and gives it life and unity.³⁸² As materialists, the Stoics perceived the relationship between God and the world as between soul and body, where God is the impersonal soul and the world is the body of God. Their view is essentially pantheistic.³⁸³

---

378. In Epicurus whose views later became popularized, σάρξ could designate the seat of emotions, especially the seat of desire (Schweizer, "σάρξ," *TDNT*, 7:99–105). Similarly, Seebass, "σάρξ," *NIDNTT*, 1:671, points out that in this thinking the cravings and lusts of the body could defile the soul, which would have a share in the divine.

379. Guthrie, *Theology*, 165.

380. Kremer, "πνεῦμα," *EDNT*, 3:118; cf. Kamlah, "πνεῦμα," *NIDNTT*, 3:689–90; Kleinknecht, "πνεῦμα," *TDNT*, 6:357.

381. In the NT, πνεῦμα can stand in opposition to that which is natural (cf. 1 Cor 2:14). See also the NT use of πνεῦμα as denoting a personal, supernatural and transcendent God (e.g., Rom 8:9, 16; 1 Cor 2:10; Heb 3:7; 1 Tim 4:1).

382. Kleinknecht, "πνεῦμα," *TDNT*, 6:357–58; cf. Kamlah, "πνεῦμα," *NIDNTT*, 3:689–90.

383. Nash, *Christianity*, 69.

6. In passages where the spirit/soul and body are mentioned together (1 Cor 5:3–5;[384] 6:20; 1 Thess 5:23;[385] cf. 2 Cor 7:1),[386] both a dualistic and holistic understanding of humanity is present. Cooper is probably right to refer to Paul's anthropology as representing "holistic dualism."[387]

---

384. The spirit, which will be saved (1 Cor 5:5), can denote the whole person (Fee, *Empowering Presence*, 127) or the "the essential, inward self" (Barrett, *First Epistle*, 126). Yet, a possible understanding of denoting *that* faculty within the human constitution that determines identity as God's children in the new eon in Christ (the spirit, which witnesses with God's Spirit, Rom 8:16), cannot be ruled out.

385. In 1 Thess 5:23, notions of dualism have to be acknowledged, for it is impossible to understand πνεῦμα here as term that denotes the whole human being (cf. Schweizer, "σάρξ," *TDNT*, 7:435).

386. In 2 Cor 7:1, σάρξ most likely refers to the physical body (BDAG, σάρξ, §2; Harris, *Second Epistle*, 512; cf. Gal 2:20, see note 83, p. 129).

387. Cooper, *Body*, 230–31.

6

"All Israel" and "the Israel of God"

ROMANS 11 (ESP. VV. 25-27) and Galatians 6:7-16 (esp. v. 16) arguably represent two of the most controversial and variously interpreted passages regarding Israel in the New Testament. Both passages constitute a climax or end in Paul's line of thought. The interpretation of Romans 11:25-27 and Galatians 6:16 presented here does not represent a majority view and will therefore largely build on the research on Paul's theological thought around identity that has been put forth up to this point of the book. Where most of the exegesis has been mainly deductive until now, the approach to Romans 11 (esp. vv. 25-27) and Galatians 6:7-16 (esp. v. 16) will lean more toward the inductive side. In other words, a different line of interpretation in comparison to conventional interpretations will be tested and evaluated against the text of these passages. This evaluation will chiefly involve semantic, structural, theological, and exegetical aspects.

Introduction to Romans 9 to 11

One of the first questions that have an influence on the understanding of Romans 9 to 11 is the one about the recipients of the letter to the Romans. This debate has developed for the most part into viewing the majority of the recipients as a gentile Christ-believing majority and a Judean Christ-believing minority.[1] The community had taken on the complexion of a gentile Christ-believing community, which had shifted from the more Judean matrix of Christ-believers to a more gentile framework. This process was accelerated by the enforced exile of Judean believers under Claudius.[2] On

---

1. Longenecker, *Introducing Romans*, 75-78; Moo, *Romans*, 13; Kümmel, *Introduction*, 309-11.

2. Moo, *Romans*, 13. This took place around 49 CE, as attested by Suetonius' (*Claud.* 25.4) statement that Claudius "expelled the Judeans from Rome because they were constantly rioting at the instigation of Chrestus [Christ]" (Carson and Moo,

the other hand, by the time Paul wrote to the church in Rome,[3] some of the dust might have settled after Claudius' expulsion. So we find for example the Judeans Aquila and Priscilla back in Rome (Rom 16:3; Acts 18:2).[4] Hagner states that "it seems clear that Jewish readers are occasionally in view."[5] In the same vein, Wright argues that

> Paul will have known of some Jewish Christians who had returned to Rome and who, alongside Gentile cobelievers, would now be facing the difficult question of how to live together as one family with those who cherished very different cultural traditions.[6]

As Dunn admits, "[w]e have little hard evidence regarding the earliest Christian groups in Rome."[7] Much of the understanding of Paul's recipients thus has to be inferred from the text of Romans itself. Dunn argues strongly (exclusively?) for gentile recipients, that he regards as obvious from passages such as 11:13-32 and 15:7-12.[8] J. H. Elliott on the other hand states that Paul had "Israelite fellow believers" in his audience to whom much of his rhetoric was directed.[9] Much of one's view of Paul's audience is thus subjected to how Romans 9 to 11 and other passages in the letter are interpreted, which accounts for a measure of circularity in this debate. Is Romans 9 to 11 solely an exhortation to gentiles to have a more positive regard for Judeans, or can it be an apology to Judeans or Judean Christ-believers for Paul's pressing for an all-inclusive gospel where there is "no difference" (Rom 10:12) between Judean and Greek? Can Romans 9 to 11 be seen as an apologetic exposition of his view of Israel who "stumbled at that stumblingstone" (Rom 9:32) and by implication have been cut off (Rom 11:22)?[10] This line of thinking corresponds to the view of some commentators who think that Paul's law-free gospel[11] to the gentiles earned him the

---

Introduction, 395).

3. This was probably around the beginning of 57 CE (Carson and Moo, *Introduction*, 394; Cranfield, *Romans*, 1:16).

4. Carson and Moo, *Introduction*, 396; cf. Wright, "Romans," 407.

5. Hagner, *New Testament*, 522.

6. Wright, "Romans," 407.

7. Dunn, *Romans*, 1:xlv.

8. Dunn, *Romans*, 1:xlv; cf. Sanders, "Paul's Jewishness."

9. Elliott, "Jesus," 147; cf. Zoccali, "All Israel," 302; Esler, *Conflict*, 119.

10. Sanday and Headlam, *Romans*, 232-33.

11. See p. 128, esp. n. 76. Contra Nanos, "Myth," 4, who argues for Paul being a Torah abiding "Jew," quoting passages such as 2 Cor 11:22; Phil 3:3-6; Gal 2:15; 5:3 and 1 Cor 7:17-24. In 2 Cor 11:22 and Phil 3:3-6, Paul employs the terms Ἰσραηλίτης and

reputation of being anti-Judean.¹² This possible view on Paul's recipients has to be kept open, and will be revisited later on.

Käsemann may be right that Romans 9 to 11 is not primarily intended as a dialogue with either Judeans or gentiles as such: "What we have is a theological reflection, which . . . is broken up by fictitious objections and answers to them."¹³ Käsemann's approach implies a dialectical relationship between, in Robbins' words, the "intertexture" and the "inner texture" of the text.¹⁴ Similarly, Moo argues that "the purpose of Paul in 1:5-6 (and 1:13) is not so much to identify the national complexion of the community as to locate it within the scope of his commission to the Gentiles."¹⁵

Moving on to the position of 9 to 11 in the letter, it needs no proof that most scholars acknowledge a break in Paul's thought after 1 to 8 and before 12 to 16, even to the point that Dodd argued that Romans 9 to 11 was a worked out sermon by Paul that he inserted into the letter at this point.¹⁶ Toward the other extreme, scholars such as Stendahl, Dunn, Fitzmyer, Wright, and Witherington have argued for viewing Romans 9 to 11 as the real climax of the letter.¹⁷

Ἰσραήλ respectively (not Ἰουδαῖος) as designation for his physical heritage and ethnicity (as argued). Paul's status as being "blameless" concerning the righteousness in the law (Phil 3:6) defines his previous identity before belief in Christ, which he rejected and considers as refuse (Phil 3:8). In Gal 2:15 Paul merely designates his ethnic status and then goes on to state that no one is made righteous from the works of the Torah, but through faith in Christ (v. 16; cf. Segal, *Paul the Convert*, 130). As argued, Paul's reference to being a Judean (v. 15) rather refers to status by birth than denoting law observance. Gal 5:3 does not put Torah observance in a positive light, but rather that if you circumcise yourself, you are in debt to do the whole law. Paul stated earlier in Galatians that the law has put those under the law under the curse of the law (3:10, 13). 1 Cor 7:19 states that circumcision is nothing and uncircumcision is nothing, but the keeping of the ἐντολῶν θεοῦ. This does not necessarily point to the full Torah as such, but can be interpreted as pointing to the will of God (Dunn, *New Perspective*, 336-37; Fee, *Corinthians*, 314; Barrett, *First Epistle*, 169) or the commandment of love (Martyn, *Galatians*, 519; Pop, *Eerste Brief*, 141). But as argued elsewhere (Du Toit, "Keeping of the Commandments"), it is likely that it has a similar meaning to that of Gal 5:3 and Rom 2:25, being a pejorative, shorthand reference (based on his teaching to the Corinthian congregation) to the consequence of placing yourself under the law by circumcision: when reverting to old-age thinking by focusing on circumcision you then might as well do the whole law.

12. E.g., Moo, *Romans*, 556; Barrett, *Romans*, 175-76; cf. Bruce, *Romans*, 183-84.
13. Käsemann, *Romans*, 261.
14. Robbins, *Texture*, 3-4.
15. Moo, *Romans*, 13.
16. Dodd, *Romans*, 161-63.
17. Stendahl, *Paul*, 4, 85; Dunn, *Romans*, 2:520; Fitzmyer, *Romans*, 541; Wright, "Romans," 620; *Climax*; Witherington and Hyatt, *Romans*, 237, 244.

Moo is concerned that viewing Romans 9 to 11 as climactic may underplay "the importance of the individual's relationship to God" in Romans 1 to 8.[18] This is not an inevitable conclusion, however. It might be that Paul wants to introduce an additional layer to his exposition in 1 to 8 from a deeper and wider perspective, not to diminish any of the individual elements in the gospel, but to understand from a salvation-historical vantage point[19] why and how there is now no difference between Judeans and Greeks (Rom 10:12). In Romans 9 to 11, both the continuity as well as the discontinuity of the gospel with Israel is highlighted and some of the underlying concerns (or probably the most fundamental concerns) regarding Israel is answered. Within his exposition, God's faithfulness is underlined in the way in which the promises have been fulfilled to Israel in the history of salvation,[20] which probably constituted a concern within the congregation.[21]

As for the structure of Romans 9 to 11, it has to be taken as a coherent unit,[22] where final conclusions have to be postponed until the end of 11. My approach will be to pursue the meaning of Rom 9 to 11 within the following order of priority: (1) from within the text of Rom 9 to 11 itself, including the way in which Paul interprets and appropriates the Old Testament, (2) then from the bigger co-text of Romans (esp. 1–8), and lastly (3) from other Pauline material.

Concerning the style of Romans 9 to 11, Paul might have appropriated some aspects of the diatribe style[23] in combination with personification and personal involvement.[24] In Paul's retelling of the story of Israel,[25] his "own role and vocation become topics within the story."[26] Paul's appro-

---

18. Moo, *Romans*, 551–52.

19. Cf. Wright, "Romans," 620; Moo, *Romans*, 561; Käsemann, *Romans*, 254; Ridderbos, *Romeinen*, 203.

20. Wright, "Romans," 622; Moo, *Romans*, 550–51, 553, 564; cf. Witherington and Hyatt, *Romans*, 236.

21. Dunn, *Romans*, 2:519.

22. Hultgren, *Romans*, 347; Dunn, *Romans*, 2:518; Cranfield, *Romans*, 2:447–48; cf. Barrett, *Romans*, 175. Rom 9–11 appears as a rounded unit with a clear beginning (9:1–5) and an end (11:33–36; Dunn, *Romans*, 2:518). The section is preceded by the climactic conclusion of 8:31–39 (cf. Hultgren, *Romans*, 347) and is followed by a more personal note (Rom 12, etc.). The theme of Israel (marked by the terms Ἰσραήλ and Ἰσραηλίτης) is prominent in Rom 9–11 and does not occur elsewhere in the letter.

23. This similarity cannot be exaggerated since Rom 9–11 does depend to a large extent on 1–8, and cannot be seen as a "completely performed unit" (Dunn, *Romans*, 2:520).

24. Witherington and Hyatt, *Romans*, 236; Dunn, *Romans*, 2:519.

25. Wright, "Romans," 622.

26. Wright, "Romans," 624.

priation of the Old Testament Scripture references, of which the amount is remarkable,[27] will be approached from the perspective that the passages quoted are not mere proof texts for his argument, but are interwoven in his exposition as part of his own argumentation.[28] In other words, his argument does not flow around the quoted passages, but goes right through them. In a sense, the quoted passages become his own words. This approach will become clearer below.[29]

Romans 9 (ABC)

Since Romans 9:3-8 has already been discussed on pp. 45-52, the results of that subsection will be incorporated here with the focus on the flow of Paul's argument.

Inner Israel Versus Kindred According to the Flesh (vv. 1-10) (AB)

Paul starts this passage with an oath (v. 1) that signifies more than solemnity[30] or sincerity,[31] but utter seriousness,[32] to the point of the shocking statement in verse 3 where he could wish to be accursed and removed from Christ (ἀνάθεμα . . . ἀπὸ τοῦ Χριστοῦ) for the sake of his "brothers," his kindred according to the flesh (τῶν συγγενῶν . . . κατὰ σάρκα). What exactly

---

27. Hultgren, *Romans*, 348, counts 35 direct quotations from the Old Testament (39% of the verses) in Rom 9-11, which includes many more allusions and summaries of OT material.

28. Cf. Hultgren, *Romans*, 348.

29. Dunn, *Romans*, 2:520, calls Paul's appropriation of Scripture "midrashic" (cf. Stegner, "Romans"). Neusner, *Midrash*, 7, argues against a general, unqualified designation such as "midrashic," since there are different approaches among the "Judaisms" of late antiquity to the systematic interpretation of Scripture: Midrash (1) as paraphrase, (2) as prophecy, and (3) as allegorical reading of Scripture. Even while one has to recognize the similarity in Paul's appropriation of Scripture and Midrash as prophecy (2), Paul did not exactly treat "the historical life of ancient Israel and the contemporary times of the exegete as essentially the same, reading the former as a prefiguring of the latter," but rather adhered to the original sense of the passage, seeing Israel as the object of the passages (cf. Moo, *Romans*, 570). Neither did Paul treat Rom 9-11 as allegory (3), which would imply a hidden or even a mystical meaning in the text of the OT (cf. Neusner, *Midrash*, 8).

30. Cranfield, *Romans*, 2:451.

31. Moo, *Romans*, 555.

32. Cf. Wright, "Romans," 627, who writes that this was not a mere "rhetorical ploy to gain a little sympathy for a while. It was truly heartfelt."

constitutes Paul's sorrow (v. 2) for his kindred according to the flesh is not yet clear, and is set to unfold during the course of Romans 9 to 11.

Some commentators[33] see a possible connection in Paul's wish to be accursed (v. 3) with Exodus 32:30–34, where Moses prayed to God to be blotted out of the book of life if the people that sinned by means of idolatry to the law in making a golden calf, could only be spared. This understanding implies that Paul might have assimilated the same mediating role as Moses for his people. This possible underlying connotation has to be kept in mind for the rest of Romans 9 to 11.

As was argued on pp. 46–50, all eight privileges mentioned in 9:3–5 (adoption; glory; covenants; legislation; service; promises; fathers and Christ according to the flesh) applied to historical Israel, and can be considered as external privileges. None of these privileges necessarily imply salvation, faith or devoutness to God. In verses 6 to 8, Paul established an important hermeneutical key in understanding the term "Israel" in Romans 9 to 11. Paul distinguished between an *outer* and an *inner* Israel. National Israel or "Israel according to the flesh" (1 Cor 10:18) constitutes outer Israel. All of the eight privileges apply to them (identity mode A) by implication. Inner Israel or "true Israel" is Israel of the promise. They constitute an inner elect Israel within national Israel (identity mode B within A, that is, identity mode AB). The reader is advised at this point to review the earlier diagram that illustrates how these two modes of identity fit together (see p. 53). It is important to note that when Paul uses the term "Israel" without further qualification in the rest of Romans 9 to 11, he has *inner* Israel in mind.

If outer or national Israel is not necessarily saved, an implicit question underneath Paul's mentioning of these external privileges would be: if being a physical Israelite does not guarantee salvation, what does? On what basis is an Israelite in the Old Testament then saved? Or even more pertinently, are they saved? As can be derived from Paul's reference to the patriarchs in his salvation-historical exposition that follows after verses 6 to 7 (vv. 8–14), these questions would be applicable to historical Israel in particular.

At the background of the Israelites' refusal to recognize the fulfillment of its promises, their history now had taken an unexpected turn.[34] This notion is surely implied after 9:1–5, since Paul mentioned all the Israelites' privileges, which even include the Messiah after the flesh. They had everything they needed. The start of verse 6 enhances this notion: "It is not as though the word of God had failed." All of what is explained in Romans 9 to

---

33. E.g., Seifrid, "Romans," 639; Osborne, *Romans*, 237; Wright, "Romans," 628; Moo, *Romans*, 558–59; contra Käsemann, *Romans*, 258.

34. Moo, *Romans*, 568.

11 fits into God's plan and His faithfulness to His Word. Dunn writes about verse 6: "The verse is therefore thematic not only for the next paragraph or two . . . but for the whole section."[35] Furthermore, if the Israelites could inherit the gospel by physical descent (by default) and not by faith, Paul's gospel would be in jeopardy.[36]

Dunn points out that there was a natural tendency, at least on the part of some, "to regard descent from the patriarchs as guarantee of salvation."[37] Yet Paul does not deny that they remain "God's people, in some sense (cf. 9:4-5; 11:1-2, 28). But he denies that this corporate election of Israel means the salvation of all Israelites."[38] Cranfield certainly works in the right direction when he writes that "the point Paul is making is that not all who are included in the comprehensive Israel are included also in the selective, special Israel."[39] Similarly, he refers to an "Israel within Israel,"[40] to "God's distinguishing within the general area of election," and to an "inner circle of election" as opposed to those who are outside of this circle.[41] Moo writes: "Within the corporate election of Israel, there is operating, Paul shows, an election of individuals."[42] The same accounts for Bruce who writes that "not all the descendants of Israel are Israelites in the inward sense" or in a "spiritual sense."[43] While agreeing with Bruce's general notion, "spiritual" could hardly denote the work of the Holy Spirit in the sense of regeneration, which would correspond to the identity in Christ. Paul in fact generally stays away from the proper designation πνεῦμα[44] when writing about Israel, which calls

---

35. Dunn, *Romans*, 2:539; cf. Wright, "Romans," 635.

36. Moo, *Romans*, 569.

37. Dunn, *Romans*, 2:539; cf. Moo, *Romans*, 573. See e.g., Matt 3:9; Luke 3:8; Justin, *Dial.* 140.

38. Moo, *Romans*, 573; cf. Ridderbos, *Romeinen*, 209.

39. Cranfield, *Romans*, 2:473.

40. Cranfield, *Romans*, 2:474, 475.

41. Cranfield, *Romans*, 2:471. Cf. Cosgrove, *Elusive Israel*, 65-72, who also distinguishes between an "Israel A" and an "Israel B," where "Israel B is in some sense *true* Israel" and "Israel A" would either refer to "children of the flesh" (v. 8) or "the twelve tribes stemming from Jacob." But on his reading of 9:6-13, Cosgrove seems to include the descendants of Esau and Ishmael under "Israel A," which would point for him to the possibility that "all human beings belong to another Israel, Abrahamic Israel" in whom all the nations of the earth would be blessed.

42. Moo, *Romans*, 738.

43. Bruce, *Romans*, 188.

44. A possible exception is Rom 2:29, yet there it seems to denote the unregenerate human spirit (as argued) and not the working of the Holy Spirit as such (as e.g. in Rom 8). Furthermore, πνεῦμα has to be distinguished from πνευματικός "spiritual," e.g., in connection with the law (Rom 7:14, see pp. 189-99).

for hesitance to speak of "spiritual Israel."[45] The context of Romans 9 constrains the identification of the "real" or "true" Israel (in Paul's definition) within the covenant people of the Old Testament.[46]

Still, the question remains: what does Paul mean by "Israel" that is not of physical descent, which are "children of the promise" or "in Isaac" (quoting Gen 21:12)? At first glance, Paul's notion not to make physical descent decisive of being Ἰσραήλ (v. 6, second occurrence), seems to be contradicted by his mention of Isaac as Israel the patriarch's (v. 6, first occurrence)[47] father, Sarah, his mother (v. 9), and Rebecca, his wife (v. 10), as if genealogy did play a role. Yet, if the distinction was merely physical and would merely point to some of the physical descendants of Israel the patriarch higher up in the genealogical line, it would render such a distinction meaningless. The reference to Isaac implies a contrast to Ishmael, the other child of Abraham, as is clear from the context of the quoted Gen 21:12 (v. 7). Even though the fulfillment of God's promise involves genealogy, Paul's ultimate contrast is between the τέκνα τῆς σαρκός and the τέκνα τῆς ἐπαγγελίας (v. 8), and is thus not foremost genealogical.[48] He has something deeper in mind. Isaac was the object of God's promise rather than Ishmael. Isaac was Abraham's σπέρμα "in the selective sense."[49] Paul's reference to Isaac as "our father" (v. 10) has to be associated with Paul's identity as Israelite, his kindred according to the flesh.[50] Verse 10 accentuates that neither Jacob nor Esau had a better claim than the other on the divine promise[51] (cf. v. 13).

At this point (end of verse 10) in Paul's discourse there are still some outstanding questions. It is still not entirely clear what is meant by "children of the promise" or by children "in Isaac." What are the criteria for them to be reckoned as true or inner "Israel"? The ἐπαγγελίας (vv. 8–9) surely alludes to the promise to Abraham in Romans 4:13, 14, 16. But in this context the notion of faith is not explicitly mentioned as in Romans 4, neither of Abraham nor of the people of Israel. As with πνεῦμα,[52] one should be hesitant to identify Paul's notion of πίστις with identity mode AB as such (cf. Rom 4). Paul rather connects the term πίστις later in 9:30, 32 to belief in Christ.[53]

---

45. Cf. Käsemann, *Romans*, 262; contra Moo, *Romans*, 573, 575.
46. Cf. Käsemann, *Romans*, 263.
47. BDAG, Ἰσραήλ, §1; Moo, *Romans*, 573; cf. Dunn, *Romans*, 2:538.
48. Cf. Cranfield, *Romans*, 2:474–75.
49. Cranfield, *Romans*, 2:476.
50. Cranfield, *Romans*, 2:477.
51. Moo, *Romans*, 580.
52. Cf. Käsemann, *Romans*, 262; contra Dunn, *Romans*, 2:541.
53. Cf. Dunn, *Romans*, 539; Ridderbos, *Romeinen*, 210.

Another question that could arise is, does being "from Isaac" and being "children of the promise" mean that *inner Israel* of the Old Testament is saved? Käsemann senses this tension when he writes: "Hasty statements are of no use at this point."[54] At this point Paul probably builds up the tension on these underlying questions intentionally.

Israel of Calling and Election: An Inner and Outer Aspect (vv. 11–23) (AB)

In verses 11 to 23 Paul elaborates on what constitutes (inner) Israel (v. 6), the "children of the promise" (v. 8). Simultaneously, Paul interprets and appropriates *salvation history*[55] within the context of his gospel of faith, which is first to the Judean, and also to the Greek (1:16).[56] The aim in this section is not to explain all the detail of each verse, and neither to attempt to answer all possible questions regarding God's purpose and/or election. The focus will be on Paul's bigger argument and only some specific questions pertaining to my enquiry will be addressed. Verses 14 to 23 can be understood as an excursion or detour to Paul's main argument,[57] where the style of diatribe is particularly evident.[58]

The eventual outcome of salvation history in Christ is rooted in κατ' ἐκλογὴν πρόθεσις τοῦ θεοῦ (v. 11): "the purpose of God according to election."[59] The primary theme here is not so much election as it is God's πρόθεσις: His *purpose*[60] or *plan*.[61] God's purpose κατ' ἐκλογὴν describes the way in which His purpose is fulfilled.[62]

In verses 11 to 23, Paul focuses on the bigger picture of the purpose of God that culminates in the inclusion of gentiles (v. 24). Verses 11 to 23 are thus not foremost a treatise on the mechanics of individual election,[63] but rather a motivation for the outcome of salvation history in terms of the for-

---

54. Käsemann, *Romans*, 263.

55. Dunn, *Romans*, 2:562, 564; Käsemann, *Romans*, 264; Cranfield, *Romans*, 2:479, 492.

56. Cf. Wright, "Romans," 638.

57. Moo, *Romans*, 589.

58. Hultgren, *Romans*, 366; Moo, *Romans*, 589; Dunn, *Romans*, 2:555; Käsemann, *Romans*, 267; Barrett, *Romans*, 185.

59. LITV; KJV.

60. E.g., NRSV; KJV.

61. BDAG, πρόθεσις, §2.

62. Cf. Käsemann, *Romans*, 264; Sanday and Headlam, *Romans*, 244.

63. Contra Moo, *Romans*, 580–609.

mer priority of Israel and the latter inclusion of the gentiles (cf. 1:16). In other words, God's calling (καλέω) was to Israel first (v. 12) and then to the gentiles (v. 24). It has more to do with the priority of nations in God's purposes and how salvation history plays out, than individual election as such. Against this backdrop, the content of these verses has to be interpreted.[64]

Some of the terminology that relate to God's purpose (πρόθεσις) are the following:

1. God's ultimate will (implied in v. 15; θέλω: vv. 16, 18) corresponds to His bigger purpose.

2. The hardening[65] (σκληρύνω: v. 18) of people culminates in a salvation-historical outcome where God's ultimate purpose is effected.

3. Certain actions or attributes of God all serve God's greater purpose: (a) God's wrath (ὀργή: v. 22), (b) the showing of mercy (ἐλεέω: vv. 15, 16, 18, 23) and (c) God's patience (μακροθυμία: v. 22).

4. Paul's use of "vessel" (σκεῦος, vv. 21–23) underlines the instrumental character of God's dealings with people in the greater scheme of salvation history[66] that would culminate in Christ.[67]

The theme of election that stands in a close relationship to God's purpose (v. 11) and stays present underneath the surface of this whole passage can be expressed in terms of two aspects:

A. *Outer election.* This has to do with the whole nation of Israelites. This functions on the level of ethnicity and a specific bloodline, which culminated in Christ according to the flesh (ὁ Χριστὸς τὸ κατὰ σάρκα, v. 5). All the privileges listed in verses 4 to 5 identify them as God's children or people in some sense, but does not necessarily imply salvation. This aspect of election corresponds to identity mode A.

B. *Inner election.* This more closely relates to God's specific purpose in salvation history. The people that share in this aspect, "stand in a positive relationship to God's purpose,"[68] which differentiates them from the outer aspect of election, or in Cranfield's words, from those who "stand outside the circle of the Israel within Israel."[69] Even though this

---

64. Cf. Wright, "Romans," 638; Dunn, *Romans*, 2:569.
65. For Israel's hardening, see esp. pp. 242–51 and pp. 262–67.
66. Cf. Cranfield, *Romans*, 2:487, 492.
67. Cf. Witherington and Hyatt, *Romans*, 256.
68. Cranfield, *Romans*, 2:481.
69. Cranfield, *Romans*, 2:481.

might imply salvation, Paul does not specifically mention salvation as such here,[70] and continues to leave the underlying question about (inner) Israel's salvation unanswered. This aspect of election corresponds to identity mode AB.

In the light of Paul's bigger scheme of salvation history, his reference to Jacob and Esau (v. 13) can be understood as representatives or types[71] of *whole nations*, where Jacob would represent historical Israel (as the patriarch carrying that name) and Esau would represent the nations outside of Israel. In other words, Paul also had the people who descended from them in mind.[72] This notion is confirmed by Paul's quotation in verse 12: Ὁ μείζων δουλεύσει τῷ ἐλάσσονι, an exact quote from Genesis 25:23 (LXX), denoting the "two nations" (δύο ἔθνη, LXX) in Rebekah's womb.[73] Even the reference to Malachi 1:2–3 in verse 13 indicates that "the nations Israel and Edom, rather than their individual ancestors Jacob and Esau" are in view.[74]

God's purpose according to election (v. 12) is based on calling (καλέω) and not on works (ἐξ ἔργων). The emphasis is on God's initiative in the calling of Israel (v. 12) and the nations (v. 24) respectively. If it was based on works, it would have been based on the initiative of human beings. The works here probably refer to the works of the law as an identity marker for being God's people rather than an attempt to earn[75] election.[76] Paul excludes the works of the law as marker for election in answer to a Judean conception of Israel's election that included the works of the law[77] or regarded physical descent as determinative of partaking in the promise.[78] It is worthy of note here that Paul neither mentions anything of Israel's faith as such as possible criterion for election nor salvation. Paul seems to reserve faith as criterion for salvation for believers in Christ (cf. Rom 4; Rom 10:1–21).

The effect of viewing God's purpose according to election here in a more generic sense as ultimately pointing to Israel and the nations (v. 24), is probably best understood as Paul's answer to sceptical Judeans that

70. Cf. Sanday and Headlam, *Romans*, 245.

71. Käsemann, *Romans*, 264.

72. Witherington and Hyatt, *Romans*, 253; Moo, *Romans*, 584; Bruce, *Romans*, 192; Käsemann, *Romans*, 265; Cranfield, *Romans*, 2:479–80; cf. Dunn, *Romans*, 2:544; Sanday and Headlam, *Romans*, 246.

73. Cranfield, *Romans*, 2:479.

74. Bruce, *Romans*, 192–93.

75. The latter notion is, however, not necessarily totally excluded.

76. Wright, "Romans," 637; Dunn, *Romans*, 2:548–49.

77. Cf. Dunn, *Romans*, 2:549, 551.

78. Barrett, *Romans*, 183; Sanday and Headlam, *Romans*, 246.

questioned Paul's inclusion of the gentiles. If seen in this way, it strengthens the possibility that Paul addressed a mixed audience, including a number of Judeans.

The Cross-Over in Salvation History (vv. 24–33) (AC)

After Paul's exposition of God's plan (πρόθεσις, v. 11) of election in salvation-historical perspective (9:11–23), which is based on calling and not on works (v. 12), he now brings the current state of affairs into the picture. The sentence starting with "what if" in verse 22 is never completed, and Paul elaborates on the vessels of mercy whom he has called (καλέω, v. 24).[79] In the light of the true (inner) Israel, defined in verse 6 and the reference to Jacob and Esau in verse 13, one might expect a reference to *inner* Israel here as vessels of mercy. But Paul now brings his retelling of salvation history into the sphere of the gospel. By utilizing the first person plural (ἡμᾶς, v. 24), he includes himself (a Judean Christ-believer) and his predominantly gentile audience as the objects of God's calling in Christ: οὐ μόνον ἐξ Ἰουδαίων ἀλλὰ καὶ ἐξ ἐθνῶν. This major turning point in the present telling of Israel's story ties what will follow to 3:21–4:25.[80]

Paul now reaches a critical point in his exposition. As noted earlier, Paul uses scripture not as mere proof texts, but appropriates them into the fabric of his exposition in a way that they become intricately interwoven within his argument (see pp. 234–35). In verses 25–29, salvation history is portrayed as making a *crossover*[81] like two parallel rails each swopping over to the other rail. Three aspects of this scenario can be identified, and will be discussed below: (1) Verses 25 to 26 describe the outcome of God's plan for the nations and (2) verses 27 to 29 describe the outcome of His plan for Israel. (3) Verses 30 to 33 describe the deeper reasoning and foundation behind this crossover, which, as I will argue, constitutes the culmination of salvation history.

The Outcome of God's Plan for the Nations (vv. 25–26)

From Paul's convergence of Hosea 2:25 and 2:1 (LXX) in verses 25 to 26, he explains that those who were previously not God's people, are now called God's people, or worded differently, those who were not loved are now

---

79. Wright, "Romans," 642.
80. Wright, "Romans," 642.
81. Cf. Wright, "Romans," 635, who refers to the mystery of Israel as being "cross-shaped, to involve being cast away that the world might be redeemed." Moo, *Romans*, 617, describes vv. 24–29 as a "surprising turn of salvation history."

beloved (v. 25). Verse 26 parallels the same theme: those who are not God's people will be called "sons of the living God." These parallel scenarios refer to the gentiles' inclusion into God's promise (vv. 8, 9), effected by His calling (καλέω, v. 26), which is the gospel.[82] The expression "sons of God" (υἱοὶ θεοῦ, v. 26) points back to the same theme in verse 8 (τέκνα τοῦ θεοῦ), constituting the children of the promise (τέκνα τῆς ἐπαγγελίας) who are reckoned as seed (σπέρμα, v. 29).[83] This means that the promise was always designated to include gentiles. But in the current scenario, the allusion might even include the earlier "sonship" (υἱοθεσία, v. 4),[84] one of the privileges of Israel according to the flesh, which would imply a reversal of the conditions for covenant membership in the sense that it is not partly based on ethnicity any longer, but open to the nations.

The Outcome of God's Plan for Israel (vv. 27–29)

Paul now moves over to Israel. He conflates Isaiah 10:20–23 in verses 27 to 28. Even though the number of the children of Israel was great, only the ὑπόλειμμα, the "remnant" will be saved. While Paul quotes from the Septuagint, the idea of a remnant comes from the Hebrew שְׁאָר, denoting a *rest or remainder*.[85] This remnant that constitutes an element of hope and salvation,[86] presupposes a *judgment*.[87] This is clear from Isaiah 10:22: "destruction has been decreed"[88] (חָרוּץ כִּלָּיוֹן בּוֹ). The participles συντελῶν and συντέμνων (v. 28, directly from Isaiah 10:20, LXX) are difficult to translate. According to BDAG, the verb συντελέω in this context means to bring something into being that has been promised,[89] but it could mean to complete or finish something.[90] The verb συντέμνω can mean to cut short, to shorten or to limit,[91] and either denotes a shortened time[92] or Israel that is

---

82. Wright, "Romans," 643.
83. Wright, "Romans," 643.; Barrett, *Romans*, 191.
84. Cf. Wright, "Romans," 643.
85. BDB, שְׁאָר.
86. Moo, *Romans*, 615–16; cf. Bruce, *Romans*, 195.
87. Moo, *Romans*, 615; Bruce, *Romans*, 195; Hasel, *Remnant*; cf. Hultgren, *Romans*, 371–72; Wright, "Romans," 643; Käsemann, *Romans*, 275–76, 278; Sanday and Headlam, *Romans*, 265.
88. NIV.
89. BDAG, συντελέω, §2.
90. BDAG, συντελέω, §1; LITV.
91. BDAG, συντέμνω.
92. BDAG, συντέμνω; e.g., Wright, "Romans," 643; NRSV; NIV.

being cut down.[93] In the context of those who remain (remnant) after an implied judgment,[94] the latter meaning (being cut down) is probably part of the overall implied connotation here.[95] Paul retains some of the ambiguity in the phrase συντελῶν καὶ συντέμνων (LXX) probably to soften some of the harshness of the outcome of God's judgment.[96] The harsh implication of God's judgment with [only][97] a remnant being saved seems to be that Israel that lived before the point of judgment is in fact not saved. If Paul still honors his distinction about who "Israel" is (v. 6), the further implication might even be that the inner, elect Israel of the promise living before the point of judgment is not saved. At this point it is worthy of note that Paul applies referred authority: "Isaiah cries" (v. 27). Even though this cry of Isaiah conveys what Paul wants to bring across at this point in his exposition, it is not Paul's last word on the matter.

Verse 29, referring to Isaiah 1:9 (LXX), describes the outcome of Israel except for the seed (σπέρμα) that the Lord leaves behind. This seed is caused "to remain or to exist after a point in time"[98] and thus denotes the remnant.[99] In the Masoretic Text (Isa 1:9) it denotes a "survivor."[100] If it was not for the remnant, Israel would have become like Sodom and Gomorrah, which was completely destroyed. The reference to these two cities here reminds of the promised seed to Abraham and Lot and his family's escape (Gen 19:29)[101] amidst God's judgment. While the focus is on the remnant and God's provision, Sodom and Gomorrah in the background implies the judgment and the cutting off of Israel itself.[102] Paul conveys his message in a way that Scripture almost speaks for itself. His readers must see for themselves what Scripture says[103] and "read between the lines." The way in which Paul appropriates Scripture seems to contribute to his euphemistic and apologetic approach in the whole of Romans 9 to 11.

---

93. BDAG, συντέμνω; e.g., Wilckens, *Römer*; Calvin, *Romans*, 323.

94. Wright, "Romans," 648.

95. Cf. Wright, "Romans," 635, 649, 651; Barrett, *Romans*, 192.

96. Dunn, *Romans*, 2:576.

97. Although not being part of the Greek text, some translations add "only" here (e.g., ISV; ESV; GW; NRSV; GNB; NAT; OAT).

98. BDAG, ἐγκαταλείπω, §1.

99. Wright, "Romans," 643.

100. BDB, שָׂרִיד, §1.

101. Wright, "Romans," 643.

102. Cf. Käsemann, *Romans*, 275; Ridderbos, *Romeinen*, 224; Calvin, *Romans*, 324.

103. Cf. Hendriksen, *Romans*, 333; Ridderbos, *Romeinen*, 224.

The Culmination of Salvation History (vv. 30–33)

The question at the beginning of verse 30 (Τί οὖν ἐροῦμεν;) is a rhetorical device to introduce the implication of Paul's exposition up to this point.[104] Paul now reverts back to the gentiles. They did not pursue or strive for[105] righteousness by definition,[106] but attained it through faith. Righteousness here denotes a "righteous status in God's sight"[107] or more specifically, "a right relationship between a person and God."[108] The phrase ἐκ πίστεως points back to the same phrase earlier (1:17; 3:26, 30; 4:16), denoting the original condition of the promise to Abraham in which all nations participate through faith in Christ. The righteousness to the gentiles within the context once again points to their inclusion into God's salvific economy, rather than denoting the righteousness of each individual gentile.[109]

Israel did pursue the νόμον δικαιοσύνης (v. 31). This unexpected phrase would evoke the typical Judean understanding of the law where the law defines righteousness.[110] Moo, however, notes that the only other instances in Romans where Paul connects righteousness language absolutely to the law stand in connection with "doing" (2:13, ποιητής; 10:5, ποιέω).[111] As noted earlier, Paul is not merely addressing an incorrect definition of identity (NPP) or *merely* an incorrect *understanding* of the law.[112] While it did involve an incorrect understanding of what the law was intended for, the connection between law and righteousness also involved *actual disobedience* to the law itself.[113] Israel could not attain or reach[114] (φθάνω, v. 31) the law. This law of righteousness is carried over to verse 31 as the object of "attain."[115] The reason given for not attaining the law was that Israel "did not

---

104. Moo, *Romans*, 621.
105. BDAG, διώκω, §4.
106. Dunn, *Romans*, 2:580.
107. Cranfield, *Romans*, 2:506.
108. Hultgren, *Romans*, 382; cf. Barrett, *Romans*, 193.
109. Cf. Wright, "Romans," 626; Dunn, *Romans*, 2:592. It is correct that only gentiles who believe will obtain righteousness (Schreiner, *Romans*, 536; Cranfield, *Romans*, 2:506), but Paul's point is here not to identify individual faith or individual inclusion, but that all gentiles are principally included into God's larger scheme of salvation.
110. Dunn, *Romans*, 2:581; cf. Wright, "Romans," 649.
111. Moo, *Romans*, 625.
112. Contra Dunn, *Romans*, 2:577, 582, 583–84.
113. Cf. Hultgren, *Romans*, 378; Rom 2:17–19; Rom 4:1–25.
114. BDAG, φθάνω, §3.
115. Moo, *Romans*, 625; Dunn, *Romans*, 2:581.

strive for it on the basis of faith, but as if it were based on works"[116] (v. 32). This means that the law was *incapable* of defining covenant membership[117] or of activating "the law's promise of righteousness."[118] Osborne states that "the law is no longer a valid approach to God."[119] It was *impossible* to adhere to the standard the law has set[120] (see 3:20; 7:6; 8:3; cf. Gal 3:21), but that did not remove Israel's responsibility. They stumbled over the stumbling stone. They disregarded the law and failed to adhere to it.[121] Further support is lended to the notion of obedience to the law from 10:5. In 10:5 Paul describes the "righteousness" that has caused Israel to stumble, namely that by keeping the law one shall live (quoting Lev 18:4–5; see δικαιοσύνη in both 9:31 and 10:5). The context of Leviticus 18 from where Paul quotes in 10:5 shows that those who violate the law's precepts will be cut off from the people (Lev 18:29).[122] What is described here in Romans 9:31–32 thus seems to be a fulfillment of Leviticus 18:29: "For whoever commits any of these abominations shall be cut off from their people."[123]

Verse 33 contains a quotation from a combination of Isaiah 8:14 and 28:16. Moo is probably right that Paul has both Israel's unbelief and an inappropriate focus on the law in mind that led Israel into stumbling.[124] The "stone of stumbling" (λίθῳ τοῦ προσκόμματος, v. 32; λίθον προσκόμματος, v. 33)[125] or the "rock that will make them fall" (πέτραν σκανδάλου, v. 33)[126] is also the object of faith (v. 33), a connotation derived from Isa-

---

116. NRSV.

117. Wright, "Romans," 649. Cf. note 229, p. 99. In terms of defining covenant membership, Wright focuses stronger on the *inability* of the law to do so whereas Dunn, *Romans*, focuses more on an *incorrect understanding* of the law (see main text).

118. Moo, *Romans*, 627; cf. Witherington and Hyatt, *Romans*, 259; Käsemann, *Romans*, 277.

119. Osborne, *Romans*, 261.

120. Hultgren, *Romans*, 379; cf. Westerholm, *Perspectives*, 380, 383, 444; Gathercole, "Justified," 150; Witherington and Hyatt, *Romans*, 259; Witherington, *Paul Quest*, 67; Räisänen, *Paul*, 95, 199.

121. Hultgren, *Romans*, 378–79; Gathercole, *Boasting*, 207; Moo, *Romans*, 626–27; Cranfield, *Romans*, 2:508; Sanday and Headlam, *Romans*, 278; cf. Hong, "Law," 154; CD; Pss. Sol.

122. Cf. Matera, *Romans*, 236.

123. NRSV.

124. Moo, *Romans*, 628.

125. Dunn, *Romans*, 2:853; Moo, *Romans*, 620; cf. BDAG, πρόσκομμα, §1.

126. NRSV; ISV; Bruce, *Romans*, 197; cf. Robinson, *Lexicon*, 754. BDAG, σκάνδαλον, lists Rom 9:33 under §2: "an action or circumstance that leads one to act contrary to a proper course of action or set of beliefs, *temptation to sin, enticement*." Given the current context, the outcome seems to lead (figuratively) to actual fatality

iah 28:16 where it denotes "a foundation stone, a tested stone, a precious cornerstone, a sure foundation."[127] Dunn[128] and others[129] note that the Targum (Str-B 3:276) gives an explicit reference to the royal messiah in its interpretation of Isaiah 28:16 (cf. 1QH 6:26–27; 1QS 8:7), which makes it unlikely that it first emerged in Christ-believing circles.[130] The stumbling stone, which is simultaneously the precious cornerstone, is thus Christ himself that God has placed in Zion[131] (cf. 10:11). While the bulk of Israel has stumbled over the stumbling stone, the faithful remnant is those who accepted the gospel by faith[132] (cf. 6:17). The judgment of Israel, which is connected to their hardening (v. 18) and their eventual stumbling (vv. 32–33), is thus effected through Christ (the stumbling stone) and through the cross by implication.[133]

There is another aspect to the remnant concept (to be elaborated upon on pp. 251–319). If the remnant indicates those who survive after judgment in Christ, it implies that those who were judged are everyone *before* the

---

as from "the *bait-stick* of a trap, *a snare*" (Abbott-Smith, *Lexicon*, 408; cf. Wright, "Romans," 649; Mounce, *Romans*, 206; Zerwick and Grosvenor, *Grammatical Analysis*, 481; Lenski, *Corinthians*, 66), which is the literal meaning (cf. BDAG, σκάνδαλον, §1). The Thayer lexicon (Thayer, *Lexicon*, 577) states that the term was figuratively "applied to Jesus Christ, whose person and career were so contrary to the expectations of the Jews concerning the Messiah, that they rejected him and by their obstinacy made shipwreck of salvation."

127. NRSV.
128. Dunn, *Romans*, 2:583.
129. E.g., Hultgren, *Romans*, 381; Cranfield, *Romans*, 2:511.
130. Cf. Käsemann, *Romans*, 278. There is reason for caution, however. Hultgren, *Romans*, 381, argues that the dating of the Targum is difficult and that the interpretations in the Targum mainly represents generations of interpreters after the rise of Christianity (see Chilton, *Isaiah Targum*, xx–xxv).
131. Hultgren, *Romans*, 382; Longenecker, *Introducing Romans*, 418; Seifrid, "Romans," 651; Osborne, *Romans*, 262; Schnelle, *Paul*, 346; Wright, "Romans," 650; Moo, *Romans*, 628–30; Dunn, *Romans*, 2:584–85, 594; Bruce, *Romans*, 198; Cranfield, *Romans*, 2:511–12; Käsemann, *Romans*, 278; Sanday and Headlam, *Romans*, 281–82. Even though Isa 8:14 as prediction of Israel's judgment was a warning that they would fall over the Lord Himself, Paul's quote differs from both the Septuagint and the MT but is identical to 1 Pet 2:8. This suggests that the understanding that Christ is the stumbling stone in Isa 8:14, formed part of an early tradition of the church (Moo, *Romans*, 629; Dunn, *Romans*, 2:584; Stanley, *Language*, 123–24; Koch, *Zeuge*, 59–60; Cranfield, *Romans*, 2:512; cf. Käsemann, *Romans*, 279). Wright, "Romans," 650, notes that at least some Rabbis understood Isa 8:14 in a messianic sense (b. Sanh. 38a).
132. Hultgren, *Romans*, 371; Dunn, *Romans*, 2:593–94.
133. Wright, "Romans," 650, 671; Sanday and Headlam, *Romans*, 280; Denney, "Romans," 668. This connotation is especially evident in 1 Cor 1:23, where Paul connects the cross directly to the σκάνδαλον for the Judeans (cf. the πέτραν σκανδάλου of Rom 9:33).

point of judgment. Most of Paul's exposition in 9:9-17 is indeed about historical (ancient) Israel,[134] and they are by implication included in the judgment, just as God's hardening did not merely involve those of Israel who did not believe in *their* Messiah[135] when He was revealed, but includes the hardening of the whole of historical Israel through the course of salvation history[136] (11:7-10, see pp. 262-67; 2 Cor 3:13-14, see pp. 180-81, esp. note 53). Isaiah's cry on behalf of Israel that [only] a remnant will be saved and that the rest would be judged by implication (v. 27; quoting Isa 10:22), could hardly point merely to a "future" (from the point in time of the prophecy) generation of Israelites.[137] Even Israel's stumbling is not meant as the stumbling of only those who did not believe in their Messiah in the gospel era. It pertains to the whole of the *historical nation of Israel* in terms of their position in salvation history. This *diachronic* perspective on Israel can be derived from Paul's appropriation of Old Testament prophecy (esp. Isa 8:14; 28:16) that is such as to display an interplay between Israel's historical situation and Paul's current situation (cf. Gal 3:14, 16, 19; 1 Cor 10:4). While Paul surely implies a reference to Christ as the stumbling stone in quoting Isaiah 8:14 in Romans 9:33 (see above), its original reference to Yahweh Himself (Isa 8:13) would not be excluded in Paul's reference. Likewise, Israel's "following after a law of righteousness" (v. 31) over the course of Israel's history corresponds to their hardening, and thus includes the whole historical Israel. Their status as "My people" (v. 25) shifted together with the shift of the nations in becoming God's people (except for the remnant), crossing each other in the cross itself. This *crossover* constitutes only a part of Paul's exposition, and does not draw the whole picture. There is more explaining due regarding Israel's position from the perspective of the gospel (10:1-11:36), and the question about historical Israel's ultimate fate is still pending.

Summary and Conclusion

To summarize, Israel's history converged on a single point in their Messiah. Christ according to the flesh (9:5) is the "goal of the entire history laid out

---

134. Gutbrod, "Ἰσραήλ," *TDNT*, 3:386.

135. Wright, "Romans," 625.

136. Cranfield, *Romans*, 2:549; cf. Munck, *Christ and Israel*, 44-45. See esp. the ἄρα οὖν in v. 18, referring back to the whole historical exposition of God's mercy and hardening in vv. 9-17.

137. Cf. the context of the quoted Isa 10, where v. 24 predicts the striking with the rod of the recipients of the prophecy on account of their sin (vv. 10-14).

here"[138] in Romans 9. Christ as culmination of the entire history of Israel, and as fulfillment of the original intention of the promise to Abraham (Rom 4), constitutes the profound *continuity* between Israel and the gospel of faith. But simultaneously, Christ represents the equally profound *crossover* in salvation history. The crossover is not necessarily to be understood as an immediate change in the election of individuals, but describes a change in the conditions or boundary markers[139] of covenant membership of God's people. Through the work of Christ, these conditions have been renewed[140] in that they are not connected to the law and ethnicity any longer (identity mode A), but now to faith alone (identity mode C). The renewal of the conditions of covenant membership is, however, not a change of God's plan (πρόθεσις, v. 11) or a change of salvation history, but the completion and fulfillment thereof in Christ. It was always heading that way. Yet the rearranged covenant and the crossover in salvation history as put forth in 9:24–33, representing the New Covenant,[141] stands in tension and thus in *discontinuity* with the old.

There exists a delicate balance in Israel's hardening and their disobedience,[142] which culminated in the resistance of belief in Christ (10:16) on the one hand, and Israel's hardening as part of God's elective purposes (9:18)[143] in the context of His salvation historical plan on the other hand. Israel's hardening is simultaneously its own responsibility and part of God's plan.[144] The bigger picture of salvation history around Israel's Messiah and the *crossover* in covenant membership (esp. 9:25–33) can be illustrated by the following diagram:

---

138. Wright, "Romans," 643.
139. Wright, "Romans," 626.
140. Cf. Wright, "Romans," 671.
141. Cf. Käsemann, *Romans*, 273.
142. Cf. Cranfield, *Romans*, 2:504; Barrett, *Romans*, 2:196.
143. Cf. Cranfield, *Romans*, 2:498.
144. Abasciano, "Paul's Use," 116; Mounce, *Romans*, 205; Bruce, *Romans*, 196; cf. Käsemann, *Romans*, 276; Ridderbos, *Romeinen*, 226.

GOD'S SAVED ISRAEL

Salvation-Historical Diagram

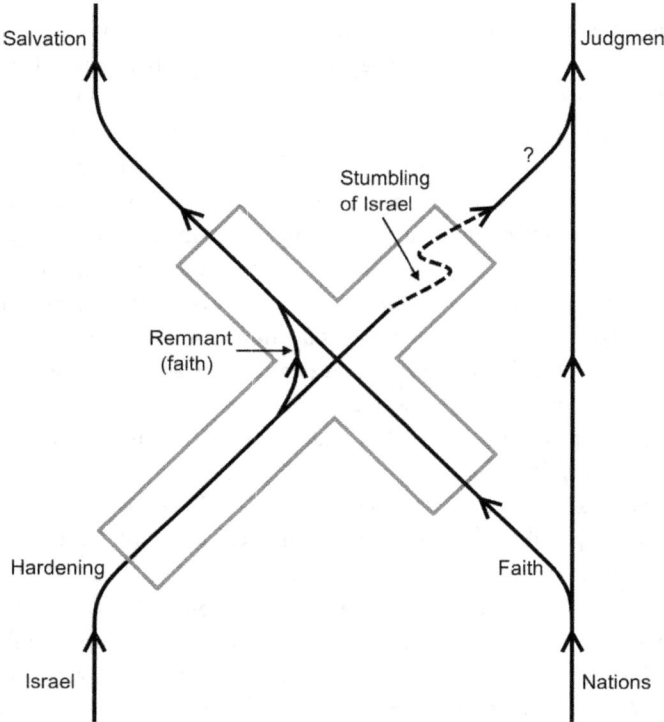

The angle of the diagram illustrates the *crossover* in salvation history, where those who were not God's people are now called His people (Rom 9:25, quoting Hos 2:23). Israel's history is portrayed by the left bottom line bending off course, representing the hardening of Israel. Their history culminates in Jesus their Messiah, represented by the grey cross. Christ is both a stumbling stone over whom Israel stumbles (dotted, s-shaped arrow), resulting in judgment of some kind (see below), and the object of faith for the believing remnant, portrayed as converging with believing gentiles (nations) unto salvation. The nations (right bottom) are principally included in Christ and partake in salvation by faith. Note that the nations may carry straight on to judgment without belief in Christ,[145] while Israel's history has no other

---

145. This is already established in Rom 1–3, where Paul described God's wrath over sin (1:18–32) and his judgment of all unrighteousness (esp. 2:2, 5–6), to which is all people have lapsed into (3:1–26). There is righteousness (escape of judgment by implication) only by faith in Christ (3:27–31).

option but to climax in their Messiah,¹⁴⁶ which represents a crossroad in their history, either unto salvation or unto judgment.

Some caution concerning Israel's judgment is warranted here (marked with a question mark: "?"). While the general thrust in this passage implies a casting away of Israel¹⁴⁷ or that they are now "outside the sphere of righteousness,"¹⁴⁸ the implication of this aspect is not explicit at this point in Paul's exposition, and is due for further clarification and qualification later on (i.e., Rom 11).

Romans 10 (AC)

Paul's "heart's desire and prayer to God"¹⁴⁹ in verse 1 is a return to the anguish in his heart for his kindred according to the flesh (9:2–3),¹⁵⁰ that they might be saved (εἰς σωτηρίαν, 10:1) in spite of their stumbling (9:32–33). But, surprising as it might appear, the salvation of historical (ancient) Israel might be included in his anguish. This possibility is introduced heuristically at this point, and will be tested and expounded upon in the rest of the discussion.

Paul's Hermeneutic as Dialectical and Diachronic

At this point in Paul's exposition, it is not entirely clear what the position of historical Israel is in terms of salvation. It does in fact appear that they as a people have been rejected in Christ,¹⁵¹ not only in terms of covenant status, but in terms of salvation too (9:25–33; see above). While Paul did identify a historical *inner* Israel as "children of the promise," a people "called" and "elected" (9:8–23), Paul never explicitly said that they were saved. He only referred to Isaiah who cried that [only] *those remaining* (those who believe in Christ, by implication) are saved (9:27–33). The absence of a specific designation for whom exactly he is concerned about (αὐτῶν, 10:1)¹⁵² may be deliberate if Paul

---

146. Wright, "Romans," 671.

147. Wright, "Romans," 635, 649, 651; cf. Barrett, *Romans*, 192; Sanday and Headlam, *Romans*, 263, 300–301.

148. Dodd, *Romans*, 175.

149. NRSV.

150. Hultgren, *Romans*, 382; Wright, "Romans," 653; cf. Käsemann, *Romans*, 280.

151. Cf. Richardson, *Introduction*, 266.

152. Some texts contain τοῦ Ἰσραήλ ἐστιν (instead of αὐτῶν) in Rom 10:1: K L 018 81 104 181 326 330 436 451 614 629 630 1241 1877 1984 1985 2200 2464 4292 𝔐. In the light of the weak external evidence and Paul's definition of Israel in 9:6, the reading

has both current unbelieving Judeans and historical Israel in mind. The basis for salvation that Paul has established up to this point in his letter, is faith in Christ (1:16; 5:9, 10; 8:24),[153] which converges with the Christ-believing remnant of Israel after judgment in Christ (9:27). The impression left by the salvation-historical *crossover* (see above) at this point in Paul's exposition, is that historical (even *inner*) Israel is in fact not saved.

As seen from the previous section, a dialectic relationship between the current hardened, unbelieving Judeans and historical Israel might be suggested by Paul's appropriation of Scripture in 9:25–33. The same hermeneutical principle might be applied here in 10:1–21. This principle might actually be engrained much deeper into Paul's use of Scripture than what might appear on the surface.[154] As discussed, a similar kind of dialectic can be detected in Galatians 3, where Paul views the gospel as being preached to Abraham (v. 14) or where he sees Christ himself as the only recipient of the promise to Abraham (vv. 16, 19). In 1 Corinthians 10:4, Paul explains the rock that Moses encountered in the desert as Christ, as if Paul is projecting Christ into the Old Testament.

In terms of Paul's engagement with Old Testament Scriptures, Cranfield comes close to identifying this hermeneutic by stating that Paul, "since he had been convinced that Jesus of Nazareth was God's Messiah, become possessed of what he saw to be key to their [OT] interpretation"[155] and "key to its proper understanding."[156] Similarly, Abasciano writes the following:

> Paul interprets the OT through the lens of Christ and the gospel even as he interprets Christ and the gospel through the lens of the OT. Very often the gospel provides the presuppositions by which to interpret the OT, and in addition to argumentative proof or illustration, the OT provides much of the content and direction of Paul's teaching within the metanarrative of the gospel and redemptive history.[157]

This hermeneutic is well accounted for in 2 Corinthians 3:14–16, where Paul sees a veil remaining over the hearts of those reading the Old Covenant/Testament, only to be removed in Christ. The gospel is so central in

---

τοῦ Ἰσραήλ εστιν is unlikely to be authentic.

153. Although Christ is not specifically mentioned in 8:24, the first person plural (ἐσώθημεν) implies salvation of the Christ-believing community, including Paul.

154. Contra Käsemann, *Romans*, 295, who argues that Paul's quotations "almost always lose their historical meaning" (cf. Sanday and Headlam, *Romans*, 303).

155. Cranfield, *Romans*, 2:866.

156. Cranfield, *Romans*, 2:869.

157. Abasciano, "Paul's Use," 374–75; cf. Carson and Moo, *Introduction*, 373.

salvation history for Paul that the gospel actually seems to have a retrojective[158] function for Paul. On one level Christ's work in his death and resurrection appears to have an actual effect into the past, spanning over the entire human history. On another level, there exists for Paul a profound *dialectic* between the epochs before and after Christ's work, in that the gospel was already locked up (hidden) in the past, only to be revealed at the fullness of time (Gal 4:4).

In terms of the letter to the Romans, the same elements of hiddenness and revelation of the gospel in Christ are evident in 16:25–26. In 2:16, there is an intricate relationship among God's judgment, hidden things of people, the gospel, and Christ. God's judgment of all people will be "according to my [Paul's] gospel" and "through Christ." While the exact implication of this verse is difficult to determine, Christ's position within salvation history and his (eschatological?)[159] judgment is central for Paul, affecting all human beings (2:11–16), including historical Israel by implication. Even Christ's righteousness affects all people (δικαιώματος εἰς πάντας ἀνθρώπους, 5:18). Although these cosmic aspects[160] of Christ's work and his lordship[161] are difficult to pin down, there appears to be a deep-seated *diachronic* aspect to the gospel that has to be kept in mind in the way Paul appropriates Scripture in Romans 10.

Law, Gospel and Israel

The notion behind οὐ κατ' ἐπίγνωσιν (v. 2) and ἀγνοοῦντες (v. 3) is that these people were ignorant and "without vital knowledge"[162] in spite of their zeal.[163] Their ignorance can be seen in their seeking to establish their "own righteousness" (ἰδίαν δικαιοσύνην, v. 3), which is contrasted to "God's righteousness" (δικαιοσύνη τοῦ θεοῦ, v. 3). The righteousness of God implies

---

158. "Retrojective" is more than "retrospective." The latter denotes "looking back on or dealing with past events or situations," but to "retroject" is to "project backwards" (Soanes and Stevenson, *Dictionary*, 1229, 1230).

159. Cf. Moo, *Romans*, 154.

160. A cosmic dimension to the gospel would correspond to Col 1:23 (Wright, "Romans," 668); Eph 1:10, 21 and 3:15–20, which would contribute to arguing for Pauline authorship of these letters.

161. Cf. Käsemann, *Romans*, 289, 294, 296.

162. Wright, "Romans," 654; cf. Cranfield, *Romans*, 2:514.

163. In this regard Osborne, *Romans*, 264, points to the period 400 BCE to 100 CE, which he interprets as "the first such extended period of zeal for God in the history of the nation."

both "being right" and "declaring right,"[164] which are God-given.[165] The verb ὑποτάσσω shows that "the righteousness of God is an active force to which one must humbly and obediently subordinate oneself."[166] Their "own righteousness" is essentially opposed to faith. The sources of righteousness are contrasted: either as originating from God and obtained through faith or as originating from human beings.[167] This reading of their "own righteousness" is strongly suggested by the parallel Philippians 3:6-9, where Paul's "own righteousness of law" is contrasted to "the righteousness from God based on faith"[168] (see pp. 135-47).

Christ is the culmination[169] and termination (v. 4)[170] of the Mosaic law.[171] This notion is underlined by the contrast between verses 3 and 4, where "Paul wants to stress the *discontinuity* between Christ and the law"[172] (cf. 9:30-32a). The similarity between 10:3-4 and 3:20-23 is striking: According to 3:20-23,

164. Moo, *Romans*, 633.
165. Cranfield, *Romans*, 2:515.
166. Moo, *Romans*, 633; cf. Cranfield, *Romans*, 2:515; Barrett, *Romans*, 197.
167. Moo, *Romans*, 633-34; Käsemann, *Romans*, 281; cf. Hultgren, *Romans*, 383, 384; Mounce, *Romans*, 206-7; Barrett, *Romans*, 196. While my reading is not principally against the NPP, contrasting God's righteousness merely to Judean exclusivism and a misunderstanding of what obedience entailed (Dunn, *Romans*, 2:595-96) undercuts the depth of this contrast (cf. Moo, "Israel," 215). Whereas Wright, "Romans," 654-55, interprets "own righteousness" similarly, he understands "God's righteousness" as God's "covenantally loyal actions."
168. NRSV; cf. Moo, *Romans*, 635; Bruce, *Romans*, 199; Käsemann, *Romans*, 281.
169. Osborne, *Romans*, 265, 269; Moo, *Romans*, 637.
170. BDAG, τέλος, §1; Moo, *Romans*, 637; Bruce, *Romans*, 200; cf. Zerwick and Grosvenor, *Grammatical Analysis*, 482; contra Wright, "Romans," 657-58. While τέλος may also denote a "goal," (BDAG, τέλος §3; Zerwick and Grosvenor, *Grammatical Analysis*, 482; Cranfield, *Romans*, 2:519-20) it does not lose its temporal meaning ("termination") in this context (cf. Moo, *Romans*, 641). My rendering "culmination and termination" is intended to incorporate both meanings (termination and goal/fulfillment; cf. Moo, *Romans*, 641; Barrett, *Romans*, 197; Bruce, *Romans*, 200), where "culmination" would convey an element of continuity and "termination" would account for an element of discontinuity. Dunn, *Romans*, 2:590-91, 596-97, argues for the end (termination) of an incorrect understanding of the law, and Wright, "Romans," 657-58, argues for a fulfillment (τέλος) of the law and a new way of keeping it. While my translation ("culmination and termination") leans more toward accentuating discontinuity with the law (contra Wright, "Romans," 657-58), some ambiguity regarding Paul's intention with τέλος arguably remains.
171. Moo, *Romans*, 636; cf. Cranfield, *Romans*, 2:516.
172. Moo, *Romans*, 640, emphasis added; cf. Hultgren, *Romans*, 384-85; contra Dunn, *Romans*, 2:591 and Cranfield, *Romans*, 2:524, who do not view Christ and the law as mutually exclusive categories.

"ALL ISRAEL" AND "THE ISRAEL OF GOD" 255

1. the works of the law cannot confer righteousness,
2. and God's righteousness has been manifested apart from the law.
3. Righteousness is for all who believe.

In 10:3-4,

1. people have not established their own righteousness in not submitting to God's righteousness,
2. and Christ is the end of the law.
3. Righteousness is for all who believe.[173]

In essence, the end of the law stands for the end of an epoch[174] (Gal 3:17-25) where one's identity of being God's people was defined by the law (identity mode A; cf. 9:4). In the new epoch in Christ, identity is being defined by faith in Christ (identity mode C) apart from the law (3:21),[175] and by not being "under the law" (6:14, 15).

Verse 5 confirms the righteousness of the law as constituted by "doing" (ποιέω) things in order to "live" (ζάω) by them (quoting Lev 18:5).[176] Although there was nothing inherently wrong with the law and its objective to give live (cf. Gal 3:12), it could not ultimately provide life or righteousness[177] for it was impossible to adhere to the law[178] (cf. 9:31-32). This "doing" according to Moses' law is being contrasted with[179] the righteousness based on faith (vv. 6-13). Moo makes the following significant remark:

173. Cf. Moo, *Romans*, 640.

174. Dunn, *Romans*, 2:600, 611-12; cf. Witherington and Hyatt, *Romans*, 261; Moo, *Romans*, 640; Käsemann, *Romans*, 286; Barrett, *Romans*, 197.

175. Dunn, *Romans*, 2:165, understands "apart from the law" in 3:21 as outside national and religious parameters marked out by the law. This notion does not have to be excluded here. Cf. Witherington and Hyatt, *Romans*, 260-61, who combine the TAP and the NPP: "righteousness is not attained nor maintained by means of the Law but by another means."

176. Cranfield, *Romans*, 2:522, argues that "the man" (ἄνθρωπος, v. 5) is Christ, the only one who could obey perfectly and earn a righteous status for himself and for those who believe in him. Although this seems to be a legitimate interpretation, it would run against the general notion in Gal 3:12, unless one interprets Gal 3:12 as pointing to Christ's obedience too (as Cranfield does). This interpretation has to be considered as a possibility or might represent a second layer to Paul's exposition.

177. Moo, *Romans*, 654; cf. Hultgren, *Romans*, 384; Witherington and Hyatt, *Romans*, 261; Bruce, *Romans*, 200; Barrett, *Romans*, 202.

178. Hultgren, *Romans*, 384; Moo, *Romans*, 654; Mounce, *Romans*, 208; Räisänen, *Paul*, 95, 199; contra Dunn, *Romans*, 2:601.

179. Hultgren, *Romans*, 386; Moo, *Romans*, 644; Barrett, *Romans*, 198; cf. Käsemann, *Romans*, 284, 286. Although defined differently, Dunn, *Romans*, 2:602, acknowledges a

> Throughout salvation history, faith and doing, "gospel" and "law" have run along side-by-side... But, as it is fatal to ignore one or the other, it is equally fatal to mix them or to use them for the wrong ends. The *OT Israelite* who sought to base his or her relationship with God on the law rather than on God's gracious election in and through the Abrahamic promise arrangement made this mistake.[180]

Apart from Moo's perspective on the relationship between law and gospel, he provides a crucial *diachronic* perspective on Israel's relationship with God and the gospel itself that is certainly present in Romans 10.

In verses 6–8, Paul refers to Deuteronomy 30:12–14 and interprets it in the light of Christ and the gospel.[181] The best explanation to Paul's referral to the text of Deuteronomy is probably that it is an expression of God's grace "in establishing a relationship with his people."[182] The ascent to heaven (v. 6) seems to allude to the incarnation of God's Son, who has been "brought down" already. Similarly, the meaning of verse 7 is probably that the fact of the resurrection can be used to deny any need to "go down to the abyss" to bring Christ up from "the realm of the dead."[183] The "word" (ῥῆμα, v. 8) that is near, is identified with the "word of faith that we proclaim" (ῥῆμα τῆς πίστεως ὃ κηρύσσομεν), and points to the gospel[184] (cf. v. 16). It is as if Paul reads the gospel back into Deuteronomy 30 in such a way that he perceives the gospel to have always been there.

Yet, in verse 9 Paul identifies belief in the gospel that leads to salvation as confession in Jesus as Lord and belief that God raised him from the dead. Most commentators recognize traces of an early confession of faith in the early church in the formula "Jesus is Lord"[185] (cf. 1 Cor 8:6; Phil 2:11; Col 2:6), which might have been present at baptism in or into the name of Jesus[186] (cf.

---

contrast here. Contra Wright, "Romans," 658–63, who argues for righteousness based on faith as "true Torah-observance." Although the gospel can be understood as the fulfillment of the Torah (especially in referring to the OT as a whole), it signifies a new mode of existence apart from the works of the law (3:21), where the law is in no way constitutive of the new identity in Christ (7:4–6)

180. Moo, *Romans*, 649, emphasis added.

181. Moo, *Romans*, 654.

182. Moo, *Romans*, 653; cf. Witherington and Hyatt, *Romans*, 262.

183. Moo, *Romans*, 656; Cranfield, *Romans*, 2:525; Barrett, *Romans*, 199; cf. Mounce, *Romans*, 208.

184. Cranfield, *Romans*, 2:526; Barrett, *Romans*, 200.

185. E.g., Moo, *Romans*, 658; Dunn, *Romans*, 2:607; Bruce, *Romans*, 202; Cranfield, *Romans*, 2:528; Barrett, *Romans*, 200–201.

186. Wright, "Romans," 664; Dunn, *Romans*, 2:608; Bruce, *Romans*, 202; Cranfield, *Romans*, 2:527.

Rom 6:3; Acts 2:38; 8:16; 10:48; 19:5). Dunn and Käsemann rightly argue for Christ's lordship as achieving a cosmic and universal quality[187] (mainly vv. 9–13). Salvation is reiterated in verse 10, which is obtained by confession, and which functions interchangeably with belief from the heart unto righteousness.[188] If righteousness, salvation and faith are linked, it might put a further question mark behind historical Israel's salvation as portrayed in 9:30–33. The undeniable universal nature of the gospel[189] for "everyone believing on Him" (v. 11, quoting Isa 28:16), for both "Judean and Greek" (v. 12) without difference (διαστολή), is evident in verses 11 to 13. The same universality can be applied to Jesus' lordship. He is the Lord (v. 12, pointing back to κύριον Ἰησοῦν in v. 9 by γάρ [x2] in vv. 10–11) who is "rich toward all the ones calling on Him." And then in verse 13 Paul substantiates salvation through Christ and his lordship with an exact quote (LXX) from Joel 2:32 ("Everyone who calls on the name of the Lord shall be saved").[190] While the quote from Isaiah 28:16 (v. 11) in its original context can be interpreted as messianic (cf. 9:33), Joel 2:32 (v. 13) refers to Yahweh (MT).[191]

Together with Jesus' designation as κύριος (v. 9), which is the same title for Yahweh in the Septuagint, and Paul's identification of Jesus with Yahweh (v. 13), Jesus is identified with God.[192] With Paul's identification of Jesus with Yahweh, Paul once again seems to read Christ back into the Old Testament. If this is what Paul intended, it might prompt serious questions. How could the gospel be read into the Old Testament? How can gospel principles be identified with Old Testament principles? But the questions might even stretch deeper. Does the universal principal of salvation through faith in Christ only, apply to historical Israel as well? If that is the case, how can it be so if they have not heard the gospel? And this is, I suggest, exactly where Paul might be at this point in his exposition (v. 14).

While the αὐτῶν in verse 1 almost certainly alludes to his kindred according to the flesh, his "brothers" (9:3) who stumbled over the cross (9:32–33) in unbelief (see above), Paul's exposition from 9:4 up to this point (10:14) has never treated them in isolation from historical Israelites, as if Paul continuously has historical Israel and their salvation on his heart as well. My approach thus does not have to exclude current Judeans that resist

---

187. Dunn, *Romans*, 2:615, 617–18; Käsemann, *Romans*, 283, 289, 294, 296.

188. Mounce, *Romans*, 210; Bruce, *Romans*, 202.

189. Moo, *Romans*, 658–60; Mounce, *Romans*, 209; Käsemann, *Romans*, 292; Cranfield, *Romans*, 2:532; Barrett, *Romans*, 202; Sanday and Headlam, *Romans*, 290.

190. NRSV.

191. Crenshaw, *Joel*, 169.

192. Osborne, *Romans*, 271; Moo, *Romans*, 660; Mounce, *Romans*, 209; Cranfield, *Romans*, 2:529.

the gospel, but it might help understand Paul's hermeneutic and the way in which he applies Scripture here. The more Scriptures Paul quotes, the more he seems to focus the attention back to historical Israel and even measure their unbelief to his gospel (see below).

Paul asks legitimate questions in verses 14 to 15a. It is unreasonable to expect people to call on Jesus as Lord if they have not believed in him, to believe in him if they have not heard of him, or hear without a preacher being sent. Whereas these questions might be applied to all people in general[193] or to Judeans who resist the gospel in Paul's time to remove any excuse,[194] these questions would make even more sense if applied to historical Israel. Then the questions would be unavoidable and hard pressed for an answer. For if Paul identifies belief in Jesus as the only universal source of salvation, how can his lordship be applied to historical Israel? Paul's quote from Isaiah 52:7 (v. 15b) legitimizes the need for a preacher of the gospel. This quote might serve as legitimization of Paul's apostolic mission,[195] but could additionally identify the gospel and its preaching within the Old Testament itself, even though in another form or with another meaning.[196] Historical Israel knew about "the gospel of peace" and those preaching it, even though they might not have had the same understanding of it as Paul has of his gospel.

In verse 16, Paul points out that not all have obeyed the gospel. Whereas most commentators see this as the disobedience of them that did not believe the gospel in Paul's time,[197] if Paul had current unbelieving Judeans in mind, the aorist indicative (ὑπήκουσαν) seems somewhat inappropriate. One might rather expect the present or perfect tense here. Normally, the aorist indicative possesses a punctiliar *Aktionsart*[198] like a snapshot in the past,[199] which in this context might point to historical Israel. Paul closely follows the Septuagint in his quote of Isaiah 53:1 (κύριε, τίς ἐπίστευσεν τῇ

---

193. Moo, *Romans*, 664.

194. Cf. Cranfield, *Romans*, 2:537.

195. Cranfield, *Romans*, 2:535; cf. Barrett, *Romans*, 204.

196. Whereas Isa 52:7 has been interpreted in terms of the messianic age in later Rabbinic literature (Cranfield, *Romans*, 2:535), the same notion as in Isaiah 52:7 occurs in Nahum 1:15 (LXX: 2:1): "Look! On the mountains the feet of one who brings good tidings, who proclaims peace! Celebrate your festivals, O Judah, fulfill your vows, for never again shall the wicked invade you; they are utterly cut off" (NRSV). This shows that the idea of "good news" (gospel) was operational within the Old Testament time itself.

197. E.g., Osborne, *Romans*, 276; Moo, *Romans*, 644–45; Dunn, *Romans*, 2:622–23; Cranfield, *Romans*, 2:536.

198. BDF §318.

199. Wallace, *Grammar*, 555.

ἀκοῇ ἡμῶν). Apart from possibly pointing forward to Israel's rejection of the gospel of Jesus, the prophet himself (Isa 53:1) probably felt that he spoke mainly to unbelieving ears[200] (cf. Isa 28:9-15; 29:10-15; 30:9-11; 42:23). In connection with the quote from Isaiah 53:1, Seifrid writes:

> That disobedience corresponds typically to the past, when Israel disbelieved the "report" of the prophet; not only the aorist tense of the verb (*hypēkousan*) but also the repeated naming of Isaiah and Moses (with the temporal marker *prōtos*, "at the start" [10:19]) mark the event as lying in the past.[201]

In Isaiah 53:1, the complaint of unbelief thus "also comes from the mouth of Israel,"[202] which is historical Israel.[203] Hultgren, Bruce and Ridderbos[204] display diachronic awareness and a sense of continuity in terms of current unbelieving Judeans and historical Israel in their treatment of verse 16. It is thus possible that Paul used εὐαγγέλιον in very much the same way as in Galatians 3:8, where he explicitly mentions that the gospel was preached before (προευαγγελίζομαι) to Abraham.

In verse 17, Paul reiterates that faith originates from hearing, and that hearing comes from the word of the Messiah (Χριστοῦ).[205] Paul's unusual use of ῥῆμα might point back to verse 8 where he quoted from Deuteronomy 30:14 (Ἐγγύς σου τὸ ῥῆμά ἐστιν) and correspond to his next quote (τὰ ῥήματα αὐτῶν) from Psalm 18:5 (LXX) in verse 18.[206] Paul's quote from Psalm 18:5 (LXX) is once again an answer to the question: "have they not heard?" (cf. v. 14). The context of Psalm 18:5 (LXX) is cosmic: the heavens are telling the glory of God and the firmament proclaims His handiwork (18:2, LXX). This is the context in which "their voice" went out into all the earth and "their words" to the ends of the world (Rom 10:18). Is Paul's allusion to the gospel that went out to the whole world simply hyperbolic?[207] Wright correctly notes that this verse "can scarcely refer to Paul's own apostolic mission"[208] because of the "universality" displayed in the Psalm.[209]

---

200. Rawlinson, *Isaiah*, 294, on Isa 53:1.
201. Seifrid, "Romans," 662.
202. Delitzsch, *Isaiah*, 286.
203. Cf. Hultgren, *Romans*, 390; Childs, *Isaiah*, 414; Oswalt, *Isaiah*, 381.
204. Hultgren, *Romans*, 390; Bruce, *Romans*, 206; Ridderbos, *Romeinen*, 241.
205. Wright, "Romans," 668; Sanday and Headlam, *Romans*, 299.
206. Wright, "Romans," 668.
207. Moo, *Romans*, 667; Dunn, *Romans*, 2:630; cf. Bruce, *Romans*, 206.
208. Wright, "Romans," 668; contra Osborne, *Romans*, 279; Dunn, *Romans*, 2:624, 630; Barrett, *Romans*, 205.
209. Cf. Ridderbos, *Romeinen*, 242-43.

But may Paul indeed connect cosmic significance to the gospel in Christ, as if the glory of God and his handiwork can be understood through the lens of the gospel? An affirmative answer has to be seen as a possibility, for even historical Israel would have a conception of the glory of God and His handiwork (Ps 18:2, LXX).

Paul now explicitly mentions Ἰσραήλ in verses 19 and 21. Since Romans 9 he has never disconnected the term Ἰσραήλ from historical Israel, and is most probably not doing it here, especially in view of the Scriptures that Paul quotes in verses 19 to 21. Paul asks if Israel did not know (γινώσκω, v. 19), echoing much of the same notion in verse 2 (ἐπίγνωσις). Cranfield shows that there is a sense in which they knew and another sense in which they did not. They have been recipients of God's special revelation, but they did not understand. Their ignorance is a blameworthy (not excusable) ignorance.[210] In Paul's exact quote from the Septuagint (Deut 32:21), Israel's provocation of God to jealousy (Deut 32:21a, not quoted) are turned against them to provoke and anger them to jealousy (Rom 10:19). Their unfaithfulness and perversity (Deut 32:20), and by implication, their resistance of God's faithfulness are historical and had been addressed historically. Even Israel's provocation to jealousy via other nations is historical, constituted mainly by the Samaritan and Babylonian nations.[211] Driver suggests the possibility that the Midianites and the "children of the East" (Judg 6:2-6), or the Arameans (2 Kgs 6:2; 6:23) at whose hands the Israelites sometimes experienced a sharp defeat could constitute the Israelite's provocation to jealousy (Deut 32:21). The Scythians who swept over Canaan under Josiah (cf. Jer 5:15-17) or even other heathen nations could be considered in the same light (cf. Isa 24:16b; 33:1). Driver argues that it is even probable that Deuteronomy 32:21 does not have a definite people in view, but pictured heathen nations in general, who Israel would disdain as a people, as instruments in God's hands of the retribution awaiting Israel.[212]

In the reference to Isaiah 65:1 in Romans 10:20, Paul at first glance seems to have gentiles in mind not seeking God and not enquiring after Him, and yet found God.[213] Paul would then contrast this to historical Israel in verse 21 (quoting Isaiah 65:2), a "contrary" (ἀντίλεγω) and "disobedient" (ἀπειθέω) people. But many Old Testament commentators[214] interpret

210. Cranfield, *Romans*, 2:538.

211. Cranfield, *Romans*, 2:539, refers to this interpretation from Jewish literature (Sir 50:25-26; Jerusalem Targum I; cf. Seifrid, "Romans," 665).

212. Driver, *Deuteronomy*, 365-66.

213. Longenecker, *Epistle to the Romans*, 859; Middendorf, *Romans*, 1049; Moo, *Romans*, 669; Dunn, *Romans*, 2:626; Cranfield, *Romans*, 2:540; Barrett, *Romans*, 206.

214. Noted by Moo, *Romans*, 669; e.g., Childs, *Isaiah*, 535.

Isaiah 65:1 in its context as God making Himself known to the people of Israel and not to gentile nations as such.[215] In the light of my proposed hermeneutic regarding Paul and Israel in Romans 10 (see pp. 251–53), it would be possible to interpret verse 20 as indeed pointing to historical Israel. The notion would be that God did manifest Himself (ἐμφανής) to them and did show or prove Himself (εὑρίσκω)[216] to them in spite of their truancy and rebellion. The significance would then be that Paul used this to show that Israel had no excuse. If this is the case, verse 21 is not a contrast to verse 20, but a further elaboration on verse 20.[217] Denney writes that God's outstretched arms (v. 21) were "the symbol of that incessant pleading love which Israel through *all its history* has consistently despised."[218] Seifrid notes that historical Israel's recalcitrance and rebellion is a condition that extended into the present for Paul (Rom 10:19–21).[219] This last verse at least thus has to "refer to Israel both in their original context and in Paul's application of them."[220] This should be an indication that Paul probably had this *diachronic* and *dialectical* perspective in mind in most (if not all) of his quotations from the Old Testament in Romans 10.

In summary, the perspective on Romans 10 that I argue for is that Paul includes historical Israel in his removal of excuse for unbelief. It has to be noted that, even though Paul has put forth Abraham's faith in Romans 4, Paul never connects faith as such to historical Israel, even though they were supposed to believe and are judged by their unbelief (Rom 9–10). The principle of faith in terms of righteousness and covenant membership seems to be reserved for believers in Christ only. Yet Paul appears to retrojectively measure historical Israel's unrighteousness and unbelief against the gospel, and removes even their excuse for not yielding to the "gospel" (even though arguably in another form). Paul might apply a hyperbolic technique in exaggerating historical Israel's unrighteousness, unbelief and lack of excuse in Romans 10 to appeal to his readers' emotions in order to enhance the effect of what he plans to say in Romans 11.

---

215. Hultgren, *Romans*, 392; Dunn, *Romans*, 2:626; Bruce, *Romans*, 208; Sanday and Headlam, *Romans*, 300.

216. These renderings ("show" or "prove" Himself) are well within semantic range here (BDAG, εὑρίσκω, §2) in line with the Hebrew נִמְצֵאתִי (Isa 65:1).

217. This interpretation would be made possible by δέ in both verses 20 and 21, which can be translated as "but" or "and" (BDAG, δέ, §1, 4).

218. Denney, "Romans," 675, emphasis added; adopted by Mounce, *Romans*, 213; cf. Bruce, *Romans*, 204; Cranfield, *Romans*, 2:541.

219. Seifrid, "Unrighteous," 144.

220. Bruce, *Romans*, 208; cf. Hultgren, *Romans*, 392.

The modes of identity are not presented explicitly in Romans 10 and are implied implicitly by Paul's contrasts between law and gospel, righteousness and unrighteousness, and belief and unbelief. These contrasts would mainly allude to identity modes A and C, while identity mode AB might be possible if Paul has *inner*, yet *unbelieving* Israel in mind in 10:16–21.

Romans 11 (ABC)

Both verses 1 and 11 start with the same formula (Λέγω οὖν), which marks verses 1 to 10 and 11 to 32 as separate literary units.[221] Verses 1 to 10 mainly answer the question whether God has rejected his people (v. 1). The themes of rejection (ἀπωθέομαι, vv. 1, 2), the remnant (vv. ὑπολείπω, v. 3, καταλείπω, v. 4, λεῖμμα, v. 5), and God's gracious (χάρις, vv. 5, 6 [x3]) election (ἐκλογή, vv. 5, 7) are prominent in verses 1 to 10.

Verses 11 to 32, which fall under the main rubric of Israel's salvation, can be broken down into three sub-units: (1) Verses 11 to 15 mainly answers the question around Israel's fall (v. 11). (2) Verses 16 to 24 represent the olive tree metaphor, which explains much of the logic behind the election of God's people in the light of faith (in Christ). (3) Verses 25 to 32 constitute the mystery of Israel's salvation and explain it in terms of the balanced logic behind the whole of salvation history.

On the high note of the mystery of Israel's salvation and God's perfect grace toward all people, Paul concludes his salvation-historical exposition[222] that started in Romans 9 with an appropriate doxology in verses 33 to 36.

The Remnant and the Hardened (vv. 1–10)

As argued on pp. 77–100, Paul has never lost historical (ancient) Israel out of sight in Romans 9 to 10. When Paul asks whether God has rejected Israel (11:1), his diachronic and dialectical hermeneutic is retained. As I will argue, Paul in fact has historical Israel in mind in most of verses 1 to 24, but extends it to unbelieving Judeans in Paul's present where he explicitly compares historical Israel with the present time (καὶ ἐν τῷ νῦν καιρῷ, v. 5), where he draws the line of Israel's "sleep" into the present (ἕως τῆς σήμερον ἡμέρας, v. 8), or where Paul wants to provoke his "own flesh" (μου τὴν σάρκα, v. 14) to jealousy in order to lead them to salvation by faith (vv. 11, 14, 23). Paul never unambiguously describes present unbelieving Judeans with the

---

221. Moo, *Romans*, 671.
222. Cf. Longenecker, *Introducing Romans*, 419.

term Ἰσραήλ or even as Ἰσραηλίτης (denoting primarily historical Israelites in 9:4 and Paul's own descent in 11:1 and 2 Cor 11:22). Conversely, he never unambiguously describes ancient Israel with the term Ἰουδαῖος. Yet there is *continuity* in terms of the hardening of historical Israel and unbelieving Judeans in Paul's present.

In answer to the question whether God has rejected His people (λαός, v. 1), the answer is emphatically negative (μὴ γένοιτο). But instead of arguing for the continued existence of Israel as such, Paul points to himself who is a Judean Christ-believer. Jewett is essentially correct that "Paul uses himself as an example that Israel has not been abandoned."[223] It seems significant, however, that he does not refer to himself as of Ἰσραήλ, but as an Ἰσραηλίτης. As can be derived from the study up to this point, in Paul the latter term leans more toward being part of national Israel than it bears connotations about being part of God's *inner* elect people (2 Cor 11:22, Rom 9:4). With Paul's use of Ἰσραηλίτης, which he qualifies as denoting his physical descent from Abraham and membership of Benjamin's tribe, he identifies his ethnic roots within national, physical Israel (identity mode A), which is on another level than *inner* (true) Israel (9:6-8). Yet through the course of Romans, Paul has redefined the decisive markers of identity as God's people in the light of the gospel, not in terms of physical descent, but in terms of faith in Christ (3:28-4:25) and the work and presence of the life-giving Spirit (7:6; 8:1-16). Elsewhere, Paul considers his ethnic heritage as insignificant in defining a righteous status with God (e.g., Phil 3:8-9; implied in Rom 9:6-8). One therefore has to acknowledge a tension between "physical" (ethnic) continuity (Paul/Judeans believing in Christ) and "spiritual" discontinuity (rejection of hardened Israel).

Verse 2 states that God has not rejected his people that He foreknew. Since God's people in general is in view (not specific individuals), God's foreknowledge (προγινώσκω, v. 2) is not to be understood in terms of individual election but "is speaking of God's election of the people as a whole"[224] (cf. 9:11-23 above). In proving this, Paul in verse 3 refers to historical Israel (Ἰσραήλ, v. 2) by quoting 1 Kings 19:10 and 1 Kings 19:18 (in Rom 11:4) respectively. Both these quotations are utilized because of their reference to the "remnant," or more specifically, those who are left

---

223. Jewett, *Romans*, 653; cf. Hultgren, *Romans*, 399; Bruce, *Romans*, 208; Käsemann, *Romans*, 299-300; Cranfield, *Romans*, 2:543; Barrett, *Romans*, 208; Ridderbos, *Romeinen*, 245.

224. Moo, *Romans*, 674; cf. Witherington and Hyatt, *Romans*, 266; Dunn, *Romans*, 2:636; Cranfield, *Romans*, 2:545.

remaining (ὑπολείπω, v. 3)[225] or those who are left over (καταλείπω, v. 4).[226] Paul's reference to the remnant recalls 9:27, where he referred to Isaiah's cry, which indicated those surviving as the [only] ones being saved after God's judgment. A similar element of judgment is present in these two verses quoted from 1 Kings.[227] The finality of that judgment seems to be enhanced by Paul's change of the future καταλείψεις (1 Kgs 19:18, LXX) to the aorist κατέλιπον. Except for Paul's reference to his ethnic descent (v. 1), which does not as such indicate his connection to true, *inner* Israel, Paul has only given a partial answer to his question in verse 1. In this answer, Paul largely repeats the notions of Romans 9:27-33, which constitutes a crossover in salvation-history. By pointing to the remainder (λεῖμμα, v. 5)[228] chosen by grace in the present time (ἐν τῷ νῦν καιρῷ), which can only be believers in Christ,[229] not much of the underlying tension regarding historical Israel and their position in salvation history is relieved. Paul's implicit answer rather implies that they are in fact rejected in terms of salvation history and do not form part of God's people any longer, for only those who believe in Christ are now God's people.

Yet, although questions remain regarding historical Israel (e.g., their salvation), one has to acknowledge that Paul's reference to those believing Judeans who remain God's people (the "remnant") after the crossover in salvation history, are in continuity with historical Israel. The cross was the culmination of their salvation history (cf. 9:33; 1 Cor 1:23, see note 133, p. 247). Jesus is their Messiah and the gospel came to them first (cf. 1:16). Those who were born under the Old Covenant as part of historical Israel and accepted their Messiah in faith, did in fact fully experience God's uninterrupted faithfulness and grace toward His people. Dunn is therefore correct to refer to the remnant as "part of the climax of salvation-history."[230]

---

225. BDAG, ὑπολείπω; Zerwick and Grosvenor, *Grammatical Analysis*, 483.

226. BDAG, καταλείπω, §4.

227. Cf. Hultgren, *Romans*, 401; Jewett, *Romans*, 659; Käsemann, *Romans*, 300.

228. Zerwick and Grosvenor, *Grammatical Analysis*, 483.

229. Witherington and Hyatt, *Romans*, 271; Wright, "Romans," 676; Moo, *Romans*, 675, 677, 679; cf. Fitzmyer, *Romans*, 605; Käsemann, *Romans*, 301. Gaston's, *Paul*, 142, proposal that the remnant would point to those who have engaged in the gentile mission, would contradict Paul's earlier submission of himself to God's righteousness in Christ (first person plural: 3:21-22; cf. 10:3-4), which on Gaston's logic would not be applicable to Judeans (Zoccali, "All Israel," 301-2). As pointed out in the introduction to Rom 9-11, the audience of the Roman church most likely consisted of a gentile majority and a Judean minority.

230. Dunn, *Romans*, 2:638.

In verse 6, God's grace is set over against "works." Here, Paul refers to "the manner by which membership in the elect remnant is achieved."[231] Much of Paul's earlier polemic against defining identity around the works of the law is recalled (3:20, 27-28; 4:2, 6; 9:32).[232] Since Paul has closely connected grace to faith (3:22-24; 4:16; 5:2), it seems reasonable that faith in Christ is implied as being part of God's grace (vv. 5-6),[233] especially in its opposition to works. It is interesting that Paul does not employ the full phrase "works of the law" here, even though he probably has the whole concept in mind (cf. Eph 2:8-9). As elsewhere, Paul's reference includes connotations to marking off Israel's exclusive identity (NPP)[234] and notions of merit (TAP, see esp. Rom 2:17-19, pp. 55-56; Rom 4:1-25, pp. 78-81).[235]

Paul states that Israel failed to attain what it was seeking (v. 7), but that the elect obtained it. Being part of national Israel does not imply election in the *inner* sense. Paul's distinction between Israel and the elect partly recalls his earlier distinction between *inner* and *outer* Israel (9:6-8). Yet in the current context Paul's reference to the elect (v. 7), which stands parallel to the remnant, refers to those believing in Christ. Election is thus a deeper criterion for being God's people than being part of the nation of Israel. Since election and the remnant correspond, belief in Christ is once again implied, which in itself erases ethnical distinctions (10:12). Gentiles are therefore in principle included in election here,[236] a notion that can additionally be derived from the contrast between Israel and the elect (v. 7).

Israel's hardening (πωρόω, v. 7)[237] is mentioned in contrast to God's election (in Christ), which includes gentiles (v. 7). Their "stupor" (κατάνυξις, v. 8)[238] and inability to see and hear (v. 8) are once again identified historically (in reference to Isa 6:9-10; 29:10 and probably Deut

---

231. Jewett, *Romans*, 660.

232. Jewett, *Romans*, 660.

233. Cf. Dunn, *Romans*, 2:675.

234. E.g., Dunn, *Romans*, 2:647.

235. E.g., Moo, *Romans*, 677; Cranfield, *Romans*, 2:548. Paul thus counters more than a mere understanding of identity in terms of "works" or a misunderstanding of the law (contra Dunn, *Romans*, 2:647, 667, 675).

236. Dunn, *Romans*, 2:640; contra Jewett, *Romans*, 661; Moo, *Romans*, 680; Fitzmyer, *Romans*, 606.

237. BDAG, πωρόω; Zerwick and Grosvenor, *Grammatical Analysis*, 484; Moo, *Romans*, 670, 679; Dunn, *Romans*, 2:640; Cranfield, *Romans*, 2:542, 549; LITV; REB; NRSV; NIV; RSV; RV. The term denotes "petrification" (BDAG, πωρόω; Witherington and Hyatt, *Romans*, 272-73; Dunn, *Romans*, 2:640; Lenski, *Romans*, 721), e.g., such as of marble or even a stone in the bladder (Dunn, *Romans*, 2:640).

238. BDAG, κατάνυξις; Käsemann, *Romans*, 302.

29:4), and are drawn into the present (ἕως τῆς σήμερον ἡμέρας).[239] Paul hereby repeats the theme of Israel's historical hardening (9:18), which he continues up to verse 10. Verses 9 and 10 refer to Psalm 68:23-24 (LXX). Although Paul retains most of the same terminology of Ps 68:23 (LXX) in a different order, he adds καὶ εἰς θήραν: "and a trap." The words παγίς and θήρα occur in a pair in the Septuagint in Psalm 34:8; 123:6-7; Proverbs 11:8-9, and Hosea 5:1-2.[240] The term σκάνδαλον evokes 9:33, where it is used in connection with Christ as "rock that will make them fall" (πέτραν σκανδάλου, see pp. 242-49). The connotations of a *"bait-stick of a trap, a snare"* inherent to the term σκάνδαλον (see note 146, p. 246)[241] is enhanced by the terms παγίς and θήρα.[242] These terms are used together to sketch the whole picture of Israel's hardening. Whether τράπεζα (v. 9) carries overtones of Israel's exclusive table fellowship,[243] their ritual practice,[244] or their dependence on the law,[245] it does not seem crucial in terms of the general imagery for Israel's hardening.[246] The general sense is that Paul uses that which is normally applied to David's enemies, and uses it against Israel.[247] Their hardening and blindness (vv. 8-10) appear to be part of God's plan in salvation history[248] with overtones of Israel's own responsibility in terms of their actions and attitude[249] (cf. 9:24-33).

Apart from the remnant who believes in Christ, Paul does not provide in verses 1 to 10 any grounds for the continuation of historical Israel *per se* as God's people into the present time. Verses 1 to 10 largely echo the notions of Romans 9:24-33. Verses 1 to 10 denote continuity with historical Israel in the Christ-believing remnant after an implied judgment (vv. 3-4). The hardening of historical Israel is confirmed (vv. 7-10), together with their failure to obtain what they were seeking (v. 5). Israel seems to have received retribution (ἀνταπόδομα, v. 9) for their hardening. The crossover in

---

239. Mounce, *Romans*, 216-17.
240. Jewett, *Romans*, 664.
241. Cf. Seifrid, "Romans," 670.
242. Cf. Käsemann, *Romans*, 301.
243. Jewett, *Romans*, 664; Seifrid, "Romans," 671; Barrett, *Romans*, 211.
244. Dunn, *Romans*, 2:642-43, 650; Käsemann, *Romans*, 302.
245. Sanday and Headlam, *Romans*, 315.
246. Cranfield, *Romans*, 2:551; cf. Moo, *Romans*, 683.
247. Dunn, *Romans*, 2:649.
248. Cf. Cranfield, *Romans*, 2:549.

249. That their hardening is also their own responsibility probably rings loudest with the term ἀνταπόδομα (v. 9, "retribution"), which would be the consequence of their own wrong.

salvation history represented by Israel's Messiah, which now includes both Judeans and non-Judeans alike, rings in the background.

The careful wording of the question in verse 1 cannot be lost out of sight. Paul does not ask if God has rejected *Israel* (Ἰσραήλ) as such, even though they are very much part of the equation, he asks if God has rejected His *people* (λαός).[250] Although gentiles are now included due to the crossover of salvation history, the crossover is not an exchange between ethnic entities as if gentiles *per se* are now the new people of God.[251] The culmination of salvation history in Israel's Messiah rather constitutes a deeper criterion for being God's people. The identity of God's people has been *redefined* away from criteria pertaining to human possibility, which Paul mainly describes around the term σάρξ, whether these criteria marked off identity (NPP) or aim to merit God's favor (TAP). The deeper criteria for marking off God's people in the light of Christ's work ultimately revolves around divine possibility, around God's grace (vv. 5, 6) and election (vv. 5, 7), which implies faith in Christ. The answer to the question whether God has rejected His people (v. 1) is thus "no" (1) in the sense that those of Israelite descent are represented in the remnant, and (2) that the deeper criteria for being God's people (grace, election) are confirmed. What is rejected (vv. 1–10) is at heart not national Israel *per se*, but any claim on being God's people apart from grace (implying faith in Christ), which Paul summarizes with the term "works" (v. 6).

Israel's Fall and the Salvation of the World (vv. 11–15)

Verse 11 introduces another question that resulted from verses 1–10: "have they stumbled so as to fall?"[252] Since historical Israel is largely in view in verses 1–10, it is most likely that they remain in view in verse 11: "Have [historical Israel] stumbled so as to fall?" Additionally, Paul's question might specifically be interpreted salvation-historically: "Have [historical Israel] stumbled [in the course of salvation history] so as to fall?" The verb πίπτω (v. 11) denotes a decisive[253] falling from the state of grace, which implies complete ruin.[254] Paul once again (cf. v. 1) denies such a notion (μὴ γένοιτο). Yet Paul immediately follows up his question by a term that lies semantically rather close to πίπτω. He uses παράπτωμα, a form that is

250. Cf. Merkle, "Romans 11," 713.
251. Witherington and Hyatt, *Romans*, 266.
252. NRSV.
253. Zerwick and Grosvenor, *Grammatical Analysis*, 484.
254. BDAG, πίπτω, §2b.

derived from παραπίπτω ("fall aside"). His play on words here implies that even though they did not stumble unto falling away completely, they did fall in terms of their false (moral) step (παράπτωμα).[255] By this offense,[256] however, salvation [has come][257] to the gentiles, which in turn is intended to make "them" (αὐτούς) jealous. The salvation of the gentiles points to their generic inclusion into salvation history: that they would become God's people through faith in Christ (cf. 9:24, 30). Those that are intended to be made jealous (αὐτούς, v. 11) points back to verses 8 to 10, which is historical Israel. The provocation to jealousy that Paul alludes to here (Deut 32:21) and earlier (10:19) thus seems to include historical Israel. As indicated on pp. 253-62, even Israel's provocation to jealousy has a historical basis in the Old Testament, constituted by the Samaritan and Babylonian nations. Yet, as indicated in verses 5 and 8, Israel's provocation to jealousy finds continuity into Paul's present. In present context (v. 11), therefore, except that historical Israel who have trespassed and hardened their hearts would be made jealous in some way by the culmination of salvation history that brought salvation to the gentiles,[258] Paul additionally has present unbelieving Judeans in mind. This diachronic and dialectical hermeneutic that Paul retains, which involves both historical Israel and unbelieving Judeans, arguably contributes to his omission of a specific designation or title for those who are to be made jealous (αὐτούς).

In view of the synonymous parallelism constituted by the first half of verse 12,[259] πλοῦτος κόσμου can be rendered as "the Gentile world."[260] The notion is that if the offense (παράπτωμα) or defeat (ἥττημα)[261] of historical Israel results in the "spiritual blessing" (πλοῦτος)[262] of the gentile world, which images "the benefit brought by the gospel,"[263] how much more their

---

255. Zerwick and Grosvenor, *Grammatical Analysis*, 484; Cranfield, *Romans*, 2:555; Godet, *Romans*, 2:236.

256. BDAG, παράπτωμα, bβ.

257. This past tense verb seems to be required by the logic of the verse (Moo, *Romans*, 687).

258. As in 7:5 and 15:8, Paul seems to use εἰς τό + aorist infinitive (καρποφορῆσαι in 7:5; παραζηλῶσαι in 11:11; βεβαιῶσαι in 15:8) in denoting a past situation. Although a possible provocation to jealousy of deceased historical Israel is strange to Western logic, the patriarchs seem to be active participants in Paul's salvation-historical exposition (see esp. the phrase διὰ τοὺς πατέρας in 11:28: "for the sake of the fathers"; cf. 4:12, 16: Abraham as "our" father; 9:10: "our father Isaac").

259. Jewett, *Romans*, 675.

260. Witherington and Hyatt, *Romans*, 267.

261. Zerwick and Grosvenor, *Grammatical Analysis*, 484; NRSV.

262. Moo, *Romans*, 688; lit. "wealth" or "abundance" (BDAG, πλοῦτος, §2).

263. Dunn, *Romans*, 2:654.

"fullness" (πλήρωμα)²⁶⁴ or "full inclusion."²⁶⁵ To what πλήρωμα refers is not entirely clear at this point and partly has to be kept in suspense until the whole picture becomes clearer (i.e., vv. 25-27, see below). The fact that verse 12 does not have a verb or a tense contributes to the uncertainty. "Their fullness" could theoretically point to historical Israel's salvation (since historical Israel is largely in view) and/or the salvation of unbelieving Judeans in Paul's present²⁶⁶ or in the future.²⁶⁷ "Their fullness" might even carry a more general sense, for example, to reach completion²⁶⁸ or "fullness" in terms of salvation history²⁶⁹ (cf. Gal 4:4).

Paul's specific address to the gentiles (v. 13) does not necessarily imply that his recipients were exclusively gentile (cf. pp. 231-35), but rather that Paul wants to catch the attention of the gentile members specifically.²⁷⁰ Inasmuch Paul is an apostle to the gentiles, he magnifies his ministry (v. 13)²⁷¹ in order to make his "flesh" jealous and save²⁷² some of them (v. 14). Salvation here is not so much Paul who saves as him being a significant figure in salvation history.²⁷³ In accordance with Paul's non-specific references to "them" (neither Ἰσραήλ nor Ἰουδαῖοι) in verses 8 to 12, he seems to utilize the ethnic "my flesh" (μου τὴν σάρκα)²⁷⁴ in verse 14 rather than any specific title (Ἰσραήλ/Ἰουδαῖοι) in order to retain his diachronic, dialectical hermeneutic (cf. v. 11 above). If Paul's role in *salvation history* is in view rather than the

264. Wright, "Romans," 681; Mounce, *Romans*, 218; NIV; LITV; RV; KJV. Dunn, *Romans*, 2:655, argues that "fullness" is a better translation here since Paul is aiming more for effect than precision (rather than e.g., "full number": Jewett, *Romans*, 678; Moo, *Romans*, 689-90; Fitzmyer, *Romans*, 611; Bruce, *Romans*, 212). BDAG (cf. Zerwick and Grosvenor, *Grammatical Analysis*, 484) lists Rom 11:12 (πλήρωμα) under both §3a ("full number") and §4 ("fulfilling, fulfillment").

265. Hultgren, *Romans*, 397, 398, 403; Bruce, *Romans*, 212; ESV; ISV; NRSV; RSV.

266. Hendriksen, *Romans*, 367-68.

267. Witherington and Hyatt, *Romans*, 267; Moo, *Romans*, 690; Dunn, *Romans*, 2:668; Ridderbos, *Romeinen*, 254.

268. This is one of the inherent connotations of πλήρωμα (BDAG, πλήρωμα, §1b, 3; L&N §59.32; Abbott-Smith, *Lexixon*, 366).

269. Moo, *Romans*, 690.

270. Dunn, *Romans*, 2:655; Hendriksen, *Romans*, 368.

271. Cf. NRSV.

272. Although the verb σώσω (v. 14) is either a future indicative or an aorist subjunctive, the latter is more likely following the εἴ πως (Jewett, *Romans*, 679; Moo, *Romans*, 685, 692).

273. Moo, *Romans*, 692; cf. Jewett, *Romans*, 680; contra Käsemann, *Romans*, 306.

274. While Paul primarily uses the expression to denote his kindred in terms of blood relationship (see L&N §10.1; Moo, *Romans*, 692; Dunn, *Romans*, 2:656; cf. BDAG, σάρξ, §4; Cranfield, *Romans*, 2:560-61), overtones of the existence before or outside of Christ is quite possible here (see pp. 220-22).

causal consequence of Paul's ministry, the salvation of "some of" historical Israel is conceivable. Yet, Paul's notion probably leans stronger toward his role in the salvation of "some of" his own kindred according to the flesh (μου τὴν σάρκα), that is unbelieving Judeans in Paul's present.

The structure of verse 15 is the same as verse 12 and carries much of the same notions.[275] This "sentence" (v. 15) is once again without a verb. As Paul argues, if the rejection[276] or casting away[277] of Israel by God[278] is the reconciliation of the world, including both Judean and gentile alike through Christ[279] (cf. καταλλαγή in 5:11), how much more Israel's acceptance by God into a relationship (πρόσληψις).[280] The phrase ζωὴ ἐκ νεκρῶν may either be understood as metaphorical, denoting spiritual quickening,[281] or as literal, denoting physical resurrection from the dead.[282] Yet Dunn is probably right that a spiritual quickening would be too much of an anti-climax after καταλλαγὴ κόσμου,[283] or as Jewett argues, it would undercut "the rhetorical force of Paul's climactic question."[284] But whether life from death points to the eschatological consummation[285] or something

275. Cf. Mounce, *Romans*, 219; Dunn, *Romans*, 2:657; Käsemann, *Romans*, 307.

276. BDAG, ἀποβολή, §1; Dunn, *Romans*, 2:657; ISV; NRSV.

277. Moo, *Romans*, 694; KJV; RV.

278. The phrase ἀποβολὴ αὐτῶν is more likely an objective genitive than a subjective genitive and thus points to rejection by God (BDAG, ἀποβολή, §1; Wright, "Romans," 682; Moo, *Romans*, 693; Dunn, *Romans*, 2:657; Cranfield, *Romans*, 2:562; GNB; RV; cf. Sanday and Headlam, *Romans*, 325) rather than their rejection of the gospel (contra Hultgren, *Romans*, 408; Fitzmyer, *Romans*, 612).

279. Dunn, *Romans*, 2:657; cf. Wright, "Romans," 677.

280. In parallel with ἀποβολή, πρόσληψις should also be taken in the passive sense (BDAG, πρόσληψις; Osborne, *Romans*, 295; Moo, *Romans*, 693; Dunn, *Romans*, 2:657; Cranfield, *Romans*, 2:562; GNB; RV; cf. Wright, "Romans," 683; Sanday and Headlam, *Romans*, 325) rather than denoting acceptance of the gospel (contra Hultgren, *Romans*, 408; Matera, *Romans*, 267; Fitzmyer, *Romans*, 612). In both ἀποβολή and πρόσληψις, Paul seems to have in mind the same "complex of divine intention and human culpability as in 9:31-33" (Dunn, *Romans*, 2:657). The same theme of *God's* rejection is implied by the question in v. 1, and is contrasted by *God's* gracious election in juxtaposition to works in vv. 5-6. The themes of election and *God's* kindness in the bigger scheme of salvation history are echoed in vv. 28-32.

281. E.g., Hultgren, *Romans*, 409; Mounce, *Romans*, 219; Fitzmyer, *Romans*, 613; Wright, "Romans," 683; *Climax*, 248; Hendriksen, *Romans*, 369.

282. E.g., Jewett, *Romans*, 681; Schreiner, *Romans*, 599; Moo, *Romans*, 694-96; Dunn, *Romans*, 2:658; Käsemann, *Romans*, 307; Cranfield, *Romans*, 2:562-63; Sanday and Headlam, *Romans*, 326.

283. Dunn, *Romans*, 2:658; cf. Cranfield, *Romans*, 2:562.

284. Jewett, *Romans*, 681.

285. E.g., Jewett, *Romans*, 681; Witherington and Hyatt, *Romans*, 269; Moo, *Romans*, 694-96; Dunn, *Romans*, 2:658; Käsemann, *Romans*, 307; Cranfield, *Romans*,

else, which involves the acceptance of historical Israel, remains open at this point. As argued on pp. 77-86, "making the dead alive" in 4:17 might be part of the intended meaning here in 11:15.

The Metaphor of the Olive Tree (vv. 16-24)

The metaphor of the olive tree represents God's people spanning both eons of salvation history before and after the Christ event. The metaphor thus involves historical Israel and the Christ-believing Judeans and gentiles.[286] These verses serve to clarify the balance within the economy of salvation history and to counter for any form of boasting, especially on the part of gentile believers.

Paul states that if the first-fruit (ἀπαρχή)[287] or initial offering[288] is set apart (ἅγιος),[289] so also the lump (cf. Num 15:17-21; Lev 23:10-11). Paul follows with a perfect parallel comparison: if the root is set apart, so also the branches. In these two "sentences" (although without verb) the first-fruit and root thus correspond, while the lump corresponds to the branches.[290]

While most commentators understand the branches as denoting Israel[291] (Ps 92:13; Jer 11:17), there is difference of opinion in what the root refers to. Whereas some understand the root (1) as referring to Judean Christ-believers[292] and some (2) as referring to Christ,[293] most understand it (3) as referring to the patriarchs.[294] Yet both the corresponding first-fruit

---

2:563; Sanday and Headlam, *Romans*, 326.

286. Moo, *Romans*, 698.

287. Zerwick and Grosvenor, *Grammatical Analysis*, 484; Jewett, *Romans*, 666; LITV; RV; KJV. In view of the singular form ἀπαρχή, a singular translation is preferable rather than the plural "first fruits" (contra Moo, *Romans*, 696, 699; Fitzmyer, *Romans*, 613; NIV; RSV).

288. Dunn, *Romans*, 2:658.

289. Witherington and Hyatt, *Romans*, 569; Moo, *Romans*, 701.

290. Jewett, *Romans*, 670, 682-83; Moo, *Romans*, 699; Sanday and Headlam, *Romans*, 326; cf. Godet, *Romans*, 2:245; contra Wright, "Romans," 683-84; Dunn, *Romans*, 2:659; Cranfield, *Romans*, 2:564.

291. E.g., Wright, "Romans," 683; Fitzmyer, *Romans*, 613; Dunn, *Romans*, 2:659; Barrett, *Romans*, 216; cf. Moo, *Romans*, 699.

292. E.g., Barrett, *Romans*, 216; considered as a possibility by Witherington and Hyatt, *Romans*, 270.

293. E.g., Wright, "Romans," 684; Ellison, *Mystery*, 86-87; considered as a possibility by Barrett, *Romans*, 216.

294. E.g., Matera, *Romans*, 267; Osborne, *Romans*, 296; Witherington and Hyatt, *Romans*, 270; Moo, *Romans*, 699; Mounce, *Romans*, 220; Fitzmyer, *Romans*, 614; Dunn, *Romans*, 2:659-60, 672; Bruce, *Romans*, 215; Käsemann, *Romans*, 308; Cranfield,

and root are most likely to refer to Abraham specifically,²⁹⁵ based on the following:

1. The corresponding singular forms (ἀπαρχή, φύραμα) would fit this interpretation.
2. Paul specifically mentions his descent from Abraham in verse 1 when he describes his pedigree as Israelite.
3. Further back (9:7), Paul mentions descent from Abraham in his distinction between *inner* and *outer* Israel (9:6–8).
4. The strongest argument for this view is probably that Paul recalls his discussion of Abraham's faith in Romans 4. As discussed, Abraham is considered as the ethnic father of Israel (v. 1) or the father of those who are circumcised (v. 12), the original recipient of God's righteousness (vv. 3, 9), and the father of all believers in Christ (vv. 12, 16). In the new eschatological eon, believers' connection with Abraham is punctiliar (4:1–25; cf. Gal 4:21–5:1) through Christ who is both a physical descendant of Abraham (9:5) and the point of believers' spiritual connection to Abraham (4:24). Christ thus forms part of the root imagery, especially in terms of being grafted into the olive tree.²⁹⁶

If Abraham is signified by the first-fruit or root, the notion of verse 16 would be that if Abraham as first to be counted for righteousness (4:3, 9) was set apart for God, then the nation of Israel would be set apart for God as well.²⁹⁷ This setting apart does not necessarily indicate salvation for every Israelite, but signifies the special identity of the people of Israel as God's people.²⁹⁸

The branches that have been broken off (v. 17) signify God's rejection of Israel. This was the inevitable result of their historical hardening and unbelief (vv. 7–10),²⁹⁹ which culminated in the death and resurrection of Christ. The wild olive tree, signifying believing gentiles, were grafted into (v. 17) the good olive tree (v. 24), which is the *people of God* spanning both the eons of

---

Romans, 2:564; Ridderbos, *Romeinen*, 257; Sanday and Headlam, *Romans*, 326; Godet, *Romans*, 2:245; John Chrysostom, "Acts of the Apostles."

295. Witherinngton, *Jesus*, 120; cf. Osborne, *Romans*, 296; Fitzmyer, *Romans*, 610. Some mention Abraham especially among the patriarchs (e.g., Moo, *Romans*, 699; Mounce, *Romans*, 220; Dunn, *Romans*, 2:659, 672; Ridderbos, *Romeinen*, 257).

296. Cf. Wright, "Romans," 684.

297. God's covenant with Abraham and His promise to be the God of Abraham and his descendants probably lies behind this (Gen 17:7–8).

298. Moo, *Romans*, 701.

299. Cf. Moo, *Romans*, 701.

salvation history before and after the Christ event[300] and not *Israel* as such.[301] Verse 17 repeats much of the notions of verses 12 and 15. At the turning point between the old and new eons (in the Christ event), that which marked off the identity of God's people irrevocably changed.[302] Those who were part of Israel before Christ, who accepted Christ in faith, continued to be God's people,[303] constituting the remnant (vv. 3-5). But historical, hardened Israel as well as those who continued in a state of hardening and unbelief when the new eschatological eon was inaugurated, were cut off from God's people[304] (cf. 9:30-33). Paul's description of "some" (τίς, v. 17) of the branches that were broken off is probably euphemistic in order to reduce the harshness of this reality.[305] Paul in fact has the majority of Israel in mind.[306] The entire identity mode A (flesh-existence, including law, works and circumcision) was "cut off" from being a *sole or co-constituting* criterion in defining God's people.[307] In other words, those who were God's people through identity mode A or even AB, resembling the old existence in flesh (7:14-25),[308] were "cut off." In terms of the current imagery, the *entire* historical Israel has thus been cut off, including Israel according to the flesh. The existence in flesh was superseded by those who believe in Christ (3:21-4:25) and partake in the Spirit (8:1-16), constituting God's people in the new eon (identity mode C). The sharing in the richness of the olive tree denotes the sharing of the gentiles in the blessings promised to Israel.[309]

---

300. Zoccali, "All Israel," 298-99; Wright, "Romans," 684; Moo, *Romans*, 698, 702, 709; Barrett, *Romans*, 217; cf. Kim, "Reading," 321; Osborne, *Romans*, 297; Fitzmyer, *Romans*, 610; Horne, "Meaning," 330. This is probably the reason why Gaston, *Paul*, 147, finds this section inconsistent with the rest of ch. 11 (noted by Zoccali, "All Israel," 298).

301. Contra Staples, "Gentiles," 385; Matera, *Romans*, 268; Bassler, *Navigating*, 81; Schnelle, *Paul*, 350; Segal, "Conversation Four," 133; Tomson, "Names," 285.

302. Cf. Dunn, *Romans*, 2:672-73, who seems to work in this direction, but somewhat more hesitantly. He states that "the implication is present that prior to this time (the Christ event) the understanding of God's purpose as focused upon and coterminous with Israel was justified. But God has now brought that stage of salvation history to an end."

303. Cf. Jewett, *Romans*, 685.

304. Cf. Wright, "Romans," 685; Moo, *Romans*, 701.

305. Cf. Dunn, *Romans*, 2:672.

306. Cf. Bell, *Jealousy*, 161; Fitzmyer, *Romans*, 614.

307. This will be further motivated on pp. 309-14.

308. The motif of "death" in Christ of all people (2 Cor 5:15; cf. the theme of "death" in Rom 5-8; Gal 2:20) would match this notion. Rom 11:15 carries the notion of the "death" of Israel in particular.

309. Wright, "Romans," 685; Mounce, *Romans*, 220.

The appeal not to boast against the branches (v. 18) is specifically aimed at gentile believers. In view of the pervading theme from verses 17 through 21, the branches in verse 18 probably refer to Israel that has been cut off apart from the believing remnant.[310] The root that carries "you" (gentile believer) and not the other way round, neither points to Israel's privileged position in terms of salvation to the world,[311] nor to a "Jewish root and a continuing Jewish element" within the people of God.[312] The root that carries the gentile believer rather points to Abraham's faith in salvation history (cf. 4:3) and the gentiles' punctiliar connection through Israel's Messiah to Abraham[313] who is the father of all believers (4:12, 16) alike without distinction (10:12). Despite Israel being cut off from being God's people, was it not for them, their Messiah according to the flesh (9:5) that became the Messiah for the world would not have been there for the gentiles[314] or any believer in Christ. Boasting against Israel would thus imply boasting against Christ.

In verses 19 to 22 Paul uses faith as argument to remove any grounds for boasting. This implicitly says something about the nature of faith. Faith in Christ is per definition not representative of any human contribution to salvation, but signifies total reliance and dependence on the work of Christ. Faith is inherently not a work for a reward, void of merit (4:4–5) and based on grace (11:5–6).[315] The branches (Israel) that were broken off were necessary within the larger scheme in salvation history in order to enable gentiles (or any Christ-believer) to become part of God's people through faith in Christ alone (v. 19). Yet, Israel's persistent unbelief throughout history (10:16; cf. their hardening: 11:7–10) inevitably resulted in being cut off (v. 20). In order to remain grafted into the good olive tree, one needs to remain in faith (v. 20–21)[316] and in God's kindness (χρηστότης, v. 22). If one strives to define your identity as God's people by anything pertaining to human possibility, whether by "works of the law" or externally observable identity markers, you step out of a position of faith and reliance on God's

---

310. Wright, "Romans," 68 and Barrett, *Romans*, 217, do not refer to "Israel" as such as being cut off, but to unbelieving "Jews." I have included them in order to distinguish the current view from those who view the branches as pointing to both unbelieving and believing "Jews" (e.g., Moo, *Romans*, 703; Dunn, *Romans*, 2:662; Cranfield, *Romans*, 2:567–68).

311. Contra Fitzmyer, *Romans*, 615.

312. Contra Moo, *Romans*, 704.

313. Cf. Wright, "Romans," 685.

314. Cf. Wright, "Romans," 685.

315. Dunn, *Romans*, 2:675; cf. Fitzmyer, *Romans*, 615.

316. Wright, "Romans," 685; Moo, *Romans*, 706; Dunn, *Romans*, 2:663, 665.

provision through Christ and the Spirit.[317] The latter would result in being cut off "yourself" (v. 22). Not being spared (φείδομαι [x2], v. 21) implies judgment[318] (cf. 9:27-29; 2 Pet 2:4-5).

"They" (ἐκεῖνοι in κἀκεῖνοι) that will be grafted in if they do not stay in unbelief (v. 23) have to be unbelieving Judeans according to the flesh in Paul's present. Paul here reiterates faith as the only basis for being God's people in the new eschatological eon after the Christ event. If Judeans in Paul's present believe and accept the gospel through faith, they *confirm the faithfulness of God to historical Israel*. The possibility of belief in Christ and consequential regrafting of former Israel (unbelieving Judeans in Paul's present) into the good olive tree (God's people), summarizes one aspect of the answer to the questions put forth in both verses 1 ("has God rejected his people?") and 11 ("have they stumbled so as to fall?"). But what about historical Israel that lived prior to the Christ event? Have they fallen and have they been rejected? As argued, an allusion to the salvation or acceptance of historical Israel remains a possibility hoped for or desired in verses 12, 14 and 15.

In anticipation of the mystery that Paul wants to share (vv. 25-27), the cutting off of gentiles ("you": σύ, v. 24) from the wild olive tree who were grafted into the good olive tree, which is God's people (v. 24a),[319] constitutes one side of Paul's overall salvation-historical perspective. This part of salvation history pertains to the inclusion of the gentiles, the fact that they are now included in God's generic election or election in terms of salvation history (9:11-24). In the second half of verse 24, Paul asks that if gentiles can be included, how much more will those "according to nature" (κατὰ φύσιν)[320] be grafted into their own olive tree. Within the logical construction of verse 24 starting with εἰ, the verb ἐγκεντρισθήσονται can be understood as a logical future:[321] if it is true that gentiles can be grafted onto the tree, it follows logically that the same can be true of those "according to nature." In accordance with Paul's dialectical, diachronic hermeneutic, where historical Israel remains in perspective and the fact that Israel has been cut off in the culmination of salvation history, the grafting of the

---

317. Cf. Wright, "Romans," 685. This way of looking at the NPP inevitably involves an element of human merit within the Judean spirituality, for trust in "flesh" or in any external marking or work in defining identity ultimately seeks a right standing with God in terms of human possibility.

318. Moo, *Romans*, 706.

319. Moo, *Romans*, 709.

320. LITV.

321. Cottrell, *Romans*; Kühl, *Römer*, 389; Denney, "Romans," 682; Weiss, *Römer*, 492; cf. Kim, "Reading," 327.

"natural branches"[322] might specifically point to historical Israel, since they were the "natural branches" in the *former* eon of salvation history. Another reason for this possibility is that Paul already stated in verse 23 on what basis current unbelieving Judeans are grafted back in (by faith). Paul's concern for unbelieving Judeans in his present is thus resolved in verse 23. But the second half of verse 24 seems to hint on another aspect of the complete answer to the questions put forth in both verses 1 and 11, that is, the salvation of ancient, historical Israel.

Six Interpretations of the Salvation of "All Israel" (vv. 25–27)[323]

What exactly Paul intended with the salvation of "all Israel" (v. 26) has often perplexed New Testament scholars,[324] and has given rise to many different interpretations. The interpretation of verses 25 to 27 normally go together. One's understanding of the salvation of "all Israel" determines the way in which specific terms and phrases are interpreted in these three verses. A measure of inductive reasoning thus seems inevitable. The bigger question is, however, how the interpretation of the salvation of "all Israel" dominates Pauline theology today, and especially how it dominates the understanding of the identity of Israel, Judeans and believers in Christ. Within the exegetical study, various instances of the dominating influence[325] of the interpretation of Romans 9 to 11 in approaching other passages have been demonstrated (esp. Gal 4:21–5:1, 1 Thess 2:13–16; Eph 2:2–22). The effect of current understandings of Romans 11:25–27 is probably more dominating than often acknowledged and arguably shapes many current debates in Pauline theology on identity. The fact that there are so many interpretations on this passage should, however, be an indicator of the unclear or even obscure nature of this passage. Methodologically, one should guard against working from the more obscure (Rom 11:25–27) to the less obscure (the rest of the Pauline corpus). It would be methodologically more rigorous to try and use that which is clearer in Paul to try and interpret that which

---

322. NRSV.

323. Although mostly in abbreviated form, most of the content of this section has been published under the title "The Salvation of 'All Israel' in Romans 11:25–27 as the Salvation of Inner-Elect, Historical Israel in Christ" in *Neotestamentica* 49.2 (2015) 417–52.

324. Zoccali, "All Israel," 289.

325. See no. 4 in Gager, *Reinventing*, 7–9, see p. 5.

seems more obscure. This latter methodology constitutes the approach to this passage in this book.

The prevailing interpretations of Romans 11:25-27, I will argue, seem to reveal a side of Paul's thought that is at odds with the rest of his writings, especially where Paul accentuates the new era in Christ in discontinuity with the old (as argued: Rom 9:24–11:1-10; 15:5-13; 1 Cor 1:21-24; Gal 1:11-23; Phil 3:1-9; 1 Thess 2:13-16; 2 Cor 3:5-16; 5:14-21; cf. Eph 2:8-22; Col 3:9-15). But before these problems can be pursued further, the prevailing interpretations of Romans 11:25-27 have to be put on the table. These interpretations can be categorized in terms of the following six main views:[326]

1. *Eschatological miracle.* This is the most popular interpretation. The historical nation Israel is understood as continuing into the future.[327] This "Israel"[328] as a whole ("all Israel") will then be saved after the full number of the elect of all the gentiles have come into the kingdom (πλήρωμα τῶν ἐθνῶν εἰσέλθῃ, v. 25), which is normally understood as at the parousia. The hardening is mostly seen as both in part (of "Israel") and as temporal. While most of these interpreters envision (a) "Israel" as turning to faith in Christ at the parousia,[329] others focus more on (b) God's gracious election of "Israel" without accentuating (albeit not necessarily excluding) belief in the gospel.[330] In both vari-

---

326. Cf. Zoccali, *Whom God Has Called*, 91-104; "All Israel." The titles (italic) of views 1, 2, 4, 5, and 6 are that of Zoccali (as cited), although in different order. I have followed most of his exposition of these 5 positions except the variants (a) and (b) in view 1 and my accentuation of some additional aspects in Nanos' (1996) view (6). I have customized the references to authors in accordance with those with whom I mostly interact in this book, including references to more recent authors.

327. This notion is not about the existence of what Paul calls "Judeans" after the Christ event. Since Paul (apart from Rom 11:25-26) never unambiguously designates current unbelieving kinsfolk as "Israel," the latter designation cannot be taken for granted as continuing into the future at this point, and is due for further evaluation.

328. Since it has not been finally determined whether historical Israel as God's people can be understood as continuing after the Christ event, I have put references to "Israel" in quotation marks when the continuation of historical Israel after the Christ is envisioned.

329. E.g., Longenecker, *Epistle to the Romans*, 899-900; Jewett, *Romans*, 694-706; Osborne, *Romans*, 306; Witherington and Hyatt, *Romans*, 273-76; Esler, *Conflict*, 305-6; Moo, *Romans*, 710-29; Mounce, *Romans*, 223-25; Fitzmyer, *Romans*, 618-25; Dunn, *Romans*, 2:677-84, 690-92; Bruce, *Romans*, 216-18; idem., *Heart Set Free*, 333; Sanders, *Jewish People*, 192-99; Hodge, *Romans*, 587-90.

330. Hultgren, *Romans*, 413-23; Käsemann, *Romans*, 311-15; Cranfield, *Romans*, 2:572-79). Zoccali, "All Israel," 290, appears to incorrectly ascribe the view that future "Israel" would "turn to Christ" (implying belief in Christ) after the ingathering of the

ants (or accentuations) of this view (a–b), Christ is understood as the Deliverer from Zion (v. 26).

2. *Ecclesiological.* In this understanding, "all Israel" represents the church consisting of both "Jew"[331] and gentile.[332] Wright does not understand the quotation from Isaiah (vv. 26b–27) as a reference to the parousia or any other future point in time. For him, it rather points to God's provision of the path and means of covenant renewal in the present time.[333] Much of this line of interpretation revolves around a redefinition of the concept "Israel" to include believers in Christ on the basis of e.g., "the Israel of God" in Galatians 6:16, believers as "the circumcision" in Philippans 3:3, "the circumcision of Christ" in Colossians 2:11–12, the seed of Abraham in Galatians 3 and Romans 4, and/or the name "Jew" in Romans 2:27–29.

3. *Two houses of Israel.* This recent interpretation of Staples[334] can be seen as a kind of variant on the ecclesiological view (above). He bases most of his interpretation on the promise to Ephraim in Genesis 48:19, which he relates in turn to the Old Testament distinction between Judah (the southern tribe, consisting of the tribes Judah, Levi and Benjamin) and Israel (the northern tribe, consisting of the rest of the tribes), where Judah represented a part of Israel.[335] On the basis of a similarity that Staples sees between καὶ τὸ σπέρμα αὐτοῦ ἔσται εἰς πλῆθος ἐθνῶν in Genesis 48:19 (LXX) and τὸ πλήρωμα τῶν ἐθνῶν εἰσέλθῃ in Romans 11:25, he argues that Ephraim's seed are the gentiles that need to be restored through the new covenant. Understood in this way, Staples asserts that the gentiles are in fact part of Israel.[336] He understands the hardening as the hardening of both houses of Israel: a hardening of both the northern tribe (gentiles, which is Ephraim's seed) and Judah (the "Jews"), which is only hardened partially (some have accepted the gospel). Both houses of Israel (the northern tribe [gentiles] and Judah, the "Jews") thus constitute "all Israel" and will be

---

gentiles to Käsemann and Cranfield (as listed).

331. In discussing the six views, I refer to "Jews" in quotation marks when they are equated with the Judeans of the NT or equated with "Israel" in Paul.

332. E.g., Middendorf, *Romans*, 1153–59; Wright, *Faithfulness*, 2:1243–44; "Romans," 687–93; *Climax*, 249–51; Jeremias, "Sprachliche Beobachtungen," 200; Barth, *Romans*, 412–17; Calvin, *Romans*, 376–79; Irenaeus, *Haer.* 4.2.7.

333. Wright, *Faithfulness*, 2:1251; "Romans," 691–93; *Climax*, 251.

334. Staples, "Gentiles"; cf. Maljaars, *Heel Israël*, 185–91, 250–51.

335. Staples, "Gentiles," 374.

336. Staples, "Gentiles," 386–87.

fulfilled according to the apocalyptic of early Judaism.[337] Staples typifies Paul's gospel as "messianic new covenant Israelitism," not wholly other than Judaism.[338]

4. *Total national elect.* This view argues for "all Israel" to refer to the complete number of elect from the historical/empirical nation.[339] According to this understanding, a specific salvation event in the future is not envisioned. Historical Israel is once again understood as continuing after the Christ event. "Israel's" hardening is understood as persisting until the end of the age without reversal, when their hardening will be fulfilled eschatologically. The remnant is understood as the elect from the nation of "Israel" in both ages before and after the Christ event. The salvation of "all Israel" is thus understood as including both historical Israel before Christ[340] *and* all of "Israel" (normally equated with "Jews") coming to belief during the Christ age.

5. *Two-covenant.* In this interpretation "all Israel" is understood as representing the historical nation of Israel irrespective of faith in Christ.[341] Soteriology is understood in terms of two covenants: while gentiles are saved through Christ, for Israel who is understood to continue to the end of the age, the Sinai covenant remains the means of salvation.[342] For Gaston, gentile believers are "co-partners alongside of Israel."[343] Stendahl argues that Paul's lack of reference to Christ in 10:18 to 11:36 removes a Christological element from "Israel's" salvation, which by implication serves to prevent gentiles from evangelizing them.[344] For Gaston, the hardening of Israel points to "Israel's" failure to understand that a way of salvation was made available through Christ.[345] The "Jews" who did believe in Christ would constitute the grounds for

---

337. Staples, "Gentiles," 387–88.

338. Staples, "Gentiles," 383.

339. E.g., Kruse, *Romans*, 441–45; Zoccali, *Whom God Has Called*, 104–16; idem., "All Israel," 303–9; Merkle, "Romans 11," 711–21; Hendriksen, *Romans*, 377–83; Horne, "Meaning," 329–34; Ridderbos, *Paulus*, 396–403; idem., *Romeinen*, 261–66; Lenski, *Romans*, 723–28.

340. Esp. Ridderbos, *Paulus*, 402.

341. E.g., Gager, *Reinventing*, 128–42; Gaston, *Paul*, 135–50; Tomson, "Names," 285; Stendahl, *Paul*, 1–5; cf. Eisenbaum, *Paul*, 253–55.

342. Eisenbaum, *Paul*, 253–55, is an exception here in that she does not argue so much for salvation as such, but rather for the reconciliation of all people.

343. Gaston, *Paul*, 149.

344. Stendahl, *Paul*, 4.

345. Gaston, *Paul*, 143.

God's salvation of "all Israel."³⁴⁶ He understands the reference to Isaiah 59:20–21 (Rom 11:26b–27a) primarily as a reference to God, although he admits that Paul might have Christ in mind. If so, Christ would be an agent of a special form of salvation for "Israel."³⁴⁷ The quotation of Isaiah 27:9 would affirm God's commitment to the Sinai covenant, applicable only to "Israel."³⁴⁸ In this view, salvation for gentiles and "Israel" in the present age is thus essentially on different terms.

6. *Roman mission.* This is the interpretation of Nanos.³⁴⁹ In Nanos' interpretation, "all Israel" are "Jews" in Rome who have both responded to the gospel (the remnant) and are hardened in Paul's present. The latter will be made jealous and believe on the basis of the success of Paul's mission to the gentiles when it commences in Rome.³⁵⁰ Nanos largely bases his interpretation on an anomaly taking place in Rome as portrayed in Acts, where some "Jews" would understand the gospel to be Israel's restoration while others do not, rejecting the promises to the patriarchs. For Nanos, those who believe are "orthodox Jews" who continue Israel's faith and keep the Torah.³⁵¹ Nanos bases his interpretation on a two-step pattern involving the restoration of (historical) Israel in each new location where Paul preaches before the gospel could come to the gentiles.³⁵² The latter notion constitutes his interpretation of verse 25, which he understands as "the time for the fullness of the gentiles to *begin.*"³⁵³ Nanos reads πλήρωμα in verse 25 as pointing to the beginning of the gentile mission in accordance with πληρόω of 15:19 (pointing to the completion of his mission in the east) and πλήρωμα in 15:29 (denoting Paul's missionary activity).³⁵⁴ Nanos understands the gospel to the gentiles as their admission into God's people as "righteous gentiles" who obey "the appropriate halakhah" (Noahide Laws) as outlined in the so called "Apostolic Decree" (Acts 15:19–29).³⁵⁵ The

---

346. Gaston, *Paul*, 148.
347. Gaston, *Paul*, 147–48.
348. Gaston, *Paul*, 143–44.
349. Nanos, *Mystery*, 239–88; idem., "Callused," 72–73.
350. Nanos, *Mystery*, 247–55, 259–61.
351. Nanos, *Mystery*, 268–69.
352. Nanos, *Mystery*, 269–72.
353. Nanos, *Mystery*, 267, emphasis original.
354. Nanos, *Mystery*, 265–67.
355. Nanos, *Mystery*, 269.

gentiles in Rome would be under the false assumption that they have replaced Israel, which Paul would want to correct.[356]

Critiquing the Prevalent Views on Romans 11:25–27

The constraints that have been put forth in the study pertaining to these 6 views can be formulated in terms of certain questions that can be asked to these views. One of the most important questions that apply to all 6 views is whether Paul envisions Israel to continue as a separate entity apart from believers in Christ after the Christ event. In other words, can "Judeans" and "Israel" be understood as exactly the same entity? If a future "Israel" is envisioned on the basis of the future tense of the salvation of "all Israel" (σωθήσεται, v. 26), it poses difficult questions in terms of Paul's thought: How could Paul envision a future unbelieving "Israel," which would clearly be an "Israel according to the flesh" (1 Cor 10:18), to still have a special place in God's salvific economy in some way, whether they remain hardened and unsaved until the end (views 1 and 2),[357] whether "Israel" remains a sub-category within the Christ-believing community (some in view 4),[358] or whether they continue to constitute God's (second) people (view 5)? How could they continue to be distinguished from other people based on external criteria and their existence in the flesh (7:14–25; identity mode A), a way of existence (of being God's people) outside of Christ that is supposed to be cut off (9:32–33; 11:7, 12, 17–24) and to have died in Christ (2 Cor 5:15–16; cf. Rom 5–8; Gal 2:20)? If God's people have been redefined in terms of the eschatological spirit over against an existence in the flesh (8:1–16), or if God's people are now eschatologically defined as being of faith in Christ without the law over against an existence "under the law" (Rom 3:19–22; Gal 3:22–25),[359] how could an "Israel according to the flesh" continue to be God's people in some way? Or, if they are not God's people, what are they

---

356. Nanos, *Mystery*, 273–74.

357. The notion that there will still be an "Israel" (who is normally identified with contemporary Jews) during the course of the Christ age who will embrace Christ in faith at will, still implies a continuance of Old Testament Israel (although remaining hardened) into the Christ age.

358. Zoccali, *Whom God Has Called*, understands "Israel" to be an ongoing ethnic designation within the Christ-believing community: "Israel" continues to be a "subordinate" identity within the over-arching identity of believers in Christ.

359. See especially how Rom 3:21–22 portrays faith as something that has "now" (νυνί, v. 21) been "revealed" (φανερόω, v. 21) in contrast to an existence "under the law" (v. 19), and how Gal 3:23 and 25 express faith as something that has "come" after an existence "under the law" (v. 23) or "under a guardian" (v. 25).

and on what Pauline criteria for identity are they kept in some way within God's salvific economy? Or is an understanding warranted where "all Israel" is understood in a redefined way (view 2 and 3),[360] especially between 11:25 (denoting historical Israel) and 11:26 (denoting redefined Israel consisting of Judeans and gentiles alike)?

A difficulty that lies adjacent to the above questions is the hermeneutical problem around the designations "Israel," "Judean" and "Jew." How can interpreters of Paul see contemporary Jews as a future "Israel" that Paul would have envisioned in verse 26 if today's Judaism as a religion (commencing at around 70 CE) is anachronistic to and to a large extent in discontinuity with the faith of Israel or the Judean people in Paul's time? If Paul's use of the term Ἰσραήλ in the rest of his letters and up to this point in his exposition in Romans leans toward the historical side, denoting ancient, historical Israel (as argued) in accordance with its prevalent use at the time (see pp. 31-39), it can be asked if Paul's use of the term Ἰσραήλ in Romans 11:26 transcends the prevalent limits of speech as Tomson suggests.[361] In other words, would Paul utilize the term Ἰσραήλ to denote the Ἰουδαῖοι in his present? I would propose a negative answer to this question in viewing the uses of these terms in the time of the Second Temple as constraints in interpreting Rom 11:26, rather than implying a continuation of ancient Israel into Paul's present and future. In other words, the point of departure is that the term Ἰσραήλ in Paul primarily denotes ancient, *historical Israel*, while the term Ἰουδαῖος primarily denotes people in Paul's *present* that are ethnically related to historical Israel. It is also noteworthy that Paul never uses the term Ἰουδαῖος to denote ancient, historical Israel. The latter in itself should make one hesitate to equate the terms Ἰσραήλ and Ἰουδαῖος too easily. All of the scholars listed above in representing the 6 views use terms such as "Jews" and "Israel" interchangeably (including Esler, albeit utilizing the term "Judean" instead of "Jew").[362]

Staples' proposal (view 3),[363] while intriguing poses numerous difficulties. Whether Paul would base his entire salvation-historical climax (Rom 11:25-27) on an apparent allusion to a passage (Gen 48:19, LXX) that does not resemble anything in Paul's thought on salvation history elsewhere, seems obscure at best. The matching between the two passages (Gen 48:19, LXX and Rom 11:25) on the basis of a near correspondence of two terms

---

360. The notion to include the church under the term "Israel" will be addressed on pp. 338-45.
361. Tomson, "Names," 287-88.
362. Esler, *Conflict*.
363. Staples, "Gentiles"; cf. Maljaars, *Heel Israël*.

only (πλήρωμα/πλῆθος and ἔθνος) is methodologically not a strong enough foundation for his thesis. The allusion to Genesis 48:19 on the basis of an apparent correspondence with some words in a single passage in the Septuagint would require almost esoteric knowledge for Paul's readers, rendering such an interpretation unlikely. Staples' view would thus involve a riddle within a riddle. Apart from the fact that the distinction between Israel (northern kingdom) and Judah (southern kingdom) cannot be held right through the Old Testament (see pp. 31–39, esp. note 4) or in Paul,[364] there is a hermeneutical distance between the earlier distinctions represented by יִשְׂרָאֵל and יְהוּדִי (in the Old Testament) compared to the usage of Ἰουδαῖοι as mostly an outsider term and Ἰσραήλ as mostly an insider term in the New Testament time, which is not accounted for in Staples' proposal (see pp. 31–39). Apart from this hermeneutical problem, the proposal is just too far removed from a plain reading of Paul's thought on the identity of gentiles, Judeans and Israel to be credible. Staple's view is thus hard to make fit to the rest of the Pauline corpus.[365] Lastly, in Staples' view of belief in Christ as "messianic new covenant Israelitism," which he does not view as wholly other than Judaism,[366] his view suffers from the same inherent problem as that of Nanos (view 6), that is, that belief in Christ would not transcend Judean exclusivism.

Nanos' view (view 6)[367] would imply that Paul would perpetuate a form of Judean exclusivism in that gentile believers in Christ would be considered as mere "guests" ("Noahides"). Apart from the anachronistic nature of the notion to make Paul's thought fit to the teachings about the Noahide Laws, the underlying or even subtle essentialist structure underneath the idea of the Noahide Laws stand in sharp contrast to the way in which Paul removes the distinction between Judean and Greek in Christ (see Rom 10:12; 1 Cor 1:24; 12:13; Gal 3:28–29; cf. Col 3:11).[368] In Christ's work on the cross, the

364. While Paul identifies himself as from the "nation/race of Israel" (Phil 3:5) or as an "Israelite" (Rom 11:1; 2 Cor 11:22), he simultaneously identifies his bloodline as being from the "tribe of Benjamin" (Phil 3:5; Rom 11:1), which goes against Staples', "Gentiles," 376, proposal that Judah (the southern kingdom) consists of the tribe of Benjamin, Judah and Levi in distinction from Israel (the northern kingdom), consisting of the rest of the tribes.

365. Numerous questions could follow. E.g., If the gentiles are in fact part of Israel, could Israel's privileges (Rom 9:4–5) be the gentiles' privileges? If Christ is from Israel according to the flesh (9:5), is Christ in fact from the gentiles? How could the patriarchs be of Israel (9:7–10) and simultaneously be of the gentiles? Etc.

366. Staples, "Gentiles," 383.

367. Nanos, *Mystery*.

368. I have argued this in some length elsewhere (Du Toit, "Noagitiese Wette"), questioning the validity of identifying the Noahide laws or an earlier form of them

distinction between Judean and gentile has been rendered redundant. All people come to God and relate to God on the same basis of faith in Christ. In terms of Nanos' understanding of Romans 11:25–27, the notions that there would be an anomaly of sorts in Rome and that the gospel to the gentiles would only begin upon his arrival in Rome are purely speculative.[369] Despite the correlations Nanos asserts to draw from Paul's travel plans in Romans 15, Paul's choice not to preach in Rome "where Christ has already been named" so as not to "build on someone else's foundation" (15:20),[370] would rather express Paul's hope to come to Rome soon to preach the gospel (1:15). Paul would not claim that his presence would be critical for the advent of a mission to the gentiles.[371] Additionally, Nanos' proposal for an anomalous state of affairs in Rome, which meant that their faith "lacked a proper foundation," which Paul wanted to set right,[372] is not warranted in view of Paul's satisfaction with the Roman church (15:14) and the fact that Paul was only "in passing" (15:24) and would not have time to do such rebuilding work to the church.[373]

The Coming in of the Fullness of the Gentiles and the Salvation of "All Israel" (vv. 25–27)

If the above six views are filled with difficulties that seem insurmountable, how does one proceed from here? As proposed initially (see pp. 16–17), when a difficult text has to be interpreted such as Romans 11:25–27, where a measure of inductive reasoning is inevitable, it seems methodologically more rigorous to work from a broader understanding of Paul's thought to fill in the gaps rather than to make single (difficult) passages dominate the rest of Paul's theology. As for the exposition of the rest of Romans 11, I will start with revisiting some grammatical and semantic aspects of verses 25 to 27 that have become entrenched within the prevailing interpretations of

---

before the Rabbinic period, including the book of *Jubilees*, Acts (15:19–32; 16:1–5; 21:25), the Didache and Paul. I argue that it is more likely that the whole idea of Noahide laws, which would make provision for including "righteous gentiles" or "God-fearers" within the Judean identity, postdates Paul altogether. Further, from Jewish and other sources it can be demonstrated that an essentialist structure underlies the whole idea of including "Noahides" on the basis of the Noahide laws.

369. Zoccali, "All Israel," 296.
370. NRSV.
371. Zoccali, "All Israel," 296–97.
372. Nanos, *Mystery*, 239.
373. Donfried, "Short Note," 45; adopted by Zoccali, *Whom God Has Called*, 99–100; "All Israel," 297; cf. Jewett, *Romans*, 916.

these verses, and appear to have caused most of these understandings to run into hermeneutical difficulties. After presenting my own interpretation of the salvation of "all Israel," the next step will be to test my interpretation against the whole of Romans 9 to 11 and the rest of my understanding of Paul's thought on identity as laid out in this book.

The core of Paul's thought in verses 25 to 27 revolves around these four clauses:

1. ὅτι πώρωσις ἀπὸ μέρους τῷ Ἰσραὴλ γέγονεν

2. ἄχρις οὗ τὸ πλήρωμα τῶν ἐθνῶν εἰσέλθῃ

3. καὶ οὕτως πᾶς Ἰσραὴλ σωθήσεται

4. καθὼς γέγραπται . . .

As I will argue, these four clauses[374] are interdependent and have to be understood in a close relationship in order to determine the whole meaning. The logic would be as follows: What is described in the first clause (1) reaches its time-limit on the basis of the condition stated in the second clause (2). The third clause (3) then results from the condition set forth in the second clause (2). Yet, as I will argue, the third clause (3) is in an equally dependent relationship with the fourth clause (4), making the second (2) and fourth clauses (4) to relate to the same event. The relationship among the clauses will be argued and elaborated upon below. The final interpretation of these four clauses and especially the meaning of "all Israel" will only follow after a closer examination of the smaller syntactical parts or words that constitute these clauses.

Within the build-up of Romans, Paul has never pertinently indicated whether Israel that lived before the Christ event (historical Israel) is saved. As argued, Paul probably created a deliberate uncertainty regarding historical Israel's salvation. This uncertainty can be formulated in terms of roughly the following question: If it was required for someone under the law (under the Old Covenant) to perfectly do the law in order to be justified (2:13; 10:5), but no one could perfectly do the law as a result of being under sin (3:19–20), including Old Testament Israel by implication, and if the only way one can be justified is through faith in Christ (3:22–26; 4:12, 16, 24; 5:1; 10:9–13), what happens to historical Israel? Are they saved?

It is especially in Romans 9:27–33 where Paul leaves the impression that historical Israel is in fact not saved after a cross-over in salvation history: If a saved remnant points to those remaining after a judgment in contrast to

---

374. Moo, *Romans*, 716, 727, describes Paul's main thought in verses 25–27 only in terms of clauses 1–3 (as listed) and understands καθὼς . . . αὐτῶν (vv. 26b–27) as a reinforcement.

"the children of Israel" whose number were like the sand of the sea (v. 27, quoting from Isa 10:20–23), and if Israel did not attain the law of righteousness (v. 31) but *stumbled* at the Stumbling stone (Christ) when salvation history culminated in the Christ event (v. 32–33) whereas the gentiles *did attain* righteousness by faith (v. 30), it seems indeed as if historical Israel has been discarded in favor of the gentiles. Strictly speaking, once those from historical Israel living at the time of the Christ-event believed in Christ, they already entered a new eschatological existence and identity in Christ and thus ceased being "Israel," but became part of Christ's body and part of the ekklesia (Gal 1:13; 2:20; Phil 3:5–8). The "remnant" thus does not need to be understood as pointing to all later descendants of historical Israel who believed in Christ, but only as pointing to those who remained *at the time of the Christ-event* and believed in Christ. If this interpretation is correct, the "elect" in Rom 11:7 would point to both Judean and gentile believers in Christ,[375] and the "rest" or "other" (λοιπός) would in fact primarily point to hardened, historical Israel, *resulting in* Judean unbelievers in Paul's present, for verse 8 points to historical Israel's hardening "until this day" (ἕως τῆς σήμερον ἡμέρας, see below). If the above-mentioned semantic distinctions between the designations Ἰσραήλ (God's people of the past) and Ἰουδαῖος (ethnic descendants of the historical people in the present) are retained in this context, it is noteworthy that Paul never directly states that the Ἰουδαῖοι are the ones who are hardened.

As proposed, the concern about historical Israel's salvation might in fact be the question of Rom 11:1, but then Paul points to himself as believer in Christ (11:2) and keeps the question about historical Israel's salvation in suspense (see p. 263). This underlying concern might even contribute to Paul's anguish expressed in 9:2 in that his concern for the salvation of ancient, historical Israel could be included in addition to his concern for unbelieving Judeans in his present. The uncertainty regarding historical Israel's salvation thus forms the contextual basis for the possibility of viewing the salvation of "all Israel" in 11:26 as pointing to the salvation of ancient, historical Israel. The question is if such an interpretation can fit the textual data in 11:25–27 and its immediate context, to which I now turn.

The Mystery (v. 25)

Dunn is correct to note "a degree of hesitancy about the arguments pursued by Paul" in his salvation-historical exposition up to this point.[376] Everything

---

375. Dunn, *Romans*, 2:640.
376. Dunn, *Romans*, 2:689.

that Paul has said since Romans 9:1 has built up to this point. In 11:26, Paul finally breaks the suspense in answer to the anguish expressed in 9:1-3 and 10:1,[377] followed by his pertinent questions regarding God's people in 11:1 and Israel's fall in 11:11. Paul's readers ought not to be ignorant (ἀγνοέω) of the mystery (μυστήριον) any longer. Paul, however, warns "against reliance on human wisdom" (ἵνα μὴ ἦτε παρ' ἑαυτοῖς φρόνιμοι)[378] in this matter.

Although the concept of μυστήριον was common in the Greco-Roman mystery cults where it denoted secret teachings and rituals only known to initiates,[379] Paul's usage of the term neither resembles intimate knowledge or interest in the vocabulary of the mysteries, nor does it bear the sense of disclosing secrets.[380] That his usage of the term is based on an Old Testament understanding of the revelation of divine secrets by divine agency is certainly possible (e.g., Dan 2:18-19, 27-30).[381] But within the Pauline corpus, including the three major disputed letters (Eph, Col, 2 Th), the term is mostly applied within the context of that which was hidden from God's people in the past but had now been revealed in the gospel (Rom 16:25; 1 Cor 2:1, 7; 4:1; Eph 1:9; 3:3, 4, 9; 6:19; Col 1:26, 27; 2:2; 4:3).[382] In all of these references a past mystery (not future) is in view. The only exception to this use is Paul's reference to those who have not died, who will be changed at the parousia (1 Cor 15:51). Barrett, however, notes that the "mystery" in 1 Corinthians 15:51 "is not essential to the understanding of the Gospel."[383]

In terms of Romans 11:25-27, Moo correctly argues that Paul did not receive a special prophetic insight, a view that "assumes more tension in Paul's argument in these chapters than is warranted. Better is the suggestion that Paul came to understand this mystery through study of the OT in light of the gospel."[384] Similarly, Wright states that Paul "intends the word to refer, not to a hidden truth open only to initiates, but to an aspect of the . . . plan and purpose of God that has now been unveiled through the gospel of Jesus the Messiah."[385] The relation between this "mystery" and the gospel is especially evident in verse 28 (εὐαγγέλιον), which points back to what has been

377. Cf. Dunn, *Romans*, 2:679.
378. Dunn, *Romans*, 2:679.
379. Dunn, *Romans*, 2:677-78.
380. Dunn, *Romans*, 2:678; cf. Fee, *Corinthians*, 104.
381. See Moo, *Romans*, 71; and Dunn, *Romans*, 2:678, for long lists of references to apocalyptic writings in support of Paul's use of the term.
382. Moo, *Romans*, 714. The word μυστήριον also occurs in 1 Cor 13:2; 14:3; Eph 5:32 and 2 Thess 2:7, but not in the technical sense as in the occurrences listed above.
383. Barret, *First Epistle*, 380.
384. Moo, *Romans*, 715; cf. Cranfield, *Romans*, 2:573-74.
385. Wright, "Romans," 687; cf. Fitzmyer, *Romans*, 621; Käsemann, *Romans*, 312.

put forth in verses 25 to 27. It is thus likely that the mystery that is revealed in "the coming in" (εἰσέρχομαι, v. 25) of the gentiles and the salvation of "all Israel" (v. 26) relates closely to the gospel, which in turn would be at odds with a view where Paul would here operate in the prophetic and receive a special revelation about a future event.[386]

A Hardening Has Come Partially on Israel (v. 25)

The next question is how the phrase ἀπὸ μέρους (v. 25) should be understood. The term πώρωσις is probably best translated as "hardening"[387] in concurrence with πωρόω of verse 7 and σκληρύνω in 9:18.[388] In the clause πώρωσις ἀπὸ μέρους τῷ Ἰσραὴλ γέγονεν, the phrase ἀπὸ μέρους can be understood as adjectival, qualifying Ἰσραήλ ("a hardening has come on [a] part of Israel"),[389] or as adverbial, modifying either the verbal concept present in πώρωσις ("a partial hardening has come on Israel")[390] or modifying

---

386. Contra Hultgren, *Romans*, 416; Campbell, *Paul*, 134; Jewett, *Romans*, 699; Schnelle, *Paul*, 352.

387. Zerwick and Grosvenor, *Grammatical Analysis*, 485; Moo, *Romans*, 711, 717; Fitzmyer, *Romans*, 621; Morris, *Romans*, 418; Cranfield, *Romans*, 2:572, 574; ISV; NRSV; REB; NIV; RSV; RV.

388. The term πώρωσις (Mark 3:5; Rom 11:25; Eph 4:18) indicates a state or condition of complete lack of understanding, dullness, insensibility, or obstinacy (BDAG, πώρωσις; cf. L&N §27.52). In the verbal form (πωρόω, Rom 11:7; 2 Cor 3:14), it denotes causing someone to have difficulty in understanding or comprehending—to "harden" or "petrify" (BDAG, πωρόω; cf. L&N §27.51). The use of πωρόω lies semantically close to σκληρύνω in 9:18 (Moo, *Romans*, 680; Cranfield, *Romans*, 2:548-49). On the basis of a post-holocaust interpretation of Paul, however, Nanos, "Callused," 53-55, wants to distinguish the hardening of the Pharaoh's heart (σκληρύνω, 9:18, reflecting the Hebrew קָשָׁה, e.g., Exod 9:12, 16) from πώρωσις or πωρόω. He resists an insensitive translation of two terms, and suggests to translate them as "callused," which he derives from medical discussions in antiquity (e.g., Hippocrates; Celsus), denoting an impairment and a form of protection that promotes healing. He claims that the connection of the term πώρωσις with the human heart (Mark 3:5; Eph 4:18) constitutes a later tradition after Paul. But the Gospel of Mark is sometimes dated quite early (late 50s to 60s CE, Köstenberger et al., *Cradle*, 298; Carson and Moo, *Introduction*, 182), and Ephesians are considered by many as Pauline (see note 95, p. 18). But more importantly, the term σκληρύνω (LXX) as well as the corresponding term קָשָׁה (MT) are often used for Israel's hardening (Deut 10:16; 2 Kgs 17:14; 2 Chr 30:8; Neh 9:16-17, 29; Ps 95:8; Jer 7:26; 17:23; 19:15) of which Deut 10:16 and Ps 95:8 explicitly involve the state of the heart.

389. Jewett, *Romans*, 699; Byrne, *Romans*, 354; Morris, *Romans*, 420; Käsemann, *Romans*, 311, 313; Barrett, *Romans*, 223; NRSV; AMP; NJB; NAT; RSV; cf. GW.

390. Dunn, *Romans*, 2:679; ESV; ISV; LITV; REB.

the verb γέγονεν ("a hardening has come partially on Israel").³⁹¹ The latter interpretation is to be preferred, for it is most likely syntactically³⁹² (cf. Rom 15:15, 24; 2 Cor 1:14; 2:5). In addition, ἀπὸ μέρους corresponds with ἄχρι οὗ, which has to be taken as "until."³⁹³ The hardening of Israel is thus limited in time (see below).³⁹⁴

As argued, the hardening of Israel can be understood as historical³⁹⁵ (cf. 2 Cor 3:14; Rom 9:18; 11:7-10), pointing to their disobedience and stubbornness throughout history (Rom 10:21), necessitating the coming of their Messiah. Such an understanding of Israel's hardening would complement the idea of a hardening that is limited in time. Here, the verb γέγονεν is in the perfect indicative tense, which normally denotes a completed action in the past with effects into the present.³⁹⁶ In Zerwick's words, the perfect tense is used for "indicating not the past action as such but the present 'state of affairs' resulting from the past action."³⁹⁷ In other words, the perfect tense could indicate that although Israel's hardening is historical, it resulted in unbelieving Judeans in Paul's present.³⁹⁸ Hardened Israel thus seems to correspond in some way to historical Israel. The implications of this understanding will be discussed below.

The Coming In of the Fullness of the Gentiles (v. 25)

How should the "coming in" (εἰσέλθῃ, v. 25) of the gentiles be understood? This subjunctive can be translated as "may come in,"³⁹⁹ "should come [in]"⁴⁰⁰

---

391. Kruse, *Romans*, 442; Osborne, *Romans*, 305; Wright, "Romans," 688; Cranfield, *Romans*, 2:575; Godet, *Romans*, 2:252; OAT; DST. The ambiguous translation "a hardening in part has come on Israel" or similar (e.g., RV; KJV) can also be interpreted in this way.

392. Cranfield, *Romans*, 2:575; admitted by Moo, *Romans*, 717; cf. BDF §272.

393. E.g., Zerwick and Grosvenor, *Grammatical Analysis*, 485; Moo, *Romans*, 711, 717; Cranfield, *Romans*, 2:575; ESV; NRSV; NIV; KJV.

394. As Schreiner, *Romans*, 617, and Fitzmyer, *Romans*, 621, note, even if ἀπὸ μέρους is understood as modifying the verbal concept present in πώρωσις, it can be understood as a hardening that is limited in time.

395. Lenski, *Romans*, 722.

396. Wallace, *Grammar*, 573; Moule, *Idom Book*, 13; cf. Kruger, *Eksegese*, 5; BDF §342; Van Rensburg, *Grammatika*, 109.

397. Zerwick, *Biblical Greek*, 96.

398. Cf. Kim, "Reading," 326.

399. YLT; cf. Jewett, *Romans*, 700.

400. Wallace, *Grammar*, 479.

or "has come in" (εἰσέλθῃ).⁴⁰¹ It is significant to note that the subjunctive (εἰσέλθῃ) does not indicate *time as such* but denotes an *open hypothetical mode*.⁴⁰² In terms of the aorist subjunctive, Robertson writes that there is "*no Time Element in the Subjunctive*. There is only relative time (future) and that is not due to the tense at all."⁴⁰³ Here, ἄχρι οὗ followed by the second aorist subjunctive (εἰσέλθῃ) is used in an "Indefinite Temporal Clause,"⁴⁰⁴ implying a temporal limit,⁴⁰⁵ constituting a limited (partial) hardening. The subjunctive εἰσέλθῃ thus denotes "a future contingency from the perspective of the time of the main verb."⁴⁰⁶ To avoid the time element, some therefore translate εἰσέλθῃ as "be come in."⁴⁰⁷ The "coming in" of the fullness of the gentiles could theoretically lie in Paul's present or even his past, depending on the fulfillment of the temporal condition (the fullness of the gentiles coming in). A noteworthy example in Paul of the possibility that ἄχρι(ς) οὗ followed by the second aorist subjunctive (as in 11:25) could denote something that already happened, is Galatians 3:19. There ἄχρις οὗ and the second aorist subjunctive ἔλθῃ is used within the context of the law that was added until the seed "would come,"⁴⁰⁸ "should come,"⁴⁰⁹ "came"⁴¹⁰ or "had come."⁴¹¹ The seed that *had come* was Christ (Gal 3:16).

In terms of the hardening itself, there is no indication within the text (Rom 11:25) that the hardening is removed, but rather that it lasts until the incoming of the fullness of the gentiles.⁴¹² Wright shows from 9:17–18 that the hardening constitutes a temporary suspension of judgment that would otherwise have fallen to allow for some to escape.⁴¹³ In the case of the Pharaoh the result was the exodus from Egypt. In this case (11:25–26) the result of the hardening is the coming in of the fullness of the gentiles and the salvation of "all Israel."

401. Morris, *Romans*, 418; ESV; ISV; NRSV; NKJV.
402. Kruger, *Eksegese*, 7; idem., "Conditions," 59–63.
403. Robertson, *Grammar*, 848.
404. Wallace, *Grammar*, 479.
405. Moo, *Romans*, 718; cf. Dunn, *Romans*, 2:680.
406. Wallace, *Grammar*, 479.
407. Murray, *Romans*, 2:91; ASV; RV; KJV.
408. NRSV.
409. Betz, *Galatians*, 164; ESV; LITV; AMP; ASV; RV; KJV.
410. ISV; GW.
411. George, *Galatians*, 250; NIV.
412. Zoccali, "All Israel," 306–8; Wright, "Romans," 677; *Climax*, 249; Merkle, "Romans 11," 716; Lenski, *Romans*, 721–23; cf. Calvin, *Romans*, 377; contra Moo, *Romans*, 717.
413. Wright, "Romans," 677.

"ALL ISRAEL" AND "THE ISRAEL OF GOD"

The verb Paul utilizes in denoting the coming in of the fullness of the gentiles is εἰσέρχομαι. The majority of scholars today interpret the word here to refer to the coming into the kingdom (βασιλεία) of God, indicating messianic salvation, a view that is largely based on the use of εἰσέρχομαι in the Gospels (esp. Matt 5:20; 7:13, 21; 19:17; Mark 9:43, 45, 47; 10:15, 23-25; Luke 13:24; John 3:5).[414] But before one reverts to a possible pre-Pauline tradition, it seems methodologically more rigorous to attempt to infer the meaning of εἰσέρχομαι from reviewing Paul's own employment of the term elsewhere. With respect to Paul's usage of the word βασιλεία, it can be observed that Paul never sees it as something to "come into" or similar, but rather something to be "inherited" (κληρονομέω, 1 Cor 6:9, 10; 15:50; Gal 5:21; cf. κληρονομία, Eph 5:5). As for the verb εἰσέρχομαι, apart from Romans 11:25, the verb occurs in only two other locations in the Pauline corpus: in Romans 5:12 and in 1 Corinthians 14:23-24, none of which indicates entering salvation or the kingdom of God:

1. In 1 Corinthians 14:23-24, the verb denotes the physical entry of uneducated people (ἰδιώτης)[415] or unbelievers (ἄπιστος, v. 23) into the believing assembly.[416] Here is thus no connotation regarding entrance into God's kingdom or salvation. At most it denotes people coming into the influential sphere of the believing community.

2. In Romans 5:12 εἰσέρχομαι denotes the entrance of sin and death into the world.[417] Here, the term is closely related to διέρχομαι, denoting "a movement toward a destination,"[418] which many translations render as "spread."[419] The notion is that sin and death came into the cosmos in terms of affecting humanity salvation-historically and corporately[420] rather than individually.[421]

---

414. E.g., Jewett, *Romans*, 701; Moo, *Romans*, 718; Dunn, *Romans*, 2:680; Käsemann, *Romans*, 313; Cranfield, *Romans*, 2:576; Sanday and Headlam, *Romans*, 313; cf. Witherington and Hyatt, *Romans*, 273.

415. ISV; cf. Zerwick and Grosvenor, *Grammatical Analysis*, 526; Fee, *Corinthians*, 684-85; REB; NIV.

416. Cf. BDAG, εἰσέρχομαι, §1aδ.

417. BDAG, εἰσέρχομαι, §1aβ.

418. BDAG, διέρχομαι, §1bβ.

419. ESV; NLT; ISV; NRSV; AMP; RSV.

420. Cf. Moo, *Romans*, 322-23; Cranfield, *Romans*, 1:274; Ridderbos, *Romeinen*, 112.

421. Although Paul refers to the individual dimension of sin in the last part of 5:12 (ἐφ' ᾧ πάντες ἥμαρτον) in addition to the corporate dimensions of the prior part (Moo, *Romans*, 323-24), it is not of relevance to square these notions here.

When the way in which εἰσέρχομαι is used in both 1 Corinthians 14:23, 24 and Romans 5:12 is taken into account in trying to infer its meaning in Romans 11:25, it could denote the gentiles as coming into the sphere of something.[422] For Fitzmyer, εἰσέρχομαι in 11:25 denotes the gentiles' "entrance into the community of salvation" rather than "entrance into the kingdom of God,"[423] which already seems closer to Paul's intention.

The prevailing interpretation of πλήρωμα, which qualifies τῶν ἐθνῶν, must also come under scrutiny. Most interpreters understand πλήρωμα τῶν ἐθνῶν as denoting "the full number of gentiles,"[424] which is said to be borrowed from "Jewish apocalyptic,"[425] referring to *4 Ezra* 4:35-37; *2 Apocalypse of Baruch* 23:4; 30:2; 75:6; and *Apocalypse of Abraham* 29:17. But apart from the danger of working anachronistically by borrowing from Jewish Apocalyptic, which postdates Paul,[426] such a methodology might hold the danger of not giving full account of Paul's own thought.

As argued in the discussion of 11:12, Paul's use of πλήρωμα would rather denote "fullness" or "full inclusion" than a "complete number" within that context (see note 264, p. 269). Against the translation "the full number of gentiles" of τὸ πλήρωμα τῶν ἐθνῶν in 11:25, Dunn argues that Paul intends "to indicate that the incoming of the Gentiles would be equivalent to that of Israel" in accordance with its use in 11:12.[427] Even Cranfield admits that "it may be wise not to rule out as altogether impossible . . . that Paul

422. It could be asked if such a methodology is justified exegetical practice. The principle behind this reasoning is largely based on the semantic approach that meaning is constituted by more than the inherent meaning of individual words (Botha, *Semeïon*, 169). One has to keep the possibility open that Paul might use εἰσέρχομαι in a different way than other New Testament writers. But given Paul's sparce usage of εἰσέρχομαι, the proposed meaning in Rom 11:25 is not intended as final, and has to be seen as largely tentative and hypothetical at this point.

423. Fitzmyer, *Romans*, 622.

424. E.g., BDAG, πλήρωμα, §3a; Zerwick and Grosvenor, *Grammatical Analysis*, 485; Newman and Nida, *Romans*, 226; Kruse, *Romans*, 441-42; Osborne, *Romans*, 305; Witherington and Hyatt, *Romans*, 272; Schreiner, *Romans*, 617; Dunn, *Paul the Apostle*, 527; Mounce, *Romans*, 224; Fitzmyer, *Romans*, 621-22; Morris, *Romans*, 420; Bruce, *Romans*, 217; Barrett, *Romans*, 223; Ridderbos, *Romeinen*, 262; ISV; NLT; NRSV; AMP; NIV; RSV; cf. Jewett, *Romans*, 700; Moo, *Romans*, 719; Käsemann, *Romans*, 313; GNB.

425. Moo, *Romans*, 718-19; cf. Jewett, *Romans*, 697; Osborne, *Romans*, 305; Käsemann, *Romans*, 313.

426. While most scholars date the book of *4 Ezra* around 81-96 CE (e.g., Aune, *Apocalypticism*, 151; Stone, *Fourth Ezra*, 10; Myers, *I and II Esdras*, 129-31), the book of *2 Baruch* is normally dated after the destruction of the temple in 70 CE (Aune, *Apocalypticism*, 151; Bogaert, *Baruch*, 270-95), probably around 110 CE (Starr, "Paraenesis," 90; Aune, *Revelation*, 1105). The *Apocalypse of Abraham* is normally dated around 70-150 CE (Rubinkiewicz, "Apocalypse of Abraham," 683).

427. Dunn, *Romans*, 2:680.

means by τὸ πλήρωμα τῶν ἐθνῶν something like 'the Gentile world as a whole' (compare πᾶς Ἰσραήλ in v. 26),"[428] which is a phrase borrowed from Sanday and Headlam.[429]

When Paul's sparse usage of πλήρωμα is probed in the undisputed letters (apart from Rom 11:12, 25), it can mean the following: "the fulfilling of the law" (Rom 13:10), "the fullness of the blessing of Christ" (Rom 15:29), "[the] fullness [that] are the Lord's" (1 Cor 10:26) and "the fullness of time" (Gal 4:4). In the disputed letters it can mean "the fullness of time" (Eph 1:10), "the fullness of him [Christ]" (Eph 1:23), "the fullness of God" (Eph 3:19; Col 1:19), "the full stature of Christ" (Eph 4:13) and "the . . . fullness of deity" (Col 2:9).[430]

A similar picture emerges when the verb πληρόω is considered. In the undisputed letters it can mean the following: "filled with every kind of wickedness" (Rom 1:29), "that the just requirement of the law might be fulfilled" (Rom 8:4), "has fulfilled the law" (Rom 13:8), "fill . . . with all joy" (Rom 15:13; cf. "filled with joy" in 2 Tim 1:4), "filled with all knowledge" (Rom 15:14), "fully proclaimed the good news" (Rom 15:19), "filled with consolation" (2 Cor 7:4), "obedience is complete" (10:6), "the . . . law is fulfilled" (Gal 5:14), "filled with the fruits of righteousness" (Phil 1:11), "make . . . joy complete" (Phil 2:2), "fully satisfied" (Phil 4:18) and "fully satisfy every need" (Phil 4:19). In the disputed letters, it can mean the following: "[Christ] who fills all in all" (Eph 1:23), "that you may be filled [πληρόω] with all the fullness [πλήρωμα] of God" (Eph 3:19), "fill all things" (Eph 4:10), "filled with the Spirit" (Eph 5:18), "filled with . . . knowledge" (Col 1:9), "make the word of God fully known" (Col 1:25), "come to fullness in him [Christ]" (Col 2:10), "complete the task" (Col 4:17) and "fulfil . . . every good resolve" (2 Thess 1:11).[431]

Apart from Romans 11, Paul thus neither uses the noun πλήρωμα nor the verb πληρόω in a quantitative or numerical sense. If the meaning of πλήρωμα here in Romans 11:25 (and 11:12) must be construed inductively, it seems once again safer to do it from Paul's own writing than to borrow

---

428. Cranfield, *Romans*, 2:575-76.

429. Sanday and Headlam, *Romans*, 335; cf. Richardson, *Introduction*, 252. Hultgren, *Romans*, 418, argues against both the translations "the full number of Gentiles" and "the Gentile world as a whole," but seems to miss the mark once again when he suggests that "'the fullness of the nations' will be ushered into the new humanity representatively *by those who believe throughout the various nations of the world*" (emphasis added).

430. All translations of πλήρωμα come from the NRSV.

431. All translations of πληρόω come from the NRSV, except Gal 5:14 and Phil 1:11 (RSV)

from Jewish apocalyptic, which evokes all the problems of the anachronistic relationship between Paul and later Judaism as already discussed. Since salvation (σῴζω, v. 26) is at stake, it seems reasonable to suggest that the "coming in of the fullness of the Gentiles" has something to do with salvation. Consequently, the reconstruction of the meaning of τὸ πλήρωμα τῶν ἐθνῶν εἰσέλθῃ (Rom 11:25) will be attempted by considering Paul's thought on the salvation of the gentiles in the whole of Romans, especially 9 to 11.

In Romans 9 God's call unto salvation is now, in the new eschatological eon in Christ, not only directed to Judean people, but to gentiles too (9:24). Those who were not God's people are now called God's people (9:25-26). Gentiles who did not strive for righteousness have now attained righteousness (9:30). In 11:11, Paul argues that by the false step of Israel, salvation has come to the gentiles. All of these notions (9:24, 25-26, 30; 11:11) do not denote righteousness or salvation to each individual gentile, but salvation or righteousness to the gentile nations as a whole in respect of their position in salvation history.[432] In his comment on 9:24, Wright states: "This is how God is keeping his word to Abraham, the word that spoke both of an ongoing selection from within his physical family and also of the worldwide people who would eventually *be brought in*."[433] Salvation is now to all who believe in Christ. There is no distinction between Judean and gentile (10:9–13), meaning that gentiles are now generically included in God's salvific purpose (cf. ἐπαγγελία in 9:9). Similarly, in Romans 11 the branches that have been broken off represent Israel as a *diachronic whole* apart from the remnant who believed in Christ: both ancient, historical Israel and unbelieving Judeans in Paul's present were cut off. As argued, the grafting of the gentiles into the good olive tree (God's people), although it contains an element of individual faith (remaining in faith), once again points to the generic inclusion of gentiles into salvation history and God's election.

In addition, the generic reach of salvation and righteousness/justification[434] that include gentiles, is well accounted for in Romans 5. Paul writes in verse 15 that "the free gift in the grace of the one man, Jesus Christ, abounded for the many."[435] The "free gift . . . brings justification" (v. 16)[436] generically. In verse 18, righteousness is depicted as a gift for all people (πάντας ἀνθρώπους). Through the obedience of one, many are made righteous (v. 19). That all

432. Cf. Moo, *Romans*, 617.

433. Wright, "Romans," 642, emphasis added.

434. The close relationship between salvation and concepts revolving around righteousness and justification is evident in Rom 5:9–10, 18–19 (σῴζω, vv. 9, 10; δικαιόω, v. 9; καταλλάσσω, v. 10; δικαίωμα, v. 18; δικαίωσις, v. 18; δίκαιος, v. 19).

435. NRSV.

436. NRSV.

people are principally included in salvation and righteousness, does not mean universalism, but that all people, including gentiles, have *come into* God's purpose (9:9) of salvation and calling (9:24) unto salvation.

This generic inclusion of the gentiles as a whole into God's salvation is in all probability what is echoed by Romans 11:25, not the salvation of each individual elect gentile. In summary, within the context of Paul's salvation-historical exposition from Romans 9 through 11, the best option seems to be that the "fullness" (πλήρωμα) of the gentiles here in 11:25 generically denotes the *gentile nations as a whole*, while εἰσέρχομαι denotes their *generic inclusion into God's salvific economy*.[437]

In This Manner All Israel Will Be Saved As Is Written (v. 26):
Grammar and Semantics

Next, how is καὶ οὕτως (v. 26) to be understood? Some scholars argue that καὶ οὕτως is to be understood as temporal, translating "and then" or similar.[438] Contrary to Fitzmyer and Moo[439] there is evidence for a temporal meaning of οὕτως in Greek.[440] Following van der Horst,[441] Jewett, although translating "and in such a manner, and so," seems to leave room for the modal and temporal senses not being mutually exclusive, which in the context might be suggested by the shift in verb tense from the perfect in the first

---

437. Cf. "the Gentiles have been admitted in full strength" (REB); they are "included" (GW). Some argue that πλήρωμα in 11:25 would indicate Paul's "fulfillment" of preaching in the eastern Mediterranean (15:16-19; cf. Col 1:17) implying that Paul's own preaching would complete the gentile mission, bring them into the kingdom and usher in the end (e.g., Aus, "Travel Plans," 235-37, 257-61; Munck, *Salvation*, 47-55; cf. Barrett, *Romans*, 276-77). But this interpretation of 15:16-19 is unlikely. It is not clear from this passage that Paul's own mission would in itself constitute the climax of salvation history. Although Paul would certainly see himself as a significant figure in salvation history, there is no indication that he would bring that mission to its conclusion based on his own efforts. Paul rather identifies Christ as working through him (v. 18). Rather than pointing to his special role as eschatological preacher that would complete the entire mission to all gentiles that would usher in the parousia, he claims completion in the regions laid out for his apostolic task of planting strategic churches (Moo, *Romans*, 718, 892-96; cf. Bruce, *Romans*, 262; Cranfield, *Romans*, 2:762; Godet, *Romans*, 2:374).

438. E.g., Witherington and Hyatt, *Romans*, 274; Van der Horst, "Critical Notes," 524; Käsemann, *Romans*, 313; Barrett, *Romans*, 223.

439. Fitzmyer, *Romans*, 622; Moo, *Romans*, 719-20.

440. As reported by Van der Horst, "Critical Notes," 523-24, and Jewett, *Romans*, 701, it is found in Plato's *Protagoras* 314c, in *Testament of Abraham* (recension A) 7.11, and in *Life of Jeremiah* 6 of the *Vitae prophetarum*.

441. Van der Horst, "Critical Notes," 524.

element of the mystery (v. 25c), to the subjunctive in the second (v. 25d), and to the future in the third (v. 26a).[442] He is however cautious to assert "definite stages" on the basis of this possibility.[443] Others understand οὕτως as denoting a consequence, translating "in consequence of this process" or similar.[444] But in accordance with its meaning in 1 Corinthians 11:28; 14:25 and 1 Thessalonians 4:17, it is more likely that οὕτως denotes *manner*:[445] "in *this manner* all Israel will be saved," especially if καὶ οὕτως is read in conjunction with καθὼς γέγραπται (v. 26, see below).

Before the meaning of "all Israel" can be determined, I propose another look at the future tense of σωθήσεται and how salvation is to be understood in Paul, especially in terms of its realization. As will be argued from a grammatical and co-textual point of view, that the salvation of "all Israel" is necessarily effected at a certain point in Paul's future, is not so obvious. As already noted, the subjunctive εἰσέλθῃ (v. 25) does not necessarily denote a future point in time relative to Paul (see above). In terms of the future tense, good arguments can be made for Paul's occasional employment of a logical or gnomic future that does not necessarily lie in Paul's future. Three examples that have been discussed are 2 Corinthians 3:8 (see p. 178), Romans 6:5, 8 (see p. 219), and Romans 11:24 (see p. 275), which by no means exhaust Paul's use of the logical future.[446]

---

442. Jewett, *Romans*, 701.

443. Jewett, *Romans*, 701.

444. E.g., Fitzmyer, *Romans*, 622–23; Dodd, *Romans*, 184; REB.

445. Zoccali, "All Israel," 309; Jewett, *Romans*, 694; Schreiner, *Romans*, 621; Byrne, *Romans*, 354; Moo, *Romans*, 720; Mounce, *Romans*, 224; Dunn, *Romans*, 2:681; Morris, *Romans*, 420; Bruce, *Romans*, 218; Beker, *Paul the Apostle*, 334; Cranfield, *Romans*, 2:576; Ridderbos, *Romeinen*, 263; Lenski, *Romans*, 724; Sanday and Headlam, *Romans*, 335; ESV; ISV; GW; GNB; NAT.

446. Other examples of future tenses that can be understood as gnomic or logical futures are the following: δικαιωθήσονται in Rom 2:13 (Bultmann, "Dikaiosynē," 15); λογισθήσεται in Rom 2:26 (Jewett, *Romans*, 233); δικαιωθήσεται in Rom 3:20 (Fung, *Galatians*, 233; Bultmann, *Theology*, 274; cf. Murray, *Romans*, 1:107); δικαιώσει in Rom 3:30 (Bell, "Myth," 31; Moo, *Romans*, 252; Fung, *Galatians*, 233; Käsemann, *Romans*, 104; Cranfield, *Romans*, 1:222; Schrenk, "δίκη," TDNT, 2:218; Bultmann, *Theology*, 274; Denney, "Romans," 614); ἀποθανεῖται in Rom 5:7 (Schreiner, *Romans*, 262; Wallace, *Grammar*, 571; BDF §349; Robertson, *Grammar*, 876; Burton, *Galatians*, 36); βασιλεύσουσιν in Rom 5:17 (Moo, *Romans*, 340; Denney, "Romans," 630; cf. Murray, *Romans*, 1:198); ζήσομεν in Rom 6:2 (Wilckens, *Römer*, 11), κυριεύσει in Rom 6:14 (Fitzmyer, *Romans*, 447); χρηματίσει in Rom 7:3 (Wallace, *Grammar*, 1996:571; Robertson, *Grammar*, 876; Burton, *Galatians*, 36; Blass, *Grammar*, 201); σωθήσῃ in Rom 10:9 (Jewett, *Romans*, 630; Osborne, *Romans*, 270; Moo, *Romans*, 658); σωρεύσεις in Rom 12:20 (Yarbrough, "Theology," 48); λήμψονται in Rom 13:2 (Käsemann, *Romans*, 357); κληρονομήσουσιν in 1 Cor 6:10 (Lewis, *Looking*, 86; Thiselton, *Corinthians*, 439); θερίσει (x2) in 2 Cor 9:6 (Harris, *Second Epistle*, 633); καυχήσομαι (x2) in 2 Cor 12:5

Robertson defines the gnomic future as follows: "In the gnomic future the act is *true of any time*." Additionally, "[i]n indirect discourse the time is relatively future to that of the principal verb, though it *may be absolutely past*."[447] Similarly, Blass and Debrunner state that the "future indicative is used ... occasionally as a *gnomic future* in order to express that which is to be expected under certain circumstances."[448]

In terms of the gnomic future, Wallace states that the "idea is not that a particular event is in view, but that such events are true of life,"[449] and then quotes Robertson: "In the gnomic future the act is true of any time."[450] But Wallace does not discuss the possibility that the future tense might denote something that is relatively future to that of the principal verb,[451] but *may be absolutely past* (as quoted above). When the two examples that Robertson provides in illustrating this possibility are considered (Matt 20:10; John 21:19),[452] it shows how the future can be used within a context where the future tense denotes something that *ultimately* (in terms of absolute time) lies in the past: (1) In Matthew 20:10, in the parable of the workers in the vineyard, Jesus says: "But when the first came, they thought they will receive [λήμψονται, fut.] more, but each of them also received [ἔλαβον, aor.] a denarius." (2) In John 21:19, *after* Jesus' death and resurrection, the text reads: "He said this to show the kind of death by which he will glorify [δοξάσει, fut.] God. After this he said to him, 'Follow me.'"

In Roberts' Greek grammar, he refers to the "[f]uture logical" by using the illustration εἰ ποιήσει ταῦτα, σχήσει καλῶς, and translates, "If he will do this, *it will be* well with him."[453] It therefore seems that the future indicative can be understood as a *logical future* where it stands in certain types of

---

(Harris, *Second Epistle*, 847) and ἔσται in 2 Cor 13:11 (Furnish, *II Corinthians*, 586); δικαιωθήσεται in Gal 2:16 (Fung, *Galatians*, 233; Bultmann, "Dikaiosynē," 15); ζήσεται in Gal 3:11 (Lenski, *Galatians*, 145); βαστάσει in Gal 6:5 (Kim, "Reading," 326; Martyn, *Galatians*, 543; Vaughan and Gideon, *Grammar*, 143; Burton, *Galatians*, 334). See Du Toit, "Overview," for a more elaborate discussion on the gnomic/logical future in Paul.

447. Robertson, *Grammar*, 876, emphasis added, cf. Wallace, *Grammar*, 571.
448. BDF §349; cf. Burton, *Moods*, 36; Blass, *Grammar*, 201.
449. Wallace, *Grammar*, 571.
450. Robertson, *Grammar*, 876.
451. In Rom 11:26, if οὕτως πᾶς Ἰσραὴλ σωθήσεται can be considered as *both* dependent on the condition denoted by the subjunctive εἰσέλθῃ in v. 25 (the coming in of the gentiles, which is not necessarily connected to a future point in time) *and* to καθὼς γέγραπται... (see main text), containing the futures ἥξει and ἀποστρέψει (v. 26, which refers to a point in time future from the prophetic language, but not necessarily in Paul's future), then the verb σωθήσεται can be considered as secondary in this context.
452. Robertson, *Grammar*, 876.
453. Roberts, *Grammar*, 140, emphasis added.

comparative or conditional sentences,⁴⁵⁴ a function that might be related to the future tense's probable descent from the aorist subjunctive.⁴⁵⁵ In the sentence, "By believing in Christ we *will be saved*," the condition (to believe) could have been met, resulting in being saved already. The verb *"will be saved"* can be understood as a "logical future" in this sentence. In terms of the current context (Rom 11:26), if the salvation of "all Israel" is to be expected *if* the fullness of the gentiles has *already* come in, then the future tense (σωθήσεται) could function as a logical future, but may be *absolutely past*. It has to be noted though that the designation "logical future" is strictly speaking not well accounted for in Greek grammars, and is therefore not so much a firm *grammatical* category⁴⁵⁶ inherent to the future tense itself as it is a category that is derived from the use of a future within a specific (conditional) *context*.⁴⁵⁷

If one considers the way in which the designations "gnomic future" and "logical future" (or similar) are applied in Greek grammars and commentaries, they seem to be applied similarly in terms of denoting *relative* time.⁴⁵⁸ The designation "gnomic future" however seems to lean more toward denoting a general truth (esp. Rom 5:7; 7:3), whereas the "logical future" seems to lean more toward denoting a logical result (derived from the context), which does not necessarily lie in the actual future (esp. Rom 5:19, see below; 6:5, 8; etc.).⁴⁵⁹ The frequency in which commentators interpret the future tense in Paul as a "logical future" or the future being "logical" (cf. note 446, etc.), suggests that a future is used in a *relative* context more often than what otherwise might be expected. It is another question whether the "logical future" could be considered as a subset or a certain variant of the "gnomic future." While Wallace's remark that the "gnomic future" is rare seems to argue against such a possibility,⁴⁶⁰ Robertson's remark about the *relative* future just after mentioning the "gnomic future" (citing Matt

---

454. This notion would correspond to Blass and Debrunner's definition of the gnomic future (that "which is expected under certain circumstances," BDF §349). Cf. Burton, *Moods*, 36; Blass, *Grammar*, 201.

455. Cf. Wallace, *Grammar*, 571; Robertson, *Grammar*, 354. See Paul's apparent interchangeable use of the future indicative and aorist subjunctive in similar syntactical constructions in Rom 5:19 (ὥσπερ ... οὕτως ... + fut. ind.) and 21 (ὥσπερ ... οὕτως ... + aor. subj.). Cf. also Paul's use of ἐάν + fut. ind., e.g., Rom 2:26; 9:27; 10:9; 11:23; 12:20; 1 Cor 14:7, 9; 2 Cor 10:8; Gal 5:2; 6:7. All of these examples bear some logical sense.

456. Cf. Stegall, *Gospel*, 449.

457. Black, *Learn to Read*, 21.

458. Cf. Blass, *Grammar*, 201; Robertson, *Grammar*, 876.

459. See Du Toit, "Overview"; cf. Roberts, *Grammar*, 140.

460. Wallace, *Grammar*, 571.

20:10; John 21:19)⁴⁶¹ does seem to leave such a possibility open, which in turn would imply that the gnomic future, if it includes a relative or logical future, is not necessarily that rare. The same possibility seems to be left open in Blass and Debrunner's more general definition for the gnomic future (that "which is expected under certain circumstances")⁴⁶² Since the designations "gnomic" and "logical" are often used interchangeably in commentaries,⁴⁶³ there seems to be a considerable amount of overlap in how these designations are used.

But apart from the logical construction of sentences, is there another reason why one can argue that Paul occasionally utilizes a logical future? As implied earlier, it can be argued from Romans 5:9–10 that "righteousness," "justification" and "salvation" (as denoted by their cognate terms) all correspond to the same new reality in Christ for those who believe. While all of these concepts have future significance in terms of awaiting eschatological fulfillment, all of them additionally contain a realized or present aspect in the Pauline corpus. Apart from the realized significance of the new creation for those in Christ (2 Cor 5:17, παρῆλθεν [second aor. ind.] and γέγονεν [second perf. ind.], see p. 160; cf. Gal 2:19–20, συνεσταύρωμαι [perf. ind.], ζῶ and ζῇ [both pres. ind.]; 2 Cor 1:20) and the present reality of the Spirit in believer's lives (Rom 8:10, see p. 204), the realized or present aspect can especially be derived from the occurrence of the verbs δικαιόω, καταλλάσσω and σῴζω in their perfect/aorist indicative or -participle forms, and their present indicative or -participle forms.⁴⁶⁴ In terms of Pauline eschatology, Hagner states:

> Contrary to popular misunderstanding, the Christian faith is far more a celebration of eschatological reality already accomplished than a celebration of future eschatology—"pie in the sky in the bye and bye." Eschatology is about the present as well as the future.⁴⁶⁵

---

461. Robertson, *Grammar*, 876.

462. BDF §349; cf. Burton, *Moods*, 36; Blass, *Grammar*, 201.

463. E.g., Fung, *Galatians*, 233; Bultmann, *Theology*, 274; cf. Kim, "Reading," 326.

464. *Aorist indicative*: δικαιόω: Rom 4:2; 8:30; 1 Cor 6:11 (cf. 1 Tim 3:16); καταλλάσσω: Rom 5:10; σῴζω: Rom 8:24 (cf. Titus 3:5). *Aorist participle* (denoting an antecedent to the controlling verb, Wallace, *Grammar*, 614): δικαιόω: Rom 5:1, 9 (cf. Titus 3:7); καταλλάσσω: 2 Cor 5:18 (cf. σῴζω: 2 Tim 1:9). *Perfect indicative*: δικαιόω: Rom 6:7 (cf. *perfect participle* [denoting an antecedent to the controlling verb, Wallace, *Grammar*, 614]: σῴζω: Eph 2:5, 8). *Present indicative*: δικαιόω: Gal 2:16; 3:8, 11; 5:4. *Present participle* (indicating contemporaneous time, Wallace, *Grammar*, 614): δικαιόω: Rom 3:24, 26; 4:5; 8:33; καταλλάσσω: 2 Cor 5:19; σῴζω: 1 Cor 1:18; 15:2; 2 Cor 2:15.

465. Hagner, *New Testament*, 403.

It is especially significant that Romans 8:24 portrays salvation as being realized[466] (σῴζω, aor. ind.) even though it carries a future component, a notion confirmed by Schreiner, Wright, Fee, Moo, Morris, Bruce, Cranfield, Foerster, and Ridderbos.[467] The modifying phrase τῇ ἐλπίδι is probably best understood in terms of an associative sense: "we were saved, *with hope* as the ever present companion of this salvation."[468] This present or realized aspect to salvation is arguably one of the most important reasons why scholars understand Paul to utilize a logical future more often than usually acknowledged. The effect of a logical future is that the reality denoted by the verb may already have come into effect even though it might await future completion.

A significant example of where Paul in all probability intends a logical future (not listed in note 446) is Romans 5:19. He states: "For just as by the one man's disobedience the many were made [aorist: κατεστάθησαν] sinners, so by the one man's obedience the many *will be made* [future: κατασταθήσονται] righteous."[469] That Paul has a logical future in mind (κατασταθήσονται) is suggested by Bell, Moo, Fitzmyer, Fung, Bultmann, Schrenk, and Lagrange.[470] Jewett regards κατασταθήσονται either as an eschatological future or a logical future without pertinently choosing for one.[471] Similarly, Cranfield states that κατασταθήσονται, "while it could refer to the final judgment . . . is probably better understood, in agreement

---

466. Cf. the phrase νῦν ἡμέρα σωτηρίας in 2 Cor 6:2.

467. Schreiner, *Romans*, 439; *Paul*, 228; Wright, "Romans," 598; Fee, *People of God*, 61; Moo, *Romans*, 521; Morris, *Romans*, 325; Bruce, *Romans*, 174; idem., *Heart Set Free*, 428; Cranfield, *Romans*, 1:419; Foerster, "σῴζω," *TDNT*, 7:994; Ridderbos, *Romeinen*, 189.

468. Moo, *Romans*, 521-22, emphasis added; cf. Schreiner, *Romans*, 439; Mounce, *Romans*, 186; Dodd, *Romans*, 148; ISV; NLT; GW; REB; NAT. Even by understanding τῇ ἐλπίδι as a modal dative: "in hope" (e.g., Fee, *People of God*, 61; Fitzmyer, *Romans*, 515; Bruce, *Romans*, 174; Käsemann, *Romans*, 439; Cranfield, *Romans*, 1:419; ESV; NRSV; NIV), the realized significance of salvation is retained (e.g., Fee, *People of God*, 61; Bruce, *Romans*, 174; Cranfield, *Romans*, 1:419). But a view that hope would be the means of salvation constituting an instrumental dative ("by/through hope", e.g., Ridderbos, *Romeinen*, 189; LITV; GNB; RV; KJV) is to be rejected since Paul does not make such an association elsewhere (Moo, *Romans*, 522). Yet, despite choosing to understand τῇ ἐλπίδι as an instrumental dative, Ridderbos, *Romeinen*, 189, states that "this hope has become the believers' preservation, for they are already adopted as children of God and heirs of God."

469. NRSV, emphasis added.

470. Bell, "Myth," 31; Moo, *Romans*, 345; Fitzmyer, *Romans*, 421; Fung, *Galatians*, 233; Bultmann, "Dikaiosynē," 15; idem., *Theology*, 274; Schrenk, "δίκη," *TDNT*, 2:218; Lagrange, *Paul*, 112.

471. Jewett, *Romans*, 386.

with 5.1 and 9, as referring to the present life of believers."[472] The logical aspect of the future can especially be derived from its parallel relationship with the aorist verb κατεστάθησαν.[473] Yet the significance of Romans 5:19 lies in its close grammatical correspondence with that of 11:26. The syntactical structure of each is demonstrated below:

Romans 5:19

ὥσπερ . . ., οὕτως + future indicative [κατασταθήσονται]

as [through the one man's disobedience] . . .,
in this manner . . . will be made

Romans 11:26

οὕτως + future indicative [σωθήσεται] . . ., καθώς

in this manner . . . will be saved . . ., as [is written]

As in Romans 11:26, οὕτως in 5:19 can be translated as "in this manner."[474] Both adverbial markers καθώς and ὥσπερ ("as") signify comparison.[475] In terms of the syntax, the difference between these two sentences is word order. Although the normal word order between the comparative adverbial marker and the future indicative is as within Romans 5:19 (ὥσπερ/καθώς/ ὡς, then οὕτως), there are exceptions in Paul (e.g., οὕτως, then καθώς: Phil 3:17 [so Rom 11:26]; οὕτως, then ὡς: 1 Cor 3:15; 4:1; 9:26; 2 Cor 9:5; 1 Thess 2:4 [καθώς . . . οὕτως . . . ὡς]; cf. Eph 5:28, 33). It is noteworthy that in these examples, οὕτως refers to that which stands *after* καθώς, and *not* to something *preceding* οὕτως. As a translated example, instead of writing "*as* (ὡς) not beating air, *so* (οὕτως) I fight," Paul writes "*so* (οὕτως) I fight, *as* (ὡς) not beating air" (1 Cor 9:26). In accordance with these examples, it seems possible that οὕτως . . . καθώς in Romans 11:26 could be read without

---

472. Cranfield, *Romans*, 1:291; cf. Wilckens, *Römer*, 328; Schlier, *Römerbrief*, 175; Schrenk, "δίκη," *TDNT*, 2:191; Murray, *Romans*, 1:206; Sanday and Headlam, *Romans*, 142; Lange and Fay, *Romans*, 187; Weiss, *Römer*, 258. Ridderbos, *Paulus*, 178, admits to both a present and future dimension of righteousness in Rom 3:20 and 5:19.

473. Although Dunn, *Romans*, 1:258, does not ultimately opt for the logical future here, he considers it as a possibility for the reason given.

474. BDAG, οὕτως, §1a.

475. BDAG, καθώς, §1. Although Rom 11:26 is not listed under this category, the clause καθὼς γέγραπται is listed here. See also BDAG, ὥσπερ, a; cf. BDAG, ὡς.

a comma after σωθήσεται, implying that οὕτως might (additionally) refer to that which stands after καθώς (that which is written). Οὕτως in 11:26 might therefore pertain to *both* the preceding condition set forth by the subjunctive εἰσέλθῃ in verse 25 (the coming in of the gentiles) *and* to καθὼς γέγραπται (that which is written), or a measure of ambiguity in terms of the referent of οὕτως might be implied. Οὕτως in 11:26 might therefore pertain to *both* the preceding condition set forth by the subjunctive εἰσέλθῃ in verse 25 (the coming in of the gentiles) *and* to καθὼς γέγραπται (that which is written). In other words, the *manner in which* (οὕτως) Israel is saved pertains to both the condition of the gentiles coming in (v. 25) *and* the way in which Israel's salvation is foretold in Scripture (vv. 26b–27). If οὕτως, therefore, *also* stands in a dependent relationship with καθὼς γέγραπται, it strengthens the notion that οὕτως (Rom 11:26) denotes *manner* (see above). In addition, the syntactical similarity between Romans 5:19 and Romans 11:26 might argue for viewing the future tense in Romans 11:26 also as a logical future (as in Rom 5:19). But although contributing to the argument, these possibilities in themselves are not conclusive yet.

With respect to Paul's use of οὕτως and καθώς in Romans 11:26, it is likely that Paul applies Scripture here in Romans 11:26–27 not merely to reinforce or confirm his teaching,[476] but to denote the *manner in which* Israel will be saved,[477] making the coming in of the fullness of the gentiles (ἄχρις... εἰσέλθῃ) and that which is written (καθὼς γέγραπται...) to relate to the same event. To conclude, it seems possible that the salvation of "all Israel" intricately stands in *both* (1) a *comparative* relationship with καθὼς γέγραπται..., which constitutes the *manner in which* salvation is effected, *and* (2) in a *conditional* relationship with ἄχρις οὗ τὸ πλήρωμα τῶν ἐθνῶν εἰσέλθῃ, which constitutes the *condition* for salvation.

The Deliverer out of Zion (v. 26b)

To whom does the "Deliverer" (v. 26b) refer? Can this deliverance be connected to the Christ-event? Despite some who understand ὁ ῥυόμενος as a reference to God in general or Yahweh,[478] it is more likely that it refers to Christ.[479] For within the context of Romans, Paul has already estab-

---

476. Contra Moo, *Romans*, 724, 727.

477. Wright, "Romans," 693. Cf. Longenecker, "Different Answers," 98, who argues that the identity of the Deliverer from Zion (v. 26b) is decisive in determining *how* Israel will be saved.

478. E.g., Gager, *Reinventing*, 141; Gaston, *Paul*, 147–48; Murray, *Romans*, 2:100.

479. Hultgren, *Romans*, 422–23; Jewett, *Romans*, 704; Witherington and Hyatt,

lished Christ as the one in whom one believes onto righteousness (3:22, 24; 4:23-25), through whom believers have access to the grace in which they stand (5:2), that righteousness unto eternal life is through Christ (5:21; 6:4, 7, 23), that life in the eschatological Spirit/spirit is effected in Christ (8:2, 9, 10), and probably most importantly, that those who believe in Christ will be saved (10:9; cf. 9:33). As argued, even in Romans 11, the believing remnant cannot be understood apart from belief in Christ (see above). It would thus be incredible to understand Paul's reference to the Deliverer as pointing to anyone but Christ[480] (cf. 1 Thess 1:10).

For Paul, the Deliverer comes ἐκ Σιών, a rendering that differs from the Septuagint version of Isaiah 59:20, which has ἕνεκεν Σιών: "for the sake of Zion."[481] Young notes that Paul's rendering ἐκ Σιών is correct grammatically, for the preposition לְ in the MT of Isaiah 59:20 may have this force.[482] But Kirk is probably right that Paul changes the preposition to tell "of the unexpected turn in salvation history he believes has taken place."[483] Another two fairly close parallels to Romans 11:26 are found in the similar Psalms 13:7 (LXX; 14:7, MT) and 52:7 (LXX; 53:6, MT) where it is described how deliverance will be given to Israel ἐκ Σιών when the Lord will return the captivity of His people, and Jacob and Israel will rejoice.[484] Although the Deliverer for the sake of Zion within the context of Isaiah 59:20 refers to Yahweh, Paul has identified Yahweh with Christ in Romans 10:9, 13 in allusion to Joel 3:32.[485] Moreover, in 9:33 Paul referred to Zion within the context of the stumbling stone, which is Christ.[486] Zion, therefore, seems to refer to Jerusalem as the place of Christ's death and resurrection[487] (cf. 15:19) rather than to the "heavenly Jerusalem."[488] If Christ is the Deliverer and comes out

---

Romans, 276; Wright, "Romans," 692; *Climax*, 250; Schreiner, *Romans*, 620; Moo, *Romans*, 728; Mounce, *Romans*, 225; Fitzmyer, *Romans*, 620, 624; Dunn, *Romans*, 2:682; Morris, *Romans*, 421; Sanders, *Jewish People*, 194-95; Käsemann, *Romans*, 314; Cranfield, *Romans*, 2:578; Ridderbos, *Romeinen*, 265; Sanday and Headlam, *Romans*, 337.

480. Cf. Jewett, *Romans*, 703-4; Wright, "Romans," 692; *Climax*, 250; Sanders, *Jewish People*, 194.

481. The MT has לְצִיּוֹן ("to Zion").

482. Young, *Isaiah*, 2:440.

483. Kirk, "Deliverer," 87.

484. The corresponding themes are as follows: ἐκ Σιών, Ἰσραήλ, Ἰακώβ in Rom 11:26 and Psalms 13:7 (LXX) and 52:7 (LXX); σωθήσεται in Rom 11:26 and σωτήριον in the two psalms; ἀποστρέψει in Rom 11:26 and ἐπιστρέψαι in the two psalms.

485. See esp. Wright, "Romans," 692.

486. Even Moo, *Romans*, 728, admits that "[i]t would make sense to interpret 'out of Zion' in 11:26 in light of this earlier text" (cf. Longenecker, "Different Answers," 117).

487. Fitzmyer, *Romans*, 625; cf. Kirk, "Deliverer," 91; Wilckens, *Römer*, 257.

488. Contra Jewett, *Romans*, 704; Witherington and Hyatt, *Romans*, 276; Schreiner,

of the earthly Jerusalem, then Paul's entire claim on Scripture in verses 26b to 27 pertains to Christ's first advent[489] and not to the parousia.

Dunn, however, argues that ὁ ῥυόμενος points to Christ's deliverance at the parousia on the basis that the verb ῥύομαι elsewhere points to Christ's final deliverance, citing Romans 7:24 and 1 Thessalonians 1:10.[490] This deduction is not obvious, however. Although 1 Thessalonians surely points to Christ's deliverance at the parousia, the cry for deliverance in Romans 7:24 rather anticipates Christ's deliverance constituted in Christ and the Spirit as effected by belief in Christ (8:1–16).[491] As argued on pp. 189–206, Romans 7:14-25 constitutes an old existence before or outside of Christ whereas 8:1–16 points to the life in the eschatological spirit as set over against an existence in flesh. The deliverance cried after in 7:24 is thus resolved in Christ in the existence in spirit (8:1–16; see esp. ἐν Χριστῷ Ἰησοῦ ἠλευθέρωσέν in 8:2). Elsewhere ῥύομαι is used in the context of deliverance from opponents (Rom 15:31; cf. 2 Thess 3:2) or from danger (2 Cor 1:10).[492] It might be noteworthy that in the letter to the Colossians, ῥύομαι is used in terms of realized deliverance in Christ (Col 1:13, aor. ind.). Nevertheless, a reference to the parousia in Romans 11:26 merely on the basis of its use in 1 Thessalonians 1:10 is not warranted, for in the context of Romans 9 to 11 there is no reference to the parousia.[493]

Romans, 619; Moo, *Romans*, 728; Käsemann, *Romans*, 314. The understanding of Zion as referring to the "heavenly Jerusalem" (Ἰερουσαλὴμ ἐπουρανίῳ) is largely based on an inference from Heb 12:22. Although Paul refers to the "Jerusalem above" (ἄνω Ἰερουσαλὴμ) in Gal 4:26, he neither draws a connection between "Zion" and "Jerusalem above" as such nor portray "Jerusalem above" as the Jerusalem of the eschaton. "Jerusalem above" is contrasted to the "current Jerusalem" (νῦν Ἰερουσαλὴμ, v. 25) and is rather to be interpreted as a juxtaposition of a "spiritual Jerusalem" (the mother of believers in Christ) against an "earthly Jerusalem" (Meyer, *Law*, 137; Fung, *Galatians*, 210; cf. De Boer, *Galatians*, 301–2). The "Jerusalem from above" is therefore a present reality (Meyer, *Law*, 137). Yet, even if the heavenly-Jerusalem-interpretation in Rom 11:26 would be possible, it is outweighed by (1) Paul's referral to the earthly Zion in 9:33, and (2) that Paul is not likely to refer to the parousia (see main text).

489. Kim, "Reading," 328, Kirk, "Deliverer," 87–91, Zoccali, "All Israel," 311–12, Wright, "Romans," 692, *Climax*, 250, and Sanders, *Jewish People*, 196, understand the prophecy as pertaining to the gentile mission, while Byrne, *Romans*, 355, Fitzmyer, *Romans*, 620, 625, and Lenski, *Romans*, 729, understand it more in terms of Christ's saving work. The latter understanding is preferred.

490. Dunn, *Paul the Apostle*, 528; idem., *Romans*, 2:682; cf. Cranfield, *Romans*, 2:578, citing only 1 Thess 1:10.

491. Cf. Fee, *Empowering Presence*, 521; Wright, "Romans," 571; Käsemann, *Romans*, 211; Ridderbos, *Romeinen*, 160, 171–73; contra Dunn, *Romans*, 2:682.

492. Cf. the use of ῥύομαι in the Pastorals: deliverance from persecution (2 Tim 3:11), danger (2 Tim 4:17) or evil works (2 Tim 4:18).

493. Fitzmyer, *Romans*, 620, 624–25; Sanders, *Jewish People*, 192–96.

"ALL ISRAEL" AND "THE ISRAEL OF GOD"

Fitzmyer is probably correct to argue toward understanding the future ἥξει (v. 26) within the quotation from Isaiah as a *futurum propheticum*. In reference to 9:33, he admits to possibly understanding the words as "somehow having been fulfilled."[494] Yet Byrne's view is more pronounced, writing:

> It is much simpler to see Paul understanding the prophecy as speaking out of its proper time reference, pointing to a 'coming' (of a 'deliverer') which for Isaiah lies in the future but which for Paul has already been realized in the original appearance and saving work of Christ.[495]

The salvation of all Israel could thus be future (σωθήσεται) of the prophecy in 11:26a and being written in the future tense to correspond with the future ἥξει of the prophecy. In other words, if the Deliverer coming out of Zion in Christ's first advent describes the *manner in which* "all Israel" will be saved, then it could follow logically that the salvation of Israel has *already been effected in Christ's first advent*.

The Removing of Ungodliness, the Taking Away of Sins, and God's Covenant (vv. 26b–27)

The underlying question of the prophetic material in verses 26b–27 is whether it has to refer to some point in Paul's future or could already have been fulfilled in the Christ event. The text states that the Deliverer will remove (ἀποστρέφω, v. 26)[496] ungodliness (ἀσέβεια, v. 26)[497] from Jacob. The plural ἀσεβείας pertain to "acts of impiety rather than a state of mind."[498] This constitutes the covenant/testament (διαθήκη, v. 27) with the people when the Deliverer will take away or remove (ἀφαιρέω, v. 27)[499] their sins. While the first part of Paul's quote (vv. 26b–27a) resembles Isaiah 59:20 (LXX), the latter part (v. 27b) resembles Isaiah 27:9 (LXX). An allusion to Jeremiah 38:31–33 (LXX; MT: 31:31–33) cannot be ruled out, especially around the

---

494. Fitzmyer, *Romans*, 625; cf. Holwerda, *Jesus and Israel*, 173.

495. Byrne, *Romans*, 355.

496. BDAG, ἀποστρέφω, §2a; ISV; GW; GNB; REB; NAT; cf. ESV; NRSV; RSV.

497. Zerwick and Grosvenor, *Grammatical Analysis*, 485; ISV; NRSV; RSV; KJV.

498. Zerwick and Grosvenor, *Grammatical Analysis*, 485.

499. BDAG, ἀφαιρέω, §2bβ; Zerwick and Grosvenor, *Grammatical Analysis*, 485; ISV; NRSV; NIV; RSV.

concept of διαθήκη.⁵⁰⁰ Bruno argues for an additional allusion to Isaiah 2:3 in Paul's mixed quote, which would suggest gentile inclusion.⁵⁰¹

It is noteworthy that in Paul's following of the Septuagint of Isaiah 59:20, the Deliverer is the subject of the "turning away" (ἀποστρέψει) whereas in the MT, those in Jacob seems to be the subject of the "turning away" (בְּיַעֲקֹב וּלְשָׁבֵי פֶשַׁע).⁵⁰² The reading from the MT (Isa 59:20) thus implies that those in Jacob have turned to the Lord and repented.⁵⁰³ In the MT of Isaiah 27:9, however, Yahweh is the subject, removing Jacob's sin (cf. Pss 13:7; 52:7, LXX). Since repentance as such is not Paul's intent and Israel seems to be passive in their deliverance,⁵⁰⁴ his overall quotation thus leans more toward the original intent of Isaiah 27:9 (MT) than that of Isaiah 59:20 (MT).⁵⁰⁵ It is thus problematic to say that "Paul aptly uses [Isa 59] v.20 in support of his hope of Jewish repentance in Romans 11:25-27."⁵⁰⁶

That Paul primarily has Isaiah 27:6-13 in mind in Romans 11:26-27 is additionally strengthened by the context of Isaiah 27:⁵⁰⁷

> (6) Those who come He shall cause to take root in Jacob; Israel shall blossom and bud, and fill the face of the world with fruit. (7) Has He struck Israel as He struck those who struck him? Or has He been slain according to the slaughter of those who were slain by Him? (8) In measure, by sending it away, You contended with it. He *removes* it by His rough wind in the day of the east wind. (9) Therefore by this the iniquity of Jacob will be covered; and this is all the fruit of *taking away his sin*: when he makes all the stones of the altar like chalkstones that are beaten to dust, wooden images and incense altars shall not stand. (10) Yet the fortified city will be desolate, the habitation forsaken and left like a wilderness; there the calf will feed, and

---

500. Osborne, *Romans*, 307; Wright, "Romans," 692; Fitzmyer, *Romans*, 625; Bruce, *Romans*, 218.

501. Bruno, "Deliverer," 129-32; cf. Kirk, "Deliverer," 85.

502. Cf. Vulgate: "eis qui redeunt ab iniquitate."

503. Cf. Young, *Isaiah*, 2:441.

504. Fitzmyer, *Romans*, 619; cf. Gager, *Reinventing*, 142; Stendahl, *Paul*, 132. Paul has ἀποστρέψει (v. 26) in the indicative form (third person singular) and ἀφέλωμαι (v. 27) in the first person singular (corresponding to ἐμοῦ διαθήκη), thus making the Deliverer the subject of all the actions.

505. This seems to be the safer option over against insisting that Paul's overall quote *has* to pertain to the original text and context of Isa 59:20, which in turn would force one to understand Paul's notion to be "a distillation of Isaianic theology" or that he "compresses new obedience and final redemption" (Seifrid, "Romans," 675).

506. Grogan, "Isaiah," 327.

507. Cf. Moo, *Romans*, 729.

> there it will lie down and consume its *branches*. (11) When its *boughs* are withered, they will be *broken off*; the women come and set them on fire. For it is a people of no understanding; therefore He who made them will not have mercy on them, and He who formed them will show them no favor. (12) And it shall come to pass in that day that the Lord will thresh, from the channel of the River to the Brook of Egypt; and you will be *gathered* one by one, o you children of Israel. (13) So it shall be in that day: the great trumpet will be blown; they will come, *who are about to perish* in the land of Assyria, and they who are *outcasts* in the land of Egypt, and *shall worship* the Lord in the holy mount at Jerusalem.[508]

If Isaiah 27:6 is read in the MT, "Jacob" is portrayed as taking root (יַשְׁרֵשׁ יַעֲקֹב)[509] and identified as Israel who shall blossom and bud (יָצִיץ וּפָרַח יִשְׂרָאֵל).[510] The question is asked if they are struck down or killed (v. 7). Verse 8 reports of their exile and their "removal" (הָגָה). Yet, verse 9 portrays the expiation and removal of Jacob's iniquity and sin "by means of"[511] this judgment. According to verse 11, the *branches* (קְצִירָהּ) of Jacob/Israel (v. 6) after becoming dry (בִּיבֹשׁ) are *broken off* (תִּשָּׁבַרְנָה). He that formed them will have no mercy (v. 11). But in spite of this judgment, there would be an ingathering (v. 12) and those "perishing" or "those being exterminated" (הָאֹבְדִים, v. 13)[512] would (paradoxically) come and worship the Lord on the holy mountain at Jerusalem (v. 13). Of this ingathering and worship, Young writes:

> In the light of this description it would seem that the verse [13] refers, not primarily to the exile, but to the return of sinners in Jesus Christ. It is in Him that God has gathered into one His people scattered throughout the earth.[513]

Whether this would be the kind of connotation that Paul would have attached to Isaiah 27:13 is quite possible. In Wright's understanding of Paul, the exile has been undone, God's people's sins are forgiven and the

---

508. Isa 27:6–13, NKJV, emphases added, capital letters in the middle of verses decapitalized.

509. The Septuagint omits a translation for יַשְׁרֵשׁ.

510. Cf. LXX: βλαστήσει καὶ ἐξανθήσει Ἰσραήλ.

511. Young, *Isaiah*, 1:246.

512. BDB, דאב, §1; cf. NIV: "those who were perishing"; NKJV: "those who were about to perish." Watts, *Isaiah*, 351, describes הָאֹבְדִים as those who "is like a living death."

513. Young, *Isaiah*, 1:252–53; cf. Grogan, "Isaiah," 171.

covenant has been renewed in Christ and the Spirit.[514] It is thus conceivable that Paul might have had the larger context of Isaiah 27 (esp. vv. 6–13) in mind when he uses the image of the *branches* (Israel) that have been *broken off* (Rom 11:17-24; cf. Isa 27:11), the hardening of Israel (Rom 11:7-8, 25; cf. the dry branches in Isa 27:11) and implies a judgment of Israel by the notion of a remnant (Rom 11:3-5; cf. Isa 27:7-8, 11). Even the reference to Jerusalem (Isa 27:13) might correspond to Σιών in Romans 11:26. In the Isaiah 27 account the themes of the Lord's judgment are almost paradoxically contrasted by expiation, the removal of sin and the worship of "those being exterminated."

Within the larger context of the Pauline corpus, it is hard to imagine how Paul in two verses (Rom 11:25–26) could anticipate another event where the sins of Israel/Jacob would be forgiven and removed apart from the saving work of Christ on the cross in death and resurrection. Such a notion would imply two ways of salvation for God's people, a notion that is hard to reconcile with the rest of the Pauline corpus.[515] If Paul, therefore, has the Christ event in mind with his quotation of Scripture, it is likely that the future tense of σωθήσεται in Romans 11:26 is to be understood as a *logical future*[516] (cf. esp. Rom 5:19, see above), and explained by its correspondence with the *futurum propheticum* of the Scripture references, which is fulfilled in Christ (ἥξει; ἀποστρέψει, v. 26):[517] "all Israel *will be saved* as is written: The Deliverer *will come* out of Zion and *will remove* all ungodliness." In a strict sense, my interpretation of σωθήσεται being a logical future is not intended as the non-negotiable bedrock by which the rest of my interpretation of Romans 11:26 stands or falls. The interpretation of σωθήσεται being a logical future must rather be viewed as the *most likely* interpretation given the theological constraints and grammatical or syntactical possibilities set forth by the immediate and larger context in Paul. Such an interpretation is further strengthened by the uncertainty about historical Israel's salvation underlying Paul's rhetoric in the letter up to this point (as argued). But apart from these considerations thus far, my interpretation of verses 26b to 32 has to be understood as *contributing substantially* toward understanding σωθήσεται in verse 26 as a logical future (see below).

---

514. Wright, "Romans," 691.

515. Cf. Zoccali, "All Israel," 229–303; Schreiner, *Romans*, 616; Fitzmyer, *Romans*, 620; Sanders, *Jewish People*, 194.

516. Although Kim, "Reading," 326, interprets σωθήσεται as a "gnomic future" here, he understands the salvation of "all Israel" as referring to gentile and Judean elect (318, 333).

517. Cf. Fitzmyer, *Romans*, 625.

If σωθήσεται in verse 26 is considered as a logical future, it will in addition correspond to ἐγκεντρισθήσονται in verse 24, which can be understood as a logical future too (see above). A future element constituting the eschatological *completion* of salvation is not necessarily hereby denied (cf. Ezek 36–37). But the point is that historical Israel's salvation is effected through the same event as for any believer in Christ, which is Christ's death and resurrection.[518]

The Mystery of the Salvation of "All Israel" Revealed (vv. 25–27)

If the above interpretation is correct and "all Israel" (πᾶς Ἰσραήλ, v. 26) has already been saved in Christ, who is "all Israel"? Paul quoted Isa 10:20-23 in Rom 9:27, indicating that those from historical Israel *remaining* (see above) will be saved *after* God's judgment in Christ, which are those who believe in Christ (see pp. 243-48). A similar notion is echoed in 11:3-7 (see p. 264). Yet here in 11:25-26 Paul reveals a mystery that seems to pertain to more than those remaining who are saved (9:27). "All Israel" who are saved in 11:26 would thus naturally be understood as those from historical Israel who lived *before* God's judgment in Christ *in addition to* those who remained and thus believed in Christ.[519] But the question could arise whether "all Israel" includes Israel according to the flesh. If Paul's use of "Israel" throughout Romans 11 has to be understood in terms of Paul's former distinction in that "Israel" is *inner* Israel (9:6-8, see p. 51), which is Israel of promise (9:8) and *inner* election, then the notion that "all Israel" would include Israel according to the flesh (ethnic Israel in general) seems incredible.[520] It is more likely that πᾶς refers to another dimension. The title Ἰακώβ (v. 26), which is used in parallel with Ἰσραήλ, evokes 9:13, where Ἰακώβ is mentioned. When Jacob is introduced in Rom 9:13 as first descen-

---

518. If Ezekiel's vision of the dry bones coming to life (Ezek 36–37) can be applied to Paul's notion that historical Israel's salvation is effected in Christ's first advent, the vision can be understood in such a way that the actual (eschatological) *completion* of this prophecy might still lie in Paul's future but has principally been effected in Christ's first advent.

519. This could explain Paul's reference in Rom 11:26-27 to both Isa 27:9 and 59:20, where Israel is portrayed as mostly passive in salvation (Isa 27:9 is passaive in both the LXX and the MT; 59:20 is passive in the LXX) but includes repentance in the MT of 59:20 (see above). This could imply that both historical Israel is saved in Christ as well as those who repented and believed in Christ in the time of the first Christ advent (MT of 59:20; cf. Rom 9:27).

520. Cf. Zoccali, "All Israel," 303-9; Merkle, "Romans 11," 711-21; Hendriksen, *Romans*, 381-82; Horne, "Meaning," 329-34; Ridderbos, *Paulus*, 396-403; idem., *Romeinen*, 261-66; Lenski, *Romans*, 723-28.

dent of Isaac, the child of the promise and true "seed" (vv. 7-8), Jacob still metaphorically represents God's *inner* election (v. 6) in distinction from His national election. The best explanation would therefore be that πᾶς refers to Israel *diachronically*,[521] which is *historical Israel* across the course of ancient Israel's history (cf. Mal 3:22, LXX).[522]

One of the crucial points where I believe many interpreters have it wrong is to understand hardened Israel throughout Romans 9 to 11 as Israel according to the flesh,[523] which is national Israel[524] (identity mode A) or contemporary unbelieving Jews,[525] even if such notions are unexpressed. As argued in the discussion of Romans 9:24-33, hardened Israel was in fact part of God's salvation-historical plan, and does not necessarily exclude inner election as Paul will later explain (11:28-32). Throughout Romans 9 to 11, *hardened Israel* is rather *historical Israel of inner election*. They are one and the same entity (esp. 11:28, see below). As argued, the cutting off of the branches points to the cutting off of all people claiming identity (being God's people) on the basis of a flesh-existence (including works, law, circumcision) even if flesh was a *co-constituting* criterion for being God's people (see p. 273). In other words, the metaphor represents the cutting off of identity mode A. This inevitably included inner historical Israel of whom identity as God's children were partly based on flesh (identity mode AB). But then comes the mystery, the paradox, the double action of God. This paradox arguably evokes the same paradoxical elements as portrayed in Isaiah 27:6-13 where God's forgiveness and removal of sin is applied to "those being exterminated" and those judged. This elect yet hardened historical Israel was cut off (Rom 11:17-24), then forgiven and their sins removed in Christ (vv. 26-27) and then regrafted (v. 24) onto the good olive tree (the people of God) through Christ. All these actions by God pertain to the same salvation-historical event in Christ. Israel's historical hardening was

---

521. Even while Fitzmyer, *Romans*, 623, understands "all Israel" as ethnic Israel, he understands "all Israel" diachronically (cf. Kruse, *Romans*, 443; Bell, *Provoked*, 141). So Campbell, "Israel," 443, who, although he envisions an eschatological Israel, cannot imagine an eschatological Israel with none of the historical Israel. He contends that "Paul's thinking is much more concrete and historically oriented than subsequent Gentile-Christian understanding makes it to be."

522. A diachronic understanding of "all Israel" is evident in Malachi 3:22 (LXX: πάντα τὸν Ἰσραὴλ; 4:4 in the MT: כָּל־יִשְׂרָאֵל), where "all Israel" is the whole diachronic nation to whom the statutes and ordinances of Moses apply (Zoccali, "All Israel," 292; cf. m. Sanh. 10.1; T. Benj. 10.11).

523. E.g., Wright, "Romans," 694.

524. George, *Galatians*, 440.

525. E.g., Käsemann, *Romans*, 316; Cranfield, *Romans*, 2:585, 588; cf. Witherington and Hyatt, *Romans*, 276.

thus not an end in itself, but a means to an end: to bring about the gospel in Christ, which would eventually result in their regrafting. But their regrafting is arguably now on a different basis.

Their regrafting can be understood as now being on the basis of grace and election only (vv. 28–32). But what would that mean? As discussed, the way of existence in flesh (Rom 7:14–25) can be understood as historical Israel under the law from the perspective of a believer in Christ. Their existence could not only be described as being "under the law" (2:12; 3:19; 6:14, 15; 7:23) but especially as being "under sin" (3:9; 7:14; cf. Gal 3:22). If their sins are forgiven (11:27) through Christ their *Deliverer* (ὁ ῥυόμενος, 11:26), their forgiveness probably implies more than forgiveness, but the *deliverance* from their old way of existence, and by implication the transformation of their old identity. If Israel's identity before Christ (7:14–25) can be understood as crying out for *deliverance* (ῥύομαι, 7:24; cf. 11:26) and those in Christ are being *delivered* (ἐλευθερόω, Rom 6:18, 22; 8:2)[526] from the old existence in flesh under the law and sin (Rom 7:14–25), then the same grace that has been applied to Israel (11:28–32) might imply that Christ the *Deliverer* (11:26) did the same for historical Israel in Christ as for the Christ-believers. In other words, as a result of Christ's saving work, historical Israel's identity can be understood as now being in Christ and their mode of identity as being transformed from identity mode AB to identity mode C. Israel's history and their identity as God's people has thus been fulfilled and completed as part of Christology, bringing a beautiful end to their history.

The collateral of the cutting off of all of inner, historical Israel, whose identity was not based on the grace in Christ, would be that all of former Israel that lived at the Christ event but did not accept the gospel in faith was cut off too. Since the Christ event God's people are marked off by faith and the Spirit only (identity mode C). Those being cut off who remained in unbelief at the Christ event are therefore not part of "all Israel" that are saved. For them there is always the option to believe in Christ and be regrafted into the good olive tree on the basis of faith (v. 23). Paul does not specify those who might believe in Christ in the future (v. 23) as Ἰσραήλ.[527] They are those of descent from Abraham after the Christ event whom Paul elsewhere calls Ἰουδαῖοι. Paul's concern for unbelieving Judeans in his present is thus resolved in v. 23. But in verse 24 Paul switches over to historical Ἰσραήλ: if gentiles can be grafted into the good olive tree against their nature (by faith),

---

526. Although most Bible translations render ἐλευθερόω in 6:18, 22 and 8:2 as "set free" (or similar), some translations translate the same term as "delivered" in 8:21 (e.g., ASV; RV; KJV).

527. Contra NRSV.

how much more could God graft in elect, historical Israel (natural branches) into the olive tree (v. 24). Verse 26 would finally answer the underlying question regarding historical Israel's salvation, regrafting them into the olive tree on the basis of God's mercy. In terms of the cut-off point of where "historical Israel" ends, one probably cannot be too dogmatic. But if Christ's death and resurrection is the cut-off point, then "historical Israel" probably involves those of "true Israel" who died before the point after Christ's resurrection when faith in Christ's salvific work became an option.

In conclusion, "all Israel" who are saved in Christ (vv. 26–27) can be understood as *historical Israel of inner election in its diachronic entirety that lived before the Christ event* who are saved in addition to those from Israel who believed in Christ at the time of the first Christ advent (9:27; 11:3–7). To summarize, this conclusion is mainly based on the following:

1. The probability that Paul throughout Romans 9 to 11 mainly has historical Israel in view (as argued throughout, see also below).
2. That Paul has never pertinently answered the question around historical Israel's salvation, which arguably lies beneath the surface throughout the build-up of Paul's rhetoric in Romans (as argued throughout), and that the answer to this question would thus be expected.
3. The connection of the mystery (v. 25) to the gospel, constituted by the Christ event.
4. The hardening (v. 25) of Israel, which is historical (esp. γέγονεν [perf. ind.]; cf. 10:19–21; 11:1–10; 2 Cor 3:14).
5. The "coming in of the fullness of the gentiles" (v. 25), pointing to the generic inclusion of the gentiles within God's salvific economy, which is already realized within the gospel in Christ.
6. The theological and grammatical possibility of Paul's language in general and in context to understand σωθήσεται as a logical future that could already be realized.
7. The prophetic language around the Deliverer (vv. 26–27) that pertains to Christ's first advent.
8. That the Deliverer is the Subject of the actions in the prophetic citation (vv. 26–27), which excludes repentance or conversion by the subjects as such (see esp. Isa 27:6–13, MT).
9. That the hardened (v. 25) and the term Ἰακώβ (v. 26) correspond to inner, elect Israel (see above and below).

10. The way in which this interpretation fits with the larger context and especially 11:28–32 (see below).

11. That Paul's understanding of Ἰσραήλ fits into a larger pattern of his thought around identity, where the identity and existence in Christ (defined by faith and the indwelling Spirit) eschatologically supersedes an identity and existence outside of Christ (defined by "flesh": law, sin and death). This excludes the possibility of a "future" Israel whose identity is (partly) based on "flesh."

12. An additional advantage of interpreting Rom 11:25–27 as pointing backward (retrojective) instead of forward (projective) is that the natural order of salvation, Israel first and the gentiles later, which was characteristic in the tradition of the nations' eschatological pilgrimage to Zion,[528] is not reversed. Then Kim's concern that Israel's salvation would for Paul imply a "'forceful remoulding' of the usual conception" of this order of salvation and that Paul would not substantiate such a reversal from Scripture,[529] is put to rest. Israel's salvation would then be completed within the first Christ advent, followed by the salvation of all who believe after that. This notion would even correspond to the gospel being the power of salvation for everyone who believes, to the Judean first (those descending from historical Israel who believed in Christ, Rom 9:27; 11:3–7), followed by the Greek (Rom 1:16).

It could be objected that the salvation of historical Israel could hardly be called a mystery, especially since the patriarchs have been presupposed to be part of God's kingdom in Israel's tradition (e.g., 4 Macc 13:17), the Gospel traditions (e.g., Mark 12:26; Matt 8:11; 22:32; Luke 13:28; 16:22–23), or the fact that Paul already stated that Abraham's faith will be reckoned for him as righteousness (Rom 4:3, 5, 9, 22; cf. Gal 3:6). Yet the mystery probably lies in the following aspects:

a. Paul indicates that the whole of historical elect Israel are saved and not only the patriarchs. The same historical hardened, inner Israel who was cut off is grafted in again. They are firstly rejected and then accepted in Christ. These opposites seem like a paradox, constituting a mystery.[530]

b. The salvation of historical Israel provides retrojective significance to Christ's salvific work. Christ would become the Savior of all who lived

---

528. Hofius, "Das Evangelium," 202.
529. Kim, "Mystery," 416; cf. Lang, *Mystery*, 45.
530. Barth, *Romans*, 412, writes: "By mystery Paul means what we call 'paradox.'"

before and after the Christ event, constituting a mystery. Lenski's notion applies that Christ's death counts for all time, past and future, and that all in the Old and New Testaments are saved through Christ.[531]

c. It can be noted that Paul never unambiguously identifies faith as the criterion for salvation of inner Israel in the Old Testament, although such a notion cannot be ruled out. Yet in a strict sense the criteria for salvation remains God's grace, purpose and election, constituting a mystery.

The mystery therefore does not only lie in the fact *that* all of elect historical Israel is saved, but in *how* (καὶ οὕτως, 11:26) they are saved: all the promises to historical Israel is fulfilled in another way that they might have anticipated. As noted earlier, the fulfillment of the promises to Israel is non-material in terms of (1) Abraham's seed, (2) the land and (3) the reign of God's people (see pp. 81–86). If the Messiah's reign is not material, the inheritance of historical Israel in terms of Romans 11:26 should also be understood as non-material. Cranfield notes that Paul did not entertain any hope "for the re-establishment of a national state in independence and political power, nor—incidentally—anything which could feasibly be interpreted as a scriptural endorsement of the modern nation-state of Israel."[532]

Testing the Salvation of Historical Israel Against Romans 9:1 to 11:27

If the interpretation is correct that the salvation of "all Israel" pertains to inner historical Israel that lived before the Christ event, it should fit the context. Such a reading will here be tested against 9:1 to 11:25. The testing of the interpretation against 11:28–32 will be integrated within the theological-exegetical discussion of those verses (see below).

It has been argued in the discussion of 9:1–10 that Paul is describing Israel of the Old Testament. Paul's anguish as expressed in 9:2–3 can, apart from his concern for unbelieving Judeans in his present, be understood as anticipating a judgment and cutting off of historical Israel. His rhetoric could thus provide for the possibility of Israel being cut off in spite of their national privileges (9:4–5). As argued, the distinction between inner and outer Israel is maintained in the interpretation of the salvation of all historical Israel. The historical account of salvation history in 9:9–18 would confirm that historical Israel is in view. The questions in 9:19–24 can be understood as pertaining to God's election of historical Israel in the

---

531. Lenski, *Corinthians*, 1031–32, see pp. 156–164.
532. Cranfield, *Romans*, 2:579; cf. Bruce, *Romans*, 217; Guthrie, *Theology*, 809.

era *prior to* the Christ event against the election of all in Christ, including gentiles in the era *after* the Christ event. It is important to note that Paul's accentuation of God's sovereignty in hardening and in using people as both vessels of mercy and destruction (9:18–23), opens the possibility of God's *hardening of even the elect.*

The crossover in salvation history as portrayed in 9:24–33 represents the culmination of salvation history, with the era before and after the Christ event on both sides of the crossover. With Paul's quotation of Isaiah in 9:27, it is noteworthy that he does not strictly exclude the possibility that Israel prior to those remaining after God's judgment in Christ can be saved. He utilizes referred authority by stating that "Isaiah cries out" that the remnant will be saved. By stating that it is Isaiah's cry, Paul does not necessarily exclude a possible mystery of the salvation of hardened, elect Israel of history. It could additionally be noted here that, although the reader might initially understand that "only" a remnant will be saved (some translations, see note 97, p. 244), Paul does not strictly use the word "only." Yet some tension remains between the mystery of salvation of historical Israel (11:26) and Isaiah's cry that the remnant would have been saved (9:27), which is precisely the kind of ingredients for a mystery. That the "all" in "all Israel" (11:26) would point to the inner elect that *died before* the Christ event and God's implied judgment, would naturally bring an element of surprise to the notion that those *remaining* after God's judgment in Christ would be saved (9:27). In this sense, the salvific notion in 11:26 would thus be the surprising, yet logical counterpart to the salvific notion in 9:27, constituting the mystery. In other words, the salvation of inner, elect, historical Israel in 11:26 can be viewed as *balancing* the salvation of the remnant in 9:27. It can additionally be argued that Paul would use the quotation of Isaiah rhetorically in order to create a deliberate tension in anticipation of resolving the mystery in 11:26. Israel's striving for righteousness in 9:31 can be identified historically. Moving on in salvation history, they stumbled over the stumbling stone, their Messiah, resulting in being cut off from being God's people (9:32–33).

As argued, Paul's hermeneutic in Romans 10 can be understood as diachronic and dialectical, involving both historical Israel and unbelieving Judeans. Christ being the end of the law for those who believe (10:4) points to Israel's Messiah as the culmination of salvation history, concluding the end of the previous age in the flesh. According to this logic, Paul would portray Christ as the universal access to salvation, even for historical Israel (10:9–13). Paul seems to acknowledge the inherent problem attached to such a notion, asking how historical Israel could have believed in Christ if they have not heard of him (10:14). Paul then denies Israel an excuse (10:16,

18) by pointing to Israel's disobedience to the gospel and that they have heard, arguably striking a double note again (diachronic), implying that both historical Israel were disobedient to the "gospel," although in another form, and that they stumbled against Christ in unbelief in the culmination of their salvation history, resulting in unbelieving Judeans in Paul's present. Verses 19 to 21 once again confirm the hardening of Israel (their disobedience and stubbornness) to be part of their history.

If the salvation of elect historical Israel is acknowledged (11:26), it answers the question of Romans 11:1. God did not eventually reject His people of the Old Testament. Yet 11:3–7 argues for the salvation and election of the remnant (cf. 9:27), leaving the question about historical Israel's salvation in suspense. Verses 7 to 10 once again confirm the hardening of Israel to be historical, culminating in the gospel coming to the nations (v. 11). A similar tension to that in 9:27 can be identified in 11:7 where the elect are set over against the hardened (elect, historical Israel), distinguishing the elect remnant (believers in Christ) from the hardened prior to the Christ event. This tension is however resolved in verse 26 although constituting a (paradoxical) mystery. The question in verse 11 is also answered. Historical Israel did not fall beyond recovery. They are eventually regrafted in Christ. As maintained on pp. 267–71, in verse 11 Paul probably alludes to both evoking the jealousy of historical Israel, which has an historical basis, and unbelieving Judeans in Paul's present. Verse 12 strongly anticipates the salvation of historical Israel. The "fullness" of Israel would imply the inclusion or regrafting of hardened Israel into being God's people again. Their rejection would eventually be reversed. The notion of making his people jealous, which is repeated in verse 14, arguably confirms Paul's diachronic, dialectical hermeneutic, including both historical Israel and unbelieving Judeans in order for them to be saved.

A significant note is struck in 11:15, where Paul contrasts both Israel's rejection and acceptance. Their acceptance would mean "life from death." The significance lies in their being dead and resurrected, which would eventually be realized in the death and resurrection of the Deliverer, their own Messiah (cf. Ezek 36–37). Paul's earlier thought, "making the dead alive, and calling the things that are not as if they were" (4:17), is echoed here. Historical Israel would thus be subject to the same pattern of death and resurrection as anyone else believing in Christ (cf. Rom 6:4–6; 2 Cor 5:15–16; Gal 2:20)[533] and would thereby participate in the new creation. If understood

---

533. A comparable notion is advanced by Wright, "Romans," 625, who writes: "Israel is also Messiah-shaped. The pattern of Israel's history (rejection, failure, and exile followed by astonishing covenant renewal) is none other than the pattern of death and resurrection . . . And that is why, when we look ahead to 11:11–16, where Paul is arguing for the restoration, the 'receiving back,' of Israel, he alludes to key steps in the

in this way, διαθήκη in 11:27 could be understood as denoting a testament rather than a covenant. Moreover, the phrase "life from death" (11:15) in itself seems to allude to historical Israel, since they would have been dead already at this point in time. As already discussed, the "cutting off" (vv. 17–24) represents the changing of the conditions for being God's people. All those who were God's people on the basis of flesh (including law, works and circumcision), including elect, hardened historical Israel who had flesh as co-constituting criterion in their identity as God's people (identity mode AB), were cut off. Inner, historical Israel was eventually regrafted (v. 26), while those who did not believe at the Christ event had the option of believing in Christ and be regrafted. As put forth already, while verse 23 anticipates the salvation of *unbelieving Judeans* in Paul's present (by faith), verse 24 anticipates the salvation of *historical Israel* (by promise and election). It would be most natural for God's elect, ancient people to be regrafted into their original position.

Understood in this way, the manner in which Paul describes God's election of historical Israel in 9:6–23 based on His promise, becomes the *criteria* for the salvation of inner, historical Israel. Ancient, historical Israel is thus saved by *promise and election* through Christ, while Judeans in Paul's time are saved by *faith* in Christ. Historical Israel's salvation based on promise and election would also relieve the inherent tension in the notion that God's righteousness has only "now" (in Christ) been revealed (νυνί, 3:21; cf. 9:30). For the latter would imply that historical Israel, although required to do the law in order to obtain righteousness (2:13), did not attain righteousness via the works of the law (3:1–20; 9:31). Such a predicament for those in the Old Testament "under the law" with respect to righteousness, is thus resolved in the salvation of "all Israel" in Christ (11:26–27).

A possible rhetorical situation behind such logic can thus be reconstructed: Paul would provide an answer for some Judean believers who might have felt that Paul's all-inclusive, universal gospel implies that their Old Testament heritage (e.g., the patriarchal history) was meaningless in itself and/or served the sole salvation-historical purpose of bringing on the Messiah. It would answer possible underlying concerns that ancient Israel in the previous age was discarded in totality in favor of believers in the present age. Such a rhetorical strategy would also apply to believing

---

argument of chap. 5." Wright, however, does not understand the regrafting of Israel as that of historical Israel, but as the option to believe in their own Messiah. The pattern of death and resurrection, which coheres with the paradox or double action of God (see above), favors a cutting off of the branches (Rom 11:17–24) rather than merely being broken (contra Nanos, "Broken Branches").

gentiles who might have thought that God has discarded Old Testament Israel in favor of them.

I have suggested earlier that Paul's anguish (9:2) might pertain to more than merely the unbelief of Judeans in Paul's present, and that the kind of concern for ancient Israel as described above might have contributed to his anguish (see pp. 235–39). A question that might arise against my interpretation on 11:25–27 is whether Paul's anguish in terms of unbelieving Judeans in Paul's present is sufficiently resolved. As a counter-question, one could ask if Paul's anguish for these unbelieving Judeans necessarily anticipates a divine miracle that bring about their righteousness or saves them apart from faith in Christ. Even if such a miracle would result in faith in Christ, such faith would then not be the primary determining factor in bringing about their righteousness or salvation, but the divine miracle. The anticipation of a divine miracle apart from or even superseding faith in Christ would, however, be hard to reconcile with the way in which Paul took pains to establish faith in Christ as the sole determining factor and point of entry in righteousness (3:21–5:2; 9:30; 10:5–7) and salvation (10:9–13). Instances in 9 to 11 can be pointed out where he did provide an answer or solution to the unbelief of Judeans in his present. Apart from Paul's emphasis on faith, which is open and free for all and does not involve any effort or achievement from their side (10:4–13), he removed any excuse for hardening against God's good news (10:14–21). In 11:1, Paul denies that God has rejected His people by pointing to himself as former Israelite who did believe in Christ. If an unbelieving Judean, which Paul was, comes to belief in Israel's Messiah, God's faithfulness to both historical Israel and such a Judean is affirmed. In 11:14, Paul anticipates evoking unbelieving Judeans to jealousy in order for them to be saved. Such a desire does not necessarily anticipate a miracle either, but rather a willing response of faith. Verse 23 explicitly anticipates an action of faith from unbelieving Judeans and is arguably Paul's last word on the matter.

Another possible objection to my interpretation would be that God would be unfair to cause or allow for Judeans in Paul's present to be hardened in order for the nations to come to faith. Paul however primarily defines the whole concept of hardening salvation-historically. In 11:8, the spirit of deep sleep is *extended to* Paul's present day ("unto this day"), which implies that the hardening is rooted historically. Furthermore, apart from the fact that human responsibility and divine sovereignty are both constitutive in hardening, Paul already addressed questions regarding God's alleged injustice regarding His salvation-historical purposes (9:14–23). Paul thus arguably does not intend to completely resolve such kind of allegations. Additionally, it could be pointed out that a view that anticipates a future divine miracle of salvation for Jews that live in the end time (notwithstanding the

"ALL ISRAEL" AND "THE ISRAEL OF GOD"

hermeneutical difficulty in identifying contemporary Jews with the Ἰουδαῖοι in Paul's time), would in fact leave both ancient Israel and the Jews living during the course history who did not partake in such an end-time miracle (a far greater group of people) deprived of the effect of such a miracle, constituting a far greater "injustice."

A Perfect Balance in Salvation History (vv. 28–32)

When the salvation of "all Israel" is understood as the salvation of historical, inner-elect Israel in Christ, as argued, Rom 11:28-32 suddenly makes complete sense. The whole of this passage can then be read from a salvation-historical perspective. Verse 28 pertains to the gospel (κατὰ … τὸ εὐαγγέλιον). Paul now explains the implications of the salvation of "all Israel." These verses (vv. 28-32) demonstrably contain some of the strongest evidence in viewing the salvation of "all Israel" as the realized salvation of elect historical Israel before the Christ event.

Verse 28 has no verb and consists of two contrasted, parallel statements:[534]

1. As far as the gospel is concerned (κατὰ τὸ εὐαγγέλιον),[535] the people of Israel[536] are hated (ἐχθρός)[537] or are enemies[538] for the sake of (διά)[539] the gentiles (ὑμᾶς).[540] God's "hate" of Israel is parallel to their historical hardening and their eventual rejection as God's people. With respect to salvation history, their rejection by God was necessary in order for the gospel to come (cf. 9:30-33).

---

534. Cranfield, *Romans*, 2:579.

535. Fitzmyer, *Romans*, 625; Morris, *Romans*, 422; ISV; NIV; cf. Dunn, *Romans*, 2:684-85; RSV; KJV.

536. Following directly after the salvation of "all Israel" in vv. 26-27, ἐχθρός logically points to them.

537. BDAG, ἐχθρός, §1; Käsemann, *Romans*, 315; cf. Cranfield, *Romans*, 2:580. The parallelism between ἐχθροί and ἀγαπητοί requires both to be understood in a passive sense (Cranfield, *Romans*, 2:580).

538. Zerwick and Grosvenor, *Grammatical Analysis*, 485; ISV; NRSV; NIV.

539. Fitzmyer, *Romans*, 625; Cranfield, *Romans*, 2:572; ESV; REB; NRSV; RSV; OAT; ASV; RV; cf. Moo, *Romans*, 711; KJV.

540. Paul does not identify ὑμᾶς in vv. 28-32, but it corresponds to σὺ ἐκ τῆς κατὰ φύσιν ἐξεκόπης ἀγριελαίου in v. 24, which is gentiles.

2. But as far as election is concerned (κατὰ τὴν ἐκλογήν),[541] the people of Israel are beloved (ἀγαπητοὶ) for the sake of[542] the "fathers," who are the patriarchs (cf. Lev 26:42).

These two parallel statements (1 and 2) seem to stand in a "hard paradox."[543] This paradox, which involves historical Israel's simultaneous hardening and election (vv. 25-27), would echo the same notions behind Isaiah 27:6-13, namely the expiation, the removal of sin and the worship of "those being exterminated." The paradox in 11:28 is also comparable with the notion of God's endurance or patience (μακροθυμία) of his objects of wrath (9:22)[544] and the idea of simultaneous rejection and acceptance by God in 11:15. The salvation of hardened, inner-elect Israel would thus seem to rectify God's salvation-historical dealings with historical Israel, which included hardening (9:9-23).[545]

If "they" in v. 28 are historical Israel (referring back to v. 26) who are enemies of God for the believers' sake, it would mean that their historical hardening (see above) during the course of salvation history ("they are enemies of God") culminated in the coming of the Messiah to bring the gospel to all ("for your sake"). Yet, if this same historical Israel paradoxically remains elect, it would mean that the same Israel who was hardened during the course of salvation history are saved *in addition to* those remaining from historical Israel who believed in Christ and are strictly not "Israel" any longer (9:27, see above). The phrase "for the sake of the fathers" perfectly fits the understanding that historical Israel is in view. The fathers who were part of inner-elect, historical Israel, themselves seem to benefit from this regrafting of ancient Israel. It confirms God's calling (cf. καλέω, 4:17; 9:7, 11)[546] and gifts

---

541. Fitzmyer, *Romans*, 626; Morris, *Romans*, 423; ISV; NIV; cf. Dunn, *Romans*, 2:684; RSV.

542. Dunn, *Romans*, 2:684; Cranfield, *Romans*, 2:572; ESV; REB; NRSV; RSV; OAT; ASV; RV; cf. Fitzmyer, *Romans*, 626; KJV.

543. Käsemann, *Romans*, 315.

544. While national Israel (cf. "Esau," 9:13) would naturally be an object of destruction (v. 22), v. 27 only states that those remaining (believers in Christ) would be saved, which implies that even "true" Israel (9:6) of history would be included in the eventual destruction (Israel being cut off), setting up the tension that would paradoxically be relieved in 11:26.

545. While national Israel would certainly have been part of the overall history of salvation in that God's privileges were entrusted to them, including Christ according to the flesh (9:4), these privileges do not necessarily imply salvation (see pp. 46-49). National Israel would therefore not constitute "true" Israel (9:6) and would thus not be part of those being saved.

546. An allusion to the calling of things that are not as if they were may be intentional here (4:17). In 9:7 and 11, calling corresponds to inner election of historical

(χαρίσματα)⁵⁴⁷ to them as irrevocable (v. 29). The same historical hardened Israel who was cut off from being God's people in Christ has been regrafted in Christ. The parallelism in verse 28 thus describes God's double action with historical Israel of rejecting and accepting them in Christ (cf. 11:15).

Verses 30 (introduced by ὥσπερ) and 31 (introduced by οὕτως καί) are the protasis and the apodosis respectively of a carefully constructed sentence, which is connected to the preceding by γάρ.⁵⁴⁸ Verse 32 is its summary and conclusion:

> (30) For as you then also disobeyed God, but now have obtained mercy by their disobedience, (31) so also they have now disobeyed, so that they also may now obtain mercy by the mercy [shown] to you. (32) For God imprisoned all in disobedience, that He may show mercy to all.⁵⁴⁹

Verse 30 pertains to all the the nations while verse 31 pertains to Israel. This sentence (vv. 30–31) can be understood as an explanation rather than a confirmation of verses 28–29.⁵⁵⁰ The ὥσπερ . . . οὕτως formula follows a similar pattern to 5:12, 19 and 21, stating a balanced conclusion.

The adverb νῦν in verse 30 indeed divides two salvation-historical epochs.⁵⁵¹ The nations who were disobedient⁵⁵² in the previous salvation-historical epoch have *now* found mercy (ἐλεέω) as a result of Israel's disobedience.⁵⁵³ Israel's disobedience corresponds to their historical hardening and eventual salvation-historical stumbling against the Stumbling Stone. The aorist indicatives of the gentiles' disobedience (ἠπειθήσατε) and their receiving of mercy (ἠλεήθητε), together with the adverb νῦν in verse 30 then constitute the *realized* significance of the Christ event. Additionally, the aorist indicatives of both the gentiles' (ἠπειθήσατε, v. 30) and

---

Israel, especially of the patriarchs.

547. Paul probably has the privileges of national Israel in mind (9:4-5; Moo, *Romans*, 732; Dunn, *Romans*, 2:686). However, it is significant that Christ their Messiah is reckoned as one of their privileges (9:5). In addition, Paul portrays *Christ* as the χάρισμα to humankind (5:15, 16; 6:23).

548. Cranfield, *Romans*, 2:582.

549. Rom 11:30–32, my own translation.

550. Cranfield, *Romans*, 2:582; cf. Moo, *Romans*, 732.

551. Moo, *Romans*, 733; Dunn, *Romans*, 2:687. Matera, *Romans*, 274, although he does not specifically mention two salvation-historical epochs, he points to "the past situation" and "the present situation."

552. BDAG, ἀπειθέω; Dunn, *Romans*, 2:687; cf. Moo, *Romans*, 711.

553. Fitzmyer, *Romans*, 626–27.

Israel's disobedience (ἠπείθησαν, v. 31) would point to their disobedience in the *previous* epoch.

The apodosis (v. 31) states the significance of the Christ event for Israel. It is precisely here where the understanding that historical Israel is already saved (vv. 26–27) fits best, while futuristic interpretations seem to be hard to fit. The verb ἠπείθησαν is aorist indicative, constituting a snapshot (punctiliar) of a past action:[554] they (Israel) have now (νῦν, first occurrence) been disobedient. The verb therefore does not point to Israel's "current disobedience."[555] The first νῦν here (as in v. 30) denotes the current state of affairs in the light of the Christ event. They were also disobedient in the previous epoch for the sake of (τῷ ὑμετέρῳ)[556] mercy to be shown to the gentiles. This happened in turn that they (Israel) may *now* (νῦν, second occurrence) receive mercy.

Although many manuscripts omit the second νῦν in verse 31 (e.g., P46 A D1 F G Ψ 1739. 1881 𝔐 latt), it is included in NA28, based on ℵ (Sinaiticus, 4 CE), B (Vaticanus, 4 CE), D*.c (Claromontanus, 6 CE, original hand, third corrector), 1506 (11 CE), *pc* bo (Bohairic) and fayms (Fayumic). The reading with the second νῦν included is followed by most commentators[557] and newer Bible translations.[558] Metzger writes:

> A preponderance of early and diverse witnesses favors the shorter reading. On the other hand, the difficulty in meaning that the second occurrence of νῦν seems to introduce may have prompted either its deletion or its replacement by the superficially more appropriate ὕστερον. In view of such conflicting considerations it seemed best to retain νῦν in the text but to enclose it within square brackets.[559]

---

554. Wallace, *Grammar*, 555; BDF §318.

555. Contra Jewett, *Romans*, 709.

556. Cf. BDAG, ἔλεος, b; BDF §196; Fitzmyer, *Romans*, 627. This translation takes the dative as a causal dative. BDF §196, translates: "because God desired to show you mercy" (cf. BDAG, ἔλεος, b). It is likely to be understood in this way (1) to retain the parallelism with v. 30, and (2) for its correspondence with a similar notion in v. 11 (Fitzmyer, *Romans*, 627–28).

557. Jewett, *Romans*, 694; Schreiner, *Romans*, 628, 630; Wright, "Romans," 694; Moo, *Romans*, 711; Mounce, *Romans*, 223; Fitzmyer, *Romans*, 628; Dunn, *Romans*, 2:687; Cranfield, *Romans*, 2:585–86; Barrett, *Romans*, 226; Sanday and Headlam, *Romans*, 338.

558. ESV; GNB; NRSV; NIV; NAT; RV.

559. Metzger, *Textual Commentary*, 465.

Wright argues that even if this νῦν would be missing, it is implied in the context.[560] The reading with the νῦν retained is not only the *lectio difficilior*[561] but it affects the meaning of οὕτως in 11:26.[562] Cranfield admits that "it seems difficult to deny the temporal significance of this νῦν."[563] It thus seems likely that the νῦν signifies that Israel has *already* received mercy. The same paradox of verse 28 (cf. 11:11, 15, 26–27) would then be repeated. Israel would then have been disobedient in the previous age while they simultaneously have received mercy in Christ. It would mean that historical, elected Israel has *now* been saved in Christ and thereby received mercy just as the nations have received mercy in Christ in that they can believe in him and be saved, confirming and complementing the interpretation argued for in verses 26 to 27.

The beauty[564] of verse 30 (the protasis) and verse 31 (the apodosis) lies in the perfect salvation-historical balance they represent. In terms of the bigger scheme of salvation history, all the nations living *after* the Christ event have received mercy through the gospel in spite of all nations' disobedience in the previous epoch (v. 30).[565] These are in perfect balance with God's people (inner elect Israel) who lived *before* the Christ event (v. 31). In spite of their disobedience in the previous epoch, which was for the sake of God's mercy in the gospel to all people (including people physically descending from historical Israel by implication), they (inner elect Israel) have received mercy in Christ. Verse 31 thus largely echoes and explains the notions behind verses 25b to 26a. In this understanding there is no end-time anticipation for a present or future "Israel" to be brought in. Such a notion would in fact disturb the salvation historical balance in that it would deprive the Christ event from its central, definitive position in salvation history.

---

560. Wright, "Romans," 694.
561. Jewett, *Romans*, 694; Fitzmyer, *Romans*, 628.
562. Fitzmyer, *Romans*, 628.
563. Cranfield, *Romans*, 2:585–86.
564. Dunn, *Romans*, 2:687) views verses 30 and 31 as "the most contrived or carefully constructed formulation which Paul ever produced in such a tight epigrammatic form."
565. The "you" (ὑμεῖς, v. 30) refers in v. 30a to all the nations who lived in the previous epoch, implying that the "you" is applied salvation-historically and thus not literally. Yet in v. 30b, historical Israel could even be included in the "you" by implication, for in the gospel age "you" could point to believers in Christ (the recipients of the letter), which do not necessarily exclude people who physically descended from historical Israel (cf. v. 23). If this same logic is pushed even further, the "you" in v. 30a could even include Israel by implication. But it is probably safer to apply v. 30 mainly to gentiles.

Verse 32 sums up Paul's salvation-historical exposition.[566] God has imprisoned[567] all in disobedience that He may be merciful to all. The inclusion of "all" (πᾶς) pertains to the disobedience of Israel and all the nations within the old epoch before the Christ event, in order to be merciful to all people in Christ. The net effect is that God has been merciful to His elect ancient Israel in the *prior* epoch, saving them (v. 26a), *and* to all people in the eschatological epoch *after* the Christ event, including them in the grace presented in the gospel (v. 25b). An allusion to the imprisonment under the law and sin in the old epoch is not impossible here, for Paul uses the same word (συγκλείω) in Galatians 3:22, 23 to describe the imprisonment under sin and the law.[568] Regarding this notion in Galatians 3, Hays writes: "at last through Christ's death the curse has been lifted, Israel has been set free, the exile has ended, so that the ingathering of the Gentiles can now begin."[569]

There is a universal aspect in that God's mercy was extended to all people in Christ (v. 32), but not universalism, which would imply that each individual is saved.[570] The latter view would be contradictory to Paul's thought elsewhere.[571] Verse 32 rather implies that "God's mercy is potentially available to all."[572]

Praising God's Wisdom, Knowledge and Judgments (vv. 33–36)

In verses 33 to 36, Paul does not communicate a sense of frustration in confrontation with the mysteries of God's election. There is rather a fine balance between God's sovereignty as manifested in His salvation-historical plan, and human responsibility (cf. the actives in vv. 30–31: ἠπειθήσατε, ἠπείθησαν), which is included in God's sovereign plan[573] (cf. Rom 9:24-33).

---

566. Cf. Fitzmyer, *Romans*, 629; Dunn, *Romans*, 2:696; Ridderbos, *Romeinen*, 269.

567. BDAG, συγκλείω, §2; NLT; NRSV; cf. GW; GNB.

568. Cf. the themes of freedom from the law (Rom 7:2; 8:2) and sin (6:18, 22), in contrast to being under the law (2:12; 3:19; 6:14-15; 7:23) and sin (3:9; 7:14).

569. Hays, "Galatians," 261.

570. Cf. Schreiner, *Romans*, 629; Moo, *Romans*, 736; Dunn, *Romans*, 2:697; Bruce, *Romans*, 219; Sanday and Headlam, *Romans*, 339. Schreiner, *Romans*, 629, is probably right that with πάντας Paul primarily has Israel and gentiles as groups in view (cf. Käsemann, *Romans*, 316; Sanday and Headlam, *Romans*, 339).

571. Cf. the individual dimension of the new creation (2 Cor 5:14-21, see pp. 156-64; cf. Col 3:9-15, see pp. 164-68) and faith being the condition for righteousness (Gal 3; Rom 4).

572. Moo, *Romans*, 736.

573. Moo, *Romans*, 740.

Paul's unusual vocabulary suggests that the passage is probably a hymn,[574] which borrows from the formulations of Old Testament wisdom traditions (esp. Job), apocalyptic writings[575] and even Stoic formulations.[576] Although some or all of these elements might be present in verses 33 to 36, it is likely that Paul composed the hymn himself.[577]

In verse 33, Paul praises the riches, wisdom and knowledge of God. God's judgments (cf. Job 40:8) are unsearchable (ἀνεξερεύνητος)[578] and His ways inscrutable (ἀνεξιχνίαστος).[579] With verse 33, Paul surely has God's salvation plan and His providential control of salvation history for all human beings in mind.[580] Verse 34 is a quote from Isaiah 40:13 (LXX). Paul rhetorically asks who has known the mind of the Lord (cf. 1 Cor 2:16) or who has been His counsellor. It has to do with the human experience of God's plan.[581] Verse 35 ("Or who has given a gift to him, to receive a gift in return?")[582] might be a quotation from Job 41:3 in the Septuagint, but corresponds closer to Job 41:11 in the MT.[583] Moo suggests that one can answer this question (v. 35): "no one, except Jesus Christ, who has revealed to us in his own person the plan of God for salvation history."[584] Although verse 36 does not point to Christ as such, it does not diminish the centrality of Christ within salvation history either.[585] It rather acknowledges God's control and supremacy spanning over both the epochs before and after the Christ event.

---

574. Jewett, *Romans*, 713; Moo, *Romans*, 740; Fitzmyer, *Romans*, 633; Cranfield, *Romans*, 2:589.

575. Moo, *Romans*, 740; Dunn, *Romans*, 2:698.

576. Cranfield, *Romans*, 2:589, 591. Fitzmyer, *Romans*, 633, shows this from *Meditation* 4:23 of Marcus Aurelius: "All that is in tune with you is in tune with me! Nothing that is on time for you is too early or too late for me! All that your seasons bring, O Nature, is fruit for me! All things come from you, subsist in you, are destined for you." Yet Paul substitutes "Nature" with "though Him," which contradicts Stoic pantheism (Hultgren, *Romans*, 433; Cranfield, *Romans*, 2:591; Ridderbos, *Romeinen*, 271).

577. Hultgren, *Romans*, 431; Schreiner, *Romans*, 632; Moo, *Romans*, 740-41; Dunn, *Romans*, 2:698; Käsemann, *Romans*, 318)

578. Moo, *Romans*, 739; NRSV; RSV; KJV.

579. BDAG, ἀνεξιχνίαστος; Moo, *Romans*, 739; NRSV; RSV.

580. Moo, *Romans*, 741-42.

581. Moo, *Romans*, 743.

582. NRSV.

583. Fitzmyer, *Romans*, 635. The MT (Job 41:11) has מִי הִקְדִּימַנִי וַאֲשַׁלֵּם ("who has preceded me that I should repay?"). The Septuagint (Job 41:3) has ἢ τίς ἀντιστήσεταί μοι καὶ ὑπομενεῖ ("or who will withstand me and survive?").

584. Moo, *Romans*, 743.

585. Cf. Wright, "Romans," 696, who observes that Paul uses similar language in 11:36 to that in 1 Cor 8:6 with reference to Christ: εἷς κύριος Ἰησοῦς Χριστός, δι' οὗ τὰ

Historical Israel's Salvation in Other Literature

If the interpretation is correct that the salvation of elect Israel of the Old Testament, their turning away of ungodliness and their taking away of sins are in view in Romans 11:26-27, one could ask if these ideas can be found in other literature in the New Testament or the early church. Subsequently, certain passages in the New Testament (Matt 27:51-53; Eph 4:9; 1 Pet 3:19-20; 4:6) will be probed for their compatibility with such an understanding. Some of the ideas found in these passages will be compared to similar ideas in mainly the writings Justin Martyr (around 160 CE), Irenaeus (around 182-188 CE) and Tertullian (around 203 CE).

Historical Israel's Salvation in the Rest of the New Testament?

While there is no explicit indication of historical Israel's salvation in the rest of the New Testament, there are statements that could be compatible with such an idea.

A controversial passage in the New Testament is found in Matthew 27:51-53, which contains the report about strange events taking place at Jesus' death: the earth shook, the rocks split, the tombs were opened and many bodies of the saints who had fallen asleep were raised. These resurrected saints came out of the tombs after Jesus' resurrection, entered the holy city and appeared to many. The opening of the tombs alludes to a similar notions in Daniel 12:2 (LXX);[586] Ezekiel 37:12-13 (LXX)[587] and Isaiah 26:19 (LXX).[588] While this passage in Matthew is seen by some as a post-Matthean gloss,[589] Talbert suggests that it is a "haggadic (narrative) type of exposition to explain the significance of Jesus's resurrection in the messianists' foundation document."[590] Talbert interprets this passage primarily as the fulfillment of Ezekiel 37's prophecy "of the eschatological age, when

---

πάντα καὶ ἡμεῖς δι' αὐτοῦ (cf. Col 1:15-20). Sanday and Headlam, *Romans*, 340, connect δι' αὐτοῦ in 11:36 to Christ. Cf. also Käsemann, *Romans*, 321.

586. Evans, *Matthew*, 466; Davies, *Matthew*, 228; France, *Matthew*, 1082; Dalton, *Proclamation*, 35.

587. Osborne, *Matthew*, 1045; Talbert, *Matthew*, 306-7; Davies, *Matthew*, 228; Turner, *Matthew*, 670; France, *Matthew*, 1082; Wright, *Resurrection*, 633; Schweizer, *Matthew*, 515.

588. France, *Matthew*, 1082; Wright, *Resurrection*, 633.

589. E.g., Evans, *Matthew*, 466; Meier, *Matthew*, 352.

590. Talbert, *Matthew*, 307.

graves are opened and a raised people are returned to their land."[591] Albright and Mann consider Matthew's scene as a dramatization of the eschatological resurrection of the dead portrayed in John 5:25–29, which indicates that those in the tomb will hear the Son of Man's voice and will come out.[592] Turner argues that "[i]f this resurrection is intended to preview the ultimate resurrection of humanity . . ., it is important that it be as genuine as that of Jesus . . . For Matthew, the association of the saints' resurrection with that of Jesus marks the decisive turning of ages."[593] Osborne sums up the meaning of this passage in a similar way:

> The opening of the tombs and resurrection of the dead continue the eschatological motif from the earthquake in two ways. (1) In Jesus' death the inauguration of the last days is sealed, the power of death is broken, and the righteous are resurrected. (2) The inauguration of the new age of salvation occurs, when life is made available to all. Both aspects are combined in apocalyptic expectation and look forward to the cosmic portents that will precede the return of Christ.[594]

While focusing on resurrection rather than salvation, it thus seems relatively assured that this passage creates a pertinent *eschatological link* between the Christ event and the *deceased saints of the Old Testament*.[595] In addition, it is noteworthy that in seeing Matthew 27:51–53 as a fulfillment of Ezekiel 37:12–14, the promise of the land to be inherited is fulfilled, yet arguably in another way than most expected (cf. Rom 4:13, see p. 85).

1 Peter 3:19–20 reports of Christ who went to preach to the disobedient "spirits in prison" (φυλακῇ πνεύμασιν) when the long-suffering of God waited in the days of Noah. Many interpreters understand φυλακῇ πνεύμασιν to refer to angelic or demonic spirits to whom Christ proclaimed his victory or their damnation, which would correspond to the account of fallen angels in Genesis 6:1–4.[596] While it is not common in the New Testament to refer to deceased believers as "spirits" (Heb 12:23; cf. 1 En. 22:6–7, 9, 11–13) and

---

591. Talbert, *Matthew*, 307; cf. Gurtner, *Torn Veil*, 178–79; Wright, *Resurrection*, 633; 2 Bar. 50:3–4.

592. Albright and Mann, *Matthew*, 351; cf. France, *Matthew*, 1083.

593. Turner, *Matthew*, 670; cf. Carson, "Matthew," 582. Defenders of the historicity of what is described in Matthew 27:51–53 includes Osborne, *Matthew*, 1044; Wilkins, *Matthew*, 905–7; Wright, *Resurrection*, 636; Morris, *Matthew*, 724–25; Carson, "Matthew," 581–82; and Wenham, "Resurrection Narratives."

594. Osborne, *Matthew*, 1045.

595. Cf. Osborne, *Matthew*, 1045; Schweizer, *Matthew*, 515–16.

596. E.g., Jobes, *1 Peter*, 243–44; Black, *1 Peter*; Achtemeier, *1 Peter*, 245–46.

while the rest of the New Testament does not describe the dead being in "prison," there are some who consider this passage as Jesus' preaching to *deceased human beings*.[597] There is evidence in the early Christian literature of "prison" being the place where souls are kept awaiting judgment.[598] In 4:5–6, gentile sinners are said to give an account to God who stands ready to judge the living and the dead. It is for this reason that "the gospel was proclaimed even to the dead" so that they might be "judged according to people in the flesh" and "live in the spirit as God does." Michaels reads the latter as a reference to those like the prophets (1:10–12) and the holy wives (3:5–6) *of the Old Covenant* to whom the gospel would have been preached as a promise of salvation while they still lived.[599] Yet Feldmeier links 4:6 to 3:18–20, which he supports from the way in which 4:6 contrasts "flesh" (the sphere of mortality in which judgment took place) with "spirit" (the sphere of activity of divine power that makes alive).[600] This contrast corresponds to a similar contrast in 3:18. If the connection between 3:18–20 and 4:5–6 could be established as pointing to the same event,[601] Michaels' notion (above) could be retained but even imply preaching to *those of the Old covenant in the realm of the dead*. Such an idea does not necessarily have to imply that the unrighteous dead received another opportunity to be saved.[602] While the spirits could point to the faithful of historical Israel awaiting salvation in Christ,[603] the passage might be understood as a proclamation to both the elect and non-elect dead that the Redeemer has come to save the elect and to condemn the non-elect without giving anyone a second chance on salvation. Yet none of these interpretations can be established beyond doubt and has to be understood as mere possibilities.

In Ephesians 4:9 there is a reference to Christ's descent into "the lower parts of the earth" (τὰ κατώτερα μέρη τῆς γῆς) in the context of (ful)filling (πληρόω) all things (4:10). Despite the various interpretations of this passage,[604] Muddiman and Thielman argue that τὰ κατώτερα μέρη τῆς γῆς

---

597. E.g., Feldmeier, *Peter*, 203–5; Calvin, *Catholic Epistles*, 77–78.

598. Cf. 2 Clem. 6.8 (αἰχμαλωσία); Herm. 1.8, Herm. Vis. 1.1 (αἰχμαλωτισμός); 105.7, Herm. Sim. 9.28 (δεσμωτήριον; in Feldmeier, *Peter*, 204).

599. Michaels, *1 Peter*, 235–38.

600. Feldmeier, *Peter*, 216.

601. So Wright, *Resurrection*, 467–68; Goppelt, *1 Peter*, 257–59; Calvin, *Catholic Epistles*, 77.

602. Contra Feldmeier, *Peter*, 203–5, 216.

603. Calvin, *Catholic Epistles*, 78.

604. These include (1) the view that argues from Christ's pre-existence that if he "ascended to the height" (Ps 68:18) at some point, he first had to descend and adopt a humble existence (in Thielman, *Ephesians*, 269; e.g., Boles, *Ephesians*; Stott, *Ephesians*;

is most naturally taken as a reference to subterranean regions, a notion that was well known in the Greco-Roman world.[605] Since it is unlikely that the readers of Ephesians would not be expected to understand by τὰ κατώτερα μέρη τῆς γῆς anything other than descent to the realm of the dead, "the ascent of Christ thus inevitably implies his descent to the earth's lower reaches, the place of the dead"[606] (cf. Rom 10:7; Ps 63:9). While this would point to God's reach to "every corner of the universe,"[607] it seems to be compatible with a view that *Christ descended to the grave*[608] *in order to appropriate his Messiahship in some way to elect, historical Israel.*

Historical Israel's Salvation in the Early Church

While the idea of historical Israel's salvation in Christ is not stated explicitly in the rest of the New Testament apart from what I have argued in Romans 11:25-27, there are statements from the Church Fathers that come very close to this idea.[609]

In Justin Martyr's *Dialogue with Trypho* 72, where he insists that parts of the Hebrew Scriptures have been removed, he contends that the following saying was cut out of the book of Jeremiah: "The Lord God remembered His dead people of Israel who lay in the graves;[610] and He descended to preach to them His own salvation."[611] This saying has become known as the Jeremiah-logion. It is remarkable that Irenaeus quotes the Jeremiah-logion or alludes to it *six times*.[612] While Bauckham ascribes one version of this saying as part of a Judean text prophesying the resurrection of the righteous at the last day (Irenaeus, *Haer.* 4.33.1; 4.33.12; 5.31.1), he

---

cf. Phil 2:5-11); (2) that it is simply a reference to Christ's incarnation (O'Brien, *Ephesians*, 296; Talbert, *Ephesians*, 112; Calvin, *Ephesians*, 350); and (3) that it denotes the descent of the Spirit at Pentecost (Lincoln, *Ephesians*, 247; Harris, "Ascent and Descent"). Hoehner, *Ephesians*, 532, however, notes that the latter view presupposes that the recipients of the letter had an acquaintance with the rabbinic material, which is anachronistic.

605. Muddiman, *Ephesians*, 192-93; Thielman, *Ephesians*, 270-71; cf. Dionysus; Aeneas; Orpheus; Pythagoras (see Bauckham, "Descent," ABD, 2:149-54).
606. Thielman, *Ephesians*, 217; cf. Wood, "Ephesians," 57.
607. Thielman, *Ephesians*, 272.
608. Hoehner, *Ephesians*, 535-36.
609. See Bauckham, "Descent," ABD, 2:145-59; Crossan, *Cross*, 374-77.
610. The Greek reads εἰς γῆν χώματος, thus describing it as being in the "ground" (Pierce, *Spirits*, 6).
611. Roberts and Donaldson, *Ante-Nicene Fathers*, 1:235.
612. *Haer.* 3.20.4; 4.22.1; 4.33.1; 4.33.12; 5.31.1; *Epid.* 78.

argues that another form of it was a Christian adaption of the text referring to Christ descending to Hades (Justin, *Dial.* 72; Irenaeus, *Haer.* 3.20.4; 4.22.1; *Epid.* 78).[613] According to Dalton, Justin certainly found the quote in his version of Jeremiah.[614] Dalton argues that "[w]e have no reason for suspecting the sincerity of Justin. Thus the entry of this interpolation into the text of Jeremiah must have occurred a good time before the writing of the *Dialogue* (about 160)."[615] Dalton maintains that it is probably a free development of Matthew 27:51–52.[616]

Although initially attributing the passage to Isaiah,[617] Irenaeus writes in *Against Heresies* 30.20.4: "And the holy Lord remembered His dead Israel, who had slept in the land of sepulture; and He came down to preach His salvation to them, that He might save them."[618] He immediately follows up the Jeremiah-logion with a quote from Micah 7:19[619] in which he contends that "the prophet declares the same" as constituted by the Jeremiah-logion: "He will turn again, and will have compassion upon us: He will destroy our iniquities, and will cast our sins into the depths of the sea." Irenaeus then specifies the place of this advent: "The Lord hath spoken from Zion, and He has uttered His voice from Jerusalem"[620] (Joel 3:16; Amos 1:2). If these three consecutive quotes are taken together, the themes show a remarkable agreement with the themes of Romans 11:26–27. The following themes correspond: Israel; salvation; the coming of the Lord/Deliverer from Zion; the destroying/turning away of iniquity/ungodliness; and the casting/taking away of sin. The combined sense of the three quotes lies very close to the interpretation that I argued for in Romans 11:26–27, especially the reference to the salvation of Israel lying in the grave. Yet when Irenaeus quotes Romans 11:26 specifically in *Against Heresies* 4.2.7 and points to "the sheep of Israel" (Matt 10:6) and the Samaritans who believed in Christ, it is not clear whether he connects the same sense to Romans 11:26–27 that he argued in 3.20.4 (dead Israel's salvation). It has to be noted though that Irenaeus attaches a deep diachronic sense to Christ's ministry earlier in *Against Heresies* 4.2 when he sees Moses' words as the words of Christ: if the Israelites

---

613. Bauckham, "Descent," *ABD*, 2.
614. Dalton, *Proclamation*, 34–35.
615. Dalton, *Proclamation*, 35.
616. Dalton, *Proclamation*, 35.
617. This is probably unintended since Irenaeus later attributes the same passage to Jeremiah.
618. Roberts and Donaldson, *Ante-Nicene Fathers*, 1:451.
619. Irenaeus incorrectly attributes the quote to Amos.
620. Roberts and Donaldson, *Ante-Nicene Fathers*, 1:451.

(of the Old Testament) believed Moses, they would have believed in Christ (4.7.3; cf. John 5:46–47). The same idea is carried forward into 4.7.4. It is as if Irenaeus sees these Old Testament Israelites who believed Moses' words as "Christians." When Irenaeus states at the beginning of 4.2.7 that those who feared God, were anxious about His law and ran to Christ, resulting in being saved, it thus seems as if elect, historical Israel who believed Christ (via Moses) is included in this salvation.

In *Against Heresies* 4.22.1, Irenaeus writes the following:

> Now in the last days, when the fulness of the time of liberty had arrived, the Word Himself did by Himself "wash away the filth of the daughters of Zion," [Isa 4:4] when He washed the disciples' feet with His own hands [John 3:5]. For this is the end of the human race inheriting God; that as in the beginning, by means of our first [parents], we were all brought into bondage, by being made subject to death; so at last, by means of the New Man, all who from the beginning [were His] disciples, having been cleansed and washed from things pertaining to death, should come to the life of God. For He who washed the feet of the disciples sanctified the entire body, and rendered it clean. For this reason, too, He administered food to them in a recumbent posture, indicating that those who were lying in the earth were they to whom He came to impart life. As Jeremiah declares, "The holy Lord remembered His dead Israel, who slept in the land of sepulture; and He descended to them to make known to them His salvation, that they might be saved." For this reason also were the eyes of the disciples weighed down when Christ's passion was approaching; and when, in the first instance, the Lord found them sleeping, He let it pass,—thus indicating the patience of God in regard to the state of slumber in which men lay; but coming the second time, He aroused them, and made them stand up, in token that His passion is the arousing of His sleeping disciples, on whose account "He also descended into the lower parts of the earth" [Eph 4:9] to behold with His eyes the state of those who were resting from their labours, in reference to whom He did also declare to the disciples: "Many prophets and righteous men have desired to see and hear what ye do see and hear" [Matt 13:17].[621]

While Irenaeus in the above quotation allegorically connects the "washing away of the filth" of historical Israel with the washing of the disciples' feet, the imparting of life and salvation to those lying in the earth with Jesus'

---

621. Roberts and Donaldson, *Ante-Nicene Fathers*, 1:493–94.

administering of food to his disciples, and Christ's descent into the lower parts of the earth with Jesus' arousal of his sleeping disciples (to arise the "sleeping disciples" of the Old Testament by implication), the idea of the salvation of historical Israel and their forgiveness of sins through Jesus' work is evident.

In *Against Heresies* 4.33.1, Irenaeus refers to Christ who

> gathered from the ends of the earth into His Father's fold the children who were scattered abroad, [Isa 11:12] and remembered His own dead ones who had formerly fallen asleep, and came down to them that He might deliver them.[622]

In 4.33.12, there is a reference to Christ being "brought down to the dust of death"[623] (cf. Ps 22:15). Shortly after, in reference to Jesus' crucifixion and suffering, Irenaeus writes:

> Others, again, when they said, "The holy Lord remembered His own dead ones who slept in the dust, and came down to them to raise them up, that He might save them," furnished us with the reason on account of which He suffered all these things.[624]

In 5.31.1 Irenaeus writes that Christ

> immediately upon His expiring on the cross, undoubtedly departed on high, leaving His body to the earth. But the case was, that for three days He dwelt in the place where the dead were, as the prophet says concerning Him: "And the Lord remembered His dead saints who slept formerly in the land of sepulture; and He descended to them, to rescue and save them." And the Lord Himself says, "As Jonas remained three days and three nights in the whale's belly, so shall the Son of man be in the heart of the earth" [Matt 12:40]. Then also the apostle says, "But when He ascended, what is it but that He also descended into the lower parts of the earth?" [Eph 4:9].[625]

Finally, in *The Demonstration of the Apostolic Preaching* 78, Irenaeus writes:

> And in Jeremiah He [Christ] thus declares His death and descent into hell, saying: And the Lord the Holy One of Israel, remembered his dead, which aforetime fell asleep in the dust of the earth; and he went down unto them, to bring the tidings of

---

622. Roberts and Donaldson, *Ante-Nicene Fathers*, 1:506.
623. Roberts and Donaldson, *Ante-Nicene Fathers*, 1:510.
624. Roberts and Donaldson, *Ante-Nicene Fathers*, 1:510.
625. Roberts and Donaldson, *Ante-Nicene Fathers*, 1:560.

his salvation, to deliver them. In this place He also renders the cause of His death: for His descent into hell was the salvation of them that had passed away.[626]

It is noteworthy that the action of the Lord in the Jeremiah-logion in *Against Heresies* 4.33.1 and *The Demonstration of the Apostolic Preaching* 78 (above) is specifically connected to "deliverance," which corresponds to the idea of a Deliverer in Romans 11:26. Elsewhere, Irenaeus (*Haer.* 5.27.2) reasons that Christ "descended into the regions beneath the earth, preaching His advent there also," and to declare "the remission of sins received by those who believe in Him." He defines these as "those who proclaimed His advent, and submitted to His dispensations, the righteous men, the prophets, and the patriarchs, to whom He remitted sins in the same way as He did to us, which sins we should not lay to their charge, if we would not despise the grace of God."[627] Similarly, Tertullian (*An.* 55) states that Christ did not "ascend into the heights of heaven before descending into the lower parts of the earth, that He might there make the patriarchs and prophets partakers of Himself."[628] These ideas are compatible with the idea that the Old Testament people hoped for Christ (Ignatius, *Magn.* 9.2).

Conclusion

The Jeremiah-logion, which refers to the Lord remembering His dead Israel who slept in the grave to whom He descended to make known their salvation and to save them, which closely resembles my interpretation of Romans 11:26–27, occurs with slight variations no less than seven times in the Church Fathers (Justin Martyr [x1]; Irenaeus [x6]). While the Jeremiah-logion's origin is unsure and does not occur in the Hebrew Scriptures that we have, it constitutes a tradition that was certainly prevalent among the Church Fathers, which arguably was part of an earlier version or versions of the Septuagint. From the quotes discussed above, the idea that Christ descended to the realm of the dead to proclaim the salvation of elect, historical Israel, resulting in their salvation, seems to be compatible with at least Justin Martyr, Irenaeus, Tertullian and possibly Ignatius. In quoting Ephesians 4:9 in *Against Heresies* 4.22.1 and 5.31.1, Irenaeus connects it to the whole notion of historical Israel's salvation (see above). Irenaeus' reference to the Lord's descent into the regions "beneath the earth" where He "preached" His advent

---

626. Robinson, *Demonstration*, 136.
627. Roberts and Donaldson, *Ante-Nicene Fathers*, 1:499.
628. Roberts and Donaldson, *Ante-Nicene Fathers*, 3:231.

there also, in order for these (including prophets and patriarchs) to receive remission of sins (*Haer.* 5.27.2), seems to resemble the basic idea behind 1 Peter 3:19–20;[629] 4:6 and Ephesians 4:9. The connection between the "preaching" and "the regions beneath the earth" defines those beneath the earth as those in the realm of the dead, *combining* the ideas behind Ephesians 4:9; 1 Peter 3:19–20 and 4:6. Similarly, Tertullian's reference to Christ's descent (*An.* 55) "into the lower parts of the earth" echoes Ephesians 4:9, while the idea to "make the patriarchs and prophets partakers of Himself" seems to resemble the idea behind 1 Peter 3:19–20[630] and arguably 4:6.

While the relationship of Matthew 27:51–52 with the Jeremiah-logion is unsure, the eschatological connection between the righteous of the Old Testament and Christ's death and resurrection is sure (cf. Ezek 37:12–14; Dan 12:2). The fusion of the ideas and terminology behind 1 Peter 3:19–20; 4:6 and Ephesians 4:9 in connection with the salvation of historical Israel in the writings of the Church Fathers discussed here, suggests that the interpretation that I am arguing for in Romans 11:26–27 is compatible with that which these Church Fathers argued for in their allusions to Ephesians 4:9; 1 Peter 3:19–20 and 4:6. This compatibility could in turn argue for the compatibility of my reading of Romans 11:25–27 with an early tradition in the early church, which arguably existed in the time of the writing of the New Testament.

Galatians 6:7–16 (ABC)

In Galatians 6, verses 7 to 10 conclude the argument that began in 5:13.[631] Verses 7 to 10 thus form part of an ethical section (5:13–6:10), while verses 11 to 16 form part of the letter's overall conclusion.[632] In the discussion of verses 7 to 16, the main aim is to outline the identities involved. Verses 7 to 16 recapitulate on many of the earlier themes in the letter and serves as a kind of summary and conclusion to the most important points Paul made in the letter.

---

629. Roberts and Donaldson, *Ante-Nicene Fathers*, 1:499.

630. Roberts and Donaldson, *Ante-Nicene Fathers*, 3:231.

631. Fee, *Empowering Presence*, 464; cf. Fung, *Galatians*, 294; Lategan, *Galasiërs*, 113.

632. Cf. Fung, *Galatians*, 284, 300.

Sowing and Reaping in Flesh and Spirit (vv. 7–10)

The image of sowing and reaping (vv. 7–8) takes Paul's readers back from a narrower horizon of specific exhortations in Galatians 6:1-6 to the broader view of the spirit-flesh dichotomy of 5:13-26.[633] In the harvest metaphor, Paul thus reunites the antinomic motifs that were dominant in the entire argument: life in the eschatological spirit against life in the flesh (see pp. 207-12).

Paul's reference to sowing "unto his own flesh" (εἰς τὴν σάρκα ἑαυτοῦ, v. 8)[634] thus involves "sowing unto" their former unregenerate identity of the old eon.[635] Yet, in accordance with Paul's fluid use of σάρξ, it also alludes to circumcision, which signifies confidence in an identity defined by "the works of the law."[636] The end result of an identity defined by flesh is corruption (φθορά, v. 8). Conversely, to "sow in the spirit"[637] (σπείρων εἰς τὸ πνεῦμα, v. 8) is another way of pressing the imperatives as implied by 5:16-26: to "walk" by the Spirit, being "led" by the Spirit and "bearing the fruit" of the Spirit.[638] In reference to "eternal life" (ζωὴν αἰώνιον, v. 8), there is an unmistakable eschatological orientation embedded within the exhortation contained within the harvest metaphor.[639] "Eternal life" is the end result of this new way of existence in spirit. Against the background of this opposition of spirit and flesh rings the contrast between human possibility that is without eternal value against divine possibility that has an eternal effect (see pp. 220-22). Doing what is good (τὸ καλὸν ποιοῦντες, v. 9; ἐργαζώμεθα τὸ ἀγαθόν, v. 10), which forms part of the ethical dimension of life in the Spirit, cannot flow from a life defined by flesh, but must flow from the life of the empowering Spirit within the lives of believers.[640]

"Those from the household of the faith" (πρὸς τοὺς οἰκείους τῆς πίστεως, v. 10) points to the believing community and include Judeans and

---

633. Fung, *Galatians*, 294; Burton, *Galatians*, 340.

634. Fee, *Empowering Presence*, 466; ASV; RV; cf. ESV; RSV.

635. Cf. Fee, *Empowering Presence*, 466-67; Lategan, *Galasiërs*, 113; Bruce, *Galatians*, 265.

636. Cf. Hays, "Galatians," 336; Dunn, *Epistle to the Galatians*, 330; Betz, *Galatians*, 308.

637. Burton, *Galatians*, 342-43, understands πνεῦμα here as the human spirit. But as conclusion to 5:13-26, Paul rather has the "spirit" as eschatological way of existence in the new eon in Christ in mind, implying a unity between God's Spirit and the human spirit (cf. Rom 8:16).

638. Fee, *Empowering Presence*, 465.

639. Fee, *Empowering Presence*, 465; cf. Hays, "Galatians," 337; Lategan, *Galasiërs*, 113; Betz, *Galatians*, 309.

640. Cf. Fee, *Empowering Presence*, 468; Lategan, *Galasiërs*, 113.

gentiles indiscriminately[641] (see 3:28; cf. Eph 2:19). For Paul, the Judean-gentile distinction was less significant than the believer-unbeliever distinction.[642] The binding characteristic of the household is *faith* rather than ethnic membership or law.[643] The priority of goodwill to fellow believers pertains to the historical context where new found Christ-believers might not have found assistance from their pagan friends.[644] This focus, however, does not exclude the wider responsibility of doing good to "all."[645]

Flesh, Law, and Circumcision Against the Cross and the New Creation (vv. 11–15)

The large letters that Paul draws attention to (v. 11) signifies importance or emphasis,[646] and probably points to the fact that he now writes this section with his own hand.[647] In verses 12 to 14, Paul contrasts a showing in the flesh (εὐπροσωπῆσαι ἐν σαρκί, v. 12) and boasting in the flesh (σαρκὶ καυχήσωνται, v. 13) to the cross of Christ (vv. 12, 14).

The "showing in the flesh" (v. 12), which pertains to circumcision and thus ethnic identity, is aimed at Paul's opponents, the Teachers of the Law who compelled others to be circumcised.[648] The persecution that these Teachers wanted to avoid is probably the same kind of persecution that Paul carried out before his conversion (1:13, 23) and experienced himself (2 Cor 11:24).[649] Dunn is probably correct that these Teachers of the Law wanted to remove the offense of the message that the cross was sufficient to remove sins (1:4) and to remove the curse of the law, so that the promise of Abraham might be obtained through faith alone by anyone regardless of circumcision.[650] Hays explains that the cross would have signified "the end of all ethnic, social, and religious privilege and distinction."[651] With Paul's

---

641. Bruce, *Galatians*, 266.
642. Fung, *Galatians*, 298.
643. Hays, "Galatians," 337; Dunn, *Epistle to the Galatians*, 333.
644. Fung, *Galatians*, 299.
645. Fung, *Galatians*, 299; Longenecker, *Galatians*, 283; Betz, *Galatians*, 311.
646. Hays, "Galatians," 342; Dunn, *Epistle to the Galatians*, 334; Fung, *Galatians*, 301.
647. Dunn, *Epistle to the Galatians*, 334; Fung, *Galatians*, 301; Bruce, *Galatians*, 268.
648. Hays, "Galatians," 342; Dunn, *Epistle to the Galatians*, 336.
649. George, *Galatians*, 434; Dunn, *Epistle to the Galatians*, 337.
650. Dunn, *Epistle to the Galatians*, 337.
651. Hays, "Galatians," 342.

opponents, the motive of boasting (v. 13) thus ran in tandem with the desire to escape persecution.[652] The motive "that they may boast in your flesh" (v. 13) probably points to the Teachers of the Law's "triumphant persuasive power" over the Galatians, which coincides with their motive to exclude (4:17) the Galatians to gain influence over them.[653] That the Teachers of the Law did not keep (φυλάσσω, v. 13) the law is here not so much about the inherent impossibility to keep the law (as in Rom 3:20; 7:6; 8:3; 9:31), but rather about their hypocrisy of compelling others to adhere to all its stipulations while not adhering to all of them themselves.[654]

The cross (vv. 12, 14) is set over against flesh (vv. 12, 13), law (v. 13) and circumcision (vv. 12, 13, 15). The cross stands against an identity that was defined around the law, especially in terms of the antinomy constituted by being circumcised or not.[655] When Paul writes that "the world has been crucified to me, and I to the world," (v. 14)[656] the cross does not only signify Paul's "crucifixion" to his former life as a Pharisee,[657] but it signifies a "watershed event for the whole cosmos, affecting everything after it."[658] For Paul, the cross denotes the transplantation from "one sphere of existence to the other."[659] The underlying notion is that the cross stands "for the Christ-event as a whole" in that it "marks the end of the old world and ushers in the new."[660] As Lategan describes it, "the cross is for Paul the central symbol to which the truth of the gospel is attached and wherein the transition of the way of existence of the world to the way of existence of the faith is expressed."[661] The implications for the understanding of identity (v. 14) can hardly be better described than by Hays:

> [Paul's] previous identity has disappeared altogether, and his new identity is given him only through his participation in Christ, who animates the life he now lives (Gal 2:19–20). That is why he can also say that the flesh has been crucified for those

---

652. Fung, *Galatians*, 304–6.

653. Hays, "Galatians," 343. The Judean believers probably withdrew from fellowship in order to put pressure on the Galatians to "live like Judeans" (Ἰουδαΐζω, 2:14, Hays, "Galatians," 295).

654. Hays, "Galatians," 343; Fung, *Galatians*, 302–3; Bruce, *Galatians*, 270; cf. Longenecker, *Galatians*, 293.

655. Cf. Martyn, *Galatians*, 560.

656. NRSV.

657. Fung, *Galatians*, 307.

658. Martyn, *Galatians*, 564; cf. George, *Galatians*, 437.

659. Fung, *Galatians*, 307; cf. Bruce, *Galatians*, 273; Betz, *Galatians*, 320.

660. Fung, *Galatians*, 307; cf. Hays, "Galatians," 344.

661. Lategan, *Galasiërs*, 115.

who belong to Christ. They participate, not just symbolically but actually, in his death; therefore, they have entered the new eschatological world where his life empowers the community to "walk in newness of life" and consider themselves "dead to sin and alive to God" (Rom 6:4, 11 NRSV).[662]

Within the new creation, although its full completion belongs to the future, those in Christ have already experienced the reality of it.[663] But the other side of this reality is just as significant for the believer. Their new eschatological identity in Christ (identity mode C) is constantly to be defined in terms of the crucifixion of the old "I" (2:20). Actualized life is not possible without actualized death. The significance of the cross and the new creation (καινὴ κτίσις, v. 15) is thus in close correspondence, signified by γάρ in verse 15. The new creation is a "new system of reality" and a "new order," which is characterized by "a new relation to God."[664] The cross constitutes the *line of demarcation* between the old world and the new creation[665] (cf. Eph 2:15-16). In this new creation, whether one is circumcised or uncircumcised is of no significance (v. 15; cf. 3:28).

In verses 11-15, the distinction between the two ways of existence is clear. The existence in the old eon in flesh, defined by law and circumcision (identity mode A) is set in *discontinuity* with the new creation by the cross (the Christ event), which signifies the new existence in the eschatological era in Christ (identity mode C).

The "Israel of God" (v. 16)[666]

In verse 16, Paul concludes the contrasts portrayed in verses 12-15 (cross, new creation vs. flesh, circumcision, law) with wishing peace and mercy to "those who will follow this rule"[667] (ὅσοι τῷ κανόνι τούτῳ στοιχήσουσιν), followed by καὶ ἐπὶ τὸν Ἰσραὴλ τοῦ θεοῦ. "Those who will follow this rule" surely points to those who live by the standard[668] or principle[669] of the new

662. Hays, "Galatians," 344.
663. Bruce, *Galatians*, 273; cf. Fung, *Galatians*, 308.
664. Fung, *Galatians*, 308.
665. Fung, *Galatians*, 309.
666. A similar version of this section was published under the title "Reading Galatians 6:16 in Line with Paul's Contrast between the New Aeon in Christ and the Old Aeon before the Christ Event" *Stellenbosch Theological Journal* 2/2 (2016) 203-25.
667. NRSV.
668. BDAG, κανών, §1; Dunn, *Epistle to the Galatians*, 343.
669. L&N §33.335; Lategan, *Galasiërs*, 166; Bruce, *Galatians*, 273; ISV; GW; REB.

creation,⁶⁷⁰ which is the new way of existence in Christ⁶⁷¹ and in the Spirit.⁶⁷² In this blessing, the reference to "the Israel of God" has puzzled many a New Testament scholar. As most interpreters point out, the elements εἰρήνη and Ἰσραήλ in Paul's blessing show resemblance to εἰρήνη ἐπὶ τὸν Ἰσραήλ in the Septuagint of Psalm 124:5 (MT: 125:5) and 127:6 (MT: 128:6; cf. Pss. Sol. 4:25; 6:6; 8:27–28; 9:8; 11:9). A blessing that appears similar to that of Paul is contained in the *Shemoneh Esreh* (Birkat ha-Shalom, 19ᵗʰ benediction), which formed part of the liturgy of the Synagogue (Babylonian Recension): "Bestow peace, happiness and blessing, grace and loving-kindness and mercy upon us and upon all Israel, your people."⁶⁷³ None of these correspondences, however, necessarily contribute much to the interpretation of Galatians 6:16. Yet, even if they might contribute, their contribution is not without interpretation and the interpreter has to guard against working too inductively at the possible expense of giving adequate account of Paul's own thought. Additionaly, the *Shemoneh Esreh* probably originated at a date after Paul.⁶⁷⁴ The other question is whether one's interpretation of Romans 9 to 11 might have a dominating effect on one's interpretation of Galatians 6:16 (see p. 276). These concerns become especially pressing if the prevalent understandings of Galatians 6:16 are considered. These understandings can be categorized within two main views:

1. *Ecclesiological.* In this view, "the Israel of God" is understood as part of the church. Two variants of this view can be identified: (a) Some interpret the third καί in verse 16 (in καὶ ἐπὶ τὸν Ἰσραὴλ τοῦ θεοῦ) as epexegetic, translating "namely the Israel of God," "that is the Israel of God" or something similar.⁶⁷⁵ Hereby "the Israel of God" is identified with "those who will follow this rule" and thus understood as the community of all believers in Christ, including believing *Judeans and gentiles*.⁶⁷⁶ A close variant to this view is to interpret καί as "even," trans-

---

670. Cowan, "Context," 78; Martyn, *Galatians*, 566; Bruce, *Galatians*, 273; cf. Betz, *Galatians*, 321.

671. Lategan, *Galasiërs*, 116.

672. Hays, "Galatians," 345.

673. In Betz, *Galatians*, 321.

674. Das, *Galatians*, 645; cf. Witherington, *Grace*, 452.

675. Cf. NLT; GW; REB; RSV.

676. Cowan, "Context," 78–85; Zoccali, *Whom God Has Called*, 78–83; Witherington, *Grace*, 453; Hays, "Galatians," 690; Martyn, *Galatians*, 567, 574–77; Longenecker, *Galatians*, 298–99; Lategan, *Galasiërs*, 114, 116; Lightfoot, *Galatians*, 225; cf. Reumann, *Philippians*, 474–75; Wright, "Romans," 690; Richardson, *Introduction*, 159, 353–54; Barth, *Reconciliation*, 671. Reumann, Wright, Richardson and Barth do not discuss their views of καί in the cited works.

lating "even unto/upon/to the Israel of God" or similar,[677] resulting to the same overall interpretation.[678] Under those who share a similar view and yet take καί in its normal copulative sense are Dunn, Fung and Calvin.[679] (b) Betz translates καί as a copulative and understands "the Israel of God" as the *Judean* Christ-believers who approve of the rule of the new creation.[680] De Boer who also takes καί as a copulative and understands "the Israel of God" as pointing to Judean Christ-believers, qualifies them as remaining law-observant. He incorporates an anticipatory element (not necessarily eschatological) wherein mercy upon law-observant, Christ-believing Judeans ("the Israel of God"), "looks to their eventual conversion to Paul's understanding of the gospel and indicates that the anathema of 1:6–9 is not eternal."[681]

2. *Eschatological.* Burton suggested that the comma in verse 16 must be placed after αὐτοὺς καί, reading ἔλεος together with the latter part of the sentence, translating "peace be upon them, and mercy upon the Israel of God."[682] He interprets "the Israel of God" as "the remnant according to the election of grace," which is "yet unenlightened."[683] P. Richardson has adopted Burton's punctuation, and translates: "May God give peace to all who will walk according to this criterion, and mercy also to his faithful people Israel."[684] Richardson keeps "the Israel of God" separate from the church and connects it to historical Israel without extending it to Judaism. For Richardson, "the Israel of God" is "those who are still to believe."[685] This future perspective, he bases on the contention that the *Shemoneh Esreh* was taken over by Paul, but that he has given it an ironical twist: "where it has 'us' and 'them' (who are an extension of 'us'), Paul turns this into 'us' and 'them', where 'they' are people who should be connected with 'us' but *are not yet.*"[686] Similarly, Bruce, although translating καί as a normal copulative seems

---

677. Cf. AMP; NIV.

678. Hendriksen, *Galatians*, 246–47.

679. Dunn, *Epistle to the Galatians*, 344–45, Fung, *Galatians*, 309–11; Calvin, *Galatians*, 152–54.

680. Betz, *Galatians*, 312, 323; cf. Gutbrod, "Ἰσραήλ," *TDNT*, 3:387–88; Ellicott, *Galatians*, 154.

681. De Boer, *Galatians*, 407–10.

682. Burton, *Galatians*, 357; cf. ISV.

683. Burton, *Galatians*, 358.

684. Richardson, *Israel*, 84.

685. Richardson, *Israel*, 81–84.

686. Richardson, *Israel*, 81, emphasis added.

"ALL ISRAEL" AND "THE ISRAEL OF GOD"

to be inclined toward Richardson's view on the translation of καί.[687] Bruce keeps Israel separate from the church and understands "the Israel of God" within an eschatological framework, which he borrows from his understanding of πᾶς Ἰσραὴλ in Romans 11:26.[688]

In terms of the epexegetic (or explanatory) interpretation of καί (in καὶ ἐπὶ τὸν Ἰσραὴλ τοῦ θεοῦ), Ellicott was probably right that it is doubtful whether καί is ever used by Paul with such an "explicative force."[689] It could be asked if the epexegetic translation of καί is controlled by a prior interpretation rather than the text and context itself.[690] As seen from the variations in interpretation in the above views (1 and 2), none of the interpretations of καί are necessarily decisive. It thus seems safest to hold onto the normal copulative meaning of καί here.[691]

In terms of the ecclesiological interpretation (view 1), it is noteworthy that Israel is nowhere in the biblical literature unambiguously connected to believers in Christ as such (not even in Rom 9:6, see p. 51).[692] In Galatians Paul does qualify the identity of believers in Christ as "of God" (e.g., Gal 1:13; 2:20; 3:26). But these references to God are not without some form of a qualifier. In Galatians 1:13, Paul refers to the ἐκκλησία of God. The term ἐκκλησία can only be understood here as a designation for believers in Christ, even though he might have the "universal church" in mind. In the other two locations, "God" is used in close proximity to another qualifier: "Son of God" (2:20), and "of God through faith in Christ Jesus" (3:26). While the designations "sons of Abraham" (3:7) and "Abraham's seed" (3:29) apply to Christ-believers (cf. terms such as "holy," "elect," "beloved"), they are still far off from being "Israel,"[693] and rather indicate the *punctiliar continuity* of believers with historical Israel (Gal 3, see p. 86; cf. Rom 4) than *equivalence* with Israel. It is therefore unlikely that "the Israel of God" in 6:16 without any other qualifier would refer to current believers in Christ (view 1).

---

687. Bruce, *Galatians*, 267, 274-75.

688. Cf. Schreiner, *Galatians*, 381-83, 386; Johnson, "Paul," 53-54; George, *Galatians*, 439-40.

689. Ellicott, *Galatians*, 154.

690. Cf. Johnson "Paul," 42.

691. De Boer, *Galatians*, 406; George, *Galatians*, 440; Dunn, *Epistle to the Galatians*, 344-45; Fung, *Galatians*, 310; Bruce, *Galatians*, 267; Betz, *Galatians*, 312; ESV; NRSV; LITV; OAT; ASV; RV; DST; KJV; cf. Richardson, *Israel*, 81-84; Burton, *Galatians*, 357.

692. Cf. Johnson, "Paul," 49; Burton, *Galatians*, 358.

693. Contra Cowan, "Context," 80.

When Paul speaks of Israel, he neither construes an "Israel according to spirit" in contrast to an "Israel according to flesh" (not even in Gal 4:29, see note 259, p. 204), nor does he explicitly designate an "Israel of faith" as opposed to national Israel (although he does not necessarily exclude such a possibility). While Paul does not explicitly differentiate between an inner, true Israel and an outer, ethnic Israel in Galatians in the same way as in Romans 9:6–13, such a distinction is probably implied with Abraham as believer in God's promise (Gal 3:6) and Isaac as child of the promise who is free (4:22–23, 28), against those in slavery (4:22, 24, 25) who are according to the flesh (4:29). If Paul has inner, true Israel of history in mind with the qualifier "of God" (6:16), such a qualifier would make sense, for he would not qualify them as "Israel according to spirit," "Christ's Israel" or even "Israel of faith." In Paul, all of these qualifiers normally pertain to the new eschatological age in Christ and the Spirit. Conversely, if Paul had the church in mind with τὸν Ἰσραὴλ τοῦ θεοῦ, the qualification "of God" seems somewhat out of step with the kind of language he implemented in defining the believers in Christ throughout Galatians, e.g., through/of faith (2:16; 3:2, 7, 14, 26; 5:5; 6:10), of/though/in/from the Spirit/spirit (3:14; 5:5, 16, 18, 25; 6:8), and in/with Christ (2:4, 16, 17, 20; 3:14, 17, 22, 26, 27, 28; 5:6; 6:15). Given these constraints it is thus more likely that the qualifier "of God" refers to historical Israel.

As for the eschatological view (view 2), it has to be considered that the term Ἰσραήλ is used only here in Galatians. Nothing within the context of Galatians gives an indication that Israel here has to be understood in terms of eschatology. Paul rather alludes to historical Israel in that he mentioned Abraham's faith (3:6), the gospel that was preached to Abraham (3:8), those who were kept under the guardianship of the law (3:23), being enslaved to the basic principles of this world while awaiting the fullness of time (4:3–4), and to Abraham's sons (4:22–23). In the rest of the Pauline corpus, where Ἰσραήλ is used in close proximity to θεός, the context is historical. In Romans 9:6–13, Israel is defined around Isaac, Sarah, Rebecca and Jacob, indicating the true, inner historical Israel in distinction from those "of Israel" (9:6), which is national historical Israel (see p. 51). In Romans 11:2, it is about Elijah's pleading against historical Israel, followed by the historical account from 1 Kings 19 of how God has left a remnant in history (11:3–4, see pp. 262–67). Despite its disputed status, Ephesians 2:12 indirectly seems to be the closest match to Galatians 6:16 in that the gentile's former status in the old eon in the flesh (Eph 2:11) is portrayed as *without God* while being alienated from *the citizenship of Israel* (v. 12).

As discussed, Galatians 6:16 is set against the same backdrop of the contrast between the old eon in the flesh (wherein historical Israel lived) as opposed to the new eon constituted by the new creation (vv. 8, 12–15). This contrast between the two ages is especially evident in the inauguration of faith and the Spirit (2:16; 3:2–3, 8–9, 13–14),[694] the opposition of faith and the Spirit to the "works of the law" (2:16; 3:2, 5, 10) and the curse of the law (3:13), Christ being the seed of Abraham that would "come" (3:16, 19), and lastly, faith itself that "came" (3:23) or "has come" (3:25). The eon of faith and the eon "under die law" (3:23) are thus contrasted as two distinct salvation-historical eons and ways of existence on either side of the Christ event.[695] According to chapter 4, Christ is pictured as being born "under the law" at the "fullness of time" that those "under the law" might be redeemed and obtain adoption unto childhood (litt. "sonship") by the Spirit who works in the hearts of people (vv. 4–5). The coming of Christ thus constitutes a new way of existence and mode of identity. As argued, the allegorical image of the free and slave woman (4:21–5:1) can be understood as a contrast between the Old and New Covenants,[696] implying two exclusive ways of existence.[697] The Jerusalem above, representing the eschatological people of God in the new (present) eon in Christ is contrasted to the present Jerusalem of the old age, the age of slavery (4:25–26). This latter contrast ends up being the key opposition in Galatians 4.[698] Yet these two exclusive, "eschatological" ways of existence is also evident in Galatians 5:16–25 and 6:8 where the contrast between "S/spirit" and "flesh" is ultimately absolute, representing two exclusive eschatological eons and ways of existence: the one before or outside of Christ and the other one in Christ wherein the eschatological Spirit has already come. Such a view seems certain from the context where life "in the flesh" is described in terms of a former way of life (5:19–21a) whose eschatological end is that they will "not inherit the kingdom of God," and from 5:24 that pictures the life of the believer such as having "crucified the flesh with its passions and desires." Similarly, in 6:8 the end result of sowing in the spirit is eternal life whereas the end result of sowing in the flesh is corruption. Christ and the Spirit thus mark the turning of the ages; and therefore "life in keeping with the flesh" and "life by the Spirit" are mutually incompatible options.[699]

---

694. Cf. Wright, *Climax*, 157–74.

695. De Boer, *Galatians*, 239; Martyn, *Galatians*, 323; Fee, *Empowering Presence*, 385; Fung, *Galatians*, 167–70; cf. Moo, *Galatians*, 22, 240–44; Schreiner, *Galatians*; Lategan, *Galasiërs*, 71; Betz, *Galatians*, 175–76.

696. E.g., Fee, *Empowering Presence*, 413, 416; George, *Galatians*, 340.

697. Meyer, *Law*, 129, 136–37.

698. De Boer, *Galatians*, 301.

699. Fee, *Empowering Presence*, 431, 438; cf. De Boer, *Galatians*, 354.

While 6:7–16 summarizes and concludes the above mentioned contrasts in the letter, those following "this rule" (the new creation) in 6:16a could thus naturally point to those in the new, eschatological eon, while "the Israel of God" in 6:16b could naturally point to historical Israel that lived in the old eon before the Christ event. Up to this point, Paul has pictured the new eon and the new covenant in sharp *discontinuity* with the former age. The only *continuity* that God's people now have with the old eon is punctiliar, by faith in the Seed of Abraham, which is Christ.[700] Paul, therefore, might have left the impression that the new eon in Christ has completely nullified the former eon wherein Israel lived.[701] In contrast to the first half of verse 16, one could therefore expect a last minute measure of balance that pertains to the old eon in the words καὶ ἐπὶ τὸν Ἰσραὴλ τοῦ θεοῦ.[702]

Against the ecclesiological interpretation (view 1) it can additionally be argued that an identification of the church with Israel (e.g., as "Israel of God") to characterize the church is absent until 160 CE in the early church.[703] Yet when it appears in Justin's *Dialogue with Trypho*, Justin renders it as "the true spiritual Israel" (11.5; cf. 100.4; 123.9),[704] which is still somewhat removed from viewing the church as "the Israel of God." This is partly the reason why Campbell writes that

> there is no clear or explicit evidence prior to Romans 9–11 that suggests either an identification of the church with "the New Israel" nor of a theory of displacement of the "old Israel" by the new. *Only historical Israel* can properly claim the title "Israel of God."[705]

But if Romans 11:26 is to be understood as the salvation of historical Israel, as argued, and if one has to transfer the meaning of Romans 11:26 to Galatians 6:16, it would make both the ecclesiological and eschatological interpretations of "the Israel of God" in Galatians 6:16 even more unlikely.

---

700. The way in which Paul describes the continuity and discontinuity in Galatians thus argues against viewing Paul as belonging to "two communities" such as the new Christ-believing community and the people of Israel (Tomson, "Names," 285).

701. Cf. Martyn, *Galatians*, 350.

702. Cf. Richardson, *Israel*, 82–83, who has a similar idea (even though he understands Israel eschatologically) when he writes that "from the way Paul has argued previously in the letter, one might infer that he was condemning everything about Israel. To forestall this inference he includes this prayer to God for mercy to be shown to Israel."

703. Campbell, "Israel," 441; Richardson, *Israel*, 12, 83.

704. In Mayer, "Israel," *NIDNTT*, 2:316.

705. Campbell, "Israel," 442, emphasis added. Although Horsley, *1 Corinthians*, 141, does not elaborate, he mentions in passing in his commentary on 1 Corinthians that "the Israel of God" in Gal 6:16 refers to "historical Israel."

In conclusion, the understanding of "the Israel of God" in Galatians 6:16 that seems to fit best within the constraints discussed, is that it denotes the *inner, elect Israel of the old eon before Christ*. In this way, the sentence would be in perfect balance, blessing all of God's elect people in both the eon *after* the Christ event (καὶ ὅσοι τῷ κανόνι τούτῳ στοιχήσουσιν) and the eon *before* the Christ event (καὶ ἐπὶ τὸν Ἰσραὴλ τοῦ θεοῦ). This interpretation implies that the blessing spans God's people over both salvation-historical eons: ancient Israel (old) and believers in Christ (new). This understanding probably best accounts for Paul's "out of the blue"[706] reference to "the Israel of God" over against approaches to this expression that either need to borrow from prevalent interpretations of Romans 9–11 (eschatological) or have to speculate about the exact (ecclesiological) entity that is involved.[707]

The above reading does not only account for Paul's juxtaposition of the old eon in the "flesh" under law with the new eon in Christ and the Spirit in Galatians, but it also accounts for Paul's view of identity in Christ beyond Galatians, where external, observable markers of identity such as ethnicity, circumcision or law observance are not constitutive of the deeper, controlling criteria for identity of God's people any longer. Christ and the Spirit constitute the new controlling criteria for identity in the new eon and render all external markers of identity in terms of demarcating God's people obsolete. This does not mean that ethnic identities in Christ are necessarily eradicated as such, but these are not constitutive in demarcating God's people in the new eon any longer (esp. 3:28–29). The idea that ancient Israel's messianic hope has been fulfilled in Christ, although renewed and redrawn,[708] strengthens the notion that Israel as God's people has been fulfilled and completed in Christ in whom a new people came into existence on the basis of new criteria for being God's people.

---

706. De Boer, *Galatians*, 407.

707. Even De Boer, *Galatians*, 407–10, who otherwise resists both a full-blown ecclesiological view and an explicit eschatological view, anticipates in Gal 6:16 Paul's "same line of thought to Israel" as in Romans 9–11, a methodology that he commendably challenges elsewhere (2; see Wright, *Faithfulness*, 2:1149).

708. Wright, *Faithfulness*, 2:1061–78; idem., "Romans," 691; idem., *People of God*, 406–7.

7

Conclusions and Implications

AFTER PURSUING PAUL'S THOUGHT on the identity of Israel, Judeans and Christ-believers throughout the Pauline corpus, the ultimate conclusion of this book is that the salvation of "all Israel" in Romans 11:25-27 involves the salvation of inner, elect, historical Israel that lived before the Christ event, who are saved in addition to those from Israel who remained and believed in Christ at the time of the first Christ advent (9:27; 11:3-7). This inner Israel is saved in spite of their hardening (disobedience and stubbornness throughout history), which culminated in the advent of their and every one else's Messiah (see pp. 309-14).

In the interpretation of Romans 11:25-27, σωθήσεται (11:26) is understood as a logical future that lies future of the prophecy (11:26b-27) but is realised in the first Christ advent. Similarly, the conclusion was reached that the "Israel of God" in Galatians 6:16 pertains to the same elect, historical Israel (see pp. 338-45). This interpretation seems to be compatible with other traditions in the New Testament (Matt 27:51-53; Eph 4:9; 1 Pet 3:19-20; 4:6) and the Church Fathers (esp. Justin Martyr; Irenaeus; Tertullian) of which the Jeremiah-logion, pointing to God that remembered his people that already died and saved them, resembles this interpretation in particular.

The conclusion on Romans 11:25-27 was reached after evaluating several areas within six of the main interpretative theories on this passage (eschatological miracle, ecclesiological, two houses of Israel, total national elect, two-covenant, Roman mission). This evaluation mainly pertains to the following: (1) The future eschatological nature of most of these interpretations (except that of Nanos)[1] have been problematized in terms of the anachronism among the identities of Israel (ancient), Judeans (in Paul's present) and Judaism (modern). (2) Nanos' interpretation has been argued to be contrary to Paul's view on the law with respect to identity, and as im-

---

1. Nanos, *Mystery*.

plausible in terms of an alleged anomaly in Rome. (3) Paul's use of specific terms in Romans 11:25–27 (e.g., μυστήριον, εἰσέρχομαι, πλήρωμα, ῥύομαι) were compared to their use elsewhere by Paul, rather than inferring their meaning (inductively) from external sources (e.g., Jewish apocalyptic). (4) Similarly, Paul's language (e.g., ὥσπερ . . . οὕτως + fut. ind., in Rom 5:19 and 11:26) and especially his use of the future tense of σωθήσεται was reassessed in terms of the use of the future tense elsewhere in the Pauline corpus. This was done in conjunction with how Paul portrays concepts such as salvation (σῴζω), righteousness (δικαιόω) and reconciliation (καταλλάσσω) elsewhere, especially with respect to their realization. (5) The interpretation of Romans 11:25–27 was tested against the context of Romans as well as the rest of the Pauline corpus (as concluded from the exegetical study), but especially in the subsequent verses (Rom 11:28–32). (6) The balance that the historical interpretation of Israel's salvation achieves in Romans 11:28–32 with respect to the old salvation-historical eon before the Christ event and the new eschatological age thereafter, constituting a fulfillment of Israel's salvation history, has been determined as the interpretation that fits these verses best.[2] This fulfillment is understood as surpassing prevalent messianic expectations and fulfilling Israel's hope in a different way than most expected, including their hope for national liberation and material inheritance of land.

While the differences between my view and the "two covenant" view or the view of Nanos is quite evident, my view has to be distinguished from the "national elect" view, which sees "Israel" as including today's Jews who come to faith, a reading that does not see the Christ-event as the fulfillment and completion of Israel as a people. While my view coheres on many points with the ecclesiological view in terms of the fulfillment of historical Israel in Christ,[3] it does not see believers in Christ as a redefined "Israel." My view differs from the majority "eschatological miracle" view in that it does not read the salvation of "all Israel" in a futuristic way, but rather *christologically*—as being already fulfilled and completed in Christ's death and resurrection.

Finally, it could be asked what the criteria would be for God's salvation of inner-elect, historical Israel. According to the language in Rom 11:26b–27 they are passive in their deliverance. Since their deliverance could not be on the basis of faith in Christ, for they lived before Christ's coming in the flesh, and since Paul in Romans defines faith as believing in Christ, their

---

2. Cf. the more detailed summary of specific arguments whereupon this conclusion is based on pp. 312–13.

3. Cf. the view of Staples, "Gentiles."

deliverance has to be based on God's mercy (cf. 9:11, 15–16, 18, 22–23; 11:28), which stands in balance with the mercy God has shown to all people in the gospel era (11:30–32). This does not necessarily mean that those of historical Israel who are saved did not trust God at all, never loved Him at all, or never obeyed Him, but that is not the focus of Paul's discourse. His focus is rather on God's mercy in spite of their hardening, which arguably contributes to the mystery (11:25).

In accordance with the interpretation of Romans 11:25–27 that is presented here, the conclusion on the meaning of "the Israel of God" in Galatians 6:16 was reached after an evaluation of the use of the third καί in this verse, Paul's use of the qualification "of God" in Galatians and other passages in the Pauline corpus where "God" is used in close proximity with "Israel," and the logical contrast of the salvation-historical eon before and after the Christ event throughout Galatians. The conclusion that "the Israel of God" denotes elect Israel of history has been argued as the best fit within the given constraints.

Israel, Judeans, and Identity

If the conclusions reached about the salvation of "all Israel" (Rom 11:26), "the Israel of God" (Gal 6:16) and Paul's use of the term Ἰσραήλ through the course of Romans 9 to 11 are correct, Paul does not seem to use the term Ἰσραήλ in denoting descendants of the patriarchs or God's people in his *present or future* but only in his *past*. The way in which Paul uses the term Ἰσραηλίτης shows somewhat more diachronic fluidity in that he uses it as a self-designation (Rom 11:1; 2 Cor 11:22).[4] It has to be noted, however, that in both Romans 11:1 and 2 Corinthians 11:22, the term rather denotes Paul's line of descent than his present identity. Together with the term's use in Romans 9:4, Paul's overall intention with the term Ἰσραηλίτης thus leans more toward the historical side. Paul's use of Ἰσραήλ and Ἰσραηλίτης therefore lies close to the prevalent use of the terms in his time. The implication of this understanding is that Paul's use of the designation Ἰσραήλ neither *transcended* the limits of Judean speech nor implies that Paul invited gentiles in his present to call the Judeans "Israel," contrary to what Tomson argued.[5] As pointed out (see pp. 31–39), the terms Ἰσραήλ and Ἰσραηλίτης mostly denoted the people of the pre-exilic period and was thus used as a designation for ancient Israel (e.g., early church

---

4. Cf. Paul's reference to being of the nation of Israel (ἐκ γένους Ἰσραήλ) in Phil 3:5.

5. Tomson, "Names," 287–88.

and Josephus) and was not applied as a self-designation for Christians until 160 CE (Justin), even though the letter was done in a qualified sense ("the true spiritual Israel"). These terms were thus mostly reserved for a part of history that was closed. Conversely, Paul never employs the term Ἰουδαῖος as a *historical* designation for the descendants of the patriarchs or the people of God. In this regard, his use of the term also corresponds to the prevalent use of his time in mostly denoting the people of the second temple. These conclusions about Paul's use of these terms (Ἰσραήλ/ Ἰουδαῖος) are however not intended as a rigid scheme, but rather as pointing out the tendencies in Paul's use of them.

In terms of identity, Paul's use of Ἰουδαῖος for the most part denotes ethnic identity, which is an identity pertaining mostly to shared biological origins or nationality. As discussed (see pp. 54–68), the only possible exception to this tendency, Romans 2:17–29, is rather to be understood as part of Paul's rhetoric, where he uses the original meaning of the term Ἰουδαῖος against their identity claim. The notion is that these Ἰουδαῖοι would have to comply with the whole law in order to live up to their claim. In this interpretation Paul would try to show them that if they really wanted to be "true Judeans" whose "praise" is from God, they would have been "circumcised in heart," meaning that they would be capable of fulfilling the whole law. A Judean who is "circumcised in heart" in terms of its true meaning, therefore, never becomes an actual designation for identity, but is rather part of Paul's rhetoric to sketch an *ideal* Judean, which he goes on to demonstrate in 3:1–20 as impossible. The aim of his rhetoric is thus to realize the dilemma inherent to Judean identity apart from Christ and eventually win them over to accept Christ. The fact that Paul uses the term Ἰουδαῖος together with belief in Christ (esp. Rom 1:16; 10:11–12; cf. Gal 3:28; 1 Cor 12:13; Col 3:11) underscores the notion that Ἰουδαῖος is largely an ethnic identity for Paul, which is identity mode A (see pp. 27–30).

Yet, being a Ἰουδαῖος is not a disadvantage as such for Paul, but rather an advantage in that God's words are entrusted to them (Rom 3:2). Although Paul attaches some form of priority to the Ἰουδαῖος, this priority is rather in terms of responsibility toward the gospel (Rom 1:16; 2:10) and even judgment (Rom 2:9), for in terms of their status before God, there is no difference over other nations before God with respect to sin (Rom 3:9), their claim on God (Rom 3:29; 9:24) or their position in Christ (Rom 10:12; 1 Cor 1:24; 12:13; Gal 3:28; cf. Col 3:11).

While the term Ἰσραηλίτης denotes external identity with respect to ethnicity or being part of national Israel (Rom 9:4; 11:1; 2 Cor 11:22; identity mode A), Paul uses the term Ἰσραήλ in connection with both a national, ethnic identity according to "flesh" (Rom 9:6; 1 Cor 10:18; 2 Cor 3:7, 13; Phil

3:5; cf. Eph 2:12; identity mode A—even though it denotes the patriarch Israel in Rom 9:6 and Phil 3:5 specifically), and historical Israel of inner election (Rom 9:6, 27, 31; 10:19, 21; 11:2, 7, 25, 26; Gal 6:16; identity mode AB; see pp. 27–30).

The Identity in Christ and the Spirit as Fulfilling the Identity According to the Flesh

As discussed on pp. 45–54, the hardening of Israel inevitably culminated in the coming of their Messiah, who became both the foundation stone onto belief in Christ for the remnant and Israel's Stumbling Stone by which they were cut off from being God's people (Rom 9:33; 11:17–21). Their cutting off coincided with the generic "coming in" of the nations (cf. Rom 11:25), constituting a crossover in salvation history. However, Israel's sins were forgiven by Christ their Deliverer in his salvific work in death and resurrection and their cutting off was reversed. In this they followed the same pattern of death and resurrection as believers in Christ. This historical Israel of promise and inner election were regrafted into their original position as God's children into a new, transformed identity in Christ (Rom 11:25–27). The implication is that Christ's work was effective for Paul's present, past (retrojective) and future (projective). The crossover in salvation history and both the projective and retrojective significance of Christ's salvific work can be illustrated by the grey, dotted arrows in the following, completed diagram:[6]

---

6. See the earlier stage of the same diagram for explanation on. p. 250.

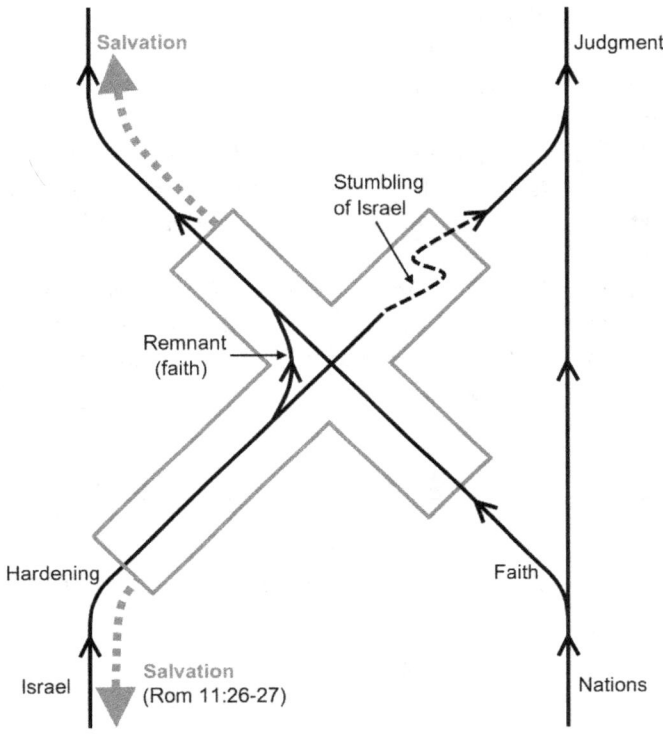

Christ as Israel's Messiah and as culmination of Israel's salvation history represents the punctiliar point of *continuity* of Christ-believers with historical Israel. The identity in Christ (identity mode C, see pp. 27–30) therefore fulfills what the external identity marked off by law and circumcision could not accomplish. Paul describes the latter identity as in- or according to "flesh" (identity mode A). The way in which the new identity accomplishes that which the old identity in flesh could not achieve, is by the empowering work of the Spirit in the life of the believer (esp. Rom 8:2). In Paul, the Spirit in unity with the human spirit (Rom 8:16; cf. Gal 3:2–5) and faith (Rom 4; Gal 3) are the markers of identity in the new eschatological eon. Paul describes the way of existence in Christ as in- or according to "spirit" (identity mode C, relating to both God's Spirit and the human spirit), which stands in *discontinuity* with the way of existence in the old eon before or outside of Christ in "flesh." In its extended meaning, both "flesh" and "spirit" can thus be understood as mutually incompatible eschatological realities, each representing a distinct mode of identity (esp. Rom 7:5–6; 8:1–16, see pp. 189–206). These eschatological realities correspond to the Old Covenant and the New Covenant respectively (2 Cor 3:5–16).

The implication of the cutting off and regrafting of inner, elect, historical Israel in Christ is that their identity has been transformed from identity mode AB, where a flesh-identity was co-constitutive of their identity as God's people, to identity mode C, which is solely defined by the work of Christ. The identity in flesh has therefore been redeemed and overcame in Christ's work. The Christ-event is therefore to be understood as eschatological in inaugurating the new creation, which will be fully completed at the parousia.

People sharing in the various modes of identity spanning both eons before and after the Christ event can be illustrated by the diagram that will follow shortly. The dotted line represents the line of demarcation between the old eon before Christ and the new creation in Christ (cf. Gal 6:11–15; 2 Cor 5:14–21; Eph 2:8–22):[7]

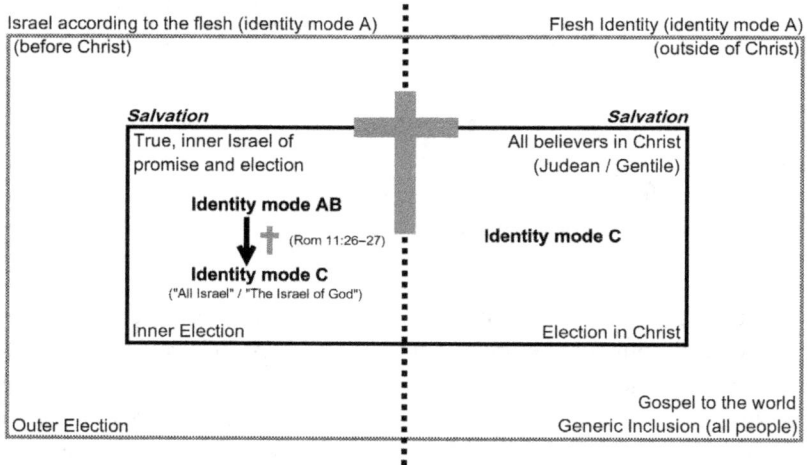

As portrayed in the above diagram, Christ represents the point of convergence among all modes of identity. Christ shared in the identity in flesh in that he was "Christ according to the flesh" (Rom 9:5): he was a physical descendant within the line of descent of the patriarch Israel. He was circumcised, born "under the law" (Gal 4:4), to redeem those under the law in order to adopt them as children (Gal 4:5). In Christ's work, therefore, the old identity (identity mode AB) is transformed into a new identity (identity mode C). In retrospect of Christ's saving work, inner, elect, historical Israel and Christ-believers stand in completed continuity through Christ.

As anticipated on pp. 262–67, in view of an eschatological understanding of identity (the change of eons), the titles "Israel" and "Judean"

7. Cf. the diagram of an earlier phase of identity in the old eon on p. 53.

can be understood as mostly representing distinct identities on either side of salvation history in Paul: *before* the Christ event ("Israel") and *after* the Christ event ("Judean"). Within this distinction, the term "Israel" is mostly used in connection with the historical *people of God*, while "Judean" is mostly applied in the context of an *ethnic identity* apart from being God's people in Paul's present.

Universal and Particular

As argued throughout the book, in Pauline terms Christ's work bears profound universal and cosmological significance (e.g., Rom 1:16–17; 10:9–13; 15:5–13; 1 Cor 1:21–24; 2 Cor 5:14–21; cf. Col 3:9–15). But as 2 Corinthians 5:14–21 shows (cf. Col 3:9–15), the new creation bears equally prominent individual significance, which is more than forensic but also has ontological implications. It is worthy of note, however, that Paul never eradicates the ethnic Judean identity as such, even though he might describe his former privileges and accomplishments as garbage (Phil 3:8). But since he does not view ethnic or cultural identity as constitutive in defining the identity in Christ, he relativizes all ethnic identities in Christ (Gal 3:28; 1 Cor 12:13; cf. Col 3:11). These ethnic identities are still acknowledged but insignificant in terms of marking off the people of God. More specifically, while the identity defined by the "works of the law" and circumcision were replaced by an identity defined by faith and spirit, Paul provides lenience in terms of sabbaths, dietary laws and feasts (e.g., Rom 14:1–15; cf. Col 2:16). These "externals" are, however, relativized in terms of the work of the Spirit (Rom 14:17) and thus considered superfluous with respect to defining identity as God's people in the new eon in Christ. While the identity in Christ can be understood as a "third entity" (cf. 1 Cor 10:32; Eph 2:14–16), it is defined on another level than ethnic identities (e.g., Judean/Greek) and thus does not so much replace them as exceed them and include them.

Ethnic identity is thus understood as a "flesh" *aspect* of identity that is subordinate to and relative to an over-arching "spiritual" *aspect* of identity, which is the identity in Christ. The latter understanding argues against RNPP approaches to identity. While it can be admitted that the concept of ethnicity could contain elements that are being constructed rather than being a predefined essence, ethnicity is not seen as the controlling category for identity in Paul. In other words, filiation to God or being God's people by faith and the Spirit is understood as the over-arching and controlling characteristic of identity and of being in Christ. The new identity in Christ in the Spirit is thus understood as the eschatological fulfillment of salvation history. This fulfillment is part of Christ's completed work in and through human beings and thus something that is *inherited* in Christ rather than something that is *negotiated*. That does not mean, however, that a process of the negotiation of aspects of identity is not acknowledged in the early church, but such a process was arguably more a process of *aligning* one's social identity to what is received in Christ than *negotiating* the whole concept of being in Christ.[8]

In respect of the main thesis of this book, it is particularly significant that the identity of historical Israel is not replaced by a "new Israel" or even a "redefined Israel." In Pauline terms, the old identity of Israel was rather terminated and completed in Christ. Christ, therefore, represents the point of continuity of the Christ-believers with Israel. But this continuity is more aptly described as "historical heritage in Christ" than "cultural indebtedness," contra Campbell.[9] Paul did thus not provide a basis for religious pluralism within the identity of the Christ-believer, but rather for relativizing culture within the identity in Christ. It has to be noted though, that in Paul things such as circumcision, dietary laws, and Sabbath observance are rather treated as being part of the old *covenant* than being mere *cultural* symbols.

Implications for Pauline Theology

The most profound implication of the conclusions reached about the identity of Israel for Pauline theology is probably that it has a *unifying effect* on Pauline theology as a whole. Rather than interpolating elements from later Jewish apocalyptic into the understanding of Romans 11:25–27 and Galatians 6:16, the interpretation of Israel's identity in these passages was inferred from examining Paul's own thought and language in the context of the respective letters (Rom and Gal) and the rest of his letters. The tendency was to argue from the more certain to the more obscure rather than the other way round. In addition, this approach results in a larger appreciation of the coherency in Paul's thought on identity across the Pauline corpus, especially between Romans and Galatians. A side-effect of this approach is that it contributes in reassessing some of the arguments about Pauline authorship with respect to Colossians and Ephesians.

The other aspect in Pauline theology that this study highlights is the interrelatedness of Pauline terms and concepts around identity, especially Paul's understanding of eschatology and how "flesh" and "spirit" (in their

8. See esp. Lim, "New Creation."
9. Campbell, *Paul*, 96–103.

extended application) fit into this understanding. The realized aspect of Paul's eschatology as expressed in "flesh" and "spirit" closely interrelates with the modes of identity that Paul perceives: "flesh" in its extended meaning corresponds mostly to ethnic identity, law, works and sin, while "spirit" in the eschatological sense mostly corresponds to and identity defined by the Spirit, deliverance, faith, and grace. One of the implications of this particular understanding of "flesh" and "spirit" is that when Paul uses πνεῦμα in terms of a *mode of existence* (esp. Rom 7:6; 8:4, 5, 9a; Gal 5:16, 25), he neither has the human spirit nor God's Spirit *per se* in mind. Where πνεῦμα can be understood as a *mode of existence*, it should relieve much of the difficulty in translating πνεῦμα, especially for those who seek to translate πνεῦμα either in terms of the human spirit or God's Spirit.[10]

Some of the specific areas in Pauline theology where this study provides other perspectives are the areas of realized eschatology,[11] Paul's use of the logical future, his use of Old Testament Scripture, and most importantly, the understanding of Christ's salvific work. The latter aspect provides not only for a more profound Christology, but for a deeper *diachronic* understanding of Christ's work in terms of having an effect on the present, past (retrojective) and future (projective). This approach in turn provides a possible key for reinterpreting passages about Christ's work in general. One such example is arguably Romans 5:17-19. The "free gift of righteousness" (v. 17), the "act of righteousness" (v. 18) and the "many who will be made righteous" (logical future, v. 19) might be understood as including ancient Israel. If understood in this way, the correspondence between Romans 11:25-27 and Romans 5:17-19 would be more than grammatical (see pp. 295-302), but theological as well (as anticipated on pp. 186-87).

Another side-effect of the retrojective interpretation of Christ's work is that it relieves the charges of double predestination that is often laid against Romans 9 (e.g., on 9:13, 22).[12] The hardening of elect Israel that resulted in their cutting off and their regrafting in Christ can be understood as God's overarching salvific plan for His elect people Israel. Their cutting off was thus not an end in itself, but a necessary step in the salvation-historical change of identity in Christ wherein identity according to flesh (even in part) has been cut off. Although all unbelieving people remaining after the Christ event have been cut off as a result of the change of the criteria of identity in Christ,

10. E.g., Du Toit, "Translating Romans," 590-95. In this understanding, to translate πνεῦμα in passages such as Rom 7:6; 8:4, 5, 9a; and Gal 5:16, 25, as *either* the human spirit *or* God's Spirit *per se*, can be understood as a category mistake.

11. Wright, "Romans," 692, is probably correct that scholars too often embrace an under-realized eschatology rather than an over-realized one.

12. E.g., Schreiner, *Romans*, 501, 522; Käsemann, *Romans*, 265, 272.

they cannot be connected to individual predestination, for they continue to have the option to believe in Christ and thereby be regrafted.

In terms of the NPP versus TAP debate, aspects of both approaches were appreciated and combined in this study. While the notions of Judean exclusivity and of marking off identity by ethnicity, law and circumcision are acknowledged (NPP), an element of merit inherent to the keeping of the law is also acknowledged, which in turn is understood as contributing to final justification (TAP). Paul argued against all of these (NPP and TAP), picturing the new, eschatological identity in Christ and the Spirit as accomplishing justification/righteousness in a way that was impossible within an existence before or outside Christ, including the identity of Israel or the Judeans.

Paul and Christianity

In sensitivity to current distinctions of identity in Pauline theology, I have employed the term "Christ-believers" or similar in reference to the identity in Christ in this book unless where I quoted others. While the discontinuity between the Judean identity and Judaism seems relatively assured, it is another matter whether the same principles should apply with respect to believers in Christ in Paul's present and Christianity. As for the institutional character of Christianity throughout history, one could indeed argue for greater discontinuity between Christ-believers in Paul and Christianity. But if "Christianity" is to be defined more in terms of a personal relationship between the believer and God as defined by the eschatological way of existence in spirit, and not so much as a "world religion," the discontinuity between Paul and Christianity is diminished. With respect to this debate, I would rather argue for a redefinition of current Christianity that is more in line with Paul's original thought. My intention is that this redefinition should involve more of a *practical realignment* in line with Paul's definitions than a re-evaluation of the current or historical data about the worldwide phenomenon of Christianity. In other words, I would argue that the problem is at heart that "Christianity" *ought to* be defined and lived out more as a *way of life* in the Spirit (in Pauline terms) than as a "religion."

Bibliography

Abasciano, Brian J. "Paul's Use of the Old Testament in Romans 9:1–9: An Intertextual and Theological Exegesis." PhD diss., University of Aberdeen, 2004.
Abbott, T. K. *A Critical and Exegetical Commentary on the Epistles to the Ephesians and to the Colossians*. ICC. New York: Schribner's, 1897.
Abbott-Smith, G. *A Manual Greek Lexicon of the New Testament*. London: T. & T. Clark, 1923.
Achtemeier, Paul J. *1 Peter*. Hermeneia. Minneapolis: Fortress, 1996.
Albright, W. F., and C. S. Mann. *Matthew*. AB. New York: Doubleday, 1971.
Arnold, Clinton E. *Ephesians*. ZECNT. Grand Rapids: Zondervan, 2010.
Aune, David E. *Apocalypticism, Prophecy and Magic in Early Christianity*. Tübingen: Mohr Siebeck, 2006.
———. *Revelation 1–5*. WBC. Dallas: Word, 1997.
Aus, Roger D. "Paul's Travel Plans to Spain and the 'Full Number of the Gentiles' of Rom. XI 25." *NovT* 21/3 (1979) 232–62.
Barclay, John M. G. *Obeying the Truth: Paul's Ethics in Galatians*. Minneapolis: Fortress, 1991.
Barnett, Paul. *The Second Epistle to the Corinthians*. NICNT. Grand Rapids: Eerdmans, 1997.
Barr, James. *The Semantics of Biblical Language*. Oxford: Oxford University Press, 1961.
Barrett, C. K. *A Commentary on the Epistle to the Romans*. BNTC. London: Adam & Charles Black, 1962.
———. *A Commentary on the First Epistle to the Corinthians*. BNTC. London: Adam & Charles Black, 1971.
———. *A Commentary on the Second Epistle to the Corinthians*. BNTC. London: Adam & Charles Black, 1973.
———. *From First Adam to Last: A Study in Pauline Theology*. New York: Scribner's, 1962.
Barth, Fredrik, ed. *Ethnic Groups and Boundaries: The Social Organization of Cultural Difference*. London: Allen & Unwin, 1969.
Barth, Karl. *The Doctrine of Reconciliation*. Translated by G. W. Bromiley. Church Dogmatics 4.1. New York: Scribner's, 1956.
———. *The Epistle to the Romans*. Translated by E. C. Hoskyns. Oxford: Oxford University Press, 1968.
Barth, Markus. *Ephesians: Introduction, Translation, and Commentary on Chapters 1–3*. AB. New York: Doubleday, 1974.

———. *Israel and the Church*. Richmond: John Knox, 1969.
Barth, Markus, and Helmut Blanke. *Colossians*. AB. New York: Doubleday, 1994.
Bassler, Jouette M. *Navigating Paul: An Introduction to Key Theological Concepts*. Louisville: Westminster John Knox, 2007.
Bauckham, Richard J. "Descent to the Underworld." *ABD* 2:145–59.
Beale, G. K. *1–2 Thessalonians*. IVPNTC. Leicester: InterVarsity, 2003.
Beare, Francis W. *A Commentary on the Epistle to the Philippians*. BNTC. New York: Harper, 1959.
Beasley-Murray, G. R. *Baptism in the New Testament*. Exeter: Paternoster, 1972.
Beet, Joseph A. *A Commentary on St. Paul's Epistle to the Romans*. 5th ed. New York: Thomas Whittaker, 1885.
Beker, J. Christiaan. *Paul the Apostle: The Triumph of God in Life and Thought*. Philadelphia: Fortress, 1980.
———. *The Triumph of God: The Essence of Paul's Thought*. Minneapolis: Fortress, 1990.
Bell, Richard H. "The Myth of Adam and the Myth of Christ in Romans 5.12–21." In *Paul, Luke and the Graeco-Roman World: Essays in Honour of Alexander J. M. Wedderburn*, edited by Carsten Claussen et al., 21–36. JSNTSup 217. Sheffield: Sheffield Academic Press, 2002.
———. *Provoked to Jealousy: The Origin and Purpose of the Jealousy Motif in Romans 9–11*. Tubingen: J. C. B. Mohr, 1994.
Belleville, Linda. *1 Timothy*. CBC. Carol Stream, IL: Tyndale, 2009.
Bernard, J. H. "The Second Epistle to the Corinthians." *EGT* 3:1–119.
Best, Ernest. *The First and Second Epistles to the Thessalonians*. BNTC. London: Adam & Charles Black, 1972.
———. *One Body in Christ: A Study in the Relationship of the Church to Christ in the Epistles of the Apostle Paul*. London: SPCK, 1955.
Betz, Hans D. *Galatians: A Commentary on Paul's Letter to the Churches in Galatia*. Hermeneia. Philadelphia: Fortress, 1979.
Betz, Otto. "ἰουδαΐζω." *EDNT* 2:192.
Black, Allen. *1 Peter*. CPNIVC. Joplin, MO: College Press, 1999.
Black, David A. *Learn to Read New Testament Greek*. 3rd ed. Nashville: B&H, 2009.
Blass, Friedrich. *Grammar of New Testament Greek*. Translated by Henry St. John Thackeray. New York: Macmillan, 1905.
Bloesch, Donald G. *The Future of Evangelical Christianity*. New York: Doubleday, 1983.
Bockmuehl, Markus. *A Commentary on the Epistle to the Philippians*. BNTC. London: Adam & Charles Black, 1997.
———. *Jewish Law in Gentile Churches*. Edinburgh: T. & T. Clark, 2000.
Bogaert, Pierre. *Apocalypse de Baruch: Introduction, Traduction du Syriaque et Commentaire*. Vol. 1. Paris: Le Cerf, 1969.
Boles, Kenneth L. *Ephesians*. CPNIVC. Joplin, MO: College Press, 1994.
Botha, Jan. "Die Louw & Nida-Woordeboek—'n Kragtige nuwe hulpmiddel vir die eksegeet, prediker en Bybelvertaler." *IDS* 23/4 (1989) 1–23.
———. *Semeïon: Inleiding tot Aspekte van die Interpretasie van die Griekse Nuwe Testament*. Pretoria: NG Kerkboekhandel, 1990.
Boyarin, Daniel. *A Radical Jew: Paul and the Politics of Identity*. Berkeley: University of California Press, 1994.

———. "Rethinking Jewish Christianity: An Argument for Dismantling a Dubious Category (to which is Appended a Correction of my Border Lines)." *JQR* 99/1 (2009) 7–36.
Bruce, F. F. *1 & 2 Thessalonians*. WBC. Waco: Word, 1982.
———. *I and II Corinthians*. London: Oliphants, 1971.
———. *The Epistle of Paul to the Galatians*. NIGTC. Exeter: Paternoster, 1982.
———. *The Epistle to the Colossians, to Philemon, and to the Ephesians*. NICNT. Grand Rapids: Eerdmans, 1984.
———. *Paul: Apostle of the Heart Set Free*. Grand Rapids: Eerdmans, 2000.
———. *Romans*. TNTC. Downers Grove, IL: InterVarsity, 1985.
Bruno, Christopher R. "The Deliverer From Zion: The Source(s) and Function of Paul's Citation in Romans 11.26–27." *TynBul* 59 (2008) 119–34.
Buell, Denise K. *Why this New Race: Ethnic Reasoning in Early Christianity*. New York: Columbia University Press, 2005.
Bultmann, Rudolph. "Dikaiosynē Theou." *JBL* 83 (1964) 12–16.
———. *The Second Letter to the Corinthians*. Translated by R. A. Harrisville. Minneapolis: Augsburg, 1985.
———. "The Significance of the Old Testament for Christian Faith." In *The Old Testament and Christian Faith*, edited by Bernhard W. Anderson, 8–35. New York: Harper & Row, 1963.
———. *Theology of the New Testament*. Vol. 1. Translated by K. Grobel. Waco: Baylor University Press, 1951.
Burton, Ernest De W. *A Critical and Exegetical Commentary on the Epistle to the Galatians*. ICC. New York: Scribner's, 1920.
———. *Moods and Tenses in New Testament Greek*. Chicago: The University Chicago Press, 1906.
Byrne, Brendan. *Romans*. SP. Collegeville, MN: Liturgical, 1996.
Calvin, John. *Commentaries on the Catholic Epistles*. Grand Rapids: Christian Classics Ethereal Library, 2018. http://www.ccel.org/ccel/calvin/calcom45.pdf.
———. *Commentary on Corinthians*. Vol. 1. Edited and translated by J. Pringle. Grand Rapids: Christian Classics Ethereal Library, 2018. http://www.ccel.org/ccel/calvin/calcom39.pdf.
———. *Commentary on Galatians and Ephesians*. Edited and translated by J. Pringle. Grand Rapids: Christian Classics Ethereal Library, 2018. http://www.ccel.org/ccel/calvin/calcom41.pdf.
———. *Commentary on Romans*. Edited and translated by John Owen. Grand Rapids: Christian Classics Ethereal Library, 2018. http://www.ccel.org/ccel/calvin/calcom38.pdf.
———. *Sermons on the Epistle to the Ephesias*. Translated by A. Golding. Edinburgh: Banner of Truth, 1973.
Campbell, William S. "Israel." *DPL* 441–46.
———. *Paul and the Creation of Christian Identity*. London: T. & T. Clark, 2008.
Carson, Donald A. "Matthew." In *The Expositor's Bible Commentary*, edited by Frank E. Gaebelein, 8:3–599. Grand Rapids: Zondervan, 1984.
Carson, Donald A., and Douglas J. Moo. *An Introduction to the New Testament*. 2nd ed. Grand Rapids: Zondervan, 2005.
Carson, Donald A., et al., eds. *Justification and Variegated Nomism: The Complexities of Second Temple Judaism*. Vol. 1. Grand Rapids: Baker Academic, 2001.

———. *Justification and Variegated Nomism: The Paradoxes in Paul.* Vol. 2. Grand Rapids: Baker Academic, 2004.

Casey, Thomas G., and Justin Taylor, eds. *Paul's Jewish Matrix: With an Introductory Essay by Karl P. Donfried.* Bible in Dialogue 2. Rome: Gregorian & Biblical, 2011.

Casurella, A. "Israel, Twelve Tribes." *DLNT* 542–44.

Charles, R. H., ed. *The Apocrypha and Pseudepigrapha of the Old Testament in English: With Introductions and Critical and Explanatory Notes to Several Books.* Vol. 2. Oxford: Claredon, 1913.

Childs, Brevard S. *Isaiah.* OTL. London: Westminster John Knox, 2001.

Chilton, Bruce D. *The Isaiah Targum: Introduction, Translation, Apparatus and Notes.* Wilmington, DE: Michael Glazier, 1987.

Ciampa, Roy E., and Brian S. Rosner. *The First Letter to the Corinthians.* PNTC. Grand Rapids: Eerdmans, 2010.

Collange, J. F. *Enigmes de la deuxième épître de Paul aux Corinthiens. Étude exégétique de 2 Cor. 2:14–7:4.* Society for New Testament Studies Monograph Series 18. Cambridge: Cambridge University Press, 1972.

Collins, A. Y. "Vilification and Self-Definition in the book of Revelation." *HTR* 79 (1986) 308–20.

Collins, Raymond F. *First Corinthians.* SP 7. Collegeville, MN: Liturgical, 1999.

———. *Second Corinthians.* PCNT. Grand Rapids: Baker Academic, 2013.

Conzelmann, Hans. *1 Corinthians.* Translated by J. W. Leitch. Hermeneia. Philadelphia: Fortress, 1975.

Cooper, John W. *Body, Soul and Life Everlasting: Biblical Anthropology and the Monism-Dualism Debate.* Grand Rapids: Eerdmans, 2000.

Cosgrove, Charles H. *Elusive Israel: The Puzzle of Election in Romans.* Louisville: Westminster John Knox, 1997.

Cottle, R. E. "All Were Baptized." *JETS* 17 (1974) 75–80.

Cottrell, Jack. *Romans.* 2 vols. CPNIVC. Joplin, MO: College Press, 1998.

Cowan, Christopher W. "Context Is Everything: 'The Israel of God' in Galatians 6:16." *SBJT* 14/3 (2010) 78–85.

Craigie, Peter C. *The Book of Deuteronomy.* NICOT. Grand Rapids: Eerdmans, 1976.

Cranfield, C. E. B. *A Critical and Exegetical Commentary on the Epistle to the Romans.* 2 vols. ICC. Edinburgh: T. & T. Clark, 1975, 1979.

Cranford, Michael. "Election and Ethnicity: Paul's View of Israel in Romans 9.1–13." *JSNT* 50/15 (1993) 27–41.

Crenshaw, James L. *Joel.* AB. New York: Doubleday, 1995.

Crook, Zeba. "A Former Jew: Paul and the Dialectics of Race: Review Article." *RelSRev* 37/1 (2011) 60.

Crossan, John D. *The Cross that Spoke: The Origins of the Passion Narrative.* San Francisco: Harper & Row, 1988.

Cullmann, Oscar. *The Christology of the New Testament.* London: SCM, 1963.

Dalton, William J. *Christ's Proclamation to the Spirits: A Study of 1 Peter 3:18—4:6.* Rome: Editrice Pontificio Istituto Biblico, 1989.

D'Angelo Mary R. *Moses in the Letter to the Hebrews.* SBL Book Series 42. Missoula: Scholars, 1979.

Danker, Frederick W. *II Corinthians.* ACNT. Minneapolis: Augsburg, 1989.

Das, A. Andrew. *Galatians.* ConcC. St. Louis: Concordia, 2014.

Davies, Margaret. *Matthew*. Readings: A New Biblical Commentary. 2nd ed. Sheffield: Sheffield Phoenix, 2009.
Davies, W. D. *Paul and Rabbinic Judaism: Some Rabbinic Elements in Pauline Theology*. 2nd ed. Philadelphia: Fortress, 1980.
De Boer, Martinus C. *Galatians: A Commentary*. NTL. Louisville: Westminster John Knox, 2011.
Delitzsch, Franz. *Biblical Commentary on the Prophecies of Isaiah*. Translated by S. R. Driver. Clark's Foreign Library 42. Edinburgh: T. & T. Clark, 1892.
Denney, James. "St. Paul's Epistle to the Romans." *EGT* 2:555–725.
De Saussure, Ferdinand. *Course in General Linguistics*. Translated by W. Baskin. New York: Philosophical Library, 1959.
Dodd, Carles H. "Ephesians." In *The Abingdon Bible Commentary*, edited by F. C. Eiselen et al., 1222–37. New York: Abingdon-Cokesbury, 1929.
———. *The Epistle to the Romans*. London: Collins Fontana, 1959.
Donfried, Karl P. *Paul, Thessalonica, and Early Christianity*. Grand Rapids: Eerdmans, 2002.
———. "Paul's Jewish Matrix: The Scope and Nature of the Contributions." In *Paul's Jewish Matrix: With an Introductory Essay by Karl P. Donfried*, edited by Thomas G. Casey and Justin Taylor, 11–49. Rome: Gregorian & Biblical, 2011.
———. "A Short Note on Romans." In *The Romans Debate*, edited by Karl P. Donfried, 44–52. Peabody, MA: Hendrickson, 1991.
Driver, Samuel R. *A Critical and Exegetical Commentary on Deuteronomy*. ICC. Edinburgh: T. & T. Clark, 1902.
Duling, Dennis. "'Whatever Gain I Had . . .': Ethnicity and Paul's Self-identification in Philippians 3:5–6." *HTS* 64/2 (2008) 799–818.
Dunn, James D. G. *Baptism in the Holy Spirit: A Re-examination of the New Testament Teaching on the Gift of the Spirit in Relation to Pentecostalism Today*. Studies in Biblical Theology, Second Series 15. London: SCM, 1970.
———. *A Commentary on the Epistle to the Galatians*. BNTC. London: Adam & Charles Black, 1993.
———. *The Epistles to the Colossians and to Philemon*. NIGTC. Grand Rapids: Carlisle: Paternoster, 1996.
———. "The New Perspective on Paul." *BJRL* 65 (1983) 95–122.
———. *The New Perspective on Paul*. Grand Rapids: Eerdmans, 2008.
———. *Romans*. 2 vols. WBC. Dallas: Word, 1988.
———. *The Theology of Paul the Apostle*. London: T. & T. Clark, 1998.
———. *The Theology of Paul's Letter to the Galatians*. Cambridge: Cambridge University Press, 1993.
———. *Unity and Diversity in the New Testament: An Inquiry into the Character of Earliest Christianity*. 3rd ed. London: SCM, 2006.
———. "Who Did Paul Think He Was? A Study of Jewish-Christian Identity." *NTS* 45/2 (1999) 174–93.
Du Toit, Andreas B. "Translating Romans: Some Persistent Headaches." *IDS* 44/3–4 (2010) 581–602.
———. "Vilification as a Pragmatic Device in Early Christian Epistolography." *Biblica* 75/3 (1994) 403–12.

Du Toit, Philip La G. "Die 'beklee-' Metafoor by Paulus: Semantiese Valensie en Teologiese Belang op Weg na 'n Gesprek oor die Doop." MTh. diss., Stellenbosch University, 2011.

———. "The 'Clothe' Metaphor in Paul and the Entity Taking the Active Role in Baptism." *NGTT* 54/1-2 (2013) 29-39.

———. "Does the New Testament Support Christian Zionism?" *IDS* 50/1 (2016) 1-9.

———. "Galatians 3 and the Redefinition of the Criteria of Covenant Membership in the New Faith-era in Christ." *Neot* 52.1 (2018) 41-67.

———. "An Overview of the Gnomic or Logical Future Tense in the Pauline Corpus." In *New Testament Philology: Essays in Honor of David Allan Black*, edited by Melton B. Winstead, 69-83. Eugene, OR: Pickwick, 2018.

———. "Paul's Radicalisation of Law-obedience in Romans 2: The Plight of Someone Under the Law." *IDS* 50/1 (2016) 1-8.

———. "Paul's Reference to the 'Keeping of the Commandments of God' in 1 Corinthians 7:19." *Neot* 49/1 (2015) 21-45.

———. "Perspektiewe op die Noagitiese Wette by Paulus, en die Belang Daarvan vir Joods-Christelike Dialoog." *Litnet Akademies* 10/1 (2013) 631-56.

———. "Reading Galatians 6:16 in Line with Paul's Contrast between the New Aeon in Christ and the Old Aeon before the Christ Event." *STJ* 2/2. (2016) 203-25.

———. "The Salvation of 'All Israel' in Romans 11:25-27 as the Salvation of Inner-Elect, Historical Israel in Christ." *Neot* 49.2 (2015) 417-52.

———. "Was Paul Fully Torah Observant According to Acts?" *HTS* 72/3 (2016) 1-9.

Eisenbaum, Pamela. "Paul as the New Abraham." In *Paul and Politics: Ekklesia, Israel, Imperium, Interpretation. Essays in Honor of Kirster Stendahl*, edited by Richard A. Horsley, 130-45. Harrisburg, PA: Trinity, 2000.

———. *Paul Was Not a Christian: The Original Message of a Misunderstood Apostle.* New York: HarperCollins, 2009.

Ellicott, Charles J. *A Commentary, Critical and Grammatical, on St. Paul's Epistle to the Galatians, with a Revised Translation.* Boston: Crosby, Nichols, Lee, 1860.

Elliott, John H. "Jesus the Israelite Was Neither a 'Jew' nor a 'Christian': On Correcting Misleading Nomenclature." *JSHJ* 5/2 (2007) 119-54.

Elliott, Neil. *Liberating Paul: The Justice of God and the Politics of the Apostle.* Minneapolis: Fortress, 1995.

Ellison, H. L. *The Mystery of Israel: An Exposition of Romans 9-11.* Grand Rapids: Eerdmans, 1966.

Eltester, Walther. "Israel im lukanischen Werk und die Nazarethperikope." In *Jesus in Nazareth*, edited by Walter Eltester, 76-147. BZNW 40. Berlin: Walter de Gruyter, 1972.

Ervin, Howard M. *Conversion-Initiation and the Baptism in the Holy Spirit: A Critique of James D. G. Dunn,* Baptism in the Holy Spirit. Peabody, MA: Hendrickson, 1984.

Esler, Philip F. *Conflict and Identity in Romans: The Social Reading of Paul's Letter.* Minneapolis: Fortress, 2003.

Evans, Craig A. *Matthew.* NCBC. Cambridge: Cambridge University Press, 2012.

Fape, M. Olusina. *Paul's Concept of Baptism and Its Present Implications for Believers: Walking in the Newness of Life.* Lewiston, NY: Edwin Mellen, 1999.

Faust, Eberhard. *Pax Christi et Pax Caesaris: Religionsgeschichtliche, traditionsgeschichtliche und sozialgeschichtliche Studien zum Epheserbrief.* Novum Testamentum et Orbis Antiquus 24. Göttingen: Vanderhoeck & Ruprecht, 1993.

Fee, Gordon D. *1 and 2 Timothy, Titus*. NIBCNT. Peabody, MA: Hendrickson, 1988.
———. *The First and Second Letters to the Thessalonians*. NICNT. Grand Rapids: Eerdmans, 2009.
———. *The First Epistle to the Corinthians*. NICNT. Grand Rapids: Eerdmans, 1987.
———. *God's Empowering Presence: The Holy Spirit in the Letters of Paul*. Grand Rapids: Baker Academic, 1994.
———. *Paul, the Spirit, and the People of God*. Grand Rapids: Baker Academic, 1996.
———. *Paul's Letter to the Philippians*. NICNT. Grand Rapids: Eerdmans, 1995.
Felder, Cain H. "The Letter to Philemon." In *The New Interpreter's Bible*, edited by Leander E. Keck, 11:881–905. Nashville: Abingdon, 2000.
Feldmeier, Reinhard. *The First Letter of Peter*. Translated by P. H. Davids. Waco: Baylor University Press, 2008.
Ferguson, Everett. *Baptism in the Early Church: History, Theology, and Liturgy in the First Five Centuries*. Grand Rapids: Eerdmans, 2009.
Fitch, David E. *The End of Evangelicalism? Discerning a New Faithfulness for Mission Towards an Evangelical Political Theology*. Eugene, OR: Cascade, 2011.
Fitzmyer, Joseph A. *First Corinthians*. AB. New Haven: Yale University Press, 2008.
———. *The Letter to Philemon*. AB. New York: Doubleday, 2000.
———. *The One Who Is to Come*. Grand Rapids: Eerdmans, 2007.
———. *Romans*. AB. New York: Doubleday, 1993.
Foerster, W. "σῴζω, σωτηρία, σωτήρ, σωτήριος." *TDNT* 7:980–1012.
Foley, Claire. "The Noachide Laws." *Studia Antiqua* 3/2 (2003) 19–49.
Foulkes, Francis. *Ephesians*. TNTC. Guildford: InterVarsity, 1963.
Frame, James E. *A Critical and Exegetical Commentary on the Epistles of St. Paul to the Thessalonians*. ICC. Edinburgh: T. & T. Clark, 1912.
France, R. T. *The Gospel of Matthew*. NICNT. Grand Rapids: Eerdmans, 2007.
Frankemölle, Hubert. "λαός." *EDNT* 2:339–44.
———. *Das Taufverständnis des Paulus: Taufe, Tod und Auferstehung nach Röm 6*. Stuttgarter Bibelstudien 47. Stuttgart: Katholisches Bibelwerk, 1970.
Freyne, Sean. "Vilifying the Other and Defining the Self: Matthew's and John's Anti-Jewish Polemic in Focus." In *"To See Ourselves As Others See Us": Christians, Jews, "Others" in Late Antiquity*, edited by Jacob Neusner and Ernest S. Frerichs, 117–43. Chico, CA: Scholars, 1985.
Frid, Bo. "Römer 6, 4–5: Εἰς τὸν Θάνατον und τῷ Ὁμοιώματι τοῦ Θανάτου Αὐτοῦ als Schlüssel zu Duktus und Gedankengang in Röm 6, 6–11." *Biblische Zeitschrift* 30 (1986) 188–203.
Fuller, Reginald H. *A Critical Introduction to the New Testament*. London: Gerald Duckworth, 1966.
Fung, Ronald Y. K. *The Epistle to the Galatians*. NICNT. Grand Rapids: Eerdmans, 1988.
Furnish, Victor P. *II Corinthians*. AB. New York: Doubleday, 1984.
Gager, John G. *Reinventing Paul*. New York: Oxford University Press, 2000.
Gagnon, Robert A. J. "Why the 'Weak' at Rome Cannot Be Non-Christian Jews." *CBQ* 62/1 (2000) 64–82.
Garland, David E. *1 Corinthians*. Ebook ed. BECNT. Grand Rapids: Baker Academic, 2003.
———. *2 Corinthians*. NAC. Nashville: B&H, 1999.
———. *Colossians and Philemon*. NIVAC. Grand Rapids: Zondervan, 1998.

Gaston, Lloyd. *Paul and the Torah*. Vancouver: University of British Columbia Press, 1987.

Gathercole, Simon J. "Justified by Faith, Justified by His Blood: The Evidence of Romans 3:21–4:25." In *Justification and Variegated Nomism: The Paradoxes in Paul*, edited by Donald A. Carson et al., 2:147–84. Grand Rapids: Baker Academic, 2004.

———. *Where Is Boasting? Early Jewish Soteriology and Paul's Response in Romans 1–5*. Grand Rapids: Eerdmans, 2002.

George, Timothy. *Galatians*. NAC. Nashville: B&H, 1994.

Gillespie, Thomas W. *The First Theologians: A Study in Early Christian Prophecy*. Grand Rapids: Eerdmans, 1994.

Gispen, W. H. *Het Boek Leviticus*. Commentaar op het Oude Testament. Kampen: Kok, 1950.

Godet, Frédéric. *Commentary on St. Paul's Epistle to the Romans*. 2 vols. Edinburgh: T. & T. Clark, 1881.

———. *Commentary on St. Paul's First Epistle to the Corinthians*. Vol. 1. Edinburgh: T. & T. Clark, 1889.

Goppelt, Leonhard. *1 Peter*. Translated by John E. Alsup. Grand Rapids: Eerdmans, 1993.

Grayston, Kenneth. "'Not Ashamed of the Gospel': Romans 1,16a and the Structure of the Epistle." *SE* 1/1 (1964) 569–73.

Green, Gene L. *The Letters to the Thessalonians*. PNTC. Leicester: Apollos, 2002.

Grogan, Geoffrey W. "Isaiah." In *The Expositor's Bible Commentary*, edited by Frank E. Gaebelein, 6:1–354. Grand Rapids: Zondervan, 1986.

Gundry, Robert H. *A Survey of the New Testament*. 5th ed. Grand Rapids: Zondervan, 2012.

Gurtner, Daniel M. *The Torn Veil: Matthew's Exposition of the Death of Jesus*. Cambridge: Cambridge University Press, 2007.

Gutbrod, Walter. "Ἰσραήλ, Ἰσραηλίτης, Ἰουδαῖος, Ἰουδαία, Ἰουδαϊκός, ἰουδαΐζω, Ἰουδαϊσμός, Ἑβραῖος, Ἑβραϊκός, ἑβραΐς, ἑβραϊστί." *TDNT* 3:369–91.

Guthrie, Donald. *New Testament Introduction*. Aylesbury: InterVarsity, 1990.

———. *New Testament Theology*. Leicester: InterVarsity, 1981.

———. *The Pastoral Epistles*. TNTC. Nottingham: InterVarsity, 1990.

Guthrie, George H. *2 Corinthians*. BECNT. Grand Rapids: Baker Academic, 2015.

Hagner, Donald A. *The New Testament: A Historical and Theological Introduction*. Grand Rapids: Baker Academic, 2012.

Hamerton-Kelly, Robert. *Sacred Violence: Paul's Hermeneutic of the Cross*. Minneapolis: Fortress, 1992.

Hansen, G. Walter. *The Letter to the Philippians*. PNTC. Grand Rapids: Eerdmans, 2009.

Hanson, Anthony T. *Studies in Paul's Technique and Theology*. Grand Rapids: Eerdmans, 1974.

Harris, Murray J. "2 Corinthians." In *The Expositor's Bible Commentary*, edited by Frank E. Gaebelein, 10:299–406. Grand Rapids: Zondervan, 1976.

———. *Colossians and Philemon: Exegetical Guide to the Greek New Testament*. Grand Rapids: Eerdmans, 1991.

———. *The Second Epistle to the Corinthians*. NIGTC. Grand Rapids: Eerdmans; Milton Keynes: Paternoster, 2005.

Harris, W. Hall. "The Ascent and Descent of Christ in Ephesians 4:9–10." *BSac* 151 (1994) 198–214.

Harrison, R. K. *Jeremiah and Lamentations*. TOTC. London: InterVarsity, 1973.
Hasel, Gerhard F. *The Remnant: The History and Theology of the Remnant Idea from Genesis to Isaiah*. Berrien Springs, MI: Andrews University Press, 1972.
Havemann, S. J. *Paul, Moses, and the History of Israel: The Letter/Spirit Contrast and the Argument from Scripture in 2 Corinthians 3*. Tübingen: J. C. B. Mohr, 1995.
Hawthorne, Gerald F. *Philippians*. WBC. Waco: Word, 1983.
Hays, Richard B. *Echoes of Scripture in the letters of Paul*. New Haven: Yale University Press, 1989.
———. *The Faith of Jesus Christ: The Narrative Structure of Galatians 3:1—4:11*. 2nd ed. Grand Rapids: Eerdmans, 2002.
———. "The Letter to the Galatians." In *The New Interpreter's Bible*, edited by Leander E. Keck, 11:181–348. Nashville: Abingdon, 2000.
Hendriksen, William. *Exposition of Colossians, and Philemon*. Baker's New Testament Commentary. Grand Rapids: Baker, 1968.
———. *Exposition of Ephesians*. Baker's New Testament Commentary. Grand Rapids: Baker, 1967
———. *Exposition of Galatians*. Baker's New Testament Commentary. Grand Rapids: Baker, 1968.
———. *Exposition of Paul's Epistle to the Romans*. 2 vols. Baker's New Testament Commentary. Grand Rapids: Baker, 1980, 1981.
Hengel, Martin. *The "Hellenization" of Judaea in the First Century after Christ*. Philadelphia: Trinity, 1989.
Herbert, Gabriel. "Faithfulness and Faith." *Theology* 58 (1955) 373–79.
Hodge, Charles. *Commentary on the Epistle to the Romans*. Rev. ed. Philadelphia: H. B. Garner, 1883.
———. *An Exposition of the Second Epistle to the Corinthians*. New York: Robert Carter, 1860.
Hoehner, Harold W. *Ephesians: An Exegetical Commentary*. Grand Rapids: Baker Academic, 2002.
Hofius, Otfried. "Das Evangelium und Israel." In *Paulusstudien*, edited by Otfried Hofius, 175–202. WUNT 51. Tübingen: Mohr-Siebeck, 1989.
Holmberg, Bengt. "Jewish *Versus* Christian Identity in the Early Church." *RB* 105 (1998) 397–425.
Holwerda, David E. *Jesus and Israel: One Covenant or Two?* Grand Rapids: Eerdmans, 1995.
Hong, In-Gyu. "The Law in Galatians." DTh. diss., Stellenbosch University, 1991.
Hooker, Morna D. "The Letter to the Philippians." In *The New Interpreter's Bible*, edited by Leander E. Keck, 11:467–549. Nashville: Abingdon, 2000.
Horne, Charles M. "The Meaning of the Phrase 'And thus all Israel will be saved' (Romans 11:26)." *JETS* 21/4 (1978) 329–34.
Horrell, David G. *Solidarity and Difference: A Contemporary Reading of Paul's Ethics*. London: T. & T. Clark, 2005.
Horsley, Richard A. *1 Corinthians*. ANTC. Nashville: Abingdon, 1998.
Hughes, Philip E. *Paul's Second Epistle to the Corinthians*. NICNT. Grand Rapids: Eerdmans, 1962.
Hultgren, Arland J. *Paul's Letter to the Romans: A Commentary*. Grand Rapids: Eerdmans, 2011.

Hunt, J. P. T. "Colossians 2:11–12, the Circumcision/Baptism Analogy, and Infant Baptism." *TynBul* 41/2 (1990) 227–44.
Hutchinson, John, and Anthony D. Smith. *Ethnicity*. Oxford Readers. Oxford: Oxford University Press, 1996.
Jeremias, Joachim. "ἄνθρωπος, ἀνθρώπινος." *TDNT* 1:364–67.
———. "Einige vorwiegend sprachliche Beobachtungen zur Römer 11.25–36." In *Die Israelfrage nach Röm 9–11*, edited by W. G. Kümmel et al., 193–203. Monographische Reihe von Benedictina, Biblisch-ökumenische Abteilung 3. Rome: Abbazia S. Paolo, 1977.
Jewett, Robert. *Paul's Anthropological Terms: A Study of Their Use in Conflict Settings*. Arbeiten zur Geschichte des antiken Judentums und des Urchristentums 10. Leiden: Brill, 1971.
———. *Romans*. Hermeneia. Minneapolis: Fortress, 2007.
———. *The Thessalonian Correspondence: Pauline Rhetoric and Millenarian Piety*. Philadelphia: Fortress, 1986.
Jipp, Joshua W. "Rereading the Story of Abraham, Isaac, and 'Us' in Romans 4." *JSNT* 32/2 (2009) 217–42.
Jobes, Karen H. *1 Peter*. BECNT. Grand Rapids: Baker Academic, 2005.
John Chrysostom. "Commentary of St. John Chrysostom, Archbishop of Constantinople, on the Epistle of St. Paul the Apostle to the Galatians." Edited by Philip Schaff. http://www.ccel.org/ccel/schaff/npnf113.
———. "Homilies on the Acts of the Apostles and the Epistle to the Romans." Edited by Philip Schaff. http://www.ccel.org/ccel/schaff/npnf111.i.html.
———. "Homily on the Epistles of Paul to the Corinthians." Edited by Philip Schaff. http://www.ccel.org/ccel/schaff/npnf112.i.html.
Johnson, Luke T. *The First and Second Letters to Timothy*. AB. New York: Doubleday, 2001.
———. *The Writings of the New Testament: An Interpretation*. Minneapolis: Fortress, 2010.
Johnson, S. Lewis, Jr. "Paul and 'The Israel of God': An Exegetical and Eschatological Case-Study." *MSJ* 20/1 (2009) 41–45.
Johnson Hodge, Caroline. *If Sons, Then Heirs: A Study of Kinship and Ethnicity in the Letters of Paul*. New York: Oxford University Press, 2007.
Jones, Ivor H. *The Epistles to the Thessalonians*. Peterborough: Epworth, 2005.
Kamlah, E. "πνεῦμα." *NIDNTT* 3:689–93.
Käsemann, Ernst. *Commentary on Romans*. Translated by Geoffrey W. Bromiley. London: SCM, 1980.
———. *Perspectives on Paul*. Translated by M. Kohl. London: SCM, 1971.
Keener, Craig S. *1–2 Corinthians*. NCBC. Cambridge: Cambridge University Press, 2005.
Kennedy, George A. *New Testament Interpretation through Rhetorical Criticism*. Chapel Hill: University of North Carolina Press, 1984.
Kim, Dongsu. "Reading Paul's καὶ οὕτως πᾶς Ἰσραὴλ σωθήσεται (Rom 11:26a) in the Context of Romans." *CTJ* 45/2 (2010) 317–34.
Kim, Sang-Hoon. "A Syntactic-Analytic New Testament Greek Study with a Newly Promoted Pedagogical Consideration." *CJET* 10 (2006) 55–75.
Kim, Seyoon. "The 'Mystery' of Rom 11.25–6 Once More." *NTS* 43/3 (1997) 412–29.
Kirby, John C. *Ephesians: Baptism and Pentecost*. Montreal: McGill University Press, 1968.

Kirk, J. R. Daniel. "Why Does the Deliverer Come ἐκ Σιών (Romans 11:26)?" *JSNT* 33/1 (2010) 81–99.

Kistemaker, Simon J. *Exposition of the Acts of the Apostles*. Baker's New Testament Commentary. Grand Rapids: Baker, 1990.

———. *Exposition of the Book of Revelation*. Baker's New Testament Commentary. Grand Rapids: Baker, 2001.

———. *Exposition of the First Epistle to the Corinthians*. Baker's New Testament Commentary. Grand Rapids: Baker, 1993.

———. *Exposition of the Second Epistle to the Corinthians*. Baker's New Testament Commentary. Grand Rapids: Baker, 1997.

Kleinknecht, Hermann. "πνεῦμα, πνευματικός, πνέω, ἐμπνέω, πνοή, ἐκπνέω, θεόπνευστος." *TDNT* 6:332–59.

Knight, George W., III. *The Pastoral Epistles*. NIGTC. Grand Rapids: Eerdmans, 1992.

Koch, Dietrich A. *Die Schrift als Zeuge des Evangeliums: Untersuchungen zur Verwendung und zum Verständnis der Schrift bei Paulus*. Beiträge zur Historischen Theologie 69. Tübingen: Mohr, 1986.

Köstenberger, Andreas J., et al. *The Cradle, the Cross, and the Crown: An Introduction to the New Testament*. Ebook ed. Nashville: B&H, 2009.

———. *Going Deeper with New Testament Greek*. Nashville: B&H, 2016.

Kremer, J. "πνεῦμα." *EDNT* 3:117–22.

Kruger, G. Van W. "Conditions in the N.T.: A Study in Their Rationale." PhD diss., University of Cambridge, 1966.

———. *Die Teorie en Eksegese van die Nuwe Testamentiese Verbum*. Stellenbosch: Universiteits-Uitgewers en –Boekhandelaars, 1981.

Kruse, Colin G. *Paul's Letter to the Romans*. PNTC. Grand Rapids: Eerdmans, 2012.

———. *The Second Epistle of Paul to the Corinthians*. TNTC. Grand Rapids: Eerdmans, 1987. Kühl, Ernst. *Der Brief des Paulus an die Römer*. Leipzig: Quell & Meyer, 1913.

Kuhli, H. "Ἰουδαῖος." *EDNT* 2:193–97.

———. "Ἰσραήλ." *EDNT* 2:202–4.

———. "Ἰσραηλίτης." *EDNT*, 2:204–5.

Kuhn, Karl G. "Ἰσραήλ, Ἰσραηλίτης, Ἰουδαῖος, Ἰουδαία, Ἰουδαϊκός, ἰουδαΐζω, Ἰουδαϊσμός, Ἑβραῖος, Ἑβραϊκός, ἑβραΐς, ἑβραϊστί." *TDNT* 3:359–69.

Kümmel, Werner G. *Introduction to the New Testament*. London: SCM, 1975.

———. *Römer 7 und die Bekehrung des Paulus*. Leipzig: Hinrichs, 1929.

Ladd, George E. *A Theology of the New Testament*. Rev. ed. Grand Rapids: Eerdmans, 1993.

Lagrange, Marie-Joseph. *Saint Paul: Epître aux Romains*. Paris: Gabalda, 1950.

Lambrecht, Jan. *The Wretched "I" and Its Liberation: Paul in Romans 7 and 8*. Leuven: Peeters, 1990.

Lang, Timothy J. *Mystery and the Making of a Christian Historical Consciousness*. Berlin: de Gruyter, 2015.

Lange, J. P., and F. R. Fay. *The Epistle of Paul to the Romans*. Translated by J. F. Hurst. New York: Schribner's, 1899.

Langer, Ruth. "Jewish Understandings of the Religious Other." *TS* 64 (2003) 255–77.

Larsson, Edvin. *Christus als Vorbild: Eine Untersuchung zu den paulinischen Tauf- und Eikontexten*. Acta Seminarii Neotestamentici Upsalensis 23. Uppsala: Almqvist & Wiksells, 1962.

Lategan, Bernard C. *Die Brief aan die Galasiërs*. Cape Town: N G Kerk-Uitgewers, 1986.
Lenski, Richard C. H. *The Interpretation of St. Paul's Epistles to the Galatians to the Ephesians and to the Philippians*. Minneapolis: Augsburg, 1937.
———. *The Interpretation of St. Paul's Epistle to the Romans 8-16*. Minneapolis: Augsburg Fortress, 1945.
———. *The Interpretation of St. Paul's First and Second Epistles to the Corinthians*. Minneapolis: Augsburg, 1963.
Levine, Amy-Jill. *The Misunderstood Jew: The Church and the Scandal of the Jewish Jesus*. San Francisco: HarperSanFrancisco, 2006.
Levison, John R. *Filled with the Spirit*. Grand Rapids: Eerdmans, 2009.
Lewis, John G. *Looking for Life: The Role of "Theo-Ethical Reasoning" in Paul's Religion*. London: T. & T. Clark, 2005.
Lieu, Judith M. *Christian Identity in the Jewish and Graeco-Roman World*. Oxford: Oxford University Press, 2004.
———. *Neither Jew nor Greek. Constructing Early Christianity*. Studies of the New Testament and Its World. London: T. & T. Clark, 2002.
Lightfoot, Joseph B. *Saint Paul's Epistles to the Colossians and to Philemon: A Revised Text with Introductions, Notes, and Books*. 9th ed. London: Macmillan, 1890.
———. *Saint Paul's Epistle to the Galatians: A Revised Text with Introduction, Notes, and Books*. London: Macmillan, 1914.
———. *Saint Paul's Epistle to the Philippians: A Revised Text with Introduction, Notes and Books*. New York: Macmillan, 1903.
Lim, Kar Y. "'If Anyone is in Christ, New Creation: The Old has Gone, the New has Come' (2 Corinthians 5.17): New Creation and Temporal Comparison in Social Identity Formation in 2 Corinthians." In *T. & T. Clark Handbook to Social Identity in the New Testament*, edited by J. Brian Tucker and Coleman A. Baker, 289-310. London: Bloomsbury, 2014.
Lincoln, Andrew T. *Ephesians*. WBC. Dallas: Word, 1990.
———. "The Letter to the Colossians." In *The New Interpreter's Bible*, edited by Leander E. Keck, 11:551-669. Nashville: Abingdon, 2000.
Lindemann, Andreas. *Die Aufhebung der Zeit: Geschichtsverständnis und Eschatologie im Epheserbrief*. Studien zum Neuen Testament 12. Gütersloh: Gert Mohn, 1975.
Lohse, Eduard. *Colossians and Philemon: A Commentary on the Epistles to the Colossians and to Philemon*. Hermeneia. Philadelphia: Fortress, 1971.
Longenecker, Richard N. "Different Answers to Different Issues: Israel, the Gentiles and Salvation History in Romans 9-11." *JSNT* 36 (1989) 95-123.
———. *The Epistle to the Romans*. NIGTC. Grand Rapids: Eerdmans, 2016.
———. *Galatians*. WBC. Dallas: Word, 1990.
———. *Introducing Romans: Critical Issues in Paul's Most Famous Letter*. Grand Rapids: Eerdmans, 2011.
Lührmann, Dieter. *Galatians: A Continental Commentary*. Translated by O. C. Dean Jr. Minneapolis: Fortress, 1992.
Luther, Martin. *On the Jews and Their Lies*. Translated by Martin H. Bertram. Luther's Works 47. Philadelphia: Fortress, 1971.
Luz, Ulrich. "Rechtfertigung bei den Paulusschülern." In *Festschrift für Ernst Käsemann zum 70. Gebturtstag*, edited by Johannes Friedrich et al., 365-83. Tübingen: Mohr Siebeck, 1976.

Lyons, George. *Pauline Autobiography: Toward a New Understanding*. Society of Biblical Literature 73. Atlanta: Scholars, 1985.
Malherbe, Abraham J. *The Letters to the Thessalonians*. AB. New York: Doubleday, 2000.
Malina, Bruce J. *The New Testament World: Insights from Cultural Anthropology*. Louisville: Westminster John Knox, 2001.
Malina, Bruce J., and Richard L. Rohrbaugh. *Social-Science Commentary on the Synoptic Gospels*. Minneapolis: Fortress, 1992.
Maljaars, Bram. *Heel Israël Zal Behouden Worden: Een Kritisch Onderzoek van de Gangbare Exegese van Romeinen 11, speciaal vs. 26*. Soesterberg Uitgeverij Aspekt, 2015.
Manson, T. W. "Paul's Letter to the Romans—and Others." In *The Romans Debate*, edited by Karl P. Donfried, 3–15. Peabody, MA: Hendrickson, 1991.
Mare, W. Harold. "1 Corinthians." In *The Expositor's Bible Commentary*, edited by Frank E. Gaebelein, 10:173–297. Grand Rapids: Zondervan, 1976.
Marshall, I. Howard. *1 and 2 Thessalonians*. NBC. Grand Rapids: Eerdmans, 1983.
———. "Salvation, Grace and Works in the Later Writings of the Pauline Corpus." *NTS* 42 (1996) 339–58.
Martin, D. Michael. *1, 2 Thessalonians*. NAC. Nashville: B&H, 1995.
Martyn, J. Louis. *Galatians*. AB. New York: Doubleday, 1997.
Mason, Steve. "Jews, Judaeans, Judaizing, Judaism: Problems of Categorization in Ancient History." *JSJ* 38 (2007) 457–512.
Maston, Jason. *Divine and Human Agency in Second Temple Judaism and Paul*. Tübingen: Mohr Siebeck, 2010.
Matera, Frank J. *II Corinthians: A Commentary*. Louisville: Westminster John Knox, 2003.
———. *Romans*. PCNT. Grand Rapids: Baker Academic, 2010.
Mayer, R. "Israel, Jew, Hebrew, Jacob, Judah." *NIDNTT* 2:304–16.
Meeks, Wayne A. "Social Function of Apocalyptic Language in Pauline Christianity." In *Apocalypticism in the Mediterranean World and the Near East*, edited by David Hellholm, 687–705. Tübingen: Mohr, 1983.
Meier, John P. *Matthew*. Wilmington, DE: Glazier, 1980.
Melick, Richar R. *Philippians, Colossians, Philemon*. NAC. Nashville: B&H, 1991.
Merkle, Ben L. "Romans 11 and the Future of Ethnic Israel." *JETS* 43/4 (2000) 709–21.
Merrill, Eugene H. *Deuteronomy*. NAC. Nashville: B&H, 1994.
Metzger, Bruce M. *A Textual Commentary on the Greek New Testament*. 2nd ed. Stuttgart: Deutsche Bibelgesellschaft, 1994.
Meyer, Heinrich A. W. *Critical and Exegetical Hand-Book to the Epistles to the Corinthians*. Translated by D. D. Bannerman. Translation revised and edited by W. P. Dickson. New York: Funk & Wagnalls, 1884.
Meyer, Jason C. *The End of the Law: Mosaic Covenant in Pauline Theology*. Ebook ed. Nashville: B&H, 2009.
Michaels, J. Ramsey. *1 Peter*. WBC. Dallas: Word, 1988.
Middendorf, Michael P. *Romans 9–16*. ConcC. Saint Louis: Concordia, 2016.
Miller, David M. "Ethnicity, Religion and the Meaning of *Ioudaios* in Ancient 'Judaism.'" *CurBR* 12 (2014) 216–65.
———. "The Meaning of *Ioudaios* and Its Relationship to Other Group Labels in Ancient 'Judaism.'" *CurBR* 9 (2010) 98–126.
Moo, Douglas J. *The Epistle to the Romans*. NICNT. Grand Rapids: Eerdmans, 1996.

———. *Galatians*. BECNT. Grand Rapids: Baker Academic, 2013.

———. "Israel and the Law in Romans 5–11: Interaction with the New Perspective." In *Justification and Variegated Nomism: The Paradoxes in Paul*, edited by Donald A. Carson et al., 2:185–216. Grand Rapids: Baker Academic, 2004.

———. *The Letters to the Colossians and to Philemon*. PNTC. Grand Rapids: Eerdmans, 2008.

Morris, Leon. *The Epistle to the Romans*. PNTC. Grand Rapids: Eerdmans, 1988.

———. *The First and Second Epistles to the Thessalonians*. NICNT. Grand Rapids: Eerdmans, 1991.

———. *The First Epistle of Paul to the Corinthians*. TNTC. Leicester: InterVarsity, 1958.

———. *The Gospel According to Matthew*. PNTC. Grand Rapids: Eerdmans, 1992.

Moule, C. F. D. *An Idiom Book of New Testament Greek*. Cambridge: Cambridge University Press, 1959.

Mounce, Robert H. *Pastoral Epistles*. BWC 46. Nashville: Thomas Nelson, 2000.

———. *Romans*. NAC. Nashville: B&H, 1995.

Muddiman, John. *A Commentary on the Epistle to the Ephesians*. BNTC. London: Continuum, 2001.

Munck, Johannes. *Christ and Israel: An Interpretation of Romans 9–11*. Philadelphia: Fortress, 1967.

———. *Paul and the Salvation of Mankind*. London: SCM, 1959.

Murray, John. *The Epistle to the Romans*. 2 vols. NICNT. Grand Rapids: Eerdmans, 1959, 1965.

Myers, Jacob M. *I and II Esdras*. AB. New York: Doubleday, 1974.

Nanos, Mark D. "'Broken Branches': A Pauline Metaphor Gone Awry? (Romans 11:11–24)." In *Between Gospel and Election: Explorations in the Interpretation of Romans 9–11*, edited by Florian Wilk and J. Ross Wagner, 339–76. Tübingen: Mohr Siebeck, 2010.

———. "'Callused,' Not 'Hardened': Paul's Revelation of Temporary Protection until All Israel Can Be Healed." In *Reading Paul in Context: Explorations in Identity Formation*, edited by Kathy Ehrensperger and J. Brian Tucker, 52–73. London: T. & T. Clark, 2010.

———. *The Mystery of Romans: The Jewish Context of Paul's Letter*. Minneapolis: Fortress, 1996.

———. "The Myth of the 'Law-Free' Paul Standing Between Christians and Jews." *Studies in Christian-Jewish Relations* 4 (2009) 1–21.

———. "Paul's Non-Jews Do Not Become 'Jews,' But Do They Become 'Jewish'?: Reading Romans 2:25–29 Within Judaism, Alongside Josephus." *Journal of the Jesus Movement in Its Jewish Setting* 1 (2014) 26–53.

———. "Paul's Relationship to Torah in Light of His Strategy 'to Become Everything to Everyone' (1 Corinthians 9.19–23)." In *Paul and Judaism: Crosscurrents in Pauline Exegesis and the Study of Jewish-Christian Relations*, edited by Reimund Bieringer and Didier Pollefeyt, 106–40. London: T. & T. Clark, 2012.

———. "Rethinking the 'Paul and Judaism' Paradigm: Why Not 'Paul's Judaism'?" www.marknanos.com/Paul'sJudaism-5-28-08.pdf.

Nash, Ronald H. *Christianity and the Hellenistic World*. Grand Rapids: Zondervan, 1984.

Nathan, Emmanuel, and Reimund Bieringer. "Paul, Moses and the Veil: Paul's Perspective on Judaism in Light of 2 Corinthians 3." In *Paul's Jewish Matrix: With an Introductory Essay by Karl P. Donfried*, edited by Thomas G. Casey and Justin Taylor, 201–28. Bible in Dialogue 2. Rome: Gregorian & Biblical, 2011.

Neusner, Jacob. *Messiah in Context: Israel's History and Destiny in Formative Judaism*. Philadelphia: Fortress, 1984.

———. *What is Midrash?* Philadelphia: Fortress, 1987.

Newman, Barclay M., and Eugene A. Nida. *A Translator's Handbook on Paul's Letter to the Romans*. Stuttgart: United Bible Societies, 1973.

Nicholl, Colin R. *From Hope to Despair in Thessalonica: Situating 1 and 2 Thessalonians*. New York: Cambridge University Press, 2004.

O'Brien, Peter T. *Colossians, Philemon*. WBC. Waco: Word, 1982.

———. *The Epistle to the Philippians*. NIGTC. Grand Rapids: Eerdmans, 1991.

———. *The Letter to the Ephesians*. PNTC. Grand Rapids: Eerdmans, 1999.

———. "Was Paul Converted?" In *Justification and Variegated Nomism: The Paradoxes in Paul*, edited by Donald A. Carson et al., 2:361–91. Grand Rapids: Baker Academic, 2004.

Oden, Thomas C. *First and Second Timothy and Titus*. Int. Louisville: John Knox, 1989.

Olson, Roger E. *The Westminster Handbook to Evangelical Theology*. Louisville: Westminster John Knox, 2004.

O'Neill, John C. *Paul's Letter to the Romans*. Middlesex: Penguin, 1975.

Osborne, Grant R. *Matthew*. ZECNT. Grand Rapids: Zondervan, 2010.

———. *Romans*. IVPNTC. Downers Grove, IL: IVP Academic, 2004.

Oswalt, John N. *The Book of Isaiah: Chapters 40–66*. NICOT. Grand Rapids: Eerdmans, 1998.

Owen, John. *The Death of Death in the Death of Christ*. The Banner of Truth Trust. Worcester: Billing, 1959.

Pao, David W. *Colossians and Philemon*. ZECNT. Grand Rapids: Zondervan, 2010.

Park, Eung C. *Either Jew or Gentile: Paul's Unfolding Theology of Inclusivity*. Louisville: Westminster John Knox, 2003.

Patterson, Paige. *Revelation*. Ebook ed. NAC. Nashville: B&H, 2012.

Pearson, Birger A. "1 Thessalonians 2:13–16: A Deutero-Pauline Interpolation." *HTR* 64 (1971) 79–94.

Perkins, Pheme. *First Corinthians*. PCNT. Grand Rapids: Baker Academic, 2012.

———. "The Letter to the Ephesians." In *The New Interpreter's Bible*, edited by Leander E. Keck, 11:349–466. Nashville: Abingdon, 2000.

Pierard, Richard V., and Walter A. Elwell. "Evangelicalism." In *Evangelical Dictionary of Theology*, edited by Walter A. Elwell, 405–10. 2nd ed. Grand Rapids: Baker Academic, 2001.

Pierce, Chad T. *Spirits and the Proclamation of Christ*. WUNT 2. Reihe 305. Tübingen: Mohr Siebeck, 2011.

Piper, John. *The Justification of God: An Exegetical and Theological Study of Romans 9:1–23*. Grand Rapids: Baker, 1983.

Plummer, Alfred. *A Commentary on St. Paul's First Epistle to the Thessalonians*. London: Robert Scott, 1918.

———. *A Critical and Exegetical Commentary on the Second Epistle of St. Paul to the Corinthians*. ICC. New York: Scribner's, 1915.

Pokorný, Petr. *Colossians: A Commentary*. Peabody, MA: Hendrickson, 1991.

Pop, F. J. *De Eerste Brief van Paulus aan de Corinthiërs*. Nijkerk: G. F. Callenbach, 1965.

———. *De Tweede Brief van Paulus aan de Corinthiërs*. Nijkerk: G. F. Callenbach, 1953.

Prior, Mihael. *Paul the Letter-Writer and the Second Letter to Timothy.* JSNTSup 23. Sheffield: JSOT, 1989.

Punt, Jeremy. "1 Corinthians 7:17–24. Identity and Human Dignity Amidst Power and Liminality." *Verbum et Ecclesia* 33/1 (2012) 1–9.

———. "Identity, Memory and Scriptural Warrant: Arguing Paul's Case." *JECH* 1/2 (2011) 152–73.

———. "A Politics of Difference in the New Testament: Identity and the Others in Paul." In *The New Testament Interpreted: Essays in Honour of Bernard C. Lategan*, edited by Cilliers Breytenbach et al., 199–225. Leiden: Brill, 2007.

Räisänen, Heikki. *Paul and the Law.* 2nd ed. Tübingen: Mohr, 1987.

Ramsey, Ian T. *Religious Language: An Empirical Placing of Theological Phrases.* London: SCM, 1957.

Rawlinson, George. *Isaiah: Exposition and Homeletics.* Vol. 2. The Pulpit Commentary. New York: Funk & Wagnalls, 1913.

Reed, Jeffrey T. "Philippians and the Epistolary Hesitation Formulas: The Literary Integrity of Philippians, Again." *JBL* (1996) 63–90.

Reumann, John. *Philippians.* AB. New Haven: Yale University Press, 2008.

Richardson, Alan. *Introduction to the Theology of the New Testament.* New York: Harper, 1958.

Richardson, Peter. *Israel in the Apostolic Church.* Cambridge: Cambridge University Press, 1969.

Ridderbos, Herman N. *Aan de Kolossenzen.* Commentaar op het Nieuwe Testament. Kampen: Kok, 1960.

———. *Aan de Romeinen.* Commentaar op het Nieuwe Testament. Kampen: Kok, 1959.

———. *Paulus: Ontwerp van zijn Theologie.* Kampen: Kok, 1966.

Robbins, Vernon K. *Exploring the Texture of Texts: A Guide to Socio-Rhetorical Interpretation.* Valley Forge, PA: Trinity, 1996.

Roberts, Alexander, and James Donaldson, eds. *The Ante-Nicene Fathers.* Vol. 1. Revised and editedy by A. C. Coxe. New York: Schribner's, 1913.

———. *The Ante-Nicene Fathers.* Vol. 3. Revised and edited by A. C. Coxe. New York: Schribner's, 1918.

Roberts, J. H. *Die Brief aan die Efesiërs.* Cape Town: NG Kerk-Uitgewers, 1983.

———. "Righteousness in Romans with Special Reference to Romans 3:19–31." *Neot* 15 (1981) 19–31.

Roberts, J. W. *A Grammar of the Greek New Testament for Beginners.* Edited by D. L. Potter. Abilene: Abilene Christian College, 1958.

Robertson, A. T. *A Grammar of the Greek New Testament in the Light of Historical Research.* New York: Hodder & Stoughton; George H. Doran Company, 1919.

Robinson, Armitage, ed. *The Demonstration of the Apostolic Preaching by St. Irenaeus, Bishop of Lyon.* New York: Macmillan, 1920.

Robinson, Edward. *A Greek and English Lexicon of the New Testament.* London: William Tegg, 1852.

Roloff, Jurcen. *The Revelation of John: A Continental Commentary.* Minneapolis: Fortress, 1993.

Rubinkiewicz, Ryszard. "Apocalypse of Abraham." In *The Old Testament Pseudepigrapha*, edited by James H. Charlesworth, 1:681–706. London: Darton; Longman & Todd, 1983.

Rudolph, David J. *A Jew to the Jews: Jewish Contours of Pauline Flexibility in 1 Corinthians 9:19–23.* Tübingen: Mohr, 2011.
Ruzer, Serge. "Paul's Stance on the Torah Revisited: Gentile Addressees and the Jewish Setting." In *Paul's Jewish Matrix: With an Introductory Essay by Karl P. Donfried*, edited by Thomas G. Casey and Justin Taylor, 75–99. Bible in Dialogue 2. Rome: Gregorian & Biblical, 2011.
Sampley, J. Paul. "The Second Letter to the Corinthians." In *The New Interpreter's Bible*, edited by Leander E. Keck, 11:1–180. Nashville: Abingdon, 2000.
Sand, Alexander. "σάρξ." *EDNT* 3:230–33.
Sanday, William, and Arthur C. Headlam. *A Critical and Exegetical Commentary on the Epistle to the Romans.* ICC. Edinburgh: T. & T. Clark, 1902.
Sanders, Ed P. *Paul and Palestinian Judaism: A Comparison of Patterns of Religion.* London: SCM, 1977.
———. *Paul: The Apostle's Life, Letters, and Thought.* Minneapolis: Fortress, 2015.
———. *Paul, the Law, and the Jewish People.* Minneapolis: Fortress, 1983.
———. "Paul's Jewishness." In *Paul's Jewish Matrix: With an Introductory Essay by Karl P. Donfried*, edited by Thomas G. Casey and Justin Taylor, 51–74. Bible in Dialogue 2. Rome: Gregorian & Biblical, 2011.
Schlier, Heinrich. *Der Römerbrief Kommentar.* HThKNT. Freiburg: Herder, 1977.
Schmidt, D. "1 Thessalonians 2:13–16: Linguistic Evidence for an Interpolation." *JBL* 102 (1983) 269–79.
Schnackenburg, Rudolf. *Baptism in the Thought of St. Paul: A Study in Pauline Theology.* Translated by G. R. Beasley-Murray. Oxford: Basil Blackwell, 1964.
———. *Ephesians: A Commentary.* Translated by H. Heron. Edinburgh: T. & T. Clark, 1991.
Schnelle, Udo. *Apostle Paul: His Life and Theology.* Translated by M. E. Boring. Grand Rapids: Baker Academic, 2003.
Schreiner, Thomas R. "The Abolition and the Fulfillment of the Law in Paul." *JSNT* 35 (1989) 54–59.
———. *Galatians.* Zondervan Exegetical Commentary on the New Testament. Grand Rapids: Zondervan, 2010.
———. *New Testament Theology: Magnifying God in Christ.* Grand Rapids: Baker Academic, 2008.
———. *Paul, Apostle of God's Glory in Christ: A Pauline Theology.* Downers Grove, IL: IVP Academic, 2001.
———. *Romans.* BECNT. Grand Rapids: Baker Academic, 1998.
Schrenk, Gottlob. "δίκη, δίκαιος, δικαιοσύνη, δικαιόω, δικαίωμα, δικαίωσις, δικαιοκρισία." *TDNT* 2:178–225.
Schüssler Fiorenza, Elisabeth. "Paul and the Politics of Interpretation." In *Paul and Politics: Ekklesia, Israel, Imperium, Interpretation. Essays in Honor of Kirster Stendahl*, edited by Richard A. Horsley, 40–57. Harrisburg, PA: Trinity, 2000.
Schweizer, Eduard. *The Good News According to Matthew.* Translated by D. E. Green. London: SPCK, 1975.
———. *The Letter to the Colossians: A Commentary.* Translated by A. Chester. London: SPCK, 1982.
———. "πνεῦμα, πνευματικός, πνέω, ἐμπνέω, πνοή, ἐκπνέω, θεόπνευστος." *TDNT* 6:389–455.
———. "σάρξ, σαρκικός, σάρκινος." *TDNT* 7:98–105, 119–51.

Sechrest, Love L. *A Former Jew: Paul and the Dialectics of Race*. London: T. & T. Clark, 2009.

Seebass, H. "σάρξ." *NIDNTT* 1:671–78.

Segal, Alan F. "Conversation Four: One Covenant or Two: Paul and Early Christianity on Universalism and Cultural Pluralism." In *Reinterpreting Revelation and Tradition: Jews and Christians in Conversation*, edited by John T. Pawlikowski and Hayim G. Perelmuter, 113–40. Franklin, WI: Sheed & Ward, 2000.

———. *Paul the Convert: The Apostolate and Apostasy of Saul the Pharisee*. New Haven: Yale University Press, 1990.

———. "Paul's Jewish Presuppositions." In *The Cambridge Companion to St Paul*, edited by James D. G. Dunn, 159–72. Cambridge: Cambridge University Press, 2003.

———. "Response: Some Aspects of Conversion and Identity Formation in the Christian Community of Paul's Time." In *Paul and Politics: Ekklesia, Israel, Imperium, Interpretation. Essays in Honor of Kirster Stendahl*, edited by Richard A. Horsley, 184–90. Harrisburg, PA: Trinity, 2000.

Seifrid, Mark A. "Romans." In *Commentary on the New Testament Use of the Old Testament*, edited by G. K. Beale and Donald A. Carson, 607–94. Grand Rapids: Baker Academic, 2007.

———. *The Second Letter to the Corinthians*. PNTC. Grand Rapids: Eerdmans, 2014.

———. "Unrighteous by Faith: Apostolic Proclamation in Romans 1:18–3:20." In *Justification and Variegated Nomism: The Paradoxes in Paul*, edited by Donald A. Carson et al., 2:105–45. Tübingen: Mohr Siebeck, 2004.

Shogren, Gary S. *1 and 2 Thessalonians*. ZECNT. Grand Rapids: Zondervan, 2012.

Silva, Moises. *Biblical Words and Their Meaning: An Introduction to Lexical Semantics*. Grand Rapids: Zondervan, 1983.

———. "Faith Versus Works of Law in Galatians." In *Justification and Variegated Nomism: The Paradoxes in Paul*, edited by Donald A. Carson et al., 2:217–48. Tübingen: Mohr Siebeck, 2004.

———. *Interpreting Galatians: Explorations in Exegetical Method*. Grand Rapids: Baker Academic, 2001.

———. *Philippians*. WEC. Chicago: Moody, 1988.

———. *Philippians*. 2nd ed. BECNT. Grand Rapids: Baker Academic, 2005.

Smith, Abraham. "The First Letter to the Thessalonians." In *The New Interpreter's Bible*, edited by Leander E. Keck, 11:671–737. Nashville: Abingdon, 2000.

Soanes, Catherine, and Angus Stevenson, eds. *Concise Oxford English Dictionary*. 11th ed. Oxford: Oxford University Press, 2008.

Stanley, Christopher D. *Paul and the Language of Scripture: Citation Technique in the Pauline Epistles and Contemporary Literature*. Cambridge: Cambridge University Press, 1992.

Staples, Jason A. "What Do the Gentiles Have to Do with 'All Israel'? A Fresh Look at Romans 11:25–27." *JBL* 130/2 (2011) 371–90.

Starr, James M. "Was Paraenesis for Beginners?" In *Early Christian Paraenesis in Context*, edited by James M. Starr and Troels Engberg-Pedersen, 73–112. Berlin: Walter de Gruyter, 2005.

Stegall, Thomas L. *The Gospel of the Christ: A Biblical Response to the Crossless Gospel Regarding the Contents of Saving Faith*. Milwaukee: Grace Gospel, 2009.

Stegner, William R. "Romans 9.6–29—a Midrash." *JSNT* 22 (1984) 37–52.

Stendahl, Kirster. "The Apostle Paul and the Introspective Conscience of the West." *HTR* 56 (1963) 199–215.

———. *Paul Among Jews and Gentiles and Other Essays*. Philadelphia: Fortress, 1976.
Stone, Michael E. *Fourth Ezra*. Hermeneia. Minneapolis: Fortress, 1990.
Stott, John. *The Message of 1 Timothy and Titus: The Life of the Local Church*. Leicester: InterVarsity, 1996.
———. *The Message of Ephesians: God's New Society*. The Bible Speaks Today. Downers Grove, IL: InterVarsity, 1979.
Suh, Robert H. "The Use of Ezekiel 37 in Ephesians 2." *JETS* 50/4 (2007) 715–33.
Swanepoel, J. "Literêre Analise van die Nuwe Testament." *Koers* 51/3 (1986) 287–327.
Talbert, Charles H. *Ephesians and Colossians*. PCNT. Grand Rapids: Baker Academic, 2007.
———. *Matthew*. PCNT. Grand Rapids: Baker Academic, 2010.
Taylor, Mark. *1 Corinthians*. Ebook ed. NAC. Nashville: B&H, 2014.
Thayer, Joseph H. *A Greek-English Lexicon of the New Testament Being Grimm's Wilke's Clavis Novi Testamenti: Translated, Revised and Enlarged*. New York: American Book Company, 1889.
Theissen, Matthew. "Paul's Argument against Gentile Circumcision in Romans 2:17–29." *NovT* 56 (2014) 373–91.
Thielman, Frank. *Ephesians*. BECNT. Grand Rapids: Baker Academic, 2010.
Thiselton, Anthony C. *1 and 2 Thessalonians through the Centuries*. Blackwell Bible Commentaries. Chichester: Blackwell, 2011.
———. *The First Epistle to the Corinthians*. NIGTC. Grand Rapids: Eerdmans, 2000.
———. *The Hermeneutics of Doctrine*. Grand Rapids: Eerdmans, 2007.
———. *New Horizons in Hermeneutics*. Grand Rapids: Zondervan, 1992.
Thomas, Robert L. "1 Thessalonians." In *The Expositor's Bible Commentary*, edited by Frank E. Gaebelein, 11:227–98. Grand Rapids: Zondervan, 1978.
———. "2 Thessalonians." In *The Expositor's Bible Commentary*, edited by Frank E. Gaebelein, 11:299–338. Grand Rapids: Zondervan, 1978.
———. "Current Hermeneutical Trends: Toward Explanation or Obfuscation?" *JETS* 39/2 (1996) 241–56.
Thompson, Marianne M. *Colossians and Philemon*. Two Horizons New Testament Commentary. Grand Rapids: Eerdmans, 2005.
Thrall, Margaret E. *A Critical and Exegetical Commentary on the Second Epistle to the Corinthians*. 2 vols. ICC. Edinburgh: T. & T. Clark, 1994, 2000.
Thyen, H. *Studien zur Südenvegebung im Neuen Testament undseinen alttestamentlichen und jüdischen Voraussetzungen*. Forshungen zur Religion und Literatur des Alten und Neuen Testaments 96. Göttingen: Vandenhoeck & Ruprecht, 1970.
Tomson, Peter J. "The Names 'Israel' and 'Jew' in Ancient Judaism and the New Testament." *Bijdr* 47 (1986) 120–40, 266–89.
———. *Paul and the Jewish Law: Halakha in the Letters of the Apostle to the Gentiles*. Assen: van Gorcum, 1990.
Towner, Philip H. *The Letters to Timothy and Titus*. NICNT. Grand Rapids: Eerdmans, 2006.
Tucker, J. Brian. *Remain in Your Calling: Paul and the Continuation of Social Identities in 1 Corinthians*. Eugene, OR: Pickwick, 2011.
———. *You Belong to Christ: Paul and the Formation of Social Identity in 1 Corinthians 1–4*. Eugene, OR: Pickwick, 2010.
Tucker, J. Brian, and Coleman A. Baker, eds. *T. & T. Clark Handbook to Social Identity in the New Testament*. London: Bloomsbury, 2014.
Turner, David L. *Matthew*. BECNT. Grand Rapids: Baker Academic, 2008.

Van der Horst, Pieter W. "Critical Notes: 'Only Then will All Israel be Saved': A Short Note on the Meaning of καὶ οὕτως in Romans 11:26." *JBL* 119/3 (2000) 521–25.
Van Houwelingen, P. H. Rob. *Tessalonicenzen: Voortgezet basisonderwijs*. Kampen: Kok, 2002.
Van Neste, Ray. "The Message of Titus: An Overview." *SBJT* 7/3 (2003) 18–30.
Van Rensburg, J. P. J. *'n Eerste Griekse Grammatika*. Stellenbosch: Universiteits-Uitgewers en –Boekhandelaars, 1953.
Van Roon, A. *The Authenticity of Ephesians*. NovTSup 39. Leiden: Brill, 1974.
Vaughan, Curtis. "Colossians." In *The Expositor's Bible Commentary*, edited by Frank E. Gaebelein, 11:161–226. Grand Rapids: Zondervan, 1978.
Vaughan, Curtis, and Virtus E. Gideon. *A Greek Grammar of the New Testament*. Nashville: Broadman, 1979.
Vincent, Marvin R. *A Critical and Exegetical Commentary on the Epistles to the Philippians and to Philemon*. ICC. New York: Scribner's, 1906.
Von Rad, Gerhard. "Ἰσραήλ, Ἰσραηλίτης, Ἰουδαῖος, Ἰουδαία, Ἰουδαϊκός, ἰουδαΐζω, Ἰουδαϊσμός, Ἑβραῖος, Ἑβραϊκός, ἑβραΐς, ἑβραϊστί." *TDNT* 3:356–59.
Wallace, Daniel B. *Greek Grammar Beyond the Basics: An Exegetical Syntax of the New Testament*. Grand Rapids: Zondervan, 1996.
Walter, Nikolaus. "ἔθνος." *EDNT* 1:381–83.
Wan, Sze-kar. "Collection for the Saints as Anticolonial Act: Implications for Paul's Ethnic Reconstruction." In *Paul and Politics: Ekklesia, Israel, Imperium, Interpretation. Essays in Honor of Kirster Stendahl*, edited by Richard A. Horsley, 191–215. Harrisburg, PA: Trinity, 2000.
Wanamaker, Charles A. *The Epistles to the Thessalonians*. NIGTC. Grand Rapids: Eerdmans, 1990.
Watson, Francis. *Paul, Judaism, and the Gentiles: Beyond the New Perspective*. Grand Rapids: Eerdmans, 2007.
Watts, John D. W. *Isaiah 1–33*. WBC. Waco: Word, 1985.
Weeks, Theodore R. "Ethnicity." In *Berkshire Encyclopedia of World History*, edited by William McNeill, 2:680–85. Great Barrington: Berkshire, 2005.
Weima, Jeffrey A. D. *1–2 Thessalonians*. Ebook ed. BECNT. Grand Rapids: Baker Academic, 2014.
Weiss, Bernhard. *Der Brief an die Römer*. 9th ed. Göttingen: Vandenhoeck & Ruprecht, 1899.
Wenham, David. "The Resurrection Narratives in Matthew's Gospel." *TynBul* 24 (1973) 21–54.
Westerholm, Stephen. *Israel's Law and the Church's Faith: Paul and His Recent Interpreters*. Grand Rapids: Eerdmans, 1988.
———. *Perspectives Old and New on Paul: The "Lutheran" Paul and His Critics*. Grand Rapids: Eerdmans, 2004.
Wilckens, Ulrich. *Der Brief an die Römer*. Vol. 2. EKKNT. Neukirchener: Neukirchen; Vluyn, 1980.
Wilkins, Michael J. *Matthew*. NIVAC. Grand Rapids: Zondervan, 2004.
Witherington, Ben, III. *1 and 2 Thessalonians: A Socio-Rhetorical Commentary*. Grand Rapids: Eerdmans, 2006.
———. *Conflict and Community in Corinth: A Socio-Rhetorical Commentary on 1 and 2 Corinthians*. Grand Rapids: Eerdmans, 1995.
———. "Contemporary Perspectives on Paul." In *The Cambridge Companion to St Paul*, edited by James D. G. Dunn, 256–69. Cambridge: Cambridge University Press, 2003.

———. *Grace in Galatia: A Commentary on Paul's Letter to the Galatians*. Grand Rapids: Eerdmans, 1998.

———. *Jesus, Paul and the End of the World: A Comparative Study in New Testament Eschatology*. Downers Grove, IL: InterVarsity, 1992.

———. *The Paul Quest: The Renewed Search For the Jew of Tarsus*. Downers Grove, IL: InterVarsity, 1998.

Witherington, Ben, III, and Darlene Hyatt. *Paul's Letter to the Romans: A Socio-Rhetorical Commentary*. Grand Rapids: Eerdmans, 2004.

Wood, A. Skevington. "Ephesians." In *The Expositor's Bible Commentary*, edited by Frank E. Gaebelein, 11:1–92. Grand Rapids: Zondervan, 1978.

Wright, Nicholas T. *The Climax of the Covenant: Christ and the Law in Pauline Theology*. Minneapolis: Fortress, 1991.

———. *The Epistles of Paul to the Colossians and to Philemon: An Introduction and Commentary*. TNTC. Grand Rapids: Eerdmans, 1986.

———. "The Letter to the Romans." In *The New Interpreter's Bible*, edited by Leander E. Keck, 10:394–770. Nashville: Abingdon, 2002.

———. *The New Testament and the People of God*. London: SPCK, 1992.

———. *Paul and the Faithfulness of God*. 2 vols. London: SPCK, 2013.

———. *Paul: In Fresh Perspective*. Minneapolis: Fortress, 2005.

———. *The Resurrection of the Son of God*. London: SPCK, 2003.

———. *What Saint Paul Really Said: Was Paul of Tarsus the Real Founder of Christianity?* Grand Rapids: Eerdmans, 1997.

Wuellner, Wilhelm. "Greek Rhetoric and Pauline Argumentation." In *Early Christian Literature and the Classical Intellectual Tradition: In Honorem Robert M. Grant*, edited by William R. Schoedel and Robert L. Wilken, 177–88. Paris: Beauchesne, 1979.

Yarbrough, Robert W. "The Theology of Romans in Future Tense." *SBJT* 11/3 (2007) 46–57.

Young, Edward J. *The Book of Isaiah*. 3 vols. NICOT. Grand Rapids: Eerdmans, 1965, 1969, 1972.

Zerwick, Maximilian. *Biblical Greek Illustrated by Examples*. Rome: Pontificii Instituti Biblici, 1963.

Zerwick, Maximilian, and Mary Grosvenor. *A Grammatical Analysis of the New Testament*. 4th ed. Rome: Editrice Prontificio Istituto Biblico, 1993.

Zetterholm, Magnus. *Approaches to Paul: A Student's Guide to Recent Scholarship*. Minneapolis: Fortress, 2009.

———. *The Formation of Christianity in Antioch: A Social-Scientific Approach to the Separation Between Judaism and Christianity*. London: Routledge, 2003.

Zoccali, Christopher. "'And so all Israel will be saved': Competing Interpretations of Romans 11.26 in Pauline Scholarship." *JSNT* 30/3 (2008) 289–318.

———. "Children of Abraham, the Restoration of Israel and the Eschatological Pilgrimage of the Nations: What Does it Mean for 'In Christ' Identity?" In *T. & T. Clark Handbook to Social Identity in the New Testament*, edited by J. Brian Tucker and Coleman A. Baker, 253–71. London: Bloomsbury, 2014.

———. "Paul and Social Identity in 1 Corinthians: Review Article." *Journal of Beliefs and Values* 34 (2013) 105–14.

———. *Whom God Has Called: The Relationship of Church and Israel in Pauline Interpretation, 1920 to the Present*. Eugene, OR: Pickwick, 2010.

Subject Index

Abraham, 28, 42, 44, 47–49, 52, 69, 76, 78–85, 90–93, 95–97, 99–100, 102, 104, 116–18, 121, 143, 163, 189, 210, 225, 238, 244–45, 249, 261, 272, 274, 278, 313–14, 336, 341–44
adoption, 47, 100, 111, 160, 171, 205, 221, 225, 227, 243, 343, 352
anachronism, 13–14, 97, 142n204, 143, 208n267, 282–83, 292, 294, 329n604, 346
anthropology, Pauline, 162, 196, 201, 203, 206n245, 211, 226–30
Antioch incident, 131–35
antisemitism, 6, 10, 147
Apostolic Decree, 143, 280

baptism, 96, 162, 167, 187n90, 212–18, 256

Christianity, 11–12, 14, 89n154, 128, 149, 356
Christology, 72, 83, 95, 124, 136, 157–59, 163, 166, 171, 182–83, 186, 203, 215, 217–18, 253, 257, 279, 311, 325, 347, 355
circumcision, 58, 60–63, 68, 81–84, 86, 88, 91–93, 97, 105, 111–12, 114–15, 117, 120, 137–42, 168, 171, 194, 206–7, 210, 215–18, 226, 233n11, 272, 278, 335–38, 353–54, 356
conversion, Paul's, 125–30, 128, 142, 146, 162, 169, 336

covenant(s), 3, 47–48, 102–7, 111, 118, 126, 133, 164, 174–85, 190, 216, 246, 249, 251–52, 279, 305–6, 308, 317, 343, 351, 354
cross, 5, 93, 98n225, 112, 123–24, 127, 157, 159, 173, 179, 216, 247–48, 250, 264, 283, 308, 332, 336–38

David, 49, 72, 79, 121–22
diachrony, 19, 31, 248, 253, 256, 259, 261–62, 268–69, 294, 310, 312, 315–16, 355
divinity of Christ, 49–50, 98, 183, 257

election, 167–68, 237–41, 263, 267, 277, 294, 310, 312, 314, 320, 352
Empire, Roman, 149
eschatology, 66, 73, 90, 93–94, 105, 139, 145, 161, 170, 176–78, 182, 187–88, 190–92, 198–99, 201–2, 204, 206–12, 217, 219–21, 223–28, 253, 270, 273, 275, 277, 279, 281, 286, 294, 299, 303, 309, 310n521, 313, 326–27, 335, 338, 340–43, 345, 347, 351–53, 355–56
ethnicity, 6, 9–11, 14, 15, 38, 56, 86, 89n154, 92, 94, 104, 109–10, 118, 120, 133, 135, 140, 143, 154, 156, 159–60, 164, 166, 168–71, 214, 218, 226, 233n11, 240, 263–65, 269, 272, 336, 345, 349, 353, 355–56
evangelical, 5

faith, 74, 76–86, 89, 90–91, 93–95, 97, 99, 107, 109, 117, 123, 130, 134–35, 143, 145, 146, 162, 169, 176–77, 201, 206, 208, 215, 217–18, 221, 225, 236, 238–39, 241, 245–50, 252, 254–55, 257–59, 261, 263, 265, 267–68, 273–77, 279, 281, 284, 286, 311, 313–15, 318, 335–36, 342–43, 346–47, 351, 353, 355

flesh, 12, 39–42, 44–47, 49–50, 52, 69, 72, 81, 84, 86, 88–89, 91–92, 103–4, 109, 110–14, 120, 137, 139, 143–46, 155–56, 159, 168, 170, 172, 181, 184–86, 188, 190–91, 193–98, 200–204, 206–12, 215–18, 220–23, 225–26, 228–29, 235–36, 238, 240, 251, 267, 269, 273, 281, 309–10, 313, 317, 328, 335–37, 342–43, 345, 349, 351–55

gnomic future tense, *See* logical future tense

halakha, 3, 143–44, 280
hardening of Israel, 154, 180–81, 240, 247–50, 252, 260, 263, 265–66, 268, 272–73, 279, 281, 288–90, 310–12, 315–22, 346, 348, 350–51, 355
Hebrew, 31, 42–43, 69, 127, 140–41
Holocaust, 1, 288n388

intermediate state, 227–28
Israel, 4, 15–16, 17, 21–22, 24, 27–41, 46, 49–53, 55, 59, 65, 68–69, 100, 108, 111–15, 118, 120–22, 128n80, 140, 154, 156, 167–68, 173, 179–81, 186, 189, 196, 218, 222, 225–26, 231, 234, 236–53, 256–324, 326, 328–34, 338–55
Israelite, 21–22, 24, 33–34, 42–44, 46–47, 50–51, 55, 69, 84, 95, 173, 195, 232n11, 237, 248, 256, 263, 272, 283n364, 318, 348–49

Judaism, 2–3, 5, 8–9, 13, 15, 89n154, 126, 128n80, 142n204, 163, 279, 293–94, 310, 346
Judean(s), 9–13, 15, 22, 24–25, 29, 32–39, 43–45, 47, 50, 53, 54–69, 72, 74, 76, 79, 82, 84, 87, 88, 90, 92–93, 94, 98, 104–6, 108, 111, 113–14, 120, 121, 123–26, 128n80, 131–32, 135, 137–39, 142–45, 148–54, 163–64, 166, 169–71, 181, 196, 214, 216, 231–34, 239, 241–42, 245, 252, 254n167, 257–59, 262–64, 268–71, 275–78, 281–84, 286, 294, 311, 314, 316–19, 335–36, 340, 346–49, 352–53, 356
justification, 74, 78, 89, 109–10, 129n88, 133–35, 179, 224, 285, 294, 299, 356

land, promised, 85, 189, 314, 327, 347
law, Mosaic, 48, 55–68, 70, 77–78, 82, 85–86, 88–89, 91–92, 94–99, 104–5, 113–14, 117, 127, 128, 132–34, 138n171, 139, 141–42, 144–46, 169, 171, 174–80, 182–203, 206–9, 221–25, 227, 233n11, 245–46, 249, 254–55, 280–81, 285, 311, 313, 315, 324, 336–37, 340, 342–43, 345, 349, 355
logical future tense, 178, 219, 275, 296–302, 308–9, 312, 346–47, 355

memory, 110
Messiah, 49, 72, 85n122, 111, 115–16, 120–22, 127, 151, 154, 159, 163, 236, 247–52, 257, 259, 264, 267, 274, 289, 314–15, 317, 350–51
midrash, 235n29
mystery, 286–88, 310, 312–15, 348

new creation, 108, 110, 112, 114, 116–17, 132, 155–65, 168, 170, 172–73, 186, 210, 217, 221, 228, 299, 338, 340, 343, 352–53

New Perspective on Paul (NPP), 1–3, 57–58, 77, 79–80, 92, 99n228, 131, 134, 146, 225, 245, 254n167, 255n175, 265, 267, 275n317, 356
Noahide Laws/Commandments, 143, 280, 283–84

othering, 138, 149, 169

paradox, 65, 307–8, 310, 313, 320
Paul Within Judaism, *See* Radical New Perspective on Paul
persecution, 36, 61, 126–27, 129, 141, 147–52, 154, 336–37
Pharisee(s), 127, 141–42, 337
promises to the fathers, 48–49, 52, 69, 71, 79–82, 84–86, 90, 94, 96–98, 104, 107, 111, 120, 138n171, 210, 238, 245, 314, 317, 336, 342

race, 14–15, 81, 124
Radical New Perspective on Paul (RNPP), 2–3, 54n180, 106n273, 142–44, 170–72, 280–81, 283, 353
redemptive history, *See* salvation history
regeneration, 162, 170, 195, 222–24, 226–27, 237
remnant, 40, 122, 243–44, 247–48, 250, 263–66, 274, 286, 309, 316, 350–51
righteousness, 75–76, 134, 145, 160, 175, 178, 187–88, 199–200, 204, 207, 219, 221, 245–46, 250n145, 251, 253–55, 257, 263, 313, 317, 347, 356

Sabbath(s), 91, 106n273, 126, 354
salvation history, 66, 73–74, 81, 84, 86, 100, 103, 109, 124, 163, 170, 173, 179–80, 182, 186–88, 190–92, 194, 199, 204, 206–8, 210–11, 220, 225–26, 234, 239–42, 248–49, 252–53, 256, 262, 264, 266–69, 271, 275–76, 282, 285–86, 294, 303, 310, 315–25, 327, 345, 347–48, 351, 353–55
salvation, 55, 72–73, 90n159, 109, 112, 123, 205, 236–37, 240–41, 250–52, 257–58, 268–69, 274, 286, 294, 296, 299–302, 308–9, 312–15, 328–34, 346–47, 351
S/spirit, 12, 27–29, 40, 47n131, 54–68, 70, 90–93, 95–97, 103–4, 107, 112, 114, 116, 118, 122, 128, 138–39, 143, 145–46, 155, 174–79, 182–85, 189–92, 194–95, 199–215, 218, 220–30, 237, 275, 303, 313, 335, 339, 343, 345, 351, 353–56
supersession, 3, 114, 118, 160n359, 163, 169, 177, 183–84, 207, 313
synchrony, 19–20, 34

third entity, 7–8, 105, 114–15, 118, 124, 129, 153, 164, 170, 353
third race, *See* third entity
Traditional Approach to Paul (TAP), 1–2, 77, 79, 131, 134, 145, 225, 255n175, 265, 267, 356

works of the law, 2, 89, 91, 109, 117, 141, 154, 160, 169, 208, 214, 221, 226, 241, 255, 265, 274, 335, 343, 353

Index of Modern Authors

Abasciano, Brian J., 252
Albright, W. F., 327

Barclay, John M. G., 87n138
Barrett, C. K., 120n9, 176n22, 188n98, 191n119, 228n374, 287
Barth, Fredrik, 14n81
Barth, Karl, 313n530
Bassler, Jouette M., 5
Beasley-Murray, G. R., 214n318, 217
Betz, Hans D., 101, 104n259, 106, 132n111, 340
Blass, Friedrich, 297, 299
Bloesch, Donald G., 5
Bockmuehl, Markus, 142
Botha, Jan, 19
Boyarin, Daniel, 13, 226n367, 227n370
Bruce, F. F., 89n155, 105–6, 127, 130, 131n106, 237, 340–41
Bruno, Christopher R., 306
Buell, Denise K., 14, 15n90
Bultmann, Rudolph, 104n260
Burton, Ernest De W., 105, 340
Byrne, Brendan, 305

Calvin, John, 340
Campbell, William S., 8, 12n68, 38, 164, 310n521, 344, 354
Chrysostom, John, 42
Ciampa, Roy E., 40
Collins, Raymond F., 124
Cooper, John W., 230
Cosgrove, Charles H., 237n41

Cranfield, C. E. B., 75, 99, 180n49, 237, 252, 255n176, 260, 292–93, 300–301, 314, 323

Dalton, William J., 330
Danker, Frederick W., 159
Das, A. Andrew, 209
De Boer, Martinus C., 92, 102n249, 130, 132, 210–11, 340, 345n707
Debrunner, Albert, 297, 299
Denney, James, 261
De Saussure, Ferdinand, 19
Driver, Samuel R., 260
Duling, Dennis, 14–15
Dunn, James D. G., 2, 48, 56n201, 57, 74–77, 80, 88, 91–92, 96n205, 98n228, 102, 121, 125n57, 126n65, 128n79–80, 130n98, 131, 167, 188n98, 191n119, 195n151, 201n198, 208n266, 209–10, 232, 237, 254n170, 255n175, 264, 269n264, 270, 273n302, 286, 292, 304, 323n564, 336, 340

Eisenbaum, Pamela, 84n117, 279n342
Ellicott, Charles J., 341
Elliott, John H., 12n72, 14, 26n110, 37, 232
Ervin, Howard M., 65n253
Esler, Philip F., 8n42, 10, 282

Fee, Gordon D., 90n182, 93, 104n259, 145, 149, 150n279, 176, 200, 206–7, 209

383

INDEX OF MODERN AUTHORS

Feldmeier, Reinhard, 328
Fitch, David E., 5
Fitzmyer, Joseph A., 41, 155, 305, 310n521, 325n576
Fung, Ronald Y. K., 95n200, 127, 131n105, 340
Furnish, Victor P., 159n354, 175

Gager, John G., 4–5, 39, 98n226
Garland, David E., 180
Gaston, Lloyd, 264n229, 273n300, 279
Gathercole, Simon J., 57
George, Timothy, 125n53
Gispen, W. H., 66n256
Gutbrod, Walter, 33, 36n44, 133
Guthrie, George H., 182

Hagner, Donald A., 232, 299
Hansen, G. Walter, 89–90
Harris, Murray J., 228n374
Hays, Richard B., 102, 125, 130, 324, 336–38
Hoehner, Harold W., 329n604
Hooker, Morna D., 139
Horrell, David G., 144
Horsley, Richard A., 344n705
Hultgren, Arland J., 72n9
Hutchinson, John, 14n83

Jewett, Robert, 48n145, 73, 82n106, 270, 300
Jipp, Joshua W., 83
Johnson Hodge, Caroline, 3n18, 15

Käsemann, Ernst, 72, 86, 197n173, 201n197, 233
Kim, Dongsu, 6
Kim, Seyoon, 313
Kirk, J. R. Daniel, 303
Kistemaker, Simon J., 40, 182
Köstenberger, Andreas J., 19
Kuhli, H., 33
Kuhn, Karl G., 32, 37

Lategan, Bernard C., 131, 208n263, 337
Lenski, Richard C. H., 42, 123n45, 158, 314
Levine, Amy-Jill, 10

Levison, John R., 224
Lightfoot, Joseph B., 130
Lim, Kar Y., 172–73
Lincoln, Andrew T., 97n215, 108–9
Longenecker, Richard N., 45n122, 58, 91, 92n174, 93, 99n238, 101, 103n254, 106, 130, 131n106, 132n111, 134, 208n267, 302n477
Louw, Johannes P., 20, 34
Luther, Martin, 1, 75, 188n98

Mann, C. S., 327
Marshall, I. Howard, 109
Martyn, J. Louis, 92, 97, 102, 107, 131–32, 208n267, 210–11
Mason, Steve, 9–11, 13, 126
Maston, Jason, 79n86
Matera, Frank J., 194, 321n551
Meeks, Wayne A., 149
Metzger, Bruce M., 322
Meyer, Jason C., 104–5, 180n53
Michaels, J. Ramsey, 328
Miller, David M., 10, 11n63, 33–34, 37, 126n65
Moo, Douglas J., 49, 57, 72, 75, 80, 121–22, 130, 155, 164n393, 171, 193n134, 200n196, 202, 204n223, 233–34, 237, 245, 246, 255–56, 285n374, 287, 325
Mounce, Robert H., 74
Muddiman, John, 328–29

Nanos, Mark D., 3n15, 232n11, 280–81, 284, 288n388, 346–47
Nathan, Emmanuel, 179n47
Neusner, Jacob, 9, 235n29
Nida, Eugene A., 20, 34

Osborne, Grant R., 78, 246, 327

Perkins, Pheme, 108, 114

Räisänen, Heikki, 95n199
Reumann, John, 138n171
Richardson, Peter, 340, 344n702
Ridderbos, Herman N., 165, 191, 300n468

Robertson, A. T., 290, 297–99
Rosner, Brian S., 40

Sampley, J. Paul, 179n43
Sanders, Ed P., 2, 79n86, 128n80
Schreiner, Thomas R., 198–99, 324n570
Sechrest, Love L., 15
Seifrid, Mark A., 259, 261
Silva, Moises, 19, 90n162–63, 94, 137–38, 146n239
Smith, Anthony D., 14n83
Staples, Jason A., 278–79, 282–83
Stendahl, Kirster, 2, 279
Suh, Robert H., 116–17

Thielman, Frank, 328–29
Thiselton, Anthony C., 16, 123n43, 124, 214n318
Thrall, Margaret E., 179n43
Tomson, Peter J., 37, 115n353, 282, 348
Towner, Philip H., 18n96

Tucker, J. Brian, 6–7
Turner, David L., 327

Von Rad, Gerhard, 37n52, 43n104

Wallace, Daniel B., 297–98
Wan, Sze-kar, 7, 15, 143
Weima, Jeffrey A. D., 147n252
Westerholm, Stephen, 57–58
Wright, Nicholas T., 2, 18n96, 30n116, 51n172, 57n202, 65, 73, 77n64, 91n170, 98nn224–25, 99n229, 122, 159, 180n49, 184, 186, 203, 232, 242n81, 254n167, 256n179, 259, 278, 287, 290, 294, 307–8, 316n533, 323, 325n585

Young, Edward J., 303, 307

Zerwick, Maximilian, 289
Zoccali, Christopher, 8n42, 68, 277n326

Index of Ancient Sources

Old Testament

Genesis

6:1–4	327
12:1–3	116
12:7	85
13:15–17	85
14:13	42
15:7	85
15:16	152
17:1–14	216
17:10	58n221
19:29	244
21:12	238
25:1–6	44
25:12–18	44
25:23 (LXX)	241
32:28	31n2, 43
35:16–18	140
41:8	62
48:19 (LXX)	278, 282–83

Exodus

4:22	205
9:12, 16	288n388
14:13	73n14
15:2	73n14
16:10	47
24:5–17	47
31:18 (LXX)	175
32:30–34	236
34:1 (LXX)	175
34:29–35 (LXX)	179
34:32–35	179
40:34–35	47

Leviticus

3:3	41
7:15	41
9:23	47
18:5	61, 66n256, 67, 246, 255
18:29	246
23:10–11	271
26:40–43	60, 320
26:41	66

Numbers

14:10	47
14:11, 22–23	180n53
15:17–21	271

Deuteronomy

2:30	62–63
4:37	168n420
7:6–8	168n420
9:22–24	180n53
10:16	216, 288n388
10:16 (LXX)	180n53
14:1	205
14:2	167n420
10:12–22	60

Deuteronomy (continued)

10:15	168n420
11:1, 8	61
29:4	180n53
29:26–29	61
30:1–16	61
30:6	216
30:12–14	256, 259
32:8–9	38n60
32:20–21	260, 268
32:43	121

Joshua

2:11	62
5:1	62
8:24 (LXX)	152
22:27	48

Judges

6:2–6	260
15:18	73n14

1 Samuel

9:1–2	140
11:9	73n14

2 Samuel

2:4–17	49
7:12	36
22:50	121
22:51	36

1 Kings

10:9	168n420
19:10, 14	150, 263–64
19:18 (LXX)	263–64

2 Kings

6:2, 23	260
17:14 (LXX)	180n53, 288n388
19:7	62

1 Chronicles

16:13 (LXX)	167n420
28:9 (LXX)	152
28:13	48

2 Chronicles

2:12 (LXX)	152
28:12	62
30:8 (LXX)	180n53, 288n388
36:15	150

Nehemiah

9:16–17 (LXX)	180n53, 288n388
9:26	150
9:29 (LXX)	180n53, 288n388

Job

7:11	62
40:8	325
41:11	325

Psalms

5:6 (LXX)	137
6:9 (LXX)	137
9:18 (LXX)	152
13:7 (LXX)	303, 306
14:7	303
17:50 (LXX)	121
18:2, 5 (LXX)	259–60
22:15	332
25:13	85
34:8 (LXX)	266
37:9	85
52:7 (LXX)	303, 306

53:6	303	27:6–13	306–8, 310, 312, 320
58:3 (LXX)	137	27:9	280, 305–6, 309n519
63:9	329		
67:19 (LXX)	50n161	28:9–15	259
68:18	328n604	28:16	246–47, 257
68:23–24 (LXX)	266	29:4	266
77:6	62	29:10–15	180n53, 259, 265
77:8 (LXX)	152	29:13	48
78:56	180n53	29:22	32n4
78:68	168n420	30:9–11	259
92:13	271	33:1	260
95:8 (LXX)	180n53, 288n388	40:13 (LXX)	325
105:6, 43 (LXX)	167n420	41:8	168n420
106:5 (LXX)	167n420	42:1	85
116:1 (LXX)	121	42:5	62
117:1	121	42:6	85
123 (LXX)	266	42:9	163
124:5 (LXX)	339	42:23	259
125:5	339	43:6	205
127:6 (LXX)	339	43:18–19	160n359, 163
128:6	339	43:20 (LXX)	167n420
148:14	115	44:18	180n53
		45:4 (LXX)	167n420
		46:13	73n14
		48:6	163
		49:5	116
		49:6	73n14, 85, 116
		52:7, 10	73n14, 258
		53:1	258–59
		54:3	85
		56:10	180n53
		57:13	85
		59:20–21	280, 303–6, 309n519
		60:21	85
		63:17 (LXX)	180n53
		65:1–2	260–61
		65:9 (LXX)	167n420
		65:17	160n359
		66:22	160n359

Proverbs

11:8–9 (LXX)	266

Isaiah

1:9 (LXX)	244
2:3	306
2:5–6	32n4
4:4	331
5:7	32n4
6:9–11	180n53, 181, 265
8:13	248
8:14	246, 248
8:18	32n4
10:20–23	243–44, 248, 286, 309
11:10	122
11:10–14	85, 332
12:2	73n14
24:16	260
25:9	73n14
26:19 (LXX)	326

Jeremiah

2:30	150
3:19	205

Jeremiah (continued)

3:17	180n53
4:1–4	62
4:2	85
4:4	216
5:15–17	260
5:21	180n53
7:24	180n53
7:26 (LXX)	180n53, 288n388
9:13–14	62
9:23–24	136n156
9:25–26	62
10:19–20	193
11:8	180n53
11:17	271
13:10	180n53
17:23 (LXX)	180n53, 288n388
19:15 (LXX)	180n53, 288n388
23:5	85
23:17	180n53
24:6	85
30:3	85
31:9	205
31:31	176
31:31–33	305–6
31:34	136n156
32:41	85
38:31–34 (LXX)	176, 199, 305–6

Ezekiel

3:7, 9	180n53
11:19 (LXX)	175
12:2	180n53
20:11, 13, 21	67
36:10–12	85
36:24–32	199, 224, 309, 316
36:26–27 (LXX)	175–76, 309, 316
37:1–27	117n361, 309, 316
37:6	224
37:12–14 (LXX)	326–27, 334
37:14	176, 224
37:25	85
44:7	216

Daniel

2:18–19	287
2:27–30	287
3:8, 12	32n9
8:23	152
12:2 (LXX)	326, 334

Hosea

2:1 (LXX)	205, 242
2:23	250
2:25 (LXX)	242
4:1	136n156
5:1–2 (LXX)	266
6:6	136n156
11:1	168n420, 205

Joel

2:32	50n161, 257, 303
3:16	330

Amos

1:2	330

Micah

1:2–3	241
2:7	32n4
2:12	32n4
3:1, 8, 9	32n4
3:11	55n189
5:1	32n4
5:6	32n4
7:7–10	193
7:19	330

Nahum

1:15 (LXX)	258n196
2:2	32n4

Habakkuk

2:4	76–77

Zechariah

8:23	32n9
9:10	85

Malachi

3:22 (LXX)	310
4:4	310n522

Old Testament Apocryphja/ Pseudepigrapha

Apocalypse of Abraham

29:17	292

2 Apocalypse of Baruch

23:4	292
30:2	292
75:6	292

The Cairo Damascus Document

2:14–16	88n146
3:2–4	79n83

Community Rule (1QS)

5:5	88n146

1 Enoch

22:6–13	327

4 Ezra

4:35–37	292

Jubilees

1:22–25	63
7:20–21	3n15
19:8–9	79n83
23:9–10	79n83

Life of Jeremiah (in Vitae prophetarum)

6	295n440

1 Maccabees

2:15	127n72
2:52	79n83
2:58	127n72

2 Maccabees

1:1–10	37
2:21	125
6:14	152
6:23	48n142
8:1	125
8:15	48n140
8:32	37
10:8	37
14:38	125

3 Maccabees

4:21	37

4 Maccabees

4:26	125–26
13:17	49, 313
17:16	48n142
18:1	33

Psalms of Solomon

4:25	339
6:6	339
8:27–28	339
9:8	339
11:9	339

1QH

6:26–27	247

1QS

8:7	247

Sirach

44:12	48n140
44:19–20	79n83
48:2	127n72
50:25–26	260n211

Testament of Abraham (recention A)

7.11	295n440

Wisdom of Solomon

4:15 (LXX)	167n420
18:4	99n238
18:22	48n140

New Testament

Matthew

2:2	35n33, 37n50
2:6	34
3:11	214n313
5:7–9	48
5:20	291
7:6	137
7:13, 21	291
8:10	35
8:11	313
10:5–6	43n106
10:6	35, 37n50, 330
12:40	332
13:17	331
15:1	35
15:12	150
15:24	35, 37n50
17:20	91n163
19:28	35
20:10	297
21:21	91n163
22:32	313
23:1–4	113
23:15–24	113
23:31–37	151, 153
27:11	37n50
27:25	150
27:29	37n50
27:37	37n50
27:42	35
27:51–53	326–27, 330, 334, 346

Mark

1:8	214n313
3:5	288n388
4:40	91n163
7:3	34
7:5–8	113
7:6	48
9:43–47	291
10:15–25	291
11:22	91n163
11:23	91n163
12:1–9	150
12:26	313
15:2, 9	37n50
15:12, 18	37n50
15:26	37n50
15:32	35

Luke

1:16	43
1:68	35
2:25, 32	35
3:16	214n313
6:12	90n163
7:9	35
11:48–51	151
13:24	291
13:28	313
13:33–34	151
15:24	35
16:22–23	313
17:6	91n163
23:3	37n50
23:37, 38	37n50
24:20	150
24:21	35

John

1:33	214n313
1:47	35
3:3–5	222, 291, 331
3:6	208n267
5:18	150
5:25–29	327
5:46–47	331
7:1	150
8:31	35
8:59	150
11:45	35
11:45–53	150
12:11	35
18:14, 31	150
18:33	35, 37n50
18:36	35
18:39	37n50
19:3	37n50
19:19, 21	37n50
21:19	297

Acts

1:5	214n313
2:22	36
2:23	150
2:36	36, 150
2:38	257
3:12	36
3:13–15	150
4:10	36, 150
5:21	43
5:30	150
5:35	36
6:1	43
7:52	150–51
8:16	257
9:1–3	126
9:17–18	183
9:22, 23	36, 163
10:28	36
10:39	150
10:48	257
11:16	214n313
12:11	36
13:16	36
13:23, 24	36
13:28	150
13:50	36
14:2	36
15:19–32	143, 280
16:1–5	143
16:3	36
17:3	163
17:5–10	149
17:5, 13	36
18:2	232
18:28	36
19:5	257
19:37	56
21:25	143
21:39	36
22:3	36, 127
22:3–5	126
22:12	36
23:6	127
26:5	127

Romans

1:1–3	72, 86, 184, 221
1:4	219
1:5–6	233
1:7	50n161
1:9	72, 293
1:15	284
1:16	109, 252, 264, 313, 349
1:16–17	64, 71–77, 239–40, 353
1:17	80–81, 124, 245
1:18–32	63, 250n145
1:25	50n161
2:1	138n169
2:1–16	54, 63, 250n145
2:8	139
2:8–9	74, 349
2:9–10	124
2:10	74, 349
2:11–16	253
2:12	66, 311
2:13	70, 190, 200, 245, 285, 296n446, 317
2:14–15	66–67, 198
2:16	253
2:17–22	55–56
2:17–29	54–55, 190, 349
2:19	139
2:22	138n169
2:23–27	57–59
2:25	68, 233n11
2:25–29	138n171, 176–77, 278
2:26	296n446
2:28–29	34, 40, 59–70, 192n126, 216
2:29	32n7, 190, 195
3:1	4, 66–67
3:1–20	64–65, 77, 190, 250n145, 317, 349, 351
3:2	74, 349
3:3	66, 90n163
3:4	54
3:7	193n132
3:8	259
3:9	66, 311
3:9–24	59, 65, 69, 198
3:19	66–67, 82, 311
3:19–20	66, 285
3:20	4, 64, 86, 109, 141, 192n126, 224, 246, 265, 296n446, 337
3:20–23	254–55
3:21	55n180, 64, 70, 81, 199–200, 255, 264n229, 317
3:21–31	59, 65–66, 68, 70, 145, 273, 285, 351
3:22	64, 81, 143, 264n229
3:22–26	83, 265, 303
3:23	67
3:24	109
3:24–26	78, 299n464
3:25–26	66, 200, 245
3:27–28	83, 265
3:27–31	77, 250n145
3:28	64, 86, 109
3:29	78, 83, 349
3:30	68, 78, 83, 245, 296n446
3:31	4, 78, 83, 177
4:1	41, 184, 221
4:1–25	77–86, 94–100, 117, 163, 241, 261, 263, 272–73, 278, 313, 341, 351
4:2, 6	265, 299n464
4:3–20	76
4:4	109, 274
4:5	91n163, 110, 274, 299n464
4:7–12	94
4:9	91n163
4:12	274, 285
4:13	85, 189, 200, 327
4:13–16	238, 245, 265, 274, 285
4:17	176, 271, 316, 320n546
4:23–24	136, 285, 303
5:1	78, 285, 299n464

INDEX OF ANCIENT SOURCES 395

5:1–2	80, 83, 265, 303	7:5	156, 203, 207, 218, 220, 224–25, 268n258, 351
5:2–21	186–87		
5:5	73n24, 224		
5:7	296n446, 298	7:5–9	177
5:9–10	73, 90n159, 199, 252, 299	7:6	64, 141, 160n358, 176, 199, 202, 206–7, 211, 220, 246, 263, 337, 351, 355
5:10	109, 113n328, 299n464		
5:11	56, 136, 199, 270		
5:12	291–92	7:7	4
5:12–21	161, 193, 194, 198–99, 294, 321, 355	7:7–12	192, 194–95, 199, 210, 224
		7:7–25	189, 200
5:14	166	7:10–11	99, 177, 224
5:15	197, 210, 224n365, 321n547	7:12	4, 225
		7:14	177, 221n355
5:16	199, 321n547	7:14–25	192–99, 222, 225, 227, 281, 304, 311
5:17	296n446		
5:18	199, 253	7:21	203
5:19	200, 300–302, 347	7:23	138n169, 200, 203, 311
5:20	224		
5:21	136, 303	7:24	210, 217, 221, 227, 304, 311
6:1–5	162		
6:2	296n446	8:1–16	199–207, 211, 218, 220, 222–23, 226–27, 263, 273, 304, 351, 355
6:2–15	187–88, 193, 197, 215		
6:3–6	167n415, 210, 257		
6:4	160n358, 223, 303, 338	8:2	177, 193–94, 222, 225, 303, 311, 351
6:4–5	165	8:3	141, 189, 221–22, 225, 246, 337
6:5, 8	219, 296		
6:6	165, 217	8:4	66, 81, 221–22, 225, 293
6:7	299n464, 303		
6:11	201, 338	8:6	212
6:12–13	194	8:7	113n328
6:14	296n446	8:7–10	227
6:14–15	64, 144, 194, 255, 311	8:8	156, 226
		8:9	193, 226, 303
6:17	247	8:10	221, 225, 299, 303
6:18–22	193, 311	8:11	176
6:19	188, 199	8:13	221
6:21–22	199	8:15	47n131, 89, 100, 160, 221, 225
6:23	303, 321n547		
7:1–6	189–92, 194, 256n179	8:16	224, 226–27, 230n384, 335n637, 351
7:3	296n446, 298		
7:3–4	138n169	8:18	47n135
7:4	160, 225	8:19–23	228

Romans (continued)

8:21	311n526	9:30–33	163, 196, 245–51, 254–55, 257, 264, 273, 281, 285–86, 315, 317–19
8:23	47n131, 160		
8:24	90n159, 252, 299n464, 300	9:31	4, 48, 337, 350
		9:32	48, 78, 232, 238, 265,
8:33	299n464		
8:38	139	9:33	266, 303–5, 350
8:39	138n169	10:1	287
9:1–10	84, 235–39, 314	10:1–4	163
9:2–3	251, 286–87, 318	10:1–21	241, 251–62, 315–16
9:3–8	45–54, 69, 110–11, 115, 120, 263, 265, 272, 283n365, 309–10, 320n545, 321n547	10:3	154n310
		10:4	81, 178, 225
		10:4–5	48, 177, 245–46, 285
9:3	17, 41, 184, 221, 225, 257	10:5–7	318, 329
		10:6	78
9:4	4, 28n115, 173, 255, 263, 348–49	10:9	296n446
		10:9–10	109, 123, 163, 303
9:5	81, 95, 100, 184, 222, 272, 274, 352	10:9–13	183, 285, 294, 303, 318, 353
9:6	34, 41, 84, 140, 341–42, 349–50	10:11	247, 349
		10:12	143, 163, 166, 232, 265, 274, 283, 349
9:6–13	49, 317, 342		
9:8	28n115, 184		
9:9	294–95	10:13	50, 121, 136
9:11–23	239–42, 263, 275, 314–15, 317–18, 320, 348	10:16	249, 274
		10:19	268, 312, 318, 350
		10:21	154n310, 196, 289, 312, 318, 350
9:13	309, 355		
9:17–18	290	11:1	4, 22n107, 55n184, 173, 287, 316, 318, 348–49
9:18	266, 288, 289		
9:22–24	154n310, 295, 314, 320, 349, 355		
		11:1–2	237, 283n364, 286, 342, 350
9:24–33	242, 266, 268, 294, 310, 315, 324		
		11:1–10	262–67, 312
9:25	22n107	11:1–36	262, 281
9:25–26	242–43	11:3	151
9:26	205	11:3–7	308–9, 312–13, 316, 342, 346
9:27	43, 252, 264, 286, 309, 312–13, 315–16, 320, 346, 350		
		11:7	286, 288n388, 350
		11:7–10	289, 308, 316
		11:8	318
9:27–29	243–44, 264, 275, 285	11:11–12	123, 234, 287, 292–94, 316
9:30	78, 238, 299n464	11:11–15	267–71, 323
		11:13–21	106

11:13–32	232	15:16–19	295n437
11:14	318	15:19	72, 280, 293
11:15	49, 316–17, 320	15:20	284
11:16–24	271–76, 310, 317, 350	15:21–24	67n257
		15:24	284, 289
11:22	232	15:25–31	132
11:24	296, 312	15:26–27	148
11:25–27	275–319, 323, 326, 330, 333, 346–47, 350, 354	15:29	72, 280, 293
		15:31	304
		16:3	232
11:26	4, 16, 30, 34, 333, 344	16:3–23	144
		16:25–26	253, 287
11:28	4, 49		
11:28–32	310–11, 319–24, 347	## 1 Corinthians	
11:30–31	199, 348	1:1	144
11:32	45, 348	1:3	136
11:33–36	324–26	1:14	144
11:36	50n161	1:18	299n464
12:1–2	167n419, 201, 227–28	1:21–24	123–24, 169, 353
		1:22–23	151, 224, 264
12:3–8	212	1:24	143, 283, 349
12:20	296n446	1:31	56
13:2	296n446	2:1, 7	287
13:3	110	2:4–5	214
13:8	138n169, 293	2:11–16	223–24, 227
13:9	138n169	2:12	89
13:11	73	2:16	325
13:12–14	194	3:1–3	195
13:20	293	3:4	138n169
14:1–2	106n273	3:15	301
14:1–15	353	4:1	287, 301
14:1–15:13	106	4:4–5	50n161
14:4	139	4:6	138n169
14:7	221	4:20	209
14:9	85	5:3–5	192n126, 230
14:14	106n273	5:12–13	138n169
14:17	209, 353	6:1	138n169
14:23	78	6:9, 10	291
15:1	106n273	6:10–11	224, 296n446, 299n464
15:1–6	159		
15:5–13	119–22, 169, 353	6:17	206
15:7–12	232	6:19	228
15:8	84–85, 268n258	6:20	230
15:12	85	7:17–24	232n11
15:13	221, 293	7:18–19	144
15:14	139, 284, 293	8:6	256, 325n585
15:15	289		

1 Corinthians (continued)

8:11	163
9:20	128n80, 144
9:21	144
9:22–23	127n72
9:26	301
10:2	213n311
10:3–4	195, 252
10:11	41, 176
10:14	41
10:15–22	39
10:16–17	41, 212
10:18	17, 39–42, 69, 140, 184, 221–22, 225, 236, 281, 349
10:24, 29	138n169
10:26	293
11:25	160n358, 176
11:28	296
11:29	212
11:31–32	193n132
10:32	124, 164, 353
12:9–10	138n169, 192n126
12:11–14	212–15
12:13	143, 166, 222, 226, 283, 349, 353
13:1–3	193n132, 287n382
14:3	287n382
14:7	138n169
14:11	193n132
14:14–15	206
14:21	138n169
14:23–24	291–92
14:25	296
15:2	90n159, 109, 299n464
15:3–5	130
15:22	166
15:40	138n169
15:44	227
15:45	166, 176
15:50–54	227, 287, 291
15:53	158
15:56	177, 200
16:19	144

2 Corinthians

1:9	139
1:10	304
1:14	289
1:16	44n117
1:20	299
1:22	89n155
2:3	139
2:15	299n464
3:1–18	174
3:2–4	175
3:5–16	174–84, 200, 225–26
3:7	349
3:13	349
3:14	288n388, 312
3:16–17	223
3:6	206
3:7	43
3:8	296
3:14	4
3:14–16	252
4:11	156
4:13	221
4:16	196
5:4	227
5:5	89n155, 224
5:10	50n161, 110
5:11	139
5:12	42
5:14–21	156–64, 170, 181, 186–87, 353
5:15	165, 172, 184, 197, 210, 223, 226–27, 273n308, 281
5:16	85, 184, 222, 281
5:17	112, 147, 155, 165–66, 168, 181, 210, 222–23, 299
5:18	171, 299n464
5:19	299n464
6:4	89
7:1	230
7:4	293
8:8	138n169
9:5	301

INDEX OF ANCIENT SOURCES   399

9:6	296n446	2:16	90n163, 92, 146n239, 297n446, 299n464, 342–43
9:8	110		
10:3	156		
10:6	293		
10:7	139	2:16–17	109, 342
10:12	156	2:19–21	88, 128–29, 157–58, 160, 165, 169, 173, 210, 299, 337–38
10:17	56		
10:18	156		
11:4	138n169		
11:5	41	2:20	156, 188, 197, 208n266, 210, 223, 227, 230n386, 273n308, 281, 286, 341–42
11:12	156, 159		
11:13	42n91		
11:15	42n91		
11:16–33	41		
11:18	192n126, 221		
11:18–24	41–45, 69, 156–57, 159, 184	3:1–5	139
		3:1–29	87–101, 117, 208, 342
11:22	55n184, 133, 173, 232n11, 263, 283n364, 348–49	3:2	92
		3:2–5	104, 185, 199, 208, 214, 221–22, 225, 343, 351
11:23	178		
11:24–26	151, 336	3:6	90n162, 313, 342
11:30	157	3:6–14	176
11:31	50n161	3:7–9	81, 144, 205, 299n464, 341, 343
12:2–4	228		
12:5, 9	157, 296n446	3:10	88, 138, 141
12:11	42n91	3:10–14	4, 177, 343
13:11	297n446	3:11	109, 297n446, 299n464
		3:12	88, 177, 224, 255

Galatians

		3:13	141, 161n366
1:1	219	3:14	120, 221, 252
1:3–4	130	3:16	81, 252, 290, 343
1:5	50n161	3:17	193–94
1:6	138n169	3:17–25	255
1:6–9	340	3:19	252, 290
1:11	208	3:21	4, 141, 177, 224, 246
1:11–14	125–29, 169		
1:13	144, 286, 336, 341	3:22	90n163, 120, 146n239, 324
1:17–24	148		
1:19	138n169	3:22–29	104
1:22–23	129–30, 169, 336	3:23, 25	66, 81, 93, 143, 177, 209, 224, 343
2:1–10	148		
2:4	342	3:24	103, 109, 225
2:7–10	132	3:25	208
2:11–16	131–35	3:26	100, 205, 341
2:15	232n11	3:26–29	163, 167

Galatians (continued)

3:27	162
3:28	73n24, 132, 143–44, 151n285, 160, 166, 210, 214, 226, 283, 336, 338, 345, 349, 353
3:29	143, 210, 341, 345
4:1	224
4:1–9	100–101
4:3–4	342
4:4–5	66, 103, 104n259, 160, 209, 222, 225, 253, 293, 343, 352
4:8–11	88, 91
4:21–5:1	100–107, 177, 206, 224–25, 272, 342–43
4:23	111, 184, 221
4:25–26	40, 304n488
4:28	111, 205, 222
4:29	184, 221, 223, 342
5:2–15	206–7
5:3	138, 232–33n11
5:4	88, 299n464
5:5	221, 342
5:6	110, 208, 342
5:13	191
5:14	293
5:16	88, 342, 355
5:16–25	206–12, 220, 225, 335, 343
5:17	191, 226
5:18	199, 209, 342
5:19	221, 343
5:21	291, 343
5:24	88, 188, 343
5:25	73n24, 342, 355
6:1	208
6:1–6	335
6:4	138n169
6:5	297n446
6:7–10	335–36
6:7–16	334, 344
6:8	211, 342–43
6:8–15	208
6:10	110, 342
6:11–15	336–38, 343
6:14	138, 157, 188
6:15	4, 112, 132, 160, 210, 342
6:16	4, 16, 30, 34, 100, 138n171, 278, 338–46, 348, 350, 354

Ephesians

1:4	168n420
1:9	287
1:10	253n160, 293
1:11–14	108
1:23	293
2:5, 8	90n159, 112, 299n464
2:8–9	265
2:8–22	107–17, 124, 164
2:11–12	218, 342, 350
2:13–16	160n358, 161, 338, 353
2:19	336
3:1	108
3:3	287
3:4	182, 287
3:9	50n161, 287
3:15–20	109, 253n160
3:16	196
3:19	293
4:1–16	109
4:9	328–29, 331–34, 346
4:10	293, 328
4:13	293
4:18	288n388
4:22–24	158, 160n358, 165, 188, 227
5:5	291
5:18	293
5:27	167n419
5:28	301
5:32	287n382
5:33	301
6:10–20	109

Philippians

1:11	293
1:18	136
1:19	192n126
1:21	165
1:22	156
1:29–30	136
2:2, 5	137, 293
2:5–21	159
2:6	50n161
2:6–11	137
2:11	256
2:15	167n419, 205
2:17, 18	136
2:19–30	136
2:21	136
2:28	136
3:1–9	135–47, 169, 173, 194, 232n11, 254, 263, 286
3:3–4	156, 185, 192n126, 216, 222, 226, 278
3:5	127, 283n364, 349–50
3:8	353
3:17	301
3:20	136, 147
3:21	227
4:1–3	136
4:2	137
4:4	136
4:10	136
4:18, 19	293

Colossians

1:2	168n420
1:9	293
1:13	304
1:15–20	326n587
1:16	50n161
1:17	295n437
1:19	293
1:21–22	167n419, 217
1:22	113
1:23	253n160
1:25	293
1:26, 27	287
2:1–10	215
2:2	287
2:6	256
2:9, 10	293
2:11	139
2:11–13	215–19, 223, 278
2:11–15	167
2:12	165
2:16	353
3:1–4	165, 227
3:9–15	156, 164–68, 170, 188, 217–19, 222–23, 227, 353
3:10	160n358
3:10–14	158
3:11	214, 226, 283, 349, 353
3:13	50n161
3:18—4:1	166
4:3	287
4:5	138n169
4:16	182
4:17	293

1 Thessalonians

1:2–3	147
1:10	303–4
1:15	148
2:1–12	147n252
2:4	301
2:13–16	147–55, 169–70
2:14	129
2:16	109
2:17—3:10	147n252
4:12	138n169
4:13, 16	227
4:17	296
5:9	73
5:15	110
5:23	230
5:27	182

2 Thessalonians

1:11	293
2:7	287n382
2:17	110
3:2	304

1 Timothy

3:16	299n464
4:13	181

2 Timothy

1:4	293
1:9	299n464

Titus

3:5	222, 299n464
3:7	299n464

Philemon

1:16	144, 155–56, 170, 222

Hebrews

12:22	304n488
12:23	327

1 Peter

1:3, 23	222
1:10–12	328
3:5–6	328
3:18–20	327–28, 334, 346
4:5–6	328, 334, 346

2 Peter

2:4–5	275

Revelation

2:9	36, 153
2:14	36
3:9	36, 153
5:5	122
7:4	36
21:12	36
22:16	122

New Testamet Apocrypha/ Pseudepigrapha

1 Clement

29.2–3	38n60

2 Clement

6.8	328n598

Shepherd of Hermas

1.8	328n598

Shepherd of Hermas, Vision(s)

1.1	328n598

Shepherd of Hermas, Similitude(s)

9.28	328n598

Church Fathers

Clement

Stromateis

6.5.41.6	114n342

Diognetus

1	114n342

Ignatius

To the Magnesians

9.2	333

Irenaeus

Against Heresies

3.20.4	330
4.2.7	330–31
4.7.3	331
4.7.4	331
4.22.1	330, 333
4.33.1	329, 332–33
4.33.12	329, 332
5.27.2	333–34
5.31.1	329, 332–33

Demonstration of the Apostolic Preaching

78	330, 332–33

Justin

Dialogue with Trypho

11.5	38n63, 344
72	329–30
100.4	38n63, 344
123.9	38n63, 344

Tertullian

The Soul

55	333–34

Other Greco-Roman Writers

Cicero

Pro Flacco

28	164n393

Epictetus

Diatribai

2.26.4	195n154

Josephus

Against Apion

2.121	152n290
2.227	99n238

Jewish Antiquities

6.6	33
6.317	33
11.169–73	33n19
12.3.4	164n393

Jewish War

2.8.14	141n197

Marcus Aurelius

Meditation

4:23	325n576

Ovid

Metamorphoses

7:21	195n154

Philo

De Vita Mosis

2.14	99n238

Philostratus

Vita Apollonii
5.33   152n290

Plato

Protagoras
314c   295n440

Suetonius

Divus Claudius
25.4   231n2

Tacitus

Historiae
5:5   152n290

Mishnah, Talmud and Related Literature

Jerusalem Targum

1   260n211

Midrash Tanhuma

107b   137n163

Sanhedrin

10.1   310n522

Targum Str-B

1:725   137n163
3:276   247

Testament of Benjamin

10.11   310n522

Shemoneh Esreh

19   339

www.ingramcontent.com/pod-product-compliance
Lightning Source LLC
Chambersburg PA
CBHW071228290426
44108CB00013B/1325